Bill Penman-Brown spent 25 years in senior management in International Banking and Financial Services in the UK, Bermuda, Canada, Jersey and Guernsey, followed by three years as the first Banking and Financial Services Commissioner in Gibraltar. He was a Council Member of the Chartered Institute of Bankers and Chief Examiner for the Associate examination in Offshore Practice and Administration.

The Decline and Fall of Banking

Bill Penman Brown

Matador
5 Weir Road
Kibworth Beauchamp
Leicester LE8 0LQ, UK
Tel: (+44) 116 279 2299
Email: books@troubador.co.uk
Web: www.troubador.co.uk/matador

ISBN 978-1848761-469

A Cataloguing-in-Publication (CIP) catalogue record for this book
is available from the British Library.

Typeset in 9.5pt Arial by Troubador Publishing Ltd, Leicester, UK
Printed in the UK by TJ International, Padstow, Cornwall

Matador is an imprint of Troubador Publishing Ltd

This book is dedicated to my wife Margaret
without whose unwavering support and encouragement
it could never have been completed

and

to my grandson Christian Anton William Wetzels
in the hope that it will help him understand some
future financial crisis when he is old enough to wonder
what it is all about.

Contents

Acknowledgements

The purpose of this book was to relate how the financial crises and credit-crunch of 2007/08 developed and to analyse it. Much of the book was written as the events described happened or very shortly afterwards. I particularly wished to limit the use of that solver of problems, hindsight.

The only way my objective could be achieved was to study official and corporate statements and documents as they became available and to read and note newspaper reports, supplemented by broadcast media reports since that is the only manner in which the average "man in the street" can judge the development of events. The study was conducted by reading both newspapers and internet websites.

We are fortunate as a community in having elements in broadcasting and the press which at least most of the time report events responsibly and as fully as they can with a proper regard for the public interest. There are many such organisations from which to make a selection. In order to create a measure of consistency and because I have been familiar with most of them for many years, in random order I selected the following as representative of sources of reliable information:

The Times and Times online, The Financial Times, The Guardian, The Banker, Investors Chronicle, Sunday Times, Thomson Financial, AP Associated Press BBC, ITV, Thomson Financial, Reuters, The New York Times, International Herald Tribune, UK Shareholders Association, Yahoo Finance, ADVFN stock trading reports, This is money.co.uk, The Telegraph, The Independent, Daily Mail, The Centre for Responsible Lending,

Background information was also obtained from a wide range of official publications and websites.

I am very grateful to have had access to all those sources and to the journalists who researched and reported on so many matters of significance to the rest of us. Without their contributions we would be even less able to make sense of such wide-ranging global financial problems as have been experienced recently and which will continue to affect us for some time to come.

Bill Penman Brown
Cramond, Edinburgh

Introduction

February 2009

"What we anticipate seldom occurs; what we least expected generally happens."
Benjamin Disraeli 1804 -1881.

When this book was first considered all the attention had been focused on Northern Rock and how it faced a liquidity problem due to an inability to access inter-bank wholesale lending markets that had "frozen" because of fears about serious problems in the US subprime mortgage markets and the associated "securitisation" of mortgages. Those are topics that will be examined in the course of the next few chapters.

From September 2007, when the Northern Rock crisis began, until March of 2008 most media and Press reports were associated with Northern Rock, latterly with its nationalization. Although references were made to problems affecting other banks and the credit crisis that had developed Northern Rock appeared to have been most affected, although as we shall see, its problems paled into insignificance alongside those that later beset other major banks, particularly in the UK and the USA. Some suffered substantial write-downs of assets, a need to re-capitalize or were subject to takeovers and government intervention. A few disappeared altogether.

That was the reported situation until July 2008 when the whole picture began to change and by September 2008 concentration had switched to a full-blown global financial crisis of proportions not seen since 1929. New problems and the stories surrounding them emerged daily as the financial abyss that had opened up appeared to have no bottom. Banks, lending institutions, regulators and governments around the world were all caught up in the maelstrom, one that totally dwarfed the original Northern Rock situation.

The Northern Rock story deserves examination as it highlighted deficiencies in the official handling of its problems and demonstrated that there was a lack of preparation for such eventualities, on the part of the Northern Rock board, the regulators and the government in the shape of HM Treasury. It also demonstrated a global unwillingness in the financial world to face up to the seriousness of the problems that gave rise to Northern Rock's lack of liquidity.

There is more than one story to be told. My original intention was to examine the relationship between Northern Rock PLC and sub-prime lending in the USA. However it became necessary to consider the Northern Rock story within the context of the wider problems of the credit crisis as it appeared up to mid-2008. After July 2008 that became no longer appropriate. The credit crisis had exploded into a global financial and economic disaster involving the collapse or need for rescue of many first rank banks in the UK, Europe (including Iceland) and the USA. It became a much more dramatic story which had to be dealt with alongside that of Northern Rock. Nevertheless the Northern Rock part of the story is still important as it alerted regulators and governments to the need for a proactive approach as the subsequent crises developed. It also meant that although they were not fully prepared for the extent of the problems that arose, they were much more conscious of their significance.

But for the funding crisis that overtook Northern Rock PLC on the 14th September 2007, it would have been some time before the general public in the UK heard anything much about sub-prime mortgages and the problems surrounding them.

In June 2007 Northern Rock issued a very positive Half-yearly Report accompanied the following month by encouraging Interim Accounts, albeit with a qualification that 2007 profits would be lower than expected because of the increase in funding costs brought about by a recent rise in Bank Rate. Northern Rock had continued to build on several years of rapid growth, probably as we can now speculate, too rapid.

From the statistics provided in the Interim Accounts, it appeared that the high quality of its loan book had been maintained and its repossession and default rates were about half the industry average. Actual losses suffered as a result of repossessions and defaults were minimal.

Furthermore investment journals wrote positively about Northern Rock's prospects. For example on 30th July 2007, "Investors Chronicle" reported under a "BUY" signal that "Northern Rock made solid progress." Its comment was that,

> *Shareholders can look forward to an increase in the dividend payout ratio to 50% of underlying earnings (much better than that of many FTSE100 companies) as a result of changes in capital rules. And while the shares have fallen from our "Buy Tip" at 1,105p (4 August 2006), they are now trading on a forward P/E ratio of 8 which seems harsh for one of the banking sector's best-run outfits. Still a medium term buy.*

No doubt influenced by such positive comments in respected investment journals many shareholders purchased shares in the period June to August 2007 and were still holding shares at the date of nationalization.

Although some professionals in the financial markets commented on the reliance Northern Rock placed on money market funding around this time, the risk was either discounted or people assumed that the Bank of England would in its role as lender of last resort step in to provide funding specifically to Northern Rock if necessary. Moreover, there were no obvious indications that Northern Rock's funding markets were about to freeze up completely, giving rise to the first run on a UK bank's deposits since 1878.

So, what went wrong?

There is no simple answer, although at the time the media offered a number of simplistic and at times erroneous reasons for the apparent downfall of what was, as far as could be determined, a solvent and efficiently administered business. The reasons did not lie solely in the failure of a complex Funding Model, as many media reports suggested.

Part of its funding model was virtually identical to that used in the USA and the UK to securitise more than twelve trillion dollar's worth of mortgages, including those emanating from what was referred to as the "sub-prime mortgage market". This meant that when the global US based securitisation market collapsed, there was a knock-on effect on other funding sources that brought down Northern Rock and quite seriously affected many other UK, US and European financial institutions, depending on the extent to which they were individually involved in the mortgage, securitisation and inter-bank wholesale markets.

The securitisation of mortgage loans to produce "derivatives" was a major factor in the creation of the financial crisis that arose in the last quarter of 2007, but "securitisation", although an established and substantial part of the investment activities of major banks and other financial institutions in recent years, is something of a mystery to the man in the street. "Securitisation" is not much more than an expression which nobody has taken the trouble to explain to him because it is a process which, in the main, involves only financial institutions, their lawyers and global professional and institutional investors. In addition the mechanisms used can be extremely complex and require extensive study if they are to be fully understood.

"Derivatives" covers a wide range of financial instruments. The futures markets deal in derivatives that can be legitimately used by financial and commercial firms to hedge future financial exposures. There are many ways in which the use of derivatives can be beneficial but our concern at present is principally with their use to leverage bank funding and to remove liabilities from bank balance sheets. Those are also legitimate uses but as we shall see a substantial part of the financial crises that arose resulted from the mis-use of derivatives.

It can be suggested that "understanding", or lack of it on the part of many of the participants in the securitisation process, including senior bank managements, played a significant role in bringing about, at least temporarily, the downfall of this method of packaging loans and using them for further leverage by issuing bonds against the security of a package of loans, hence the expression "securitisation". At the same time fear within banks about the uncertainties arising in the securitisation market and a complete lack of transparency brought inter-bank wholesale lending markets to a virtual standstill.

Although the US "sub-prime mortgage market" has its equivalent in the UK, the size of the US market is many times greater. "Sub-prime" is a description which has been applied to it in media reports, and it is a category of mortgage lending which is well known to financial institutions and investment bankers but not specifically identified as such at the point of sale by either lenders or borrowers. However, those factors that are peculiar to this specific market were instrumental in starting the widely experienced financial crisis that has resulted in the more or less total collapse of the derivatives markets and of a number of banks.

The British media also made much of the perceived shortcomings of the British financial regulatory system after the Northern Rock problems emerged, particularly in relation to the run on that Bank. The media were also critical of the management of Northern Rock and those criticisms are two of the factors that have to be examined if we are to understand what went wrong. Interestingly when the crisis widened to take in other banks, there was little or no reference to regulatory deficiencies.

Although the run on Northern Rock deposits happened overnight, the wider story had its origins several years before, and appeared to reach crisis proportions during the third quarter of 2007. However, that was only a foretaste of what was to come later in 2008. There are periodic crises in one or another part of the international financial system, but the events in 2007/8 spread much more widely through global financial markets and impacted many areas of financial activity in a manner that had no precedent and its extent appears to have been totally unforeseen. As a result, the initial crisis was not handled in a pre-planned and effective manner in any country, by the institutions involved, the Regulators and Central Banks, or even by national Governments. As we shall see many of the parties involved were in denial, they refused to acknowledge facts that almost daily became more obvious.

That does not necessarily imply that everyone involved should be severely criticized. This financial crisis was the result of many factors coming together at one time. It was described by one senior banker as being a "low probability, high impact" situation. It was out-with the experience of those involved, whether investment or banking executives, governments or regulators, and not least the media which reported on it. If one single cause is to be identified, it was the avarice of the participants and of their bonus driven managements who for a decade or so not only believed in their own infallibility but that they had uncovered the secrets of financial alchemy.

If lessons are to be learned from the credit crisis (and that is always the cry), we have to examine how it developed and what steps were, or were not taken, to counter its effects as they happened and what has been changed so that there is much less likelihood of a recurrence. For anyone to believe that we shall be able to ensure that that there will never be a recurrence is to live in a fool's paradise.

In order to appreciate what brought about the crisis and the manner in which all the parties involved handled it over a period of time, in this case less than fifteen months, we have to turn to the available sources of information, the media, government agencies and the financial institutions caught up in the crisis.

However, a disadvantage of such an approach is that each of these sources has its own agenda and only makes available the information that it wishes to make public, which in part explains why the story changed almost from day to day as more and more facts trickled slowly out. Some took more than a year to do so.

Recording the story can be tackled in two different ways. Firstly as author I can acquire and read through all the available materials. I can then make my personal assessment of events and create a record that will be my interpretation of what happened, and probably subject to my private agenda. The second method is to relate what happened as it was recorded in a selection of contemporary reports and announcements from a variety of sources normally recognized as being reliable.

By adopting the second method, the reader is presented with a record of events as they were reported at the time they happened. The value of this approach is that when one creates a record in this manner one avoids the constant use of hindsight that could distort the story of what actually happened. This method provides a record "warts and all", since progress through the crisis was far from perfect, nor was it at times logical. There were many mistakes made by the participating parties who also failed to anticipate the manner in which aspects of the crisis would develop and spread.

Even if there was no actual change in the overall situation from day to day, there was much media comment on a daily basis, as one would expect during a financial crisis of this significance. It follows that the best way in which to learn how it developed, the palliative steps which were being taken (or were not being taken), and the new developments which were taking place, is by recording the daily progress as it was presented in newspapers and periodicals, on the internet, and on television and radio.

A number of works have been published that deal with the financial crises of 2007/8 and their economic aftermath. Some propose solutions for the avoidance of future crises, others concentrate on particular aspects. Some are opinionated, others are sensationalist in character.

This book is intended to be a record of what happened. It is not my interpretation of events although when we come to examine the after-effects it is necessary that an analysis is made based on personal opinions, in this case mine, which may differ from the pronouncements of parties more directly involved such as the bank managements, regulators and politicians, each of whom will have his own agenda. I have endeavoured to produce a text that is both readable and informative for investors and other interested parties but also of sufficient depth to be of value to finance industry professionals.

In order to achieve my objectives the presentation of some chapters has been arranged chronologically. It is important that we see the development of the story in this manner if we are to understand why mistakes were made and the arbitrary manner in which the crisis spread to financial institutions that initially appeared to have no direct involvement. It is also important that we examine each facet in detail, in particular the official announcements and background statutory instruments that formed part of the story.

Media reporting of events of this nature is the only source of information available to the man in the street. His opinions and actions are formed by what he reads, hears and sees. He has little or no access to what is going on behind the scenes, whether it is in Government and its agencies, or in the financial markets and institutions, at home or abroad. Even more importantly he is not privy to the outpourings of the rumour mill that permeates all major financial communities.

We live in a media dominated age where the cult of celebrity is paramount. There tends to be a concentration on personalities rather than facts. It is all too easy in such an environment to point the finger at specific people, discuss their short-comings and even heap blame on them personally rather than concentrate on the broader underlying causes.

Looked at from another perspective, there are those who seek to be recognized as "celebrities". This distorts their perception of what is gong on around them and may cause them to make mistakes. It follows that with greater celebrity status, the potential for errors of judgment increases, possibly followed by a need to save face.

Personalities featured greatly in media reporting of the credit crunch and Northern Rock's woes as we shall see, but the real story was not about personalities or celebrities, it was about events brought about by a social and business culture that had lost sight of basic principles and the concept of a service to the public. For that reason it is important that everyone involved in retail and wholesale financial activities, whether as a provider or as a consumer or as a regulatory authoritiy learns lessons from what is undoubtedly the biggest financial upheaval in nearly one hundred years. The last comparable financial crisis was that which started in 1929. Whilst the root causes may have been different, they were both brought about by over-optimism, over-confidence, and let us face it – sheer greed.

It is very easy to concentrate entirely on the downsides of this financial crisis but it should not be forgotten that the expansion of credit, including the availability of mortgage funds that was enabled, also produced a number of years of rapid economic growth and prosperity in many countries. Unfortunately a balance was not maintained between desirable expansion and excessive optimism.

At this point I should declare a personal interest – I am a Northern Rock shareholder. Furthermore, for many years I was involved in the management of subsidiaries of international banks and finished my financial career as poacher turned gamekeeper, in other words I became a financial services regulator.

Readers may find traces of duplication in the text. That has been brought about by the need to examine the same topics for different reasons in succeeding chapters.

This is a fascinating story, but at the same time it is a cautionary tale, indeed at times it is a very sorry tale.

1 Northern Rock Plc.

Background

In common with many other Building Societies, Northern Rock had its origins in the 1850's, at a time when there was a rapid expansion in industrialization, growth of towns to accommodate factory workers and a consequent need of workers for housing. It grew out of the Northern Community Fund, formed by a group of shopkeepers as a means of bringing together those who had cash to invest with others who required financial assistance.

Eventually, as the result of a merger between Northern Counties Permanent Building Society (established 1850) and Rock Building Society (established 1865) Northern Rock Building Society emerged on 1st July 1965. In total, Northern Rock Building Society was the result of an amalgamation of 53 small local building societies.

In 1997 its term as a Building Society ended when it converted from a Building Society to a public limited company, Northern Rock PLC, achieved a listing on the London Stock Exchange and also acquired Authorized Bank status, regulated by the Financial Services Authority. It expanded its number of branches beyond the North East of England into other parts of the country, including London and Scotland.

By 1997 Northern Rock had become a well known local institution in and around Newcastle-upon-Tyne and in order to preserve the image it had acquired as a community benefactor and supporter of local charities, the new company set up the "**Northern Rock Foundation**" as a charity and made a commitment to contribute 5% of its annual pre-tax profits to the Foundation.

In the last ten years the Foundation has received distributions amounting to £190 million. The Foundation is particularly interested in helping to promote programmes that tackle disadvantage and improve the quality of life in Northeast England and Cumbria.

In addition Northern Rock has been a strong financial sponsor of a number of local sports, including Newcastle United football club.

Building Societies are "mutual" societies, each is owned by its members who are also its customers. The Societies have no "share capital" as such, but gain strength from the accumulation of a reserve of funds from their annual profits. They do not have to pay dividends to shareholders in the same way as companies are expected to pay dividends.

However, as Building Societies have to rely principally on new depositors and monthly repayments of capital and interest on existing mortgage loans for funds to lend, there are constraints on the rate at which they can grow their business. There are many smaller building societies whose activities are restricted to a particular region, but a number of larger building societies operating nationally have chosen to convert to public limited liability companies with a Stock Exchange quotation in order to free themselves from operational constraints and to compete more effectively with high street banks for mortgage business.

Of course, in order to do so they have to seek the approval of their Members, but this has not proved difficult since at the time of the conversion, and because of the reserves which societies had accumulated, they were able to offer Members attractive cash payouts or free share allocations, commonly referred to as "windfalls". In the case of Northern Rock this amounted to 500 shares in the new company for every Member, valued at £4.51 p. each, a windfall of £2255.

But societies did not convert to public limited companies for the benefit of Members, the real purpose was to avail themselves of new opportunities to borrow funds in the wholesale markets and leverage their ability to finance a greater volume of mortgage lending. They were also enabled to conduct other forms of banking, for example they could issue credit cards and provide other banking services.

Since they also registered and were authorised as "banks", this gave them access to a range of financial options that were not available to them as building societies.

An example of the apparent advantages that accrue from conversion can be seen in Northern Rock PLC by examination of its growth from 2002 to June 2007. This period was one of general expansion in financial services, growth in the economy, and more particularly in the housing market where prices rose rapidly, and an increasing number of people borrowed by taking advantage of relatively low interest rates, in fact the lowest interest rates in 20 years.

Excerpts from a summary of Northern Rock PLC results issued as part of the Annual Accounts in December 2006 are shown in Table 1.

The excerpts from the accounts in Table 1 demonstrate a rate of growth that reflects fairly aggressive management policies during a lengthy period of economic "good times".

Table 1

Note: net lending for the year represents the total amount of new lending less redemptions

	2002	2003	2004	2005	2006
£millions					
Net interest income	391.2	450.7	612.7	706.8	823.0
Other income and charges	169.8	209.0	111.8	129.0	152.8
Total income	561.0	659.7	724.5	835.8	975.8
Operating expenses	169.8	194.5	216.9	249.4	277.5
Other expenses , etc.	65.8	78.6	66.1	81.8	100.6
After Tax Profit for year	228.9	274.4	313.8	356.7	415.5
Profit attributable to shareholders	**228.9**	**274.4**	**271.2**	**308.1**	**367.0**
Total assets	41,875	51,944	64,711	81,057	100,468
% Growth in total assets	35	24	25	25	24
Average Interest Earning assets	36,036	46,435	57,222	72,730	88,788
Retail Deposits	15,336	16,343	17,290	20,104	22,631
Net lending (see note)	6,697	8,514	12,932	14,555	16,621
Earnings per Ordinary share	**55.4**	**66.6**	**65.7**	**74.3**	**88.1**

In each of the areas quoted, namely interest income, other income, total assets, retail deposits and the net annual increase in lending, there has been a consistent rate of growth. The figures indicate that there has been a substantial increase in income earning assets that has in turn produced a very satisfactory growth in net income. Net lending increased substantially, having more than doubled in five years.

Two lines in the table that are worth noting are those listing "Profit attributable to shareholders" and " Earnings per Ordinary share." These are the figures of most immediate interest to shareholders in any company. They play a significant role in setting share price growth and determine the rate of dividend return received by shareholders.

In the case of Northern Rock PLC., the "Profit attributable to shareholders" has to be read bearing in mind that the Issued Ordinary share capital of the Company is only 421,200,000 shares. *"Only"*, because in 2006, for example, "Profit attributable to shareholders" amounted to £ 364,000,000. In other words annual net after tax profit of £364,000,000 technically belonged to the holders of no more than 421,200,000 shares. In the June 2007 Half Yearly Interim accounts it was stated that the payout ratio for 2007 and beyond would be 50% of attributable profits, resulting in an increase of 33.3% in the interim dividend which was due to have been paid on 26th October 2007.

The other line of figures that deserves attention is "Retail Deposits." If we compare this line with that for "Total Assets", we find that in December 2006 there were only £22,631,000,000 of retail Deposits, against "Total Assets" of £100,468,000,000. We shall return to this ratio later as it is the manner in which Northern Rock funded its expansion that brought about the problems that climaxed in September 2007.

In order to properly examine the quality of business in a mortgage lending company it is appropriate to look at the different categories of lending which it undertakes so that we can evaluate the level of security underlying the mortgage loans. In this connection one should also look at the "loan to value" ratio for each category, and the capacity of the borrower to maintain monthly payments.

Both of these can affect the rate of arrears experienced in borrower's monthly payments and in the number of re-possessions that have to be undertaken.

In Northern Rock's case, for the half year to June 2007 (and for the previous twelve months), the volume of accounts 3 months or more in arrears was only 0.47% of total loans outstanding, (stated to be around half of the industry average), and repossessions amounted to 1314. That number represented 0.17% of all accounts.

Repossessions were made in accordance with an active management policy where it was clear that the borrower was unwilling to maintain payments and where it was considered that the risk was higher than normal.

It must be borne in mind, however, that repossession of a property by the lender does not necessarily result in a loss to the lender. Northern Rock write-offs in the first half of 2007 amounted to £8 million, representing only 0.01% of outstanding residential mortgage balances. It is important to note these figures. Later on we shall see how media commentators implied and in some cases stated categorically that Northern Rock's record and future prospects in relation to defaults and re-possessions were much worse.

Mortgage loans that adhere to industry "best practice" benchmarks are considered amongst the most secure loans made by financial institutions. This is why they have been used extensively for securitisation purposes, an important element in charting Northern Rock's problems, to which we shall return in a later Chapter

Table 2 details the values of loans made for residential, including "buy to let", commercial, unsecured and a total. It can be seen that most of Northern Rock's lending falls into the conventional residential category. Unsecured lending amounted to approximately 8% of total lending in June 2007.

Commercial lending at that time amounted to no more than 0.85% and in fact in the half

Table 2
Analysis of lending by category

2006 Full Yr (£ millions)	Residential	Buy to let	Total Residential	Commercial	Unsecured	Total
Gross	26,745	2,227	28,972	423	3,594	32,989
Net	13,592	1,408	15,090	40	1,491	16,531
Closing balance	72,011	5,281	77,292	1,560	7,277	86,129
2007 - First Half year						
Gross	15,979	1,455	17,434	188	1,704	19,326
Net	9,170	899	10,069	(748)	554	9,875
Closing balance	81,210	6,285	87,495	818	7,829	96,142

year statement issued in July 2007 the Company advised that it had decided to exit the commercial market for balance sheet purposes (following the application of revised Basel 2 based regulatory rules which had the effect of adversely changing the relative capital efficiency of loans secured on commercial property).

Northern Rock planned to continue to offer commercial property loans, but would pass them directly through to third parties. An arrangement had been agreed with Lehman Brothers (investment bankers) for one of its subsidiaries to acquire higher risk weighted loans including commercial property loans. This explains the drop in value of commercial loans between December 2006 and June 2007.

Another influence on the annual profitability of mortgage lenders is the manner in which interest rates fluctuate. When rates are low, there is a natural tendency for borrowers to take out, and lenders to make, more and larger loans. Because of fluctuations in Bank Base Rate, which influences most other lending rates, mortgage lenders are unwilling to offer long term fixed rate loans.

It is common practice however for them to offer two year Fixed Rate loans, particularly to new borrowers, and often at favourable rates, sometimes referred to as "teaser rates" because they are the bait used to "hook" prospective borrowers.

If during the period these two-year Fixed Rates have been taken up by borrowers the Bank Rate rises the lending institution is faced with increased costs to keep them financed either through having to pay more to its depositors, or because obtaining money in the wholesale inter-bank markets will have become more expensive. The immediate effect on the lender's accounts will be to decrease its profit margin and reduce profitability. This provides another reason for considering the securitisation of loans, a topic we shall follow up in a later chapter.

Northern Rock's 2006 annual accounts were attractively presented and started off with a representation of "The Virtuous Circle", a diagram which the company frequently featured in its advertising as shown in Figure 1.

The diagram followed a "Mission statement" which read,

> *Northern Rock is a specialized lending and savings bank which aims to deliver superior value to customers and shareholders through excellent products, efficiency and growth.*

As at December 2006 we were presented with a company which appeared to experience consistent and substantial growth year by year, which kept its running costs under control, which did very well for its shareholders and its local community, which appeared to have a well trained staff and which anticipated continued growth on the same lines.

Strategy and current position

- "Virtuous circle" of volume growth, cost control, efficiency and profitability
- Most cost efficient UK mortgage lender
- Diversified funding mix
- 5th largest UK mortgage lender by stock

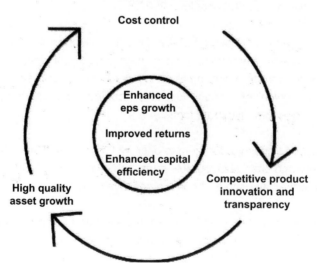

Figure 1

In support of this glowing report the Board also noted in the "Funding" section of the accounts

> *In recognition of our broad and innovative access to a cost effective and diverse capital markets investor base, Northern rock was awarded the prestigious International Financing Review's 2006 Financial Institution Group Borrower of the year award.*

Why is it prestigious? This is what the Review says about itself:

With International Financing Review (IFR), you can:

- Guarantee the commentary and analysis you receive is the most authoritative, unbiased and reliable there is.

- Stay fully up-to-date with developments in bonds, equities, loans, structured finance, leveraged finance, derivatives and emerging markets.

- Judge market sentiment, structure and market forthcoming transactions and make better, more informed, decisions.

The award has been noted since it was possibly one of the factors that reassured the FSA examiners that all was well. Northern Rock was in good company, Goldman Sachs, Citigroup, Lehman Bros, Deutsche Bank, JP Morgan Chase, Barclays Capital and RBS were only a few of the many which received the 92 awards of one sort or another at an Annual Dinner attended by 1500 senior investment bankers.

Perhaps the dinner was what the award ceremony was really about.

That was the situation Northern Rock presented in its 2006 Report and Annual Accounts.

As late as July 2007 the "*Outlook*" in the interim accounts for 2007 was described as follows:

> *The core Northern Rock strategy of growth in our residential lending business continues. Spreads will be squeezed in 2007 as a result of the interest rate environment together with our decision to continue to lend as swap rates rose. This will also affect spreads in 2008, but even so we continue to expect good revenue growth from our core business. - - - - Our strategic target for growth in underlying profit attributable to equity shareholders is 20%, +/- 5%. The drag through impact of 2007 into 2008 means at this very early stage we expect to be at the bottom of this range for 2008, broadly in line with current mean consensus. The final outcome*

*will be affected by how the interest rate and credit risk environments emerge and the prospects for the mortgage market. Further guidance will be provided at the year end. - - - - **We remain positive on our outlook for the medium term.***

The Management of the Company also reiterated that Northern Rock PLC was the 5th largest mortgage lender in Britain; the largest financial institution based in the North East of England; and it was one of the most cost efficient UK mortgage lenders based on key performance ratios. The Company had opened offices in Guernsey to tap the substantial market there for overseas and expatriate deposits; it also had opened another in Dublin and an online savings bank in Denmark, with a view to generating new depositors from these countries.

In later months there were numerous media references to poor quality mortgage loans. Commentators concentrated on anything that would support their inferred suggestions that Northern Rock was a reckless, cowboy outfit. As noted earlier, those accusations were not borne out by the statistics published in the company's 2006 Annual Report and Accounts which were, of course approved by the external auditor, PriceWaterhouseCoopers, as presenting a true and fair record of the group's and the company's financial affairs, profit and cash flow.

Whatever other failings there were, and there were serious failings, the company appeared to have been well run as far as administration was concerned, in particular it appeared, or claimed to maintain strict control over borrowers arrears positions as and when they arose. In a presentation prepared for investors in the 2007 Series 3 UK Prime Residential Mortgage Securitisation Issue by Granite Master Issuer (see Chapter 5) in September of that year, it presented the following:-

Behavioral scoring as a pro-active arrears prevention tool

All applications are credit scored at origination and existing borrowers are re-scored on a monthly basis.

Predicts which borrowers are most likely to go two or more months in arrears in the next six months

The behavioural scoring system allows Northern Rock to :

*   Undertake intelligent marketing and cross-selling
*   Target retention of high quality existing customers
*   Predict future arrears issues and concentrate arrears management

-    Conduct financial modeling and loss provisioning.

Of course, that could all have been promotional hype or a *"wish list"* but the fact was that Northern Rock's arrears record was a good one at half the industry average.

The 2007-3 Series of securitised bonds was due to be issued just as the credit crunch and the run on Northern Rock's deposits happened and as a result the bank had to retain the whole issue as there was no market for it.

After the run on its deposits, Northern Rock was the subject of numerous media reports, some of which as time went by commented on the fact that "many in the City" had been uneasy about Northern Rock's financial situation and indeed had predicted that there was trouble ahead. It was the case, as it later transpired, that City professionals had misgivings about Northern Rock's financial strategies, but how could the man in the street, its personal investors and depositors be expected to realize that Northern Rock was vulnerable? After all it was regulated by the Financial Services Authority.

Publications emanating from the Company were, as has been noted, wholly positive (except for the profit warning based on interest rate mis-matches, something which was explained and was understandable, and at the end of the day it was anticipated that they would have only a moderate influence on medium term growth and results). None of the share analysts, credit rating organizations, the Financial Services Authority (FSA) and the Bank of England appeared to have adverse views on Northern Rock's short / medium term future. The 2007 interim dividend was to be increased by 33 1/3%, a £200 million share buy-back was planned. Why, therefore would ordinary people have any reason to doubt, prior to the 13th September 2007 that Northern Rock was not as solid as it presented itself?

Admittedly, the share price had been falling since the beginning of 2007 but even that appeared to be related to general market trends.

The share price had reached a peak of 1224 pence on 5th January but fell back after publication of the annual accounts in January 2007 to around 1175p. On the release of a Stock Market announcement from the Company on 27th June 2007, the price fell further to around 850p, apparently because of the caveat that

> *we have a structural mismatch between Libor (London Interbank Offered Rate) and Bank Base Rates.- - - - As forward interest rates have moved higher, it takes time for new retail fixed rate mortgage prices to adjust upwards. - - - - In times of rising interest rates this dampens revenue growth with the opposite occurring as rates fall.*

The half-year accounts on 25th July 2007 brought the share price down further to around 750p.

The share price falls were perhaps not unreasonable bearing in mind that they were from an all time high when stock markets generally were in a euphoric mood, and possibly to be expected in view of the changes taking place in the general economic outlook. To some extent Northern Rock's experience was mirrored by falls in the share prices of other banks.

Although as we shall see, it would have been reasonable to have expected someone to have interpreted the warning signals, the Board of Northern Rock did not anticipate that there would be a total collapse of the Company's share price within a matter of a few weeks and that there would be a run on the Bank by its Depositors, on a scale not seen in Britain for more than 130 years.

Both the company's Chairman and its Chief Executive when they were later interviewed by the Parliamentary Select Committee protested that no one foresaw what was about to happen and they regarded that as a justification for why they had not anticipated a collapse in the inter-bank lending markets which precipitated the credit crunch. So what about the stress testing of their strategies? Furthermore, what about the "Corporate governance" controls, the description of which took up five pages in the 2006 accounts. We shall return to that topic later when we consider the culpability of the directors.

As we shall see, the FSA and the Bank of England also appear to have been caught wrong-footed when the run on Northern Rock's deposits took off.

We shall now examine in the succeeding chapters what brought about a complete change in the fortunes of Northern Rock PLC.

2 The Sub-prime Mortgage Market in the USA

It is necessary to examine the US sub-prime lending market in some detail as the serious problems which affected it, and which surfaced in 2006 but did not become critical until 2007, were instrumental in bringing about the downfall of Northern Rock Plc in the United Kingdom, followed in 2008 by at least twenty other banks worldwide, proof if ever it was needed that in globalised financial markets, no one can be an island.

So, what is a "sub-prime mortgage loan"?

Actually, it is more accurate to identify the category of borrower, because it is the borrower who falls into a sub-prime classification rather than the loan. It is the below average creditworthiness of the borrower which primarily determines what is a sub-prime loan

If he is in a low-income group there may be uncertainty over his longer- term employment prospects, or he may have a tarnished credit record, or perhaps he is unable to fund a conventional level of up-front deposit (20%). As a result, he does not qualify for a loan from a mainstream lender.

Although we speak of "sub-prime loans and lenders", they are very seldom identified as such at the point of sale for the simple reason that it is considered bad for marketing to mention the "sub-prime" word.

Whilst there has always been some access to a non-prime mortgage loan, in the last five years "sub-prime" lending mushroomed into a substantial, identifiable and separate market, although from the beginning of 2008 activity in it dropped dramatically as a result of the virtual disaster which struck in 2007.

The current sub-prime lending problems developed in recent years, but the concept of making loans available to borrowers who could not meet normal mortgage lending criteria is not new in the USA. In 1938 under President Franklin D Roosevelt the Federal Government created The Federal National Mortgage Corporation (FNMC or Fannie Mae as it is more commonly known) at a time when millions of families could not become homeowners or risked losing their homes because of the lack of a consistent supply of mortgage funds across the country.

Later the National Housing Act of 1968 (President Lyndon Johnson) provided government subsidized loans (Section 235 loans) and the Federal Home Loans Mortgage Corporation (FHLMC or Freddie Mac) was set up by government at this time to extend the operations of Fannie Mae and to provide a degree of competition.

Neither of those bodies made loans directly to borrowers. Their role was to raise funds that they could provide to lenders in exchange for the transfer of mortgages granted by the lenders. They also provided guarantees to the lenders as an encouragement to them to lend funds to poorer borrowers.

This was all done in an effort to enable poor Americans, African Americans in particular, to achieve home ownership and was part of a Federal Government campaign to extend home ownership throughout the country, particularly in traditionally poor urban and country areas.

The terms were such that a poor family could obtain a mortgage of up to $24,000 from a lending institution with as little as $200 down payment and at the same time pay only a portion of the interest. As long as the borrower made his payments on time, the government met all of the loan's interest above 1%. In the event of a default, the government paid off the balance of the loan.

In an effort to improve the effectiveness of the 1968 Act, Congress enacted the Home Mortgage Disclosure Act 1975 (HMDA) that was a legislative response to the still commonly practiced exclusion of African American and other ethnic neighbourhoods when marketing or granting home loans.

This Act was followed by the Community Reinvestment Act (CRA) to encourage lending in what had previously been neglected communities. At the same time, the Equal Credit Opportunity Act (ECOA) prohibited discrimination on various criteria, including race and national origin (largely Hispanic and Latino immigrants).

The CRA required financial institutions to help to meet the credit needs of entire communities and ECOA backed this up by making discrimination in the extension of financial credit illegal. By requiring registered lending institutions to submit returns which included summaries of their mortgage lending by census tracts, HMDA lent support to the aims of the other two Acts and enabled a nationwide snapshot of mortgage lending to be compiled.

The Monetary Control Act (MCA) pre-empted State laws limiting interest rates on first-lien loans unless States specifically opted out of the law. As a result the MCA effectively prepared the ground for the later development of a high priced mortgage refinance market under which lenders were enabled to introduce a wider range of loan pricing and other charges than had been envisaged up to that time in what was a burgeoning market. At the time these Acts came into force, they concentrated, not on the cost of borrowing, but on the *access* that potential borrowers had to credit.

Predatory or discriminatory credit pricing, although in evidence, did not begin to be an issue until after the passing in 1980 of the Depository Institutions Deregulation Act which gave rise to a differentiation between a "prime" loan market and a "sub-prime" loan market.

These Acts improved the ability of Government and private agencies to monitor mortgage lending generally, but it took some years before the requirements were extended to non-depository institutions, such as mortgage corporations. Those, and an army of mortgage brokers, mushroomed into existence as the potential profitability of dealing in sub-prime loans selling at much higher than normal conventional prime loan rates became more and more apparent.

It was not until 2004 that HMDA introduced a requirement for the disclosure of the annual percentage rate (APR) of some loans. In respect of loans originating in 2004, lenders in Metropolitan areas with assets valued at more than $33 million were required to report the spread between the APR of designated loans and the yield on US Treasury securities of comparable maturities.

This produced even more statistics on mortgage lending, but still excluded large areas of the country that were serviced by relatively small lending corporations that were not included in the reporting regime. The information required related to first lien (first mortgage) loans if the spread was at or above 3% over the one-year Treasury Bill Rate, and on subordinate (2nd mortgage) loans if the spread was 5% or more. Loans in these categories were regarded as "sub-prime".

This reporting requirement did not extend to the other charges generally applied to sub-prime loans, as we shall learn later, therefore it did not present the whole picture. Loans where the spread was lower than these figures were "prime" loans and exempt from reporting requirements.

Additionally, a growing source of business in the sub-prime market was for second loans, to finance house repairs, etc., or to provide cash for other family purposes. Those loans were enabled because of the equity borrowers had built up in their homes.

A private institution, **The Centre for Responsible Lending** summarized much of the above information on its website in 2006 and carried out an analysis of its findings, parts of which are quoted later in this chapter.

Notwithstanding those legislative measures, the reality of the situation was that sub-prime loans were not adequately monitored and those measures did not prevent the sub-prime crisis arising, despite the fact that a number of people in senior Federal and Treasury positions tried to draw attention to what they saw as an impending disaster area.

Consumer protection organisations and university sponsored programmes also produced critical surveys of the sub-prime market, some as far back as 1995/96. As early as 2000 and 2001, there were warnings that the new style unregulated lending corporations were making loans to too many borrowers who were unable to afford them, and who did not properly understand the nature of the mortgage agreements that they were signing.

Mortgage Lending in minority communities

Those organisations also stressed the inequality in lending markets where black and minority groups could be clearly shown to be disadvantaged when seeking mortgage loans.

Although there were many criticisms of the sub-prime mortgage market, it also had its defenders. It all depends which aspect one chooses to highlight, the dubious practices of some sub-prime lenders that are described later in this chapter, or the benefits to whole communities that had no hope of access to conventional prime mortgage lending institutions.

As early as November 1999 "The New York Times" printed an article describing a study, carried out by the Woodstock Institute, which identified disadvantages for black people seeking home mortgages. This study was carried out in Chicago, and was one of many similar studies conducted throughout the nation in the ensuing years.

The findings of this study included the following:-

9 out of 10 whites in Chicago borrow from mainstream banks and mortgage companies. They were assessed as having an "A" credit rating.

Even in "middle-income" neighbourhoods, 5 out of 10 middle-income blacks borrow from sub-prime lenders, having been assessed as " A—, B or C " credit ratings.

The study found that race was a stronger factor in determining the pattern of loans than household income, home value, real estate debt, education and location in the city or its suburbs.

As a follow up to this study, other organizations conducted surveys concentrating on racial discrimination in 34 other cities using a selection of homeowners, black, white, and Hispanic, all of whom were considered to have comparable credit ratings as "applicants" for mortgages. Creditworthy whites were referred more often to prime lenders, but blacks were not given this advice.

Other examples were given of "predatory lending", high-pressure salesmanship, high fees and repeated refinancing, especially where the applicant was vulnerable to such tactics.

On the other hand, industry officials said that they did not single out minorities and had added codes of ethics to stop abusive practices by a few lenders. They claimed to be performing a socially responsible function and were extending credit to people who had often been ignored or rejected by banks.

J.L. Zeltzer, an Executive Director of the National Home Equity Mortgage Association was quoted as saying

> *Non-prime lenders have brought democracy to credit markets. We've made a real difference in peoples lives. We have no intention of apologizing for that.*

It is true that a wider range of people had been given access to mortgage facilities.

The study in Chicago referred to above identified that between 1993 and 1998 home equity loans by sub-prime lenders grew by 30 times in black areas, whilst those in white areas only increased by 2.5 times. The study further recorded that in 1998 58% of such loans in black neighbourhoods were made by sub-prime lenders, compared with 10% in white areas.

This pattern of distribution held up when applied to middle income areas in 1998. Sub-prime lenders made 53% of the loans in black areas (2,090 out of 3,923 loans), compared with 12% in middle-income white areas (5,537 out of 46,022).

The study also found that generally lenders operated only in communities of one race or the other, but not in both. Of the 20 lenders who received the most applications in white areas, 17 were prime lenders, whereas 18 of the top 20 lenders in black areas were sub-prime.

A few other observations in the study are worth noting in the light of the crisis which arose in 2007, bearing in mind that the observations were made as long ago as 1999. This was no sudden revelation just as the storm broke.

In many cases, sub-prime and prime lenders were owned in the same corporate Group. Wide margins on interest rates, pre-payment clauses and other fees common in this business in recent years made it potentially very profitable. That attracted affiliates of mainstream lenders such as large regional and even foreign banks, but operating under different names. They had taken an ever-increasing share of the market. One could be forgiven for believing that the involvement of household name banks in this market would improve the quality of the lending process, but that has not always been the case, despite the protestations of some of the participants to the contrary.

One can only conclude that the parent companies were more interested in the abnormally high returns achieved by sub-prime lenders than in the methods practiced in the sub-prime market to achieve them. As will be seen later, banks around the world bid for and acquired sub-prime lenders after the initial surge in sub-prime lending took place. There was another factor. As a general rule, regulated banks had to confine their activities to one State. However, if they acquired or created unregulated mortgage lending or finance companies those companies could operate anywhere in the USA.

Because the Democrat administration of Bill Clinton was making home ownership in minority communities a priority, with aggressive investigations of lending discrimination, home buying by blacks and Hispanics rose twice as fast as buying by whites.

Notwithstanding Clinton's efforts, the Chicago study found that abusive mortgage lending had grown (in 1999) to a scale that threatened to reverse the impact of his administration's achievements. The investigators were more concerned to increase the numbers of borrowers than to examine the terms of the lending. A telling comment made by Mr Zeltzer and reported at the time by *The New York Times* was that the industry preferred self-regulation.

> *We need to root out any bad practices. Customers have to shop, shop,*
> *shop. The practicality is that most people don't shop.*

Repeatedly in the history of sub-prime lending we find the practitioners protesting that their self-regulation was adequate protection for borrowers and at the same time we also find them throwing the onus onto borrowers to look out for themselves. Remember that more often than not, these were poorly educated people with very limited experience of financial matters, at the bottom of the social pyramid.

So much for self-regulation, in other words " caveat emptor". The development of the 2007 crisis tells the real story.

The Growth of the Sub-Prime market

Anyone researching the history of sub-prime lending has no difficulty turning up a myriad of examples and anecdotal instances of faults, greed, sharp practices and outright fraud in the story of the growth of sub-prime lending.

There are many descriptions of the direction in which the industry was heading.

> *We are sitting on a time bomb*, one mortgage analyst said, *a huge increase in unconventional home loans like balloon mortgages (interest only, with capital repayment at the end of the mortgage term) taken out by consumers who cannot qualify for regular mortgages. The high payments,* he continued, *are just beginning to come due and a lot of people who were betting on interest rates coming down by now risk losing their homes because they can't pay the debt.*

Once again, this quote was reported in *The New York Times*, and it would have been very apposite, had it referred to the 2007 sub-prime crisis, but it was recorded in 1981, twenty-six years earlier.

It is necessary to concentrate on the negatives in the operation of the sub-prime lending market, because they contributed substantially to the 2007 crisis, but they were not the only cause.

There was much speculative buying in some areas, Florida and California being only two examples of areas where there was an over-optimistic boom in new building, creating a dream world in which speculators, many of whom were ordinary, normally sane people, who were now convinced that property prices, which had been rising exponentially, would keep on going. In the short term therefore the cost of a mortgage did not matter. The expectation was that the loan could be refinanced at cheaper rates when the value of the property increased far beyond the original mortgage. That was not all. It would happen within a very short period.

Lenders made (sub-prime) loans freely available and tens of thousands of people were sucked into what turned out to be nothing less than a vortex from which the only escape was foreclosure. Sub-prime and other lenders fed the demand but were not wholly responsible for its outcome.

What appears to have brought about the crisis was a combination of factors, not the least being the sheer size of the sub-prime market. By 2007, as we shall see later, it had grown to $1,300 billion.

It is necessary to understand the part played by the size of the market when it has been estimated that prior to 2007 fewer than 15% of "sub-prime" borrowers had been delinquent on their payments, much less defaulted.

It has to be borne in mind that when contemplating ways including legislative means to prevent the granting of excessive mortgages for the 14% or so of borrowers (Federal Reserve Board statistics) whose loans turned sour, we have to be careful not to deny the ability of the other 86% to obtain mortgages, in other words, don't throw the baby out with the bath water!

Who were the sub-prime lenders?

The property against which the mortgage is secured is not a sub-standard property, the value of individual properties only comes into question when there has been a general fall in property prices in a particular area or region after the mortgage loan has been granted. The only clear indication that a lender operates in a sub-prime environment is in its pricing of loans, and in its target borrowers. The interest rate is always higher than the rates one expects from a mainstream lending institution. Much of the subprime lending was to be found in the industrialized States and in the South

By way of example, Cleveland, Ohio, an industrial city of declining industries has been dubbed the "sub-prime capital of America". By late 2007 it was calculated that one in ten homes in greater Cleveland had been repossessed and that Deutsche Bank Trust acting on behalf of bondholders had become the largest property owner in the city.

The man in the street in Great Britain could be forgiven if he had never heard of sub-prime lending before the latter part of 2007. There are a few U.K. specialist lenders that can be classified as "sub-prime" lenders for all practical purposes, but the bulk of all mortgage lending in the UK has traditionally been carried on by long established and conservative Building Societies, latterly joined by major banks, including those which were formerly building societies.

However it is not a new phenomenon in the USA.

As indicated earlier, it was with the very best intentions that the Federal Government introduced the concept. However it was not until after the very high US interest rates of the 1980's on one-year Treasury bonds and the lower but still relatively high rates of the 1990's fell to 2% or less between 2002 and 2005 that conditions were right for growth in the sub-prime market to accelerate. Low official rates left room for wider than normal margins to be factored into lending rates.

Perhaps all would have been well, or at least it would not have grown to crisis proportions if lenders had not pressed borrowers so much on interest rates, particularly the hike in rates which they applied to most mortgages at the end of an initial two year "low rate" introductory period, many of such periods were coming to an end from 2005 onwards. Federal interest rates increased several times after 2005, but the related increases applied by lenders were excessive.

"Sub-prime" had grown from modest beginnings to being a major industry that served a large market. Borrowers who had to look for "sub-prime" loans were those who did not qualify for prime financing terms due to their low credit ratings, probably based on a poor credit record, an inability to document income and assets, or an inability to produce much by way of a down payment as noted above.

Such borrowers may have been rejected by mainstream lenders, but could be accepted by a lender specializing in sub-prime loans, indeed many sub-prime lenders had aggressive marketing and cold calling programmes in place to seek out potential borrowers, particularly in low income group neighbourhoods, especially if they had large communities of African Americans or were minority populated communities.

Basically, qualification for a mortgage should be down to an assessment of the degree of risk involved. Prime lenders work on reasonably narrow margins, dictated by market competition for prime borrowers. They set fairly high assessment criteria before offering loans. By maintaining high standards lenders should acquire a preferred status when they sell their mortgages into the secondary markets where they are "securitized" to raise funds to finance more mortgages, as we shall see in the next chapter.

Lenders achieved higher margins based on "risk based pricing", and as has been shown in a number of studies, by predatory discretionary pricing which was not necessarily disclosed to borrowers, particularly when lending to vulnerable people such as the financially unsophisticated.

Sub-prime lenders compensated for the extra potential risks they incurred. Each borrower was assessed on an individual basis, but in many cases with an eye to maximizing profitability, rather than with a concern that the borrower should be provided with the best, or even just a fair deal.

Their rates should have been based on much the same factors as those used by prime lenders. However, the lower the credit-score of the borrower and the smaller the down payment, the higher would be the rate that was charged. The lender justifies the high rates applied because of the need to cover higher administration costs since a larger percentage of applications are rejected and marketing costs are higher. There is also a potential that a greater number of loans will go into default.

Credit Rating agencies in the USA have a well-defined system for the application of ratings. Each person for whom a record exists has a rating of between approximately 300 and 900 points, the majority of persons with an acceptable credit rating for mortgage lending purposes fall into the 600 —700 bracket. Those with a rating below about 620 are unlikely to obtain credit except from a sub-prime lender.

The USA is a vast country and the market for mortgage loans is huge, illustrated by the following information listed in Table 3, published in November 2007 by the "**Center for Responsible Lending**", and based principally on official statistics.

The significance of the last statistic is that without Federal insurance there is no protection if the lender goes into bankruptcy. It also illustrates that about half of all sub-prime mortgages are sold by lenders affiliated with a Federally insured bank, but not necessarily insured in their own right. One would expect an acceptable degree of ethical practice from such affiliated institutions, but that is not always the borrower's experience as we can see elsewhere in this chapter.

Figures for total residential mortgage lending as at November 2007 were not available at the time of writing, but $1,300 billion of sub-prime loans can be related to a residential mortgage loan total of $10,921.3 billion as at the end of 2006.

Table 3

Number of families holding a sub-prime mortgage:	7.2 million
Proportion of sub-prime mortgages in default :	14.44%
(equates to approx. 1,040,000 families)	
Dollar amount of loans outstanding in 2003 :	$332 billion
Dollar amount of sub-prime loans outstanding at Nov 2007:	$1,300 billion
Percentage increase from 2003 to Nov 2007	292%
Sub-prime share of all home loans outstanding as at end 2006:	12%
Estimated proportion of sub-prime loans made by independent Mortgage lenders not affiliated with a Federally insured bank :	
In 2004 :	51%
In 2005 :	52%
In 2006 :	46%

In other words the sub-prime market had grown to represent almost 12% of the total mortgage market, which helps to explain the part it has played in the disarray which has been experienced in the residential mortgage backed securities (RMBS) market of which we shall learn more in chapter 3.

Of note also is the dramatic surge in lending between 2003 and November 2007, 292% or $968 billion. In a decade the sub-prime market has experienced a profound transformation in every respect - including size and mortgage type. It has been enabled to expand at such a rate because of investor demand for the resulting residential mortgage backed securities that provided a higher than normal rate of return for investors.

Securitising mortgages into RMBS was the engine which drove the enormous expansion in mortgage transactions, even more so than borrower demand which could not have developed as quickly had it not been for the greater use of securitisation together with the development of automated processing systems and the reputation and global reach of the big Wall Street investment bankers.

We shall study the role of securitisation in the next chapter.

The changes in mortgage interest rates were other factors that acted as a catalyst in the growth of the sub-prime market. The rates charged on individual sub-prime adjustable rate mortgages (ARM's) are variable and cannot be meaningfully tabulated, however the following rates (Table 4) are derived from official statistics for conventional *prime* mortgages, compared with Treasury bonds. Unless there was at least a 20% down payment rates would be higher.

The value of residential mortgage loans originated for multi-occupation - 1 to 4 families

Table 4

	ARM	One Yr Treasury	Fixed Rate
Average % for ten years			
1990 - 1999	5.36%	8.02%	5.99%
Average % for three years			
2003 - 2005	2.25%	5.84%	4.05%

The one year Treasury Bond rate is the index rate for ARM mortgages, fixed rate mortgage rates are allied to longer maturities.

Table 5

Housing_production(no.of units)	Single family	Multi-family	Total
In 1990	894,800	72,900	1,381,000
In 2005	1,715,800	352,500	2,215,100

- homes in 1990 was $458.4 billion and increased fairly steadily during the next ten years to $1354.9 billion but for the low interest rate years between 2003 and 2005 the annual figures were $3851.9, $2790.4, and $3033.8 billion, respectively.

Lower interest rates in these last three years undoubtedly encouraged the growth in mortgage volume, both in numbers and average size of loan. The growth in the housing stock during this period was also significantly greater than in earlier years, in large measure due to almost frenetic speculative building, particularly in Florida and California, the "sunshine states".

The "Total" column includes shipments of manufactured housing units that have not been allocated between single and multi-family (condominium or apartment) units

The peak years were 2003, 2004 and 2005. During this period the housing stock of single-family homes increased by 4,825,300, and the multi-family homes increase was 1,046,500.

Various organizations have produced figures relating to sub-prime mortgages, based on official statistics. The figures in Table 6 are taken from a table published in November 2007 by the **Centre for Responsible Lending** (www.responsiblelending.org).

If the statistics in Table 6 are examined in detail, a number of issues can be identified which help towards a better understanding of what has contributed to the 2007 crisis in the sub-prime market.

The first point to note is that the statistics, in the main, are applicable to the years 2003 to 2007, the period when the whole mortgage industry, prime and sub-prime, experienced an unusually rapid rate of growth and during which time serious problems began to emerge.

It should also be borne in mind that this is only a consideration of the residential property market, major problems also arose in the commercial property market, but as in the main they affected corporations and institutional investors, they did not have the serious consequences for individuals that have been experienced in the residential market.

Table 6

Proportion of sub-prime mortgages made from 2004 to 2006 that come with "exploding" adjustable interest rates :	89 -93%
Percentage increase of interest rate on an "exploding" adjustable rate mortgages resetting from 7% to 12%	70%
Typical increase in monthly payment (3rd year) :	30 -50%
Proportion of completed foreclosures attributable to adjustable rate loans out of all sub-prime loans made in 2006 and bundled in sub-prime mortgage backed securities :	93%
Sub-prime share of all mortgage originations in 2006 :	28%
Sub-prime share of all mortgage originations in 2003 :	8%
Sub-prime share of all home loans outstanding (Nov 2007) :	14%
Sub-prime share of foreclosure filings in the 12 months to June 30 2007:	64%
Number of sub-prime mortgages made in 2005 -2006 projected to end in foreclosure :	1 in 5
Year-on- year increase in foreclosure filings on sub-prime loans with Adjustable rates (2nd Quarter 2006 to 2007):	90%
Increase in foreclosure filings on prime fixed rate loans during same period :	23%
Proportion of sub-prime mortgages with prepayment penalties :	70%
Proportion of prime mortgages with prepayment penalties :	2%
Families with a sub-prime loan made from 1998 through 2006 that have lost or will lose their home to foreclosure in the next few years :	2.2million
Projected maximum equity that will be lost through foreclosure by families holding sub-prime mortgages :	$164 billion
Sub-prime mortgages set for an interest rate reset in 2007and 2008 :	1.8 million
Valued at :	$450billions

The first batch of figures relates to one particular and as it turned out very damaging aspect of residential mortgages namely the aptly named "exploding" Adjustable interest Rate Mortgages, or "ARM's".

According to statistics provided by Freddie Mac, in September 2006, out of its total prime mortgage portfolio of $ 1,500 billion, only 7% of residential mortgages financed by it were ARM, whilst 23% were 15year fixed rate and 62% were 30 year fixed rate.

Compare this with the sub-prime figures listed above, where 88–93% of mortgages issued between 2004 and 2006 were ARM's. Why was this percentage so high when compared with the figures for conventional mortgages?

The reason is quite simply that borrowers were steered by brokers and loan agents towards lenders operating in the sub-prime market where they could be offered so called "2—28 ARM" loans. Lenders emphasized the relatively low starter rates, commonly referred to in the industry as "teaser rates" which lasted only for the first two years of the mortgage and which were pitched at a level that borrowers could be encouraged to believe were affordable.

The problems only arose when that rate came to an end and for the remaining 28 years a much higher rate was applied to the mortgage, a rate which was itself variable to take account of fluctuations in general interest rates, in particular the one year US Treasury Bond rate to which conventional ARM's are indexed.

In the case of sub-prime borrowers, the increase in rate at the end of the "teaser period" was generally quite substantial, 5% being not untypical. As noted in Table 6, 70% of borrowers experienced an average reset from 7% to 12%. For the borrower this translated into something equal to a 30–50 % increase in monthly payments.

The next statistic in Table 6 is an important one, because it relates to the global problems experienced in the "freezing" and collapse of the mortgage backed securities market, as will be seen in the next chapter.

The proportion of <u>completed</u> foreclosures attributable to ARM sub-prime mortgages made in 2006 was 93% which, when linked to the timing of the collapse in 2007, demonstrates fairly conclusively that the biggest problem facing borrowers was the substantial increase in the interest rate that was applied to their loans at the end of the two year initial period. Furthermore, this increase was magnified by the increase in official base rates experienced in 2007.

Despite all the evidence of the existence of predatory pricing policies in the sub-prime market, most borrowers were able to cope with the expenses immediately attaching to their loan, and during the first two years, met the monthly interest payments, bearing in mind that few of the mortgage loans would include monthly capital amortization payments. Borrowers only had to pay the interest instalment. Most mortgages were written as "balloon" type mortgages where the capital sum borrowed only became due for repayment when the mortgage term expired.

A comparable British style mortgage would be an "interest only mortgage", which would have to be backed up by satisfactory arrangements for repayment of the loan capital at maturity. This would normally be an endowment or unit linked endowment policy with a third party insurer approved by the lender.

It is not logical that the sub-prime market, which in 2007 accounted for no more than 14% of total residential mortgage lending, should be capable on its own of causing the level of problems in the financial markets that has been experienced since mid-2007. It follows that the prime loans market also contributed to the turmoil.

In January 2008 Freddie Mac released the results of its 24th Annual ARM Survey. The survey revealed that the Mortgage Bankers Association had reported that delinquency rates on prime ARM loans moved sharply higher during 2007 and were well above rates on fixed prime loans. Serious delinquency (i.e. leading towards foreclosure proceedings) on prime ARM's was 3.1%, compared with 0.8% for fixed rate loans and compared with 1.1% on prime ARM's a year earlier.

The survey also noted that notwithstanding a decrease in the Federal Funds target rate from 5.25% to 4.25%, the starting rates for ARM's were close to or above rates of a year earlier.

Based on rates charged during part of December 2007, the fully indexed rate, which is the rate on the index (one year Treasury Bonds) plus the ARM margin, averaged about 2.75% across the prime ARM products surveyed.

Freddie Mac also noted that the share of ARM's in loan applications in October 2007 (after the collapse of the mortgage backed securities market) was still 17%, compared with 11% in 1998 and a high of 33% in 2004. 33% of the total loans originated in 2004 amounts to $928.32 billion. This gives some idea of the size of the potential problems with which markets and investors had to deal.

The next batch of figures in Table 6 illustrates the significant growth in the sub-prime market between 2003 and 2006, when the sub-prime share of the total mortgage originations in those years rose from 8% to 28%. As at November 2007, it was estimated that about 14% of the total market was made up of sub-prime loans.

Also quoted in Table 6 is the proportion of mortgages with "prepayment" clauses.

Prepayment requirements in loans consist of a provision that calls for what in most cases amounts to a penalty payment to be made if the loan is paid off before maturity, bearing in mind that most of these loans had a contractual life of 30 years.

The penalty may be expressed as, say six months interest, which in most cases would amount to a substantial sum. The real purpose of the prepayment penalty, although lenders will deny it, was to ensure that most borrowers in the sub-prime market would find difficulty in attempting to refinance elsewhere at cheaper rates.

They were therefore obliged to try to maintain their mortgage and at the end of the first two years pay the higher reset variable rate of interest. The significant statistic here is that 70% of sub-prime loans incorporated a prepayment clause, whilst only 2% of prime loans had one.

The last group of figures in Table 6 relates to foreclosure statistics. Foreclosures were not confined to sub-prime mortgages, but the sub-prime share in the twelve months to the end of June 2007 was 64%.

One of the problems that faced financial markets at the end of 2007 was the uncertainty over the depth of the credit crisis, because it was clearly recognized at that time that the bottom had not been reached. The estimate quoted in Table 6, that one in five mortgage loans originated in 2006 (a total of approximately $550 billion) would probably end up in foreclosure within three to four years gives some idea of the extent of the problem. Another indicator of future problems is that 1.8 million sub-prime mortgages with a total estimated value of $450 billion were due to "reset" rates in 2007 and 2008. Translating those matters into the effect on real people, it is estimated that of families that took out a sub-prime loan between 1998 and 2006, 2.2 million of them have lost, or will lose their homes. Put in money terms, they will additionally have lost as a result of foreclosures up to $164billion of equity in their homes.

Foreclosures have always featured in mortgage lending, but foreclosures do not in normal times result in a 100% loss for the lender and the borrower. The mortgaged property will have a resale value, and there may be some equity left in it for the defaulting borrower. One expects, as with any form of extended credit, that a proportion of borrowers will be unable to meet interest and repayments. Persons in default try to hang on as long as possible, hoping that Mr. McCawber's philosophy that "something will turn up", will eventually rescue them.

If it does not, then, at least in the sub-prime market, foreclosure may become inevitable.

Historically, during normal times in the prime mortgage market, foreclosures account for less than 1% of total lending, so why have there been so many foreclosures bringing about the 2007 crisis? Part of the answer lies in the changing pattern of mortgage financing in recent years.

It is necessary to understand that banking in the USA is quite different from that in Europe, and more particularly, in the United Kingdom. In Europe and the UK the principal market place for mortgages consists of a small number of large banks operating through a centrally controlled nationwide branch system subject to a government sponsored supervisory regime (The Financial Services Authority in the UK).

In the USA the system is different.

The United States favoured a system of "unit banks", i.e., banks with offices in only one town. There are over 4000 such banks in the USA, further divided into two types, national banks (authorized by Federal legislation), and state banks, regulated by state authorities. Fifty years ago there were more than 13,000 such banks.

There are some large banks, but they also operate in the wholesale and global international financial markets and to a large extent that accounts for their greater size. Their retail banking business, whilst substantial, is normally confined to the State within the USA in which they are based.

In general, State and Federal Laws prevent banks from operating across State boundaries. In other words each bank has to confine its operations to one State, and indeed many smaller banks only operate in one city within the State. The relatively small size and localized nature of many of these banks means that their operations are restricted to meeting the needs of a local community, although they can effectively carry out inter-state transactions through correspondent relationships with banks in other states. It follows that they can operate on a much more personalized basis vis -vis their retail customers, compared to the more impersonal approach of large banks.

When these regulated local banks held a mortgage loan, bankers knew the home owners and the values of their properties and it was in everyone's interest to avoid foreclosures, with its associated costs and possible losses from falling house values. They were familiar with property values within their operating area. They also financed the greater part, if not all of their lending by taking in deposits from local savers.

However, once securitisation was introduced, and became the accepted method of financing the growth of mortgage business, local banks which continued to observe high standards of risk assessment were unable to maintain their status as the principle source of residential mortgage (and other) loans, and lost out to a plethora of unregulated lenders that spread rapidly through most States, often operating from a central office in some other part of the nation.

The mechanisms used to obtain a mortgage then changed. Instead of visiting the local bank prospective property purchasers, particularly those who were not in good standing with a local bank, (possibly only because they had no real prior need for a bank account), obtained loans through a mortgage broker acting for one or more of those new mortgage lending corporations which were principally interested in what became the "sub-prime market". As growth in lending accelerated, the largest sub-prime lenders developed selling techniques through networks of "call centres" manned by hundreds of so-called "loan officers".

So much for the personal touch, that was once so highly prized.

Although the situation has changed to some extent, an important point to note here is that those lending corporations were not licensed or regulated as were the banks at the time.

Banking laws and regulation did not apply to them.

They could therefore spread their operations throughout the USA to any extent they chose. Once they became established, this made them attractive acquisitions for some of the larger banks who were unable to extend their own operations beyond their State boundaries, but which wanted a nationwide share of this lucrative new business.

The mortgage-lending corporations sold their mortgages on to securitising banks, mostly those on Wall Street in New York and in a number of cases, to their own parent bank. Those banks in turn marketed the resulting Residential Mortgage Backed securities (RMBS) as bonds or notes to US and global investors, which were principally, as we shall learn later, other banks or institutional investors including hedge funds.

At the same time, the RMBS structure had been devised in such a manner as to shift the credit risk for the loan from the original lender to the end investor, or at the least to any intermediary institution that purchased or held the bonds or notes. It is most important that this aspect, the shifting of risk is recognized and understood as it was a primary factor in the credit crises that arose later.

Once the securitisation process became well established, the mortgage lending corporations had a virtually unlimited supply of funds and they were therefore enabled to grow their business rapidly through aggressive marketing and handsome commissions to employees, brokers and other agents.

Whereas the banks had previously left borrowers to approach the bank, those new lenders were very pro-active in searching out potential borrowers, in many instances even resorting to "cold calling" from call centres as noted above. The nature of their market was such that the borrowers were gathered from lower income neighbourhoods and frequently included persons unlikely to possess any degree of financial sophistication. Since the lending organization obtained much of its business through brokers and real estate agencies, the lending process was impersonalized and borrowers could have no face-to-face contact with the lender.

The scene was therefore set for an "anything goes" bonanza.

That is what happened until 2007 when the bubble burst.

The ability to offload the credit risk from the original lending institution to the bond purchaser is a major factor contributing to the exponential increase in the number of foreclosures recorded. The mortgage-lending corporations no longer had a vested interest in keeping borrowers afloat by seeking a compromise solution when borrowers found themselves in difficulty meeting monthly payments. The simplest solution (and importantly for the lender, least costly to administer) was to foreclose on the property.

If the resulting sale of the property did not cover the amount outstanding on the mortgage, it would be the RMBS investor, or the corporation guaranteeing the loan that would have to stand the loss, not the lender.

As noted above foreclosure should not necessarily mean a total loss of the sum lent, or even a partial loss. However, the number of foreclosures in 2007 (and likely to continue through 2008 and 2009) has been such that in some cities whole neighbourhoods have experienced a situation whereby up to 50% or more of the homes in the district have been subject to foreclosure, and there will be no secondary market of buyers for those homes until such time as the market picks up and they can sell on at a profit. As always there will be exceptions such as speculators picking up cheaply priced properties at auction with a view to renting them to, amongst others, the former homeowners.

An indication that the problem lay with loans granted after 2003, lies in the fact that year on year there was a 90% increase in foreclosure filings connected to ARM sub-prime loans between 2nd quarter 2006 and 2007.

The increase in foreclosure filings for prime mortgages during the same period was a much lower 23%, but still much higher than would have been expected in normal times.

The sub-prime mortgage market is enormous but, if operated on sound lines, provides a very much-needed facility to persons who cannot aspire to a prime borrower credit rating. It is a risky market for lenders, but just as with other forms of personal and commercial credit lending, and as has been illustrated, although not wholly successfully by Freddie Mac and Fannie Mae, it can be structured in such a manner as to be viable and profitable whilst still providing a service which many borrowers need and can afford.

However, the reality is that as so often happens when business is conducted on the "fringes" of a market, less scrupulous operators are attracted, and their employees and agents (loan brokers) are encouraged to achieve sales, for which they are rewarded by bonuses for each loan sold. In itself this should not be a problem but this was an industry that over-reached itself and earned a very poor reputation. It achieved this fall in status by using a number of different techniques, of which some examples follow.

It is important to recognize that it is not sub-prime lending on its own that has given rise to all the major problems within the finance and investment industries, rather it is the widespread departures from good practice in both the sub-prime and prime markets, and let's face it greed and a desire to maximize profits that have contributed most to the crisis which erupted in 2007.

Those departures were by no means new, having been identified and commented upon some years ago, without meaningful intervention either by regulatory bodies, or by Federal and State legislators. By the nature of the business, a higher proportion of sub-prime loans than of prime loans goes into default, and a higher proportion pre-pay early and seek to refinance, notwithstanding the penalties involved.

An additional catalyst for this state of affairs is the common practice, described above, of selling an adjustable rate mortgage on which the rate is fixed for two years and then reset with a link to a rate index (in Britain it would be Bank Rate, in the US, Treasury Bonds), plus a margin.

Sub-prime market margins are high. Rates are deliberately structured to rise sharply at the two-year mark, even if market rates do not change. Adjustable rate mortgages (ARM's), as we have noted earlier, are much more common in the sub-prime market than in the conventional prime market. Typically, the initial rate may be 8% for the first two years, when the index rate is 4%. If the margin after the second year becomes 6% and the index rate remains at 4% after two years, the loan rate will rise to 10%. If the index rate rises after the two year period to, say, 6%, the new rate payable by the borrower will be 12%.

What set the stage for the collapse of the mortgage markets in the USA was the number of increases in the Federal Interest Rate in a relatively short period of time, less than one year, after several years of an unchanged very low rate. Neither borrowers nor lenders anticipated that this would happen.

The substantial increases that borrowers have had to bear at the end of the first two years when the interest rate was reset, has contributed to the number of defaults which have been experienced during the latter part of 2006 and into 2007 with the expectation that there will be many more in the following two years.

It is also a fact that it was the high rates of interest on sub-prime mortgages that were in place before widespread defaults became the norm, that were the attraction for banks carrying out the securitisation process.

Statistics were not available for the percentages of sub-prime loans involved in refinancing or in ARM loans, but the figures for all 1–4 family residential property loans were as in Table 7.

An important point to note in Table 7 is the manner in which the USA mortgage market differs from the UK market.

In the UK borrowers are attracted by an initial fixed "teaser" rate period of two, or possibly three years, the understanding being that when this period ends, the lender will almost invariably offer to renew the mortgage, but only on variable (adjustable) rate terms.

If the borrower wishes to seek a further fixed "teaser" rate elsewhere he is free to do so, and until very recent years, prepayment in most cases was not a problem, although it was also part of the marketing strategy of all lenders to encourage borrowers to refinance with them. UK mortgages were not structured on the 2 + 28 ARM principle in the USA, which locks the borrower in for 30 years, unless he pays a substantial pre-payment penalty.

Fixed rate mortgages that extend beyond five years or possibly at the most, ten years, are very difficult to obtain in the UK, although Prime Minister Gordon Brown when he was Chancellor, indicated a desire to see longer fixed rate mortgages. That has not happened because the mortgage products on offer in the UK are dictated by market forces and the funding strategies used by lenders.

However, other than in the sub-prime market, the norm for a conventional residential single home mortgage in the USA is a fixed rate term of 30 years and it is not unusual for the mortgage to be transferred with the house if the property is sold.

Table 7

	% refinanced	% ARM
1990	22.8%	5%
2006	47.6%	28%

It may be assumed therefore that the substantial jump in both the percentage of loans refinanced and offered as ARM loans in the USA relates to the growth in recent years of the sub-prime sector. It can be further deduced that the ARM loans are possibly responsible for the increase in refinancing deals.

Some borrowers who are obliged by their poor credit rating to take a sub-prime loan do so in the expectation that they will be able to improve their credit rating during the two-year initial period and refinance at a better rate. To circumvent this aspiration lenders commonly incorporate a prepayment penalty that runs past the initial two years of the loan. Such prepayment clauses are usually sufficiently costly or penal that they restrict the borrower's ability to refinance at a cheaper rate.

Another ploy, reported by the Center for Responsible Lending as long ago as 2004, and which is believed to apply to around 85 - 90% of sub-prime mortgage loans, involves what are called "yield spread premiums" (YSP's), which is industry-speak for "kickbacks". They are cash bonuses to employees, brokers and intermediaries who place borrowers in a loan with a higher rate of interest than the lender would have been prepared to offer. These kickbacks provide brokers with a strong incentive to propose a higher rate to borrowers when they could qualify for a less expensive loan.

Not all loans that incorporate YSP's are abusive, but because YSP's are permitted and easy to hide, unscrupulous brokers can make excessive profits at the expense of borrowers. Brokers and lenders frequently overcharge borrowers through a practice known as "interest rate steering", i.e. setting rates on the basis of perceived financial sophistication (or rather - lack of it!) instead of on an assessment of risk. Elderly, minority and low-income homeowners have been shown to be the prime targets.

Extensive studies have shown that a significant percentage of sub-prime borrowers (75%) could qualify for mainstream mortgage loans if they were properly advised. In one study of 50,000 sub-prime mortgages it was estimated that on average borrowers paid $1,850 each, making these kickbacks by far the largest source of compensation for brokers. The estimated cost to all affected borrowers was around $3 billion per year, yet there was no legal requirement to inform borrowers about the connection between the YSP and the interest rate charged on a loan.

The findings of the Center for Responsible Lending as noted earlier, and a number of university studies take these matters even further. They are critical of the predatory nature of the tactics used, such as aggressive marketing of second mortgages to homeowners who already have mortgages. A major pitch was the cash that borrowers could take out of their equity in their properties through "cash-out" refinance. Lenders targeted groups and areas that promised to have many sub-prime borrowers, such as lower income black neighbourhoods.

Yet another predatory tactic was to pressure a homeowner to refinance the mortgage frequently, charging high closing fees each time that are rolled into the mortgage amount so that the borrower does not have to find ready cash, (a ploy that was also used by UK mortgage lenders).

There is also evidence that loans were made regardless of the borrower's ability to repay. When the borrower inevitably defaults, the predatory lender forecloses and sells the property, at least he did before foreclosures reached extreme levels and the property market collapsed. By 2007 the number of foreclosures in some cities and urban areas was so great that it became impossible to find new buyers, although as we shall see shortly, even that situation played into the hands of unscrupulous operators and criminal gangs.

Ample evidence has been gathered to demonstrate that African Americans, Hispanic and Latino Americans, plus native (Indian) Americans, are all much more likely to become involved with a sub-prime lender than white Americans, even although there may be no difference in their respective credit ratings.This is illustrated in Table 8.

Although the sub-prime market is substantial in size, the total US residential mortgage market is much larger, and has grown exponentially as can be seen from Table 9.

Table 9 demonstrates how overall mortgage lending, both prime and sub-prime has grown over ten years, in fact threefold. Of particular note also is the huge increase in securitisation of mortgages into mortgage-backed securities, from $1776 billion to $5899 billion.

Table 9 also points up the change in the market shares of each of the Lending institutions. The notable statistic here is the growth in the share of "others", i.e., the unregulated lenders. Their share of whole (or retained) loans increased by 74%, with an even greater increase of 78% in the mortgages that they passed through for securitisation.

Table 10 lists the "boom" years for the origination of residential mortgage loans and illustrates those years during which exceptionally high growth took place.

Table 8

Proportion of 2006 sub-prime Home Loans to African Americans :	52.44%
Proportion of 2006 sub-prime Home Loans to Hispanic and Latinos:	25.36%
Proportion of 2006 sub-prime Home Loans to white non-Hispanic :	22.20%a

Table 9   Residential Mortgage Debt Outstanding (Billions of US dollars)

	Total	as whole loans	as mortgage related securities (MBS)
1995	3,726.7	1,950.7	1,776.0
2006	10,921.3	5,022.3	5,899.0
Of which			
Commercial banks			
1995		689.1	329.0
2006		2,213.2	972.3
S & L's			
1995		544.3	215.7
2006		965.1	223.4
Fannie Mae			
1995		178.3	75.2
2006		279.0	445.4
Freddie Mac			
1995		43.8	63.7
2006		65.8	637.8
Others			
1995		495.3	1092.4
2006		1499.2	3620.1

Table 10   Residential mortgage loans originated (per annum) — 1 - 4 Family homes
(billions of US$)

	1990	491.0
Peak years:	**2001**	**2,210.1**
	2002	**2,835.2**
	2003	**3,851.9**
	2004	**2,790.4**
	2005	**3,033.8**
	2006	**2,760.7**

Does not include multi-family homes for which figures are not available.

Automated underwriting and loan processing

There is one element that has played a significant role in the ability of lenders to process huge volumes of loan applications, and has almost certainly been a contributory factor that brought about the sub-prime crisis. It is the procedural change in the processing of loan applications from face to face meetings with an experienced loan officer, which was the traditional, but time consuming and costly method of processing, to a fully automated system based on computer programmes and algorithms. The story of the development of these programmes, and their usage is worth studying since without them it is doubtful if lenders could have processed such large volumes of mortgage loans, the total value of which in turn brought about the credit crisis.

Software had been available from 1995 and was in use at both Fannie Mae and Freddie Mac, but a specific programme had not been produced for sub-prime lenders.

A journalist, Lynnley Browning, researched the subject in an article that was published in March 2007 in *The New York Times.* The following is essentially a paraphrased version of that article.

A Mr Edward N Jones of Austin, Texas and his son, through their private software company Arc Systems, recognized the particular needs of sub-prime lenders and designed a programme that used the internet to screen borrowers with weak credit histories in seconds. The software was the first of its kind, although other programmes have been developed and put to use since. According to Mr Jones, using Arc software the lender does not need to chase every lead, just green light them!

In early 1999 he obtained his first big customer, First Franklin Financial, one of the principal lenders to home buyers with weak or sub-prime credit ratings. First Franklin has since been acquired by Merrill Lynch and has changed over to an in-house developed programme. Considering Merrill Lynch's downfall in 2008, it perhaps was not developed far enough.

Under the traditional method of processing mortgages an experienced loan officer conducted a personal interview, collected income statements, identification documents, ordered credit histories from Credit Agencies, etc., typically over days, if not weeks. Such a process requires trained personnel and is relatively costly, although many lenders charge up-front processing fees to defray the cost. The new computerized processes were estimated in 2001 by Fannie Mae to reduce the average loan processing cost by $916. There is no mention as to whether this saving was passed to the borrower. Most probably it was not.

The new computerized programmes enabled operatives, many of whom were employed in call centres and who had a limited experience of mortgage processing, to retrieve real-time credit reports online, followed by using algorithms to gauge the risks of default and so process applications in minutes. This new procedure was adopted by First Franklin Financial and by 2005, at the height of the housing boom, it had increased the number of sub-prime loan applications seven-fold to 50,000 every month. By mid-2004, Countrywide Financial, another major lender used another automated programme to double the number of loans it made to 150,000 monthly.

It has been estimated that since 1999 Mr Jones' software has been used to process $450 billion in sub-prime loans and that each time a borrower submits a loan application companies like Arc Systems can earn $10–$30 in royalties.

Automated underwriting programmes like this one helped to make the big sub-prime boom possible. Conversely it could also be said to have been one of the factors instrumental in bringing about the collapse of the mortgage markets.

Automating the process made it possible to create an array of different sub-prime mortgage packages, such as those that required no down payment, or interest only "balloon type" mortgages. Computer software helped to change what was a niche product into a mainstream industry. It was estimated that by late 2007 as many as 40% of all sub-prime loans were generated in this manner.

Another major sub-prime lender, New Century Financial promised mortgage brokers on its website that with its FastQual (the name says it all) automated system "We'll give you loan answers in just 12 seconds." It is little wonder that as early as March 2007 it was on the brink of bankruptcy.

This type of software is only one facet of computerization that has revolutionized the ability of financial institutions and other corporations to process a wide range of services quickly and accurately. Credit Cards, hire purchase, Internet Banking, supermarket check-outs, telephone and internet insurance sales, etc., have all depended on the development of specialised computer software.

The software used in these applications, including mortgage processing, cannot be blamed for lowering standards or the creation of lax controls. However there can be little doubt that the pursuit of ever increasing volumes of business, undertaken to produce exceptional bottom line figures, influenced many lenders to take shortcuts, ignore warning signs or focus entirely on credit scores that did not necessarily tell an adequate story. In itself, automated underwriting is evolutionary and necessary, the problems arise when it is massaged to change underwriting standards adversely.

Deception and fraud

The fundamental causes of the sub-prime crisis have been described in this chapter, but deception and fraud also played a significant role.

Whether intentional or by default, the deception of borrowers was practiced by many sub-prime lenders. It may have been manifest when lenders omitted to discuss the dangers inherent in the rate increases which were a feature of ARM loans; or when the lender omitted to describe the nature and size of pre-payment clauses; or because the application process was carried out through a call centre and no documentation was produced until after the loan had been made and accepted.

There are many other variations on what would have constituted deception, bearing in mind also that most sub-prime borrowers were low income families, financially naive with little understanding of the mortgage scene and having only one dream, to become a house owner. Such people were vulnerable targets.

One can find numerous examples on a variety of websites of borrowers who consider that they were deceived. One, known as " the bad business bureau", that also publishes the "Ripoff Report" noted in <u>2004</u> that apart from the cases quoted on its website, it had a further 437 reports against the same company, Household Finance Company, which later became a subsidiary one of the world's largest banks, HSBC, without actually halting the flow of complaints against it. On the other hand, if one looked up the company's website in 2007, one would have discovered that the company saw itself quite differently, in fact as the saviour of poor, hardworking people: "mandated to listen and treat customers with courtesy and respect, HFC account executives are here to help".

An example of "I say therefore it must be so".

Although much deception and fraud was directed at sub-prime borrowers there were also a significant number of fraudsters taking advantage of the frenetic markets that had developed. Most of the frauds that were perpetrated on the lenders were carried out by both professional criminals and rings of people connected with the mortgage and housing industries who were not necessarily full-time professional criminals.

State courts and police forces have been involved together with the FBI in pursuit of the fraudsters and bringing them to justice. Two main types of fraud have been identified, although there are variations on each theme.

The first has been referred to as "fraud for profit". This happens when one or more persons seek to make off with the funds from a loan. Firstly they buy a house from a legitimate seller perhaps using a stolen identity, then immediately put the house up for sale. Their associates in the crime ring then pose as buyers and work with a corrupt appraiser to produce an inflated valuation of the property. After finding a mortgage at the inflated value, the "sellers" split the proceeds of the fraudulent mortgage with their associated "buyers". The scam may be rounded off when the "buyer" defaults and disappears and the house falls into foreclosure proceedings, leaving the lender with any loss.

The second category has been described as a "fraud for property". In this type of case, the borrowers inflate their incomes on the mortgage application in order to qualify for a mortgage to which they would otherwise not be entitled. "Stated income" had become commonplace in the sub-prime market and lenders had limited means of verifying the declared income, and frequently had no wish to verify it. Equally often the borrowers had no intention of repaying the loan.

In the case of professional criminals, the amounts involved have increased in size and by early 2007, the FBI found that in 54% of the cases reported to it, over one million dollars was lost.

Cases involving fraud grew rapidly in numbers during the sub-prime bonanza of 2004-2007. This was principally because of the lax vetting conditions that existed, particularly in the earlier years. Lenders eventually applied stricter examination to applications in an effort to prevent fraud. At the same time, according to statistics from the FBI and the Financial Crimes Enforcement Network of the Treasury Department, such crime was (in 2007) a growing problem. Their figures were as noted in Table 11.

Not all cases were confined to the sub-prime market.

Having limited resources, law enforcement agencies have been overwhelmed by the number of cases. Because of the complexity of many of these crimes which led to long investigations and difficulty in finding and identifying the perpetrators in many cases, the agencies have had to concentrate on those areas where they consider they were most able to produce convictions. They also have taken into account that this is a type of

Table 11

2002	Number of cases reported	5623
2007		21994
2007		36000
2007		47,717

crime where the victims (Federally insured banks and other lenders) could afford to write off losses that in 2007 were estimated at $813 million. The Mortgage Bankers Association has pointed out that these figures only tell part of the story because they did not include mortgage brokers who were responsible for arranging half of new mortgages. It estimated that the total loss in 2007 could have amounted to $4 Billion.

Those are the frauds perpetrated against lenders, but the FBI announced in January 2008 that it had opened criminal investigations into 14 companies that had played a part in the mortgage bonanza, they included lenders, mortgage brokers and banks that carried out the securitisation of mortgages. Their investigations were aimed at uncovering accounting fraud and possible insider trading.

Other events, which in ethical terms could be described as "frauds" result from the huge number of foreclosures that gave rise to auction sales of homes nationwide. Examples reported in the "New York Times" of 22nd October 2007 included the following.

> In Minneapolis 700 people gathered to participate in what was said to be the largest auction of foreclosed properties ever in Minnesota, more than 300 houses and apartments for sale over two days. They were all expecting to pick up real bargains of properties. Although it was reckoned to be the largest sale of its kind ever held, it still only accounted for a fraction of the 20,000 foreclosures in the State in 2007, nearly double the number for 2006 according to data from sheriffs' sales.

An irony of this sale was that representatives of Countrywide Financial and Bear Stearns, two big sub-prime mortgage lenders that had been hard hit by the crisis, were on hand to provide mortgages to the sale buyers! They were also amongst the lenders selling repossessed properties at the auction.

A further irony was that it was believed that many of the properties had to be auctioned off because speculators tried to make a killing on them and failed. It was estimated that 55% of foreclosures in the State in 2007 involved properties that were not occupied by their owners, i.e., they were "buy to let" investments.

"The New York Times" article goes on to describe the scene at this auction as bedlam, and described experiences at other auctions elsewhere, all very typical of what was taking place throughout the nation, with buyers scrambling to acquire properties at what they considered were bargain prices which just had to go up and produce a handsome profit given a little time for the markets to settle.

It reminds me of a cartoon published by the UK *Telegraph* newspaper in the early 1990's after the conviction of Peter Clowes an investment fund manager who set up Barlow

Clowes International, supposedly investing in British Government Gilts. However, he fraudulently used subscriptions for his personal benefit, living a life of Reilly, with yachts, planes and a Chateau in France. He was jailed for 10 years.

The cartoon is of a jailor handing a fistful of bank-notes through the bars of a cell to Mr Clowes saying, "and can you really treble it for me before you get out Mr Clowes? "

3 Securitisation

Securitisation is a blanket term that covers a wide variety of financial strategies each tailored to particular financing needs. Some of the techniques used have been in existence for many years, but the rapid growth of securitisation within different branches of finance only took place in the last ten years, to such an extent that it became a major industry in its own right.

What creates difficulties for anyone trying to understand its workings is that it is a world that contains a huge variety of differently structured products, all described by different acronyms. As the terms can be set to suit the issuer and the requirements of the end investors there can be many variations that are only spelled out in the "small print". That means, therefore, that one has to study the documentation very carefully in order to fully understand the true nature of each individual securitisation.

One must also appreciate that the legal and financial structures used in most securitisation processes are complex and there is no simple way of describing them. However, if one starts with the basics it is possible to build up an understanding of some of the intricacies of the processes involved in the one branch of securitisation in which we are interested. It is known as the "asset backed commercial paper market" (ABCP). We can narrow this further to a section known as "residential mortgage backed securities" (RMBS).

Asset Backed Commercial Paper market

The asset backed commercial paper market had its origins several centuries ago in the use of "commercial paper", or " bills", in commerce. The bills, which eventually became known as "Bills of Exchange" were used to settle commercial transactions and in essence they provided a method by means of which a supplier gave credit to a customer. The customer agreed on the bill to pay a sum certain of money on demand or at a fixed or determinable future time, with or without interest.

Suppliers then held the bill to maturity when it would be presented to the customer for payment. Alternatively, a practice grew up whereby the bill could be taken to the supplier's banker who, if satisfied that the bill was likely to be paid at maturity, would offer to discount it and pay the supplier the discounted value.

The rate of discount would depend on the status of the bank's customer and the time to maturity. Such bills were not secured by specific assets but the supplier (or his banker) would be able to use the bill as proof that he was a creditor of the customer.

Although a much simpler financial instrument than its later cousin, asset backed paper, it nevertheless was capable of giving rise to similar problems to those recently experienced in the mortgage backed securities market. In fact discounting too many bills of high values for a small number of supposedly important corporate customers was the root cause of the failure of the City of Glasgow Bank in 1878, the last occasion on which there was a catastrophic run on the deposits of a British bank. So, perhaps we shall never learn!

As our concern at present is with the securitisation of mortgages, we can examine how securitisation is used in this context.

The basic concept is to use debt assets, such as mortgage loans issued by a bank or other mortgage lender, to generate further funds based on using the debt assets without actually selling them to a third party. This is achieved by using the steady flow of funds received on the mortgage loans by way of monthly payments of interest and instalments of capital repayments to service new borrowings created from bond (or note) issues.

The investors interested in such bonds are principally made up of global institutional investors such as banks, pension funds, insurance companies, investment fund managers and sovereign states. They are all looking for both a good rate of return and capital security. The issuers of these bonds seek to meet both requirements by a range of methods, which is where the complications arise.

Special Purpose Vehicles

For over twenty years it has been common practice for mortgage lenders, particularly in the USA, to parcel large numbers of individual residential mortgage loans which they should ensure will meet certain minimum quality standards specified in the bond documentation. Those parcels of mortgage loans are assigned to a "special purpose vehicle" (referred to as an SPV or "conduit") that in turn, probably through one or more associated companies, issues securities (bonds or notes). A typical process is described in Chapter 5 which deals with Granite Master Issuer, Northern Rock's conduit.

The proceeds of the sale of the bonds to investors are paid to the originator who will be the mortgage lender or the bank carrying out the securitisation. The SPV meets the interest and capital repayments on its issued bonds or notes by using the interest and capital repayments derived from the original residential mortgages. The SPV has first call on the mortgages in the event that a default situation arises.

Bond investors have the security of knowing that if the mortgagees default on their monthly payments they could, through the intervention of the SPV, have access to the value of the underlying property when it has been repossessed. Alternatively, and this would be the normal course of action, the originator will replace the mortgage in default with another or others of equal value.

The whole structure is based on a number of assumptions:

- The "package" of mortgages is of the quality declared by the originator (the mortgage lending institution).

- At market value the package as a whole is worth in excess of the amount of the bond issue, providing a "cushion" of additional security.

- There will only ever be a small incidence of defaults by mortgagees.

- The values of the underlying properties will not fall substantially so that the properties are worth less than the mortgage on them.

- The mortgagees will make their payments regularly and on time.

The security aspect of each of these points is necessary because it is a primary feature of securitizations that the default risk has been transferred from the originator to the bond investor. Apart from this last considerable benefit, several other advantages accrue from this arrangement to the lender initiating the individual mortgages (the originator) including :-

It obtains tranches of new funds arising from the transfer of the mortgage loans and the consequent issue of bonds. This enables it to finance further lending to mortgage customers.

The bonds issued by the SPV are secured by its parcel of mortgages. This in turn enables it to issue bonds that carry a lower rate of interest than would be the case if the bonds were issued without security. It is customary also for the issuer to arrange default insurance cover with a monoline insurer. This is known as a Credit Default Swap (CDS).

There will also be a difference between the interest rate on the mortgage loans and the rate paid on the bonds issued by the conduit. This is because it is usually cheaper to borrow short-term money (the bonds issued by the SPV may only have a life of between one to three years), than long-term borrowing (the mortgage loans, which may be for as long as twenty-five years or more). The interest rate differential may be increased if a change of currency is involved.

By way of example, for some time interest rates on US dollars were lower than the rates on Sterling. Many residential mortgage backed securities (RMBS) were created for sale in international markets, therefore the associated bonds were issued in US dollars. However, changes of currency introduce an additional complication in that the foreign exchange risk has to be taken into account and protected against.

The SPV that arranges for the mortgages to be held in trust uses the income and capital repayments from the mortgage loans to service its own bond issues. Surpluses are returned to the originator.

It is a feature of the structuring of asset backed commercial paper (ABCP) vehicles, as noted above, that the originator of the individual mortgage loans is relieved of the risks of default by borrowers. In other words, the risk of a default by borrowers is removed from its balance sheet.

The originator has reduced the risk exposure on its lending and improved its capital / debt ratios. This enables it to make further loans in compliance with banking regulations without requiring an increase in its regulatory capital requirements.

We shall return to this last advantage since it has a bearing on the problems that beset Northern Rock.

It is already beginning to sound complicated and we have only just scratched the surface. The scenario just described could lead one to assume that the underlying mortgages are all similar in type and credit worthiness, but that is far from being the case. In a description of its US Residential Mortgage Backed Securities (RMBS) research service, Moody's Investors Service describes the range of asset classes covered by it as including those listed in Table 12.

The headings in Table 12 relate to mortgages in the US market and each represents a specific type of mortgage, and the list is by no means exhaustive.

In early 2008 British mortgage lenders culled the number of different mortgages on offer. Across the board they collectively reduced the variety of mortgages available by 6400, although many of these would be variations of similar types on offer by a range of lenders. They included those listed in Table 13.

Table 12

Alt-A	construction loans	Re-performing
High LTV	FHA/VA guaranteed	Scratch and dent
HELOC	First lien, high LTV	Lot Loans
Jumbo-A	High net worth	sub-prime
Relocation	Home improvements	other
Conforming	Manufactured	housing

Table 13

Base Rate tracker	Adverse Credit	Buy to Let
First Time buyer	Refinance mortgages	Endowment
Pension mortgages	Cash Back	Variable rate
Self employed	Current Account mortgage	Re-mortgage
Fixed Rate buy to let	Bad credit mortgage	Interest only
Second mortgage	Investment mortgages	Flexible
Offset mortgages	Discounted variable rate	Capped Rate
Equity Release	Self build mortgage	Self Certification
Overseas mortgages	100% mortgages	125% mortgages

The last category, 125% mortgages, which had been the subject of much criticism as the mortgage crisis developed, became unavailable on 22nd February 2008 when the last few banks offering them ceased to do so. Although there was not the same degree of publicity, many of the other categories became less available after underwriting standards were tightened by all mortgage lenders in the latter half of 2008.

In both the USA and the UK, borrowers were presented with a bewildering array of mortgages and individual terms that varied just sufficiently from lender to lender to make a choice, or even a viable comparison very difficult if not impossible.

Because there was a wide range of mortgages, securitising banks could include more than one type in its RMBS package. The mortgages in a package may also be acquired from different originators. It follows that an investor in RMBS has to examine the "small print" very carefully in any Offer of Bonds, to be quite certain that he understands what it is he is acquiring. The 2007 credit crunch highlighted the point that investors could not rely on the credit ratings awarded by major credit rating agencies, who classified RMBS almost universally as A to triple A, with insufficient regard to the type, and therefore the quality of mortgages backing the RMBS bonds.

Not only is it possible to use a wide variety of mortgages within a RMBS package, the bonds issued through the conduit are frequently arranged in different categories, with different credit ratings and degrees of priority for payment. This enables slightly higher rates of interest to be paid on those bonds that have lower priority, thus catering for a wider range of investors.

Another factor that influenced the high credit ratings was the fact that part of the RMBS package included the credit default swap (CDS) guarantee mentioned above. Normally this insurance is provided by a monoline insurer (so called because it only insures this one type of business). In fact general insurers and casualty and life insurers are prohibited by US law from engaging directly in this type of business although they may provide underwriting facilities or act through a dedicated subsidiary.

In the same way as covered bonds were at one time principally issued in connection with high quality public sector borrowers, the main business of the monoline insurers was to insure municipal and public sector bonds. As these were high quality and seldom defaulted, this was good business for the insurers. However as the RMBS market became more dominant, there was a need to provide insurance guarantees for bondholders in order to ensure the coveted high AAA credit rating that was important in the selling process.

Mortgage backed securities were considered pretty safe, global economies were booming, so the monoline insurers saw another profitable source of good business. They therefore stepped up to fill the need and their volume of this business expanded very rapidly over a few years - during a period when mortgage defaults appeared to be at a very manageable level. As we know that situation did not last, the sub-prime crisis came along, markets seized up and the insurers faced mounting claims, to the extent that their own solvency was jeopardized as we shall see later on.

So, not only were bondholders unable to rely on the rating agencies, the insurance guarantees they had been given began to seem unreliable. Those two factors were material in the disastrous collapse of the RMBS collateralized bond markets.

It is worth noting that in the case of the bonds issued by Granite Master Issuer Plc, the off-balance sheet vehicle used by Northern Rock, only high quality mortgages were securitised and the explanations and detail given to prospective investors in the prospectus and its supplements cannot be faulted, all of which was registered with, and presumably approved by the UK Financial Services Authority and Securities and Exchange Commission in the USA as most of the notes or bonds were issued in US dollars. At the same time this meant that the offer documents ran to over 300 pages, which meant that the bond-holder would have to be pretty dedicated to read through it all, and more importantly understand it.

It is important to appreciate the total size of these markets, and the rate of growth within them, as it is the sheer size and rate of growth that has transformed the sub-prime crisis and the freezing of credit markets into such a serious global financial problem. Twenty years ago the derivatives market hardly existed. The asset backed commercial paper market in its many forms, were collectively known as "derivatives". By October 2008 the derivatives market was said to be worth $531 trillion, (i.e. $531,000,000 million) up from $106 trillion in 2002.

The total notional amounts insured by monoline insurers has risen rapidly as illustrated in Table 14.

Only a small percentage of these sums in Table 14 related to RMBS contracts, but as they were the ones that started to produce defaults, by the end of 2007 they were causing serious concerns in financial markets, as we shall learn when we come to examine other aspects of the financial crisis.

The 2007 amount of insurance was written by the mono-line insurers against the backing of about $34 billion of capitalization.

For some years commercial lawyers and bankers have applied a great deal of ingenuity directed at the creation of "financially engineered" products such as RMBS that will provide off balance sheet benefits.

As mortgage lenders in most countries (particularly if they are banks) are subject to regulatory requirements in relation to liquidity and capital, it is a significant benefit to be able to conduct as much of the financing activities as possible "off balance sheet" in other vehicles which are not directly connected to or owned by the lender, thus legitimately circumventing the then current regulatory restrictions and enabling a much larger volume of loan business to be conducted without requiring mandatory increases in capital funds cover.

Table 14

As at end -	2005	US $ 13,900 Billion
	2006	28,900 Billion
	2007	45,000 Billion

Those benefits soon proved illusory for the banks that had adopted them.

In addition, the use of off balance sheet vehicles enabled corporations to conduct their activities, financial and otherwise, in a manner which may preserve secrecy, including protection of the identity of the originator of the vehicles. If not complete secrecy, then without being readily subject to scrutiny by third parties, including regulators. The off-balance sheet vehicles almost always bear a name that is un-associated with that of the originating corporation and until late 2007 their existence was virtually unknown to those outside the principal financial centres, or even to many within them.

The disadvantage from the point of view of persons dealing with the corporation is that there is a lack of transparency that can be abused by the corporation that is using off balance sheet vehicles.

The most significant example of this in recent years (prior to the sub-prime crisis) was the collapse of the mammoth US corporation, Enron, in 2001. Off-balance sheet offshore vehicles that had been structured, at least in part, by officers of a department of the UK National Westminster Bank (part of The Royal Bank of Scotland Group), played a significant role in the fraudulent activities that took place within Enron.

This was recognized in February 2008 after a lengthy trial, when three former officers of National Westminster Bank, who had been extradited to the USA to stand trial, were convicted and sentenced to thirty-seven months imprisonment each.

Although the Enron case may have been a one-off fraudulent use of conduits (Special Purpose Vehicles or SPVs), banks and other commercial corporations have quite legitimately but questionably turned to the use of off balance sheet vehicles in increasing numbers. However, at least in the case of banks, regulatory authorities have in recent times become more conscious of the potential dangers that may arise from the use of these vehicles, although as we shall see later, in 2007 the regulators were not as well clued–up on the use of off-balance sheet vehicles as they ought to have been.

As far back as January 2002, "The Banker" magazine published a review of the asset backed commercial paper market (ABCP) which is a generic description of a market which is sub-divided into a variety of specialties of which the residential mortgage backed securities (RMBS) is the branch in which we are principally interested.

"The Banker" article noted that according to the US Federal Reserve Board, the ABPC market had grown since 1994 at a compound average annual rate of 40% to reach by end 2001 total outstanding issues of $710 billion, a figure that is almost insignificant by 2008 standards, when the sub-prime RMBS sector alone had out-standings of $1,300 billion.

The magazine also noted in 1994 that the market was primarily a United States one, used by half the world's largest banks that between them had created around 300 off balance sheet SPV's or conduits. Since then banks and other lenders created many hundreds more conduits and the market became a global one, but the major Wall Street investment banks still remained the big players at the centre of it.

So what were the attractions of this market?

The first had an influence on Northern Rock's downfall, namely the ability to finance long term assets (mortgages) by relatively short term paper and create extra profits on the way, notwithstanding the additional administrative and legal costs involved. In addition a secondary market was operated by investment banks and others in which this short term paper (or bonds) could be sold on at a market determined price.

Securitisation enabled Northern Rock to take around 50% of its mortgages off balance sheet. Had it not been able to do so, it is unlikely that it would have been able to grow its business (and until 2006, its profitability) at an annual rate in excess of 20%, since its core capital would not have supported such rapid expansion and neither its deposit taking business nor its ability to raise additional capital and other funds in the short- term inter-bank loan market could have been extended sufficiently fast to accommodate that rate of growth.

By 2002 the global asset backed commercial paper market was growing rapidly.

It was not a new concept, as we noted earlier in this chapter, but more sophisticated ways of using it were being devised all the time. In the jargon of finance, Lehman Brothers were quoted (in 2002) as saying "the heightened focus of European and US banks on risk based capital gave rise to the promotion of ABCP programmes for use as a tool to help banks improve balance sheet and capital management and achieve more efficient lending". What this really means is that more lending at cheaper cost can be undertaken without the normally associated need for and expense of raising and servicing more regulatorily required capital resources.

It was generally recognized that this was the catalyst underpinning the rapid expansion of borrowing, which in turn engendered increased economic growth on a global basis, particularly in Europe (including the UK) and North America. Although our concern now is to identify the causes of the credit crisis, it must also be recognized that the rapid expansion in mortgage and other types of lending facilitated by the securitization processes played a very significant role in economic development in a number of countries in the ten years prior to 2007.

It was not all bad news – at least for a time. Once the concept of using assets to create new funds from off balance sheet sources became truly established, all manner of ways of putting it to use were devised.

The creation by banks and others of off balance sheet vehicles or conduits was, and is an expensive business. It is accepted that for less than one billion dollars, or equivalent worth of funds it is not an economically viable option. This led to the creation by large banks of conduits that could be "rented " to smaller banks, or even to commercial customers, whose assets would be pooled within the conduit to give the necessary economies of scale. These were known as "multi-seller" conduits.

Set up by banks, they could purchase quantities of supposedly good quality trade receivables from a bank's corporate clients. A few commonly encountered examples are car loans, credit card payments, equipment leases, and of course, mortgages. Other assets securitized in such transactions have included trade receivables, builder loan receivables, farm loan receivables, premium finance receivables, structured settlements, life settlements, tobacco legal fees and football club takings.

These were then funded, within the conduit, in the commercial paper market. In other words, corporate clients obtained funding which in practice could be rolled over and therefore be semi-permanent in nature, although that would not be a strictly legal characterization of it, and as we shall see, it breaks the basic banking tenet of not borrowing short to lend long.

The danger that arises from reliance on such a strategy is precisely the one that brought about the downfall of Northern Rock, a lack of liquidity caused by an inability to re-finance short-term borrowing. At the same time, in the case of Northern Rock the problem did not arise primarily in its RMBS conduit but in its funding operations in the inter-bank market, where maturities tend to be short, one year to one month or less, and where it had obtained and had been able to regularly roll over upwards of £25 billion in short term inter-bank loans. That market dried up in August 2007 when banks became too fearful to lend to each other because they were not able to assess the downside risks attaching to the ABCP holdings of fellow banks.

By using conduits corporations could achieve a continuous source of funding without resorting to the issue of loan capital in the form, for example, of bonds which on each occasion require prospectuses to be registered and issued to potential investors, a marketing campaign, etc., all of which adds up in time spent and expense. Even more importantly, funds raised by such methods had to be retained as liabilities on the balance sheet.

Credit enhancement

An additional advantage that was devised was "Credit enhancement". The securitisation process was capable of creating a security that had a higher rating than the issuing corporation, which allowed the issuing corporation to use its assets to raise new money while paying a lower rate of interest than would have been possible via a secured bank loan or debt issuance by the issuing company.

Although there are substantial costs involved in the organization of a securitized bond structure, it tends to be "one-off", as the same pool of mortgage assets can be increased and used for several issues of bonds, and over a period of more than one year. What tends to be forgotten is that the securitisation process introduces a "leveraging" element, i.e., existing loans are used to create new loans. As always with "leveraging" or "gearing" operations they work well as long as nothing goes wrong, but can be disastrous when something does go wrong.

The ABCP route therefore produced cheaper financing for corporations, helped banks' balance sheets and as a bonus, provided the banks with a regular fee income from the provision of conduits and for their administration.

The head of asset securitisation at the Bank of America was quoted in 2002 as saying

> The ABCP market generally trades well below LIBOR (the London inter-bank offered rate) because it is recognized as a very safe liquid product. (My underlining). This is why it is so attractive to blue chip borrowers or, at least those with good quality receivables that form the collateral for the ABCP.

He may have been right at the time, but by 2006 it had become apparent that the "good quality collateral" stipulation had become much too flexible and one could maintain that it was not the concept that was faulty, rather it was the diminution of standards that brought about the downfall of several sectors of the market.

Almost certainly greed and the need to maintain or increase market share also played a substantial part since the concept was a great money-spinner for banks, accountants, rating agencies, insurers, lawyers and other intermediaries.

Partly because of the "rent-a-conduit" concept, it would become increasingly difficult to identify precisely the actual composition of the asset mix backing the commercial paper or bonds. In many cases they could also include collateralized bond or loan obligations, which means that one has a "conduit within a conduit". These became known as "squared conduits". Squared conduits are particularly vulnerable. They can be related to the problems that arose some years ago with "Split Capital Trusts". When those hit a crisis and substantial loss of value, it was in large part because they invested in each other, therefore when one went down, others followed almost automatically.

In order to counter criticisms of a lack of transparency that surrounds many ABCP conduits, and also with an eye to a triple A rating, collateralized issues are substantially over-collateralized relative to the amount of bonds or notes issued by them. They are also backed by a liquidity facility by way of an insurance backed guarantee also known as a credit default swap (CDS). It was not intended that this guarantee should be regarded as an insurance against the default of the issuer. It is a guarantee that the bond holder will get paid if the market is disrupted to such an extent that he cannot be repaid when the bond falls due, but in practice that also includes defaults by mortgagees whose mortgages are in the conduit "*pool*".

Covered Bonds

Securitisation is not the only way in which an institution such as a mortgage lender can utilize its portfolio of mortgage assets to fund further lending.

It can issue "covered bonds". Covered bond issues may have variable or fixed rates of interest and they will be redeemable after a specified period of time, usually between one and five years, although it is not unknown for shorter or longer terms to be issued.

The concept of covered bonds is similar to the securitisation technique which produces residential mortgage backed securities with the important exception that the individual mortgage loans which are used to back the covered bond are segregated into "pools" but remain on the balance sheet of the issuing institution. The issuer retains full management of the mortgage assets for its own account and the bonds are obligations of the issuer.

Covered bonds differ from straight bonds (i.e. bonds which are general unsecured liabilities of the issuing company) in that they are backed by a dedicated group of mortgage loans described as a "cover pool" which sets the assets in it apart from the general assets of a company in the event that the company goes into bankruptcy.

The credit rating applied to the covered bonds will depend on the quality of the mortgages in the "cover pool". Within limits decreed by market competition, the higher the rating the lower the rate of interest is likely to be on the bonds. Issuers can change the make up of the "cover pool" in order to maintain the credit quality supporting the bonds, i.e. they can add to the cover pool, or substitute new mortgages for those which they believe to have declined in value.

Traditionally, covered bonds have been backed by high quality assets. Until the bundling of mortgages to back covered bonds, they were used almost exclusively in continental European countries for Public Sector borrowing.

Covered bonds are issued within a well-established legal and regulatory framework administered by the European Covered Bond Council (ECBC). As a result they have been highly liquid within a widely established market and have usually enjoyed triple A credit ratings. The types of loan assets typically backing covered bonds relate to shipping, the public sector and mortgage loans.

Having said that, investors need to take care to ensure that the law of the country in which the bonds are issued permits the segregation of assets that are in the "cover pool". Many European countries have specific laws that govern covered bonds, although the provisions of the applicable law can differ from one country to another.

The European Union (EU) has tried to introduce a measure of standardization to the law by including covered bonds in the provisions of the Directive on Undertakings for Collective Investments in Transferable Securities (UCITS), 1988. If the criteria in the Directive are met, investment in covered bonds of any single issuer may be made by investment funds up to 25% of their assets.

The introduction in 2006 of new bank capital requirements promulgated by Basel 2 also allowed banks which invest in covered bonds which meet the EU criteria to apply a risk weighting of 10% instead of 20% when calculating their capital reserves against covered bonds. This was an added advantage that accrued to covered bonds. Basel 2 is part of the internationally accepted bank regulatory regime adopted, in addition to their own requirements, by bank regulators in most countries throughout the world.

As mortgages often have a potentially long life, the covered bonds can have a range of maturities to suit market requirements at the time of issue. Two to ten years would not be uncommon, but longer maturities are not unknown although after all the turmoil in other bond markets in late 2007, there has been a move towards shorter, safer covered bonds.

Banks and other lenders favour the issue of covered bonds since they offer several advantages over straight bonds. Because of the strict regulatory requirements affecting covered bonds they will generally qualify for a high credit rating that is attractive to investors, even although it also enables the issuer to attach a lower interest coupon to them. They also enable issuers wishing to obtain funding to reach a wider range of investors than would be possible if only straight bonds are issued. An even wider range of investors can be tapped if the bank or mortgage lender also includes mortgage-backed covered bonds in its offerings.

Another advantage of covered bonds, from both the issuer's and the investor's point of view, is that they do not automatically become due if the issuer becomes insolvent. Furthermore under some legal systems should the cover pool default the bondholders still have equal rights with unsecured creditors of the issuer.

Covered bonds denominated in euros are much used in continental European countries, particularly Germany which at the end of 2006 accounted for about one half of the total European market of 1.900 billion Euros. They make up the second largest segment of the European bond market, the largest being government bonds.

Northern Rock used covered bonds as part of its financing strategies, and as at 30th June 2007 had £8.1billion outstanding. This was a relatively modest amount compared with its use of RMBS issues that accounted for £45 billion at that time.

As mentioned above covered bonds remained as liabilities on the issuer's balance sheet, whereas residential mortgage backed securities (RMBS), after they have been produced by the securitisation process, were off-balance sheet transactions where the risks attaching to the underlying mortgage loans were removed from the lender's balance sheet. At the same time, the loans still appeared on the bank's balance sheet as assets.

Perhaps this was an ultimate form of financial alchemy.

Whilst our principal interest is with RMBS structures, securitisation covers many other forms of financial activity. They all contribute to the creation of an enormous market that now not only outstrips conventional commercial banking in global money volumes but one that has been estimated to be twice as large as the GDP of the United States.

It is all part of what is known as "the derivatives" market and the name applies to many different forms of structured securities. It is far beyond the scope of this chapter to review the workings of the derivatives markets or to attempt to explain how the various components are structured or used.

The fact is that this is a highly specialized area where even the participants may only be familiar with specific products or specific parts of the processing procedures and the manner in which they can be used. It can also be suggested that one of the reasons for the credit crunch which happened in 2007 was that not enough of the participants, and in particular their senior managements had a sufficient understanding of the markets in which their institutions were operating, or for that matter, the extent to which they were committed. They appear to have failed to fully identify the extent of the potential risks involved.

This was not for the first time and Union Bank of Switzerland (UBS) and Royal Bank of Scotland were prime examples as we shall see.

One critic even made the point that the problem in at least one major bank, which had to write down several billion on its holdings of collateralized debt obligations, was that its senior management officers were not even aware that their bank held those securities.

These may be pretty unpalatable suggestions, but there is just too much supporting evidence. If it was otherwise, one is at a loss to find an explanation as to why bank managements would allow their institutions throughout the world to engage so heavily in a business that would rack up such huge losses in 2007-08 and even bring about the downfall of a number of major banks, as we shall see in later chapters.

What is of particular interest to us, however, is the manner in which Northern Rock used the derivatives market. We shall study this in Chapter 5.

4 Fannie Mae and Freddie Mac

As mentioned earlier, prime lenders in the USA are afforded access to the secondary markets for securitisation and funding services through the medium of two **Federal Government Sponsored Enterprises** (GSE's), Fannie Mae (**Federal National Mortgage Corporation** or FNMC) and Freddie Mac (**Federal Home Loan Mortgage Corporation** or FHLMC), which purchase conforming loans from mortgage lenders including banks and either retain them on their own balance sheets or package them into residential mortgage backed securities (RMBS) which they sell on to banks and investors. In this manner they obtain additional funds to make available to prime lenders – principally banks.

Both entities also issue lenders with guarantees on qualifying loans. In this way lenders are relieved of the principal risks attaching to their loans.

Those two entities were created by the Federal Government to fill a void, namely, the need to provide loans for lower income families. As part of the package with which they were endowed, the Charters gave them exemption from state and local taxes (but not from Federal taxation), an ability to borrow money to finance their activities at lower than normal market rates and as we shall see later, an implied government guarantee.

Although jointly they have financed almost half of the overall US mortgage market of 10-12 trillion dollars, their ability to fulfill their original role has been overshadowed by the growth in recent years of both bank lending (by-passing Fannie and Freddie and going straight to securitising banks and insurers on Wall Street) and the "other" category of lenders noted in Chapter 2 that were courted by the same Wall Street banks who, in order to satisfy investor demand, were in search of even higher returns on their RMBS packages for both themselves and their investment clients.

Prime loans normally fall into two categories, "conforming" loans and "jumbo" loans, the first being much more common.

"Conforming" in this context means mortgages that conform to the standards set, both as to risk assessment and maximum amount loaned, by the GSE's. Both GSE's are regulated by the US Department of Housing and Urban Development (HUD) and its Office of Federal Housing Enterprise Oversight (OFHEO), but The Federal Housing Finance Reform Act of 2007 already passed by the United States House of Representatives, when finally approved is intended to consolidate oversight for Freddie Mac, Fannie Mae and the Federal Home Loan Banks into a single regulator.

"Jumbo " loans are those that exceed the GSEs' upper lending limits that are set from time to time and linked to general inflationary increases in property prices. They will be prime loans agreed in appropriate circumstances for qualifying borrowers.

Fannie Mae and Freddie Mac both started life sponsored by the US Federal Government. In 1968 first Fannie Mae and then in 1970 Freddie Mac became listed corporations owned by shareholders. Neither they, nor securities issued by them, were funded or protected by the US Government. This was explicitly stated in the law that authorized GSE's, on the securities themselves and in public communications issued by the GSE's.

However, they enjoyed the confidence of Government and also a general perception by investors and others that they were backed by an implicit Government guarantee. In addition, although they broadened their activities into all sectors of the mortgage market except (at least by direct involvement) the subprime area, they retained the advantages given to them in their original Charters, something that competitors regarded as giving the two companies unfair and unwarranted advantages.

By March 2008, the collapse of the securitisation markets generally began to reverberate through Freddie and Fannie's world, leading a number of commentators to speculate on just how "implicit" the federal government guarantee might be. As we shall see later, this "implicit guarantee" was put to the test in July 2008.

How do they operate and how do they compare?

Fannie Mae

Fannie Mae's website describing itself (early 2008) included the following descriptions of its role:

> Fannie Mae was created by Charter in 1938 under President Franklin D Roosevelt at a time when millions of families could not become homeowners or risked losing their homes for lack of a consistent supply of mortgage funds across the country. The Government established Fannie Mae in order to expand the flow of mortgage funds in all communities, at

all times, under all economic conditions, and to help lower the costs to buy a home.

In 1968 Fannie Mae was re-chartered by Congress as a shareholder owned company, funded solely with private capital raised from investors on Wall Street and around the world.

Fannie Mae has a unique duty to the public it serves—and the private investors that fuel its service—to be a model company focused on service, reliability and value.

It does not lend money directly to home buyers but it makes sure mortgage funds are consistently available and affordable by buying mortgages from a variety of institutional lenders. The primary lenders with which it has business associations include mortgage companies, savings and loan associations, commercial banks, credit unions and State and local housing finance agencies.

Mortgages that comply with its guidelines and loan limits can be sold to Fannie Mae. This is in keeping with Fannie Mae's mission to help more low, moderate and middle income people to buy homes.

Its loan limits are adjusted each year, in response to changes in housing affordability nationwide.

As part of the secondary market, Fannie Mae's role in providing a steady stream of mortgage funds to lenders across the country is complemented by new tautologies that make the process of buying a home quicker, easier and less expensive. It has developed automated systems that lenders are using nationwide, which allow many of their home buying customers to get approved for a mortgage loan more quickly and affordably than ever before.

What Fannie Mae's website does not choose to mention are its shortcomings, which demonstrate that whilst it could have been said that for a long time it carried out an important role fairly effectively, it was not immune to the buccaneering ploys that have permeated many parts of the financial services industry.

In 2004 the Office of Federal Housing Enterprise Oversight, in conjunction with several other bodies, carried out an investigation into Fannie Mae's accounting practices. It published a preliminary report in September 2004 alleging widespread accounting errors, including shifting losses for no better reason than to ensure that senior executives qualified for large bonuses. The Report was a comprehensive one running to 195 pages and identified a number of areas of sufficiently serious concern that the Company was required to restate its published accounts for all the periods between January 2001 and second quarter 2004 (its fiscal year 2004 accounts were not filed with the Securities and Exchange Commission (SEC Form 10K) until October 2006, such was the extent of the reworking of the accounts).

In the eventually published 2004 accounts the Company recorded that it started restatement in December 2004 and changes were also made in senior management when in December 2004 US regulators filed 101 civil charges against three top executive officers accused of manipulating Fannie Mae's earnings to maximize their bonuses. The law-suit sought to recoup $115 million in bonus payments collectively accrued by the three senior officers between 1998 and 2004, plus about $100 million in penalties.

Due to the complexities and the lack of effective internal control over financial reporting, it was reported that the restatement process required an extensive effort by thousands of financial and accounting professionals, including both employees and external consultants (which explains why the Company expected to spend more than $1billion up to 2006 to complete its internal audit and bring it closer to compliance). Adjustments to the accounts involved restatement of retained earnings to show a decrease of about $6.3 billion and other substantial adjustments.

In August 2007 Fannie Mae sought approval to extend its mortgage holdings by 10% in an effort to ease concerns about credit shortages and to provide help to the depressed housing market. This extension would have enabled the company to make another $72 billion available for the purchase of mortgages into its portfolio, but it was turned down by the Office of Federal Housing Enterprise Oversight on the basis that Freddie Mac's principle market for mortgages was liquid and working. At the same time, the regulator indicated that it would keep the situation under review.

The reason for its refusal was because the issues of liquidity and availability of credit were concentrated in the sub-prime, jumbo and Alt-A loan markets that were not markets in which Fannie Mae normally operated.

Although both Fannie Mae and Freddie Mac have limits applied by the regulators on the extent of the loans they are allowed to hold, those limits do not apply to mortgages which they package into securities. It followed therefore that by using that route they continued to ensure that conventional mortgages were made available for home-buyers without regulatory restriction.

That situation lasted until March 2008 when the regulator allowed an increase of up to $200 billion in the purchase of home loans by the two companies. Part of this would be found from the release of funds that the two companies had in hand as reserves against losses. Congress also increased the capacity of the two companies to acquire mortgages by temporarily increasing the "conforming loan limit" from $417,000 to $730,000 for the rest of 2008.

Not everyone supported the decision. Some considered that the capitalization of Fannie Mae ($45 billion) and Freddie Mac ($37 billion) was insufficient during times of market turmoil to support $1.4 trillion of combined debt and debt guarantees.

In political circles the "*U-turn*" by the regulator was very controversial. Some politicians were concerned that investors dealing with the two companies may have been placing too much reliance on the implicit guarantees of government backing and too little on the actual strength of the companies. Both critics and rivals expressed longstanding opinions that the so-called implicit guarantee meant that the risk would end up in the public sector while the profits of the two companies accrued to the private sector.

As noted elsewhere, the Federal administration has repeatedly said that no such implicit guarantee exists, but investors, particularly overseas investors in the securities packaged by the two companies were encouraged to believe that if the worst happened, the Government would provide a bail-out. Overall, Fannie Mae's operations are otherwise on much the same lines as those of Freddie Mac, as described below.

Freddie Mac

In the same manner as Fannie Mae, Freddie Mac does not itself make loans directly to would be house buyers. Its role is to set standards, fund lenders and so enable them to make conforming mortgage loans, and to buy the resulting mortgages from the lenders so that it can package them into saleable securities in order to raise further funds for its lending activities. It also retains a proportion of the loans on its own books.

Another very important role it undertakes is the issue of guarantees on the loans it processes, for which it charges fees. Loans carrying a Freddie Mac guarantee were considered to be very desirable in the securitisation markets, partly because of the perception of an implicit Federal Government guarantee, as mentioned above. Senior officers on overseas marketing trips were understood to have encouraged investors to believe that Fannie and Freddie paper was as good as US Treasuries.

Despite the general collapse in the RMBS markets in the latter part of 2007 (and continuing into 2008), in January 2008 Fannie Mae marketed three year and five year tranches of notes amounting to $4 billion each through a consortium of Wall Street issuing banks. Bearing in mind that the RMBS securitisation market world-wide had been frozen for several months, that was quite an achievement. Northern Rock had to retain its September 2007 issue of about £5 billion as there were no takers for it.

Non-GSE loans that pass through the securitisation process are normally guaranteed by third party insurers, but as we shall see later, those insuring corporations, and there are only a handful which conduct most of this guarantee business, found themselves in serious financial difficulties by late 2007.

The Website of Freddie Mac from which the following quotes are taken, describes all aspects of its operations, its objectives and also produces comprehensive statistics on mortgage lending.

> *Created by Congress, Freddie Mac's job is to ensure a reliable supply of funds to mortgage lenders in support of home ownership and rental housing. It attracts capital from around the world to finance housing in America, and it constantly innovates to deliver it as effectively as possible. As a result, mortgage rates are lower, 30-year fixed rate financing is plentiful, and borrowers get loan approvals in minutes.*

This last piece of information, "borrowers get loan approvals in minutes" is an interesting one that flowed from the automated underwriting and loan processing computer programmes described in Chapter 2.

> *Freddie Mac achieves its aims through partnerships with other similarly committed groups which include local and State government entities, non-profit organizations and non-lender participants in the housing industry. It claims to be dedicated to working with these and other organizations to provide the service and innovation necessary to continue the record growth of home ownership in America.*

> *It states that the nation's home ownership rate had reached a record high, with record numbers of families of all racial and ethnic backgrounds owning homes. Playing a vital role in the nation's mortgage markets, Freddie Mac has opened doors for more than 50 million families. Still, less than half of America's minority households have achieved the dream of home ownership.*

> *Freddie Mac's "Expanding Markets" products and services are more accessible than ever before, providing lenders with the solutions they need to reach more borrowers and make a difference in their communities. Together we work with community housing organizations and non-profit agencies to strengthen communities.*

We're up to the challenge of doing more. Building on our strong record of expanding access to the mortgage market, Freddie Mac has launched a number of high impact initiatives to accelerate the growth in minority home -ownership. Our initiatives range from best in class homebuyer outreach and education to new technologies and mortgage products designed to put families into homes they can afford and keep.

Making the rental housing market more affordable is another part of Freddie Mac's business. From investing in low-income housing tax credit partnerships to developing mortgage products that speed the construction and rental of very low income housing, the multi-family division has made affordable housing possible for more than 4 million families.

On a separate page Freddie Mac published a "Mission statement".

Freddie Mac's mission is to provide liquidity, stability and affordability to the housing market.

Congress defined this mission in our 1970 Charter, which lays the foundation of our business and the ideals that power our goals.

Our mission forms the framework for our business lines, shapes the products we bring to the market and drives the services we provide to the nation's housing and mortgage industry. Everything we do comes back to making America's mortgage markets liquid and stable and increasing opportunities for home ownership and affordable rental housing across the nation.

Our mission strives to create:

Stability: *Freddie Mac's retained portfolio plays an important role in making sure there's a stable supply of money for lenders to make the home loans that new homebuyers need and an available supply of workforce housing in our communities.*

Affordability: *Financing housing for low and moderate-income families has been a key part of Freddie Mac's business since we opened our doors. Freddie Mac's vision is that families must be able both to afford to purchase a home and to keep that home.*

Liquidity: *Freddie Mac makes sure there's a stable supply of money for lenders to make the loans new homeowners need. This gives everyone* *better access to home financing, raising the roof on home owning opportunity in America."*

It all sounded great, but was it?

The mission statement read as if it had been compiled by a Saint Freddie. Like so many corporate mission statements it turned out to be more of a wish list rather than a statement of applied policies. The management of corporate bodies does not seem to realize that it is never sufficient just to believe in "I say, therefore it is so". As we shall see later, even as late as August 2008 both companies refused to publicly acknowledge what became a fast deterioration in their ability to operate normally.

In September 2007 Freddie Mac claimed to have toughened its lending standards by imposing additional restrictions with a view to improving sub-prime lending practices. In this manner it sought to set stricter rules relating to the mortgages which would qualify for purchase by it. Freddie Mac did not purchase sub-prime mortgages, however it appeared to participate in the sub-prime market by investing in,

> *highly rated triple A bonds backed by sub-prime mortgages- - - - given our role as a GSE, we chose this financing strategy <u>as a prudent way</u>* (my underlining) *to provide liquidity to a largely untested segment of the mortgage market. These investments have been critical to our ability to meet our annual affordable housing goals.*

The person who said that on behalf of Freddie's management must have regretted that he ever thought it up. The credit rating of RMBS and other derivatives will be considered in Chapter 6.

The release went on to say,

> *"Beginning September 2007, Freddie Mac is restricting our sub-prime investments in securities backed by short term hybrid adjustable rate mortgages (ARM's) to those that have been underwritten to a fully-indexed, fully-amortizing level. We are also significantly restricting the use of stated income in lieu of more traditional documentation standards for sub-prime mortgages backing the securities we purchase. As an additional consumer protection, we are encouraging sub-prime lenders to escrow borrower funds for taxes and insurance. Since 2000, Freddie Mac has taken unilateral, voluntary leadership positions that have helped improve sub-prime market practices.*

But not by enough.

Undoubtedly, Freddie Mac, and its sister Fannie Mae with the support of State and Federal laws, and oversight by HUD (US Dept of Housing and Urban Development), oversight that for some years was too lax and was subject to serious criticism, has done much to improve the conduct and availability of reasonably priced mortgages. However, it begs the question, if a major part of its mission was to ensure financing of housing for low and moderate income families, why did the parallel sub-prime market grow to such an extent during the same period that it brought about the collapse of the mortgage finance market, both its own market and the prime market?

In November 2007 "The New York Times" examined information releases from Freddie Mac from which the reporter noted that although Freddie Mac did not buy sub-prime loans, it appeared to have acquired enough poor quality loans to noticeably affect its 2007 results. Its chief financial officer, Anthony S Piszel, was quoted as saying,

> *The underwriting standards declined, across the board. Those who made loans and expected to sell them quickly did not care much about assuring that the loans would be repaid. It turns out that the financial wizards who made it easy to transfer risk also assured that more risks would be taken. They produced innovations like "nina" loans, which,* Mr Piszel said, *found their way into prime space.*

"Found their way into prime space" could possibly be interpreted as "our controls were not good enough to identify them", or perhaps it was a euphemism for "we looked the other way".

The newspaper report continued, "Nina" stands for " no income, no assets". It does not mean that the loans went to people without either assets or income, only that borrowers were not asked if they had either. The reporter went on to say that although he had known about "stated income" loans (self certification loans in the UK), also commonly referred to in the trade as "liars loans", for which the bank or lender took a borrower's word for how much income he earned, the reporter had not realized that one could borrow money without even being asked about one's income.

There was also a third category colloquially referred to as "ninja" loans—"no income, no job and no assets"!

Freddie Mac appears to have taken on such loans routinely, because it eventually identified them and in November 2007 it stopped giving a guarantee on them.

The newspaper reporter also recorded that enough borrowers were defaulting on loans, none of them classified as sub-prime, to cause Freddie Mac to mark down the value its portfolio in 2007 by $1.2 billion. Furthermore, for the third quarter of 2007 it reported a

$2 billion loss that created a need for it to contemplate raising large amounts of new capital if it was to keep buying loans.

The report continued by suggesting that a kinder interpretation would be that competition forced Freddie Mac to lower its standards. Either way, the information released by Freddie Mac demonstrated that its standards had been eroded. None of the loans on its books from 2003 or earlier called for payments of interest only. Almost a quarter of the loans it bought in 2007 had that characteristic.

It also appears, from the same article, that whilst Freddie Mac did not guarantee any sub-prime loans, it did help to finance them by purchasing over $19 billion of securities backed by sub-prime mortgages. It did not plan (early 2008) to sell the securities and expected them to be paid off eventually, therefore it did not see a need to report a loss on them. At the same time, it could not possibly sell them in the market existing in 2007 or in 2008 for anything like what they cost. What that decision meant is that it saw no need to apply an "impairment charge" as part of a "fair market value valuation" in accordance with accepted accounting practices, although at the same time it maintained that its actions were within accounting rules. That did not prevent some analysts suggesting in July 2008 that the company was technically insolvent under fair value accounting rules if the company put a market value on its assets as if it had to sell them.

It was by no means alone amongst financial institutions in adopting an attitude that could possibly be described as "if I shut my eyes it will go away".

The story did not end there. On 11th November 2007 it was reported that Freddie Mac would suffer a credit hit of $12 billion as a result of a "cool down" in sub-prime mortgage payments in the United States. Its chief executive, Richard F Syron told investors that "credit losses would total approximately between $10 billion and $12 billion", which is difficult to reconcile with the positive mission statements regarded as current less than three months earlier.

In an earlier year, 2003, the company revealed that earnings had been understated by almost $5 billion, one of the largest corporate re-statements (at that time - pre Enron) in US corporate history. As a result it was fined $125 millions. The Office of Federal Housing Enterprise Oversight indicated in a 200 page report that the company's records had been manipulated to meet Wall Street earnings expectations. The corporation was required to sign a consent order promising to improve internal controls and corporate governance. Yet in mid-2008 the regulator was still complaining about the need to improve internal controls

Following that episode, in April 2006 Freddie Mac agreed to pay a $3.8 million fine to settle allegations that it had made illegal electoral campaign contributions. No doubt as part of its extensive political lobbying efforts.

After reading of the problems discovered at both Fannie Mae and Freddie Mac and the comments of outsiders one has to question the extent to which they have lived up to their mission statements although we must not decry them altogether.

They both did much to improve and steady US mortgage markets and they managed to maintain an active and always available supply of funds for prime conforming mortgages through the troubled times of 2006 and 2007 into 2008, but they were obviously not immune to the general canker that had spread through the mortgage industry at all levels, including the "securitization" processes. There was far too much concentration on increasing "shareholder value" and thereby ensuring that big executive bonuses would be paid. Between 2003 and 2004, Richard F. Syron, Freddie Mac's CEO picked up $38 million.

If we continue the Freddie and Fannie story into 2008 we find a disastrous deterioration in the fortunes and performance of both Freddie and Fannie.

During April 2008 the Federal Reserve Chairman Ben S Bernanke and the Treasury Secretary Henry M Paulson Jr both urged Freddie Mac and Fannie Mae to raise additional capital from investors. On May 14 Freddie Mac announced that it intended to raise $2.75 billion in new common stock from investors that was additional to the $25 billion Freddie and Fannie had already asked investors for since December 2007. However as the share prices of the companies declined week by week, raising new funds became increasingly difficult.

It was also noted in May that the two companies had guaranteed or had invested in a very substantial amount of sub-prime and ALT-A loans. Bad news about the operations of the two companies seemed to filter out daily. Public pronouncements by senior executives of the two companies maintained that the concerns expressed by government, regulators and the media all overstated the extent of their problems.

On July 7 shares of both plummeted. After falling almost continuously over the previous month, in just one day Freddie Mac tumbled another 18 percent, and Fannie Mae lost 16 percent resulting in a loss in share values of more than 60 percent of its market value since the beginning of 2008. Freddie closed on July 7 at $11.91, the company's lowest price since 1994. Fannie fell to $15.74, its lowest level since 1992. As a result of their falling stock prices, both organizations were finding that their ability to borrow in the market place was becoming more expensive. In addition it was costing three times more to buy insurance on a two-year Fannie bond than it had three years previously.

On July 11 Shares of Freddie and Fannie plummeted again into single figure prices as it became known that President Bush's administration officials were considering a plan to have the government take over one or both of the companies and place them in a "conservatorship" if their problems worsened. Under a conservatorship, the shares of Fannie and Freddie would be worth little or nothing, and any losses on mortgages they owned or guaranteed would be paid by taxpayers. As Freddie and Fannie were involved with about $5 trillion of mortgage debt that included the sub-prime and ALT-A loans mentioned above, the bill which taxpayers could be called upon to meet under this plan was potentially enormous.

Government officials said that the administration had also considered calling for legislation that would offer an explicit government guarantee on the $5 trillion of debt owned or guaranteed by the companies. But that was a far less attractive option, they said, because it would effectively double the size of the public debt.

Notwithstanding those announcements, in July 2008 government officials stressed that no action by the administration was imminent as Freddie and Fannie were not considered to be in a crisis situation. Because the mortgage backed securities issued by Freddie and Fannie were held by a variety of overseas financial institutions and by investors such as sovereign funds and central banks, the US authorities were concerned at the potential damage that a collapse of Freddie and Fannie would inflict on economies worldwide and on international perception of the financial condition of the USA.

There were strong political connotations to Freddie and Fannie's problems. Senator John McCain, the presumptive Republican nominee for President, said he supported federal intervention to save Fannie or Freddie from collapsing.

> *Those institutions, Fannie and Freddie, have been responsible for millions of Americans to be able to own their own homes, and they will not fail, we will not allow them to fail. They are vital to Americans' ability to own their own homes and we will do what's necessary to make sure that they continue that function.*

It became increasingly apparent that the political fallout from a collapse of Freddie and/or Fannie had become the primary consideration. Concern was expressed that in the event of a government bail-out taxpayer's money should not be used to prop up private shareholders. However, Mr. Bush implied a willingness to do just that. At a news conference he indicated that as long as shareholders owned Fannie and Freddie, any new government aid would not be deemed a "bail-out."

A government rescue would have to take control of Fannie and Freddie until the housing crisis passed, something that could take several years, and then consider how best to sever the links between the government and the companies. The risk to taxpayers was seen to be too great to allow them to continue in their then current form.

If a "bail-out" became necessary, the government would have to consider how it could continue the companies' original mission, namely, to ensure that underserved groups have access to mortgages and that low-income housing needs are met. The perception, in some quarters, was that the country needed a Fannie and Freddie (or at least one of them) to continue to perform their functions, which were central to the smooth functioning of the wider financial markets in the US. That view was not shared by many Senators and other political figures whose opinions were that Freddie and Fannie were not essential in their then current form. They should be allowed to slowly run down their activities over a period of 5–10 years during which time market forces would ensure that their business would be taken up by other financial institutions. Little did those senators and others realize that within three months many "other financial institutions" would themselves disappear.

Neither company granted mortgages directly to borrowers. Their business was essentially one of either guaranteeing and holding mortgages that they purchased from lenders and raising funds, much of it in international markets, against the security of the mortgages that they had purchased. By way of illustration, by July 2008 Asian institutions and investors held $800 billion of Freddie and Fannie securities, of which $376 billion was held by China and $228 billion by Japan. Luxembourg investment companies held $39 billion and in Belgium $33 billion, whilst investors in Russia held $75 billion and in the UK $28 billion. Middle East and other sovereign wealth funds were also large holders of unspecified amounts.

Whatever changes had become necessary, one thing was certain, the future of Fannie and Freddie would have to be quite different from their past.

Why would this be necessary?

Both had a long history of extensive, and expensive political lobbying at the highest levels. In the previous six years they spent $170 million on such activities and in contributions to political parties. As a result it could be said that they were able to fend off regulators and legislation mooted from time to time to prescribe their activities. Regulators had been subject to criticism for lax or indifferent supervision. Senators and Representatives in government were said to have placed a higher value on campaign contributions than on their duty to legislate against the excesses of the financial markets and those of Freddie and Fannie.

Why was there little or no attempt made to curtail the activities of the two companies to ensure that the extent of the liabilities they incurred bore an appropriate relationship to their capital and assets?

The answer that was repeated year after year was that Freddie and Fannie were doing a great job enabling more Americans to realize the American dream of every man owning his own home. Remember, that was their original *raison d'etre*. The problem was that by 2004 or so they had grown to such a size that they were vulnerable to any downturn in the economy or the housing markets.

It was considered by some that it would have been preferable if the bulk of the business that they conducted had been spread over a larger number of market players. In that way, if one or two got into trouble there would not be a systemic risk to the whole financial system. Furthermore, the regulatory supervision of a fragmented industry would probably have been much more effective since the regulators would not have had to battle with two giants that were protected by their size and an effective political lobbying organization.

Freddie and Fannie, when they were first created fulfilled a very necessary purpose on a manageable scale. As the US economy expanded after World War 2 the two agencies increased the volumes of business undertaken. In 1968-70 it was decided that they should become stock market quoted companies rather than government agencies. From then on they had a succession of ambitious CEO's anxious to expand the business for the benefit of shareholders (and of course, themselves). By the 1990's and early 2000's the economy was booming and the need for housing finance expanded rapidly, as we have seen in Chapters 2 and 3. Freddie and Fannie were at the center of this and their businesses grew exponentially without intervention by either legislators or industry regulators.

Executives at Freddie and Fannie appear to have subscribed to the general view that house prices would keep rising forever and as indicated earlier, paid insufficient attention to the deterioration in the quality of the mortgages they acquired and to the problems in the subprime market that from early 2006 became increasingly evident.

In 2003 a "New York Times " article included the following:

> *Lax regulatory oversight of these companies is made more worrisome by confusion over the extent to which Uncle Sam backs them up. An "implied guarantee" gives Freddie and Fannie a competitive advantage in the marketplace, part of which is passed on to home- buyers. But there is a danger in having the market place complacently assume that normal risk assessments need not apply to these players. Their current regulator is ill equipped to keep tabs on Freddie and Fannie's sophisticated hedging strategies and other financial moves they use to manage their huge investments.* (My underlining)

In February <u>2004</u> *the* "New York Times" published another article that discussed suggestions that a Bill would be presented to better regulate the activities of Freddie and Fannie. A comment made was that,

> *There is a low probability that a bill which is hostile to Fannie and Freddie will be passed. Unless the Congress is confident that they are doing something that is not harmful to the housing market, they will do nothing.*

Also in 2004 David A. Andrukonis, then the company's risk officer had warned the new CEO of Freddie Mac, Richard Syron that Freddie Mac was buying loans that,

> *Would likely pose an enormous financial and reputational risk to the company and the country.*

His warning was ignored.

Freddie and Fannie's woes were not an overnight happening, they had been building up for many years.

Not everyone ignored the signs. Alan Greenspan, the former Federal Reserve chairman, testified year after year that Fannie and Freddie had become so large, and took so much risk, that they could one day damage the nation's financial system but he was ignored by the same members of Congress that usually regarded him as a fount of all wisdom in financial matters.

In the summer of 2005, a bill emerged from the senate Banking Committee that considerably tightened regulations on Fannie and Freddie, including controls over their capital and their ability to hold portfolios of mortgages or mortgage-backed securities. All the Republicans voted for the bill in its committee stage; all the Democrats voted against it.

Although Freddie and Fannie had "missions" (As noted earlier in this chapter), their executives concentrated more on growth that would be reflected in improved share prices and, of course, in their cash bonuses and generous stock options. Executive remuneration had been substantial for many years. In 2003 it was calculated that the then CEO, Franklin D. Raines (although about to lose his job) made $90 million in his six years as CEO, notwithstanding the serious accounting scandal on his watch, as related earlier. Although Fannie was fined, Mr. Raines never gave up any of his bounty. In 2007, despite all the problems that were surfacing at the two companies, their CEO's jointly pocketed $30 million of cash and stock.

The Bail Out

The stories of Freddie and Fannie, their growth, activities and problems could quite easily fill a book by themselves. What has been presented in this Chapter is a snapshot of the two companies and their involvement in the general credit crisis by tracing their histories up to mid-2008, terminating in the rescue package that President Bush, although he had initially resisted the proposals, signed into law on 30th July 2008, notwithstanding that as recently as 11th July 2008 the Treasury Secretary and the Chairman of the Federal Reserve both said that Fannie and Freddie were "adequately capitalized", implying that they had sufficient cash and other assets to withstand the turbulence in the markets.

The package was intended to achieve two objectives. Firstly to authorize the Treasury to take whatever steps became necessary to rescue Freddie and Fannie should it appear that they were on the verge of collapse. At the same time it appears to have been believed in some quarters that these powers would not actually need to be activated. Their mere existence was thought to be sufficient to reassure investors and the financial markets

The second part of the package was intended to provide an opportunity for about 400,000 deserving homeowners to pay off mortgages with which they had become unable to cope and replace them with more affordable government insured loans. The proposals required lenders to agree to take losses by reducing the principal of each loan prior to its being refinanced by the government.

There were provisions in the proposals for the Federal Housing Administration (FHA) to insure up to $300 billion of such loans, although it was not anticipated that the take-up would amount to that much. Other provisions meant that the original lenders would have to contribute to an insurance fund and borrowers would have an annual 1.5% fee to pay.

Other provisions were for limited housing-related tax breaks and grants to local authorities to acquire and refurbish foreclosed properties. The new law and some of its provisions were highly controversial in political circles, but as well as helping mortgagees in trouble they were intended to protect the US economy and US international standing.

Early in September 2008 the CEO's of the two companies met with bankers in New York to seek assurances regarding the continuity of funding and the provision of additional capital resources from financial markets, but their efforts proved unsuccessful.

They had reached the end of the line.

As a result, the crunch came on Sunday, 7th September 2008 when the Treasury Secretary, Mr. Paulson, announced that the government plan to deal with Freddie and Fannie's problems would be implemented and that with immediate effect he was placing the two companies into conservatorship, somewhat akin to a bankruptcy reorganization under Chapter 11. The plan also provided for the replacement of the two CEO's by Mr. Paulson's appointees. The plan had been worked out over several months and was extensive in its scope. The following are some of its provisions.

It would not involve immediate taxpayer loans or investments.

- The two CEO's would remain during an unspecified transition period.

- It would enable the Treasury to ultimately purchase the companies outright at little cost.

- There would be no more dividends to shareholders, although the shares would continue to be traded.

- Principal and interest payments on the companies' debt would be protected.

- Both companies would be forced to reduce the size of their portfolios by 10% per year beginning in 2010.

- The Treasury would purchase significant amounts of their mortgage backed securities on the open market. As a start, it was proposed to purchase $5 billion during September.

There was further detail as to the manner in which the Treasury would endeavour to limit potential taxpayer losses and at the same time benefit from the restructuring of the two companies, whose long-term future would be decided by the new administration some time after the Presidential elections in November 2008.

Mr. Paulson ended by saying,

> Market discipline is best served when shareholders bear both the risk and the reward of their investment. Whilst conservatorship does not eliminate the common stock, it does place common shareholders last in terms of claims on the assets of the enterprise.

This has been a rather lengthy review of the activities of Freddie and Fannie, but they each played a very significant role in the US mortgage markets with such disastrous effects in the USA, UK and elsewhere. It is important that we understand the part that these two companies played in the credit crisis.

Because they became too large, because they far exceeded their original brief and because they allowed too great a deterioration in their operating standards, they were instrumental in extending the subprime crisis into one that encompassed the entire mortgage and RMBS industry.

They virtually destroyed themselves.

5 Granite Master Issuer PLC

The off balance sheet conduit or Special Purpose Vehicle (SPV) used by Northern Rock is known as **Granite Master Issuer PLC**. It formed the core of the RMBS securitization structure used by Northern Rock to raise funds in the derivatives market.

Nothing better demonstrates the mystery that surrounds the use of derivatives than the 2007 history of Granite Master Issuer Plc. It was clear at the time from press comment, and even the initial questioning of the Northern Rock Chief Executive, Adam Applegarth by the House of Commons Select Committee, that its structure was not understood.

That there was a lack of general understanding was apparent from the following excerpts quoted from an article headlined "**Revealed: massive hole in Northern Rock's Assets**" in the "Guardian" Newspaper on 23rd November 2007. The article was in relation to the (at that date) £23 billion "lender of last resort" borrowing by Northern Rock from the Bank of England,

> *Fresh doubts emerged last night about Northern Rock's ability to repay the £23bn of taxpayer's money it has been lent by the Bank of England.*
>
> *A Guardian examination of Northern Rock's books has found that £53 bn of mortgages - over 70% of its mortgage portfolio - is not owned by the beleaguered bank, but by a separate offshore company - - - -.*
>
> *The mortgages are now owned by a Jersey-based trust company and have been used to underpin a series of bond issues to raise cash for Northern Rock. It means that the pool of assets available to provide collateral for Northern Rock's creditors, including the Bank of England, is dramatically reduced, calling into question the government claims that tax payers' money is safe.*
>
> *This week the Chancellor, Alistair Darling, told parliament taxpayers' money was safeguarded. "Bank of England lending is secured against*

assets held by Northern Rock.   These assets include high quality mortgages with a significant protection margin built in and high quality securities with the highest quality of rating" he said.

The article then went on to describe, in detail, how the reporter, Ian Griffiths, found evidence of a deterioration in the quality of business undertaken, in support of his statement that,

A number of bidders have expressed an interest in buying Northern Rock but the offers have been below the stock market price of the shares suggesting that there are concerns about the bank's underlying value.

The Guardian analysis has also discovered that Northern Rock has admitted being in breach of the conditions of the securities it has sold through its Jersey-based Granite Master Issuer, the company which packages and sells mortgage backed securities, but it has decided to ignore the breach. The breach occurred in September when Fitch, one of the main ratings agencies, downgraded Northern Rock's long term credit ratings.

The article did not explain the reason why Northern Rock had decided that the breach was not significant for note holders, namely that as it had unlimited access to funds from the Bank of England, the breach could be regarded as a technicality arising from circumstances which had not been envisaged in the Notes Prospectus. Fitch did not downgrade the notes issued by the Granite conduit, which remained AAA.

Richard Murphy, a forensic accountant and director of Tax Research and who has followed the Northern Rock affair and scrutinized its relationship with Granite, is concerned that the division between Northern Rock and Granite has been blurred, creating uncertainty over its mortgage portfolio.

This should be a concern for the Bank and the Treasury particularly if the emergency loans have actually been used to finance the activities of Granite rather than Northern Rock. It would be harder for the government to secure preferential treatment over other creditors if it is shown that the money was actually for Granite's benefit, he said.

Focus of attention in the Northern Rock saga has shifted to a web of offshore companies under the Granite name used by the bank to raise funds to support its mortgage lending. The credit crunch stopped further fundraising through Granite and forced its management to seek emergency funding from the Bank.

In addition to its funding activities through Granite, Northern Rock had also funded about £25 billion through relatively short loans raised in the inter-bank markets. Although such loans are normally granted for short periods, this is a commonly used method of financing by banks amongst themselves and it is normal for loans to more or less automatically roll over into new loans at maturity. The inability to roll over or renew these loans because the entire market had "frozen" and banks were unwilling to make loans to each other was a very unusual occurrence. In consequence Northern Rock was obliged to seek assistance from the Bank of England. It was not due primarily to an inability to make further issues through the Granite conduit, although that also had an affect on its immediate liquidity problem.

The article continued,

> Critics said the complex web of assets held in the Granite scheme blurred the ownership of the bank's mortgages, making it unclear how much of the assets the Bank (of England) would have a claim to if Northern Rock was wound up.

A response from Northern Rock was then quoted:

> Our Granite structure and programme reporting are open and transparent.

> Northern Rock has assets of over £100bn. Only around half of those assets are securitized as part of the Granite programme, leaving around £50bn of unencumbered assets.

> Against claims that Northern Rock's loan with the Bank of England is in the order of £23bn, this would therefore suggest that Northern Rock is able to cover such a figure by around two-fold.

Although it was true that only £23 billion had been borrowed (against the security of mortgages and other assets, and at a penal rate of interest), the bank also held around £24 Billion of depositors money and it was the withdrawal of a substantial but undisclosed amount of those deposits over a period of a week or two that gave rise to an immediate requirement for funds from the Bank of England. Further funds were drawn upon from the Bank of England over several weeks as it became virtually impossible to renew maturing loans in the inter-bank market.

With regard to the withdrawal of deposits, possibly £1–3 billion was withdrawn in a few days but the main problem was that even after the Government guaranteed all deposits then in the bank, depositors continued to withdraw large sums, possibly up to £10 billion more over ensuing weeks. The problem seemed to be partly because depositors had no faith in the Government guarantee. Alternatively they believed that if the bank went down, it would take some time to recover funds under the guarantee. A secondary influence was that the management of Northern Rock appeared to be paralysed as it did very little to reassure depositors or to make it worth their while to keep deposits with the bank.

Apart from vague references to "over-reliance on wholesale funding" there were no other media comments about the use of derivatives in the weeks following 14th September 2007. Variations on the Guardian newspaper report were quoted by other media sources and included such headlines as " **New Worries over Northern Rock Assets**", **"Northern Rock has 53 Bn Sterling of mortgages owned by offshore company"**. A second article published by the Guardian on the same day carried the headline

"How bidders took fright at the hole in Rock's books. Doubts over whether the Bank of England's loan would be supported by assets."

To say the least, the Guardian reports contained a number of inaccuracies which demonstrated a lack of understanding by the reporter, and also seemed to be more concerned at hinting at the use of some form of underhand and secret "web" of offshore companies which had cast into doubt Northern Rock's ability to repay the Bank of England borrowings amounting to £23 billion, than explaining an established and commonly used funding technique.

Because that is what it was at the time, a well established and universally used method by which mortgage lenders used existing mortgage loans to raise new funds to finance more mortgages, as was explained in the last chapter. Northern Rock may have used the facility to excess in its pre-occupation with growing its business rapidly and positioning itself ever higher in industry league tables, and the whole securitization process had serious questions hanging over it as to the conduct of some of the major banks that promoted it, but we shall return to those aspects later.

So, how does the Granite conduit structure operate?

We have examined some of the benefits bestowed by RMBS conduits in the previous chapter but it is appropriate now to take a look at the particular structure used by Northern Rock. This is best achieved by an examination of the chart in Table 16 and then considering the role of each of the constituent parts.

Anyone interested in a full examination of what is typical of an RMBS structure should look up a Prospectus for a Granite Master Issuer PLC Note Issue, of which there were a number. One can be obtained by typing "Granite Master Issuer" into Google, or from the Northern Rock Treasury website.

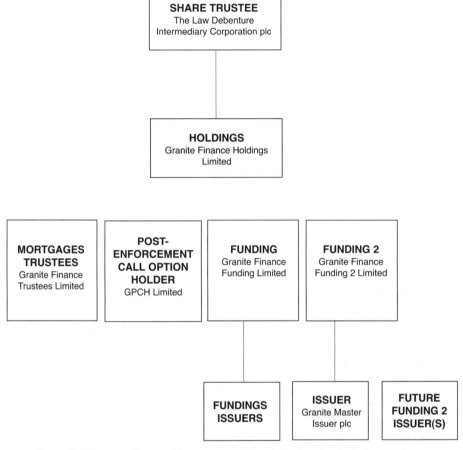

Figure 2 Diagram of ownership structure of the principal parties to the transaction

The base company is Granite Finance Holdings Ltd. (Holdings). The entire share capital of this company is held on trust by The Law Debenture Intermediary Corporation PLC, a professional trust company unaffiliated to Northern Rock PLC, under the terms of a Discretionary Settlement for the ultimate benefit of one or more charities. Holdings is organized as a special purpose company whose principal objects are set out in its memorandum of association and are:

> *To acquire and hold, by way of investments or otherwise and to deal in or exploit in such manner as may from time to time be considered expedient, all or any of the shares stocks, debenture stocks, debentures or other interests of or in any company (including the mortgages trustee, Funding 1, Funding 2 and the Post-enforcement Call Option Holder).*

Any profits received by Granite Finance Holdings Ltd, after payment of its costs and expenses, will be paid for the benefit of the Down's Syndrome North East Association (UK) and for other charitable purposes selected at the discretion of the professional trust company.

This arrangement has no effect on payments due to note (bond) holders.

A point which has to be understood is that Discretionary Settlements (Trusts) which are usually set up in an offshore jurisdiction, are regularly used where it is desired to keep an investment holding company separate from the persons or corporation that would otherwise be the shareholders or beneficial owners. Although the shares in the company are held for the ultimate benefit of charitable bodies, the reality is that in most such cases very few shares are issued and therefore their value is quite limited.

The company may acquire other funds including those derived from profits that are applicable to shareholders but the assets of the company used in the conduct of its business would not be included. As the company is essentially a conduit for funds, it is not likely to produce much by way of profits attributable to the beneficiaries of the Discretionary Settlement.

For those reasons it was appropriate to record that the trust arrangements would have no effect on note holders.

We can now consider how the Granite structure operates.

Granite Finance Holdings Ltd has four wholly owned subsidiaries as follows:

The first is **Granite Finance Trustees Ltd** and it is a special purpose private limited company incorporated in, and with its registered office in Jersey, Channel Islands. This and other companies in the structure are created as "special purpose" companies, that is to say, each undertakes a specific type of business function in the securitization process and will not be used for any other purpose. It is quite common to provide such a limitation within the Memorandum of Association of private investment holding companies.

Granite Finance Trustees Ltd is identified as "the Mortgages Trustee". Its purpose is to acquire from time to time additional trust property (qualifying mortgages) from Northern Rock (the "seller") and to hold all of the trust property on trust for the seller, Funding and Funding 2 (see below) under the terms of the mortgages trust deed. It is mostly passive in nature.

To explain this in simple terms, when Northern Rock wishes to raise new funds from

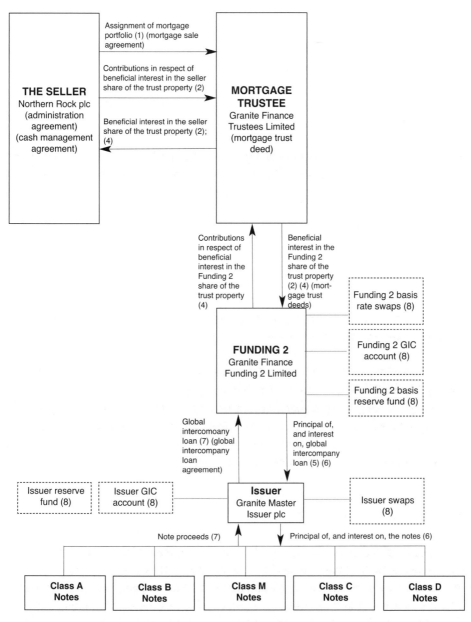

Figure 3 Structural diagram of the securitisation transaction

which to finance further mortgage loans, it does so by transferring a package of mortgages (which individually have to meet specified standards for inclusion in the package) to the Mortgages Trustee. The Mortgages Trustee does not <u>own</u> the package but holds the capital value of the mortgages on trust as follows:

- Firstly, as security backing for the issues of notes for the benefit of the note-holders.

- Secondly, as security backing for the operations of Funding and Funding 2.

- Lastly, to the extent that these obligations have been fully met, for the benefit of Northern Rock.

Northern Rock has a residuary entitlement over the mortgages because it is in the nature of securitization structures that the liabilities arising from the issue of Notes are initially secured to a far greater extent than is strictly necessary. This is in order to ensure adequate cover in the event of mortgagees defaulting or the underlying properties securing the mortgages falling in value below the amount of the mortgage loans.

In addition, it is a feature of the securitization structure that the obligations to note-holders are satisfied out of the monthly instalments of interest and capital repayments made by mortgagees and which are collected by Northern Rock and passed through the conduit to note or bond-holders as appropriate.

Other subsidiaries, **Granite Finance Funding Ltd** (Funding) and **Granite Finance Funding 2 Ltd** ("Funding 2") are special purpose UK incorporated private companies. Funding and Funding 2, which each have a beneficial interest in the mortgages trust, have each established and may establish issuers that have issued and will issue notes which are ultimately secured by the same trust property (primarily consisting of the mortgage portfolio) as the notes offered by Granite Master Issuer. Subject to certain exceptions, allocations of the proceeds of the trust property, including receipts of principal and interest on the mortgage loans, will be made *pari passu* and *pro rata* as between Funding and Funding 2.

Their function is to borrow money from Granite Master Issuer PLC in accordance with the terms of the Global Inter-company Loan Agreement. They use the borrowed money to pay contributions to the mortgages trustee for the Funding and Funding 2 shares of the trust property pursuant to the trust deed or to re-finance existing loans made by Granite Master Issuer to Funding or Funding 2. They are mostly passive and have no employees. Funding 2 has one subsidiary, **Granite Master Issuer PLC**.

The **Global Inter-company Loan Agreement** is a complex one that is described in the Granite Master Issuer prospectus, but its *raison d'étre* is to regulate the purposes to which loans between Granite Master Issuer and Funding 2 are put. It is an essential part of the mechanisms for passing through the proceeds of sales of Notes to the other parties in the structure, when and in such amounts as they are entitled.

GPCH Ltd – the post enforcement call option holder is the fourth wholly owned subsidiary of Granite Finance Holdings Ltd. It is organized as a special purpose UK incorporated private company. Its objectives are set out in its memorandum of association

Granite Master Issuer PLC is a public limited company incorporated in England and Wales. It has its registered office in London. It is another special purpose company and is a wholly owned subsidiary of Granite Finance Funding 2 Ltd. Its purpose is to issue notes from time to time that represent its mortgage backed obligations. It uses the proceeds of the note issues to lend amounts equal to the proceeds of the notes to Granite Finance Funding 2 Ltd. It does not engage in any activities unrelated to its declared purpose.

The Notes or bonds issued under the securitization programme are sold globally through agents to international investors who will include sovereign investors, corporations, pension funds, hedge funds, insurance companies and other investors with substantial funds to invest (it is common practice to issue notes with a minimum denomination of $100.000, and for investors to take them up in tranches counted in millions). Such investors customarily invest through the Eurobond markets where periodic interest on their bond investments is paid without deduction of an income or withholding tax. Eurobonds issued on behalf of (principally) multi-national commercial corporations and other institutions have been available for over fifty years and form a major investment market organized principally out of jurisdictions such as Luxembourg, Jersey, Netherlands Antilles and Grand Cayman.

In order to achieve gross payment of interest, the bonds or notes have to be issued by a company incorporated in a jurisdiction that does not deduct tax on distributions of interest. These are, for all practical purposes, "offshore" financial centres of which Jersey is an example. This is the principal reason why the Granite conduit for the securitization of assets by Northern Rock is based in Jersey.

There was no underlying questionable motive.

Another important objective of the securitization process is to transfer risk. If a company such as Northern Rock issues notes (or bonds) directly to investors, the notes would remain as a liability on its balance sheet. It would have full corporate responsibility for payment of periodic interest and for repayment of the notes at maturity, and being a bank, would have to maintain the appropriate level of approved capital funds in order to meet regulatory capitalization requirements.

The legal structures created in the securitization process are designed to remove the notes from Northern Rock's balance sheet and thereby transfer the risks attaching to the notes, namely that interest on them will not be paid on the due dates and that the notes may not be repaid in full at maturity.

Once the risk has been transferred off Northern Rock's balance sheet, it has to be borne elsewhere. Typically, securitization processes transfer all the risks attaching to the notes to the note-holders. Naturally the investor will expect to be given some form of assurance that his investment is of good quality. This is achieved by "credit enhancement" in the shape of a Credit Default Swap (CDS) arrangement. This is arranged by the swap provider that purchases a financial guarantee, much the same as an insurance, to cover the default risk. The cost of CDS cover will depend on the rating of the issuer of the bonds. CDS guarantees are generally provided by monoline insurers as described in Chapter 6.

This guarantee, together with the fact that the issue of notes will be secured by a package of quality mortgages of much higher total value than the note issue, is sufficient to ensure that the notes will be awarded a "AAA" rating by a major credit rating agency such as Moodies, Fitch or Standard and Poors.

It follows, therefore, that the real purpose of transferring risk from the bank that arranged the securitization to the note-holders is not simply to saddle the note-holders with risk, but rather to remove the liabilities from the bank's balance sheet and so to reduce the amount of qualifying capital that has to be held for regulatory reasons.

The sub-prime crisis changed all that.

In addition to the foregoing company structure, there are a number of other functions that have to be undertaken by someone. As these companies are passive in nature and do not have their own staffs, Northern Rock contracts with them as appropriate to function as seller, administrator, cash manager, issuer cash manager, account bank and as a Swap Provider.

The seller originates each of the mortgage loans that it assigns to the mortgages trustee. It is apparent from media coverage over several months in 2007-8 that this has been a misunderstood part of the securitization process. The originating bank, Northern Rock in this case, does not sell the mortgages to Granite Master Issuer, which has no beneficial interest in the mortgages *per se*. The mortgages are assigned to the mortgages trustee (Granite Finance Trustees Ltd) as security for the note issues. Interest payable on the notes, and eventual repayment of them at maturity, as noted above, is paid out of the accumulation of monthly interest and capital repayments paid by the original mortgage borrowers and passed through by Northern Rock to Funding 2.

The seller, on behalf of the mortgages trustees and the beneficiaries (the note-holders), also acts as administrator of the mortgage portfolio under the terms of an administrative agreement. It collects the monthly payments on the mortgages and takes whatever steps are necessary to recover arrears. There are provisions of the agreement that cover its resignation, removal and replacement.

The seller is also appointed as cash manager for the mortgages trustee, Funding and Funding2 to manage their bank accounts, determine the amounts of payments due to them, arrange for payments to be made to them, and to keep records on their behalf. It also acts as banker to Granite Master Issuer and in that capacity determines the amounts of and arranges payments to be made by it and keeps records on its behalf.

Other financial institutions were involved in a variety of capacities.

Citibank NA was appointed an account bank to provide banking services to Granite Master Issuer. In addition Citibank NA in London and New York act as paying agents who make payments on the Notes to note-holders. The London office also acts as the agent bank that calculates the interest rate on the floating rate notes and index linked interest notes. Its last function is to act as registrar and transfer agent. It maintains the register in respect of the notes and is responsible for administering any transfer of notes.

LloydsTSB Bank PLC, Jersey, was appointed as Jersey account bank to provide banking services to the mortgages trustee.

The London office of The Bank of New York acts as trustee for the Funding 2 secured creditors (which includes Granite master Issuer) under the Funding 2 Deed of Charge. It also acts as Note trustee under the trust deed on behalf of the note-holders and it functions as the issuer security trustee, acting for the issuer secured creditors (including the note-holders) under the issuer Deed of Charge.

Northern Rock acts as the basis rate swap provider, having entered into the Funding 2 **Basis Rate Swap Agreement** with Funding 2. The swap agreements (there are several) are described in the Prospectus, but the following gives some idea of their complexity and content.

> *Each series and class of notes to be issued by us (Granite Master Issuer) from time to time may be denominated in different currencies and have a fixed or floating rate of interest (as specified in the relevant prospectus supplement. To hedge certain interest rate, currency and/or other risks in respect of amounts received by us from Funding 2 under the global intercompany loan agreement and amounts payable by us in respect of each series and class of notes, on the closing date for any series and class of notes we may enter into an issuer swap agreement with an issuer swap*

provider in relation to such series and class of notes. Each prospectus supplement will provide details of any issuer swap agreement in respect of the related series and class of notes including the name of the issuer swap provider.

The issues of notes are complicated further because notes are issued in series in respect of each tranche of notes issued. As Northern Rock accumulates a sufficient value of new mortgages over a period of some months, it finds itself in a position to arrange for the issue of a new series of notes. Each series has its own set of documentation that has to be registered with, and approved by the relevant regulatory authorities in the UK, USA (US dollar issues) and possibly in other countries where it is proposed to sell notes.

Each series of new notes issued on a single issue date typically consists of several classes of note, class A, and classes B, M, C or D.

A class designation determines the relative seniority for receipt of cash flows. The notes of a particular class in different series (and the notes of differing sub-classes of the same class and series) will not necessarily have all the same terms. Differences may include principal amount, interest rates, interest rate calculations, currency, permitted redemption dates, final maturity dates, and/or ratings. Each series and class of notes will be secured over the same property as the notes offered by this prospectus. The terms of each series and class of notes will be set forth in the related prospectus supplement.

*Some series and classes of notes will be paid ahead of others, regardless of the ranking of the notes. For example, some payments on some series of class B notes, class M notes, class C and class D notes may be paid before some series of class A notes, as described in –" **Payment priority and ranking of notes".***

*References in the prospectus to a " **series**" of notes refer to all classes of notes issued on a given day and any class of notes issued on any other day which: A). is expressed to be consolidated; and B). is identical in all respects (including as to listing) except for closing date, interest commencement date and issue price, with any of the classes of notes issued on such given day.*

*A class of notes of a given series may comprise one or more sub-classes. If a class of notes of a given series does comprise more than one sub-class, references to "**series and class**" will refer to a particular sub-class within such class.*

*Unless otherwise specified in the related prospectus supplement for the series and class of notes we may only issue such series and class of notes on the satisfaction of 12 certain tests, referred to as the "**issuance tests**", which are set out in **"Issuance of Notes – Issuance"**. In particular a note may be issued only if there is sufficient credit enhancement on that date in the form of outstanding subordinated loan tranches and reserves or other forms of credit enhancement, equal to or greater than the required subordinated amount for each outstanding class of notes. The required subordinated percentage for each class of notes will be specified in the applicable prospectus supplement. The required subordination for a class of notes may, subject to certain conditions, be increased or decreased without note-holder consent.*

In addition to the series and classes of notes, the supplement also lists the types of notes that may be issued within a series. They include Fixed Rate, Floating Rate, Index linked, Dual currency, Zero coupon Pass-through, Controlled amortisation, Scheduled redemption, Bullet redemption and Money market notes. This demonstrates the real need to pay close attention to all the terms and conditions before investing.

The various classes and sub-classes of notes are issued with differing interest rates and / or other terms in order to appeal to a wide range of investors who will typically have different objectives and investment criteria.

Additionally the various classes are subject to payment priorities and ranking of the notes. The highest-ranking issue is normally Class A, other classes ranking in succession below it. The purpose of ranking in each series is to give each class entitlement to prior payment of interest and principal ahead of the class ranked immediately below it. As a general rule, the lower the class in the ranking table, the higher the rate of interest it earns. Investors can therefore choose a higher level of security at the expense of acquiring a lower rate of interest. The differences are not great since it is an objective of the issuer that the whole of a series qualifies for a AAA or close credit rating.

There are many more pages in the Prospectus supplement that deal with the terms relating to notes and their issue but the foregoing gives some flavour of the complexity and depth of explanations contained in a typical prospectus.

In all, up to September 2007 Northern Rock used the Granite structures to process twenty-three RMBS issues.

The base cause of the sub-prime mortgage market crisis was the poor quality of the loans, not necessarily because of low quality real estate assets, but rather the frequently deliberate lack of proper assessment of the creditworthiness of the home-owners. This led to poor quality backing for the notes issued by the banks involved in the securitization process. It is worth noting that the two US companies Freddie Mac and Fannie Mae conducted a very substantial volume of Mortgage backed securitisation business but did not directly securitise sub-prime mortgages. It follows that somewhere in the even larger volume of securitisation carried out by the Wall Street investment banks there must be found the sub-prime mortgages that were at the root of the credit crunch and which were patently of inferior quality to prime mortgage loans. At the same time, the total volume of subprime mortgages in issue or in default was insufficient to account for the total collapse of values in the RMBS markets.

The notes issued through Northern Rock's Granite programme on the other hand were backed by high quality mortgage loans secured against properties that had all been professionally and independently valued. All of the mortgages held by the mortgages trustee were claimed to meet the high qualifying standards specified in the note prospectus for each issue. Contrary to the inferences found in some media reporting, Northern Rock appeared to have followed standards that were beyond criticism.

Under practically any circumstances one would be entitled to assume that the well-known banks that played the various roles described above each carried out due diligence on the Granite structure before they became involved and put their name to the process. But perhaps they didn't, perhaps they were just interested in the fees that were to be made.

The paragraphs in "italics" have been taken from one of the Granite prospectus supplements and could be supplemented by many other quotes if every topic is to be covered. A typical Granite prospectus supplement runs to 300 or more pages and it is quite beyond the scope of this book to cover them all.

The objective has been to give a flavour of the securitization process so that the average person can gain an outline understanding of what is involved. As will be discussed later, it was either a deliberate omission or an unwillingness to have proper regard for the processes involved which played a substantial role in the creation of the sub-prime crisis and the associated credit crunch.

The foregoing includes an abbreviated description of the Northern Rock securitisation structures, which are very typical of many such conduit structures used by banks in a number of countries, particularly in the USA, UK and Europe. As described in Chapter 3 such structures are used for the securitisation of other types of assets as well as for mortgages. The range of companies and the trust arrangements that are used has to be complex in order to separate the various functions and so to create the legal ownership structure necessary to achieve all the objectives.

If one is to understand what went wrong and what created the sub-prime crisis and the associated credit crunch, one must have a reasonable knowledge of why the securitisation process was created and how it is applied. Very few people, including senior finance professionals, acquire an adequate knowledge of the securitisation process as there are many, many variations on the basic concept. The documentation supporting the structures involved normally runs to several hundred pages of Prospectus, with a huge range of supporting and reporting documents.

It should be borne in mind also that all this documentation has to be lodged with the FSC (in the UK) and if the notes are being offered in the USA, with the Securities and Exchange Commission there, and the requisite regulatory approvals obtained. Which leads to another question that will be addressed in a later chapter, to what extent did the authorities examine and question the securitisation processes, and if not, why not? Both in the UK and the USA, they seemed perfectly content to let it all happen without question until a crisis point was reached.

The Granite Master Issuer and associated documentation for each of its Note Issues is very comprehensive in its description of the companies and trusts used, their locations and operation. It also provides many tables which analyze Northern Rock's operating criteria, voluminous information on mortgages and other relevant matters including, by way of example, in the case of one of its Issues 27 pages of explanations of possible risks to investors. There can be no doubt that as far as possible, Northern Rock and the law firms which drafted the documentation of Granite's note issues endeavoured to give a clear and complete description of the securitization process for the benefit of regulators, investors in the notes and other interested parties. On the other hand, perhaps what they intended was to "blind investors with science" or in other words, leave them to rely on the cleverness of the creators of the securitised bonds because there was too much information for investors to digest.

Although he can be criticized on several counts, Mr. Applegarth the Chief Executive of Northern Rock up to December 2007, was fully justified when he said that the Granite structure and reporting were open and transparent. The problem, particularly post-September 2007, was that those people commenting including self-styled financial journalists seem to have examined it very selectively if at all and many obviously did not understand the processes followed. Nor did they appear to be aware that securitisation was a much-used method of raising finance on a global basis.

There were literally thousands of ABCP issues. Many of them were issued through a few major Wall Street investment banks and the sheer volume would make it difficult to make assessments of their individual worthiness as investments.

6 Monoline Insurers and Credit Rating Agencies

Monoline Insurers

The term "monoline" was coined in 1989 when the State of New York, home state of most guarantors at the time, introduced new requirements for the capital structure of those insurers and restricted the type of risk they could take on to only one business line, i.e. the insurance of repayment of third-party debt. Those restrictive business policies typically earn monoliners a triple A rating.

However, financial guaranty insurance is generally acknowledged to have begun in 1971 with the insurance of a $650,000 obligation bond in Alaska. The first time a guarantee was called was in 1983 when the Washington Public Power Supply System defaulted on its debt repayments but insured bondholders were paid out in full and on time.

The bond insurance business carried on by these monoline insurers is that of insuring against bond defaults. It is a line of business which (in the USA) other insurers are not allowed to undertake directly. It was a little-known industry conducted by a small number of players until problems started to emerge late in 2007. It had a low profile because it was originally created to provide credit default swap (CDS) insurance by guaranteeing municipal bonds that were generally of high quality and defaults were rare. It enabled state and local governments to issue bonds in the capital markets at lower interest rate cost, even after paying insurance premiums to a monoline insurer.

This type of insurance was therefore an attractive and lucrative form of business.

As happened elsewhere in the financial world, the monoline insurers saw new business opportunities as the securitisation of mortgage backed securities mushroomed. The widely held view in the finance industry was that nothing could be safer than a property-secured mortgage loan. For a similar reason twenty-five years earlier, the big multi-national US banks plunged into sovereign loans (ie. Loans to foreign governments, many in the "third world"). The mantra of the banks was that "governments don't go bust".

Maybe they did not, but the bank's money often disappeared anyway, giving rise to substantial write-offs. An exception was Mexico that defaulted on about $90 billion of debt, principally to US banks which then had to "restructure" the loans – a euphemism for trying to salvage as much as possible on new terms.

From about 2003 the housing loan market expanded rapidly, there was a general consensus amongst financial professionals and estate agents that there would be never ending rises in underlying property values and all the time there was an endless queue of borrowers.

For all those reasons the monoline insurers identified a new market, which by US law, only they could service – an additional bonus, so over a few years before 2007 they entered the market in a big way, insuring hundreds of billions of dollars of bonds secured by, amongst the prime loans, a substantial amount of sub-prime borrowings.

Typical securitisation programmes for the creation of notes or bonds backed by residential mortgage loans, etc., as described in Chapter 3 require two additional "sales aids" – default insurance from a monoline insurer and a triple A credit rating (or close) from one or more of the principal rating agencies.

Credit Enhancement

Securitised bonds are structured in such a manner that the default risks attaching to the underlying mortgage loan and the originating lender are transferred to the note (or bond) holder. The note holder therefore seeks reassurance that the risk of default by the mortgage borrower has been minimized as far as possible. This is known as "credit enhancement".

Bond issuers that choose to buy insurance want to enhance the bond issue's rating to triple A in order to reduce net interest costs (after fees to the insurer) and secure a wider distribution. In practical terms, the triple A guarantor "wraps" its own credit rating around a debt obligation and guarantees its timely payment of interest and principal for a fee.

The distinguishing feature of monoliners is that their guarantee is unconditional and irrevocable and that a verifiable failure to pay by the issuer of the insured debt is all that is required for the protection buyer to be able to claim under the insurance policy.

Possession of these two facilities, default insurance from a third party insurer (rather than from a loan originator that could become insolvent) and a triple A credit rating was considered sufficient to ensure that default risks were fully covered.

That was the perceived wisdom and until 2007 it went unchallenged.

Expansion beyond the customarily safe municipal (muni) bond guarantee business into structured finance underwriting was driven by increasingly competitive industry conditions and tight credit spreads that reduced the potential premium income in their traditional "muni" business during the 1990s. By 1999 the new volume of more remuneratively insured asset-backed securities (ABS) for the first time exceeded that of insured munis.

To provide some idea of the size of the monoliner's market, as at the end of 2006, Fitch estimated that eight or nine principal monoline insurers had $ 2,515 billion ($2.5 trillion) of guaranty insurance on their books, of which only $273 billion was reinsured with other insurance companies.

The total was more or less equally divided between "muni-bond" business and a combination of international and structured finance that included RMBS as a component.

Capitalization by way of shareholder's funds of the eight principal monoliners at end 2006 was estimated at $24 billion.

Banks' total holdings of structured securities enhanced and hedged with insurers amounted to $820 billion and it was estimated by S & P that the monoliners guaranteed $127 billion of collateralized debt obligations (CDOs) linked to subprime mortgages.

The complexity of this market renders it difficult to make a meaningful analysis of the risks involved. Although our concern is with RMBS based exposures, the insurers also wrote business on many other forms of structured credit, or CDO's. However, RMBS were the second largest component representing 14% of the total, or $65billion.

As noted above, monoline insurers provide "external credit enhancement", meaning that their insurance cover for a RMBS or CDO tranche raised the tranche's rating to triple A. This was achieved because at the time the monoliners themselves enjoyed a Triple A rating therefore any RMBS issue they guaranteed inherited it.

A bank, for example, buys insurance from monoliners in order to hedge an open AAA position on its books. The financial guaranty shields the bank from mark-to-market losses, allows accounting for the position at par, and frees up regulatory capital. The quality of those hedges depends crucially on the counterparty's credit quality, i.e. monoliners themselves require a triple A rating if they are to operate effectively.

Until 2006, everything seemed to be going according to plan – profitability was good and default claims were low.

During 2007 sub-prime mortgagees in the USA began to default in ever increasing numbers as their two year fixed rate deals at relatively low interest rates ran off and they were required to re-mortgage at much higher rates. Questions began to arise as to the justifiability of the credit ratings that had been assigned to the RMBS bonds and also regarding the credit agencies themselves.

The two most important factors attaching to banks and most investment media are confidence and trust. Default insurance from the monoline insurers and AAA rating by the rating agencies was intended to enable investors to have complete confidence in their investments.

At the same time, bear in mind that the investors in securitised bonds are classed as being "sophisticated", in that they are major banks, pension funds, hedge funds, insurance companies, sovereign investment funds (of wealthy foreign governments) and other institutional investors, most of whom, if not all, can be expected to employ experienced analysts and investment managers.

Along came the collapse of the sub-prime market in 2007 and the insurers found themselves faced with very substantial potential losses with the prospect of even more losses in following years.

In February 2007 several large mortgage lenders involved in the sub-prime market collapsed and gave rise to a loss of confidence in the security of sub-prime backed notes. That was the beginning of the end, at least for the foreseeable future, of the sub-prime market and a real shake-up for the rest of the financial world.

We can now follow developments more or less as they happened.

16th June 2007.

The "New York Times" published an article which reported a further loss of confidence brought about by a surge in Treasury Bond yields due to a sizeable liquidation of bonds by hedge funds, and by rising delinquencies in home loans to people with weak or sub-prime credit. A loss of confidence was further highlighted when two hedge funds, sponsored by Bear Stearns, a major Wall Street investment bank, large underwriter of sub-prime bonds and one of the biggest traders in securities, sought bids for $4 Billion worth of sub-prime bonds after the funds faced substantial redemption requests.

This sale appeared to confirm the fears of many investors that losses would steadily increase as more sub-prime loans defaulted and more homes were foreclosed. Confirmation came from the Mortgage Bankers Association which reported that nearly 19% of all sub-prime loans were either past due or in foreclosure at the end of March

2007. It also recorded that the recent increase in interest rates and a glut of unsold properties available for sale would make it more difficult for borrowers to refinance or sell their homes.

Although bond holders may have started to worry, the financial "experts" in the banks seemed less bothered. Karen Weaver, the global head of securitization research at Deutsche Bank, was quoted as saying "This is not a cataclysmic event, it's a slow bleed". I wonder if she still has a job?

The "New York Times" continued,

> It remains to be seen whether the liquidation of sub-prime bonds by some funds will force others to sell to cover margin calls or to meet redemption demands by jittery investors looking to minimize their losses

> The paper then quoted Timothy D Rowe, a portfolio manager at Smith Breedon Associates, as saying, "that would depend on what kind of prices bonds being auctioned now fetch. The pressure to liquidate will be greatest on investors who borrowed heavily to trade those bonds, rather than the buy–to-hold fund managers." He also noted that while (mortgage) loans made last year are performing poorly, demand for bonds backed by mortgages made this year (2007), which have been made with more caution, appear to be holding up well. "A lot of the sub-prime market is still in good shape, its going to be around."

It sounds very much as if he was whistling in the wind.

Perhaps the best way to understand what monoline insurance claimed to provide is to consider the description given on the website of the Association of Financial Guaranty Insurers in the USA, as follows. The underlining has been applied to highlight matters where monoline insurers fell short during 2007/8.

> The monoline bond insurance industry provides services to one industry - the capital markets. _The complex nature of the capital markets requires that all participants develop a deep understanding of the strategic, tactical, regulatory, and technical aspects of the industry._ The monoline structure ensures that our full attention is given to adding value to our capital markets customers.

> By providing credit enhancement to capital markets transactions, monoline insurers provide investors and issuers with _financial security and liquidity_. Core benefits of monoline credit enhancement include:

confidence that an insured security will pay in full, even under worst-case stress scenarios,

an expertise in credit analysis allowing for the application of conservative, zero-loss underwriting criteria to insured transactions,

monitoring of collateral and servicer performance in order to take any action necessary to avoid deterioration of assets or underlying credit quality,

a level of scrutiny and analysis beyond the rating agencies, ensuring that most transactions are believed to be investment-grade before they are wrapped.

Our singular focus on serving the capital markets sets monoline insurance companies apart from traditional insurance providers. This focus has allowed us to develop financial guaranty policies that meet the unique needs of our customers. From underwriting to claims, every aspect of the monoline business is shaped around the needs and expectations of the issuer and investor communities. Thus, there are key attributes of a monoline guaranty that differentiate the monoline enhancement from traditional forms of insurance:

Timeliness of payment *- monoline insurance companies make debt service payments whenever an issuer is unable to do so. This is in contrast to multi-line insurance companies which may require a lengthy and unpredictable claims submission and adjustment process*

Experienced surveillance *- securities that carry a monoline insurance guaranty are monitored to detect and remediate problems before they occur*

Specialized reinsurance relationships *- monoline insurers have relationships with monoline and multiline reinsurance companies that help them to effectively spread risk and ensure that capacity is available for new policies. Multiline insurance companies may not always have these reinsurance relationships in place.*

That was the official industry view of itself. It was a pity that it may have been little more than another example of "I say, therefore it must be so".

20ᵗʰ December 2007

An article by Jim Willie on the "Kitco" website concentrated on one monoline insurer that even in the following months received little or no publicity. Even if his article is biased and only partially reflects the true situation, it is something of a revelation, although it has to be said that the remainder of his article was somewhat alarmist and was not confirmed by events over the following few months (but even in November 2008 it is early days, his prophesies may yet come true).

The opinions expressed may be somewhat skewed, but Jim Willy was possibly closer to the truth than the banks and monoliners cared to admit

The hidden bond insurers used by Wall Street firms are in the news. The list includes ACA Capital, MBIA, Ambac Financial, and Financial Guaranty Insurance. ACA Capital has only $1.1 billion in cash for payout of bond failure claims, but has lost $1 billion in the most recent quarter. Bear Stearns, the fifth largest US securities firm, owns a 39% stake in ACA Capital." (This is an interesting twist that does not appear to be featured in the later collapse of Bear Stearns.)

More losses are assured. Implications are huge, with monumental ripple effects. Financial press reporting of the bond insurers is woefully inadequate. Moodys and Fitch are giving analysis review to nine 'AAA' rated bond insurers to see if they have sufficient capital to conduct their insurance operations.

They have faced a likely downgrade by Moodys for weeks, sure to put in grave doubt the status of $652 billion of structured finance bonds, as well as state and municipal bonds that they insure. The world's largest bond insurer, MBIA beat the market to the punch in a surprising admission of having $8.1 billion in CDO bond exposure. They also opened the door to discussion of 'CDO Squared' derivatives, which are leveraged instruments built recklessly atop other leveraged mortgage bond securities. Expect the MBIA actual losses will ultimately be three to five times larger. MBIA, ACA Capital, and six other bond insurers sweat bullets over debt rating agency downgrades. A loss of their top rating would cast serious doubt on $2400 billion in asset backed debt securities collectively. Given the size of their total insured bond portfolios, Bloomberg Data estimates the downgrades could result in $200 billion in bond losses and bank write-downs.

The group of bond insurers combine to insure over 80,000 bonds and related securities. The insurers wrote contracts on almost $100 billion in risky CDO bonds backed by subprime mortgages as of mid-June 2007

according to Fitch. In June (2007), the value of bonds linked to credit default swaps rose to a staggering $42.6 trillion, up from only $6.4 trillion at year end 2004. Those figures are supplied by the Bank for International Settlements in Switzerland.

This part of the story covers the period beginning December 2007 and carrying through to August 2008. During that time there were many news reports of which most speculatively foretold the path that events would follow, and of course many merely repeated what had been related elsewhere. Those included here have been randomly selected from what were believed to be representative and reliable sources.

However, without seeing how the problems developed in such an *ad hoc* manner, we are not likely to understand why the problems became so serious and spread so widely and went unrecognized for so long. After all, it was initially a US domestic problem in a relatively modest sized part of the US financial markets.

23rd January 2008

The "New York Times" reported that Ambac Financial Group, one of the largest monoline insurers had announced that it "was exploring strategic alternatives" after a $3.6 billion loss for its 4th quarter of 2007.

Even a single quarter loss of that magnitude did not dampen speculators' enthusiasm. In Wall Street parlance, the newspaper reported, strategic alternatives means, amongst other things, a potential sale or outside investment. This caused the shares to recover by 28% on the disclosure that it was in talks with "potential parties".

Be that as it may, it has become increasingly difficult in recent years in financial and investment circles to separate rumour, sometimes deliberately spread around, from fact and so to identify proper justification for such substantial share price fluctuations.

In this particular case, the cause of the company's losses was a $5.21 billion write-down on its portfolio of credit derivatives, of which $1.11 billion related to sub-prime backed bonds.

As mentioned earlier, in order to function properly as an insurer, Ambac needed to retain a triple A credit rating on its own shares, but what happens if it or another monoline insurer loses its AAA-Rating?

First, the issuer's obligation is "wrapped" with the guarantor's rating which means that if the guarantor is downgraded, all the insured paper faces pressure for downgrades as well. "The Economist" reported that Fitch had proceeded to downgrade 137,500 bonds. The direct effect was a widening of spreads and higher interest payments on the insured paper by the issuer. In the $1.2 trillion muni-bond market the losses incurred through this channel are estimated to amount to $200 billion.

Secondly there was the effect on hedged and credit enhanced structured finance positions. Barclays Bank reported that, based on an estimated $820billion hedged structured finance positions with monoliners, banks would need at least $22 billion if the credit rating of bonds covered by insurers led by MBIA Inc. and Ambac Financial Group Inc. were cut from AAA, By way of an example, when ACA Capital was downgraded from A to CCC by S&P in December, Merrill Lynch was forced to write off $1.9billion of positions hedged with ACA.

Thirdly, as reported by *Fitch*, financial guarantors are net sellers of credit protection via CDS to the tune of $463billion, $287billion of which is written on corporate issues. This makes them important counter-parties in the financial system. Taking again the case of the ACA Capital downgrade as an example, the company on January 21 won a month's grace to unwind *$60 billion* of credit-default swap contracts that it can't pay.

To return to AMBAC, when it abandoned a plan to raise $1 billion in new capital, it lost its triple A rating. Fitch Ratings downgraded it, whilst Standard and Poor's and Moody's threatened downgrades. All of which resulted in a loss of three quarters of its capital value and in the dismissal of its chief executive.

Once again, however, one has to wonder just how seriously the company's Board viewed the situation. Its new chairman and acting chief executive, Michael A Callen was quoted as having said,

> We view the current perceptions of Ambac's business by both the market and rating agencies as underestimating Ambac's strengths and future potential. As the market normalizes and perceptions correspond more closely to reality, the market will more accurately assess our assets and strengths.

So what were those assets and strengths? Let us follow the course of Ambac over the next few weeks

The insurers were not the only organizations that were affected. State and local government bonds insured by them dropped in value, and those public bodies found it more expensive to issue new debt instruments. The contagion spread to major banks, Merrill Lynch and Canadian Bank of Commerce being named by the "New York Times" as two banks affected, in that sub-prime backed bonds issued by them and insured by Ambac dropped in value, raising the prospect, at that time, of greater losses for these banks.

24ᵗʰ January 2008

The "New York Times" recorded,

> *Officials began moving to defuse another potential time bomb in the markets: the weakened condition of two large (monoline) insurance companies that have guaranteed buyers against losses on more than $1 trillion of bonds. Regulators fear a possible chain of events in which the troubled bond insurers, MBIA and Ambac, might be unable to keep their promise to pay investors if borrowers default on their debt.*
>
> *That could leave the buyers of the bonds – including many banks and pension funds – on the hook for untold billions of dollars in losses, shaking confidence in the financial system.*

At last the penny seems to have dropped!

The "New York Times" article continued,

> *To avoid a possible crisis, insurance regulators met with representatives of about a dozen banks to discuss ways to shore up the insurers by injecting fresh capital, much as the Wall Street firms have turned to outside investors recently, after suffering steep losses related to sub-prime mortgages - - - - the talks focused on raising as much as $15 billion for the (two) companies. - - - - The notion that the failure of even one big bond insurer might touch off a chain reaction of losses across the financial world has unnerved Wall Street and Washington.*

The information coming out on the monoline problems seldom mentions that although the principal liabilities would fall on them, other insurers were involved as re-insurers to the monoline companies, although as noted earlier, less than 11% of the business had been re-insured. One article recorded that Assured Guaranty, a Bermuda-based financial services company that provides "credit enhancement products" to other financial institutions, announced that it was reinsuring $29 billion already insured by AMBAC which of course, apart from being an insurer, was also in the credit enhancement business.

As European insurers were heavily involved in the reinsurance industry, reports were coming out in mid-January of potential losses. French-Belgian bank Dexia said it and its bond insurance unit FSA had indirect financial exposure to Ambac totalling billions of euros. (Dexia had to be bailed out by the French, Belgian and Luxemburg governments in October 2008). Swiss Re, which also reinsured the business of the US monoliners, was hardest hit among Europe's insurers, losing 9.4 per cent of its market value. In December it said it had 2.8 billion Swiss francs in exposure to monoline insurers, 17 per cent of which was with Ambac. Of the total exposure, 1.7 billion Swiss francs was sub-prime.

Other European and British insurers mentioned included Allianz, stock price 9.1 per cent weaker, ING Group down 9 per cent, Zurich Financial 5.5 per cent off and Standard Life falling around 7 per cent. But a sector analyst thought the insurance sector was now oversold: "I think it is completely incorrect as the European insurers have very little exposure to the monolines."

Returning to the "New York Times", the newspaper then described at length the efforts of regulators to come up with solutions at meetings with executives of the insurers and of banks.

There were two principal regulators involved, Eric R Dinallo, the New York insurance superintendent who regulated MBIA, and Sean Dilweg the commissioner of insurance for Wisconsin, where Ambac is regulated. He is quoted as saying, *Eric (Dinallo) is looking at the overall issue, but I am pretty confident that we will work through Ambac's specific issues. They are a stable and well-capitalised company but they have some choices to make.*

Such as what?

> *Other options open to the banks include providing lines of credit and other backup financing to the guarantors. A chief goal of any rescue would be to help the companies regain or keep triple-A credit ratings which are seen as vital to their business.*

The article continued,

> *Whilst $15 billion might seem like a large amount of money for banks to commit to bond guarantors at a time when many investors have lost faith in them, it would be smaller than the billions the banks might have to write down if the companies lost their top ratings (in fact AMBAC had already done so) or incurred major losses. It's a calculated kind of risk.*

Whatever that means.

Notably, neither MBIA nor AMBAC were prepared to comment on their situations.

30th January 2008
Another article which appeared on the website of "The Street.com" and which quoted a review by Oppenheimer & Co, related how,

Bank write-downs related to monoline bond insurers will be concentrated largely at the firms UBS, Citigroup and Merrill Lynch. Oppenheimer financial analyst Meredith Whitney estimates that the risk of downgrades by rating agencies of monoline names MBIA and Ambac Financial would rack up at least $40 billion in write-downs and as much as $75 billion. UBS, Citi and Merrill would be among the hardest hit because those institutions hold about 44% to 45% of the risk exposure. As a result, Whitney notes that a systemic banking crisis caused by monoline downgrades might not be as great a risk as many believe, given the disproportionate exposures at the three banks.

Importantly, because we estimate that almost half of this risk is concentrated amongst three financial institutions with the remainder broadly distributed amongst many, there is no systemic risk at hand or immediate justification for a system-wide bailout, in our view. Whitney wrote in her note.

The article continued,

Merrill and its peers typically sell a large portion of the CDOs originated, but held onto what was considered the highest-rated pieces, known as super-senior triple-A paper. Those arcane securities, which should be valued at 100 cents on the dollar, however, have already plummeted in value to as little as 20 cents on the dollar in some cases amid the mounting mortgage crisis. The massive decline in value so far has served up huge losses on the balance sheets of investment banks and financial firms, and a downgrade of monoliners means further pain.

It also recorded that,

Merrill originated $31 billion in CDO paper last year, representing 18% of the total origination volume. Citi grabbed CDO origination market share of 16%, issuing $28 billion. UBS kicked in $21 billion for a share representing 10%, the analyst estimates.

The market share of origination was so skewed toward the top three that they encompassed the equivalent of 13 of the top 20 issuers' volume between three companies, Whitney writes in her report.

Whitney estimates that Merrill, Citi and UBS's heavy origination in 2007 of funky mortgage paper known as collateralized debt obligations account for the trio's massive exposures to monoline bond downgrades. CDOs are pools of debt that has been sliced and diced into pieces that are then rated by Fitch Ratings, Moody's Investors Service and Standard & Poor's and sold to investors.

Whitney's research report comes on the heels of Zurich-based UBS' warning of a fourth-quarter net loss of $11.4 billion or 12.5 billion Swiss francs. The bank said the loss was driven by write-downs of about $14 billion to U.S. subprime paper.

French bank BNP Paribas also posted a 42% decrease in fourth-quarter profit to $1.47 billion, along with a write-down equivalent to about $870 million on its exposure to monoline insurers.

While we had previously believed the monoline insurers MBIA and Ambac were too important to fail due to the threat of systemic risk and thus would likely be bailed out, we no longer think systemic risk is even realistic or a bailout of the monolines even viable, Whitney wrote, as quoted in a *"Dow Jones Market Watch"* report.

Although the issue of bonds was centred on the banks mentioned above, many other banks and institutions bought the bonds and held them as "assets for sale" or treasury assets. Those institutions holding the bonds were, in general, writing down their value by up to 80% because the market for such bonds had, at least temporarily, ceased to exist. At the same time, subprime bonds at $1.3 trillion represented only 10% of the whole RMBS market and in the subprime area only 20-25% of mortgages had defaulted. Even then losses were recouped in a fair number of cases when the repossessed properties were sold. This makes one question why there were such huge write-downs of the value of these bonds and in the share values of banks, monoliners and hedge funds, etc., the write-downs in share values appear to far exceed the extent of the potential losses, much of which have been written-down, or written-off out of current profits.

It was all down to a loss of confidence in the banks and of the banks in each other and had very little to do with the actual situation.

Returning to the "New York Times" article, it then reviewed a range of relative, if speculative comment by various parties, before commenting on the defence put up by the insurers.

The companies have defended their assumptions. They also note that losses on the bonds that they insure would have to rise substantially before they would have to pay claims, and even then they would make interest *and principal payments over the life of the bond, not all at once. MBIA has estimated that in the worst case, which it described as a one in 10,000 event, it expects to incur losses of $10billion, a fraction of the $673 billion it has insured.*

If the regulators had seen the penny drop, it did not seem as if the insurers chose to do so.

Other comments, by Walter B Kielholz chairman of Credit Suisse were quoted,

I am not sure that discipline was maintained, also, there was a rapid turnover of young analysts at the agencies, giving rise to problems.

He also argued that blame should be spread around,

What happened to caveat emptor? There seems to be an entitlement that rating agencies be right, and that the highly compensated analysts for institutional investors not be expected to do their own analysis.

If we take the documentation of Northern Rock's bond issues as an example, it contained very comprehensive information on the issuer, the back up mortgages for the bonds and on the terms of the bonds themselves, such as would enable a bond holder or its analyst to make a full assessment of the degree of risk being undertaken by the bond holder independently of a credit rating agency rating, provided he was willing to read through the several hundred pages of documentation that was available to every investor..

Whilst there is considerable merit in Kielholtz' last comment, there seems to be a game of "pass the parcel" going on in which every player hopes that it will not land in his lap when the music stops.

1st February2008
The "Times" newspaper ran an article headed "**Stakes in the ratings game are still rising**".

The piece pointed out that without their triple A rating, AMBAC and MBIA, the two biggest monoline insurers would no longer be able to charge for their guarantees. Without the guarantees, more than $2000 billion worth of bonds that carried bond guarantees could also be downgraded, forcing investors who prize security to sell.

A lack of guarantees would also affect banks such as Citigroup, Merrill Lynch and UBS whose derivatives contracts with the bond insurers could look more risky, forcing huge write-downs. The article then covered some of the subject matter of the "New York

Times" articles noted above, before ending with a quote from an anonymous banker,

> *All the parties are in a frenzy, but it is all within the context of potential downgrade. The rating agencies risk downgrading too soon, and looking stupid, or downgrading too late, and looking stupid. We think they are more likely to take the risk of acting too soon in the current environment.*

That not untypically ambiguous style of comment was of very debatable use to anyone studying the nature of the market problems.

2ⁿᵈ February 2008

"The Times" reported that Royal Bank of Scotland and Barclays Bank had joined six other banks to work on a $15 billion rescue plan for the struggling mortgage bond insurance industry. This was the same plan as "The New York Times" had mentioned on the 24ᵗʰ January, as noted above.

The article reviewed the situation in much the same way as "The New York Times" coverage, but added,

> *If they are to survive, the insurers need multi-billion dollar cash injections or to find a buyer, analysts argue. Merrill Lynch, Citigroup and UBS are among the banks that have taken hefty write-downs this year on the prospect that insurers of its bond portfolio will not be able to pay up. However, the losses would be far bigger and more widespread if the insurers start to withhold claims payments, as further declines in confidence would push the bottom out of an already fragile bond market. A meltdown among the key bond insurers (bear in mind that there are only half a dozen of them) could easily lead to a further $100 billion of losses at banks worldwide, on top of the $135 billion that they have already taken, S & P said.*

The article concluded by quoting "experts" as believing that as much as $200 billion, not $15 billion is needed.

"All parties declined to comment on the bailout consortium".

2ⁿᵈ February 2008

"The New York Times" also returned to this topic and in addition to re-iterating part of the information it had covered earlier, pointed out that,

> *The banks participating in the Ambac talks are said to be those that have most direct exposure to that company, people briefed on the talks said.*

> *Likewise other banks that have heavier involvements with MBIA and Financial Guaranty are working on plans to help those companies.*

> *Generally speaking these deals are being commercially driven, said one person briefed on the negotiations, It is related to each bank's own situation.*

Which amounts to "financial speak" for "the banks were looking after number one".

Later in the article the newspaper recorded that,

> *The insurers' problems also raise questions about how closely the companies were supervised in recent years when they insured tens of billions of dollars of complex investments tied to risky mortgages and consumer loans.*

So where were the regulators?

The Wisconsin regulator, Dilweg, said,

> *He was confident that the company (AMBAC) was in sound financial health but was working with the company as it develops and implements its business plan in response to current market conditions. For the protection of policyholders, Wisconsin has substantial financial requirements pertaining to municipal bond insurers, he said in a statement. AMBAC meets and exceeds all these statutory requirements.*

Behind the long running problems besetting the financial world runs another story. The story relates to the company executives who appear to be cocooned in a world of their own. This is only a minor sample, wait until we see how the real winners fared.

Contemporaneously with the announcement of its capitalization problems, AMBAC disclosed in a regulatory filing (not in a public or stockholder announcement, that would have been indelicate), that it was granting cash bonuses of $700,000 and $800,000 to four senior executives, who also received stock options and restricted stock awards that will vest in three years time.

The cash will come in handy, but they had better work very hard during the next three years if the options are to be worth anything.

3rd February 2008
The "Financial Times" recorded that,

Leading private equity firms are unlikely to participate in any recapitalization of AMBAC and MBIA, increasing the pressure on banks to come up with a rescue package.

The reason for non-participation was that they concluded that the risks were far too great.

There is another aspect to this. Private equity firms, if they assisted, would do so by investing in equity and would stand to lose their investment if the insurer became insolvent. The banks are more likely to structure their aid in such a manner as will at least leave them as creditors of a bankrupt insurer, and maybe even as a preferred creditor if they financed through something like a "covered bond".

The managing director in charge of financial service investments for one of the leading private equity funds was quoted as saying,

If we worry that we can get shot from the shadows by something we can't see coming, it is not for us. The financial guarantors pass neither the shadow test nor the ability to understand test.

The paper ended by suggesting that,

The next two to four weeks will be vital for the bond insurers because the biggest ratings agencies have made it clear they are very close to cutting their ratings. Fitch, a smaller ratings agency has already cut the triple A ratings of AMBAC and MBIA.

When different ratings agencies can award different ratings at the same time, one has to question the accuracy and validity of their rating procedures.

5th February 2008
"The New York Times" carried a heading **"Bond Insurer Trials Threaten Banks as Ross Circles".** This article demonstrates the manner in which the whole financial scene can be likened to a pool of water into which a relatively small pebble is thrown. The ripples spread out until they have covered the whole pool.

In this case the "pebble" is represented by the monoline insurers, the "ripples" by the affect on each area of financial activity. In this case, the banks made up the first ripple. The newspaper reported that,

Commercial and investment banks could see their credit ratings cut if the bond insurers which hedge some of their assets were themselves

*downgraded, Standard and Poors said, as billionaire investor Wilbur Ross
mulled whether to invest $1 billion or more in the sector.*

*The S & P report drove home the importance of the bond insurer's financial
health to the wider financial services industry, which has already taken
more than $100 billion in write-downs on sub-prime related assets and bad
loans.*

The paper went on to describe how Wilbur Ross, who often sought opportunities in
troubled industries, expected to reach a decision on an investment "very shortly".

Following the analogy of the ever-increasing circles, the paper dwelt on the ways in
which some banks could be affected.

*S & P said the highest potential losses for banks, stemming from bond
insurer down-grades might be in hedges that bond insurers provide for
pieces of collateralized debt obligations – complex debt comprised of a
variety of assets, such as sub-prime mortgages. To date, losses that banks
have reported on the CDO exposures have predominantly been on un-
hedged exposures. However, $125 billion of sub-prime related CDOs
hedged by bond insurers remains concentrated in the hands of a relatively
small number of banks. Few banks have disclosed how much that
exposure is.*

*In the municipal bond market, banks have also provided liquidity lines to
some special-purpose entities that fund muni (municipal) bond investments
wrapped by bond insurers. With investors skittish about the strength of the
bond insurers that guaranteed such investments, banks are being forced
to take some of the bonds back on their own balance sheets. That could
curtail the amount of liquidity banks have available for other needs*

This article gave some idea as to just how far the ripples could spread, although at the
same time, the complexity and particularly the lack of transparency in the securitization
markets managed by major banks, plus the reticence of the banks in the provision of
meaningful information made it very difficult to assess the true situation.

However, what is one man's poison, is another man's meat, which is particularly true in
the world of high finance. Take this "blog" published on the "**Money**" website by "ED"
about the report that Warren Buffet had offered an escape route to Ambac and MBIA.

*Warren Buffet spent half an hour on the phone with CNBC on TV this
morning, talking about an offer he made last week to the top three*

"monoline" bond insurers (MBIA, AMBAC, FGIC) to reinsure their municipal bond business — but not their far riskier and depressed structured finance (CDOs and the like) business.

The insurers' stocks are up on the comments at the moment, but for no good reason. Buffet's refusal to capitalize them means they're dead meat, and probably sooner than later.

And once they fall (or merely lose their triple A ratings), a body of structured finance bonds they insure, larger than the body of failed sub-prime mortgage bonds, will sweep banks and insurance companies worldwide up in another, deeper round of losses, approaching systemic insolvency.

The price Buffet's asking from the bond insurers for this reinsurance is all the income (cumulative incoming premiums on an ongoing basis) on their munipal bond business plus another 50%. Thus, the insurers would pass thru to Buffet all their income on their muni business and pay him another 50% for the privilege.

Buffet justified this 150% take by noting that his new bond insurance company, formed late last year, is already receiving 200% from individual muni bond issuers to reinsure their bonds. So his offer to do it wholesale — to reinsure the entire $800 billion of munis that these three monolines currently insure — for 150% is, from one angle, cheap.

Nevertheless, by stripping the insurers of their reliable, secure muni income, and doing nothing to fix their bleeding s-f (structured finance = mortgage backed bonds) business — which almost certainly will bankrupt them unless somebody gives them a ton of support, which Buffet has now publicly declined to do — the plan is no better, for the insurers, than a vulturous bankruptcy wind up.

It is better for the muni bondholders currently insured by the distressed monos, in that they would know they've got the Buffet backstop regardless of what happens to the monos.

But there seems no reason for the bond insurers or their shareholders to celebrate here. They are indeed being picked over by a (gentlemanly, salt of the earth) vulture.

None of the insurers have accepted this lousy offer. One suspects Buffet has now gone public with it in a spectacular way (the half hour call on TV)

*because he wants the world to know he's waiting outside the door when
the bond insurers get drawn into bankruptcy or similar regulatory regimes.
At that point regulators one way or another will cut the municipal bond
business from the carcass.*

This article may be a bit "over the top" but it is also close to the mark in places. Such articles have been quoted as being illustrative of the influences to which the public (including investors) were subjected daily at the time. Their principle effect was not to tell us how bad things were but rather to unnecessarily undermine confidence in the financial situation.

6th February 2008

"Reuters" reported on a British Government plan to restore confidence in the covered bonds and mortgage backed securities market. This was described as a partially politically motivated attempt for the Labour Government to regain the initiative after the freezing of the securitized debt markets and Northern Rock damaged its reputation for economic prowess.

The report then quoted from the text of a speech by Alistair Darling, Chancellor, at a businessmen's conference,

> *The Government will consult on a new "gold standard" for covered bonds
> and mortgage-backed securities—which will help not just the housing
> market but wider economic growth in these uncertain times.*

In view of the record of the regulators, Governments and the global banking industry during 2007, one wonders if such a consultation would not be a case of "the blind leading the blind".

14th February 2008

The "Financial Times" ran a heading "**Bond insurer FGIC tells regulator it will split**". The story read,

> *Privately held bond insurer Financial Guaranty Insurance Company
> confirmed on Friday that it wished to split into two companies. The news
> follows moves by Eliot Spitzer, New York Governor, (and former NY
> Attorney General and "bête noir" of the finance industry) who on Thursday
> gave bond insurers three to five business days to find fresh capital, or face
> a potential break-up by state regulators who want to safeguard the
> municipal bond markets.*
>
> *Mr Spitzer's warning came shortly before Moody's highlighted concerns*

about the bond insurers by withdrawing its triple A rating from FGIC. Eric Dinallo, New York's superintendent of insurance confirmed on CNBC TV that FGIC had told the regulator that it wished to be split into two. Investors had expected the move.

However, the sting of Moody's downgrade was mitigated by its more positive comments about MBIA and Ambac, the two largest bond insurers, which helped to send their shares up 8.4% and 12.4% respectively, in New York trading.

This last comment on the trading of shares in the two insurers was typical of stock market activity throughout the sub-prime crisis. Virtually on a daily basis, a piece of good (or better) news was almost immediately reflected in a noticeable general stock price rise, and equally, less good news resulted in a fall. Those price movements did not always signal activity by genuine investors. They were short term movements carried out by speculators, who much of the time, sat at the trading desks of banks, hedge funds and other institutional investors, trading and "shorting" large volumes of shares all day long, every day, in affected companies.

That topic will be examined in detail in the Chapter on the trading, or possibly more appropriately, the gambling in Northern Rock shares.

The article covered other aspects of the immediate problems of the monoline insurers and concluded,

Mr Dinallo said the regulator would allow bond insurers to split into two companies. - - - - If we do not take effective action, this could be a financial tsunami that causes substantial damage throughout our economy.

Mr.Dinallo also said "he was considering rewriting the rules for bond insurance to prevent companies taking inappropriate risks".

The main purpose of the "split" into two companies was to insulate the municipal bond business from the now seen to be much riskier mortgage backed bond issues. If defaults on the latter continued to be experienced, as seemed most likely, the capitalization of the monoline insurers would be insufficient to enable, amongst other problems, a triple-A rating for the insurers. Without it, they would be unable to conduct the muni-bond business, which in truth, was their only profitable business following the crisis in the sub-prime market. A key factor in making the split was how capital funds would be apportioned between the two companies.

By mid-March 2008 the current state of play in relation to the losses both projected and actually suffered by the monoline insurers were compared to insurers' losses from the Katrina hurricane, recorded as the worst natural disaster in US history. Katrina was said to have cost insurers $41.1 billion. Asset write-downs and credit losses reported in connection with the sub-prime related financial business were estimated to have reached at least $38 billion.

A problem that will exist for some time arises from "write-downs". Write-downs are not necessarily the same as "write-offs" where losses are recognized and deducted from profits and/or reserves.

Write-downs also affect the balance sheet, but are deductions made from asset values to reflect what is regarded as a realistic re-assessment of particular asset values on a current basis. They are in effect, unrealized losses. Should the realizable value of assets increase, another revaluation will take place that will be reflected in enhanced asset values in the company accounts. This is a standard *"mark to market"* procedure that is applied to many classes of asset, both in banking and commerce.

The biggest problem faced in late 2007 and the early part of 2008 was that the markets for structured financial products had completely seized up, there was no trading in these instruments and therefore it was impossible to attribute a realistic "market" value to them.

Initially, banks were very reluctant to acknowledge this situation, partly no doubt because of the affect it would have on their accounts, share prices and executive egos, not to mention public perception of their stability, following upon the Northern Rock episode, and partly because, McCawber-like, they hoped that "something will turn up".

As there was no benchmark market, and in this unprecedented situation, no real regulatory or audit guidance, banks were left to self-assess the extent of the valuation downgrades without being under an obligation to publicize what actions had or had not been taken. Far from being helpful to them this state of affairs made the situation worse.

Because no one in the banking world knew the extent of the losses that individual banks may have been harbouring, the interbank markets then froze solid, banks being too afraid to lend to each other. This was precisely what brought about (unnecessarily) the downfall of Northern Rock.

A report listed the losses of a number of insurers, as follows:—

American International Group Inc, noted as the world's biggest insurer, reported the largest loss in its 89-year history because of the decline in its investments linked to mortgages, so not necessarily as a result of direct involvement with the monoline industry. **AIG** reported $6.7 billion losses on residential mortgage backed securities and

$11 billion from credit default swaps, designed to protect fixed-income investors. Those were revised figures after its auditors found that it had originally used the wrong formula to value its holdings and had understated losses. (In September 2008 AIG had to be rescued by one of the largest US Treasury bail-outs up to that time, $140 billion in total).

AMBAC had $6 billion of write-downs

MBIA's losses amounted to $3 billion.

In all there were 15 publicly traded companies based in the USA and Bermuda which contributed to the industry total of $38 billion, but this number excludes "captive insurance companies" (policy-holder owned companies) and European companies.

Prudential Financial Inc recorded unrealized losses of $2.86 billion on fixed–maturity investments of which $1.1 billion related to sub-prime mortgages.

Met Life posted $4.45 billion unrealized losses, but only $219 million from subprime

Whether realized or not, those credit related write-downs badly affected the share prices not only of the companies listed, but many others which were possibly not directly involved in the credit crisis.

Another factor that increased the uncertainties, concerned the mono-liners' acceptance of insurance of CDS contracts (credit default swaps). For example it was reported in June 2008 that MBIA had written $137 billion in swaps. The problem lay in the fact that these contracts usually stipulated that if MBIA's bond insurance unit became insolvent or was taken over by State regulators, buyers of the contracts could demand payment immediately. That would affect the insurer's ability to honour its municipal bond contracts.

There were so many uncertainties involved that nobody was sure of the true situation, but press comment at the time mostly predicted worse to come in 2008/9. That may have been a justified prediction, but it did not help the situation.

The plight of the mono-line insurers occupied the Press, almost daily, for about three months into March 2008. From then on there was virtually no comment on mono-liners or their prospects. A possible reason for this was that government intervention in the banking scene meant that it was increasingly likely that, at least in the short term, governments would replace the insurers as guarantors.

Query? Were the insurers still being paid for cover?

However in August 2008 there was a report of a ray of sunshine for Ambac. It was that the two biggest rating agencies down rated Ambac Assurance in June, making it harder for the company to do business. But the ray of sunshine lay in the fact that the downgrade allowed Ambac to record a $961.6 million accounting gain because the company is theoretically less able to make good on some of its insurance contracts, making those liabilities less onerous.

Who can deny that one can prove anything with figures?

Credit Rating Agencies

In the second quarter of 2007, Fitch Ratings issued 404 downgrades of sub-prime bonds, and 113 upgrades. This followed 127 downgrades in the first three months of the year.

In July 2007 Fitch Ratings announced that it might downgrade bonds valued at $7.1 billion because of rising delinquencies and defaults on sub-prime mortgages. It was putting 170 sub-prime transactions "under analysis", indicating that they might be cut.

Standard and Poor's, another major rating agency, placed 612 classes of sub-prime bonds on watch for downgrade, involving $7.4 billion, representing 1.2% of the $565.3 billion of sub-prime bonds issued from the fourth quarter of 2005 through 2006.

Moody's downgraded 399 sub-prime mortgage backed securities and said it might cut another 32, in all $5 billion, representing 6.8% of the sub-prime bonds rated by Moody's in 2006.

Most of this downgrading was of a relatively small proportion of the bonds issued by a few lenders, of which one had filed for bankruptcy protection three months earlier and another had been forced by state regulators to cease sub-prime business four months earlier.

All of this presaged the subprime market turmoil that was about to manifest itself.

The ratings agencies were not necessarily acting voluntarily in downgrading tranches of bonds. Investors had come to realize that perhaps the rating system was not as reliable as they had previously thought since it did not seem to properly reflect the accelerating rate of increase in defaults.

Progress in acknowledging the development of adverse trends was slow. "The New York Times" reported that Kathleen Corbet, president of Standard and Poor's resigned on 31st August 2007 after lawmakers and investors criticized the company for failing to judge the risks of securities backed by sub-prime mortgages. McGraw Hill, the parent company of Standard and Poor's issued a statement that M/s Corbet's departure was to enable her "to spend more time with her family and was not related to the current credit market turmoil". Whether that was true or merely a repetition of an oft-repeated excuse used by chief executives heading away from trouble (or being pushed) is anyone's guess.

There were reports that both S & P and Moody's failed, until July 2007, to downgrade bonds backed by loans to borrowers with a poor credit history, notwithstanding that some of the bonds had already lost more than 50cents on the dollar.

The Senate Banking Committee Chairman, Christopher J Dodd was quoted as saying that credit rating agencies must explain why they assigned "AAA" ratings to securities that never deserved them.

26th January 2008
If we move on, the "New York Times" again published an article on the credit rating companies.

> *The chief executive of Moody's* (whilst enjoying a break at the World Economic Forum in Davos, Switzerland) *conceded that his agency had made significant mistakes in the rating of the structured finance products, but added that the agency had been deceived by people who put together the products.*

(and of course, who paid them to award the triple A rating that they were giving).

The article continued,

> *Many such products backed by sub-prime mortgages have been downgraded from the top triple A sometimes to junk status, and their prices have collapsed, to the anger of investors. - - - -*

An executive, Raymond W McDaniel, Jr. (presumably of Moody's) was then quoted,

> *In hindsight, it is pretty clear that there was a failure in some key assumptions that were supporting our analytics and our models.*

He told a panel at the World Economic Forum (whilst he was also relaxing in Davos, where he heard complaints about conflicts of interest and suggestions that large fees had influenced the ratings).

> *One reason for the failure was that the information quality given to Moody's, both the completeness and veracity, was deteriorating as the sub-prime mortgage market grew.*

In other words, some clients were telling them "porkies", but they were not too bothered about it. This is another example of a company executive who prefers not to unequivocally admit to the facts.

After receiving more criticism he vigorously defended Moody's saying its work was *"not in some way corrupted by the business model"*.

Strange that he should say that. A business model is intended to set standards, not to corrupt them.

As the newspaper noted,

> *Rating agencies are paid by the companies they rate, a fact that has been harshly criticized here and elsewhere - - - -.*

Regulators in the USA were taking a greater interest in what was a deteriorating situation. In a review of proposals released by the rating agencies, Andrew M Cuomo, the New York Attorney General said,

> *both S& P and Moody's are attempting to make piecemeal changes that seems more like public relations window dressing than systemic reform.*

Mr Cuomo's office was looking into how the ratings agencies assigned triple-A ratings to many bonds backed by risky sub-prime home loans. He wanted to know if the firms asked for and received information that would have warned them about specific risks associated with home mortgages.

One could be forgiven for believing that such information was a fundamental requirement of the rating process.

At the same time the Securities and Exchange Commission had also started an enquiry into the ratings agencies, sending in teams of examiners and collecting documents.

This was not the first time agency ratings had been called into question. After the collapse of Enron in 2001 and the earlier bankruptcy of Orange County, California, in 1994, questions were raised about the quality and depth of rating agencies' research, as well as their independence since the ratings agencies were paid by the corporations and banks. In the case of some securitised bonds, a strong ranking makes it easier (and cheaper) to raise money in the capital markets.

Although there were similarities with the Enron situation where the debts amounted to $13 billion the 2007/08 crises were many times greater.

In their response to Mr.Cuomo's criticisms S & P executives stopped short of saying their methods of analyzing mortgage-linked and other structured securities were flawed. Deven Sharma, President of S & P was quoted,

> In any business you have to continue to look at how you can do things better. Some of the issues we have been hearing in the marketplace are that if investors had had more information, they could make more informed decisions. We think our actions may give them more confidence to get back into the market. The actions taken by S & P are meaningful and will be important measures". Amongst other things it planned to "collect more information about the processes used by the issuers and originators to assess the accuracy of their data and their fraud detection measures.

But, as noted above, should it not always have been collecting that information anyway?

The S & P announcements included undertakings to address growing concerns about potential conflicts of interest with issuers by hiring an independent ombudsman to investigate complaints and by periodically bringing in an outside firm to conduct independent reviews of how the firm managed potential conflicts of interest and to review the work of any analyst who left the firm for a job with an issuer or investment bank.

One of the principal complaints against the rating agencies was that because they are paid by the institutions whose bonds they rate, they cannot be trusted to be independent.

So, what does S & P do now? It proposes to hire an ombudsman (ie. pay him) to mediate on complaints brought against S & P!

Surely it is a primary responsibility of senior management in any company to ensure that its policies are carried out fully and that the rules they set are observed at all times. Employing ombudsmen and outside agents to check what is going on in a company (external auditors should already do a lot of this), is yet another example of the way in which the managements of corporations absolve themselves from their responsibilities. It is all part of a modern corporate culture of ensuring that there is always someone else who can be blamed. All too often company executives can be seen to have outsourced their responsibilities to others, so-called "experts", although it seems to have no adverse effect on their pay packet or bonuses.

Following on S & P's statement, Moody's said it was weighing proposals to change its ratings for structured-finance bonds that were backed by mortgages and other loans. The measures it was considering included adding the suffix "sf," signifying "structured finance", to the letter-grade ratings it already uses, serving as a notice that a bond would not be the equal of others with the same letter-grade rating.

Surely this defeats the purpose of grading – a desire to create a uniform range of standards of credit-worthiness. Triple A should mean just that, it should not have to be construed as "maybe not triple-A." There is a wide range of other gradings below triple-A from which to choose, if the structured bonds did not merit a proper triple-A rating. Whilst structured bonds are different from straight bonds, it is not their nature that is being rated, but the ultimate credit-worthiness of both types of bonds.

These statements by S & P and Moody's appear to have formed a large part of their response to Mr. Cuomo's criticism that they were only window dressing and one has to agree that he appeared to be right. It is difficult to see how the proposals put forward by either company would assist prospective bond holders to feel more comfortable about the accuracy of credit ratings awarded by these agencies.

Furthermore, if each credit rating agency applies different credit assessment methods and standards, how can an investor relate differently structured ratings to each other?

A Moody's spokesman later added that In response to Mr. Cuomo's criticisms the firm welcomed feedback from all participants and that it looked forward to a "continued constructive dialogue" with regulators.

By which he no doubt meant that Moody's would tell the regulators what they proposed, which would still enable them to rate new bond issues as triple A, and they would expect the regulator to agree with what they proposed.

The problem which regulators in general face is that they are often in reality only empowered to hold "continued constructive dialogue", but are not sufficiently empowered to enforce their side of the dialogue on the other party. When criticism of the performance of regulators is expressed, that fact should be brought into the consideration.

Not everyone subscribed to the criticisms of the credit raters. Donald Brownstein, chief executive of Structured Portfolio Management, a hedge fund based in Stamford, Connecticut said,

Rating agencies should not bear the brunt of the blame for the mortgage crisis. The bonds backed by home loans were sold to sophisticated investors who should have done better analysis on the securities they were buying. This is a land of grown-ups, and this is not munchkin land, people have to respect the old saying, caveat emptor.

As a postscript, last year Mr. Brownstein profitably foresaw that mortgage securities would fall in value as housing defaults rose.

It's an ill-wind that blows no good!

About this time "The Times" reported from Davos that the credit ratings agencies faced a crackdown by the EU's Commissioner for Internal Markets, Charlie McCreevy, after he received the report of an enquiry into their activities that he had commissioned from the EU Committee of Securities Regulators. The Chairman of this committee had already voiced the opinion that the rating agencies were less culpable for the sub-prime crisis than Wall Street investment banks and investors.

Notwithstanding, Mr McCreevy was quoted as saying that the status quo was unacceptable and that he would over-rule the findings of the Committee if he thought necessary. He also criticized the fact that the agencies were paid by those whose products they were rating, in other words by the Wall Street investment banks and other issuers.

Many commentators highlighted the fact that an overhaul of the manner in which rating agencies operated and the way in which they were remunerated for their rating services should be a priority, particularly in respect of securitised bonds where part of the sales pitch required the bonds to be rated as highly as possible as part of the "credit enhancement" process.

As with the monoliners, Press interest in the Credit Rating Agencies ceased after the few months to April 2008. Despite all the criticisms aired, it has not been possible to identify any meaningful official action to improve matters.

7 Northern Rock PLC The Fall

In Chapter 2 we traced the rise of Northern Rock. It is now time to examine its fall.

The value of shares in Northern Rock peaked at the end of 2006 and not long afterwards, started a slide downwards, a slide which during the next eight months was attributed by the Company to tightening market conditions and the effect of rising interest rates. Northern Rock stated that the delays in passing higher borrowing rates on to the majority of its 700,000 mortgage customers would be responsible for an anticipated £200 million shortfall on net interest income for 2007. A decrease in share values was only to be expected in such conditions.

"We get squeezed when rates rise and we have now had rising rates for a year and the expectations for interest rates have changed notably since the first quarter" (2007), Adam Applegarth, the bank's Chief Executive was quoted as saying in a "Times" newspaper article on 27th June 2007. Stockbrokers responded by downgrading the shares from "buy" to "hold".

Mr.Applegarth insisted that, "the group was continuing to trade strongly despite an adverse interest environment." Northern Rock also had an increased dividend payout in prospect and a £200 million share buy-back planned, both based on the anticipated level of earnings for 2007 after taking into account the anticipated £200 million shortfall in interest income.

The share buy-back was partly as a result of changes in the regulatory capital requirements introduced by the Basle 2 proposals, but was basically dependent on sufficient earnings being generated.

On 27th June 2007, Northern Rock issued a Stock Exchange announcement headed "pre close statement and Basle 2 strategic update". The Company newsroom release covered strategy, market outlook, costs (in relation to cost efficiency), income and profits, lending and comments by the Chief Executive.

This press release whilst acknowledging the adverse interest rate environment, was positive about the outlook for the company and there were no indications that its core strategies were not on track.

The next announcement from the company came on 25th July 2007, when it published its half-year interim results. Operating performance was recorded as:-

- Record H1 (first half year) gross lending of £19.3 billion, an increase of 30.5%, with record H1 net lending of £10.7 billion, an increase of 47.3%

- Share of UK gross mortgage lending of 9.7% and net mortgage lending of 18.9%

- Total underlying assets of £113.0 billion, an increase of 28.3% from June 2006.

- Credit quality remains robust, 0.47% of mortgage accounts 3 months or more in arrears – around half the industry average.

- Underlying profit before tax, including gains on disposals £346.6 million, up by 0.7%. Underlying profit attributable to equity shareholders of £223.7 million, up by 28%.

The rest of the report provided a range of statistics supporting these, on the face of it, very satisfactory results.

Mr Applegarth stated,

> *Operationally Northern Rock had a good first half in 2007. Mortgage lending has been particularly strong with a gross market share of 9.7% and a net market share of 18.9%, helped by improvements in retention of home moving customers, keeping customers coming to the end of their product deals, and a strong mortgage market. Credit quality remains robust.*

> *The outlook for the full year is being impacted by sharp increases in money market and swap rates seen in the first half. This has resulted in a negative impact on net interest income as mortgage pricing in the market generally has lagged behind increases in funding costs in the year to date. Action has been taken with changes in our swap transaction policies to minimise exposures in the future to significant changes in interest rates.*

> *We are pleased to have achieved approval for use of our Basle 2 rating systems. This means that the benefits of Basle 2 enable us to increase*

our 2007 dividend by 30%.   Going forward our dividend payout rate increased to 50% of underlying EPS from around 40%.   Future capital planning, including the reduction of capital hungry assets, will allow us to return capital to shareholders through a share buyback programme.

The medium term outlook for the Company is very positive.

The rest of the report appeared to justify the positive nature of Mr Applegarth's commentary.

Yet less than eight weeks later Northern Rock had foundered and was on the rocks. How did it get there?

Why did it happen?

The answers to those questions are both simple and complex. The crisis was within the Company's power to avoid, but at a much earlier stage in its development, possibly as much as five years earlier.

On the other hand, structured as it then was in 2007, there was no way for the company to avoid the problems brought about by a range of events that were out-with its control. At the same time, we have to examine why it was that the directors of Northern Rock apparently failed to see the crisis coming. Were they keeping their fingers crossed (and doing little else) or had they just buried their heads in the sand? Or was it reasonable that they could have anticipated what was about to happen?

Their performance after the15th September was less than inspiring.

Professional observers described the Northern Rock management / board as being weak and timid. The Chairman of the company, a well-known local personality but not a banker and his successor Bryan Sanderson (who possibly spent too much of his time in London, away from the center of the action) did nothing to inspire confidence by depositors in the company. They made very few public statements and did not appear to understand the importance of good P R in times of stress.

They did not write to depositors or shareholders to keep them posted on what was going on, although that may have been on the advice of their lawyers who possibly advised them to say as little as possible. The problem with not doing so however was that it left a news vacuum that the Press filled with lurid and at times inaccurate headlines. Another factor may have been the direct involvement of the FSA, the Bank of England and then HM Treasury who very quickly after their initial inertia appeared to be running the show behind the scenes, thus inhibiting what the management could do or say.

Financial institutions are expected, indeed are required by regulators, to carry out "stress testing" of their operating policies. After the credit crunch happened there was discussion of the extent to which this was carried out effectively by the Board of Directors and executive officers of Northern Rock. In simple terms, "stress testing" means applying computerised models to determine where a breaking point or seizure will occur in relation to a company's financial strategies. It requires assumptions to be made. The extent to which these assumptions encompass a "worst case scenario" and also the circumstances in which liquidity based problems, as opposed to solvency problems, are likely to arise, governs how effective the stress testing is in identifying financial and strategic weaknesses.

The Chief Executive of Northern Rock, Adam Applegarth later maintained (*inter alia*, before a Parliamentary Select Committee) that the freezing of the capital and inter-bank markets following the severe problems which had emerged in the sub-prime market were unforeseeable. If we examine the financial crisis over the following twelve months the one fact that stands out is that it developed globally and piecemeal. There was absolutely no evidence that anyone in the world's major banks, the regulators or governments foretold how and the extent to which the crisis would develop. There were those, hedge funds and other market traders who used the uncertainties and the continuing worsening of the situation to their own advantage. But they did so on a day-to-day basis, it is doubtful that they exhibited "second sight".

Nevertheless, what indications of a pending collapse were to be gleaned from falls in the price of Northern Rock shares? Table 15 traces some of the share price movements from the beginning of 2007.

Table 15   Northern Rock PLC Average share Prices

2007	January		1175 pence
	February		1200
	March		1160
	April		1120
	May		1070
	June		1030
	July		820
	August		725
	September	3	737
		10	654
		14	520
		17	320

The progress of the share price after the run on deposits in September will be the subject of later chapters.

The steady fall in share price during the first six months of 2007 reflected the adverse market conditions in which Northern Rock was operating, and to some extent the views of some professional investors who suspected that Northern Rock might run into liquidity problems, but it must also be taken into account that over the same period there was a general fall affecting bank shares and also in global stock market indices. Northern Rock was not alone in reaching a peak share price early in 2007 and then falling away from it. Over a twelve- month period to end October 2007 share prices in the UK banking sector generally fell by upwards of 30-50% as a result of the turmoil in financial markets and uncertainty over the extent of banks' exposures to the sub-prime problems in the USA. By September 2008 most UK bank share prices had crashed in a spectacular and totally unforeseen manner.

Northern Rock, however, was the first casualty and gave rise to a day which will go down in British banking history as one of the most significant in many years —14th September 2007, the day that there was the first serious run on deposits in a British Bank in the 130 years since the City of Glasgow Bank had to close its doors after a panic run of withdrawals by depositors. That is to say the only occasion, if we ignore the run that started 5 th July 1991 on the Bank of Credit and Commerce International (BCCI), which technically was not a British Bank.

However, it is worth noting that in 1878, as with the run on Northern Rock deposits, not a single penny was lost by depositors. Both panic stricken runs were unnecessary, but reflected depositors' perceptions of the situation, their herd instincts and their natural fears for their savings.

Neither was there any need to call on a Deposit Protection Fund, although the UK Treasury Department did issue on the 17th September 2007 a guarantee of all deposits that were in the bank as at close of normal business hours on that day.

In the case of Northern Rock the run was sparked by what can only be regarded as sensationalist, ill-informed, and speculative media headlines and comment on 14/15th September which is difficult to dignify as responsible financial "reporting". It followed several days of widely reported short-term difficulties in financial markets as a result of temporary market conditions, but not with specific reference to Northern Rock. The short-term difficulties were those of the inter-bank loan market and bond markets generally and were not specifically linked to problems at Northern Rock.

Although it later emerged that there was concern at the Bank of England, FSA and Treasury as early as 14th August that Northern Rock might have imminent potential liquidity problems arising from the wider market situation, that knowledge was not generally available in the public domain, and does not appear to have been acted upon in any meaningful way by the authorities prior to 13th September when it was agreed that the B of E would make funds available to cope with Northern Rock's prospective liquidity problem.

Northern Rock's particular situation was only "revealed" on the evening of Thursday the 13th September by Robert Peston of the BBC in a news broadcast.

He revealed that,

> *Northern Rock has asked for and been granted emergency financial support from the Bank of England, in the latter's role as lender of last resort.*

BBC Business editor Robert Peston says,

> *Northern Rock is not in danger of going bust and there is no reason for its customers to panic.*

But he adds that,

> *Although the firm remains profitable, the fact that it has had to go cap in hand to the Bank is the most tangible sign that the crisis in financial markets is spilling over into businesses that touch most of our lives.*

The influence of the media on events should not be underestimated. It was recognized by a bank General Manager, George Rae, in a classic banking handbook, "The Country Banker" that he wrote in 1885:-

> *The panics of the future will be influenced to some extent in their direction and force by the application of the public press. Its universal eye will always be upon us. What any leading newspaper says today, as to the monetary outlook, will be repeated throughout the land in a million or so of broadsheets tomorrow morning. The Press cannot, it is true, prevent the fabrication of malicious and mischievous rumour, but it can refuse to give it circulation. In the strained condition of things which precedes and heralds panic, what is to be said, for example, of some such paragraph as this —*
> *— "Two banks in ——-shire are freely spoken about"? What advantage such a paragraph can yield to anyone passes comprehension; but the evil it may do is not difficult to estimate. Before night of the day of publication, not two, but half-a-score of banks will be freely spoken about, their depositors and shareholders needlessly alarmed, and fresh fuel added to the prevailing excitement.*

When he wrote that piece, George Rae knew nothing of the added powers of radio, television and the internet that we have to face today.

Returning to Northern Rock, it has also to be borne in mind that until late in the afternoon of 14th September 2007, there was no reassuring message coming from any of Northern Rock, the Bank of England, The Treasury or the Government itself. Depositors had to make up their minds on action quickly as the 14th was a Friday and the weekend was approaching. The reassurance from the Northern Rock board was poorly presented and did little or nothing to assuage investors' fears.

Mr Peston was later subject to severe criticism for his revelations that were based on leaked information from an undeclared source and which were made in advance of any official announcement by either Northern Rock or the authorities. He decided to respond to that criticism in his blog entitled "Peston's Picks" which he put on the BBC website on 16th October 2007. As it is only fair that his point of view should be available for consideration, it is set out below.

> *At 8.30pm on 13th September I disclosed on BBC News 24 that Northern Rock had approached the Bank of England for emergency financial support – and then spent the rest of that evening elaborating on that <u>scoop</u> in reports for the Ten o'clock News, radio bulletins, BBC online and so on.*

> *Since then I have been criticised by readers of this blog and others for being in some way being responsible for the run at Northern Rock, which began the following morning.*

> *I've not responded to the criticism, largely because it goes against the grain to write about my stories. As a journalist, I broadcast and write about things in the world that seem to me to be important, not about myself.*

This was perhaps a noble sentiment but one that was hardly supported as he continued to write about his actions for another two and a half pages.

> *But since the Chairman and Chief Executive of Northern Rock both today told the Treasury Select Committee that they believed the "leak" to me had exacerbated the woes of their bank, I felt I could no longer keep schtoom.*

> *The first thing to say is that I cannot possibly know whether anyone decided to take their money out of Northern Rock as a direct result of seeing my broadcasts.*

> *But here are a few thoughts that seem to me to be relevant:*

1. I was in a position to broadcast many hours before I actually did that the Bank of England, in its role as a lender of last resort, had been approached for help by the Rock. The reason I held off was because I wanted to ascertain whether Northern Rock was insolvent – whether its loans were bad—in addition to having got itself into the parlous state of finding it impossible to finance itself in the normal way.

Having been given the assurance that there was nothing seriously wrong with Northern Rock's loan book (by the "leaker"?), I then felt able to broadcast. Why? Because I was then able to give appropriate context to the story. I was able to say that there was both bad news and good news.

The bad news was that Northern Rock had committed a cardinal sin for a bank, which was that it had failed to ensure that its sources of funding would continue in all market conditions. But the better news was that with the Bank of England stepping into the breach, depositors ought not to lose any money.

I've reviewed our broadcasts of the night of September 13th. And if I have any doubts about what I said it is that – in the light of the subsequent run on the bank- I may have given too much reassurance to depositors rather than too little. Because, as the Governor of the Bank of England, has pointed out, it was rational for depositors to remove their funds.

2. This was a story I had been working on for weeks, if not years. I first expressed concerns about Northern Rock's business model in July 2003, when I was City editor of the Sunday Telegraph. And when money markets seized up on August 9th, I and other journalists, and many in the City- identified Northern Rock as being vulnerable. For example, Numis, the stockbroking firm, in mid-August stopped giving any kind of recommendation on the Rock's shares, because it felt unable to value the company while there were doubts about how it was going to raise finance.

And on August 16th, in my blog, I wrote that Northern Rock was "the stock to watch" because it was "heavily dependent on funding from the bond market".

I took my own advice. I watched what was happening to this bank closely, because of the likelihood that it would generate news of a substantial nature.

Also, as Adam Applegarth, the chief executive of Northern Rock, pointed out today (16th October) vast numbers of bankers, officials, regulators and corporate advisers knew both that Northern Rock had run into serious difficulties and that it was approaching the Bank of England for succour. In other words, it was immensely unlikely that the Rock would be able to keep its plight secret.

In those circumstances, it is extraordinary that it and the Bank of England started the detailed negotiations on the terms of the emergency loan on September 13th (though it was not signed off till the early hours of September 14th) with a view to announcing what had happened the following Monday, September 17th. How could it possibly believe it could keep the news out of the public domain all through the Friday and the weekend?

What's more, the Rock formally told the Bank of England it needed to tap it for help on September 10th, the Monday. It almost beggars belief that the Rock and the Bank thought they could keep a lid on what was going on till a full week later.

Of course I understand that Northern Rock and the authorities feel that if they had made the announcement of the Bank's support in their own time and in their own way, depositors might not have been quite so alarmed. But none of them are actually claiming that the run would not have happened. Because when they ask themselves whether they would have kept their savings in a bank which had been forced to ask the bank of England for emergency help, they know what the answer is.

Mr Peston's blog, to the extent that it explains his long term interest in, and examination of Northern Rock's business strategies, is factual and accurate. He had access to sources of information, and an "ear to the ground" in the City that were not available to the average depositor in Northern Rock. He also appears to have been kept informed of pending developments by his personal "leaker". (Who was within HM Treasury? We shall never know because the Chancellor refused to hold an investigation into the "leak".)

Depositors, and the average "man in the street", were completely unaware of the information that Peston was able to piece together. News emanating from the Rock, earlier in the year, whilst acknowledging market place problems, was essentially positive. That also extended to its Stock Exchange Announcement on 14th September, which of course, would not come readily to the notice of ordinary depositors, many of whom were in the North East of England, far removed from City gossip and intrigue. The Company's announcement was issued for London Stock Exchange information and as a precursor to a same day internet conference for analysts and (institutional) investors.

What Mr Peston chose to ignore is the fact that as at 13th September when he "revealed" what was happening, there was a world of difference between what financial journalists, the authorities and some people working in the City may have known, or guessed at, and what the general public, and more particularly, individual depositors in Northern Rock knew.

There can be no doubt that his comments on the shortcomings in official behaviour and news dissemination are justified, but as there were no official announcements made publicly before the 14th September, why did a run on Northern Rock escalate so rapidly from first thing on the morning of the 14th? Indeed it appeared to be the case that the Northern Rock website crashed under the pressure from a high rate of traffic during the evening / night of the 13th.

There is only one credible answer, that depositors were spooked by the constant repetitions of Peston's "revelation" the night before –

> *At 8.30pm on 13th September I disclosed on BBC News 24 that Northern Rock had approached the Bank of England for emergency financial support – and then spent the rest of that evening elaborating on that scoop in reports for the Ten o'clock News, radio bulletins, BBC online and so on.*

Of course no one can be certain that a run on the bank could have been averted if the information available to depositors had been initially derived from appropriately worded news releases from Northern Rock, the Bank of England or another official source, but it is a fact that the run began before any such announcements were made on the 14th September. It is also the case that other observers have commented on Mr. Peston's style of delivery that is usually a mix of hesitation and excitement, presented in a manner likely to agitate listeners. It is a style that has the effect of adding an extra dimension to his spoken words.

The point at issue here is not that Northern Rock was suffering severe liquidity problems brought about by its extreme business model and the "freezing" of credit markets. It is whether the run on deposits was brought about by that situation, or by the premature exposure of its lack of liquidity. In fact there was no general public awareness of the full extent of the lack of liquidity until five or six weeks later. In any event it is doubtful if the average personal depositor would have any understanding of bank liquidity problems. In the event depositors that queued to withdraw their savings did so because they did not differentiate between a liquidity problem and insolvency. They appeared to have been motivated by fear of the latter.

Mr.Peston tried to cover himself,

> *I may have given too much reassurance to depositors rather than too little.*

> *Because, as the Governor of the Bank of England, has pointed out, it was*
> *rational for depositors to remove their funds.*

It would only have been rational for depositors to remove their funds if they thought there was a reason for doing so and the only one they had first thing on Friday morning was Mr Peston's much repeated "revelation" —

> *BBC Business editor Robert Peston says Northern Rock is not in danger*
> *of going bust and there is no reason for its customers to panic.*

But he adds that

> *the fact it has had to go cap in hand to the Bank is the most tangible sign*
> *that the crisis in financial markets is spilling over into businesses that touch*
> *most of our lives.*

One can speculate as to whether Peston was more interested in making the most of a "scoop" that was the culmination of his long watch over Northern Rock, than giving consideration to the effect his revelations might have on depositors, the bank and the financial scene in general.

There is another aspect that was never addressed, either officially or in Press comment. He was disclosing confidential information. As an experienced financial journalist he clearly would have been aware that this was price sensitive information and that premature disclosure could be enormously damaging to the company's share trading.

Peston dwelt on the fact that it was unrealistic to believe that a lid could have been kept on this information for a week or more. That may have been true at the time. Mervyn King, Governor of the Bank of England later said that he would have liked to have been in a position to make the loans available covertly but could not see how this would have been feasible. What we have to remember is that the run on the bank came out of the blue, it had never happened before in many years. The extent of the aid being offered to Northern Rock was also very much greater than had been experienced at any time in the past. It therefore was bound to attract attention when it became known and the figures — in tens of billions — were sufficient to spook most people.

The most significant factor, however, was that all of the players, at the bank, the FSA, the B of E, HM Treasury or in wider government circles were unaccustomed to dealing with such a situation and they quite obviously had no plans in place to deal with it. Much has happened since then and as at November 2008 the authorities have had an opportunity to plan proposed actions for assistance in a much more co-ordinated manner. In fact between April and October 2008 the Bank of England / HM Treasury offered banks up to £200 billion of official support on a completely confidential basis. The names of those banks taking advantage of this offer were not disclosed and the B of E has said that they will not be made public. Neither was there a disclosure of the total amount taken up by banks during that period.

Which goes to show that had the authorities been ready for the Northern Rock situation, it might have been possible to have made the loans in confidence. In a later chapter we shall examine the official developments that took place in dealing with the catastrophic financial situation that impacted on the UK banks and those elsewhere in the world.

Presenting a scoop is a dream cherished by all reporters, therefore Peston can hardly be blamed for making the most of it. In fact, on 18th March 2008 he appeared in the course of a BBC News 24 promotion of its broadcasts alongside a headline "RTS Scoop of the Year Award 2007" saying, in relation to this statement "we were ahead of the game". Later, on 12th April 2008, and probably on other occasions, Robert Peston appeared on a BBC "trailer" promoting its news coverage. He talked about Northern Rock, mentioned that it was the fifth largest mortgage lender in the UK and then ended with, "this was our story, this was our scoop".

After all that, it is not difficult to determine which priorities were his driving force.

Other media coverage on 14th and 15th September appeared to wallow in the mess, rather than try to explain it in a reasoned manner. It is therefore no wonder that depositors formed long queues outside Northern Rock branches, driven into action by pictures of the queues in frequent TV news bulletins on all channels during Thursday 14th and on the front pages of newspapers etc the following morning.

One expects the tabloid press to dramatize such stories, but a "Times" newspaper front page on Saturday the 15th read in huge type *"***Run on the Bank***"* with sub headings : **"Thousands queue to withdraw savings from Northern Rock**" and *"***Pleas for calm as website crashes under scramble to transfer cash**."

On the same day, in its Business Section, Patrick Hosking wrote a half-page "commentary", which started off "Northern Crock. Northern Wreck. Northern Pebble. The nicknames dished out to Northern Rock yesterday (by whom?) speak volumes about the future of Britain's fifth biggest mortgage lender."

> *It is unlikely to have one –at least not in anything like its present guise —*
> *——.*

Readers of that introduction, if they were Northern Rock depositors, would be trying to get to a Northern Rock branch as quickly as possible.

The article then became more serious. However, in the absence of reliable sources of information, either from Northern Rock itself (which seemed for all practical purposes to have shut down its public relations department) or official regulatory / government sources, Mr Hosking of necessity had to speculate somewhat as all other media sources were obliged to do at the time. Nevertheless he produced a thought-provoking article that made a number of useful comments and explanations.

The article continued with a perceptive comment on what was the crux of the run on deposits:

> But in the world of retail banking –where confidence is everything – the Rock's reputation is tarnished. Most people queuing in Northern Rock branches yesterday probably did not really believe that their nest eggs were going to vanish but will have thought, "Why take the risk?" The psychology of bank runs has more to do with herd behaviour than cool logic.

After reviewing a range of pertinent matters, the article ended,

> Why did the stress testing supposedly used to ensure that banks are able to withstand any hurricanes thrown at them fail to spot the weakness? Has there been too much emphasis on balance sheet strength and too little on retaining big enough pools of liquidity? Banks are different. Their survival cannot just be left to market forces and the law of the financial jungle. Some have too special a place in the heart of the financial system to be allowed to fail. The wider question for policymakers, as they witness the agonies of Northern Rock and others, is whether they have been abusing that privileged position.

A question we shall return to later when considering how blame should be apportioned.

This chapter is about the fall of Northern Rock and although the run on deposits, speculatively estimated at times to amount to almost one half of total deposits, may have contributed to the panic which brought about its downfall, the predominant factor was the much more significant problem of an inability to maintain its funding in the by then, shut down interbank markets.

In Chapter 1 it was noted that in December 2006 Northern Rock had total assets of £100.468 billion and retail deposits (or liabilities of the bank) of £22.631 billion. Clearly there must have been other liabilities to balance the books, in fact £77.837 billion of them, and therein lay Northern Rock's "Achilles heel".

In order to raise this last amount, necessary to finance its acquisition of assets (through making mortgage loans), it resorted to other methods of funding.

The first was to borrow in the inter-bank markets.

The core business of a bank—any bank – is to seek deposits and make loans. Of course nowadays banks conduct many other types of financial business, but that is not relevant in the present context other than that it enables them to spread risk more widely than a bank like Northern Rock, the only significant business of which was to grant mortgages.

Banks carry on their lending business to customers, both personal and corporate, but they also lend to each other through what is known as the inter-bank market. Because to some extent banks are lending reserve cash in this market, loans are generally of short term, often as short a period as "over-night". In fact there has always been a substantial recognized "over-night" market in the City of London.

The only other alternative is for a bank to invest in government short-term securities (in Britain - Gilts).

In a country such as the UK, which has an established and regulated banking system, in normal times lending to another established bank is probably as risk free as lending gets. However, the banking system is periodically hit by a major trauma that tends to disprove the "risk free" proposition, but such traumas have not previously spread through the entire system, bringing it to a halt.

Nevertheless that is what happened not only in the UK but globally in 2007.

At the end of 2006, Northern Rock had borrowed £24.240 billion from other banks through the inter-bank market and this had risen to £26.710 billion by mid–2007. From mid–2007 onwards, the inter–bank market gradually became harder and more expensive to access and in August / September, certainly as far Northern Rock was concerned, it dried up altogether.

This meant that Northern Rock had *circa* £26.710 billion pounds of borrowings falling due for repayment within relatively short periods of time and no way of repaying them. In the normal course of events, much of this borrowing would have "rolled over" (i.e. been renewed automatically by the lending institution), or would have been replaced by new borrowing from other banks. But those options were not available to Northern Rock due to the general unease, one could even say panic that permeated the financial world.

The man in the street reading the Northern Rock 2006 annual accounts, all 103 pages of them, (in the unlikely event that he actually did so) would have had considerable difficulty understanding and interpreting them. On the other hand investment analysts, institutional investors and banks who understood the nature of the funding liabilities on its balance sheet, would certainly have noted that Northern Rock's liquidity and ability to keep lending depended on regular access to the inter-bank and securitisation markets, and the word circulating behind the scenes in City circles was that Northern Rock could be heading for difficulties.

Did this mean that Northern Rock became insolvent?

No. Because it still had its £100.468 billion of assets, comprised of the mortgage loans it had made secured by the properties against which it had made loans, and other assets. Despite insinuations in the Press to the contrary, at least 70% of those mortgage loans were of high quality and fully secured.

The Press made much of Northern Rock's "Together" mortgages because they were capable of increasing borrowing up to 125% of the property valuation. In the 2007 Annual Accounts one finds that the "unsecured" element of those loans amounted to 14% of the total borrowed. This meant that on average the unsecured part of a loan was not 25% but 14%. The unsecured element of all the "Together" mortgages was shown as £3.371 billion out of a total lending for this class of mortgage of £24 billion. It follows that the percentage of "together" loans to the total of mortgage loans was 37%, which it has to be admitted was quite high. However the 2007 Accounts also showed the following statistics:

Total residential mortgages	£90.777 billion
Past due, but not impaired	£2.154 billion
Past due and impaired	£143 million

As at the beginning of 2008 it follows that the "Together" mortgages had not given rise to much concern by way of arrears and write-offs.

So, what was the problem?

It was one of a lack of liquidity. From time immemorial, bankers have known the maxim "banks do not lend long and borrow short". Prudently operated banks try to "match" their liabilities and assets, that is to say, they endeavour to ensure that when liabilities fall due, they have access to liquid assets to settle them.

At the same time it has always been a tenet of banking that if a bank gathers in deposits from a wide range of relatively small depositors, it is highly unlikely that all the depositors will seek to withdraw all their money at the same time, even although bank deposits are repayable on demand in the absence of an agreement with the depositor to the contrary. In other words, there is unlikely to be a "run" on the bank. It is therefore safe to lend a reasonable proportion of the deposits for longer terms such as on mortgage loans.

That is a situation that exists for all traditional "high street" banks, but Northern Rock, much as it tried to emulate one, was not a traditional high street bank. Northern Rock had only one option available to it, to approach the Bank of England for assistance, but because of the size of its short and medium term funding needs, the Treasury had to become involved as one of the Tripartite regulators interested in the maintenance of economic stability in the banking system.

The Treasury's take on the protection of the banking system as a whole and the immediate needs of Northern Rock in particular were subject to much speculative reporting and was not officially made public until the Chancellor made this statement in parliament on 10th October 2007:

Extract from a Statement by Alistair Darling, Chancellor of the Exchequer to the Commons

> *Northern Rock, because of its business model, faced particular problems: it has a large share of Britain's mortgages, but they are primarily financed through the wholesale markets, including a significant proportion from securitisation. This meant Northern Rock was particularly vulnerable to the virtual closing of this market over the summer.*
>
> *On 14 August the FSA told the Bank and the Treasury about their concerns on Northern Rock and its vulnerability in the current market circumstances. During August it became increasingly clear that Northern Rock was having difficulty getting access to the financing it needed, and that the cost of doing so was increasing.*
>
> *The general situation and Northern Rock's position in particular were monitored on a daily basis. On 5 September the Bank announced £4.4 billion of extra support to provide increased liquidity to the wider market. As Northern Rock's position deteriorated, it became clear that specific support was likely to be needed for it.*
>
> *On the 13 September the Governor and the Chairman of the FSA recommended that I authorise the Bank to provide special liquidity support and I agreed because I believed this was justified.*
>
> *There are clear principles governing such support, which are set out in the*

memorandum of understanding, between the Treasury, Bank and FSA, first signed in 1997: such support should only be undertaken where there is a genuine threat to the stability of the financial system and in order to avoid a serious disturbance in the wider economy. That was the case here.

The provision of this support was announced on the 14 September. Although the FSA had assured the public that Northern Rock was solvent and that if depositors wanted to get their money out they could do so, it became clear that further assurance was needed.

So on 17 September, again on the advice and with the agreement of the FSA and Bank of England, I announced that during the current instability in the financial markets and should it prove necessary, I would put in place arrangements that would guarantee all the existing deposits in Northern Rock. This undertaking was explained and extended on 20 and 21 September.

The Bank of England is the UK Central Bank, that is to say it has responsibilities for managing various aspects of the country's economic well-being. It maintains the country's bullion and monetary reserves, issues its banknotes and coin, and sets the interest Base Rate to which most UK interest rates are linked. Until 1997 it was also responsible for the regulation of the entire banking system in the UK and was responsible for the issue of Banking Licences and the regulation of licensed banks. (the actual legislation referred to "Licensed Deposit Takers").

In addition, the Bank of England is banker to the Government and to all other Banks in Britain. In this last capacity it serves, when the need arises, as a "lender of last resort". What this means is that when an otherwise solvent bank finds itself in temporary liquidity difficulties, it can approach the Bank of England for funding assistance, at a price, in the knowledge that it will not be refused.

That is what Northern Rock did *circa* Monday 10th September 2007, a fact which was publicized from an unofficial source as noted above at peak TV viewing times on the evening of Thursday, 13th September.

Unfortunately, the tenor of the general media reporting of the approach to the Bank of England led the average man in the street (or depositor) to believe that "last resort" meant just that, the bank was on its last legs, about to collapse.

Had the report emanated in the first instance from the Bank of England, the FSA or HM Treasury, it would probably have been with some form of reassurance that the loans were no more than short term funding to see the bank through a temporary difficulty that was unrelated to the solvency of the bank, which was assured. That was the message that eventually trickled out from the authorities.

However, the picture which emerged from media and press reporting was one of enormous quantities of "tax-payer's" money, yours and mine, being thrown at a failing or failed bank. Which all added to the general sense of panic that gripped depositors, not only those in Northern Rock, but also depositors in other banks that also became the subject of publicized rumours as to their stability.

The rock on which all banking is built is trust. Whenever that trust is questioned, even if only on the basis of rumours – which by definition, one does not know to be true or false – it is a very short step to a run on a bank. It is not the reality of a situation that matters, but the public perception of it. That has always been the case since banks were first formed.

Robert Peston quoted the Governor of the Bank of England as saying "it was rational for depositors to remove their funds". That comment was made in the light of the only information people had available to them on 14th and 15th September, the first days of the run on deposits. Had the authorities made the initial announcement in a more measured and timely manner, together with an earlier undertaking to guarantee deposits, the situation might have been different. The authorities were faced with a situation which had not happened before in the working lifetimes of any of the officials involved and it is all too easy to determine what should have happened with hindsight after the event.

However, it was generally acknowledged within a few weeks that there were serious shortcomings in the planning put in place by the authorities for a contingency of this nature, and although Northern Rock was at the centre of the storm, a tempest had been brewing in global financial markets for some months, therefore the authorities should have been carrying out their own "*stress-testing*" of contingency plans. In the event it appeared that the only emergency the regulators had planned for (whether effectively or not is open to question in the light of subsequent events) was the anticipated fall-out from a terrorist attack on the scale of the 9/11 Twin Towers disaster in the USA. Many of the offices in the World Trade center had been banks, brokers and other important financial firms.

There were other relevant factors that should have provided clues as to what might happen to Northern Rock to which we shall return in the chapter that examines blame.

The second major source of funding which Northern Rock used was its securitisation programme. By mid–2007 it had raised £45.698 billion in this manner.

Its securitisation programme through the Granite Master Issuer conduit described in

Chapter 5 produced new funding in the first half of 2007, however the problems which had chrystalized in the US mortgage backed securities market in Wall Street closed off this avenue of financing for Northern Rock, although it has to be stressed that there was nothing intrinsically wrong with Northern Rock's own RMBS issues.

The last, and much smaller source of funding used by Northern Rock was the issue of "covered bonds" (explained in Chapter 3). Northern Rock had issued £8.105 billion of those, as reported in its 2007 mid-year interim accounts.

It can be seen, therefore, that Northern Rock used a variety of methods to raise finance to fund its very ambitious lending programme. So what did it do wrong to land itself in such a dire situation?

The answer is still the same – a mis-match of liquidity terms coupled with too many eggs in one basket. It can be argued that money market funding is no more vulnerable than funding through retail deposits. Most banks use both methods. However despite its efforts to obtain a variety of sources of funding Northern Rock did not achieve an appropriate balance between the sources. It has been noted earlier that UK Building Societies normally restrict non-retail funding to around 30% of total funding, with a maximum of 50%. Northern Rock at 77% greatly exceeded those figures.

This imbalance left Northern Rock vulnerable to the freezing of wholesale lending markets, a happening which one senior banker described as a "low probability, high risk" situation. As we discovered later in 2008 Northern Rock was not alone in having an undesirable business model.

8 The Rescue Phase One

For some days from 14th September 2007 the press and media concentrated on the scenes outside Northern Rock branches as depositors queued to withdraw savings, and Northern Rock certainly dominated the news headlines during this period.

Comment on Northern Rock continued to occupy pride of place in financial news on a daily basis for several months, comprised of rumours and reports of rescue efforts. Unfortunately we live in an era of headline grabbing, one-liners and sound bites and much of the reporting during this period was more interested in sensationalizing the problems than in the usefulness of the information that was relayed.

This was a story which rumbled on week after week into February 2008, but it is only by following it through that we can either make sense of it, or learn lessons from it, whichever happens to be our objective. The story has been followed virtually on a day -by-day basis that some readers may find tedious and be inclined to skip through. If they do, they will still be able to follow the remainder of the story, but they will not appreciate the major differences between the Northern Rock story and that which will be covered in Chapters 15 and 16, the story of the second and much more serious financial crisis that peaked in September/October 2008.

It was partly – but only partly – because of the long drawn out efforts to find a solution to Northern Rock's situation and because of the concentration on it by the authorities, the media and the financial industry in the UK, that it took so long for the problems to emerge from the other financial institutions that suffered in the ensuing crisis.

Quotes from broadcasts and newspaper reports mentioned below are not necessarily complete, but the most significant points relating to the day's news have been selected. There has been no policy of "*cherry picking*" and the selection of particularly relevant parts that constitute a new development in the story has been done in good faith and with no intention to distort the content of any of the reports. Not unexpectedly, many of the daily reports carried repetitions of information produced earlier or in other publications.

The process took much longer than was initially envisaged by all the parties, but that was probably because there was no previous event of this type and magnitude that could have been used as a guide. Because there was no previous guidance, the persons involved in providing solutions, particularly those on the side of the authorities, were faced with an entirely new experience, out-with their normal daily responsibilities. At the same time one would have expected that somewhere in official circles a measure of pre-planned action would have been available for implementation. No evidence emerged that there was any such plan in place.

The first six weeks or so after 14th September were, in a way, a period of exploration of the possibilities, without actually producing any solutions.

Friday, 14th September
TV news bulletins featured pictures of queues outside Northern Rock branches, with savers anxious to withdraw deposits, the related commentary was of a run on the Bank following disclosure of the "bailout" by the Bank of England.

In an announcement Northern Rock said that because of extreme global conditions it had taken action to preserve liquidity. This was a four-page release made at opening of business on the 14th; produced for Stock Exchange information; and intended for institutional investors and analysts. It was not until the bottom of the first page was reached that there was any mention of the key factor, that Northern rock had approached the Bank of England for standby liquidity arrangements.

Private investors and the public generally would only become aware of this announcement when mention was made of it in media reports.

Saturday 15th September
Newspapers carried even more pictures of queues at branches with copious reporting and comment, in some cases, covering several pages.

In Chapter 7 comments were quoted from a full page article in "The Times" by Patrick Hoskins that related to the fall of Northern Rock, but the article went on to discuss not only how the Rock might be rescued, but some of the difficulties that would be faced by bidders.

After a somewhat facetious start, the article continued,

> *Ideally a larger, stronger institution may be persuaded or even tempted to take it over. It is strongly capitalised, has a good portfolio of solid prime mortgages and a useful branch network.*

That was practically the only media acknowledgement published up to 15th September, and in fact at any time subsequently other than by the Treasury, which acknowledged that Northern Rock was not an irredeemable basket case. The article then reviewed a range of major financial institutions that could have benefited from the acquisition of Northern Rock. The potential candidates included US and European banks as well as British ones.

It then continued,

> *If no white knight comes along, the Rock may just wither away. The B of E is providing the lender of last resort facility to ensure that every cash withdrawal request can be honoured. But it is hard to see the bank doing much new business while such a shadow hangs over it*

> *For the moment the role of Adam Applegarth, chief executive, is little more than logistical, making sure that enough lorry loads of banknotes are delivered to the back door of his branches to be taken out of the front door by anxious customers.*

> *Short of a miraculous reverse in its fortunes, the name Northern Rock is likely to enter folklore as an institution to be uttered in the same breath as Barings and BCCI. That will not be fair.*

> *There has been no fraud. Until recently the bank was being applauded as a model of solid low-cost lending. It has dabbled no more irresponsibly in US sub-prime than most of its rivals.*

This last comment, although well meant, was inaccurate. Northern Rock was far less directly involved in investment in sub-prime securities mortgages than any other bank with such problems. Its Treasury department had invested in a very small amount of such bonds as part of the investment of its capital and reserve funds. Its own securitised bonds were of genuine AAA quality, which is more than could be said for many of the others in that market.

Monday, 17th September
Pictures and coverage of the Northern Rock problems continued to dominate the news.

Despite the long queues portrayed in the media and the unending publicity given to the "run", the amount withdrawn in the three days was reported to be about £2 Billion. It was a large amount, but less than 10% of total deposits. It was reported later in the week that up to 75,000 depositors, out of 1.5 million had withdrawn their funds, in other words, only 5% of depositors.

As Northern Rock also provided internet accounts, they too experienced such a volume of attempted withdrawals that the system crashed as early as Thursday night, exacerbating the problems and increasing the general sense of panic.

Other news on this day included a note about growing fears that the Northern Rock run might spill over into the rest of the banking system and undermine confidence in it, particularly in the mortgage sector. Shares in Alliance and Leicester fell 30% (it had been subject to earlier rumours) and those in Bradford and Bingley by 15%.

Just before 6.00 pm, and as a response to the rising level of concern about the stability of the UK financial system, Alistair Darling, the UK Chancellor of the Exchequer announced that the Government would guarantee all deposits held in Northern Rock at that time. This guarantee would last as long as the emergency and he promised that if it was to be withdrawn, three months notice would be given of the Government's intentions.

The statement by the Chancellor was backed by the Prime Minister, Gordon Brown who said that the government's actions were decisive and that the UK economy remained strong.

Tuesday and Wednesday, 18th and 19th September
The run on Northern Rock gradually subsided. In the USA, the Federal Reserve cut interest rates by ½ % to 4.75% in an effort to rejuvenate the flagging financial markets there. The Bank of England acted differently by offering a £10 billion injection into the money markets in an attempt to bring down the cost of inter-bank lending. As it transpired this did not have the intended affect as none of the money was taken up by banks.

In order to ease access by banks to Bank of England funding and in particular to cope with Northern Rock's needs, the Bank widened the range of assets acceptable as collateral and included mortgage debt.

Political commentators attacked these measures as being a "u-turn" and too late to solve the problems. Which of course was true, although nevertheless they made some sense.

"Thomson Financial", (as reported on Yahoo Financial News, and quoted from a "Daily Telegraph" article citing a Bank of England spokesman), relayed the story behind the previously announced revelation that Lloyds TSB, in discussions with the Bank of England and Northern Rock sought a £30 billion two year loan from the Bank of England, without a penalty rate of interest, in order to assist its bid for Northern Rock. This negotiation was said to have taken place over the weekend of 8th September and the details were discussed with the Tri-partite authorities (the banking regulators) who agreed that it would have been inappropriate to assist the financing of a bid in this manner. Apparently neither Northern Rock nor LloydsTSB were prepared to comment on the story.

This was one of many reports over the ensuing weeks where it was difficult to differentiate between rumours and facts. There were also at this time pronouncements by Mervyn King, Governor of the Bank of England of the "moral hazard" associated with making government funds available to bail out errant financial institutions. The problem facing the authorities on this occasion was whether it was a lesser evil to bail out individual institutions as necessary, or risk watching the whole financial system descend into chaos.

It should be noted that whilst a systemic collapse of the financial system in the UK was on the minds of the Chancellor, his colleagues and Mr. King, Governor of the Bank of England, the prospect – at least to the public and the financial institutions themselves – did not seem a likely scenario. It took more than nine months before a serious financial crisis became a reality.

Thursday 20th September
The Treasury stated that its guarantee of deposits would extend only to those accounts existing at mid-night that day, but it would be extended to include all former depositors who had withdrawn their funds if they replaced them in a similar type of account with Northern Rock. It would not extend to new deposits placed after 20th September.

Mervyn King, responding to the Parliamentary Select Committee on Banking and Finance, defended the manner in which he had tackled the banking crisis. He was accused of "being asleep at the wheel", but responded that it would have been irresponsible to have intervened earlier to save Northern Rock, although he would have liked to have been in a position to offer financial support in secret but was prevented from doing so by a combination of UK and EU regulations.

This view was challenged by the Committee but the fact was that whilst in an earlier age the Bank of England would have dealt with the problems in that manner, the amounts involved would have been much smaller and it would have been up against a much less formidable press and media power than exists today. Furthermore, the reach of communications technology then was nothing like what is available today in our global environment

Those comments are a matter of opinion, but the bottom line was that even if the regulations allowed, it would have been difficult, when only one bank was involved, to keep such a secret behind closed doors. After all, everything seems to be "leaked" nowadays. Nevertheless, as noted earlier in chapter 7, the Bank of England later managed to make substantial funds available to a number of banks on a confidential basis.

Sunday 23rd September
There was comment that the Board of Northern Rock was likely to come under pressure from shareholders to seek a sale of the Bank as soon as possible, the reason being that

it seemed unlikely that a takeover of the whole Group would emerge. This comment was probably based on the knowledge that Lloyds TSB had been in exploratory takeover talks that ended a week before the first run on deposits, but had withdrawn any interest. It was known that Northern Rock had engaged Merrill Lynch to try to find another buyer.

At this time we had the first speculations about an interest in Northern Rock by private equity firms. The names being mentioned included Citadel, Cerberus, Ripplewood, Lone Star and Chris Flowers of J C Flowers. It was suggested that the reputation of the last named gentleman was such that it would be relatively easy for him to structure a deal quickly.

In view of the size of Northern Rock's book, it could be that a deal would not encompass the whole of Northern Rock. There was further speculation that if a comprehensive bid did not materialise within a few weeks, there might have to be a break-up of the Bank.

The last piece of speculation was that Northern Rock could continue to trade, but gradually "run down" its book until it became a much smaller operation. An option described as not being to the liking of shareholders.

A theme emerged, which was repeated regularly over the next few weeks, that Northern Rock had been guilty of irresponsible lending. "Times Online" carried a headline **"Northern Rock still lending recklessly",** the report being that,

> *it emerged this weekend that the beleaguered bank is still offering mortgages of six times salary to potential customers.*

This comment appears to have its basis on an offer made to a reporter posing as a potential customer. The report further stated that,

> *Financial experts were this weekend stunned that Northern Rock is offering such loans a week after it was forced to turn to the Bank of England for emergency funding.*

Market place competition was such in the years leading up to the 2007 crisis that Northern Rock and most lenders funded a range of mortgages out-with conventional terms, but the Northern Rock 2007 Interim Accounts recorded unsecured loans at 8% of the total and 70% of mortgage loans below an 80% LTV (Loan to Value ratio), with an average loan book figure of 59% LTV. Hardly a picture of reckless lending, bearing in mind also that Northern Rock's three month default rate was 0.47% of its total mortgage book and was only half the published industry average. Such a headline, although no doubt true of one mortgage applicant was completely unjustified as being representative of most of Northern Rock's mortgage lending.

At that time Northern Rock had only received £3 billion of Bank of England aid. A large sum, yes, but hardly enough to generate all the media concern, particularly in view of the much larger sums which Central banks in the USA, Europe and the UK were pumping into the financial markets to support them. Northern Rock's immediate need for aid was brought about by the run on deposits, it was not at that time in respect of the underlying liquidity problems. The bank's CEO had earlier declared that the bank had two – three months of funding available to it in September.

The article continued on another theme, the controversy likely to arise if Northern Rock went ahead with a plan to pay a £59 million dividend to shareholders that same week - a dividend that had been announced in July. It was described as being available because the FSA had given,

> A special dispensation to the Bank in July to dip into its assets to pay out a dividend - which is 30% higher than last year's payout.

The proposed dividend was certainly controversial in the circumstances and after the announcement provoked adverse publicity the Board voluntarily cancelled it but it would have been paid out of increased annual earnings attributable to shareholders. At the time the Bank was solvent and meeting all its liabilities, including the payment of a penal rate of interest on the Bank of England loans that were also fully secured (with an excess margin) by a deposit of Northern Rock assets with the B of E.

Another aspect of the problems relating to Northern Rock was the political one. Northern Rock's troubles and the credit crisis generally provided scope for a great deal of partisan politically based comment which had very little to do with solving financial crises.

The "Times Online" article quoted above continued,

> Politicians yesterday expressed dismay that the Government and its regulators had not stepped in to supervise Northern Rock's business practices following the Government bailout. George Osborne, Shadow Chancellor, said "One week Alistair Darling is attacking the lending culture in this country and the next he is issuing emergency guarantees for people's mortgages and savings." George Mudie, a Labour member of the Treasury Select Committee said, "Of all the people, have Northern Rock learned nothing? It is reckless".

It is difficult to see any helpful, or even sensible element in either of those two statements.

More significantly, on 23rd September "BBC News" drew attention, to what was going on in the background. It reported that hedge funds and city traders in some of the big investment banks had been betting heavily for months that Northern Rock was facing serious funding problems and that its shares "were on the way south".

The article described their strategy as being to "short" shares they believe are over-valued. Hedge funds borrow shares from long term investors such as pension funds and insurers for a rental fee and sell them. Later, they buy back the same number of shares and return them to the lender on an agreed date.

We shall return to this aspect of the trading in Northern Rock shares later, but to put it in context, and by way of example, it was recorded on 12th October 2007 that 52.33 million shares in Northern Rock were on loan. These were shares held in the "CREST" electronic trading system of the London Stock Exchange.

There were 319.91 million Northern Rock shares held in Crest accounts, so 52.33 million shares represented 16.36% of that total. Northern Rock had 421.23 million ordinary shares in issue at the time, which means that 75.95% of its shares were held in Crest accounts and 12.42% of shares in issue were being borrowed to speculate on price movements in Northern Rock shares. As we shall see later, the daily share trading charts after 14th September show that the trading activity was many times greater than it had been in the previous nine months. The average "*short*" position across other bank shares was believed to be about 3.5%.

This was not a sudden development. In June, as we have noted earlier, Northern Rock issued a profits warning brought about by rising interest rates. Up till then it had been estimated that about 7% of Northern Rock's shares were subject to "shorting". By the end of July that figure had more than doubled to 15%, and in October 2007 it had increased at times to 20%, with one un-named hedge fund being responsible for almost half of that amount. Of course hedge funds were not the only financial institutions engaged in "shorting" shares, bank trading desks joined in the share gambling.

Naturally it is difficult to obtain a meaningful estimate of the profits accruing to the hedge funds from those activities in 2007 (which of course continued in 2008). Estimates have varied from more than £100 million to a billion, but only the managers know the true position.

When one considers that it has been estimated that about 40% of trading on the London Stock Exchange on any business day is conducted by hedge funds, this form of speculative trading, although it is claimed that it improves liquidity in markets, cannot do other than distort the operation of stock markets. The scale on which it is conducted also means that those operations have a strong self-fulfilling influence on stock market price movements.

Monday 24th September

The "UK Shareholders Association" issued a Press release announcing that it was forming a Shareholder Action Group for Northern Rock shareholders to promote the interests of shareholders since it believed that many private shareholders were persuaded to invest in shares in Northern Rock in recent months on the apparent strength of the business when in reality the company was in great financial difficulty. Information about its financial difficulties had not been made publicly available as it should have been. Shareholders had suffered major financial losses as a result and in addition, longer standing shareholders would also suffer loss if the company was sold quickly at an unrealistic value.

Speculation had been circulating of it being necessary to find a buyer for the company as quickly as possible in order to preserve "what was left of it", essentially without regard to a valuation basis that took into account the underlying strength and assets of the company. The Association's view was that more value would accrue to shareholders if the Company was permitted to stabilize and rebuild its franchise with customers as opposed to being subjected to a "fire sale".

The press release covered a number of other relevant points including a suggestion that changes should be made to the composition of the Board of Directors in order to re-establish confidence in the management of the company.

The Association pointed out that the Bank of England had been aware of an impending funding crisis at Northern Rock by 14th August 2007, if not earlier.

> *But the Company made no announcements until 14th September when the "rescue funding" by the Bank of England was announced. Why was no announcement made prior to that time? Companies have an obligation to announce significant price sensitive information as soon as possible and we believe that the lack of any such announcements led to a false market in the shares of the company. In addition, while private investors might have been buying, many institutional investors were selling or even "shorting" the stock with constant rumours of impending profits warnings going round the city. In addition the stock fell substantially on the 13th September (the day before the announcement) which suggests possible insider trading so we will be complaining to both the LSE and FSA about these events as it suggests that they would fall into the category of "market abuse".*

The Association release went on to raise a number of other questions that required an answer before ending,

> *The directors should also explain to shareholders why they had apparently*

failed to anticipate the funding crisis, and exactly what steps they took to avoid the impending crisis once it became apparent.

This last statement is a very valid one to which the Board of Northern Rock never produced an answer. In fact the Investor Relations page of its website produced very little information after the publication of the Interim Accounts in July 2007.

The Company was very well acquainted with what was going on in the US mortgage markets. That must have been so because of its deep involvement through its Granite securitisation programme. As recently as the beginning of September 2007 it registered a new issue of Notes with the Securities and Exchange Commission (SEC) in the US, although as noted elsewhere it failed to sell any of them.

Other news reported on 24th September by "Times Online" was that Northern Rock "proposed to pay £59 million to shareholders - Including the Chief Executive - in a post-profit-warning dividend increase". As noted above this dividend was subsequently cancelled.

There was a certain "red rag to a bull" element in the dividend proposal, particularly when it emerged that the architect of Northern Rock's woes, its Chief Executive, Adam Applegarth would have received £14,000 as his share.

The article also noted that,

> *It emerged over the weekend that about twelve financial institutions had brushed off an approach from Northern Rock to acquire the troubled bank while hedge funds including JC Flowers and Cerberus are eyeing the business.*

Tuesday, 25th September

The "Financial Times" is a highly respected purveyor of business news but on this day it printed a lengthy Editorial Comment about Northern Rock and its troubles which some observers may consider had too narrow a base for some of the views expressed.

It was headed, " **Fast sale of troubled UK bank's operations is the priority** " and continued,

> *The British taxpayer has been in the home mortgage business for a couple of weeks but it is already time to move on. The bail out of Northern Rock by the Bank of England, which extended a large line of credit to the bank, and the Treasury, which guaranteed its deposits, has halted a run and restored a measure of confidence. The next step is to get rid of Northern Rock, quickly*

The troubled lender loses value with every minute it spends in the central bank's intensive care unit. Borrowers, depositors and suppliers will steadily withdraw their business. Northern Rock's systems, staff and branch network, built to handle a certain volume of business will become a liability rather than an asset. The greater the erosion of Northern Rock's asset base, the greater the chance of loss to the public purse, most likely from the guarantee extended to depositors.

As a forecast those comments proved, months later, to be way off the mark. None of the predictions actually happened, despite the fact that there was very little improvement in Northern Rock's overall prospects.

The comment continued,

The Treasury, the Bank and Northern Rock's Board have three main options: sell Northern Rock as a going concern, break it up and sell off the pieces, or put the bank into run-off (which means making staff redundant and then waiting while debtors repay their loans).

Selling the bank as a going concern is most attractive, although hard to engineer, because any buyer would have to fill a £30 billions funding gap. The authorities should sell to anybody willing to pay more than zero - be it private equity or another bank.

A piecemeal sale of the branch network, systems, and deposit base would capture at least some value from Northern Rock's franchise, and is preferable to shutting it down. It should be tried if the bank cannot be sold as a whole.

Bear in mind that this "shooting from the hip" style assessment of solutions to the problem came within fourteen days of the Bank of England funding and the run on the bank. Takeovers or amalgamations of this size are normally conducted over a period of months and involve the immediate parties, their lawyers and professional advisors, plus the banks that will eventually fund the deal. So why insist on such haste on this occasion?

It is interesting to compare this rhetoric, concerned as it was with what by October 2008 can be seen as almost a minor event when compared with the hundreds of billions of pounds, euros and dollars that have since been poured into the rest of the global banking system, practically the only press comment being to accept that it "was necessary".

Apart from its liquidity mis-matching Northern Rock had a sound and apparently well administered business base. Yet at this time no possibility was being suggested, by anybody, that it had any hope of replacing its funding by returning to the inter-bank markets.

Until the impact of the US sub-prime crisis in which Northern Rock had no direct involvement over a period of 4 - 5 years (at least), Northern Rock had experienced no difficulty obtaining continuous funding of around £26 billion from this source. The banks lending it (or whichever institutions were involved) had been perfectly comfortable with Northern Rock, so why was there no effort (for example persuasion by the Bank of England, as might have happened thirty years earlier in similar circumstances) to renew those lines of funding, even if on the understanding that Northern Rock would systematically reduce its overall borrowings from this source over a period of time, which in fact is what happened later.

Within three months after 14th September 2007 inter-bank lending as a source of funding had dried up completely, for any borrower. That is what necessitated the increase to £23 billion in the Bank of England's loans to Northern Rock.

It is a poor reflection on the trust, integrity and professionalism of the financial markets that the same banks who had been happily lending to Northern Rock (and making money out of it) did not have the ability to determine that the quality of Northern Rock's portfolio which they had regarded as perfectly satisfactory before, had not changed materially, and that they could safely continue to lend to Northern Rock at a time when they could not identify other homes for their funds. As we shall see later, part of the problem lay in the fact that many banks had their own problems and wished to hang on to their cash.

It is inconceivable in the circumstances in which it found itself that Northern Rock would not have co-operated in the determination of the continuing quality of its mortgage book.

Or was there a darker motive? Perhaps the banks were not unhappy to witness the demise of an also ran which had become a serious and successful competitor.

None of which wholly excuses the Northern Rock Board for having approved and adopted an extreme business strategy.

The "FT" comment continued,

> That leaves the bank's loan book. It would be a mistake to try to auction
> off those mortgage assets now, when they would only fetch fire-sale prices,
> and doubtless leave the Treasury nursing a loss. But the Bank of England
> cannot finance them indefinitely. If Northern Rock has to be broken up then
> the best option would be to wait a few months before trying to sell.

> *Northern Rock's Board has indicated that it will do its bit by postponing the bank's interim dividend. To pay either that or the coupons on its other Tier 1 capital securities would send completely the wrong message: that the Rock is more interested in shovelling shareholder's cash out than in making responsible use of public money to weather the storm.*

> *That Northern Rock is still extending loans and still has the power to pay dividends, despite being dependent on the Bank of England, is troubling. The authorities need to move it off their books.*

I was a regular reader of the Financial Times for over forty years and held it in the highest regard for the accuracy and unsensational manner in which it recorded and disseminated business news in a manner which could be trusted. I do not know if the Editor was proud of his "Comment" on this occasion, but I cannot believe that it maintained the paper's usual standards. I can think of a few tabloids where it may have made more appropriate reading, and in that respect, the "Comment" has been related in full as it was typical of many unhelpful newspaper articles on Northern Rock that were rife at the time.

In everyday life we frequently refer to "trial by media". Northern Rock's plight over the following months was a prime example.

25th September was a busy day for newspaper coverage of Northern Rock.

"Yahoo Finance", in its banking section, printed a lengthy and well-considered article by Sarah Medlock headed "**Northern Rock - your questions answered".**

Unlike so many "advisory" articles which appeared at the time, this was a well considered and helpful piece, following headings such as, " What's happened?", "Is my money safe?", "What about Northern Rock shares?", "Any chance of this happenings to other banks?" and " What does the future hold for Northern Rock?"

Under this last heading an interesting factor was discussed, which had not appeared in any other report. It was that,

> *There were mutterings about a fine from FSA in the future but it could be some time before more is known about this.*

The prospect of a fine appeared some months later to have died. Not surprisingly in view of the criticisms that emerged over subsequent weeks of the FSA's failed regulatory oversight of Northern Rock

Rumours of pending takeover interest in Northern Rock were repeated regularly during these early weeks, and on this day it was the turn of a Spanish group of investors headed by a company, Nueva Rumasa. The owner of this company was reported as having written to Northern Rock that,

> He would be interested in acquiring a package of shares in Northern Rock large enough to give him direction of the bank.

Northern Rock was said not to have responded, but the bank itself would not comment on the report.

Another piece of news which emerged on the 25th was that "a source " told Reuters that "the US investment bank, Goldman Sachs is advising the Treasury on some matters relating to Northern Rock." Goldman were said later to be advising the Government on some of the mechanics of the guarantee (of deposits), should it be required.

27th September
A report from Madrid claimed that Nueva Rumasa planned to bid for 10% of Northern Rock ordinary shares in the "next few days". Snr. Ruiz-Mateos, the owner of Nueva Rumasa was said to believe that with a 10% stake, he could head up the bank, supported by a "steering committee" made up from other Northern Rock shareholders. Northern Rock's only comment was that it had received approaches from a number of potential buyers.

This particular proposal sank without trace.

29th September
Radio 4's Money Box programme devoted time to a discussion of Northern Rock, starting off with the "UK Shareholder's Association" (UKSA) circular issued on 24th September (see above). The programme quoted UKSA's "plea" made to the BBC that " Northern Rock shareholders should be protected against further losses by the Government".

This was on the basis that it would stabilize the business and give it a long-term future, but BBC's business editor Robert Peston said Northern Rock could not survive as an independent bank. He told the Money Programme,

> It seems probable that Northern Rock's days of independence are well and truly over. Investment banks have been appointed by the company and the Treasury to examine a sale

He continued,

> Each side had different objectives. The Treasury and Chancellor - even

the Prime Minister - would like this resolved as soon as possible and Northern Rock put into safe hands. But Northern Rock believes it is a viable business, and ought to be able to conduct disposal in an orderly way that maximises shareholder value.

Roger Lawson of UKSA contributed,

We do not want the Government or the Bank of England pushing the company into a fire sale. We would like the Government to provide reasonable support to the company so it stabilizes its business and has a long-term future.

His concerns were expressed as being that shareholders could lose what little remained of the value of their shares.

There was further discussion of the interests of shareholders and the value at various times of their shares and the programme ended on the note that it was not clear what value could be placed on the shares, a lot of damage had been done to the company. It had suffered a tremendous blow to its reputation and it was thought that it would take two or three weeks more before the future of the bank could be determined.

This was actually about the first reference to the shareholders, the owners of Northern Rock. For all practical purposes their interests had been ignored. Of course shareholders are essentially risk takers. If a company fails, they have to suffer the loss. But in the case of Northern Rock, the company had not failed, it had run into serious temporary liquidity problems which were only partly of its making, and it was not the shareholders that were to blame, it was the Board of Directors who had failed to keep their shareholders fully advised of the company's situation, and indeed could have been accused of misleading them.

As we shall see as the story develops, the interests of Northern Rock shareholders were very low down on the list of priorities considered by the media, Treasury, Government and regulators. In fact, but for UKSA, Northern rock shareholders might as well have been non-existent.

The beginning of October brought about more concrete proposals for the rescue of Northern Rock, although much of the reporting was still speculative.

3rd October
An "FT" report by Jane Croft and Thai Larsen started with the JC Flowers bid, first mentioned above on 23rd September. The article recorded that JC Flowers, a private equity group, had secured about £15 Billion of funding which could be used to refinance

Northern Rock. It was understood by the reporters that Chris Flowers, its Chairman (who was a former Goldman Sachs banker) would soon be meeting Northern Rock advisers to discuss a transaction after which it could start due diligence.

Flowers was noted as one of several bidders who expressed an interest in buying all or part of Northern Rock's business. The hedge fund Cerebus was mentioned again. JC Flowers was, in the previous week, given access to Northern Rocks books where it could examine "commercially sensitive details about its financial performance". Flowers was being advised by Credit Suisse.

It was also disclosed that Northern Rock was on the verge of hiring Citigroup to work with Merrill Lynch as its investment banking advisors. It was also noted that the bank's regulators had urged it to explore all avenues in an effort to resolve its liquidity problems that had caused it to borrow up to £8 billion at this date. This raised expectations that there would be a speedy sale or break-up of the bank.

It is a reflection of the fact that to bring about an end to Northern Rock's predicament concentration was on the need for a rapid repayment of the B of E loans (which as noted above amounted to no more than £8 billion) and a sale or break up of the bank. When one compares that panicked reaction to the actions a year later when the B of E offered other banks in extreme difficulties (that were almost entirely of their own making) £200 billion with a guarantee that it would be available for at least three years, one can only conclude that Northern Rock was unfairly treated.

Why was that so?

It was because of the inexperience of everyone in dealing with such matters at the time. Amongst other reasons including the run on the bank's deposits, they were panicked by the frequently sensationalist media reporting.

4th October
"Times Online" reported that Citigroup was ready to provide,

> well in excess of £5 billion in financing to ease the way for a takeover of Northern Rock.

The website recorded an understanding that at least four serious bidders remained in the auction of the Northern Rock, referred to as "the troubled Newcastle based bank"

The background to this story was explained as,

> Given the scarcity of banks able to provide multi-billion pound liquidity lines

in the current credit crisis, Northern Rock was thought to be concerned that one bidder would tie up most of the City's advisors, depriving rival acquirers of funding. To level the playing field Citigroup was brought in to provide financing to bidders. It is thought that it is ready to offer significantly more than £5 billion in funding. The credit line provided by the American banking giant will be secured in part on Northern Rock's mortgage assets. The final terms of the deal are still being hammered out, but it is thought that Citigroup will also provide some advisory services to the Rock.

A source said that although the Bank of England is providing liquidity, it's important that Northern Rock is seen to be able to secure its own funding for a deal.

The article continued,

It is thought that the bank has stabilised its business after a £2 billion run on its coffers, and the need for an immediate sale is less pressing.

It is not clear just how much of this article was based on credible sources of information and how much was no more than wishful thinking, but the Citigroup monies, together with other offers of funding described elsewhere evaporated. In Citgroup's case, not surprisingly when we see later on the extent of its own losses in the mortgage backed/ sub-prime securities markets.

The article concluded with a review of the Northern Rock Foundation's interest in what was happening to Northern Rock.

A Mr. Balls, Chairman of the Foundation's trustees was quoted as saying,

that whilst we understand the need for an early resolution - - - - we are concerned that a transaction is not concluded on unfavourable terms simply to meet a self-imposed timetable to the detriment of the charity, its work and jobs in the North.

It was noted that the Foundation held non-voting shares in Northern Rock that would convert into a 15% holding in the Bank in a takeover.

The foundation's presence was seen as a poison pill to an acquisition attempt.

7th October
The Business Section of the "Sunday Times" reviewed the then current status of takeover interest and started off by saying that Citigroup, the world's largest bank was planning to

bail out Northern Rock by "throwing" a £10 billion lifeline to the stricken mortgage group. It was expected that the deal would be completed within a week. It was considered that it would send a powerful signal that Britain's fifth-largest mortgage lender was on a more stable footing and able to raise funds in the wholesale markets, although the reality at the time was that no commercial lenders had been prepared to deal with it.

This report has to be viewed against the fact that, as the paper recorded, Northern Rock at this date had borrowed £10.9 billion from the Bank of England. In the light of what happened later, in September / October 2008, it is almost unbelievable that the only solution that was being considered for Northern Rock was a break-up or, in essence, a fire sale at a time when, but for the inter-bank crisis which by then affected nearly every bank, it was still trading normally and making satisfactory profits. However, as we shall see later its government appointed Chairman and CEO managed to write off enough provisions against potential losses to produce a revenue loss for 2007. All that was for what in late 2008 we would have to regard as a paltry sum, namely £10.8 billion.

The article then commented on the involvement of JC Flowers, describing him as a "billionaire financier". He was said to wish to keep Northern Rock intact and had approached senior British bankers and several former government figures about running the bank

Cerberus was then noted as being interested in parts of Northern Rock's £105 billion mortgage book.

The paper made what appeared to be a first mention of what was described as Northern Rock's "Tier 2 debt" amounting to about £1 billion of junior bonds not covered by the Treasury guarantee of deposits in the bank. It was also noted that in the previous week both JC Flowers and Cerberus were looking for cash injections from investors (existing shareholders?) and sovereign wealth funds. Blackstone and Apax, private equity firms were also listed as being interested in Northern Rock.

10ᵗʰ October
This was the day of the first public intimation of the involvement of Jon Wood and his US$ 3 billion hedge fund, SRM Global. He was credited with being one of the City's shrewdest traders, and it was stated that he had built up a 4% stake in Northern Rock shares.

Jon Wood was quoted as saying that there was still significant value in Northern Rock for bondholders and shareholders. It was said that his stake was significant because he and other investors, such as RAB Capital, another hedge fund, could block a takeover of the bank.

One of the reasons for a 66 ¾ % rise in the Northern Rock share price on this day was that hedge funds which had been borrowing shares to "short " them, had to close short positions as it became more difficult to keep borrowing shares. As we shall see when we examine trading patterns for the shares, although they did not bring about the downfall of Northern Rock, these "shorting" activities were largely responsible for the wildly fluctuating market price of Northern Rock shares over several months. Unfortunately, it was only when other major banks suffered the same shorting treatment during 2008 that H M Treasury stepped in and banned the shorting of bank shares.

A Swedish pension fund, Andra AP-Fonden had increased its investment to 1.3%, and JC Flowers, Cerberus, Apollo, Blackstone and Lone Star were all said to be "circling the bank".

The Bank of England also announced that it would accept a wider range of collateral against its lending to Northern Rock, including its controversial "Together" product which combines a mortgage and an unsecured loan in one package. Although seen as "controversial", this product only accounted for 3.47% of the June 2007 total lending. The extension of the Treasury's "cast iron" guarantee to protect depositor's who put money in the bank after 19th September also had a beneficial affect on the share price.

This article linked the Northern Rock news to the broader picture in financial markets by saying that the Chancellor, Alistair Darling, would the following day make a statement on "banks in difficulty" and the fact that Northern Rock had borrowed £11 billion from the Bank of England. At the same time, the article noted that,

> The Wednesday term auction held by the Bank of England was again shunned by the banks for a third week, the Bank receiving no bids for the £10 billion of three month loans available under its emergency facility.

Friday 12th October
The "*FT*", through Jane Croft, Thai Larsen and Ben Fenton published one of the first articles announcing that Sir Richard Branson, of Virgin fame, had announced a plan to rescue Northern Rock.

> His plan had the backing of a group of "heavyweight investors and banking figures," which included AIG, a US insurance group, Wilbur Ross, "the distressed debt investor", First Eastern Investment Group, run by a Hong Kong businessman, Victor Chu and Toscafund, a hedge fund chain chaired by Sir George Mathewson, former Chairman of Royal Bank of Scotland.

The plan was based on merging Northern Rock with his Virgin Money financial services business, injecting up to £1 billion of new capital at a discount to the then current share price in exchange for a controlling interest in the company which he intended to re-brand under the Virgin name, which was said to be more attractive to investors and consumers than the by then discredited Northern Rock brand. There was also a suggestion that Virgin would earn a fee for the use of its brand name.

The writers noted that the proposed new equity investment was relatively small compared with the challenge of re-financing Northern Rock that now had B of E borrowings of £13 billion, and no details were given as to how this task would be accomplished.

Sir Richard Branson also proposed to provide new top management for the re-branded bank in the shape of Jayne Anne Gadhia, the Chief Executive of Virgin Money and a former director of RBS Mortgages. An opinion was expressed that it was doubtful if this background prepared her to restore confidence in Britain's ninth-largest bank.

The article carried on with descriptions of various aspects of Virgin's business activities that were interesting as background, but not relevant to the Northern Rock situation.

The FT ran a separate article about M/s Gahdia entitled **"A new face prepares to dominate the stock market".**

The article made the point that M/s Ghadia had never run a public company before and Virgin's success with Northern Rock's recovery would depend on her ability to execute the new strategy. It pointed out that whilst her credentials were impressive, they were,

> an imperfect fit to the challenges ahead.- - - - She had not previously run
> a branch Network and the central plank of her recovery plan for Northern
> Rock - substituting retail deposits for wholesale funding - would mark a
> relatively new departure for her.

The article continued,

> Then there is dealing with the City. The new Virgin-branded company
> would remain on the stock market. This will be the greatest ever baptism
> of fire in the field of investor relations.

It was then noted that,

> Help is at hand from the intimidating bunch of big-wigs involved in Virgin's
> consortium - - - there followed a list, then - - - their collective wisdom provides
> some comfort, but they are not going to be the core management team - - - -.

One gets an impression that there was less than full-hearted media support for Branson's proposals, and certainly they did not appeal to existing shareholders. The proposals appeared to have been structured to give the consortium "most bangs for its buck".

There was a range of other reports on Branson's entry into the fray and it all amounted to the most significant news concerning Northern Rock for two weeks or so. This was what everyone was waiting for, concrete plans for the rehabilitation of Northern Rock.

BBC News 24 carried full coverage and quoted Virgin as saying that its proposal was the "quickest possible solution" to restore public confidence in Northern Rock. The Virgin consortium was not looking to buy Northern Rock, but would inject "hundreds of millions of pounds" in return for a substantial stake, which as reported above in the FT, was a controlling stake.

Robert Peston pointed out that the problem of the B of E loans amounting to £13 billion had to be solved by a successful bidder and he was of the opinion that in current market conditions that might be too difficult for any buyer unless the Treasury continued its support.

Sir Richard insisted that the consortium's business plan would deal with this problem and it was later reported that Virgin wanted three years to repay the B of E loans in full.

The news bulletin then commented on the competition from a number of possible rival bidders. Reports were that JC Flowers had set aside £15 Billion to buy the bank. There was also further speculation that Flowers and rival Cerberus were planning to break up the bank and buy its lucrative home loan book.

This was an interesting report in that it highlighted the fact that Northern Rock actually had a "lucrative" mortgage book, whereas until then most comment tried to downgrade it.

"The Times Business Section" also ran a lengthy article on the Branson proposals covering much the same ground as the others, but suggesting that the inclusion of AIG insurers was a key element because additional funding for Northern Rock could come from the establishment of more Special Purpose Vehicles (SPVs), similar to the Granite structure already in place, which would issue mortgage-backed securities. AIG Financial Products, which specialises in the provision of credit guarantees, could offer insurance to buyers of Northern Rock's securities, increasing their attractiveness. As we shall see, less than a year later AIG had more than enough problems with which to cope in order to avoid its own bankruptcy.

At this time, Northern Rock shares were still quoted at 273.25 pence.

In a separate analysis of the Branson bid, James Harding suggested that,

Like so many of Sir Richard's gambits, the publicity has already promised more than the venture may ultimately deliver: the Virgin consortium is still a long way from rescuing Northern Rock.

His piece ended with,

But if the Rock rescue works, it could well be seen as Sir Richard Branson's most audacious gamble yet. Virgin is looking to inject a relatively small credit card business with a £25 million annual profit and possibly, a little cash to get control of a huge mortgage business and £115 billion worth of assets. In the absence of other bidders, Virgin is offering a lifeline to the Rock's employees and its charitable Foundation. But, make no mistake, this is not altruism, it's opportunism.

Elsewhere "The Times" had extensive cover of Mr. Christopher Flowers of J C Flowers, relating his background and the growth of his financial activities. Mr. Flowers was quoted as having said his business philosophy was,

Finding good partners and being co-operative where you can. There is a style of investing that is much more adversarial, but it doesn't work for me.

The article also speculated meaningfully on the nature and extent of the financial problems besetting Northern Rock, together with various options which might be available to provide a solution to them, most of which have been covered elsewhere in this chapter.

Sunday 14th September
Less cheerful news emerged today. "Yahoo Finance" put together an article from Thomson Financial, also based on Sunday Telegraph reports. The heading read **"Three Northern Rock suitors offer close to zero for shares"**

It then went on to say that Virgin, Flowers and Cerberus have all indicated to the Government that they would offer close to zero for the shareholder equity.

"The Telegraph" was quoted as saying,

Sources close to the sale, however, warned that Northern Rock shareholders could still fight a sale, believing a gradual Government backed wind-down of the bank would deliver them more cash, it said.

The real issue, according to sources, remains the bidders' inability to raise debt for a new line of funding for the bank, the newspaper said.

A quote from "The Mail on Sunday" read,

> *Under European Commission rules, the Government's 28 billion Sterling guarantees to savers count as "rescue aid" and so could only continue for six months, limiting the amount of time bidders would have to stabilize the business.*

Where did the £28 billion of guarantees to savers come from when it had been established that Northern rock had lost about half of its £24 billion of retail deposits?

The article also suggested that the Government view was that a total of about £30 billion would be needed to ensure survival of the bank without its State guarantees.

Another "Yahoo Financial News" page dwelt on the various people who were being approached by Virgin to act as Chairman of its proposed new bank, quoting several newspaper reports. "The Sunday Times" suggested Sir Brian Pitman, a former Chairman of Lloyds TSB, Sir Peter Ellwood, a former Chief Executive of the same bank and James Crosby, a former Chief Executive of HBOS

"The Sunday Telegraph" added to the list, Sir Peter Burt, a former CEO of Bank of Scotland.

Whilst the newspapers were working from the "word on the street", and no doubt had the best of intentions, this was largely speculative comment, which at the end of the day came to nothing. The article was padded out with more repetitions of earlier news and speculation that was not particularly helpful.

Monday 15th October
Today brought an "FT" article by Ben Fenton, carrying the headline

> **"Rock plunges as it confirms talks"**
> *Shares in Northern Rock plunged in early trading after a statement from the bank that disappointed investors hoping for firmer news of a takeover.*

The company confirmed that talks were taking place, but were only "preliminary". The "plunge" was of about 25% to 203 pence, before recovering to 225.75 pence. The full story of the price movements in Northern Rock shares forms the subject of a later Chapter.

The article stated that,

> *Although the potential bidders could easily buy Northern Rock, the big*

question is whether any are able to meet the huge commitments required.

That seems to be a contradiction of terms. A bidder was not just acquiring the ordinary share capital of Northern Rock, which only amounted to 421.2 million shares. That would achieve nothing. What was being bid for was the business of Northern Rock as a going concern, and that would take substantial funds, as noted elsewhere.

In fact, Virgin's bid provided a pointer to what was behind all the interest in Northern Rock. Its existing holders of 421.2 million shares actually owned a business with assets worth over £100 billion, if only the liquidity problems could be resolved. Even if a quick solution could not be found, there was only £23 billion or so of Treasury funding to be repaid out of these assets. Assuming the Treasury was prepared to wait until maturing mortgage loans provided sufficient funds to pay off its loans, a process that could realistically happen over two-three years at most, the shareholders could still be left as owners of £75-80 billion of assets and the income stream that they would generate.

That was what was attracting the bidders for the company, and if they could buy out the existing shareholders cheaply they would eventually show handsome profits within a year or two.

It has also to be borne in mind that the Bank of England / Treasury temporary funding was not a free gift. It was actually costing the shareholders of Northern Rock more than it would have cost had it been able to source the funds in the financial markets.

The FT article ended with comment that,

> *Adam Applegarth, the Chief Executive and Matt Ridley, the author and journalist who sits as non-executive chairman, have been summoned to explain to the Treasury select committee on Tuesday how they got into the position where the bank had to turn to the Bank of England to remain solvent. The MPs are expected to concentrate on the Newcastle based bank's practice of using short-term money raised in wholesale markets to balance its books against long term mortgage loans.*

The "Investors Chronicle" published an article by Jonas Crosland that was mostly concerned with the news as it had a bearing on a valuation of the shares. The article made three points that were negative in that context.

Firstly,

> *In the longer term, the bank may be forced to align the amount that it lends*

with its deposit base, which some are suggesting would mean a reduction in annual lending from £30 billion to just £3 billion.

This implied an assumption that Northern Rock would be unable to increase its deposit base.

Secondly,

Much of its savings business comes through the internet, so any reduction in business that would follow withdrawal of Government Guarantees on deposits would call into question the need for 6500 employees and 76 branches, especially as a majority of its mortgage and deposit business is conducted through brokers and the internet.

This is a valid assessment as far as staffing level is concerned, borne out in February 2008 when the bank was nationalised and it was indicated that there would be a reduction in staff through natural wastage of about 3000. At that time also it was expected that the branch network would be retained to improve the prospects for increased deposits.

The third comment was that,

Ultimately, any potential buyer will have to consider how it can raise funds cheaply enough to continue offering mortgages, There is also some doubt over the timing of any potential bid, given the mounting evidence that demand for mortgages is set to decline.

As the bank will operate in a competitive commercial market place, there is no reason why it should not be able to raise funds at the "going rate" in the same way as its competitors. As far as demand is concerned, it is not demand that is likely to fall away by very much, it is supply that will prove to be a problem. Northern Rock will certainly not be able to grow at its previous annual 20% rate, but should be able to attract an appropriate share of the market in keeping with any new business plan it adopts.

The article concluded that,

Northern Rock may have a quality loan book but its name is tarnished beyond repair. With such negative sentiment closing in on the bank, the shares are a sell.

One could argue with the negativity of the piece, but not with the "sell" conclusion, after all the purpose of the article was to determine whether the shares were a "hold" or a "sell".

Although Investors Chronicle saw the shares as a sell, not everyone was so minded. Today's news was that Northern Rock announced that UBS AG, the big Swiss investment bank had bought 22.81 million shares in the bank, representing 5.41% of the share capital.

Friday 19th October

A *"Reuters"* report was quoted on Yahoo Finance that the Northern Rock Chairman, Matt Ridley had resigned and had been replaced by Bryan Sanderson, a former Standard Chartered Bank chairman, subject to approval by the FSA. Ian Gibson, the senior non-executive director of the bank was quoted as saying that Sanderson's experience of banking and of working with the Government "will prove invaluable to Northern Rock when considering future strategic options"

It was also noted that Northern Rock had until the end of February to assess its options, which were expected to end in a sale.

Ridley's resignation came after his "grilling" by the Parliamentary Select Committee earlier in the week when a member of the Committee, Michael Fallon MP asked him,

> *Does no one have any honour? Has no one offered to resign?*

To which Mr Ridley replied,

> *I have made it clear that my resignation is available as soon as it is decided it is in the best interests of shareholders and stakeholders that I go.*

The article also commented that Mr Ridley had been criticized for his low profile as the crisis grew and that the Chief Executive and all other directors also offered to resign last month, but investors and advisers wanted the board to stay on to steer the bank through its crisis.

Wednesday 24th October

The magazine, "The Business", reported that there had been very few developments in the plans for Virgin to save Northern Rock. The only real news was that the bank had borrowed another £3 billion from the B of E.

It continued,

> *It seems that due diligence takes time. And it is not just Virgin's, the bank may have allowed a leading high street bank (Lloyds TSB) to reach the brink of failure once, but it is not going to repeat the error. Just as the Virgin consortium is going to have to eventually persuade shareholders of the merits of its transaction, so now it will have to show the regulatory*

triamvirate, comprising the Bank of England, The Treasury and the FSA, of the merits of its approach.

The article considered various other aspects of the bid and concluded that,

If Northern Rock capital value remains at around £800 million (just under 32 pence per share), Virgin will try to buy it at a much lower price than currently expected. A controlling stake in Northern Rock on Virgin's terms may cost closer to £300 million. Virgin, after all, is buying damaged goods.

As was the case at the time, there was a fair amount of speculation and the expression of a contestable opinion in this article.

On the 18th October the U K Shareholders Association (UKSA) issued a press release headed, " **How Much are the Shares in Northern Rock Worth?**"

The following are extracts:

Recent comments in the press suggest that the bidders who have approached Northern Rock may attach zero value to the shares. Even the Virgin consortium's offer is rumoured to involve heavy dilution of existing shareholders. Should shareholders take those reports at face value, or is this more likely to be a case of the bidders trying to lower expectations?

The UK Shareholders Association (UKSA) cannot give investment advice and neither do we think it wise to try to put any valuation on the business at this time. But we would like to point out a few salient pieces of information to try and stop the current speculation about valuation.

The Press Release then described how it was not possible to place a value on the company without access to up to date financial information which at that time was not publicly available. It then continued,

Clearly though the problems of Northern Rock stem not from a lack of profits, or a deficit in assets but from a temporary cash flow crisis. The last relevant announcement by the company (on the 14th September) indicated that profits would exceed £500 million for the current year and it has been stated elsewhere that the assets exceeded the liabilities. Although the exodus of depositors due to the panic thereafter will no doubt have impacted prospective profits, as will the reliance on more expensive funds from the Bank of England, it is worth pointing out that these impacts may be only temporary or short term.

Businesses are valued ultimately on their long term cash flows over several years, so just because there is a temporary erosion of profits and assets does not mean that the equity in the business instantly becomes worthless.

Ways to replace the funding currently supplied by the Bank of England need to be examined. This might be achieved from Northern Rock's own resources by gradually running down its mortgage book until the Bank of England loan is repaid. This would only require the liquidation of around 12% of the mortgage book and could be probably achieved in around 6 months as interest is paid on mortgages and the mortgages are redeemed.

How would the bidders replace the Bank of England funding? This is not clear. In fact some have indicated that they would probably need it in place initially.

Alternatively they might obtain funding from other sources but it seems pretty clear that they need third party assistance and are not promising to fund it from their own cash resources. Well if the bidders can obtain third party funding secured against the assets held by Northern Rock, so can Northern Rock itself. It appears these bidders are simply seeking to acquire a valuable business at close to zero cost. The losers will be the thousands of loyal shareholders and staff.

As noted elsewhere, UKSA Press Releases, whilst issued with the interests of shareholders in mind, always presented reasoned and un-sensationalized points for consideration.

Friday 26th October

"The Financial Times" reported that Blackstone, a private equity group had won a mandate to advise Northern Rock's board on funding options and the sale process for the "embattled mortgage bank", brought in by the new Northern Rock chairman, Bryan Sanderson. Blackstone would be working alongside Citigroup and Merrill Lynch, also advising on the sale process.

With such a bevy of reputedly expert (and very expensive) advisors, it was difficult to understand why a better outcome could not have been achieved. However, by October 2008 we learned that some of the advisers seemed to have been incapable of managing their own businesses, far less advise others.

The article also covered the point that bidders were looking for the B of E to undertake to maintain its financial support for some time after a successful bid. It also reported that

Paul Myers, earmarked as a Chairman for Northern Rock in the event of a successful bid by JC Flowers, stepped aside as a member of the Court of the Bank of England for as long as any potential conflict of interest remained.

Saturday, 27th October

"The Times" newspaper repeated the story about Paul Myers. The remainder of the article covered old ground, but added a whole host of City names that were being tipped for one job or other in the event that one of the several bidders clinched a deal to takeover Northern Rock.

It almost seemed as if everyone of former note in banking circles was happy to join the party. "The Times" even ran an illustrated half-page article listing the main contenders and their CVs.

Monday 28th October

The "FT" published an article by Jane Croft reviewing the then current situation in relation to the bidders, in particular, JC Flowers, following a meeting at Northern Rock with its advisers the previous week.

The advisers were understood to have indicated that,

> J C Flowers' proposal was not as developed as it might have been on the financing side and that it is expected to return with greater detail. Northern Rock was reported as being keen to slow down the sale to make for a more competitive auction as it explored alternative funding options and restructuring prospects. It is notable that some bidders believe Northern Rock had delayed the process by being slow to provide key information at its start.

A final snippet of information was that Cerberus, a private equity group tipped as a bidder, owned a stake in a US mortgage lender, GMAC which has operations in the UK which could be combined with those of Northern Rock. In fact it later transpired that not only did GMAC have an agreement to channel its business through Bradford and Bingley but its business was unlikely to appeal to any right-thinking CEO.

This brings us to the end of Phase One, the beginning of November seemed to represent a watershed, after which there was much more activity which at the time seemed to be positive, but as we shall see failed to produce any desired results.

9 The Rescue Phase Two

This is a continuation of the story of the so-called rescue attempts. It is a chronological selection of reports and as such illustrates how the story developed day by day.

If lessons are to be learned from Northern Rock's problems, they can only be achieved by following the story as it developed. To relate the story introducing hindsight derived from knowing the end result would prevent us from seeing just <u>how </u>that end result came about.

Most newspapers and TV stations were giving full coverage to Northern Rock and to a much lesser extent at this time, the sub-prime crisis and the credit crunch brought about by the seized-up inter-bank markets. Much of the reporting was of necessity repetitive, therefore by following a few selected reports we get as complete a picture as is necessary to understand what was going on during the period covered. We may also be able to spot the mistakes that were made. Much of the comment was necessarily speculative, but nevertheless it would influence public perception of Northern Rock's situation.

An element that requires close examination is the time factor. Undoubtedly the saga of Northern Rock went on for far too long, although it has to be accepted that the particular circumstances of the case, that is to say the manner in which Northern Rock was part of the fallout from a much bigger problem, played a significant role. This made it difficult to engineer a private-sector solution, as we shall see. The fact that Northern Rock was the first bank to publicly run into trouble and was therefore somewhat of a "guinea pig" for the authorities to "cut their teeth" on (if we can mix metaphors) also contributed to the delay in reaching a conclusion.

Having said all that, however, one of the first articles that appeared during this second phase suggested that the Government (and the taxpayer) were making money out of Northern Rock, so why hurry? The author was Professor Tim Congdon.

Professor Tim Congdon is one of Britain's leading economic commentators and the founder of Lombard Street Research. Between 1992 and 1997 he was a member of the Treasury Panel of Independent Forecasters (the so-called "wise men") who advised the Chancellor of the Exchequer on economic policy. In 1997 he was awarded the CBE for services to economic debate. He is currently a member of the Shadow Monetary Policy Committee.

The article, in "The Times" was headed, **"Northern Rock is making money for taxpayers"**, was published 2nd November and read,

> *Alistair Darling, the chancellor, has said he expects the bank's directors to come up with proposals by February to end its reliance on government support.*

> *But what is the rush? Is there a serious threat to Britain's public finances? Is a large sum of public money at risk? The precise terms of the Bank's facility to Northern Rock are secret. -Everyone knows that the loan is on penalty terms and that Northern Rock is losing money on it. Nevertheless, as Northern Rock ought at least to be breaking even on its remaining funds, the bulk of its capital must be intact. Even if no bidder emerges, Northern Rock should be able to repay the £21bn in due course.*

> *Suppose that the affair drags on, that the loan exceeds £30bn at its peak, that the loan averages £30bn for a full year and that the interest rate is 6¾ per cent. In these circumstances - apparently so shocking and disgraceful for British banking - what will be the effect on the Bank of England's profits and the wider ramifications for our public finances?*

> *Suppose that Northern Rock has a loss equal to 1½ per cent a year on the £30bn loan and suppose that the rest of its operations break even. Plainly, it will still have substantial positive capital in the autumn of 2008. (The loss of £450m is less than the capital of £2.3bn.) The central assumption has therefore to be that - as the Bank and the Financial Services Authority have insisted several times - Northern Rock is solvent and can repay the loan in full. If so, what is the damage to the Bank of England and the public finances? The answer - paradoxically - is: there is no damage at all. On the contrary, the £30bn rescue of Northern Rock will boost the Central bank's profits and reduce - yes, reduce - the budget deficit by £2bn.*

> *The explanation is that the Bank of England can create money "by a stroke of the pen". Parliament has made it the UK's only issuer of legal-tender notes, and it can expand the note issue or credit a balance convertible into*

notes at virtually nil cost. Because of these special powers, the Bank does not need to borrow in the interbank market at a positive interest rate. Instead the interest cost on its £21bn loan (and indeed its £30bn loan if it reaches that level) is zero. So the Bank's profit on the operation in the circumstances discussed would amount to about £2bn (that is, 6¾ per cent on £30bn).

The crisis arose because a well-capitalised bank with sound assets found, very suddenly, that it could no longer fund those assets. By setting a deadline of February 2008 for proposals to end its loan, the Bank of England is giving a bargaining counter to the bidders who want to acquire Northern Rock assets on the cheap. As things stand, Northern Rock and its customers are in fact making a large contribution to the Bank of England's profits and, at a further remove, to the government's coffers. The more time the various players are given to think, the better is the likely outcome for everyone.

The article covered other points including the EU state aid rules but the foregoing extract is of interest because it represented a positive approach that was quite contrary to what was being published elsewhere, and certainly did not reflect H M Treasury's public pronouncements. Nevertheless, in view of who was the author of this piece, it must be accorded credibility.

Monday 29th October

"Yahoo Finance" posted an article based on a report from "Sky News",

There are fresh fears about the future of up to 2000 staff at the troubled bank, Sky News has learned. The struggling mortgage lender is understood to be considering a business plan that could see up to one-third of the workforce losing their jobs. - - - - Northern Rock has said it has no plans for compulsory redundancies—although it has put a freeze on hiring.

The report then commented that,

A third possible suitor for Northern Rock is looking at the company's books ahead of a possible takeover. Private equity company Cerberus is understood to be putting together a bid for the bank. It is being backed by GMAC, the finance firm half-owned by General Motors.

We later discovered, in January 2009 that GMAC required, and received, $5 billion by way of a government bail-out, and General Motors received over $14 billion.

Monday 5th November

This was "Guy Fox" day, but no fireworks to celebrate the rescue of Northern Rock. In fact, quite the opposite was the case. A "Reuters" story related how Northern Rock shares tumbled by 6% amid concerns that potential bidders will steer clear as the turmoil in global financial markets deepens.

In this and the previous Chapter concentration has been on those matters which have a direct bearing on Northern Rock's immediate situation, but as we shall see in Chapter 15 those events, as they developed, were impacted by what was happening on the global financial scene. Northern Rock was not the only bank facing difficulties and its shares were not the only bank shares at that time that suffered substantial falls, in the UK, the USA and elsewhere, notably at that time, in Germany and Switzerland.

There was concern that the more general problems that had affected many banks in the UK, USA and elsewhere would deter Northern Rock bidders and hamper their financing plans. Bidders all wanted the Treasury funding to remain largely in place until such time as they could refinance it in the financial markets. A time scale of three years was being suggested. They were unlikely to complete their bids unless this was agreed.

For practical and political reasons the Treasury was anxious to see the B of E loans repaid as soon as possible. The only way that these opposing points of view could be reconciled was if financial markets, in particular the UK inter-bank market, returned to normal fairly quickly.

At that point in time there were no indications that this would happen any time soon. All the talk in the City was of more problems to come. The inter-bank markets had seized up because nobody, particularly the banks themselves, could be sure that banks had fully identified the extent of their possible losses from involvement in the sub-prime and securitisation markets in which many banks had substantial investment. They were terrified to lend to each other.

The situation was not helped by the fact that banks were "self-certifying" the perceived value of their holdings of RMBS bonds and other derivatives in the absence of a functioning market. It was a fact that there was literally no functioning market in these products at this time because the usual range of investors for derivatives had lost confidence in them and had withdrawn their interest. Any secondary market that may have been operating was doing so at "fire sale" prices. This led to more uncertainty amongst the banks, and also to a reluctance to commit funds in the inter-bank markets and even to corporate customers.

It was also a fact that because investors had ceased to buy those bonds, banks were left holding much more of them than they may have wished to do.

The "Reuters" report continued,

> *Advisers for Northern Rock have sent out a broad information memorandum to potential bidders, seen as an attempt to revive interest from trade buyers or elsewhere in a break-up or other solution of the bank, which has been engulfed in crisis since needing emergency funding from the B of E six weeks ago.*

The report continued on a different topic,

> *A weekend report said as much as 14 billion pounds had been withdrawn by Northern Rock Depositors since the crisis broke, far higher than other estimates. A spokesman said that was a "significant overestimate", but declined to comment further.*

One of the problems facing the media in its efforts to keep abreast of the upheavals in the financial world was a lack of reliable information. Northern Rock produced very little, and those involved in bids for the bank and their advisers obviously had to play their cards very close to their chests in order to maintain competition-induced confidentiality.

Tuesday 6th November
"Reuters" recorded a " Financial Times" report that Northern Rock "had seen a dramatic fall in mortgage lending over the last two months."

The report also included,

> *Ray Boulger, technical director of mortgage broker Charcol, estimates that Northern Rock has been doing around 20% of the business it was doing before the start of the summer.*

Thursday 8th November
"Reuters" again reported, this time on the fact that "Documents sent to potential buyers for Northern Rock show savers have withdrawn £10.5 billion since the bank asked the Bank of England for assistance.

The immediate reaction was a drop of 12% in Northern Rock's share price although much of the fall was recovered.

The article then mentioned that a separate report from "The Financial Times" had recorded that advisers had approached up to 50 potential bidders, including Asian banks - - - - as they stepped up efforts to find a buyer.

Sunday, 11ᵗʰ November

"The Sunday Times" today reported a new entrant to the bidding arena, described by it as "One of the City's most experienced bankers, Luqman Arnold has secretly assembled a crack team to rescue Northern Rock, the stricken mortgage bank."

> *Arnold (through his investment vehicle Olivant) is proposing a salvage plan for the Newcastle-based bank which does not involve a sale or break-up. Details of his proposal are expected to be finalized ahead of this Friday's deadline set by Northern Rock's advisers for bids to be submitted.*
>
> *The ambitious plan is believed to have the support of a number of Northern Rock investors, particularly those who have been buying shares in recent weeks. One recent buyer, Philip Richards at RAB Capital said, "This is a credible solution with a proven management team." The proposal is thought to involve acquiring a stake of between 10% and 20%. Arnold would become interim chief executive, replacing Adam Applegarth, who would leave the company.*
>
> *Arnold's team would not receive any executive remuneration or fee. Their reward would come from attempting the Herculean task of restoring Northern Rock's share price.*

That Arnold's team would not receive any executive remuneration or fee (if true) was a departure from what was happening elsewhere. Everyone else involved in any capacity whatever was milking the company for every penny they could extract—collectively amounting to many million pounds.

> *The plan is expected to be well received in North-east England, where the Group's customers remain loyal despite the crisis that has engulfed their local bank.*
>
> *Arnold is thought to have sounded out Bryan Sanderson, who has recently been installed as Northern Rock's Chairman. Sanderson is believed to be supportive. Arnold is also understood to have had detailed conversations with the B of E, the FSA and the Treasury.*

The article then went on to describe Arnold's background and reputation, and the fact that he was backed by a number of wealthy investors, and was being advised by Ken Costa at Lazards (a London investment bank). It also listed a string of big-name financial people who were believed to be part of Arnold's team.

Monday 12ᵗʰ November

"Thomson Financial" was quoted in Yahoo Finance as reporting that SRM Global Master Fund held 22.99 million units of CFD's (Contracts for Difference) in Northern Rock, which gave it a 5.46% holding in Northern Rock.

Tuesday, 13ᵗʰ November

"Yahoo Finance" again quoted a "Sharecast" publication covering some apparent details relating to the takeover and other bids.

> *Parties interested in making a bid for the Tyneside based firm have been sent a briefing which reveals the firm could still owe the central bank £5.9 billion in 2010. The leaked document, issued under a confidentiality agreement, but seen by the Financial Times, assumes the bank will report a £378 million profit in 2008 and £519 million by 2010.*

It was also reported that Northern Rock's advisers, Merrill Lynch, Citigroup, and Blackstone had codenamed the bank "Blackbird" in the memo and referred to the hunt for a buyer as "Project Wing." This was all very James Bond style stuff!

The leaked memorandum was said to have set out three options, one of which, the "preferred" option, was to sell of the company as a whole. The other two options involved the sale of assets and the banking infrastructure, leaving shareholders invested in a rump company. The aim would be to run down the balance sheet, repay creditors and then "if appropriate" return the residual value of the company to shareholders.

"Advisers have set an informal deadline of Friday for approaches to be made." What were we to understand by "informal deadline"? Did it mean that there was really no deadline?

The article also disclosed that Arnold wanted a minority stake for Olivant but did not intend to make an offer for the group.

"The Times" repeated the Luqman Arnold story under the heading, *"**Lucky Luqie may be the Rock's best hope"***

> *He acquired the soubriquet "Lucky Luqie" thanks to his effortless rise through the ranks of City investment banks in the Eighties and Nineties.*

> *Unlike other bidders for the stricken bank, which want to take over Northern Rock more or less in its entirety, Mr. Arnold and his boutique investment company Olivant propose injecting a little fresh capital in return for a 10 - 20 % stake.*

The article continued with a review of some good and bad points in this proposal and the manner in which Mr Luqman dealt with the rejuvenation of Abbey National, the former building society that got into difficulties after trying to become a "real" bank operating in wholesale and corporate markets.

The article ended,

> *Mr. Arnold has won support from some Rock shareholders. That's the easy part. More difficult will be to convince Ministers that his proposal will get tax-payers off the hook any more reliably than the other bidders. That is what should decide the winning proposal.*

Wednesday, 14th November

"Yahoo Finance" had another article from "Sharecast" about the confidential memorandum issued by Northern Rock's advisers. The article was based on material from The Financial Times. It noted that Northern Rock had obtained a Court injunction restricting publication of information contained in a memorandum sent to parties interested in buying the mortgage bank.

It then quoted a statement from Northern Rock:

Further speculative reporting based on the illustrative information in the memorandum may jeopardize the complex discussions and negotiations taking place in connection with its strategic review. None of the information reported as being in the memorandum should be viewed as guidance to the market as to future outcomes of the strategic review or as an accurate representation of future results. The memorandum was not prepared with view to public disclosure or in compliance with rules, guidelines or policies relating to public disclosure.

The preferred option of the three that were available was reported as being a sale of the company, although it was believed that "many now view the chance of finding a buyer for the whole company as slim."

On the same day Yahoo Finance recorded "Thomson Financial" as having reported that,

Prime Minister Gordon Brown has come under fire for refusing to divulge details of when the troubled bank Northern Rock PLC would repay the taxpayer's cash used to bail it out during the run on deposits in September. Liberal Democrat acting leader Vince Cable launched a furious assault on Brown, demanding he confirm the figure lent to "this small mortgage bank" was £24 billion—twice the amount of public expenditure every year on primary schools.

> *Brown said he could not reveal the figure, claiming it was a matter of "commercial confidentiality". It would not be in the best interest of Northern Rock or its investors to speculate, he said.*

> *Cable labelled this defence as "bogus" and demanded a guarantee that the loan be repaid with interest. Why should the taxpayer have inferior rights to the managers, the directors and the shareholders of this company, Cable said.*

Is it any wonder that the public perception of politicians is so low when that is a not untypical example of the quality of exchanges between senior MPs?

The article continued,

> *In a separate statement, Cable accused the Chancellor Alistair Darling of a "cover-up". We are now in the absurd situation where banks can take ludicrous gambles with their customer's money, knowing that if it all goes wrong the taxpayer will bail them out.*

Handy chap, the "taxpayer"!

> *If banks are to have the benefit of the British public acting as a lender of last resort they must put an end to unsustainable lending practices.*

Is that not what the taxpayer, indirectly as a bank customer or investor, has paid the FSA to do?

> *When things do go wrong, the boards and management must be held responsible.*

Noble sentiments, but not all of them very well thought through in this particular instance. Also, although it may be a question of semantics, is it the "British taxpayer" or the Bank of England that is acting as a lender of last resort? It seems that when many billions of pounds by way of general support is being pumped into the banking system, it is Bank of England money but when much the same is being done for Northern Rock, it is "taxpayers" who have provided the funds.

Another article on the 14th came from "The Financial Times."— **Darling comments fuel Rock row"**, read the headline.

> *Alistair Darling, Chancellor, has admitted for the first time that the taxpayer could end up losing money in the multi-billion pound rescue of Northern*

Rock, a senior MP claimed.

Mr Darling has written that one of his key objectives is "minimizing the cost to the public purse of the bail out, an apparent recognition that the bank's crisis could end up costing the taxpayer money.

Since the Bank (of England) is lending money to Northern Rock at punitive rates and its loans are secured against the bank's assets, some speculate that the taxpayer could reap windfall profits from the rescue. Mr. Darling's comments, in a letter to Vince Cable suggest that he is far from confident that the loans and interest will be repaid in full.

Mr. Cable said this is the first time the government has acknowledged in print that its investment in Northern Rock could cost the taxpayer. Potentially the taxpayer could suffer enormous losses in this bail-out.

Mr. Cable said the answer betrayed the Treasury fears that a potential buyer of Northern Rock could ask for the interest bill of an estimated £2 billion to be waived, or that it was unsure of the quality of Northern Rock's assets.

This was a fine example of scare-mongering speculation for no other reason than to score political points off a fellow politician. Fortunately, later on in the crisis Mr. Cable's comments on various aspects of the broader financial crisis were less politically inspired and after he appeared to don his former mantle as an economist, he made many helpful and perceptive comments as the situation developed. At times he could be seen to be well ahead of the game.

Treasury officials insisted that Mr Darling was not signalling a change of position and said that he still expected the loan plus interest to be repaid, but admitted that the language he had used was "slightly different".

There was a little filler piece at the end of the article, "Mervyn King, Bank of England governor, said that he was not considering resigning over his role."

Thursday, 15th November

Jane Croft of "The Financial Times" produced an article that summarized the state of play amongst the bidders, from whom there were thought to be eight proposals - "some priced aggressively low - for buying the stricken bank".

It was also stated that Northern Rock's advisers had set this day as the deadline for indicative proposals, and that "one or two" banks from continental Europe and Asia were also considering the submission of proposals.

The article continued:

> *Northern Rock may issue a statement detailing where it is in the auction process as early as next week. - - - - Some bidders are thought to have lodged low bids and are expecting the UK Government to provide Northern Rock with some form of support after any takeover. The memorandum not only sets out a possible sale of the whole bank but outlines two other options - splitting it up or selling off basic infrastructure such as branches and leaving some assets and liabilities behind for an orderly run off.*

> *However, it is thought that one or two bidders have come along with bank backers which are prepared to refund the B of E over a period of time if, for example, the Government were to keep in place its guarantees for retail savers. - - - - the idea is that this reverts to the private sector as quickly as possible, said a person familiar with the situation.*

> *It is thought that Northern Rock has no plans to suspend its shares in spite of the huge volatility in the price, because it would add to the "crisis mentality" that continues to surround the company.*

The volatility in Northern Rock share prices, brought about by the sheer number of speculative trades being undertaken daily will be the subject of Chapter 11.

The article ended with,

> *Mr. Darling knows that a private equity sale could be politically awkward, particularly if it is underwritten - as expected - by tax-payer backed loans and then subsequently sold on by "fat cat bosses" at a big profit.*

This was a sentiment expressed frequently during this period by a number of commentators (and politicians) and it possibly influenced later Treasury decisions much more than was justified. It should not have been beyond the abilities of the bevy of highly paid advisers engaged by all the parties, including the Treasury, to have devised a satisfactory degree of protection for both the "tax-payer's" interests and those of the shareholders.

Friday, 16th November 2007
"Yahoo Finance" today recorded that,

> *Northern Rock is facing a critical day with the group having to weigh up rescue proposals for the crisis-hit business. Today was the deadline for proposals, although the company has said it will make an announcement when there is "greater clarity" on its future.*

The article continued with a summary of some of the ground already covered many times elsewhere, but did add a new piece of "information", namely that it was thought that Northern Rock's advisers had been trying to "drum up would be buyers from as far a field as China".

"The Financial Times" carried an article that was a follow up to its piece on 14th November. Commenting on the injunction which Northern Rock had sought, it reported that the High Court had granted a limited injunction preventing further reporting of material, but rejected a much more sweeping prohibition sought by the bank after much of the FT's report was followed up in other media.

The article reviewed again some of the information gleaned from, and already publicized from the leaked memorandum, which it noted had been sent to about 50 potential bidders. It may be more accurate to suggest it was sent to 50 institutions that were sufficiently well endowed financially to be capable of becoming involved. Where the 50 were coming from is difficult to identify, up to this time there have only been reports of a much smaller number of interested parties, in fact less than ten.

It then reviewed options (also mentioned above), the first being a sale of the basic infrastructure of the business - such as the branches, IT and call centre that might or might not include Northern Rock's £13.5 billion of retail deposits and matching assets.

Another option was described as a sale of the infrastructure plus secured mortgages, leaving behind some assets and liabilities for an orderly run-off. Both these scenarios would leave Northern Rock as a listed entity with assets that could be used to repay the B of E.

It is not clear where either of these options originated, from the Northern Rock advisors, through the "leaked "memorandum, the bidders camps, or in the mind of a journalist.

Wherever they came from they have the appearance of fantasy solutions far removed from the more down to earth solutions that would have reflected the realities of the situation.

The plain facts were that Northern Rock was not suffering from a shortage of funds. It had plenty, but some (the B of E loans) were from a source that was only available to those banks requiring short term funding in periods of economic or financial stress. Those loans were short term and had to be repaid, and in Northern Rock's case there was very little question that they would be repaid, given a reasonable time scale. What constituted "a reasonable repayment period" had to be related to the expectations of a turn round in the stressed (or distressed) money markets. The problems in these markets were not of Northern Rock's making, although as noted elsewhere, Northern

Rock may have placed too much reliance on the availability of the wholesale money market.

The Treasury, the Chancellor, the Government and the Bank of England stressed on a number of occasions that the aid had been provided, not simply to solve Northern Rock's temporary liquidity problems, but much more importantly to prevent contagion spreading throughout the country's financial system. That was the Treasury's principle objective, repeated on many occasions and it is important to keep it in mind. As events developed it will be seen that it became all too easy to concentrate on a "Northern Rock" problem and forget, once the immediate panic had subsided that the real objective had been and needed to be, preservation of a fragile banking system as a whole.

Taking full account of all of these different aspects, a repayment period dependent on Northern Rock's ability to access normally functioning inter-bank markets, or to re-activate its securitisation programmes (again depending on how long it took for sanity to return to that market), would determine the period required to repay the B of E lending.

The alternative was for Northern Rock to use the proceeds of maturing policies and of those re-financed elsewhere towards repayment of the loans.

Much has been made in media reports (and official statements from government and Treasury sources) of the dangers to which the "tax-payer" was exposed by allowing these loans to run on but the fact was that there could only be a minimal risk. A risk that would only arise if the entire UK housing market started to collapse and the inter-bank markets remained "frozen" indefinitely. That was a highly unlikely prospect that had never happened in the past, despite several severe economic and financial downturns, a repeat of which was not, at that time, anticipated in the period 2008-10, the period during which Northern Rock could reasonably be expected to repay the B of E loans.

At this time weaknesses were apparent in the UK housing markets, with sales slower and, according to the mortgage banks and building societies, a reduction in average house prices. The reductions were referred to as "falls", but in fact the average fall in any one month was less than one percent, whereas for years the market had been rising at an annual rate of 20% or more. The modest reductions in average prices did not represent a "collapse" of the housing market as some were predicting, although some borrowers at the margin would undoubtedly suffer from negative equity and increased interest rates.

The article concluded by stating,

> *Most of the bidders for Northern Rock are thought to have concluded that the shares are worth next to nothing. However, several hedge funds have*

built substantial stakes in the bank and would be expected to resist any
proposal to undermine the value of "their shares".

This report was phrased as if the shares owned by the "hedge funds" were somehow different from the 85% or so of shares owned by other shareholders at the time. Although never subject to public mention, there were also a number of insurance / pension funds and major banks, British and foreign, that had substantial holdings of shares as investments for their own account.

Sunday, 18th November
"The Sunday Times" had an article by Louise Armitstead and John Waples headed, **"Shareholders to fight Rock "fire Sale"**.

It described how the two biggest shareholders in Northern Rock were calling for the auction of the bank to be abandoned. RAB Capital and SRM Global, two hedge funds that account for 13% of the bank's equity, were quoted as saying that the company should not be sold or broken up. The reporters expressed the opinion that such a suggestion could upset the sale process that had attracted up to eight first-round offers, amongst them was one from is a consortium led Sir Richard Branson's Virgin Group that had assembled a funding syndicate led by Royal Bank of Scotland by means of which to immediately repay £ 10 billion of Northern Rock's government borrowings. According to bankers, the RBS team included Citi, and there is an intention to provide £ 20 billion.

Much of this was based on speculation rumour. There is a question one is obliged to ask. If RBS, etc., is able to produce £20 or £30 billion by way of finance (the actual amount was not clear from the article) to finance a "bid " by another consortium which presumably would be the beneficiary of any profit made out of the resuscitation of Northern Rock, why are the same banks not in a position to make the loans direct to Northern Rock against virtually the same security with possibly a "sweetener" in the deal to acknowledge their assistance. These same banks were very adept at arranging "sweeteners" in deals that they set up.

Jon Wood, head of SRM Global said,

> *Now is not the time to sell the bank or any part of its operations. We have*
> *repeatedly made it clear to the board that this sale process should be*
> *stopped. The process has become a farce that is damaging the franchise*
> *of Northern Rock and the UK banking system. Just as other banks have*
> *used facilities provided by other central banks, the Bank of England should*
> *continue to support Northern Rock in its role as lender of last resort. We*
> *need to end the process in which self-interested parties are trying to buy*
> *the company on the cheap.*

The RAB chief executive, Philip Richards added,

> *Forcing a fire sale right now is equivalent to when Gordon Brown ordered the sale of gold at the bottom of the cycle, when he was Chancellor. (perhaps this was not the most diplomatic comment he might have made) The correct response is to give Northern Rock time, and to have proven leadership.*

There were suggestions that mainstream institutional investors were disillusioned with the bank's management. This comment should be extended to all investors. Private investors were equally disillusioned, but had no effective voice other than through the UK Shareholders Association.

One institutional investor voiced the opinion that the most frustrating and worrying thing about Northern Rock now was that there seemed to be absolutely no one at the company who was acting on behalf of shareholders. This situation had few precedents but he had never witnessed such a shambles.

Another voiced the view as far as dealing with investors is concerned, the board appeared to have handed all responsibility to the investment bankers. Bryan Sanderson, its chairman, appeared not to understand the situation at all and it seemed that he was more interested in dealing with politicians and advisers.

These were comments that would be shared by many, including non-shareholders. As far as the media was concerned in its reporting, and the statements emanating from Government, Treasury and regulatory sources, the shareholders might as well have been non-existent, except for the "hedge fund" investors who occupied a status as "marked men". They were not just shareholders, they were targets for both the media and the Government.

Shareholders were considered to be either opportunists who stupidly did not get out at the 1200 pence plus share peak, or speculators who bought in cheaply after 14th September and who deserved no sympathy.

Nobody stopped to consider that those two shareholder stereotypes accounted for a very small proportion of shareholders. The others, including institutional shareholders representing pension funds and insurance policy holders, were genuine long-term investors in the company. In other words 70% or more fell into the latter category.

What seems to have been overlooked is that whilst the so-called "bidders" were circling round the carcass of Northern Rock, trying to work out the cheapest way (for them) of disposing of it and making money out of the carcass, the two hedge fund managers had put their money into Northern Rock, and lots of it, showing faith in the basic integrity of the company (but not in its management) at a difficult time. The only way they would get their money back was if Northern Rock could return to a normal operating environment on a conventional commercial basis under new management.

Of course they were no more altruistic in their motives than the bidders, but at least they put their money into Northern Rock and stood to lose it whereas the bidders had next to nothing at stake unless one of their bids was successful. At the same time they enjoyed a great deal of free publicity.

"The Sunday Times " also ran an article headed **"Rock rescue cannot ignore shareholders".** The thrust of it was that the B of E, Treasury and the FSA were about to stumble into another disaster. In their rush to try to drum up an auction for Northern Rock, they appeared to have underestimated one of the biggest obstacles to a rescue—the bank's shareholders. The Treasury was desperate to find a solution so that it could get back the £23 billion it was owed by Northern Rock but the shareholders were equally keen to see their holdings protected as well. The newspaper repeated that if the shareholders were arguing that a sale should be abandoned until markets returned to more normal conditions, perhaps the government should listen to them.

Hurrah for the beleaguered shareholders, at long last a champion had appeared!

Monday 19th November
The Treasury published the principles on which the Tripartite Authorities "currently expect to approach proposals for the future of Northern Rock and its business, in particular considering the objectives against which the Tripartite Authorities expect to assess proposals received by Northern Rock."

> In undertaking the assessment the Tripartite Authorities have taken and will continue to take actions in pursuit of wider public interest objectives.

Those objectives were noted as,

a)   to protect taxpayers

b)   to promote financial stability

c)   to protect consumers

The statement ran to three pages elaborating on these objectives and their observance and on a review of EC related "state aid" considerations.

Northern Rock issued another "strategic review update". In essence it repeated earlier statements without adding much clarification to them. Perhaps if the management and its advisers could have recognized that it was not a euphemistic "strategic review" that was required, but rather a "rescue plan", they could have achieved greater success.

In the opinion of some interested observers the management decision to spend time on a "strategic review" which is management speak for "putting the business up for sale" was a serious mistake because it resulted in a diversion of management concentration from its real job of managing the company to dealing with the army of accountants, lawyers and financial advisers that descended on the company (at the invitation of management, of course). In this case management had also to cope with the FSA and other parts of government having their say, in what was possibly a forceful manner. All of this left Northern Rock's management virtually impotent.

Why highly paid senior managements and boards of directors are unable to reach their own decisions on the appropriate actions that need to be adopted for their companies is beyond comprehension. That is particularly the case when one is dealing with a company that has only one, fairly straightforward objective.

To some observers the concept of a strategic review was unlikely to produce viable "external" options. The in-house solution, when the management got round to it (after recruiting someone to devise it) was probably the best. There was a simple reason for this. No other institutions were going to be any more successful at raising funds to re-finance the business than Northern Rock itself because the inter-bank markets remained frozen and banks were afraid to lend substantial sums to other banks.

Furthermore, the uncertainties that were spreading almost daily through financial markets and the "poison pill " of the B of E loans meant that there was unlikely to be a takeover on normal commercial terms. The only bidders for the company were those committed to picking up a bargain at the lowest possible cost.

When we see in later chapters the lengths that the government, through H M Treasury and the Bank of England were prepared to go to deal with the September 2008 financial crisis particularly, and for a long time unsuccessfully, in trying to kick-start the inter-bank lending markets, one has to wonder why there was so much "agro" attached to dealing with Northern Rock's situation.

The only logical conclusion is that at the time, nobody knew what to do.

Tuesday, 20th November

There were various media reports that JC Flowers had submitted a takeover bid for (once again) "the stricken" British home loan provider, Northern Rock. JC Flowers was quoted ("by a source familiar with the situation") to have offered to repay £15 billion to the B of E, should its bid be successful, repaying the rest of the loans over the next three years. Under the terms of the offer, JC Flowers would buy Northern Rock and take it private, investing one billion pounds into the business. Of this, existing shareholders would be offered a "nominal sum", although the precise figure had not yet been determined. The bank would continue to operate as a British mortgage lender under the Northern Rock brand.

Wednesday, 21st November

There were reports that at least two more firm bids for Northern Rock had emerged. However it was suggested yet again that "taxpayers" could still end up propping up the company for up to three years.

As it looked as if there was no alternative to the B of E loans staying in place for a time, at least in part, this problem of the "taxpayer propping up the company for several years" was one that was repeated time after time. But it was little more than rhetoric. The true situation was that HM Treasury (or, as it should have been, the Bank of England) was paid a higher than market rate for loans that were more than fully secured. All banks borrowing from official sources during the crisis had to put up an excess margin of assets acceptable to the authorities to an extent determined by the authorities. The taxpayer, if we return to him as the ultimate source of the funds enjoyed a pretty good and risk-free deal. The only uncertainty was the length of time the loans would have to last.

On the same day, the Corporate Relations department of Northern Rock issued a statement.

> *The Board confirms that, following its announcement on 19th November, the Company has received additional indicative expressions of interest covering a range of options for the business, one of which does contemplate an offer for the Company materially below the market price at close of business on Tuesday, 20th November2007*
>
> *The Company's advisers have begun discussions with a number of selected interested parties to clarify their proposals. The Company is aware that all stakeholders in the Company want clarity on the outcome of the strategic review as soon as possible and is therefore progressing the process as quickly as possible.*
>
> *As previously announced, the strategic review will be completed by February 2008, although the Company expects to make an announcement of the preferred outcome for the company and its stakeholders in advance of that.*

Northern Rock reminds all stakeholders that there can be no certainty that the discussions with interested parties will lead to an investment in or offer for the Company or for all or any part of its business or that such investment or offer will be implemented.

The Company statement (or more likely that prepared by its lawyers) continued with a number of "housekeeping matters."

There seems to be a deliberate use of "stakeholders" to apply to HM Treasury and the shareholders in Northern Rock, rather than to mention each by name, since those were the only parties with a financial interest in Northern Rock, apart from depositors who had been secured by the Government. As will be seen shortly, the Board of Northern Rock (or possibly its advisers) appeared to have discounted the views and rights of shareholders in deciding what should happen to Northern Rock.

Monday, 26th November

Northern Rock Corporate Relations department issued another of its rare updates on its "strategic review". The Northern Rock board insisted throughout this process that it be glossed over as a "strategic review" rather than as a rescue plan, which would have implied fault on its part. Here we have yet another example of a management referring to a spade as a "digging instrument".

Following receipt of indicative expressions of interest covering a range of options in respect of its business, the Company and its advisors have engaged in discussions with a limited number of selected interested parties to clarify their proposals. As a result, and following discussions with the Tripartite Authorities, the Board has concluded that it wishes to take forward discussions on an accelerated basis with a consortium comprising Virgin Group, WL Ross and Co, Toscafund Asset Management and First Eastern Investment Group, (the "Virgin" consortium).

Brian Sanderson, Chairman of Northern Rock said, "This is very good news for Northern Rock. Over the last few weeks and months we have looked at the issues from the perspective of all the stakeholders. I am grateful for the support that we have had from customers and employees who have stayed loyal to us during those difficult times - and pleased that a solution that firmly restores the Company's prospects has been identified. Furthermore our retail depositors can be fully reassured that the Government has said it will ensure saver's money is safe whatever the outcome.

The statement then went on to describe the Virgin proposals in detail.

Note once again there was no mention of shareholders, many of whom had been just as loyal to the Company as its customers and employees.

The statement also recorded that the Virgin consortium confirmed to HM Treasury and the Bank of England that any transaction will be predicated, *inter alia,* on the following principles

> *Its equity and debt financing proposals will, at the point of announcement of a definitive transaction, be full underwritten.*

> *As included in the Virgin Consortium's proposal, the private sector debt financing must be comparable in scale to any public sector debt financing required following closing.*

> *Returns on equity investments made by members of the Virgin Consortium and other holders of ordinary shares must be restricted until the public sector loans have been paid back with interest and all other public sector commitments are at an end.*

The statement continued to cover other aspects of the "strategic review" including a note that,

> *The Company had agreed to cover certain out of pocket expenses, not exceeding £5 million (plus applicable VAT) in connection with the "indicative proposal", (of the Virgin Consortium) including meeting the professional advisory costs of the financing banks on the basis that the Company expects to be able to make use of such finance whether or not the transaction proceeds.*

There can be few occasions in the course of normal commercial practice where a bidder, expressing only "an <u>indicative</u> expression of interest" on terms that are entirely in its favour, gets its preliminary expenses paid by the target company out of shareholder funds. How was that for a "sweetener"?

The second part that,

> *The company expects to make use of such finance whether or not the transaction proceeds* appeared, some months later, to have sunk without trace.

Finally the company statement ended with a reluctant acknowledgement of a notice to convene an Extraordinary General Meeting of shareholders to consider a shareholder special resolution "requiring shareholder approval for a disposal in any twelve month period of more than 5% of the aggregate book value of the Company's assets". The statement made it clear that the Board did not support such a resolution and considered it unwarranted and inappropriate. Why? Because it would have been obliged to pay some attention to the shareholders the existence of whom it, the Chairman and his advisers, preferred to ignore.

On the same day "Associated Press" produced a report by Robert Barr under the headline **"Virgin takes the lead in Northern Rock Bids".**

The article related how Northern Rock PLC planned to hold accelerated takeover discussions with the consortium led by Virgin Group. Virgin, wanted to re-brand Northern Rock as part of Virgin Money business and said that its consortium would repay 11 billion pounds of the 25 billion pounds the B of E has loaned to Northern Rock on the completion of the transaction, the remainder of the money being paid in due course. In an announcement (not to the shareholders, but to the London Stock Exchange), Northern Rock said that the Virgin consortium also promised additional funding facilities to support the business. The announcements resulted in a 29% increase in the share price.

Nick Clarke, an analyst at Charles Stanley, stockbrokers, was quoted as saying,

> *The share price has rebounded because some investors have taken the view that with shareholders keeping potentially 45% of a company re-energized under a powerful brand like Virgin, it could be worth substantially more in a couple of years than the 25 pence nominal value a share that some had predicted would be all that shareholders would receive.*

However, he cautioned that the future for Northern Rock was not sealed, that the stock was not for the fainthearted and the range of outcomes for shareholders was very wide.

The article continued,

> *Hedge Fund RAB Capital holds a 7% stake in Northern Rock and RAB's chief executive, Philip Richards has backed the Virgin offer, which would allow shareholders to retain around a third of the business and also offer them a share of any future profits.*

The Northern Rock Small Shareholders Group representing a group of private shareholders (not to be confused with the UK Shareholders Association, a much larger and more widely based Association) said they were opposed to any "fire sale" of the assets. A letter signed by Lord Stevens of Kirkwhelpington, the honorary president continued,

The options which we would oppose would be the sale of the company as a whole or piecemeal, or any move such as administration or nationalization, which would expropriate the shareholders' stake or so dilute it as to be the equivalent. We very much deprecate the driving down of the share price to meet expectations about future price, which seems to favour the interests of some potential bidders above existing shareholders.

The sentiments expressed in this letter probably reflected the views of shareholders in the company, but other than relying on the concepts enshrined in UK company law, the Group had no means of giving teeth to these utterings and as we shall see the protestations of the Group and the UK Shareholders Association were ignored by the Treasury, and for that matter, by the various bidders and the Board of the Company.

The article ended,

Northern Rock said there was no certainty that the Virgin proposal would be accepted.

As far as acceptance was concerned, the board appeared set to determine the acceptance or otherwise of any of the bids by itself, without consulting shareholders.

More comments on this subject appear later in the story.

The "Financial Times" also produced a piece headed **"Virgin approved for Northern Rock".**

It started off that it's good for Virgin, its good for the Government, but is it good for anyone else. It then recorded a share price rise on the news that Virgin was the "preferred bidder" but expressed the view that the reasons for the rise may have been based on technical issues. It was suggested that investors hoped that the proposed deal ruled out the worst-case scenario – bankruptcy - and therefore allowed the parties to refocus on the values of Northern Rock's assets, a value that fluctuated daily. In September, Northern Rock's net assets - deducting those attributable to the Northern Rock Foundation and assuming £1.94 a share of mark to market losses on certain assets, were estimated at about £ 1.90 a share. It was proposed that under the deal, Northern Rock would be merged with Virgin Money, Virgin's consumer finance business, which the consortium valued at £250 million. The bidders planned to inject £650 million of cash and raise another £650 million from existing shareholders, who would pay 25pence a share for a diluted stake (up to 45%) in the new entity. This suggested that the current shareholders' stake in the new entity, including Virgin Money and after deducting the rights price could be worth 86 pence a share.

It was suggested that re-branding was a crucial first step towards restoring confidence in the business and was thought to be a factor that swayed the Government in favour of the Virgin consortium rather than other potential bidders.

It was looked upon as a gamble. If it paid off, current shareholders would share in future growth. If it didn't, Virgin was thought to be in a better position than Northern Rock's management to sell assets. Interested parties are certainly not lacking.

This last comment "interested parties are certainly not lacking" was little more than a throw away line. The root cause of Northern Rock's problems as has been noted elsewhere, was a liquidity imbalance between its assets and liabilities with no alternative funding source readily available. If "interested parties are certainly not lacking" had been true, its problems might have been solved overnight.

In a second article by Chris Giles and George Parker, the "Financial Times" expanded on the situation of the Treasury in relation to the Virgin and other bids.

It recorded that John Kingman, the second most important Treasury official, had told friends that sorting out the Northern Rock mess was the hardest thing he has ever had to do. It is easy to see why. The Treasury's task, after getting more than £20 billion involved in the mortgage business, was to find an exit route that satisfied six tough conditions. The first three came from the government, to get the tax payer out without losing money, to safeguard financial stability, and to protect depositors.

Three additional goals were listed as, to secure agreement from Northern Rock's shareholders who can reject any bid (in theory); to protect jobs in the politically sensitive north-east of England; and to meet EU rules designed to prevent governments distorting competition across Europe.

The journalists made the point that the Virgin bid appeared to have a chance to meet all six criteria, particularly as Sir Richard Branson would be at the front of the queue to lose money if the bank suffered from rising defaults on its loan book. Not quite true, the consortium backing him would be the first to lose out. However, the bank's asset position was such that defaults were unlikely to become a significant factor, even in the then deteriorating market conditions.

Concern was expressed in various quarters (including by other banks) that the continuance of the 100% guarantee would fall foul of EU competition rules. However, the Treasury proposed to charge Northern Rock a premium for this facility, and if the premium was at commercial rates, which would not be too difficult to establish, the competition rules would be satisfied. Furthermore the depositor protection schemes in other E C countries were not on all fours with the UK scheme, therefore it would be difficult to determine the extent to which a guarantee of Northern Rock deposits would be in breach of EU rules.

Whilst the guarantee was put in place at the outset of the problems in order to halt the run on deposits, it would not really be essential to the reinstatement of Northern Rock if depositors could be convinced that Northern Rock was going to be and always had been a "going concern."

If, as reported above and on many other occasions, the Treasury's prime concern was to safeguard financial stability of the UK banking system, the deposit guarantee was a side issue and a small price to pay towards the achievement of that objective. In any event, it was possible that the importance of this additional guarantee had been over-emphasized since it only benefited depositors with more than £34,000 in the bank, later increased to £50,000. Depositors who had less than that sum were already protected under the existing Depositor Protection provisions.

The article continued,

> Northern Rock shareholders may be a tougher group to satisfy, since their shareholdings would be highly diluted under the proposals. Their reaction is yet to be tested and the bid could easily come a cropper if they feel they are getting a raw deal. But the Treasury can still threaten administration under which they would probably secure even less.

> But that threat will not necessarily appear credible. Alistair Darling, the Chancellor, was due to tell the CBI employers' organisation on Tuesday: "There were always going to be critics when the going got tough, but that is not the point. Far worse would have been to do nothing, to have allowed that bank to have gone under.

> Virgin's bid secures jobs in the north-east and has gained support from local members of parliament. Labour's north-east caucus of MP's is highly influential and Jim Cousins a Labour MP in the bank's Newcastle heartland, said Virgin had been clear about maintaining Northern Rock as a company whose head-quarters were on Tyneside. He added "This is the best option from the government point of view and best from the point of view of getting the tax-payers' money out again.

> Finally, it was recorded that it appeared that the European Commission was taking a sympathetic position on the issue of State aid, especially as the Government would be lending on terms identical to those of the private sector.

"Neelie Kroes, EU Competition Commissioner, discussed the Virgin bid with Mr Darling at the Treasury, as part of regular British contact with Brussels since the bank's near collapse in September. M/s Kroes' spokesman said Brussels' state aid rules would normally not apply if Bank of England loans to Northern Rock were charged at a commercial rate - as envisaged under the deal (and actually in place prior to it). "We would have to be satisfied the loans were on commercial terms," she said. Others however (who were they?)*, were less sure that the Treasury had got round all the obstacles.*

The political overtones surfaced once again in comments from the Liberal Democrats. Chris Hulme, a contender for the party leadership, said the Virgin bid was almost bound to be bad news for tax-payers.

By getting preferred bidder status, they actually exclude rival bids. They will then look at the books in detail and tell the Treasury that things were far worse than they expected, and they need a much better deal from the tax-payer. I could write the script."

Vince Cable, Lib Dem Treasury spokesman (who had a lot to say in Parliament over the weeks, mostly of a very critical nature) said,

The temporary nationalization of Northern Rock could still be better than the Virgin bid. Mr. Cable said he believed the Treasury and its adviser, Goldman Sachs, were continuing to look at that option.

If there was one sentence that came to the fore in nearly every review, from media and government / political sources, it was "tax-payers' money is at risk and it is paramount that their interests be protected." The need to protect taxpayers is not disputed but as indicated above and in the light of all the facts it was a card that was very much overplayed, possibly for vote-generating reasons.

That was a record of the Virgin bid as seen from the outside. However, in his recent book, "Business Stripped Bare", Sir Richard Branson included a chapter on his bid for Northern Rock that viewed it from the inside.

What was interesting to those who were not part of the "magic Circle" of financial luminaries was the insight it gave into some of the relationships that existed between the parties. A long time adviser to Virgin was Peter Norris, former Chairman of Baring Brothers at the time it gave so much of its money to Nick Leeson to gamble away in Singapore that the bank had to be sold off for £1. Matt Ridley, Chairman of Northern Rock was quoted as saying that Virgin was just what Northern Rock needed. Virgin

Direct had been a joint venture with Royal Bank of Scotland. How many other connections were there? Jayne-Anne Ghadia worked for RBS and later headed up Virgin Direct and Virgin Money. Sir George Mathewson headed up RBS at that time. He later advised Virgin on the Northern Rock bid. He also acted as senior adviser to Tosca Fund, one of the Virgin consortium members and was on its board. RBS teamed up with Deutsche Bank and Citigroup to put together the finance that Virgin needed to finalize a bid, although in the end this loan did not materialize probably due to the conditions in the finance markets later in the year.

Sir Brian Pitman was nominated by Virgin to be Chairman of Northern Rock should the bid succeed. Sir Brian was on Virgin's board. Sir Richard wrote an interesting little piece into his book about Sir Brian. Apparently Sir Brian remembered how, during the miners' strike in the 1980's, Northern Rock allowed monthly payments due from striking miners to be rolled over. He recorded how, after the strike, the miners made up their due payments and Northern Rock did not lose a penny as a result.

Sir Richard also recorded that there was a lot to admire in Northern Rock. Staff were very good and when the run on deposits happened they all came in to branches to help and to deal with customers in an exemplary manner. He also noted that it had very modern systems in place. He appeared to be genuinely interested in "saving" Northern Rock, but of course like all good entrepreneurs any deal had to make sense for him.

It is not suggested that there was anything amiss in the relationships described above, merely that they demonstrate the value of "networking".

Tuesday, November 27th
There were reports that SRM Global had increased its stake to 8.5% or 35.8 million shares to become its biggest shareholder and that SRM had said that Northern Rock should allow shareholders to vote on a sale of all or part of the bank to prevent any bidders purchasing assets at " fire sale prices."

The two principal hedge fund investors were naturally concerned because it was becoming increasingly apparent that the Board of Northern Rock, which had changed its composition from the pre-September Board, was intent on deciding on the choice of bidders without a ballot of shareholders to ascertain their wishes in the matter, as required by company law.

It was becoming increasingly apparent that normal corporate procedures were receiving scant attention from the Board, from those advising them and by those with whom they were negotiating. There was an overwhelming sense that the shareholders were an irrelevance. That the only interests which mattered were those of the Treasury, or more precisely, the (Labour) Government and "the taxpayer", and that the Government would decide on the course of action to be adopted, and notify the Board accordingly.

Notwithstanding, the existing shareholders were expected, under the Virgin offer, to subscribe for a rights issue as part of the Virgin takeover. Existing shareholders would be expected to produce about £650 million of new capital. As the shares have a nominal value of 25pence, this meant the issue of 2.6 billion new shares, in other words, 6.2 new shares for every existing Northern Rock share at 25 pence per share.

There was no incentive for existing shareholders to subscribe for these new shares. At the time of the Virgin bid, existing shares were trading around 110 pence. Each member of the former Northern Rock Building Society, a total of 885,764, received 500 shares at the time of the conversion to a PLC. The proposals would mean that a holder of 500 shares, worth 110 pence each would have a holding worth £550. To protect this investment which in any event would be diluted, and with no certainty that the Virgin bid, if successful would produce the desired result, each such shareholder was expected to invest another £775. Of course many of those original shareholders would have long since sold their shares. However, the same line of reasoning applied to all existing shareholders.

At a time when the widely expressed (but unsubstantiated) view was that the existing shares were actually worthless, it hardly seemed logical that existing shareholders would flock to subscribe an additional amount which was more than their existing shares were worth (at best) to save the original investment.

This proposal did not seem to add up. It also meant that if Virgin subscribed for its projected majority stake in the company it would have obtained it at 25 pence per share when the market value was quoted at 110 pence. That was a pretty good deal!

Of course it was also a fact that not all investors were "small" investors sitting on their original gift of 500 shares. As noted earlier, there were many institutional investors with much larger holdings who would have to consider whether to risk a further large investment in Northern Rock (or more correctly, in Virgin Money). "Small" investors was an expression used to describe individuals as investors. The fact was that many were not "small" investors as they had holdings that were substantial enough to cause them concern.

There were also the two big hedge fund holdings. They would have to contribute very large sums of money, and whilst they subsequently indicated a willingness to invest more money in Northern Rock, that commitment was not in support of the Virgin bid.

For this proposal to be successful it would have to be underwritten, and in the circumstances surrounding Northern Rock at the time, and the difficult market conditions pertaining, that would have been a difficult and expensive process to arrange. There was also the question as to whether such a cost would be borne by Northern Rock (shareholders) or by the Virgin consortium.

Wednesday 28th November
Today's "Financial Times" headline was, " **Rock seeks fully financed plan from Olivant**", again an article by Jane Croft and Thai Larsen.

> *Northern Rock today urged Olivant, the private equity group interested in making a bid for the embattled bank, to come up with a fully-financed business plan. The stricken (yet again) Newcastle bank has selected a consortium led by Virgin Group as preferred bidder but is not in exclusive talks. Olivant has met Northern Rock's advisers to discuss its plan.*

> *Olivant, led by Luqman Arnold, the former chief executive of Abbey National, proposes to inject new management into Northern Rock and run the bank as a going concern.*

> *Mr. Arnold's plans have won the support of leading shareholders, notably Jon Wood's SRM hedge fund which wants Northern Rock's board to look at other suitors in addition to Virgin. SRM has upped its stake from 8.5% to 9.1%.*

> *However, a source close to Northern Rock said Mr. Arnold was some way behind the other bidders. "If he's going to run it, he's got to come up with his own business plan", the person said.*

The article continued,

> *There have been suggestions that any credible bidder, including Olivant and Virgin, would be able to access a package of financing from banks secured against Northern Rock's asset base. However, people close to the bid process have said that this is an oversimplification.*

As noted earlier, there were others who failed to comprehend why bidders should expect to be able to access markets that were not available to Northern Rock directly. The subject of financing from banks kept coming up, based on speculation rather than on knowledge of firm commitments. The article suggested that,

> *The Virgin led consortium is in the process of finalising its financing with Royal Bank of Scotland, Deutsche bank and Citigroup, although a deal is by no means certain.*

In other words, it must have been a fifty-fifty situation at best.

It was suggested that Virgin had only secured financing from the banks, (or more correctly a commitment from them to <u>consider</u> the provision of finance) because it had appointed Sir Brian Pitman, the former head of Lloyds TSB, to be its chairman if its bid was successful. Sir Brian told "The Financial Times"that the financing banks "were very committed." At the same time the banks involved were saying nothing.

Another FT article reported that,

> *Opposition is growing to plans by Sir Richard Branson to take control of Northern Rock. The second meeting of small shareholders in three days has come out against Virgin Money's takeover offer, claiming the offer is far too low.*

> *Just yesterday, it was revealed that investment firms SRM Global and RAB Capital, both of which want the sell-off scrapped, now own 15% of Northern Rock. If the separate groups of investors show a united front they could block the Virgin deal and force the government to come back with a better deal.*

Let us indulge in a bit of hindsight here. In the light of the Government's subsequent actions that was wishful thinking that showed a lack of understanding of what was going on behind the scenes.

What has dogged the whole process over the weeks since 14th September is the manner in which the descriptions "the Government", "the Treasury " and the "Bank of England " have been used indiscriminately. In particular, "the Government" has been used to link in "the taxpayer".

The state of the financial markets as a whole, and particularly those in the UK was undoubtedly a concern for the Government. However the plight of Northern Rock was one for the Bank of England in conjunction with the Treasury. All the talk of "the Government" and " the tax-payer" was a way of hyping-up publicity of the Northern Rock problems, by both politicians and the media and of generating public indignation from those not financially involved.

SRM was reported as having said it wanted to introduce rules obliging Northern Rock to consult shareholders over all disposals involving the sale of more than 5% of its assets, in an attempt to prevent a deal at "fire sale" prices.

Friday 30th November
There were further reports on the J C Flowers offer. The bidder had offered to improve its bid but also gave warning that it would walk away if the government did not enter into

talks with it. J C Flowers had addressed two concerns the government had with its initial proposal. The government wished to ensure that all the money it has lent to Northern Rock would be repaid on a par with other creditors and that shareholders were offered some exposure to any turnaround. However, the Treasury had not been willing to discuss the issues since expressing an interest in the consortium led by Virgin Group.

It is worth taking note of this and similar reports since they give cause for concern as to the impartiality of the various negotiators, the Northern Rock Board (or more probably its advisers), the Bank of England, the Treasury and its adviser and of course, No 10 Downing Street.

Vince Cable, Liberal Democrat acting leader held the view that the government needed to consider nationalization. He said,

> *I am concerned the borrowing was running out of control. Shareholders holding little more than £50 million in equity were determining the outcome when it was the taxpayer (*him again*) that should be dictating events.*

True up to a point except that the government had no intention of allowing the shareholders to dictate events.

If we turn this idea around, we can pinpoint why there were bidders that were interested in acquiring Northern Rock. For little more than an injection of a modest amount of additional capital, they could acquire a business and sort out its illiquidity problems when markets returned to at least near normality by utilizing funds from maturing mortgages, by selling off part of its mortgage book, by raising funds in the inter-bank market or by securitising more mortgages. By one or any combination of these methods the Bank of England loans would be repaid (given a reasonable time scale). The bidder would then own a business, properly structured and worth £60 – 70 billion or more that was capable of earning several hundred million pounds per annum in profits.

It might take a year or two to achieve, but it was a worthwhile prize.

That was the attraction of Northern Rock. The bank was solvent, very much so and only needed that one key element, to rebalance its liquidity position.

Friday 7th December
Luqman Arnold of Olivant made a proposal to raise up to £800 million in new equity through a rights issue of between £450 million and £650 million and a new equity subscription from Olivant. Olivant would also be issued with high premium warrants over 7% of the enlarged equity capital. It said that it had agreement from institutional shareholders representing approximately 23% of the shareholder base to take up pro

rata rights and sub-underwrite approximately £440 million of any rights issue at or around the current share price. If successful with its rescue plan, Olivant added it would immediately refinance between £10 - 15 million of the emergency government loans and aim to pay back the rest by the end of 2009. The Bank of England would also be given high premium warrants on the same terms as Olivant over 5% of the enlarged equity capital.

The article did not provide details of the terms of the warrants, but it can be assumed that they would enable the holders to acquire shares in Northern Rock at some future date at a price much below the then current market price – assuming that the rescue was successful.

Reports elsewhere on the same day elaborated on the Olivant proposals and noted that J C Flowers had withdrawn interest because it could not find a way of meeting the government's requirements in a manner that would also achieve its own investment objectives.

Sunday, 9ᵗʰ December

There was a return to the story about the three banks, Citigroup, Royal Bank of Scotland and Deutsche Bank, that were being lined up to provide the £15 billion required by bidders for Northern Rock. They were refusing to sign off on any bail-out deal until the New Year at the earliest, or until the turbulence in the inter-bank lending markets had subsided. The banks were also understood to be attempting to demand better quality assets as collateral against their funding.

The accuracy of this last statement may be questionable since Northern Rock's book of mortgages was generally accepted to be of good quality, a fact confirmed by the FSA, and it had very few other treasury assets to put up. However, as we shall see later, H M Treasury had a plan that might have resolved that problem.

The question of funding from commercial banks was a bit of a "chicken and egg" situation. Without a firm bid deal in place, no commitment to provide funding was forthcoming. Without firm funding, a deal could not be finalised. If the various proposals all foundered, it was because commercial banks globally were too frightened to lend in other than absolutely "cast iron" circumstances.

The following day Northern Rock's Chairman was quoted as saying that a decision on the future of the bank was not likely before Christmas.

Monday 10ᵗʰ December

Northern Rock was reported as having upped its efforts to attract new savers, while retrenching from the mortgage market. The bank was also offering loyalty bonuses and improved interest rates on a range of savings accounts to try and stem the exodus of savers and bolster the funds held on deposit. At the same time it had withdrawn certain mortgages, loans and a credit card and increased borrowing rates to dissuade new customers.

On several occasions in the past three months commentators had pointed out that the best place in Britain to have a bank deposit was Northern Rock as it was the only bank covered by a 100% government guarantee.

Tuesday 12th December
The FTSE Group at the London Stock Exchange regularly revises the list of companies eligible to be listed as constituents of the FTSE 100 Index. On this day, Northern Rock was one of seven companies removed and replaced by others, effective 24th December 2007.

A quotation in the FTSE 100 is based on the capitalization of the company and is regarded as prestigious therefore deletion from the list was looked upon as another blow to Northern Rock.

Wednesday 13th December
Today Adam Applegarth, the Chief Executive of Northern Rock left the bank. The bank also revealed that the growing financial crisis had cut the value of its treasury investments by £281 million. It was also announced that Andy Kuipers formerly responsible for sales and marketing would replace Applegarth.

It was announced that Applegarth would receive a pay-off, but that it would be substantially less than the sum he was contractually entitled to. The payment would be made in monthly instalments rather than one lump sum.

It later transpired in April 2008 that Applegarth would receive one year's salary (£834,000) provided he was not in employment for the rest of 2008, hence the reason for the monthly payments.

Thursday 14th December
There were various reports that the government had rejected suggestions that a private sale Northern Rock was unlikely to succeed, but did admit that all options were open. Reports were that the government was speeding up plans for a bill to nationalize Northern Rock.

When suggestions that a private sale were diminishing and public ownership was the only realistic option, Prime Minister, Gordon Brown's spokesman said, "I don't think we should accept the premise of the question".

Monday 17ᵗʰ December

Information emerged from the bidders' camps about their bids. Olivant was said to have been prepared to offer a higher cash injection of £800 million, whilst Virgin had identified two senior City figures to add to its management team. It was also announced that the Chancellor had appointed Goldman Sachs to put together a financing package that could be offered to bidders.

Also today SRM Global Master Fund raised its holding of Northern Rock shares to 9.29% or 39.143 million shares.

Tuesday 18ᵗʰ December

The Treasury today issued a statement in which it extended the guarantees for customers and creditors of Northern Rock. The guarantees were extended to cover:

- all uncollateralised and unsubordinated wholesale deposits, and other borrowings outside the previously announced guarantee arrangements, whether existing or arising in the future.

- all payment obligations under uncollateralised derivative transactions.

- in respect of all collateralised derivatives and all wholesale borrowings which are collateralised (including without limitation, covered bonds of Northern Rock to the extent that these obligations exceed the available proceeds of the realized collateral for the relevant derivative or borrowing.

- all obligations of Northern Rock PLC to make payments on the repurchase of mortgages under the Granite securitization programme..

The purpose of these extensions, apparently made at the request of Northern Rock, was to maintain the credit ratings on the bank's subordinate debt. The amount involved was relatively small, such obligations amounting to no more than several hundred million pounds, big enough, but hardly significant in relation to the overall liabilities of Northern Rock or the problems that were appearing elsewhere.

Any downgrading of the bank's credit ratings would have made it more difficult for it to eventually raise the funding required to repay the government loans and to keep it operational. A downgrading would also have affected the ability of a successful bidder to obtain funding related to its Northern Rock acquisition or involvement.

Those new guarantees were generous and intended to make a private sector solution to the bank's problems more realizable, since it was the reluctance of other banks to lend to Northern Rock through the inter-bank wholesale markets that prevented achievement of a solution.

With such guarantees in place, covering existing or future obligations, it is difficult to understand why the banks were so reluctant to commit themselves to lending to Northern Rock. Unless the answer was that they had no funds available to lend. The question arises once again, were the banks more interested in seeing a major competitor, such as Northern Rock had been, sink without trace? However as we shall see later the deterioration in global financial markets was sufficient to increase the concerns banks had about rejuvenating the inter-bank market or lending specifically to northern Rock.

Whilst the guarantees were generous, the Treasury and the Bank of England knew that Northern Rock was basically a good quality operation, albeit with a flawed and collapsed business strategy. The added risk to the "taxpayer" as a result of granting them was very slight, unless other calamitous disasters happened to the British economy.

With an eye on alternatives there were reports that the Government had drawn up plans to nationalize the lender and divide it up between the UK's major banks should a private sector takeover fail to materialize. This was the first mention of a "carve-up". It is not clear whether the Treasury actually had such a plan or whether the report was based on rumours. Of course the nationalization bit was accurate.

A "BBC" report elaborated on the Treasury statement, estimating that,

> *The government's aid package for the bank now amounts to about £57 billion. It also pointed out that this was equivalent to each "taxpayer" having a £2000 exposure to Northern Rock.*

This was yet another mention of the poor "taxpayer", beloved of the BBC and the rest of the media.

Vince Cable again, still wearing his politician's mantle voiced the opinion that the government seemed to have got the worst of all possible worlds. It had effectively nationalized the liabilities of the bank, while at the same time it didn't control it, it didn't own it and should it be sold then all of the upside, all of the capital gains would accrue to speculative investors and not to taxpayers, an assessment that was close to the reality of the situation.

All that notwithstanding, at least Olivant proposed a structure that would endeavour to provide a fair and equitable result for all parties. What really seemed to inflame the politicians was the involvement of the two principal hedge fund investors. Their involvement may have been opportunistic but at least they had sunk substantial amounts of their investors' funds in Northern Rock at a time when no one else was prepared to commit to the bank. They jointly owned a little less than 25% of the company but were only two of a number of institutional investors who bought sizeable stakes in Northern

Rock as investments, not speculations, both before and after September 2007 but who did not attract the degree of publicity and media ire that the hedge funds generated.

Even as late as October 2008, there was still an 80% chance that they had all lost their investment, together of course with all the other smaller investors.

Those who deserved to be castigated were the short-selling speculators, principally a few hedge funds, trading rooms of the large banks and other institutions who traded vast numbers of Northern Rock shares daily as we shall see in Chapter 11. Give him his due, Vince Cable severely criticized the "shorting" speculators on a number of occasions.

Thursday 20th December

Notwithstanding the Treasury's efforts to provide guarantees, Fitch, the credit rating agency, in a research note suggested that it may cut its ratings on some Northern Rock bonds, citing concerns that the bank may be forced to sell assets cheaply if a buyer for the group was not found soon. In a research note, Fitch said it had placed its ratings on the lender's hybrid capital and subordinated bond issues on "rating watch negative". The proposed downgrading did not affect the Granite bond issues.

Bearing in mind that all the parties involved in solving Northern Rock's problems were working on solutions that were intended to avoid a "fire sale" outcome, the reasoning at Fitch was questionable and possibly more concerned with deflecting the flack that Credit Rating Agencies had to suffer at that time. Bear in mind also that Fitch was one of the rating agencies which had no problem with allocating a Triple A rating to much of the worthless US sub-prime backed bonds which had been of debatable value from the outset.

Saturday 22nd December

There were indications that the Board of Northern Rock was considering mounting its own rescue bid as an alternative to and eschewing the two proposals put forward by Virgin Money and Olivant. Northern Rock was talking to several high-level bankers to strengthen its top management team and to bring in individuals to work alongside its new chief executive, Andy Kuipers. The bank told several shareholders that an in-house rescue was a credible option and an alternative to nationalization.

Brian Sanderson, the group's chairman, said that he believed that if a financing package was open to both Olivant and Virgin, then it was also available for the incumbent management. At the same time the Treasury had concerns about the depth of management should Virgin or Olivant succeed.

An outline of how the in-house option could be developed included a rights issue or placing that would be would be used to raise the £1 billion or so needed. The two hedge fund investors would agree to underwrite a rights issue, in anticipation of which they had applied to the FSA for approval to increase their holdings above 10% each, although they were not acting in concert.

Those two most important shareholders explained that they were trying to maintain shareholder rights at a time when they were concerned that political pressure could lead to a deal without shareholders being properly consulted. This was the reason for their call to the board to convene an Extraordinary General Meeting of shareholders, as noted earlier. At last the Northern Rock board agreed to hold an extraordinary meeting on January 15th. 2008.

The following day the new rescue plan from an in-house management team in Northern Rock received media coverage. Whilst they had been working on a plan for some weeks, this was the first public indication that it had been developed, and so brought the story of the rescue into a new, third phase.

10 The Rescue Phase Three

The new entrant into the efforts to find a solution to Northern Rock's problems came from in-house, from where one would have expected it to have emerged some time before. That possibly did not happen because rescue talk all centred on a third-party takeover that would produce an input of sufficient new funds to repay the Bank of England loans, something that an in-house plan could not do within a short time-span and because of the unavailability of inter-bank funding.

Sunday 23rd December
" FT.com" ran an article reviewing the position reached in the story of the Northern Rock "rescue", starting with the news that the bank was "considering a plan to run the stricken mortgage lender as a smaller entity if efforts to find a buyer prove unsuccessful"

This was the first publicized plan that included "downsizing" Northern Rock as a major element of a solution. It did not mean, however that the other "outside" proposals had been put aside. They were still very much in the frame and it was considered highly unlikely that the in-house plan would be activated unless attempts to sell Northern rock fell through. It was also the case that the government was drawing up plans to nationalize Northern Rock and there was a general belief that state ownership was the most likely outcome.

The only real solution to Northern Rock's basic problem was a downsizing by selling off some of its mortgages currently backing the government loans. Replacing these loans with commercial ones would not solve the liquidity problem other than temporarily. The bank had to downsize so that the proportion of retail deposits to mortgages became a lot higher and much closer to the industry average.

Over the next few days between Christmas and early January, RAB Capital kept increasing its shareholding stake progressively from 6.7% to 7.59%, doesn't sound like much, but it meant a holding of 32.22 million shares. SRM Global at that time held 9.1%.

Wednesday 2nd January 2008

As far as Northern Rock was concerned the New Year started with a letter to all shareholders from SRM Global Fund concerning the proposed Resolutions to be put to an EGM on 15th January. That letter was followed up by another one from RAB Capital PLC on 3rd January covering much the same ground. The UK Shareholders Association also circularized its members, putting forward much the same proposals as the hedge funds had circulated. They all urged Northern Rock's 180,000 shareholders to back the resolutions to be proposed at the EGM amid signs that the following three weeks could be critical to the bank's future. SRM was concerned that there was a risk that the exceptional circumstances could mean that the usual shareholder checks and balances were going to be set aside.

Monday 7th January

Other reports appearing today were that the Chairman of Northern Rock expressed strong contrary views to those put forward by the two main shareholders, but there is little doubt that all the evidence to date pointed to the fact that the board was paying very little attention to the views of shareholders. It was also a fact that the recently appointed Chairman and other directors had no financial commitment to the company since they were not shareholders. Furthermore, the Chairman was very much an appointee of H M Treasury.

Whatever the media view of the two hedge fund shareholders, they were genuinely interested in seeing the best possible outcome for all parties, a proper return to the government for the important role it had assumed, but also fairness for the ordinary shareholders. As pointed out earlier, they were the only parties who had actually risked substantial sums to help achieve such an outcome. Perhaps they could not be credited with purely altruistic motives but they were certainly not there merely as speculators.

Tuesday 8th January

A corporate governance lobbying organization, Pensions and Investment Research Consultants (PIRC) recommended that shareholders should withhold support from proposals aimed at preventing a fire sale of Northern Rock's assets. The reason given was that it was not persuaded that existing takeover rules were inadequate. That must have been good news for the Chairman of Northern Rock who strongly disagreed with the proposed resolutions and also recommended shareholders not to support them.

The same day another report suggested that the government had asked Goldman Sachs (adviser to the Treasury on Northern Rock) to deliver a report by the end of the week so that it could reach a decision on Northern Rock's future by mid-January.

Thursday 10th January

Appearing before a Treasury Select Committee meeting, the Chancellor made a number of points:

- A possible nationalization would be a stepping-stone to a sale.

- He underlined the government's position that all options for Northern Rock were still on the table.

- It was not surprising that it had been difficult to find a private sector solution given the current economic climate.

He was questioned also on his plans to give more powers to the FSA, a subject that would receive attention in the Committee's report on the supervision of Northern Rock.

Also on this day, on the BBC News, Robert Peston reported that Goldman Sachs was trying to structure a plan to convert the taxpayer loans to Northern Rock into bonds for sale to investors. The bonds would require a Triple A rating in order to sell therefore they would have to carry a Government guarantee that put them on a par with the Government's own Gilts issues.

Peston believed that if the bonds were guaranteed by the government, the EC would see such a deal as state aid and therefore illegal. He suggested that if one or more of the global re-insurers took over some or the whole of the government guarantee, this problem might be solved.

Later on he said,

> Goldman's success or failure in securitising this debt will decide the very future of Northern Rock. - - - - - Full nationalization seems to have been more or less ruled out.

There was more on the future prospects for Northern Rock, but as with the comments related above, they were of a purely speculative nature.

Elsewhere, "FT.com" extended much the same story by adding, inter alia,

> The financing package (that Goldman Sachs was working on) has been developed independently, which would enable the bank's board to make it available to the winning bidder.

The central point, of which nobody seemed to be taking heed, was that unless there was to be some kind of "fire sale" the Treasury loan would have to remain in place one way or another possibly for two to three years, although no matter which solution was eventually adopted, not necessarily for the whole amount.

The reason for this was that there were no indications that the markets would return to normal fairly quickly, partly because no one knew the extent of losses or write-downs that lay within individual banks. As we shall learn later, nearly all the major UK banks at this point in time harboured substantial undeclared losses.

Whilst funds for the repayment of the loans could be generated by requiring those mortgagees whose two year deals come to an end to refinance elsewhere, that would not be an instantaneous solution. In some respects the government, the bidders and Northern Rock itself were in a "catch 22" situation.

Elsewhere a media report suggested that Goldman Sachs had widened the search for a bidder to include wealthy Middle East sovereign wealth funds, naming Abu Dhabi Investment Authority and the Quatari Investment Authority. Even if successful, and there were precedents in the shape of such investors taking multi-billion dollar stakes in Citigroup and UBS. In each case, the amounts involved would probably lead to partial solutions only. Furthermore, based on the Citigroup experience this could be an expensive option.

Friday 11th January
At an interview by the Treasury Select Committee the Chancellor said that the process of trying to find new finance to replace the £26 billion lent by the Treasury was reaching a stage when we had to come to a conclusion. He stressed that the government was operating in extremely difficult circumstances where many financial institutions cannot borrow or lend therefore it might become necessary for the bank to be nationalized. A private sector solution would be highly desirable, but if nationalization has to be considered it would only be for a temporary period before the assets could be sold, either wholesale or in piecemeal to the private sector.

The indications were that the interests of shareholders were not high up on the Chancellor's priority list.

The same day there were reports that Northern Rock expected to raise £2.25 billion through the sale of its portfolio of Lifetime Home Equity release mortgages to JP Morgan Chase at a premium of 2.25% to its balance sheet value. Northern Rock also retained an ability to continue to sell its Lifetime mortgage products and to service existing loans on behalf of the US bank. This was considered to be an encouraging sign that buyers were beginning to emerge for mortgage assets owned by Northern Rock that are regarded as good quality.

This "good quality" phrase is one that the media have returned to time after time, the inference always being that Northern Rock was a reckless bank with a sizeable proportion of "poor quality" assets.

That was not the case. If the Northern Rock Annual Accounts, the auditor's reports and the prospectuses issued through Granite Master Issuer in connection with the securitisation programme are to be believed, they demonstrated that this was clearly not so. Like all lenders it had some bad loans, but the percentage was below the industry average, and bad loans, if they are mortgage loans do not necessarily result in complete write-offs. Northern Rock's situation in relation to mortgages three months or more in default was also below the industry average.

Those points have been stressed elsewhere.

Saturday 12ᵗʰ January

Today's news was that Northern Rock's pension fund had a £100 million hole in it. The significance of this was that bidders would have to find extra money to plug the hole. It was suggested that this might place the pension fund trustees in a more powerful position where they could exercise substantial influence over any agreement between the Rock, the Government and potential bidders on clinching a rescue package.

That was wishful thinking!

Also on this day the reports were that the Government had almost ruled out a commercial rescue for Northern Rock after conceding that funding for a deal could not be found.

Sunday 13ᵗʰ January

Today's reports concentrated on matters relating to the proposed EGM of Northern Rock shareholders, and included the following points:

- the Board would issue a conciliatory statement on Monday prior to the EGM on Tuesday. (It was not issued).

- Ron Sandler confirmed that he would be appointed CEO of Northern Rock by HM Treasury in the event that nationalization went ahead.

- the Goldman Sachs financing proposal might be approved before the EGM by the Treasury and the Prime Minister. (This must have been speculation).

- Northern Rock confirmed that it would pay retention bonuses, capped at £25,000 per quarter to selected key staff but not to executive directors.

Tuesday 15ᵗʰ January

The EGM went ahead but only one of the shareholder Resolutions was passed—that which obliged the bank to consult shareholders before issuing new shares worth more than £5 million. At the same time, the other resolutions were only very narrowly defeated, the reason being that "Special resolutions" required a 75% majority and they only reached 64%. The voting result may also possibly have been influenced by the number of open proxy votes that were given to the Board by shareholders unable to attend the Meeting.

Another factor may have been that many private shareholders had shares held in nominee company names by CREST and therefore had no ready access to voting unless they contacted the operators of the nominee companies.

The UK Shareholders Association issued a number of Press Reports immediately following the meeting in which it recorded proceedings at the meeting in a comprehensive and unbiased manner. At a later date, Roger Lawson, Communications Director of UKSA suggested that one of the key points everyone seems to have missed was the importance of the EGM. Because three out of four of the requisitioning resolutions were not passed, the meeting was generally looked upon as being a "damp squib". In addition the turnout physically (about 700) and by proxy was low. However, it showed that the shareholders (including SRM, RAB and UKSA) could easily block any resolution that required a 75% majority – and any major re-structuring or disposal would almost certainly require that. His view was that although the Press reported it as a "victory" for the board, the reality was very different.

Thursday 17th January
The bidding game still continued despite the generally held impression that nationalization was coming closer day by day. Virgin group was said to be making adjustments to its proposals in order to stay in the game. Despite the fact that it was unpopular with existing shareholders, it was favoured by the government, and more particularly according to Press comment, by the Prime Minister who was said to be a close friend of Sir Richard Branson. Part of the outcome was that:

•   A Virgin team chaired by Brian Pitman a former Chairman of Lloyds TSB made a
      presentation to the FSA during the previous week.

•   He and Sir Richard Branson were still apparently expecting the Goldman Sachs
      financing package to be produced within a few days.

•   The latter proposals would have to be approved by the EC in Brussels as it would
      represent "state aid" for the bank.

•   The Prime Minister promised to exhaust all options to find a private buyer but he
      had admitted that nationalization, desired before mid-February, may be the only
      option in the current market conditions.

As a tailpiece, it was reported that the Government was now trying to work out the value of the company to pay shareholders what they deserve and avoid going to court. This was a quote from "a person close to the situation".

In the light of what happened not long afterwards, that person could not have been as close to the situation as he (or she) thought.

It may have been accidental, but the use of "what they deserve" rather than "to which they are entitled" was in keeping with previously expressed media comments regarding shareholders.

Gordon Brown, Prime Minister, interviewed for ITV News at Ten said,

> *Because stability (of the financial system) is the issue we will look at every option and that includes taking the company into public ownership and then moving it back later into the private sector.*

Friday 18th January
Northern Rock Chairman, Brian Sanderson announced,

> *I am delighted to welcome Paul Thomson who will add further skills and experience to the Board that will be invaluable to our ongoing strategic review.*

Thomson, an accountant, took over at Resolution (insurance) after its merger with Britannic Assurance, but left subsequently when Pearl Assurance acquired the company.

Elsewhere it was suggested that Mr. Thomson had been tipped as being key to Northern Rock's plans for finding a private buyer rather than to be nationalized by the Government. It was rather late in the day to be appointing a saviour, particularly one who later announced that the "bidders" plans were more likely to succeed than his own.

Saturday 19th January
There was yet another twist in the plot when it was reported that a private sale of Northern Rock was still a possibility after the Government told bidders it was prepared to clear a major obstacle by turning billions of pounds of "tax-payers' loans to the bank into bonds. The Prime Minister confirmed that talks were taking place with firms who had expressed an interest based on financing proposals drawn up by Goldman Sachs, the Government's advisers.

Although this appeared as a positive development it was noted that Goldman Sach's proposals would leave Northern Rock on the Government's books for a number of years, but that at the same time it would meet Brussels' state aid rules.

It also noted that while a private sale would ease political pressures on the Prime Minister, the Conservatives regarded nationalization as a "monumental failure" on his part.

Monday 21st January

News reports returned today to the prospects for the nationalization of Northern Rock and the question of compensation for shareholders. This was in anticipation of a statement from Alistair Darling who was expected to argue that if Northern Rock was nationalized it would be treated as if the government guarantee had never been made— rendering the shares almost worthless. Against this it was argued that any potential challenges to the nationalization of Northern Rock would also focus on whether the process was lawful—in other words, a proportionate means of achieving the government's objectives and an appropriate level of compensation for shareholders.

Friday 25th January

It seemed that the in-house rescue proposals had been simmering away in the background without much information coming into the public domain. It was thought that an in-house solution would benefit from the latest government bond proposals that were to become available to all bidders. An analyst, Bruce Packard was quoted as saying that "Closing to new business and putting up prices would be the fastest way to shrink the asset side of the balance sheet, with taxpayers paid in full.

That may be so up to a point, but it was only part of what needed to be done. The article recorded that the government had set 4th February as the deadline for rescue plans to be submitted and that the bank would be nationalized if the right deal could not be struck.

Sunday 27th January

Northern Rock's annual accounts had been due earlier in the week and there were comments on the delay in publishing them. It was reported that they would not become available until the end of March, although directors of the company, and the two main bidders, Virgin and Olivant would have access to the figures. It was pointed out that the lack of published accounts was likely to raise concerns that the market in Northern Rock shares was a false one and that the shares should be suspended.

The reality was that the market in Northern Rock's shares had been a false one for at least four months and that there had been several calls for the shares to have been suspended, a move which the directors of Northern Rock and the FSA considered to be inappropriate and unnecessary.

We shall return to the claims about a false market in Chapter 11.

Two earlier bids had resurfaced. Cerebus and Five Mile, US private equity funds that had previously shown an interest in a rescue on their own account, now proposed to take an equity stake in support of the Northern Rock management rescue package. This was a short-lived proposal.

Monday, 28th January 2008

Edwin Coe, a Lincoln's Inn, London commercial law firm, had gathered together 6000 Northern Rock shareholders and was considering legal action, despite the Government's bail-out plan. David Greene, the partner who headed litigation at the firm was quoted as saying that it is probably going to lead to further private bids for the bank. Shareholders want to see the company succeed and the possibility of group litigation over Northern Rock's breakdown is not ruled out.

The statement of this last possibility was intended to make public that in the event of nationalization there was a willingness by shareholders to consider legal action. To the extent that this intention was noted, government seemed to have got the impression that it would only have to deal with RAB and SRM if nationalization went ahead. The reality was that there was a strong sense of solidarity amongst shareholders generally.

Part of Mr.Greene's concern was that the management and the Government were aware of the availability of inside information that wasn't announced to the market for a month which clearly had an affect on share prices and that was what he was examining.

On other fronts a sign that improvements had taken place in the wholesale inter-bank markets was the fact that as at this date the three month London Interbank Offered Rate (LIBOR) was 5.58%, compared to the B of E Bank Rate at 5.50 %, but expected to drop to 5.25% within the following two weeks. In September, at the time of the run on Northern Rock, LIBOR had reached 6.90% in a restricted market.

Tuesday 29th January

Although the previous day had produced that technically good news, it was diluted by a warning that the FSA had warned that another Northern Rock crisis was possible and that nearly half-a-million households faced potentially serious debt problems over the coming year. The FSA, which had been widely blamed for the Northern Rock crisis, reported that the credit crunch may have exposed the business models of some firms as being "potentially unsuitable" in more stressed financial conditions, where for example access to liquidity is restricted. This had put pressure on measures of prudential risk for some firms, such as capital and liquidity ratios.

All this came in the FSA 2008 Financial Risk Outlook publication, a bit late in the day, one could suggest. At the same time it came a lot earlier than the banks that the FSA had in mind disclosed their true status.

Thursday 31ˢᵗ January
Various reports provided an update on the bidders' plans for Northern Rock.

The following is a synopsis.

The three bidders, Virgin, Olivant and the Northern Rock management plan were set to submit highly risk-averse business plans that could lead to job losses at the bank.

Each of the proposals would see Northern Rock initially shrink in size and write far less new mortgage lending, which was likely to be funded from new retail deposits.

The plans reflected the Government's need to comply with EU rules on state aid, that prevent a new owner from gaining an unfair advantage, something which was a concern to competitor banks.

Each of the proposals could use the government sponsored financing package under which the £28 billion Bank of England loan that was keeping Northern Rock afloat was converted into bonds backed by a government guarantee.

A less aggressive business plan would require less new capital, between £500 and £750 million instead of the £1.5 billion previously thought to be necessary.

None of the plans have made public the scale of projected job losses, although everyone, including government, anticipates that there will have to be substantial redundancies if the business was to be "shrunk".

A full-blown takeover by another bank was considered to be unlikely, but nationalization remained an option. The bid process was more concerned with a restructuring plan than a takeover.

The Chancellor and the authorities were expected to reach a decision by the end of February on which bid, if any, should succeed.

During the first two weeks of February Northern Rock made the news every day.

Friday 1ˢᵗ February
One report was about Jon Wood of SRM Global, the hedge fund that had built up a substantial stake in Northern Rock shares over a number of weeks in the belief that the bank could be salvaged. Mr. Wood was described as a former UBS trader who in his six years with that bank made $2.4 billion for it and now saw himself as a Robin Hood figure, fighting for the rights of minority shareholders against potentially unjust actions of companies.

It is open to conjecture that the involvement of these two funds, SRM Global and RAB Capital, when allied with all the talk about "taxpayers money at risk", influenced the government decision to nationalize the bank in order to prevent them profiting from their investment, as they undoubtedly hoped to do whilst fully accepting the substantial risks along the way.

Virgin Group also featured in the news portrayed as the government's preferred bidder, although many shareholders supported Arnold, and the in-house proposal had gained credibility in the past month.

Monday 4th February
"Then there were two" as the nursery rhyme puts it. The news was that the Olivant Investment Group had withdrawn its bid as it had failed to come up with an offer that could satisfy the Government's financing terms, the interests of Northern Rock shareholders, and its own investment needs.

Vince Cable returned to the fray by calling on ministers to make sure taxpayers got value for money from the successful bidder. He continued by saying that Mr. Darling should not allow his desire for a speedy private sale to over-ride the high risk to the taxpayer. Taxpayers now faced years of supporting Northern Rock while any new private owner makes an absolute killing, assuming that the EU decides that the Government position of guarantor is even legal.

This was all stirring political rhetoric of the type that had dogged all the efforts to find a solution to Northern Rock's predicament all of which probably had a substantial influence on the decision to nationalize the bank.

The *"Financial Times"* published a lengthy and informative, although at times speculative summary of the bid situation as it appeared to be at this time.

Leading newspapers and other media were attempting to update the public on developments in the Northern Rock saga, but had very little reliable information on which to work. They speculated that the authorities were likely to examine the strengths of their business plans before deciding which proposals were eligible to use the financing package. It was considered that Northern Rock's board must then decide which was the best proposal for investors, staff and other stakeholders. It was believed possible that the authorities would back just one proposal. Such a decision would back shareholders into a corner and force them to choose between that and nationalization.

This was one of the few mentions of "shareholders" as having any say in what was going on with their company. As we shall see, the suggestion – based on applicable UK Company Law – that the board would play a determining role in the decision was wishful thinking.

Elsewhere it was suggested that Alistair Darling's hopes of a vigorous bidding war had been dealt a serious blow on Monday night after Olivant's withdrawal from the auction revived speculation that the Chancellor might yet have to nationalize the bank. The Prime Minister was said to be desperate to avoid nationalization, an outcome that the Conservatives have said would be a "monumental failure of government policy" an outcome that they seemed to stress at every opportunity.

There was speculation that the proposed bond issue while deemed excessively generous by Mr. Darling's critics was still not enough to attract any other big financial operators to make a bid. Mr. Darling wanted the taxpayer to have a stake in the bank in order to enjoy a share of future profits, and was demanding a heavy fee for the guarantee of the bond issue

After quoting the by now well established Conservative and Liberal Democrat criticisms of the process and its adverse consequences for "taxpayers", news articles turned to a speculative review of some of the detail of the rescue plans in so far as they had been made publicly available.

Tuesday 5th February
Lex, writing in the "Financial Times" attempted to analyze the figures behind the bids. This was one of the few newspaper articles that dealt at length with some of the underlying factors of the bids and the arithmetic involved in them. At the same time it presented a somewhat biased view and made no mention of nationalization other than to say that it remained a possibility

Wednesday 6th February
On a "BBC Radio 4" Money programme Jayne-Anne Gadhia, the CEO of Virgin Money who would run Northern Rock in the event of a successful Virgin bid said,

> As many as 1000 jobs could be under threat at Northern Rock if Virgin takes control of the Northern Rock. We can't continue to make the promise that there will be no redundancies but we would aim very much to minimize any reductions.

This news came after earlier comments from the group that it would not cut jobs as part of the in-house rescue plan.

It was generally considered that whoever took over the bank would be faced with a prospect of a softening economy and weaker housing market, near record levels of insolvencies and rising unemployment.

Details of Virgin's plans were then relayed. It was the intention of the Virgin consortium partners to provide £500 million cash, while the Virgin Money business, which would be merged into the bank was deemed to be worth £250 million. The remainder that was required would be raised through a £500 million, 4.7 for 1 rights issue of new shares priced at 25 pence each, to make a total injection of £1.25 billion.

Another article disclosed that Paul Thomson the leader of the in-house team that hoped to revive Northern Rock was afraid that the government would favour Virgin because voters may see it as a better option. The article then described Thompson's fears that the public, familiar with the Virgin Group would consider it the only real private sector solution notwithstanding that earlier in the week, RAB Capital had said there was only one "strong and independent solution available" – the in-house proposal, which it backed.

Thompson also said that the two bids were not wholly private sector solutions, but public-private partnerships between bidder and Government until after the Bank of England loans had been repaid. That fact had to be accepted if a private sector solution was to prevail over nationalization. Thompson saw the problem as being one of public perception rather than of an understanding of the problem. This from the man who was paid £100,000 for what turned out to be no more than one month's work heading up the failed in-house rescue plan.

According to Thompson, both Olivant and Virgin had early access to the in-house salvage plan that had been developed with the authorities and had been involved in its development through the FSA and B of E. The plan had been tested and changed in response to some of the bidders suggestions. A warrant had been factored into Thompson's plan that could produce a 5 –10 % return for the Government.

It should be borne in mind that this 5 – 10% return would be in addition to the interest paid to the Bank of England on its loans, the Treasury fee for the provision of that assistance and the fees charged by the Treasury for guaranteeing deposits and other liabilities of Northern Rock. The "taxpayer" would not do too badly out of the deal, certainly when compared to what shareholders could expect over the same period. Somewhere along the line it had been forgotten that the Bank of England had a duty to provide its "lender of last resort" loans to otherwise solvent British banks.

Another article on the same day made the point that although those representing the shareholders were very vocal about shareholder rights, not much attention was being paid to them. Sir Brian Pitman, leading the Virgin consortium suggested even new investors could only expect unexciting returns. He added that, like their customers the previous September, the bank's 6500 employees were in line for disappointments because Northern Rock was staffed for a strategic vision from a golden, pre-credit squeeze era. Even the bank's own restructuring plan envisaged paring the bank back to a 2003 level that was roughly half its current size. At the end of that year Northern Rock employed fewer than 3,500 full time staff. Given that the board's plan could become a template for nationalization, it was hard to see how government ownership could offer much reassurance to employees.

The continuing loyalty of employees to the bank was one of the few bright spots in the whole story but as far back as November, potential bidders were already fretting in private about the staff's sinking morale as the government dithered.

What those reviews pinpointed was the fact that the in-house plan was the one most likely to form the template for a government plan under nationalization of the bank.

Thursday 7th February
The "Financial Times" reported a new development today.

> *Northern Rock was officially classed as a public sector company on Thursday, bringing its debts on to the Government's books and blowing apart one of the Treasury's cherished budgetary rules.*

This action was determined by the Office for National Statistics (ONS) which considered that the government had so much control over Northern Rock that it should be classified in the same way as other nationalized entities. The ONS opinion was that on the basis of Northern Rock's published accounts for the end of 2006, £90 billion should be classed as public debt. This was likely to increase public sector net debt so that it represented 6.7% of gross domestic product. If added to the current level of debt, the total public sector net debt would rise to 44.4% of GDP, far above the government's self-imposed ceiling of 40%. Much was made of this breaking through the "ceiling" at the time but within six months there was talk of public borrowing exceeding 60%, then 80% and eventually a 100% figure was being bandied about.

Whilst the ONS may have been technically correct in its pronouncements, and that is by no means certain, one cannot help feeling that it unnecessarily complicated an already tricky situation, and apart from providing some more political ammunition for opposition parties, which they grasped with both hands, served no real purpose. It was a ruling that appeared to have ignored the asset backing to all of Northern Rock's government debt.

A press release from Abbey, the major UK mortgage lender owned by Bank Santander of Spain reported a 12% rise in full year net mortgage lending in 2007, saying that,

> *It benefited from the changing competitive environment in the mortgage market and the virtual disappearance of one of the main UK mortgage lenders.*

This last comment reinforced the theory expressed earlier in this book that other UK mortgage lenders were not at all sorry to see the demise of a main competitor, a fact that may have contributed to Northern Rock's inability to renew loans in the inter-bank market, as suggested earlier.

In a separate report from "Thomson Financial" RAB Capital was noted as having added 215,000 shares to its holding, making a new total of 33,469,299 shares or 7.94% of Northern Rock's issued capital.

It did not appear that RAB was convinced that nationalization was on the cards.

Friday 8th February

The "Financial Times" reported another new development, this time that the Tyne consortium, which included Five Mile, the US private equity group, indicated that it would be willing to back Paul Thompson, the bank's non-executive director by underwriting £200 million of a rights issue needed to re-capitalize the lender, in addition to the £500 million for which Mr. Thomson had already signed up investors who were willing to underwrite it.

It was considered that the widespread support Mr. Thompson had attracted from investors had dealt a blow to the rival proposal from the Virgin consortium. Virgin's plan had failed to gain all-important shareholder support because it would have heavily diluted their holdings. Virgin proposed to raise £1.25 billion of new equity, which would protect the taxpayer because shareholders would be the first to suffer any potential losses. The same would have applied to the in-house solution. Virgin also proposed to re-brand Northern Rock.

The conclusion was that Virgin still appeared to be in the lead. Treasury officials said its bid was more advanced than that of the bank's in-house team. The management proposal was way behind in terms of capital and people, one person familiar with the situation suggested.

This was another case of "leaked information" and possibly inaccurate as it was not an official Treasury viewpoint.

There was some more media speculation on this topic. The focal point of the negotiations was the fee that the bidders were prepared to pay for the loan guarantee, estimated to be as much as £400 million, and the amount of equity to be made available to the taxpayer to share in any upturn in the Rock's fortunes. It was considered that unless the bidders made good offers to the Treasury on those two points, The Treasury (some reports named the Prime Minister) could be left with no option but to nationalize the bank – providing more ammunition for the Conservatives.

This last paragraph covers two points to which we shall return later because the last, the amount of equity for the taxpayer, is controversial and will certainly be examined when the shareholders contest the government's proposals for assessing their compensation, as we shall see shortly.

It has been the politicization of this whole saga against a background of a "frozen" inter-bank market that prevented a private sector solution from being reached at a much earlier time. What has dogged genuine attempts to reach a solution was that what was essentially a routine (albeit, up to that time, a very large and rare) "lender of last resort loan" by the Bank of England was transmuted by politicians and the media into the emotive sounding "taxpayers loan", where it was even apportioned out to individual "taxpayers" as a debt owing to them of as much as £2000 per head, as noted earlier.

Bid fever was reaching a climax as Paul Thompson announced that Northern Rock was to cut its £113 billion mortgage book in half under its in-house rescue plan, in a bid to see off a rival proposal from Sir Richard Branson's Virgin Group. He also promised to address the bank's business model by doubling the customer deposit base to £20 billion within three years, at the same time repaying the government's £25 billion loan and "releasing the taxpayer of its £30 billion deposit guarantee".

This last comment, "releasing the taxpayer of its £30 billion deposit guarantee", as mentioned earlier, was something of a red herring. By the time these comments were being made, there were practically no other British deposit taking banks that one could have looked at and said " my money will be perfectly safe there". Most had written off large amounts, their share prices had tumbled to the lowest levels seen for years. Others were the subject of recurring rumours, with much worse to come later in 2008. Northern Rock with the Bank of England loans in place and unlikely to be removed, was as safe a haven as any for depositor's money even without the backup of the Treasury's deposit guarantees. In any event, later in the year the government made it known that whatever the state of banks in the country, it would not allow depositors to lose any money and it never mentioned a price for that guarantee.

Saturday 9th February 2008
There were reports that the Prime Minister was expected to step up his involvement the following week. His office was said to be already engaged on this but would hold meetings the following week when some decisions might be made.

The newspapers suggested that a decision was expected before the end of February in time for submission of a written report to Brussels seeking approval for the government sponsored financing package (the bond issue detailed elsewhere).

Monday 11th February

The "Financial Times" introduced a new topic which was that a number of banks had approached the Treasury with a proposal to securitise up to half of the Bank of England's £25 billion loan to Northern Rock. The latest idea to securitise some of Northern Rock's assets had been put forward by Royal Bank of Scotland, and two others, believed to be Citigroup and Barclays. It was being proposed as a contingency plan in case the government's own financing package failed to get regulatory approval from Brussels. There was a constant concern expressed that "Brussels" may not have agreed the government's plans for dealing with Northern Rock.

Significantly, the three banks were not available for comment.

Separately it emerged that RAB Capital had once again increased its investment in Northern Rock to 34,264,299 shares or 8.13% of the issued capital.

Thursday 14th February

The hedge fund SRM Global that was the largest shareholder in Northern Rock at the time argued that the financial aid plan provided by the Bank of England and the Treasury was flawed.

SRM issued a statement that claimed that,

> *The European State Aid regime had been misapplied to Northern Rock. The government incorrectly conceded that measures were state aid and had not made any appeal of the Commission's decision. As a consequence, the criteria set out by the Treasury for continuing liquidity support were flawed. It would be a mistake for the government to take a decision on private sector bids and the future of Northern Rock without re-visiting the appropriateness of its criteria.*

This criticism, for which there appeared to have been good grounds, appears to have been ignored by officialdom since it never resurfaced.

In relation to observance of EC Directives on financial (and other) matters, Britain has a long history of carrying out observance within the strict letter of the law, notwithstanding that several prominent EU member countries take what at best could be called a more relaxed interpretation of the spirit of the law. Bearing in mind that the purpose behind EC Directives was to ensure the creation of a level playing field, having two such different approaches to the implementation of Directives somewhat defeated the objective, to the UK's disadvantage.

Friday 15th February

As a follow up to earlier reports there were suggestions that the two remaining bidders were told to submit revised offers so that the Treasury could make a decision the following week. Rumours indicated that the Chancellor might make an announcement as early as Monday. Nationalization was still seen as an option as the Treasury was thought to view the current rescue packages as a bad deal for the taxpayer.

There was another report that RAB Capital and SRM Global, between them holding 19.68% were preparing to vote down a rescue proposal from Sir Richard Branson's Virgin Group despite the looming threat that the bank would be nationalized if a deal failed. Legal and General Investment Management was the third largest owner of Rock shares, with a stake of 4.79%. Together the three investors had almost the 25% required to block a Virgin led rescue.

What those reports did not take into account was the fact that there were 120,000 private individual shareholders represented by the UK Shareholders Association who collectively accounted for another 25% of shareholders. UKSA's objectives were very much in line with those of the two hedge fund investors. The EGM vote clearly indicated that the private shareholders represented by UKSA managed to have a significant impact on the vote and the longer the saga dragged out the more influence UKSA would have obtained.

There was much speculation concerning nationalization issues. SRM argued that the only way the Government could bypass a Northern Rock shareholder vote would be to force the bank into administration, but that would be a legal minefield. – It planned to make a formal submission to the Treasury in which it will claim that the Bank of England was acting as a central bank liquidity provider and that any move to nationalize the bank would be an abuse of power.

Legal advice taken by SRM indicated that if the government nationalized Northern Rock, it must pay shareholders the book value of the bank, estimated to be 400 pence a share. This ran counter to the government's legal advice, which stated that shareholders should receive the market value of the bank, less the value of support so far offered through emergency loans from the Bank of England. The submitted paper (from SRM) is understood to have also made the point that the government was acting as a shadow director of the bank. That was thought to open the way for potential legal action from the shareholders.

The Government had previously indicated that the valuation to be placed on the bank's shares should be calculated on the basis that the bank was in administration or that it was not a "going concern". That was the basis that the Treasury subsequently stipulated after the bank was nationalized

Another article reported that the government was asking Virgin Group for a £200 million fee in the event the bidder succeeded in turning round Northern Rock within three years.

The money would be in return for the use of its guarantee of the Bank of England's £25 billion loan."

There were numerous reports flying around at this time, some were speculative. One, attributed to insiders said an announcement would be made following a Northern Rock board meeting, a briefing from the government's advisers Goldman Sachs, and discussions between the Treasury and officials at number 10. Another speculated that Nationalization for Northern Rock looked to be closer due to the government's firm stance and the fact that the Treasury had told Northern Rock's in-house management team that it lacked sufficient resources to take over the bank.

How much of all this was a case of putting "two and two together", and how much was fact is difficult to assess. One reviewed the then current situation, adding its own comments that the government was fearful that a private sector bidder could make millions of pounds from Northern Rock using taxpayers' money. However, Virgin and the bank's management team were believed to have little scope for an improvement in their offers thus making a private sector solution less likely. Yet again one of those "close to the situation" related that both proposals were finding it difficult to achieve the figures the government was demanding. He was quoted as having said that Ministers have shown little sympathy for shareholders who bought Northern Rock shares when the bank teetered on the brink of collapse. Mr. Darling had made clear that any compensation should represent the value of the company without state support, rather than the book value or share price.

What all this illustrates is that the concern of most of the parties involved, with the exception of the in-house management team, was not the future of Northern Rock, but who was going to make most money from its resuscitation.

The government was concerned that it be seen to be looking after the ubiquitous "taxpayer", and that is a matter which will receive our attention in a later chapter. There can be little doubt also that at least some of the official objectives were influenced by a need to be seen to be thwarting the expectations of the hedge fund and other late-comer "speculative" investors, with the emphasis placed on the two hedge funds.

It was becoming obvious by this time that despite its apparently genuine efforts to facilitate a private sector solution, the Government was heading rapidly towards nationalization, in which event the result would be a legal battle waged between groups of shareholders and the government. It would be an expensive and long-drawn out fight, and we can all guess who the real winners will be – the lawyers.

Sunday 17th February 2008
Today HM Treasury announced the temporary nationalization of Northern Rock. The

announcement was made on a Sunday, when markets were closed, in order to ensure that trading in Northern Rock shares would cease from the opening of business on the London Stock Exchange on Monday morning.

So ended the long-drawn out process of searching for a solution to Northern Rock's liquidity problems. The process and ramifications of nationalization will be considered in Chapter 12.

11 Northern Rock Share Trading

Although it may not have had a direct influence on what happened to Northern Rock in the latter part of 2007, it is nevertheless important that consideration is given to the nature of the share trading which took place in Northern Rock Ordinary shares on the London Stock Exchange and the volumes of shares that were being traded, not just on a daily basis but during every second of the time the LSE was open for trading, bearing in mind that on a peak day a new trade was being conducted, on average, every two seconds.

Before we do so, and to put the Northern Rock share trading in some sort of context, it is worth noting a few general facts about the ownership of shares on the UK stock market. The Office of National Statistics produced the following figures that relate to year-end 2006 and compared them with those in the last analysis in December 2004.

During the period the value of shares held by private investors had risen by 15% to £239 billion. At the same time, the total market capitalisation of quoted companies rose by 25% to £1858 billion, which means that the share of the market owned by private investors actually declined from 14% to 12.8%.

The proportion held by pension funds (£236 billion) and insurance companies (£273 billion) also declined, whilst the proportion held by foreign investors rose from 16% in 2004 to 41%, (£742 billion), a very substantial increase.

Other major holdings were:

UK banks, £63 billion,

UK Unit Trusts, £30 billion,

UK Investment Trusts, £45 billion,

UK Charities, £16 billion,

other UK financial institutions, £179 billion.

There are no recent statistics readily available for the average size of trade, or for the proportion of trades carried out by private investors, but the London Stock Exchange produced some in 2000 from which it can be gleaned that at that time private clients created 65% of trades by number, but only 8% by value. The average trade size for private investors was £7800, but for institutional trades the figure was £200,000, and can be assumed to be much higher now.

A more recent factor, which is not apparent from the above quoted statistics is the part now played by hedge funds in stock exchange trading volumes. It has been recently estimated that up to 40% of each day's trading was carried out by hedge funds. This brings us to a consideration of the manner in which hedge funds carry on their activities in stock markets.

Stock market trading has for decades been comprised of two different types. The original purpose of listed stock markets was to provide a medium by which investors had a ready market for the acquisition or disposal of their shares in quoted companies. That is still an important role for stock markets, but increasingly they cater for the activities of short-term investors or to describe them more appropriately, speculators. Computerisation of trading activities, the ready availability of global market and economic information in an electronic age and an ability by all dealers in professional trading rooms to monitor and analyse trading patterns in "*real time*" on a computer screen has resulted in a massive increase in the volume of short term speculative trading, much of it very short term.

In the week following the run on Northern Rock by its depositors, a number of stock-broking firms reported substantial increases in new individual investor accounts and a much higher than usual volume of trading, most of it in Northern rock shares supplemented by trades in one or two other banks that were suffering credit crunch related swings in their share prices from day to day.

In "normal" times some short term speculative trading is carried on by private investors but by far the greatest proportion of trading is conducted by institutional investors, including hedge funds. That this is so is evidenced by the size of the trading rooms in banks and other financial institutions.

Their activities were all too evident when one studies the trading that took place in Northern Rock shares, prior to 13th September2007 and afterwards until nationalisation in February 2008.

Whenever a large volume of trading takes place in a particular share, it may be accompanied by changes in the share price. Whether this happens, or the extent to which it happens depends on the nature of the trades. If sales and purchases are more or less balanced out by each other, there may be little or no change in the quoted share price. However, if there is a large volume of either sales or purchases that is not immediately counterbalanced by opposite trades, adjustments to share prices will take place. A large volume of shares sold, without counterbalancing purchases will tend to drive prices down, whilst prices will rise if purchases are made in volume without corresponding sales taking place. To some extent therefore it is possible for price changes in one direction or the other to become induced by the actions of speculators or genuine investors.

"BBC News 24" on 23rd September 2007 produced an interesting piece that concentrated on hedge fund and bank trading in Northern Rock shares. It suggested that hedge fund and big City investment banks had been betting heavily for months that Northern Rock faced serious funding problems that would be reflected in a falling share price.

It then noted how the share price had spiralled downwards "since the BBC revealed that the Newcastle based lender had applied to the Bank of England for emergency funding."

The article went on to describe the techniques employed by hedge funds,

> One of the most common strategies is to "short" shares they believe are over-valued. Hedge funds borrow shares from long-term investors such as pension funds or insurers, for a "rental" fee and sell them. Later, they buy back the same number of shares and return them to the lender on an agreed date. If the price has fallen, the difference between the share price at which the hedge funds sold the shares and bought them back is profit.

There was then a discussion as to how Northern Rock shares were being "shorted".

> Last Thursday, Mervyn King, the Governor of the Bank of England, said that he became aware that Northern Rock was facing serious difficulties only in August. The hedge fund community seems to have sensed that something was seriously awry much sooner. At the end of June, rising interest rates triggered a profits warning from Northern Rock and promptly renewed questions about the bank's business model. At that time (end June) only about 7% of Northern Rock's shares had been shorted, according to figures from Data Explorers, which collects securities lending information for investors.

> By the end of July, that short-position had grown to some 15% Of the bank's shares, and ahead of last week's announcement from the Bank of England it has passed the 20% mark (with a single hedge fund said to have been behind almost half of that position. That compares to an average short-position (at that time) of about 3.5% across the banking sector as a whole.

It next described how it had been estimated by Data Explorers that the overall profits in June from shorting Northern Rock shares was more than £100 million. It also stated that others in the hedge fund community reckoned that the overall profits from shorting Northern Rock shares was much higher, as much as £1 billion. It quoted the Managing Director of Data Explorers, Julian Pittam,

> *This may be a new story for many people, but it's not new for some sophisticated investors. They've been sceptical about Northern Rock's funding model for some time. When it came to funding, Northern Rock was a one trick pony.*

It was in fact a very old story that was addressed in George Rae's classic banking handbook written in 1885. He wrote,

> *It is a fallacy to contend that the market has the same moral right to speculative dealings in the shares of banks as in those of railway companies* (the big thing at the time*). However much you may depreciate the price of any railway stock by "bearing" operations* (shorting today)*, the undertaking itself remains intact but it may be far otherwise with a bank. It depends for its existence on credit. Sap that by fictitious sales of its shares in a time of monetary excitement, and bring its depositors upon it in a rush, and you smash up, it may be, a perfectly solvent institution.*

We are always seeking to "learn lessons", why is it that we have not learned this one so far?

There were abnormal price movements during a period of several weeks Northern Rock was in discussions with the Bank of England leading to the eventual decision to provide support. Although there was no mention in the Press, one has to question whether there was any "insider knowledge" involved in the trading of Northern Rock shares that would have given rise to market abuse. That is a reasonable question in view of the fact that "shorting" activity increased to 20% of the shares in issue during the days before the announcement and that one hedge fund was identified as being responsible for half the activity.

The presentation followed up by quoting an anonymous senior banker as having said,

> *Hedge funds actively drove down Rock's share price, and contributed to the panic and the problems. Some of these guys have made shed loads of money out of other people's misery and have imperilled the UK banking system.*

Mr Pittam disagreed,

In no way did the activity of short sellers have any effect on Northern Rock's eventual demise. The root cause of the problem is they couldn't meet their obligations. A better run bank would have had the ability to fund itself in a crisis.

The discussion continued by noting that rights and wrongs aside, short-selling of Northern Rock had slowed to a crawl by the end of the previous week after pension funds grew increasingly reluctant to lend the bank's shares.

Mr.Pittam may be correct in that the short-selling of itself did not contribute to Northern Rock's problems, but it certainly did exacerbate the losses suffered by Northern Rock's investors in the months after September 14th and created an artificial and distorted market in Northern Rock shares that none of the Bank's board, the FSA or the London Stock Exchange thought fit to tackle.

Mr.Pittam was also correct when he suggested that, "this may be a new story for many, but not for sophisticated investors". His company is one of a number that provides services to his so-called "sophisticated investors". Gamblers in a company's stock would be a more apt description.

There is an Association, The International Securities Lending Association (ISLA). Its website describes it as a trade association established in 1989 to represent the common interests of participants in the securities lending industry. ISLA works closely with European regulators and in the United Kingdom has representation on the Securities Lending and Repo Committee, a committee of market practitioners chaired by the Bank of England. The Association has contributed to a number of major market initiatives, including the development of the UK Stock Borrowing and Lending Code of Guidance and the industry standard lending agreement, the Global Master Securities Lending Agreement (GMSLA). ISLA's priorities for 2007/08 include:

- *Working with regulators to provide a safe and efficient framework for securities lending.*

- *Providing information to members about securities lending market developments.*

- *Opening up new markets for securities lending.*

- *Developing good industry practices.*

- *Reviewing the GMSLA.*

- *Enhancing the public profile of the securities lending industry.*

ISLA has more than 90 members comprising insurance companies, pension funds, asset managers, banks and securities dealers representing more than 4,000 clients. Although based in London, ISLA represents members from more than twenty countries in Europe and North America. It also has an elected Board of twelve industry professionals representing firms from all parts of the industry. The current Chairman is Laurence Marshall of UBS Investment Bank. ISLA appointed David Rule as its first Chief Executive in 2007. The website also provides a list of its member institutions which includes many major international banks.

What ISLA contributes to the efficient and useful conduct of legitimate trading in stock markets is debatable. Hedge funds using its facilities claim to act as a "lubricant", enabling better liquidity in the trading of shares on stock markets. Another point of view is that It does nothing more than lend a veneer of credence to an activity that is little more than legalized gambling. There can be few days when trading in FTSE 100 and even FTSE250 shares is not brisk without requiring the intervention of shorting activities.

As an example of how Northern Rock shares were being lent for short term trading purposes, statistics for 9th October 2007 provided the following detail:-

Shares on loan   — 52.33 million,

as a % of shares held in "Crest" — 16.36%

Shares held in Crest   — 319.91 million,

as a % of shares in issue   — 75.95%

Shares in issue   — 421.23 million,

On loan as a % of shares in issue — 12.42%

That was the position on a day selected at random. It gives an indication of the extent of shorting which was taking place in Northern Rock shares on a day-to-day basis in the latter months of 2007 and into 2008.

Apart from *shorting* shares, hedge funds were not the only professional traders dealing extensively in Northern Rock shares, before and after the September crisis. A number of banks were dealing in quite substantial numbers of Northern Rock's shares, dealings that were sufficiently large that they had to be disclosed to the London Stock Exchange under its rules (Rule 8.3 and others).

By October 2007 it was apparent to any investor that Northern Rock's problems were not going to go away or to be readily solved in the foreseeable future. Although there must have been sales activity by investors in Northern Rock wishing to dispose of their holdings, it was much less likely that new investors would be buying large numbers of shares in the company, although the on-line broker, T D Waterhouse produced figures that showed that Northern Rock was the most traded share in Britain during the previous two months. A spokesman for it also said, "We've had people opening accounts just to trade Northern Rock."

Nevertheless one is drawn to the conclusion that the high volume of daily dealing was such that much of it could only have been conducted by speculators and "shorters", institutions or other professional investors acting either for their own account or for clients.

Examples on 8th October 2007, a date chosen at random included the following, but almost any date would have produced a broadly similar result. Those were transactions which the rules of the London Stock Exchange required traders to report:-

Barclays Bank PLC reported holding the following positions in Northern Rock shares:

Securities held —- long position	24,125,030 shares
Short position	244,836 shares
Derivatives other than options — long	3,915,361
Short	3,356,354

Options and agreements to purchase 22,319

On that one day Barclays Bank carried out 289 separate purchases and 199 sales. This was not untypical of the type of trading being carried on by a number of institutions, content to speculate in, and presumably make money out of Northern Rock shares, yet at the same time unwilling to lend to Northern Rock in the inter-bank market.

Other traders on the same day were:

Abn Amro Bank NV

Securities held —- long position	605,258 shares
Short position	752,141 shares
Derivatives (other than options), Long	1,000,000
Options and agreements to purchase/sell, Long	700,000
Short	700,000

<u>Merrill Lynch International</u>

   Purchased   1,466,039 shares

   Sold   !,420,943 shares

Later on 14th November 2007 other LSE filings disclosed that:

UBS AG, London Branch had a holding of 25,969,152 shares, 6.17% of Northern Rock's issued capital.

Schroders bank noted a holding of 4,943,227 shares equal to 1.174%.

HBOS declared a holding of 3,617,177 shares, 0.859%, after having sold 1,100,590 shares.

An overseas investor, Second Swedish National Pension Fund (Anda AP Fonden or AP2) declared a holding of 6,525,798 shares equal to 1.55% that it later increased to 1.8%.

These reports are quoted as representative examples of the size of trading in Northern Rock shares. They were not the only ones. As noted in the chapters on the "Rescue" the two hedge funds interested in the rescue process were also regular purchasers of substantial numbers of shares that they still held as investments at the nationalisation date.

On 10th October 2007, "The Times" disclosed that,

> *Europe's second-largest hedge fund yesterday mistakenly exposed its large-scale shorting of shares in Northern Rock after a miscommunication with the Takeover Panel.*
>
> *GLG Partners, a $19 billion fund manager with Sir Howard Davies, the former Financial Services Authority chairman, on its advisory board, (nota bene) yesterday told the London Stock Exchange that it had failed to make trading disclosures between September 26 and October 5.*
>
> *The hedge fund manager blamed "human error" for its lapse and disclosed that it held short positions on more than 3 per cent of Northern Rock stock via contracts for difference. It is thought that up to 50 per cent of Rock's stock is currently being shorted.*

Note the estimate that up to 50% of Northern Rock's stock was being shorted.

The article went on to explain that there was actually no need to disclose, the Takeover Panel mistakenly advised GLG that it should have made disclosures, which are required where an investor has interests of 1% or more of a company's shares if the company is subject to takeover discussions. However, this rule does not apply to short-selling.

As we shall see, The Chancellor later brought short-selling within the rules.

The article continued,

> Regulators have been jumpy about trading in bank shares during recent market turmoil, amid fears of insider dealing.

> Philip Richards, a co-founder of RAB Capital and the biggest shareholder in Rock, last month attacked some rival hedge funds for fomenting panic about Rock and accused the Financial Services Authority (FSA) of failing to regulate trading in its shares.

> The FSA has taken just one notable disciplinary action against market abuse.

> In August 2006 it fined GLG and Philippe Jabre, the former managing partner, £750,000.

> GLG has also been fined by French and American regulators in the past 14 months.

Table 16 is a representative summary of the extent of the daily trading which went on, both before and after 14th September 2007:

The <u>daily</u> volume of shares traded from mid October until nationalisation in February gradually diminished, with a minimum of 1,250,000 and a maximum of 35,100,000.

To appreciate more fully the significance of these statistics, one needs to look at the number of individual trades per day and also the spread in the quoted prices each day. Unfortunately, I only collected the number of trades and the prices at which they were conducted for part of the period and those are detailed in Table 16.

From 27/09/07 to 18/10/07 the number of trades each day was within the range 6,405 to 14,186.

The daily average was 8,800 and the total number of trades during this period was 132,126.

Table 16

In the 23 weeks from 16/01/07 to 16/06/07

Total volume of shares traded	525,824,965
Average daily volume	4,572,391
Daily volume as a percentage of shares in issue	1.08%

These figures could be regarded as representative of what was "*normal*" trading in Northern Rock shares.

In the 43 working days from 12/07/07 to 12/09/07

Total volume of shares traded	558,576,000
Average daily volume	12,990.139
Daily volume as a percentage of shares in issue	3.08%

These figures bear out the statement, noted elsewhere that professional investors were shorting and trading Northern Rock shares vigorously.

In the 7 working days from 14/09/07 to 24/09/07

Total volume of shares traded	1,144,550,000
Average daily volume	163,507,142
Daily volume as a percentage of shares in issue	38.82%

This was the "peak period in speculative trading.

In the 15 working days from 27/09/07 to 18/10/07

Total volume of shares traded		596,490,000
Average daily volume	Buys	19,013,000
	Sales	20,753,000
	Average daily total	39,766,000
	Daily volume as a percentage of shares in issue	9.5%

From 19/10/07 to 30/11/07 the number of trades each day was lower – between 1,502 and 6,756.

It never dropped below 1,000 trades per day until December.

In January and February 2008 the daily numbers remained in a range 429 to 2,137, the lower figures being in the few days prior to nationalisation.

The price spread varied considerably from day to day, but the following figures give some idea of how it fluctuated on a daily basis:

During	August 2007 from	—- 16 pence to 72 pence
	September	—- 9 pence (one day) to 96 pence

October	— 7 pence to 87 pence
November	— 4.4 pence to 64.7 pence
December	— 2.5 pence to 15.7 pence

Generally speaking, the broadest daily spreads occurred on days of high dealing activity, particularly in August, September and October, which were also the months of greatest uncertainty as to Northern Rock's future. They were also affected by particular items of news relating to the progress of the "rescue".

There were a number of media comments on different aspects of Northern Rock share dealing during the period, including speculation as to whether it was time to buy Northern Rock shares.

In varying degrees experts were cautioning investors against using the turmoil affecting Northern Rock as a potential buying opportunity. A wide range of opinions was being expressed, most of them veering towards a negative viewpoint but one independent financial adviser was apparently investing although he recognised it as a risky bet. He based the decision on the fact that Northern Rock had a lot of mortgage borrowers on its books and that had to be worth something. His opinion was that someone was going to make money out of it therefore he saw it as a reasonable gamble.

The general opinion as far as existing shareholders were concerned was that they might as well hang on to see what happened in regard to any potential take-over. This was based at the time on a calculation that the worth of the group's mortgage book was about 180 pence a share which suggested that any offer would need to value Northern Rock at more than 200 pence a share to win shareholder approval.

All this speculation was being reported early on after the run on the bank and before an assessment had been made of Northern Rock's underlying liquidity problem. However, it was interesting in view of the fact that the Government subsequently decided that the shares should be treated as valueless, an opinion which was naturally not shared by anyone with a financial interest in the shares.

By October 2007 it was obvious to most observers that very little genuine long term trading was being conducted in Northern Rock shares and there were a number of calls for the shares to be suspended. Vince Cable of the Liberal Democrats said so on more than one occasion. There were other articles, one by John Waples, Business Editor of The Times calling for the suspension of the shares as it was a false market. This was a particularly relevant comment at the time

The article started,

Why, six weeks after Northern Rock went cap in hand to the Bank of England, are shares in Britain's fifth-biggest mortgage lender still allowed to trade? Buying and selling shares in the bank has become nothing more than a lottery. The bidders don't even know how to value the bank's equity, and neither do the Bank of England or the Treasury.

If you are unable to quantify the risks, what is being created is a false market. If this is the case, and I think it is, then the shares should be suspended.

He then proceeded by detailing his five reasons for this conclusion, two of which were,

One has to assume that the Bank (of England) and the Treasury have detailed knowledge of Northern Rock's books and have shared some of this information with the bidders. Wouldn't it be better to suspend the shares while these negotiations are taking place?

The second was,

Given that the Bank's rescue talks with Northern Rock were leaked, how certain can we be that more price sensitive information will not emanate from Treasury quarters.

These were very valid points. Northern Rock's collapse was the most publicly visual evidence of the global credit crisis affecting UK financial markets at that time.

The article carried on,

Mervyn King, the Bank's Governor, Sir Callum McCarthy, the head of the FSA and Alistair Darling must get a grip of the situation. They have already moved to safeguard the deposits of Northern Rock retail investors, but they appear to have no regard to the dubious morality of allowing the shares to continue trading. - - - - If King wants the City to become a glorified betting shop he is going the right way about it. The Bank is full of some very clever economists but it appears to have no one with any market nous. In the meantime private investors are being sucked into a Northern Rock recovery story and buying the shares.

Some private investors may have been "sucked into buying shares" but it is likely that they accounted for a very small percentage of total trading described above.

The article by John Waples was one of the few that commented on what was going on with Northern Rock shares. The Northern Rock directors, the FSA and the London Stock Exchange had all decided around this time that trading in Northern Rock shares should be allowed to continue, but Waples and the earlier BBC News programme quoted above correctly identified that the dealing that was taking place in Northern Rock shares was no different from casino gambling. Most of it had nothing to do with investment.

The purpose of the Bank of England and Treasury intervention was not to save Northern Rock and that may be part of the reason why there was no official interest in stopping trading. Its principal interest, perhaps its only interest, was to prevent a panic such as Northern Rock suffered on the 14th September from spreading to other banks and mortgage lenders.

As the BBC reported, "some people are making shed loads of money out of other people's misery."

Not only were they doing so, they did not observe Stock Exchange rules. The London Stock Exchange issued a statement that urged investors who had bought or sold shares in Northern Rock to settle their trades. It noted that "a very large number" of transactions had not been completed by the due date. An LSE spokesperson said the percentage of unsettled Northern Rock trades since the end of September currently stood in double figures, against a typical average of 1 - 2% for a FTSE 100 stock over the same period. Unsettled trades could include transactions where investors (if that is what they were) sold borrowed shares in the expectation of a fall in their price, allowing them to be bought back more cheaply.

Vince Cable was more pointed in his comments,

> Trading in Northern Rock shares should be suspended, as enormous positions are being taken on by the spivs and sharks in the City at the expense of the small shareholder.

These views formed part of Mr Cable's general comments on the Northern Rock situation issued in a News Release by the Liberal Democrats on 26th November 2007.

Whether or not Northern Rock shares should have been suspended was controversial. There were people close to the operation of the markets who were opposed to the suspension of shares in such circumstances as it would prejudice the right of existing shareholders to sell their shares, and there must have been some who did not wish to accept the risk of default or nationalisation or whose financial circumstances dictated that they should not remain invested in risky assets.

There was so much comment on those aspects of speculative trading in Northern Rock shares that it must have been a hot topic in City circles even if it was less obvious to the man in the street.

This part of the Northern Rock story, which was replicated by the high volumes of trading in other stocks during this period particularly in the shares of major banks, leads one to question the role of stock exchanges that operate what are in effect dual facilities without differentiating between them.

As noted earlier, the original purpose of stock exchanges was to enable the creation of active markets in the shares of listed companies, in other words to facilitate buying and selling transactions by genuine medium / long-term investors. The secondary role which developed and which could be said to have almost become the primary role, is to enable speculative gambling in shares and other instruments based on shares and bonds.

If the secondary role remains a minority activity in volumes and value, then it is acceptable when operated on the same market. However, it has now reached proportions where it has a significant affect on the pricing of shares, frequently to the disadvantage of conventional investors, particularly private investors who unless they operate regularly through an advisory stock-broker have very little opportunity to properly assess what is actually happening in the market.

It has become popular in the media to make references such as "the market says———" or "the market sentiment is ———" but one has to question if "the market" as an entity is capable of being quoted in this manner. What are really being described are the sentiments, etc of sections of unidentified groups of participants in the market place.

This substantial change in the nature of market activity leads one to question whether private investors can actually carry out stock market deals with any real confidence in the market place.

If markets are to be depended upon to provide a fair and open dealing service, where supply is regulated by the relative demands of purchasers and sellers who base their pricing assessment on the intrinsic worth and future prospects of quoted companies there needs to be change. That was the way stock markets, particularly the London Stock Exchange operated 40 - 50 years ago. Since then there have been many changes that may often be beneficial for investors and evolutionary, but that is not always the case.

Today we have an equity stock market that is used for short term gambling in stocks and shares. Trading is no longer only in the stock of listed companies, but in a variety of other derivative products which may be used for hedging purposes but are also used as pure gambles on market movements, frequently by shorting which opens a door to the deliberate manipulation of market share prices by some professional traders, either in individual shares or generally. Whilst one would like to believe that they are very much a minority the practices are becoming too common for that to be the case. When coupled to trading with the benefit of insider information the problem becomes a very real one, as has now been recognized in official quarters.

It has to be borne in mind that the primary purpose of stock markets was to provide a reliable and orderly market through which investors could buy and sell their investment holdings. Every stockbroker's newsletter, and advertisements seeking investors, invariably stress that investors should be looking at the medium – long term prospects of their investments. Apart from "boiler room" sales, none encourage investment on the basis of short-term gains.

Investors - corporate or private - need to have confidence in the integrity of markets through which they invest. Not only is the problem created by deliberate manipulation, possibly not by a relatively small number of people or investment managers but by large numbers of traders, and there are thousands working for banks and investment holding companies in the City and elsewhere, who are constantly dealing in stock markets all day long, that is their sole occupation. The sheer number and value of trades has an effect on market pricing, particularly when traders are shorting shares, i.e. selling shares they have borrowed or in fact do not possess, in the expectation of a price fall which will enable them, often on the same day, to buy shares back at a lower price and so to square their positions.

These strategies can, and frequently do become self-fulfilling. Because of the volumes involved, small movements of a few pence are sufficient to enable traders to achieve their purposes.

Add the activities of hedge funds which, as mentioned above, are estimated to account for 40% of trading activity on the London Stock Exchange where their objectives are to make profits whether markets are rising or falling, as long as they are moving, without taking "long" positions (i.e. investing to hold). In those circumstances market movements become even more distorted from the point of view of longer-term investors.

The sheer volume of hedge fund money in the UK market at any one time, running into billions of pounds Sterling (and even more in dollars in the US markets) must influence the creation of artificial stock pricing in markets.

All this happens before we even consider the activities of Private Equity Companies who also target specific quoted company shares when mounting takeovers. Here again the volumes of money involved are sufficiently large to affect market pricing.

Although the foregoing examination of market activity expresses criticisms of some of the developments in stock markets, it is not the intention to infer that much of the business is conducted improperly. At the same time, as has been noted there is, and always has been, a core of operators who break rules and ought to be penalized. The difficulty has always been to investigate such transgressions fully and to apply legal sanctions.

The Financial Services Authority, as financial regulator now has a duty to investigate such matters and bring the culprits to justice, but the City environment is such that they are seldom successful in their efforts to prove illegal market intervention. This is particularly the case when insider-trading accusations are being investigated.

In recognition of these facts the Chancellor, Alistair Darling, on the 28th March 2008, announced plans to create for the FSA new plea-bargaining powers to be known as "specified prosecutor status", powers that are already in use by the Serious Fraud Office.

The Chancellor was quoted as having said,

> I can't allow us to get into a situation where people quite deliberately manipulate markets for personal gain with the potential to destabilize the financial system. People are getting away with it and the time has come for us to start looking at it again. If a handful of people are up to no good, we have to make sure the authorities have the tools to do the job.

Consideration of proposed new legislation was revived by events the previous week when HBOS shares suffered a 20% drop within an hour following the circulation of what at the time were declared to be unfounded rumours about the bank needing emergency funding. Although the FSA started an investigation, it was generally considered in the City that they were unlikely to identify those who started the rumours.

This type of situation arose again in June 2008 when a serious "insider trading" incident affecting the shares of Bradford and Bingley was reported. It was recorded that the company saw 14% wiped off its share price in the three working days immediately preceding a profits warning. This is a serious and frequently occurring problem that tends not to receive publicity. In this case it was suggested that a hedge fund with no obvious previous interest in B & B had taken a large short position in the shares during the afternoon prior to the profits warning. In those circumstances it ought not to be too difficult to prove that its actions were motivated by inside information.

This revelation was only one of many. In previous months, and even with greater intensity later on in the year, there were some apparently flagrant abuses, such as the short selling and false rumours that undermined HBOS shares earlier. When market prices were fluctuating wildly, almost from hour to hour, it was a simple matter to carry out those raids. Yet the FSA seemed powerless to act and said that the tribunal deciding market abuse cases appeared to be applying a far higher burden of proof than the 51:49 required. As the tribunal included City practitioners (club members?) sitting in judgment on their peers, a long-standing arrangement, there was no more prospect now than there had been in the past of achieving a cessation of insider trading.

In consequence the FSA has had to resort to more difficult criminal action. However, in addition, the FSA now has access to proposed new plea-bargaining legislation coupled with immunity for whistle-blowers. Although one of the FSA's recommendations is to keep the number of insiders to a minimum that might be difficult in many circumstances where a number of parties have to be privy to price sensitive information. For example, on the B&B profit warning / rights issue reorganization there were four banks involved. On Strictly Come Dancing, "It takes two", and so it is with "leaks" - one to make the leak and another to act upon it. There were so many individuals involved with the B & B example that it was not surprising that the confidentiality of the arrangements was lost.

The Chancellor responded very quickly to at least temporarily ban shorting in a list of specified financial services companies. There was much resistance to that so a permanent or more extensive ban will take some fairly heavy-handed action on the part of the government and the FSA.

But any one who thinks that this is a recent phenomenon is not in touch with reality. I was Trust Manager of a bank in the City in the 1960's, and insider trading and "leaks" were rife then. Why therefore when they are so obviously unacceptable practices are they if anything more widespread now, forty-odd years later?

The answer lies in what The Times described in an article as "a cosy tribunal of City practitioners sitting in judgment on their peers". Forty years ago such events were "investigated" behind closed doors by the Council of the London Stock Exchange effectively comprised of Members of the Exchange, in other words self-regulation. If there is one thing I learned in later life as head of a Financial Services Commission it is that self-regulation is a useless sham whenever business and money making come together. There is seldom any real will in such self-regulating bodies to pursue a transgression or to ensure that justice is served.

No one should underestimate the "cosy" club that exists in financial circles in the City. Once again, forty years ago when I was leaving the City to work overseas, my senior manager (nowadays he would be a "Chief Executive") when making his farewells told me "the City is a village, we all know each other and we all know what is going on in the village". It is a much larger village now, but not much has changed, certainly not for the better.

As can be seen from the events related in this chapter, there was much that gave cause for concern. Why was gambling in Northern Rock shares allowed to continue for so long after the bank's problems became general knowledge and it became apparent that, nationalization aside, there could be no ready solution to them?

One can reasonably accept that September 2007 was a time when there was considerable confusion surrounding Northern Rock's future and the full extent of its problems were not properly understood by investors. However, for the four and one-half months after that, up to nationalization and the cessation of trading in the shares on 18th February 2008 there can be no credible explanation of the volume of daily trading that was carried on, other than that it was being undertaken by professional (and some amateur) speculators. What makes this even less acceptable was the fact that some of it was conducted from the trading rooms of our big banks, as the examples quoted earlier illustrate.

Of course, as Northern Rock was, for all intents and purposes, operating "normally" it was the duty of its Board to take the lead in this matter. They apparently decided that it might exacerbate the bank's situation to call for trading to cease. But was that a valid reason, compared to the huge volume of speculative trading that was taking place, of which they must have been aware, and aware also that it affected the legitimate interests of genuine investors in the company. However, as we have seen in an earlier chapter, concerns about the company's shareholders seemed to have been very much on the boardroom back-burner.

How about the FSA? If the company's board did not favour suspension of trading, was it appropriate for them to intervene? Perhaps not, but at the same time the FSA is charged with maintaining orderly markets, and the market in Northern Rock shares for much of the relative period was far from orderly, as the sample figures quoted above illustrate very clearly.

What about the London Stock Exchange itself? They would in circumstances such as those of Northern Rock expect to receive a reasoned request from the company's board for suspension of the company's shares, and that was not forthcoming. Alternatively, it would have to come to the LSE's attention that circumstances had arisen which made it difficult or impossible to conduct an orderly market in the shares. There is a range of circumstances that would have lead the LSE to suspend trading on its own initiative.

One or more such circumstances may well have arisen during the period in question but the simple fact was that none of the trading was being conducted out-with the Stock Exchange rules. Undesirable as it may be that what was going on was within the rules, that is the way in which our financial markets have evolved and unless sterner regulatory legislation is introduced by government that situation will continue and what took place in the latter part of 2007 will be repeated time after time. It reappeared in the second and third quarters of 2008. Members of the Stock Exchange and their professional clients were making lots of money out of Northern Rock's situation, as many observers commented at the time.

The Treasury and the Bank of England made references to the special nature of banks. They are not the same as other commercial companies and their financial problems can have a wide-ranging affect on other parts of the country's economy. For that reason it is suggested that it is important to treat them differently in a number of areas. One of those areas should be the trading of and more particularly speculation in their shares in times of real stress.

12 The Nationalization of Northern Rock

The run on Northern Rock deposits began on 14th September 2007 and for the rest of that month, as we have seen in Chapter 8 there was speculation on Northern Rock's future, much of it that "a white knight" would have to be found to rescue it.

It was not until the beginning of October, at least to public knowledge that knights of one sort or another began to take an interest in Northern Rock. As has been recorded in earlier chapters interest continued with varying degrees of intensity for a further three months and more, during which time the Treasury was being pressed by a number of MPs from parliamentary opposition parties to get on with the nationalization of the company as being the only solution that would ensure that "tax-payers' interests" would be protected.

From time to time, possibly as a stick shaking exercise, the Government had threatened nationalization although it appeared that it hoped that a satisfactory private sector solution would emerge. At the same time, having been caught wrong-footed when the run on Northern Rock deposits started, it was busy preparing the groundwork for a possible nationalization, which included the selection of Ron Sandler a well known City figure as prospective CEO, and Ann Godbehere, previously of Royal Bank of Scotland and Swiss-re insurers who would act as Finance Director.

The rescue bids and proposals have been detailed in Chapters 8, 9 and 10. The stumbling block for all of them was the fact that there were no signs of an early recovery in the inter-bank lending markets which would enable them to raise the £25 billion or so required to pay off the Bank of England loans and set the company on a reasonable footing from which it could go forward. In the course of negotiations the Treasury had indicated that, subject to EC agreement, the B of E loans could remain available to bidders during a restructuring for a limited period of time, at most two-to-three years.

The Bank of England loans were at a penal rate and of course, there was also the question of the Government guarantee of deposits, for which Northern Rock was paying a fee. In the event of a private takeover of Northern Rock, there were fears that if the guarantee remained in place it could give the bank a competitive advantage. If it did not remain in place, it was questionable whether the deposit base could be relied upon to remain with the bank.

There was also a lot of talk about "taxpayers' money" propping up a "fat-cat takeover", with none of the profits from a successful turn-round coming to the poor "taxpayers". This is an aspect that resurfaced at a later stage in the nationalization saga. Another concern expressed time and again in the media, was with "rebellious shareholders" who were only looking out for their own interests and who were considered to be nothing better than market gamblers who did not deserve to be bailed out.

The "rebellious shareholders" were not always precisely identified, although the inferences led one to RAB Capital and SRM Global, two hedge fund managers that had built up substantial share holdings, 6.66% and 11.5% respectively. Being hedge fund managers was enough to put them on the wrong side of the fence, but the truth was that they were two of a very few "speculators" who actually put a meaningful amount of money into the purchase of shares in the ailing Northern Rock and left it in. Interestingly, although it never seemed to reach media reports, Barclays Bank PLC was noted in Northern Rock's 2007 Annual Report as holding 5.01%. It was the third largest shareholder in Northern Rock at the date of nationalization.

All the others, and as we have seen in Chapter 11 there were many, including major banks and other professional market players, traded and shorted Northern Rock shares daily in large volumes until well into January 2008, with no other purpose than to profit from the constant fluctuations in share price throughout each day. Those fluctuations were not generated by anything other than their activities and the circulation of rumours. T D Waterhouse, a major online stockbroker, recorded that Northern Rock was the most traded share on the London Stock Exchange for over two months. It also said that many new accounts were opened just to trade Northern Rock shares. Chapter 11 examined the share trading patterns prior to nationalization.

Announcement of the nationalization of Northern Rock was a very controversial step for the Government to take, but it came in an HM Treasury Press release, followed the same day by an HM Treasury statement released by the Chancellor of the Exchequer, Alistair Darling on Sunday, 17th February 2008.

The Press release set out the reasoning behind the decision to nationalize the bank together with an explanation of how the nationalized bank would operate, and read as follows:-

1. The Government has today decided to bring forward legislation that will enable Northern Rock plc to be taken into a period of temporary public ownership. The Government has taken this decision after full consultation with the Bank of England and the Financial Services Authority. The Government's financial adviser, Goldman Sachs, has concluded from a financial point of view that a temporary period of public ownership better meets the Government's objective of protecting taxpayers.

2. Northern Rock will be open for business as usual tomorrow morning and thereafter. Branches will be open; internet and call centre services will operate as normal. All Northern Rock employees remain employed by the company. Depositors' money remains absolutely safe and secure. The Government's guarantee arrangements remain in place and will continue to do so. Borrowers will continue to make their payments in the normal way. The Financial Services Authority have advised that Northern Rock remains solvent.

3. The Government set out its objectives last year that would guide its actions in relation to Northern Rock: the protection of depositors' money; protection of the taxpayer; and maintaining wider financial stability.

4. The Government has consistently and successfully taken action to meet these objectives. Last year the Government agreed to provide support to Northern Rock because, in the prevailing market conditions, there was a serious risk that other parts of the banking system in Britain could have been destabilised. That support was successful and prevented further contagion. The Government was also determined to safeguard depositors' money and took action to put in place arrangements which have been successful in doing so. None of the guarantees have been called and therefore there has been no cost to the taxpayer.

5. While in September and October uncertainty in the market place made it difficult to attract potential buyers for Northern Rock, in November and December the board of Northern Rock received a number of expressions of interest. The Government decided to test these proposals. However, it became clear that no institution was prepared to make an offer for Northern Rock without some form of public support because of prevailing market conditions.

6. The Government was, therefore, prepared to consider a backstop guarantee arrangement to allow the Board and shareholders to explore a private sector solution, provided the terms and conditions were acceptable and met the principles set out by the Government. In the meantime, the

Chancellor made clear that a temporary period of public ownership remained an option, and that any solution would need to represent good value for money for the taxpayer.

7. Two detailed private sector proposals were received: one from the Virgin Consortium and the other, a Northern Rock led restructuring plan. These were considered alongside temporary public ownership.

8. The Government is very grateful to the bidders for their work to establish whether a private sector-led solution on acceptable terms could be found.

9. Both proposals involve a degree of risk for taxpayers and very significant implicit subsidy from the Treasury, involving a payment below the market rate to the Government for continuation of its guarantee arrangements and for the financing the Government would be putting in place.

10. Each proposal has pros and cons. The Virgin proposal would have brought a new brand and management. However, the taxpayer would only have seen any share of the private sector's return if the value of the business to its investors had reached at least £2.7bn.

11. The Board's proposal would have involved a similar level of subsidy. But it had other disadvantages, compared with Virgin, including: it would bring in less new capital, providing less "buffer" protecting the taxpayer from risk; and the business would have been dependent on Government guarantees for new retail deposits for longer.

12. A subsidy on the scale required would not, in the Government's judgement, provide value for money for the taxpayer, in circumstances where the private sector rather than the taxpayer would secure the vast majority of the value created over the period ahead. This would be a poor reflection of the balance of risk borne by the two sides.

13. By contrast, under public ownership the Government will secure the entire proceeds from the future sale of the business in return for bearing the risks in this period of market uncertainty.

14. The Government has concluded that the private sector alternatives do not meet the test of protecting the taxpayer's interest, when compared with the alternative. Accordingly, and taking all the wider considerations into account, the Government has concluded that the right approach is to take the company into a period of temporary public ownership.

15. It is also the Government's clear assessment that, under the approach the Government is taking, the taxpayer will see its outstanding loans to Northern Rock repaid in full, with interest - and that the business can and will be returned to the private sector as financial markets stabilise.

16. Tomorrow, before the markets open, it is expected that the UK Listing Authority will announce that Northern Rock's shares will be suspended from listing prior to the opening of the London Stock Exchange.

17. The Government will tomorrow also introduce a Bill that will enable the bank to be brought into temporary public ownership. Full details will be provided to Parliament.

18. The legislation will enable the Government to acquire the bank's shares. It will provide for compensation to be determined by an independent valuer. It will allow for the running of the bank and for the eventual transfer back into the private sector as soon as it is right to do so.

19. The Bill gives the Government a general power to acquire the shares in, or assets and liabilities, of institutions. But the Government is clear that this legislation is only being introduced now because there is a need to bring Northern Rock into temporary public ownership.

20. The Bill has deliberately been drafted to ensure that a bank can only be acquired in certain tightly defined circumstances. And that power will only last for twelve months. The Chancellor has previously announced a consultation which will lead to permanent legislation to deal with situations like this in the future.

21. Northern Rock will be managed on arms' length terms, as a commercial entity, by a newly appointed experienced and professional management team.

22. The Government has appointed appointed Ron Sandler CBE, former Chief Operating Officer of NatWest Group and Chief Executive of Lloyd's of London, who will be Executive Chairman of the company immediately upon the legislation coming into force. Mr Sandler will in due course recruit a new Chief Executive, at which point he will become Non-Executive Chairman.

23. Ann Godbehere, former Chief Financial Officer of Swiss Re, will be appointed as Chief Financial Officer of the company for the initial phase of public ownership.

24. Subject to the passing of the Bill, the Treasury intends to make an Order which would transfer all of the shares in Northern Rock to the Treasury Solicitor, as the Treasury's nominee. The Order would also, among other things, extinguish the existing share options; convert the foundation shares to ordinary shares and terminate the existing Foundation deed; make limited technical adjustments to the provisions of certain Tier 1 securities; provide for the rights or obligations of lenders, bondholders, swap counterparties or suppliers which would be triggered by the act of bringing Northern Rock into temporary public ownership not to be triggered; facilitate board changes; deal with the issue of liability of those directors appointed to or continuing on the board of Northern Rock whilst it is in public ownership; modify the application of certain provisions of the Financial Services and Markets Act 2000 to the company; and disapply shadow directorship provisions to specified public sector persons. A separate Order would be made which would set out the detail of a compensation scheme called for under the Bill.

Notes to editors

1. It is expected that the company's ordinary and preference shares will be suspended from listing tomorrow prior to the opening of the London Stock Exchange. The company's debt securities, which are not being transferred, will continue to trade.

2. The suspension of shares will have no effect on the rights or obligations of lenders, bondholders, swap counterparties or suppliers to Northern Rock, except for modifications principally aimed at ensuring that arrangements continue as before and that no counterparty triggers additional payments in public ownership.

3. The Northern Rock Foundation will be guaranteed a minimum income of £15m per year in 2008, 2009 and 2010. This will be paid directly by Northern Rock, and would be a condition of any sale if it were sold in this time. The new board will be asked to identify a viable long-term future for the foundation.

4. The proposed legislation provides for the assessment by an independent valuer of compensation which may be payable to any holder of shares transferred to HM Treasury. The principles for assessing compensation, set out in the legislation, reflect that Government should not be required to compensate shareholders for value which is dependent on taxpayers' support. A compensation order will be made under the legislation setting out some further details of the arrangements for compensating shareholders and others whose rights may have been affected by the transfer into public ownership. The independent valuer will set their own, more detailed, procedures.

5. The FSA has confirmed that Mr Sandler and Ms Godbehere are suitable persons to direct the business.

6. Ron Sandler, CBE, has over two decades of experience in the financial services

industry. He was Chief Executive of Lloyd's of London from 1995-1999. In 1999 he became Chief Operating Officer of NatWest Group up to its takeover by Royal Bank of Scotland. He currently chairs a number of companies. In 2002 he led a Government-sponsored review of the UK Long Term Savings Industry, which led to the creation of a new suite of simplified, lower cost savings and pension products for consumers. He has an MA from Queens' College, Cambridge and an MBA from Stanford University.

7. Ann Godbehere has extensive experience of the financial services sector having moved to London as Chief Financial Officer of Swiss Re Life & Health Division in 1998 and joined the Property & Casualty Business Group, based out of Zurich, as Chief Financial Officer on its establishment in 2001. In 2003 she was appointed Chief Financial Officer of the Swiss Re Group. Ann has also been an independent non-executive director of Prudential since 2 August 2007.

8. Ron Sandler will receive £90,000 per month and Ann Godbehere will be paid £75,000 per month. These are flat rates. No additional incentives will be discussed until the new board has discussed its business strategy with the Government.

The press Release was accompanied shortly afterwards by a statement by the Chancellor of the Exchequer, Alistair Darling.

The Statement ran to four pages and 68 sections and preceded a full statement by the Chancellor scheduled for the following day in the House of Commons. It is available on HM Treasury website, but the following are the salient points in which we should be particularly interested. The numbers are those used in the release.

1.   The preliminary announcement was being made prior to the opening of the markets the following morning.

4.   We do not believe that they (two detailed proposals for a private sector rescue) deliver sufficient value for money for the taxpayer.

5.   Our financial adviser, Goldman Sachs has concluded from a financial point of view that a temporary period of public ownership better meets our objectives of protecting taxpayers.

7.   We have done so (taken Northern Rock into temporary public ownership) after full consultation with the B of E and the FSA.

8.   Northern Rock will continue operating on a commercial basis.

9.   Importantly savers' and depositors' money remains safe and secure.

10. The Government guarantee arrangements I announced last year remain in place and will continue to do so.

14.   The FSA continue to assure me that the bank is solvent. It believes that the mortgage book is of good quality and the FSA will continue to regulate it

26.   It was right and necessary for the Government to intervene (in September 2007) because of the need to preserve financial stability in the system. That support was successful and prevented further contagion.

33.   It became clear that no institution was prepared to make an offer for Northern Rock without some form of public support because of prevailing market conditions.

38.   Both proposals (from bidders) involve a degree of risk for taxpayers and very significant implicit subsidy from the Treasury, involving a payment below the market rate to the Government for continuation of its guarantee arrangements and for the financing we would be putting in place.

40.   However, the taxpayer would only have seen any share of the private sector's return if the value of the business to its investors had reached at least £2.7 billion.

43.   By contrast, under public ownership the Government will secure the entire proceeds from the future sale of the business in return for bearing the risks in this period of market.

50.   The legislation will enable the Government to acquire the bank's shares and its assets. It will provide for compensation to be determined by an independent valuer.

51.   It will allow for the running of the bank and for the eventual transfer back into the private sector as soon as it is right to do so.

62.   The new Board and the company will operate at arm's length from the Government with complete autonomy for their decisions.

63.   As agreed in the Memorandum of understanding all operational decisions will be made by the Board with no interference from Government.

66.   At every stage the stability of the economy and the interests of depositors and taxpayers have been - and remain - our first concern.

The Treasury statement was quite straightforward and, in all the circumstances, reasonable. There was no reference to existing shareholders except indirectly in section No. 50 above, "The legislation will enable the government to acquire the bank's shares and its assets. It will provide for compensation to be determined by an independent valuer."

At face value, that provision was fine, except that HM Treasury and The Chancellor had stated on a number of occasions the basis on which an "independent" valuer would be required to make his assessment. The details were set out in a Statutory Instrument, **"The Northern Rock Plc Compensation Scheme Order 2008"** that was eventually published on 12th March 2008, as we shall see.

There are two main threads to the story of the nationalization. The first concerns all those matters related to the operations and future of the newly nationalized Northern Rock. The second relates to the compensation of shareholders, a very controversial topic.

We shall trace developments as they related to the operation of the nationalized Northern Rock prior to considering the compensation aspects. It was unlikely that the Chancellor, his government colleagues and advisers expected a meek acceptance of the proposals, and he certainly did not get one.

Nationalisation

The "Financial Times" started things off the following day with a headline,

> **"Fury over Rock Nationalization".**
> *Alistair Darling on Sunday announced the first nationalization of a sizeable British bank in a quarter of a century as he put Northern Rock into public ownership, infuriating shareholders and shocking the two private bidders hoping to take over the stricken mortgage lender. - - - - Shares in the bank, which closed at 90 pence on Friday, will be suspended on Monday morning and shareholders can expect virtually no compensation for their equity.*
>
> *- - - - The government's move stunned shareholders, who were last night considering action. Jon Wood of the SRM hedge fund, the bank's biggest shareholder, said "This is a very sad day for the stock market, banking industry and the reputation of the UK as a financial center. Noting that the chancellor insisted that the bank was solvent, he added "we will pursue all avenues to protect that value for shareholders. - - - - Robin Ashby, founder of the Northern Rock Small Shareholders Group said he was shocked and appalled that shareholders were having the bank stolen away from them.*

The Chancellor was quoted as saying, "I have a duty to the taxpayers of this country to make sure that I do the right thing by them and that is what I have done."

The article covered other aspects of the government statement before ending with another political comment, this time from the Shadow Chancellor, George Osborne, "We will not back nationalization. We will not help Gordon Brown to take this country back to the 1970's."

The "Times" newspaper followed up with an article by Anatole Kaletsky, its principal Economic Commentator and Associate Editor, and who for many years has been an economic consultant. The piece was headed, **"Absolutely, incredibly, utterly wrong!"** **"The Northern Rock fiasco will run and run".**

With that extreme heading, one knows immediately that he vehemently disagreed with the Chancellor's actions. But was he right to do so? As principal economic commentator for the newspaper, one would expect his views to be soundly based, but they appear to be, in keeping with the heading, fairly extreme personal views, some of which reflected the actualities of the situation, but others were more an exercise in rhetoric than anything else. Nevertheless, it is worth studying as an example of the media influence directed at its readers. It is also illustrative of the range of views that were being expressed over ensuing weeks and months.

> *It was clear from the start that some form of nationalisation would inevitably end the Northern Rock saga. But yesterday's announcement, far from ending this fiasco, threatened to push Gordon Brown even deeper in the hole he has dug. The purpose of nationalisation should not have been to continue "business as usual", with Northern Rock continuing to lend more money and attract retail deposits, with the backing of Treasury guarantees. The purpose should have been to secure £100 billion of taxpayers' money and to prevent any further damage to the British financial system.*
>
> *What the Chancellor should have announced are the politically difficult but financially sound decisions he will probably have to concede in the end anyway, under pressure from the financial markets, from European regulations and from lawsuits by the shareholders of Northern Rock.*
>
> *He should have announced that Northern Rock would be nationalised not to keep it in business, but to close it down; that the bank would stop lending new money or accepting new deposits as of tomorrow; that all the company's retail deposits would be shifted immediately to the National Savings system, while all the wholesale bonds would be replaced with Government gilts. The company would then be put into run-off, with the Treasury recouping its money gradually as existing borrowers repaid their mortgages over the years.*

Nationalisation, in other words, made sense only as a necessary legal stepping-stone to the orderly liquidation that Northern Rock required as soon as it ran out of money in September.

To use nationalisation to keep the bank in business and its staff in state-subsidised employment would be a travesty of all the economic principles that "new" Labour has claimed to believe in. It would represent a grossly unfair distortion of Britain's banking business and would make a mockery of all the arguments Mr Brown has vociferously advanced in Brussels against state subsidies and protectionism elsewhere in Europe. Worst of all, the provision of £100 billion of state guarantees to a grossly mismanaged and insolvent mortgage bank would be a gross insult to the hundreds of thousands of workers in businesses from coal, steel and textiles to performance cars and advanced electronics whose jobs could have been saved with Government guarantees or "temporary" nationalisations costing one-tenth or even one-hundredth of the £100 billion that the Government is now devoting to just 6,000 jobs at Northern Rock.

Nobody in Parliament has yet drawn the obvious comparisons between the largesse being directed at Northern Rock and the tough love practised on far more important and famous British companies such as Rover, Leyland and GEC-Marconi. But this silence merely testifies to the political bafflement and financial confusion created by the disaster. Now that the financial uncertainties about who will own and control the company have been resolved, the question is why it should continue to stay in business with public support.

Why should a Government that has consistently refused to offer public funding for potentially viable commercial projects of real national importance - aerospace, public transport, nuclear power - now be spending tens of billions on supporting a bust mortgage bank? Is it because Britain is short of mortgage lenders, lacks employment opportunities for bankers or suffers a deficiency of financial innovation?

Even if politicians at Westminster are unwilling to ask such questions there can be no doubt that others will. It is quite likely that the European Commission will veto the business plans for Northern Rock unless these provide for a rapid rundown of both its lending and deposit-taking operations.

To judge by previous provisional and inchoate Treasury announcements, at least since Mr Darling became Chancellor, there can be no presumption that Government legal and financial "experts" have thoroughly checked the compatibility of yesterday's announcement with EU rules on state aid. And even in the unlikely event that the Commission does approve this unprecedented state subsidy, the Treasury's problems will only just have begun.

For if it turns out that the European Commission does permit Northern Rock to continue doing business as usual, collecting deposits and lending our money, while enjoying unlimited state support, it is almost certain that other banks will demand comparable treatment. Indeed, the entire British mortgage industry has already put forward proposals for the Treasury to guarantee on a new type of mortgage bonds - and given warning of a collapse in loans to homeowners if the Government does not oblige. And almost as ominous there will be Northern Rock's former shareholders demanding compensation in the courts.

If the Government tells the European Commission that Northern Rock was a fundamentally viable company, capable of long-term survival without state support, then the same argument will be used by Northern Rock shareholders to accuse the Government of unjust expropriation and of deliberately engineering the company's failure. And behind, in the long queue of potential litigants and self-avowed victims of Government incompetence and conniving will stand the citizens of Newcastle, deprived of their largest charitable institution, as well as the Northern Rock workers, who sooner or later will surely lose their jobs.

All in all, what Mr Darling announced yesterday was a financial and political disaster of almost unimaginable proportions. The Northern Rock saga did not end yesterday; the fiasco has only just started, with the Government now officially in charge.

One would not expect Ron Sandler, the new executive chairman of Northern Rock to reach the same conclusions and at a press conference, he said that turning round the bank and repaying the £25 billion Bank of England loans would take years. He described how the nationalization programme was intended to revitalise Northern Rock and return it to the private sector as a vibrant, thriving enterprise. He saw no reason to believe that the bank could not go forward with the Northern Rock brand. He declined to comment on whether there would be redundancies.

The press conference was reported in a number of newspapers, all covering more or less the same points. On the 18th February Northern Rock also issued a Strategic Review Update.

The Board of Northern Rock notes the Government's announcement of its intention to take the Company into temporary public ownership by legislation under which it will acquire all of the shares in the Company, including the preference shares. The Government expects temporary public ownership to become effective within the next few days.

It has been important to have had the time to ensure there were a number of private sector solutions available. The Board hoped that at least one of those options would succeed and is very disappointed that the Government concluded that it was unable to provide funding to support a private sector solution and, in particular, the proposal put forward by the Company, which the Board believed satisfied the interests of all stakeholders.

The Company has been informed that the listing of its ordinary and preference shares has been suspended with immediate effect by the UK Listing Authority and that trading of these shares on the London Stock Exchange has ceased. The Government has said that it will be providing details shortly of the independent valuation process that will be established to assess compensation due to shareholders. The Company understands that the listing and trading of the debt instruments of the Company and its financing vehicles remain unaffected

The Government has also announced that it intends to appoint Ron Sandler as the new Executive Chairman of the Company and Ann Godbehere as the new Chief Financial Officer to work with the existing management team to determine the appropriate business strategy for the Company whilst in temporary public ownership. It is not possible at this stage to give any guidance on the nature of such changes or on the impact of any changes which may be made to the business, on employees of the Company.

The Government's announcement makes clear that the Company and its new management will be expected to operate at arm's length from the Government with commercial autonomy for its decisions and with the aim of returning the Company to the private sector at the earliest opportunity.

The Government has indicated that the new management of the Company will be asked to identify a viable long-term future for The Northern Rock Foundation and, in the meantime, that the proposals being developed by Mr. Sandler envisage the Company paying to the Foundation a minimum of £15 million per year in each of 2008, 2009 and 2010.

The Government has confirmed that the Company will remain fully open for business, working normal hours and operating as usual and that customers will not be affected by this development. It has also confirmed that HM Treasury's guarantee arrangements remain in place and depositors' money continues to be safe and secure. All branches, call centres, and other operations remain open for business to ensure the Company continues to provide a high standard of service to its customers.

Compared to Mr Kaletsky's piece, this Strategic Review was all very gentlemanly and restrained. Perhaps we should be thankful for the Kaletsky's of this world who stir things up, even if their opinions may sometimes be too extreme to be of real value.

Mr Sandler seemed satisfied that everything would carry on smoothly at Northern Rock, others were less satisfied. The "FT.com In Depth" website on the same day published the fact that other banks warned that public ownership of Northern Rock could put them at a competitive disadvantage. There were banking executives who were of the opinion that Northern Rock should face strict guidelines on how it can operate in the mortgage and savings markets to prevent rivals from being unfairly disadvantaged.

The article also quoted rival bankers as believing that the government's ambitions should be limited to running down Northern Rock's business in order to ensure taxpayers do not lose out. In other words were they still hoping, as they possibly did in earlier months, that Northern Rock could be made to just disappear?

The article reviewed the comments of a number of other interested parties, including George Osborne of the Conservatives who rejected the idea that Northern Rock could operate fairly in the banking sector. He claimed it could borrow and lend more cheaply than its rivals because of government backing. His reading of the situation was off-the-mark considering that the only reason Northern Rock was in a predicament was because it could not borrow in the inter-bank market, its Bank of England loans were at a penal rate above market rates (the actual rate charged was not made public) and its only advantage was the guarantee of deposits that accrued automatically through government ownership and was at no cost to the government since a fee was being charged for the facility.

As Northern Rock was now a Government owned entity in much the same way as National Savings and Investments and therefore its deposits carried an explicit government guarantee, why was it necessary for Northern Rock to be charged a fee for this facility when the government planned to retain all the profits from its continued operation?

The article also recorded the appointment of Stephen Hester, Chief Executive of British

Land and a former finance director of Abbey National as non-executive deputy chairman. (He later joined the Royal bank of Scotland board and then replaced Sir Fred Goodwin as CEO as we shall learn in chapter 16).

On this day also Standard and Poor's Rating Agency changed various Northern Rock short term credit ratings by upgrading them. Standard and Poor's added,

> *The positive outlook reflects the potential for the long-term counterparty credit rating to be upgraded once further information is available on the support that will be provided to Northern Rock whilst it remains in public ownership.*

In another release from Standard and Poor's it was said that the nationalisation of Northern Rock would have no impact on the sovereign ratings of the UK, rated AAA/A-1+ with a stable outlook. That was very reassuring!

Two days later, on the 20th February the House of Commons voted by 293 to 167 to give a third reading to the Bill to nationalize Northern Rock. It was expected to become law by the end of the week.

Defending the bill in the Commons debate, Darling insisted the government would not be involved in the day-to-day management of the bank, but it did need to approve its business plan. He wanted to make sure it was prudent, that it was sensible and protected the interests of the taxpayer. But he also wanted to make sure it avoided distortions in the banking sector. Mr. Darling also suggested that Northern Rock's shareholders should expect little in return for their investment. If the government had not intervened in September 2007 the bank would have gone bankrupt, he told the Commons.

The validity and justification for this last statement by the Chancellor should be judged in the light of what the Bank of England and the Chancellor were later prepared to do for other banks as we shall see in Chapter 16.

What had happened to the Bank of England's duty to act as a "lender of last resort" for Northern Rock?

George Osborne was then quoted,

> *He argued that it was not known how much we are buying this bank for, we don't know what we are buying in terms of its assets and liabilities, we don't know how long we are buying it for.*

Comments like those were hardly likely to inspire confidence in the Conservative party's analysis of the nationalization, or anything else, for that matter.

Also on the 20th February Vince Cable, Liberal Democrat spokesman wrote to the Chancellor, seeking clarification on why Granite (Master Issuer) held Northern Rock's best mortgages, saddling the taxpayer with the worst.

Granite was said to hold about £45 billion of the most profitable mortgages, but it would not be nationalized under the Bill going through parliament.

> In simple terms, what seems to have happened is that bondholders, who have the benefit of the best security the bank can offer, are being elevated above the taxpayer," Mr. Cable wrote. "In effect there has been an asset stripping operation designed to protect this segment of the bank's activities while the taxpayer is being left with the poor quality assets, unsecured loans and high risk mortgages.

Michael Ellam a spokesman for the Prime Minister said,

> Granite was a financing vehicle used by Northern Rock to raise money. - - - - Granite is a separate commercial and legal entity. It is not owned by Northern Rock. This is a long standing commercial relationship which stretches back to 1999. No new mortgages have been transferred into Granite since the Bank of England started bailing out Northern Rock last year, and Granite does not have any claim over Northern Rock's assets.

Mr Cable's comments, whilst no doubt expressed in good faith, amounted to little more than political posturing. There was and always has been a wealth of information available on the operations conducted through Granite and the quality of the mortgages assigned to trustees as back up for its bond issues. There was also plenty of information, confirmed by the external auditors and the FSA (for what that was worth), as to the quality of Northern Rock's mortgage assets generally. Nevertheless his point had some truth in it as the Granite conduit had always been accorded good quality loans, as its offer terms required. It follows that lesser quality loans would be amongst those left in Northern Rock, including the much-maligned up to125% loans which accounted for up to 30% of total mortgage loans.

As with every mortgage lender, Northern Rock had mortgage loans on its books that were less than top quality, but the proportion of the total mortgage assets that could be described as "under par" was no different from those of other major mortgage lenders, and better than most. It was also a fact that Northern Rock had a policy of selling on to a subsidiary of the investment banker Lehman Brothers its portfolio of commercial property loans that could be described as higher risk loans. Those are documented facts.

Any attempt to present a different picture is a distortion of the facts.

Mr Cable also seems to have missed the point, in his apparent over-ruling concern for the taxpayer, that if all the other Triple A rated securitised bonds (RMBS only) which had been issued, all $1,300 billion of them, had the quality of backing which Northern Rock's enjoyed, the turmoil in the financial markets which brought down Northern Rock would never have happened.

The fact was that a large proportion of them were put together in packages that did not contain what it said on the tin, whereas Northern Rock's did so. Furthermore, it is inconceivable that the purveyors of the bonds based on these packages were unaware that the quality of the packages did not always warrant the Triple A ratings accorded to most of them.

Later in February 2009 before the Treasury Select Committee, Sir Fred Goodwin, CEO of The Royal Bank of Scotland made a significant comment when explaining his bank's role in the derivatives markets. It acted as a "packager" or intermediary by parcelling up mortgages from "originators", paying for a Triple A rating for the packages and selling them on to investors. He said that the bank was aware that the packages contained subprime mortgages and that it placed its own valuation rating on them, but investors required an "independent" Triple A rating. He indicated that it was not RBS's concern as a mere intermediary to consider the value of the underlying mortgages. Their packages were rated Triple A and sold as such to investors.

That was no doubt an industry-wide view taken by other "packagers", including the Wall Street investment banks at the centre of securitisation. Sir Fred indicated as much.

Another article from "The Times" bore the leader **"Darling is no saint but his sins are exaggerated"**.

After a short review of Labour's problems in recent months, which extended beyond Northern Rock, the article continued,

> Talk of a £100 billion plus of taxpayer exposure is utter nonsense. That assumes the value of the houses on which the bank has lent is zero. Even a sharp fall in house prices would result in losses of a small fraction of that amount, still possibly in billions but not in the stratosphere.

That was the first time since the previous September that anyone has pointed out the fallacy behind the constant talk of "£100 billion of tax payers money at risk." An additional point here is that some of the property value underlying those mortgages that had been assigned for the benefit of Granite's bond holders would only cease to accrue to Northern

Rock if mortgagees defaulted on their mortgages en masse.

If that were to happen the associated risks had already been transferred to the bondholders who had no recourse to Northern Rock's other assets. That is the way in which the securitised bonds were structured. Northern Rock had a responsibility to supply the Granite structure with other suitable mortgages to replace defaulting mortgages, but in a total collapse of the mortgage market scenario, that would have been an academic requirement.

As a bit of light relief, although possibly not intended as such, "The Times" ran an article disclosing that the two people selected by the government to run Northern Rock, Ron Sandler (monthly Rock pay, £90,000) and Ann Godbehere (£75.000) were both "Non-domiciliaries", and as such were two of the 115,000 people in Britain who, for tax purposes, are not domiciled in the UK.

To understand the significance of this, the Government had been embroiled for some time in fiercely contested proposals to change the tax rules so that non- domiciled residents of the UK would be subject to more UK taxation. They were already liable to tax on UK source income, but not on their foreign income and assets if they were kept out of the UK.

Vince Cable could not miss the opportunity to put in his oar,

> *Mr. Sandler presumably is now becoming the second best paid person in Newcastle after Michael Owen*, adding, *at least Michael Owen pays taxes here.*

A few other people were canvassed for their (critical) comments.

The following day, 21st February, Mr. Brown was in Brussels on his first visit to the European Commission as Prime Minister, where he said that Britain would meet the conditions of the state aid regime in the EC. He was also quoted as saying that he was confident that the aid was within the rules. This had been a hotly debated political point amongst British politicians, one on which the EC was unlikely to pronounce until late in 2008 but in fact was still undecided in early 2009.

There were always people intent on finding flaws in the nationalization process and "The Times" article reported that,

> *An offshore fund with charitable status to raise money for Down's syndrome sufferers in the North East of England has emerged as the first potential barrier to a smooth nationalization of Northern Rock.*

The article described how the fund, called Granite, owned £49 billion of mortgages that were sold by Northern Rock and moved offshore to the tax-haven of Jersey. Comment has been made elsewhere on the stressing of "tax-haven" in descriptions of the Granite set-up. As we know from chapter 5, Granite sold bonds to investors and used the proceeds to issue new mortgages.

The thrust of The Times article was that claims on the fund could be in danger if Northern Rock failed keep up a flow of the new mortgage business needed to keep Granite running smoothly. It cited "one unnamed source" as saying, if you stopped writing new mortgages then Granite would have to be dissolved and all the Granite bond (holders) would have to be paid. The conclusion seemed to be that the Government would be shooting itself in the foot.

Whilst there may be some element of truth in it in places, the article showed a lack of understanding of the Granite structure, and in particular of the discretionary settlement that was the holding vehicle for the mortgages.

The statement that the Granite set up was "moved offshore to the tax-haven of Jersey" was obviously intended to infer that something shady was going on, whereas the fact was that Granite Master Issuer PLC was a UK company with a registered office in London, but whose business was structured through other Jersey companies as part of a necessary process to achieve "Euro-bond" status for the bonds it was involved in issuing because that was the only way they could acquire the status necessary for them to issue bonds that pay interest without deduction of a with-holding tax. Receiving gross interest, i.e. without deduction of tax at source, is a standard requirement of international investors.

The Down's Syndrome charity was a residuary beneficiary of the discretionary settlement at the heart of the securitization programme and would only (potentially) benefit when the whole scheme was wound up, and even then it was unlikely to receive very much. Its potential entitlement was not allied to the success or failure of the Granite operation.

Next day, "The Times" returned to the fray with an article by Martin Waller entitled, **"Guarantee for Guernsey's Rock depositors taxes belief".**

His amazement was that "tax-dodgers" who had placed their money in the Guernsey subsidiary of Northern Rock had their deposits guaranteed under the Chancellor's UK arrangements. He noted that the Guernsey subsidiary was,

> *Legally independent of the UK parent. Depositors are not, one might think, the sort of people the UK Government should stand behind, as there is but one compelling reason to have money invested in such places as*

Guernsey. But given the unwillingness of recent senior arrivals on the Rock board to pay tax, perhaps we shouldn't be too surprised.

I am told this by a good source and ring the Treasury to confirm. "The deposits in the Guernsey branch aren't covered by the guarantee." Strictly accurate, perhaps, but the Guernsey Financial Services Commission, the equivalent of the FSA, confirms to me, "HM Treasury has informed the Commission that the deposit of Northern Rock (Guernsey Ltd) with its UK parent PLC is included within the Chancellor's guarantee arrangements as an existing wholesale deposit. It is because Northern Rock (Guernsey)'s assets are placed in the form of that deposit with its parent that they are protected.

In other words, if I understand it correctly, and the Treasury isn't being too helpful here, the money is invested offshore for tax purposes, shipped back to the UK, and so protected. Extraordinary.

It is difficult to judge whether this article is a serious contribution to the nationalization story, tongue-in-cheek, or just a sarcastic tilt at the Government. What can be deduced, if the article was meant to be serious comment, is that Martin Waller did not appear to understand his subject matter.

It is a misconception that bank deposits in the Channel Islands are made up solely from deposits by UK tax evaders, depositors who are not just tax "avoiders" as stated. There is a difference.

As I managed banks in both Channel Islands over a twenty-five year period, I am very familiar with the banking scene in the Channel Islands. By way of an example, the level of bank customer deposits in Guernsey as at the end of 2007 was the equivalent of £117.893 billion, equivalent because a substantial part of it is in other currencies. Of course some part of the deposits comes from UK tax evaders, but for some time Channel Island banks with UK affiliations have been required to provide the UK tax authorities with particulars of customers with UK addresses. Anyone in the UK with a Channel Islands' bank account will be aware that the Inland Revenue has been following up those disclosures, and in fact, for a short period offered a partial amnesty to those who declared the existence of their accounts voluntarily. It is also a fact that much of the Sterling monies deposited in the Islands comes quite legitimately from UK expatriates and other overseas depositors with no liability to UK taxation on interest earned there.

Furthermore it is not always recognized that places like Jersey and Guernsey legitimately collect overseas deposits and channel them into the London money markets, thus helping to provide inward investment into the UK, something that in 2008 and early 2009 was much diminished, a fact that contributed substantially to the shutting down of the UK inter-bank market.

Lastly, the whole purpose of a subsidiary bank (not a branch as stated) in Guernsey is to gather those expatriate and other deposits for the benefit of the parent Northern Rock in the UK, a standard practice amongst UK, and other countries' banks with offshore offices.

Did Mr. Waller find out if his same reasoning applied to the deposits in Northern Rock, Dublin?

Nevertheless the government guarantee of deposits was controversial. On the 16th March, "The Times" printed an article about a complaint from Denmark's largest banks to the European Commission about the Danish office of Northern Rock, whose deposit with the UK parent would be protected in the same manner as the Guernsey one. This was said to be an unfair competitive advantage.

Northern Rock closed its Danish operations after nationalization.

The article also recorded that British banks were becoming increasingly concerned on the same grounds, with the British Bankers' Association calling for regulated interest rates on Northern Rock's savings products. The Building Societies' Association adopted the same stance.

Although the savings account rates Northern Rock offered were good, other mortgage lenders were offering much the same rates. It would have been unreasonable to cap Northern Rock's offered rates at uncompetitive levels.

One has to wonder whether the objections were all being raised as a matter of course, rather than because of a real fear of unfair competition.

On the 18th March Northern Rock issued a press release entitled, **"NORTHERN ROCK OUTLINES INTENTIONS FOR FUTURE DIRECTION OF THE BUSINESS"**.

It read as follows:

> *Smaller, more focused, financially viable mortgage and savings bank*
> *Staffing levels reduced by around a third by 2011*
> *Asset base reduced by around a half*

> *All forms of public support progressively phased out over the next three to four years*

> *The Board of Northern Rock is today setting out its intentions for the future*

direction of the business during the period of temporary public ownership. These are being worked up into a full business plan, which will be submitted to HM Treasury (HMT) for approval by the end of the month. The Government has today confirmed that it has sent the European Commission the necessary formal notification of its intention to continue to provide the existing restructuring aid to Northern Rock to support this process.

The Board of Northern Rock will be submitting to HMT a plan which will set out the basis for the removal of Government support through the creation of a smaller, more focused, financially viable mortgage and savings bank which will be returned to the private sector.

The proposed plan will be designed to deliver the Government's previously stated objectives to protect UK taxpayers, promote financial stability and protect depositors, and will be based around four strategic priorities:

Contracting to a smaller, sustainable business through a reduction in the asset base of around a half by 2011, whilst maintaining a modest level of new loan origination.

Progressive repayment of the Bank of England loan and release of the Government guarantees over the next three to four years, while increasing the level of retail deposits to form a larger share of total funding.

Restructuring the organisation and its operations so that these are aligned to the business objectives. The initial assessment is that this will involve staffing levels falling by around a third by 2011, though the final figure will depend on the business plan ultimately adopted, and the evolution of the business in the light of market and economic developments.

Strengthening risk management in key business areas.

Ron Sandler, Executive Chairman said,

I am pleased that we are making good progress developing our provisional business plan. This will be a robust plan to create a smaller mortgage and savings bank that will be tightly focused and financially viable.

It will be a demanding plan, and one that will carry a number of financial and operational risks. Market conditions remain uncertain and a protracted downturn in the housing market would clearly present challenges to its achievement. But we are testing it carefully across a range of scenarios and are confident that we can produce a plan that will be delivered.

As regards the organizational restructuring, we will work sensitively with our staff and UNITE to minimize the extent and impact of job losses. We are already closely engaged with local agencies, including One North-East, to ensure that affected staff are offered as much support as possible. I am determined that Northern Rock will remain a major employer in the North East with sufficient financial strength and stability to allow it to return, in due course, to the private sector.

The "Times" carried an article on the report in which it quoted the Chairman as saying,

We recognize that we're supported by government and we don't wish to abuse that support by competing unfairly. We'll ensure that we strike a sensible balance. Things are being said that are not always accurate. Our headline rates are between 6% and 6.25% and that's well within the basic band.

There were other articles on much the same topic over a number of days, but a change of emphasis came on 30th March when "The SundayTimes" headed an article **"Architect of Northern Rock failure may get £760,000 pay off"**

This was recorded as being double what was announced when Adam Applegarth, the Northern Rock Chief Executive, left in December 2007. The information came from the company's annual accounts, due to be published the following day.

The payment represented one year's salary and was to be paid in monthly instalments for as long as he did not accept further employment before the end of 2008. The article also recorded that he received a bonus of £660,000 for 2006, and then it moved to the FSA. It recorded that "senior directors at the FSA could pick up bonuses of more than £250,000." This despite the fact that the previous week the FSA had admitted that it had failed to provide adequate oversight of the troubled bank and would review its procedures, matters which are addressed in Chapter 13. The newspaper reported that,

Documents show that the FSA hit more than 2/3rds of its key targets, a similar proportion to last year (2006) when four senior directors shared "performance related" bonuses of £296,000.

It also suggested that,

Senior FSA officials are likely to come under pressure not to accept their bonuses this year. A spokeswoman for the FSA said any bonuses would

be disclosed later in the year, but would not comment further on the directors' remuneration.

We appear to have inherited an ethos in business generally whereunder company executives are paid a salary for just turning up. When they actually do the job properly as we believed they were paid to do, even if they only carry out two-thirds of their task, they are paid bonuses.

Returning to Applegarth's payoff, the paper quoted Vince Cable of the Liberal Democrats as having said that any compensation package for Applegarth would be "an insult to the millions of Northern Rock customers, shareholders and employees who have suffered due to his incompetence."

An apt comment considering that the following day an article in "The Times" stated that in addition to one year's salary, he received a £346,000 pension "top-up" and retained his cut-price staff mortgage. A later article in another publication added that Northern Rock paid for security guards at Mr Applegarth's home after his departure and also paid £5000 towards his legal expenses so that he could ensure payment of his contractual rights from the Bank.

In other articles, "The Sunday Times" and "The Times" the following day, dealt with the annual accounts of Northern Rock. Some points of general interest included the following:

Bryan Sanderson who was Chairman for four months received a £315,000 fee and £85,000 for office costs incurred in London.

Paul Thompson, a temporary non-executive director of the bank, appointed on 17th January 2008 for one year, but whose appointment was ended by nationalization on 22nd February, was contractually entitled to, and paid his full year remuneration of £100,000. He was said to have led the team working on the company's in-house rescue package. In addition the bank ran up fees and expenses of £28.8 million whilst carrying out its "strategic review" after September 2007.

Allocation of the fees and expenses was not disclosed but advisers working on the strategic review included Merrill Lynch and Citigroup both of which were major architects of the securitization fiasco that contributed to the creation of Northern Rock's woes. Blackstone, a private equity group was also an adviser.

The newspaper reported that,

Although the bank claimed in September that it was on-track to make profits of more than £500 million, soaring charges have pushed it into the red, to the tune of £167.6 million pre-tax losses.

It also recorded that Ron Sandler, the chairman, was keen to write off as much as possible with the first set of results.

Other points included:

Bad-debt charges against the loan book were expected to rise as British homeowners fall further behind with mortgage payments. It was not made clear if that statement was in relation to Northern Rock's expectations, or just a general comment on mortgage markets.

Arrears in the bank's mortgage book climbed almost 20% between January and February. It has to be remembered however, that this was 20% of a very low starting figure of 0.42% of total residential mortgages that rose to only 0.57%. The average figure for mortgage companies recorded by the Council of Mortgage Lenders as at end 2007 was 1.1%. Northern Rock's figures had therefore been maintained at about one-half the industry average. There were other comparisons for the various categories of lending but they related to much smaller values of loans compared with the mainstream residential mortgage lending.

If one examines the basis on which provisions for losses was made in the 2007 annual accounts one finds that although the incidence of arrears "climbed" by 20%, the provisions made at the end of 2007 were effectively increased by 375% more than the 2006 provisions, whereas one could have expected them to be increased by 20%, or possibly a little more to take account of the potentially adverse conditions in the housing markets to which the report referred.

Bear in mind that although house prices and the volume of mortgage lending both dropped in the second and third quarter of 2008, the extent of the falls was not envisaged at that earlier point in time.

The bank had also taken £120 million in write-downs to cover its exposure to sub-prime investments held as Treasury assets and other write-downs representing "impairment of values".

"Impairment" is an expression that has come to the fore fairly recently in company annual accounts. Originally, when it was coined a few years ago, it was intended to apply to the write-down of "goodwill" in balance sheets. It is a separate concept from that of depreciation or amortization that allocate an asset's purchase price over its useful life.

However, sometimes the value of an asset can decline suddenly. In such cases the asset is said to be impaired, and the accounting treatment depends on the type of asset and the accounting standards in use. In the present consideration we are only concerned with the treatment of tangible assets held for use (in the business) and tangible assets held for sale.

Assets held for use require impairment when the undiscounted value of expected future cash flows is less than the carrying value of the asset. Once this is determined, the cash flows are discounted to arrive at the appropriate asset value and the impairment charge represents the difference between the revaluation and the carrying value. The impairment test should be performed whenever events suggest impairment is possible.

Assets Held for Sale are tested for impairment when the decision is made to sell the asset. A requirement to apply these impairment accounting provisions although appropriate is, in the main, what has brought about a loss in the Northern Rock 2007 Income Statement.

The 2007 Annual accounts show net interest, fees, commission and other income plus gain on disposal of a loan book as being £923.9 million. The principal non-recurring deductions from that income figure are shown in Table 17.

The expenses, write-off and impairment charges amounted to £1047.7 million. After the remaining accounting entries and adjustments have been taken into account, the accounts showed a loss of £167.6 million compared with a profit of £443 million for 2006.

It is worthwhile considering the concept of impairment charges in greater detail. Once impaired, under U.S. standards an asset cannot be revalued upward even if the conditions of impairment are reversed. However, under International Accounting

Table 17

	(£millions)
Losses on available for sale securities	136.6
Net losses on change in fair values	21.1
Impairment on mortgage loans	239.7
Impairment on unsecured investment loans	232.2
Non-recurring fees and expenses	127.2
Admin expenses	247.2
Depreciation and amortisation	28.9
Covenant to Foundation	14.8

Standards (IAS), upward revaluations are permitted, and in the case of previously impaired assets the reversal would increase profits in the period the reversal occurs. IAS applied to the Northern Rock accounts.

If we take this a stage further, for any company the assessment of the degree of impairment appropriate in respect of each asset or asset class is determined by the company's Board in consultation with its Finance Director and advisers. The final figure is an assessment only, made in accordance with the views of the company's officers. There is no magically correct formula.

It is important to remember this fact since it was uncertainty over the nature and extent of impairment charges for which financial institutions made provision, particularly in the UK and the USA, that was one of the principal causes of the freezing up of the inter-bank lending markets. There was a lack of transparency that gave rise to a general unwillingness for banks to deal with each other. There was another aspect in that a bank may be uncertain as to the completeness of any impairment charges it has applied and therefore wishes to conserve its resources.

Of course there are accounting guidelines and formulae that can be applied to assist in the determination of the extent of impairment but they are very flexible and their application is on a voluntary basis.

For all those reasons the level of impairment and write-offs or write-downs applied in the Northern Rock case may be questionable, when taken together with the reported factor (rightly or wrongly) that the new Chairman of Northern Rock wished to take all the hits as early as possible, i.e. in the 2007 accounts. It is not suggested that the impairment charges were made in bad faith, but they are only estimates and could have been over-generous.

This is what was said in the notes to the annual accounts,

> The shortfall in 2007 underlying profit relative to (old) management's expectations at the end of last year is primarily due to the increase in expected losses on impaired loans. The deterioration described above reflects a number of factors emerging from the fourth quarter of 2007 including falling house prices and much lower anticipated recoveries on impaired loans.

Another note read,

> However, it is expected there will be a negative impact on loan loss impairment charges in future as the propensity of customers to default

increases and recoveries in defaulted loans reduce further.

The declared impairment charges are therefore predicated on events that have still to happen and may not materialize at the level for which charge-offs have been made. In particular the effect of "recoveries in defaulted loans reduce further" may have been overstated. That situation is related to a fall in the market value of properties but it has to be considered in the context of the average "loan to value" of the Northern Rock portfolio of mortgages.

Bearing in mind that impairment charges represent reductions applied to the value of assets by means of charges against income, they have the immediate effect of reducing the value of the company. If however asset values recover at a future time, they can be revalued in the accounts of that period. In Northern Rock's case it would be somewhat ironic to say the least if the impairment (and other charges) were applied liberally to lower the value of the shareholders' interests in the company now for compensation purposes and a recovery in value of the assets at a later date operated to increase the disposal value of the company for the Government.

Tuesday 1st April 2008
After months of becoming accustomed to commentators talking down Northern Rock and relegating it to "Basket case" status, the "Independent" newspaper published an article by Jeremy Warner that expressed a much more positive view under the headline, **" Now there's a surprise. Inside Northern Rock, there's a perfectly viable business".**

The essence of his piece was that the published accounts of Northern Rock showed that, despite the generous write-downs, etc., Northern Rock remained a company with a substantial book-value that would be largely unaffected by the plan to halve the size of the balance sheet over the next three years.

It was pointed out that although a picture had been drawn of a company in serious difficulty, subject to a high-risk rescue strategy, the reality was quite different. Mr Sandler's rescue plan under nationalization was virtually the same as that proposed by the in-house team.

The article continued with a prescient observation,

> *Assuming the Treasury doesn't cock it up – which is all too possible – the Government will then realize a big fat profit out of the endeavour and Gordon Brown, assuming he is still in power, will be made to look extremely clever. Yet the only cleverness has been in persuading the public that stealing the company from its owners is a perfectly reasonable course of*

action. The Government's defence is that the company would not have been able to carry on trading without its support, and otherwise would have gone into administration.

What is conveniently ignored is the Bank of England's duty as lender of last resort to provide facilities to otherwise solvent banks which have run into financial difficulties. Northern Rock availed itself of these arrangements, and, with the markets for mortgage securitisation remaining closed for much longer than anyone anticipated, has paid a terrible price for so-doing.

Yet as is now evident from the plans unveiled yesterday, it is going to be easily possible to repay all the Bank of England support together with a penalty rate of interest and still have a perfectly viable business at the end of it simply by shrinking the book.

Other newspapers covered points from the accounts, but not as positively as the Independent. They also covered Applegarth's payoff, Vince Cable being quoted,

(It was) a straightforward case of reward for failure.

The following day, 2nd April 2008, the "Times" carried an article about the EU opening an enquiry into the Northern Rock "bail out", " expected to run for several months." The article was a lengthy, factual and helpful one bringing together all aspects, although some of them had been discussed in earlier weeks.

Tuesday 20th May 2008
Today we were presented with two examples of how the Press presents the same piece of news. Under a headline, **"Northern Rock to repay 25% of B of E loan this year"**, "Reuters" published a piece dealing with announcements from the nationalized Northern Rock's new management about the time scale for repayment of the Bank of England loans. The article recorded that,

Northern Rock plans to repay almost £7 billion this year (2008) and should fully repay the loan in the next three years even if there is a recession.

Ann Godbehere, chief financial officer was quoted,

Even under that recession scenario the loan would be repaid with only a short delay. The delay would only be about six months in that scenario.

At least 25% of the loan should be repaid by the end of this year, and 75%

should be paid back by the end of 2009 and the remainder in 2010.

This was a very positive statement about the repayment of the B of E loans. It was within the timescale anticipated by the government and it was a report that accurately presented the thrust of M/s. Godbehere's announcement.

The "Guardian" newspaper ran an article on the same topic the same day, headed, **"Northern Rock could miss target date to repay £24 billion taxpayer loan".**

The article continued,

> *Northern Rock will miss its target for repaying the £24 billion taxpayer loan if the housing market deteriorates further and plunges into a 1992-style recession, the government owned bank warned today. - - - - Sandler said if house prices were to fall 5 to 10 % it would put a great deal of stress in our plan but I can't give you a single figure on which it would fall over.*

Other comments quoted from Mr. Sandler were hardly calculated to reassure his boss, "the taxpayer" (or the rest of us) that his £1 million a year salary (plus additional remuneration yet to be determined) was money well spent.

But perhaps he had been quoted out of context.

The article continued,

> *The bank has stress-tested its model against the 1992 recession – when mortgage rates soared to 15% and house prices fell by a similar amount, and even more in the South-east. Ann Godbehere said that if such conditions returned there could be a delay in repaying the loan and no certainty about when the guarantees extended to the bank could be released. Even under that recession scenario, the loan would be repaid with only a short delay from the original timetable. The delay would be about six months.*

The delay referred to by M/s Godbehere possibly related to a scenario where interest rates reached 15% (a highly unlikely scenario taking Government policies and international economic prospects into account), and a 15% or more fall in house prices which was not generally anticipated at that time.

For the first six months of 2008, Nationwide Building Society, which tracks UK house price movements, recorded a fall of 4.7%. Bear in mind also that the average indexed Northern Rock "loan to value" (LTV) ratio at the year-end remained at 60% as noted in the much depressed 2007 Annual Accounts published on 31st March 2008. According to the operating and financial review included in the accounts, this figure represented current loan balances as a percentage of updated property valuations of the mortgage book. In other words, the mortgaged properties had been revalued at around current market values.

The accounts also recorded that the average LTV ratio of new lending in 2007 increased by 1% to 79%, whilst new lending at or below 90% LTV reduced by 1% to 77%.

A fair number of Northern Rock's borrowers could be affected by even modest increases in interest rates, say above 2%, but with these LTV values it would take much more than a 4.7% fall in house prices to put borrowers into negative equity, and just as importantly, for the bank to suffer losses on forced re-possessions. Conditions did deteriorate by the end of the third quarter of 2008, the house price fall being noted by Nationwide Building Society to have been16% for the year to that time. Later in November 2008 the Chancellor declared the drop to have been no more than 11%. The longer term significance of those statistics is debatable when one notes that an increase of 1.4% in house prices was recorded for January 2009.

It is to be doubted that M/s Godbehere intended the Press to concentrate on the downside aspects of her statement to such an extent. This episode reminds me of an incident many years ago when I was one of the managers setting up a new bank in Bermuda.

The bank's shares had been floated on the Bermuda Stock Exchange and purchased by local people. Shortly afterwards I was interviewed by a reporter from the local newspaper. In the course of a half-hour interview, and many questions, he asked, "When did I think the new bank would show a profit for its shareholders." I responded that in the case of a new operation, it might take three years or more to reach profitability. Next day I opened the newspaper and was confronted by a banner headline across the whole page, " **No profit for three years, says Manager.**"

I still have that newspaper. I kept it as an object lesson on dealing with the Press.

Another factor that has a bearing on the likelihood of the bank meeting its repayment schedule is that according to the 2007 Accounts mortgage loans at the end of the year amounted to £98.445 billion, of which 92.2% of loans were residential secured loans and 7.5% personal unsecured loans.

The Accounts also showed that gross lending during 2007 amounted to £32.251 billion, the net lending figure being £12.211 billion. This means that during the year £20.040 billion of loans were redeemed one way or another. This was not an exceptional scenario for the bank. In 2006 the figures were £32.989 billion and £16.621 billion net, producing

£16.368 billion of redemptions. If 43% of total residential loans of £90.778 billion are due to be redeemed or reset within two years, that is equal to £39.034 billion becoming available for repayment of the B of E loans of £26.9 billion, assuming all the mortgage loans are redeemed in full by being refinanced elsewhere which as has been noted above is not too over-optimistic an expectation.

M/s. Godbehere's projections seemed perfectly feasible. Even in a realistic worst-case scenario that would be highly unlikely to be as bad as in1992.

In fact only a few months later, by end September 2008 it was announced that Northern Rock had repaid £15.4 billion of the outstanding £26.9 billion of B of E loans as at the beginning of 2008. The balance outstanding was £11.5 billion. Additionally at that time, retail funding balances had recovered to £17.2 billion and new wholesale funding amounted to £927 million.

The third quarter results statement also disclosed that the quality of new lending had been high at an average 60% LTV ratio.

Those results could hardly have been achieved by a "basket case".

There was very little news coming out of Northern Rock apart from the facts that firstly, Northern Rock was being cautious about the rates of interest it was paying on retail deposit accounts. Secondly, that it had tightened its lending requirements to reduce the amount of new mortgage business it was writing and that it was encouraging customers whose mortgages were due to be reset to transfer to another lender (partly by increasing its variable lending rates).

One extra piece of information, however, was that the bank had made an agreement with Lloyds TSB bank that it would pay a commission to Lloyds TSB for re-financing Northern Rock borrowers seeking an alternative mortgage loan.

Compensation

On 15th February when Northern Rock was nationalized, the announcement included a reference to the compensation of shareholders, since a nationalization without provision for compensation would amount to expropriation, something with which no reputable democratic government could afford to be associated nowadays. The following day details of the proposed legislation to enable the nationalization of Northern Rock were released.

They included the following:

*The legislation will enable the Government to acquire the bank's shares
and its assets. It will provide for compensation to be determined by an
independent valuer.*

There was no other reference to the compensation of shareholders, although it was clear
from earlier announcements that the Treasury was of the opinion that a valuation of the
bank's shares had to be considered on the basis that without the Bof E / Treasury loans,
the bank was not a "going concern" and would have had to be placed in administration.
A valuation would have to be calculated based on those two assumptions.

Over the following week there were numerous press comments on the compensation
issue. On 17th February the "Times" wrote of **"A bruising battle ahead over value of
shares",** making the point that it was a battle that could drag on after the next General
Election and was likely to produce a very low valuation. The article also recorded that
SRM Global and RAB Capital believed,

*There was significant value in Northern Rock and that they would pursue
all avenues to protect that value for shareholders.*

Robin Ashby of the Small Shareholders' Group was quoted as saying,

he was shocked and appalled at the Government's decision. He added,
*This will be hanging round the government for years to come, right up to
the next general election.*

The article also noted that the prospect of nationalization had sent bankers, lawyers and
civil servants scurrying to the history books to study precedents, pointing to the
nationalization of the aircraft, ship-building industries and Railtrack. Shareholders were
also considering taking the case to the European Court of Human Rights.

It ended by stating that the UK Shareholders Association and the Northern Rock Small
Shareholders Group were of the opinion that a valuation around £4 per share would be
appropriate. That figure came from a public quotation from Jon Wood of SRM that was
reported in the press. His figure was based on the net asset value of the company (ie.
assets per share) at the time.

The UK Shareholders Association had made no claims as to a valuation.

The Comment column in the "Financial Times" of 19th February carried the heading,
"Treasury cannot be allowed to rob bank investors."

The article was written by Professor Tim Congdon, a holder of a small number of shares in Northern Rock. Another article by him was quoted in Chapter 9.

The article has been quoted in full because it was one of the few that presented a reasoned argument about the nationalization and compensation issues at the time. It may not have been his complete argument but it was essentially very soundly based.

> For all its travails, Northern Rock in public ownership will have to publish audited accounts. Alistair Darling, Chancellor of the Exchequer, has said the mortgage lender will return to the private sector in due course. Suppose that, when the last set of accounts before its re-privatisation appears, these show that the loan from the State, (originally from the Bank of England but now presumably to be assumed by the Treasury) is repaid in full at a market interest rate or above.

> Suppose in other words, that Northern Rock repays the loan on the same terms as billions of transactions on the Sterling inter-bank market. The economic substance of the loan to Northern Rock would be difficult to distinguish from such loans, except that – at least in the early stages when it took the form of a lender-of-last-resort loan from the Bank of England – it was at a penalty rate (i.e. above market rates).

> Should the proceeds from the re-privatisation of Northern Rock belong to the government or the original shareholders? That is the key question.

> Mr Darling has made clear he does not intend to compensate shareholders at anywhere near the book value of the bank's capital, which was about £2 billion (or £4 per share) in mid-2007 and must still be above £1.5 billion. The plan –if the government's behaviour can be dignified with the word - seems to be the shareholders are to get nothing.

> The proceeds from the re-privatization (presumably a few years from now) may be deemed to belong to the government. If so, would the government have robbed the shareholders of £1.5 – 2 billion? Mr Darling has no doubt been told by his advisers that the government's approach is legally valid. But the shareholders can also recruit advisers to demonstrate that it is legally invalid and morally outrageous.

> Their central point will be that, in a nation proud of its respect for the rule of law, the government would have violated the principles of private property.

> Mr Darling and his advisers would no doubt say this is preposterous. They must think again. They ought, for example, to listen to the senior

executives in the British banking industry who nine months ago took it for granted that the Bank of England was their bank, from which they could obtain cash in much the same way as commercial banks in other countries. Those executives have been dismayed that in recent weeks Spanish banks have been able to obtain finance easily from the European Central bank (but actually from the Bank of Spain) on collateral that the bank of England has questioned.

These Spanish banks have in many respects the same business model as Northern Rock; in autumn 2007 they faced the same difficulty in financing their assets. But they have not been punished by the Spanish authorities as Northern Rock has been punished by the UK authorities and the government. The Spanish government has not threatened to nationalise them, in spite of the huge advances they have received from the ECB.

The one correct point in the argument for nationalizing Northern Rock was that the value of its assets, and hence its continued solvency, depended on the Bank of England loan. If Northern Rock had been forced last September to dispose of its assets as quickly as its depositors were withdrawing cash, those assets would have been sold at far less than their true value in normal circumstances and Northern Rock would have gone bust.

But Central banks exist for the purpose of preventing runs, or at any rate, ensuring that runs are met by lender-of-last-resort loans so the hurried liquidation of assets can be avoided. That is what is meant by the proposition, repeated in hundreds of text-books, that "the central bank is the lender of last resort to the banking system".

Western governments have deplored the Russian state's expropriation of privately owned oil companies. What the British government has done with Northern Rock – by falsely representing a business transaction at market rates or above as "state aid", encouraging a frenzy of hostile and largely silly press comment, cajoling the management and shareholders, and finally imposing a compulsory nationalization without compensation – bears comparison with President Vladimir Putin's devices to steal assets in the former Soviet Union.

If Northern Rock does repay its loan from the state in full but its shareholders receive nothing, the British government's actions would amount to robbery under the law.

Some of Professor Congdon's points will be followed up later in this chapter. His comments were made in the light of knowledge of the financial crisis at the time.

If we move forward six months or so we shall find that HM Treasury had to one way or another "bail out" all but two or three British Banks, including some of the largest in the land, to the extent of £600 billion or more That made a mockery of the panicked reaction to Northern Rock's liquidity problems which in the context of the later bail-out commitments by the government pale into insignificance. Although the "nationalization" word was bandied about there was no attempt to deprive shareholders of their interests in those banks, except for the treatment of Bradford and Bingley (which happened to be the next rescue attempt after Northern Rock) other than to place restrictions on the payment of dividends.

Those developments will be studied in Chapter 16.

Wednesday 20th February 2008
Other reports on the compensation issue included one from "Reuters" relayed on Yahoo Finance. It was headed, **"N Rock investors slam compensation plan",**

> A group of small shareholders has attacked as "grossly unethical" the terms set by the Treasury to determine the compensation they will receive after the embattled bank is nationalized.

> The Treasury, which announced plans to bring the lender into public ownership this week, confirmed that it should not be required to compensate investors for value which is dependent on tax-payers' support.

The article covered other aspects of the nationalization, then related that,

> Big and small investors in the bank have reacted angrily to a nationalization of Northern Rock which looks set to leave them little or nothing, and a legal battle seems inevitable, though few expect the funds and retail shareholders to win out.

The article continued with a discussion of the situation before closing with,

> The Treasury also said that it could not prevent bilateral off-market or over-the-counter trades in Northern Rock shares, but warned any compensation would only be paid to the person who held the shares just before nationalization, meaning buyers now may not be entitled to claim damages.

There are frequent references in Press articles to "the small shareholders", of whom there were said to be about 140,000. Those references are really intended to be to the "private shareholders", as opposed to the institutional shareholders of various descriptions. However it should be recognized that those private shareholders were not always "small" shareholders holding 500 or so shares from the original flotation of the company, many private shareholders had holdings of thousands of shares, holdings which in relation to their total invested worth would be quite substantial and therefore important to them and bought at a time when Northern Rock was generally recognized in the investment world as highly successful and was promoted as "a good buy".

There were many newspaper articles at this time that reported the Government's views on compensation, or rather lack of it, and which described the ire of shareholders, generally without expressing any sympathy for their plight.

Throughout the Northern Rock saga there were two sources of information that were less polarized than all the others. The first was the report of the Commons Select Committee on Banking and Finance. Its findings related to the official handling of the crisis and did not deal with nationalization aspects. The other source was the UK Shareholders Association, a body that described itself as "The independent voice of the private shareholder". It obviously championed the shareholders' viewpoint but always presented it in a reasoned manner. It was also prominent in promoting legal action on behalf of Northern Rock shareholders' rights.

Here is a synopsis of the more significant points in its Update Number 26 issued on 3rd March 2008.

> *Although the government is setting up an independent valuation of the shares which have been confiscated from you, they have set the terms of reference so that you will not get a fair and unbiased figure. Because of the terms of reference, the answer will almost certainly be very little or nothing, when Northern Rock was in essence a valuable business that will soon recover from its difficulties.*

> *We consider the whole sequence of events to be prejudicial because the government is benefiting from its own actions and inactions. It should not be permitted to purchase Northern Rock cheaply when it has played a major role in the erosion of the value of this business.*

> *Just such evidence of Government incompetence that affected Northern Rock (and damaged the interests of shareholders) was the comment last week from - - - - the FSA, "The standard of supervision of Northern Rock was not acceptable to us and certainly not to myself."" (This was from the*

Chief Executive, Hector Sants who, it should be noted only assumed his position on 19th July 2007 although he had been a divisional director and connected with the FSA for several years before that.)

One concern is that it is in the government's interest to have the worse possible set of figures in the 2007 accounts as it might affect the valuation."
(This aspect of the published accounts was dealt with earlier in this chapter.)

One or two publications have printed editorial comments recently that have criticized shareholders for complaining about the terms of nationalization and the basis of compensation. Here is one response that UKSA has sent out to put a stop to such ill-informed views,

To suggest we are "whingeing" when the government has outrageously set the terms for the evaluation of compensation to shareholders that bear no relation to reality is grossly unfair. All we are asking for is a fair and independent valuation of the company to be paid to shareholders as a result of the confiscation of their property (which of course is enshrined in the European Convention on Human Rights.)

In addition to suggest that the company was "bust" when it could no longer fund itself from the money markets is nonsense. Firstly, the Bank of England has a duty under the Banking Act to act as a lender of last resort and it was obvious to everyone that the government would not let Northern Rock go bust by refusing such support – there were a lot of practical reasons why they should provide such support. In any case, when they first asked for such support they probably didn't in reality need it, but the subsequent leak (the media have a lot to blame in this regard) and the mis-handling of the crisis by the Bank of England precipitated the run on the bank which was the root of the problem. In essence the Government (in the form of the Tri-partite Authorities) was as much to blame for the ultimate debacle at Northern Rock as were the company directors for any mis-guided business strategy.

The Update then commented on the offers for the company and then to more general matters concerning the Association, but two other points were mentioned in relation to compensation, in particular to a member's question as to how much compensation would be offered.

We don't know because this will be based on the "independent" valuation (but) the terms of reference for the valuation make the whole exercise a nonsense.

In answer to a question about the possible award from a truly independent valuer it was suggested,

> *It would be for the Government to argue that their funding was prejudicial to that valuation* (of £4 per share plus) *but as it was given at market rates of interest I think that would be a difficult justification.*

We had to wait until 12th March 2008 until **"The Northern Rock PLC compensation scheme order 2008"** was published before details were available about the government's intentions.

The Order ran to nine pages, from which the following are the main points of immediate interest.

(1)   The amount of any compensation payable by the Treasury to persons who held shares in Northern Rock immediately before they were transferred by the Transfer Order shall be determined in accordance with this paragraph.

(2)   The amount of compensation payable to a person shall be an amount equal to the value immediately before the transfer time of all shares in Northern Rock held immediately before the transfer time by that person.

In determining the amount of any compensation payable by the Treasury to any person in accordance with paragraphs 3 to 5, it must be assumed (in addition to the assumptions required to be made by section 5(4) of the Act (compensation etc. for securities transferred etc.) that NorthernRock :-

(a) is unable to continue as a going concern; and
(b) is in administration.

(1) The Treasury shall appoint an independent valuer for the purposes of this scheme.
(2) The valuer so appointed shall determine the amount of any compensation payable by the Treasury in accordance with Part 2 of this Scheme.
(3) The valuer is to hold and vacate office in accordance with the terms of his appointment.
(4) The Treasury may remove the valuer only on the ground of incapacity or serious misbehaviour.
(5) Before making any appointment under sub-paragraph (1) the Treasury must consult the Institute of Chartered Accountants in England and Wales.

(1) The valuer may make such rules as to the procedure in relation to the

assessment of any compensation (including the procedure for the reconsideration of any decisions relating to the assessment of compensation) as he or she considers appropriate.

(2) Where the valuer has assessed the amount of any compensation payable by the Treasury—

(a) to any porcon; or

(b) in respect of a class or description of shares or rights,

he or she shall issue an assessment notice.

(2) An assessment notice shall contain the following information—

(a the date on which the notice is issued;

(b) the amount of any compensation determined by the valuer as being payable; and

(c) the reasons for the valuer's decision.

(3) The valuer shall send a copy of the assessment notice to the Treasury.

Reconsideration of assessment notice

(1) If —

(a) the Treasury; or

(b) any person who is affected by the determination of the amount of any compensation which is contained in an assessment notice, are dissatisfied with the assessment notice, the Treasury or any such person may require the valuer to reconsider his or her determination.

(2) Where the valuer is required to reconsider his or her determination in accordance with subparagraph he or she shall issue a revised assessment notice.

(3) A revised assessment notice shall contain the following information—

(a) the date on which the notice is issued;

(b) either—

　(i) notification that the valuer has upheld the assessment notice; or

　(ii) notification that the valuer has varied the assessment notice;

(c) the amount of any compensation determined by the valuer as being payable; and

(d) the reasons for the valuer's decision.

(4) The valuer shall send a copy of the revised assessment notice to the Treasury.

Right to refer to the Tribunal

13. If—

(a) the Treasury; or

(b) any person who is affected by the determination of the amount of any compensation which is contained in the revised assessment notice, are dissatisfied with the revised assessment notice, the Treasury or any such person may refer the matter to the Tribunal.

Payment of compensation

The Treasury shall pay the amount of any compensation determined by the valuer to be payable—

(a) to any person; or

(b) in respect of a class or description of shares or rights.

(2) The Treasury shall not be required to make a payment in accordance with sub-paragraph (1) until—

(a) they have received a copy of the assessment notice or revised assessment notice, as the case may be; or

(b) if there is a reference to the Tribunal, the matter has been finally disposed of.

There followed a detailed description of the legal and procedural principles that were to govern proceedings under the order.

The "tribunal" referred to in the Order is **"The Financial Services and Markets Tribunal"** which has its own rules of procedure, some of which were modified by the Compensation Order.

To suggest that the Order was controversial would be a gross understatement, despite the fact that it provides for determination by an independent valuer, but one approved by and appointed by the Treasury. How can the valuer reach an independent valuation if the basis on which he is required to reach a determination is prescribed by the Treasury and furthermore he is required to determine a valuation on grounds which are considered to be at variance with established accounting rules, company law and insolvency practice.

As late as mid-August 2008, nearly five months after the Order was published, there was no confirmation of the appointment of a valuer by the Treasury and the job was still being advertised.

Why had there been a delay?

Firstly, the answer appears to be that there were no takers for the job. Part of the answer may have lain in the fact that one of the clauses in the Order reads, "the Treasury must consult the Institute of Chartered Accountants in England and Wales" before making an appointment. In view of the fact that the terms of reference could be considered to be in conflict with the standards that Chartered Accountants are expected to apply and were at variance with prior-existing Company Law on the subject, it may have been very difficult to recruit one of its Members for the job. If a professionally unqualified person was to be appointed, the proceedings would have lost all credibility.

An alternative reason may have been that the Treasury did not wish to advance matters whilst the Compensation Order and Nationalization was under challenge from various shareholder groups that were calling for a Judicial Review.

However, the matter was resolved when it was announced on 8th September 2008 that Andrew Caldwell, Valuations Partner at BDO Stoy Hayward had been appointed following a recommendation from an independent panel. An expert team from BDO Stoy Hayward and from outside professional firms would support him.

Tuesday 18th March 2008
UKSA issued another Update for its members following publication of the Compensation Order. It commented on the parliamentary debate and the views of some individual politicians. The following is a synopsis of excerpts from it.

In general terms the view of most politicians in the debates (from all political parties) seemed to be that the Government was right to restrict the compensation payable to shareholders, primarily on the principle that taxpayers should not be paying more, and that most shareholders were short term speculators anyway, not true, but an allegation that has been repeatedly made in the Press.

Even the Conservatives seemed to concentrate on raising technical points rather than attacking the Government's actions directly, presumably in fear that they would be seen to be supporting a bail out of those hedge funds that had holdings in Northern Rock. (Note: prior to nationalization George Osborne the Conservative shadow chancellor was adamant that his party would not support the nationalization of Northern Rock. It may not have supported it but neither did it oppose.)

A UKSA comment on SRM and RAB (the hedge funds concerned) was that,

We believe both acted ethically and reasonably during their involvement with Northern Rock. They offered support to the company and were prepared to subscribe for and underwrite a major rights issue. - - - - There are no grounds for criticizing their actions.

The Compensation Order was passed without opposition so it was then clear that shareholders would have to resort to legal action to establish their proper rights and if they were to gain fair compensation for the confiscation of their property.

The Update reported on questions from individual Members of parliament, including:-

Peter Atkinson MP raised the question of why the valuer is being told to assume the company is unable to continue as a going concern and is in administration when clearly it is a going concern and not in administration. Government Minister Angela Eagle replied that these are fair assumptions because,

> It is clear that Northern Rock would have been unable to secure the substantial amount of alternative funding that would have been required if the financial assistance provided by the Government and the Bank of England had been withdrawn.

The UKSA response was that,

Of course the Government did not withdraw its financial assistance and once they had made the decision to support the company it is unreasonable for them to later attempt to value it on some other basis. Valuations should be done on the real circumstances and taking all the known factors into account, not done on some artificially created criteria.

Mark Hoban, MP raised an interesting issue. He pointed out that "Administration" as defined in the relevant Act of Parliament can be used to "rescue the company as a going concern" as an alternative to simply protecting creditors. Therefore the valuer appointed by the Government may have to consider not simply the "liquidation" value of the business which is what everybody assumed from the terms of reference, i.e. that it would not necessarily be a "fire sale" valuation. They might instead have to consider the value of the business based on its likely recovery.

The eventual answer from Angela Eagle was,

> It is for the valuer to value Northern Rock shares with the assumptions I have set out – not that it is particularly going to be wound up, but she later said, the valuer would still have to value the business as if it was a "gone concern",

implying that it had no value, of course.

How the valuer is going to reconcile these comments with valuing it "not as a going concern" as in the Order is anyone's guess. It is certainly outside the normal principles of commercial company valuation so it is going to be enormously difficult for him to make sense of this conundrum.

Mr. Hoban raised the issue of the Granite vehicle and whether the assets/liabilities of that "associated" business would be included when valuing Northern Rock. Granite was not nationalized but was consolidated into the last set of Northern Rock accounts.

Mr. Hoban also raised the problem that some countries had treaties with the UK that cover the expropriation of assets of foreign investors. (This would be particularly relevant to the situation of the Granite structure as most of the bond investors were foreign, and powerful foreigners at that). Mr Hoban pointed out that not only do those treaties cover fair compensation but any dispute on the compensation goes to an international arbitration tribunal and would therefore fall outside the terms of the compensation order.

SRM Global, with 48,452,655 shares in Northern Rock (11.5% of its issued shares), is a foreign shareholder, based in Monaco but unfortunately without the benefit of a Tax Treaty with the UK.

It was noted that Mr. Hoban's points were not answered.

In the House of Lords, Lord Newby said that based on the assumptions proposed, the value of the shares must be zero. Why therefore did the valuer need a staff, how long would it take and how much would the valuation process cost? A Government Minister replied that the "valuer had a challenging role to play" and that it is not going to be done in a matter of weeks.

According to a Government budget announced at this time, it expected the debts owed by Northern Rock to shrink to £14 billion over the coming year. This supported what the UKSA has been saying all along that Northern Rock could recover relatively rapidly and repay the Government loans, which is what it should have been allowed to do under its own steam.

The more one reads of this story the more it resembles a Gilbert and Sullivan operetta, at times it is beyond belief that a responsible Government in a democracy could have created such a situation.

It is said that one can prove anything with figures but it also seems to be equally true that one can prove anything with words. Yet another example of "I say, therefore it shall be so".

The following day, UKSA issued a Press Note explaining the basis of the Association's case and commenting on the government's valuation rules. In particular it suggested that,

As the selection of the valuers is solely at the discretion of the Treasury there is no guarantee that they will be unbiased and impartial.

It also commented on,

The general principle that anyone who damages the value of a business should not benefit as a result in any subsequent valuation of the business. But here the Government and its agencies caused many of the problems that Northern Rock faced.

UKSA believed that a legal challenge was justifiable, that the proposed valuation approach was unlawful, immoral and unethical. The Association had taken legal advice on these issues and believed there were good grounds to pursue legal action. The UKSA believed also that shareholders have a *prima facie* case that their human rights have been violated under the Human Rights Act 1998 and the European Convention on Human Rights. In particular, it said, the Act and Convention protect rights in property from the type of action that had been taken by the Government.

UKSA did not presume to prejudge a valuation, all it was seeking was that the valuation be carried out on a normal commercial basis with shareholders and the Government being able to make submissions about the factors that may affect the conclusion. The Association did not believe that it was natural justice that a buyer of any business, in this case the Government, should dictate the terms of reference for the determination of the purchase price.

Thursday 20th March 2008
The "Times" had a lengthy article reporting how various shareholder groups were planning court challenges to the government's valuation criteria.

Northern Rock's army of small shareholders took their campaign for compensation to the courts yesterday as they accused the Government of abusing their human rights by nationalizing the stricken mortgage lender.

At the same time, SRM Global, the Monaco based hedge fund that is the biggest institutional owner of the Rock, served notice to the Treasury that it was launching a legal action of its own. SRM also plans to question the legality of the nationalization with the European Commission.

UKSA was reported as representing 7000 Rock shareholders and was raising a fighting fund for a lawsuit. RAB Capital had still to decide on a course of action but the Legal & General Investment Management Activist Fund with a substantial holding in the bank also said it was exploring its options. It later announced that it would not take part in a legal challenge, but would be watching developments carefully as a sideline "interested party".

Sunday 23rd March 2008

"Scotland on Sunday" reported a meeting called at the legal chambers of Edwin Coe, the lawyer representing the UKSA members in a legal challenge of the Government's position. It noted that a letter had been lodged with the Treasury giving ministers 21 days to respond, after which it would seek a judicial review of the compensation process.

The article covered other aspects as had already been released by UKSA and noted above.

Fast forward to April 24th, 2008 when the "Times" updated us on the progress of the judicial review proposals now that the Treasury had rejected a claim for compensation. It was said that it had also rejected similar claims from RAB and SRM. UKSA was reported as having said that it would submit an application to the Administrative Court, part of the High Court by 22nd May for a judicial review. A judicial review is a process that allows members of the public to challenge the legality of government legislation.

The article then listed all the legal firms involved as at that date.

Lord Grabiner QC, a Labour Law Lord for the Treasury, in addition to Slaughter & May a prominent City law firm led by partner Charles Randell

Nabarro, equally prominent City law firm for RAB CAPITAL

White and Case, described as an Anglo-American legal giant for SRM Global, with David Pannick, a leading human rights advocate

UKSA is being advised by David Greene of Edwin Coe

Also noted was the fact that the Treasury would soon tender for independent arbitrators to value the Rock's shares. That appears to have been inaccurate as the Compensation Order called for the appointment of a valuer with the Financial Services and Markets Tribunal to arbitrate any appeals against a valuation determined by the valuer.

On 5th of June the Treasury issued the Terms of Appointment that would be applied to applications for appointment as the valuer acting in accordance with the Compensation Order. Details of the Terms of Appointment ran to 16 pages.

Extracts of interest include:

Compensation to be determined

The valuer is required to determine the amount of any compensation payable by the Treasury to:–

Those who held ordinary, foundation or preference shares in Northern Rock immediately before they were transferred by the Transfer Order;

Those whose rights to receive shares in Northern Rock (whether by subscription, conversion or otherwise) were extinguished by article 4 of the Transfer Order; and

Those whose consequential rights were extinguished by article 12 of the Transfer Order.

Statutory valuation assumptions

Section 5(4) of the Act sets out certain assumptions to be made in determining the amount of any compensation payable by the Treasury. The assumptions are that all financial assistance provided by the Bank of England or the Treasury to the deposit-taker in question has been withdrawn (whether by the making of a demand for repayment or otherwise) and that no financial assistance would in future be provided by the Bank of England or the Treasury to the deposit-taker in question, apart from the Bank of England's ordinary market assistance subject to its usual terms.

The Compensation Scheme Order, as permitted by section 9 of the Act, sets out two further valuation assumptions to be made about Northern Rock. The two additional assumptions to be made in determining the amount of any compensation payable by the Treasury to any relevant person are:

that Northern Rock is unable to continue as a going concern; and

that it is in administration.

Criteria for appointment

The following criteria are required to be satisfied in order for an applicant to be considered for appointment as valuer:

a) **Demonstrable independence** from Government and interested parties.
b) **Freedom from conflicts of interest**: given the number of organisations that have been involved in advising parties in relation to Northern Rock to

date, some potential candidates may be ruled out because of actual or potential conflicts of interest.

In considering which person to appoint, the following additional criteria will be relevant:

a) **Professional skills and experience**: the primary qualification for the valuer is extensive professional financial company valuation skills. The valuer is likely to need to draw on a range of professional expertise, notably accountancy, investment banking and legal.

We would expect the valuer to have high standing and credibility in their profession.

b) Experience and ability to carry out a high profile public process:

in addition to being able to carry out the professional task of assessing any compensation, the valuer will need to have the capacity, resources, personal bearing and robustness to -

i) manage a high-profile, potentially multi-stage, public process involving some 200,000 former shareholders (individual and institutional, domestic and international) and other affected parties in a timely and efficient manner; and
ii) explain his or her assessment to a range of different audiences (from individuals to potentially the Tribunal) in writing, in person and through professional intermediaries such as lawyers if necessary.

c) **Track record of timely delivery**: applicants will need to demonstrate by reference to an existing track record that they will be adequately resourced and capable of discharging the function of independent valuer in a timely and efficient manner in the absence of conventional contract performance management by a client.

d) Overall **value for money** is also an important criterion against which applications will be judged.

Staff and resources
Applicants must provide details of any resources, which may include investment banking, legal and administrative resources, available to them to enable them to assist in the exercise of their function as valuer, if appointed.

The administrative resources required for communications with shareholders are discussed separately below.

If the valuer is a member of a firm, please identify whether those resources will come from within the same firm and also areas where it may be necessary to seek external advice.

For the avoidance of doubt, for these purposes staff means staff appointed as employees of the valuer, whether on a temporary or permanent basis. If the valuer is a member of a firm, it will not include the use of staff or other resources within that firm. Any charges incurred for the use of such resources will be considered to form part of the valuer's expenses.

The selection process will have two stages: short-listing and presentation.

The valuer will be appointed on the basis of the information contained in his or her application and the presentation that short-listed candidates will be asked to make.

A panel, which will be chaired by the Chief Executive of the Institute of Chartered Accountants of England and Wales, will produce a shortlist from the applications. Shortlisted applicants will be invited to present their case to the panel, including how they meet the criteria in Section C, in person, with their proposed most senior assistants.

The panel will make recommendations to Treasury Ministers who will make the final decision as to the appointment.

Duties
You are required to discharge the functions of independent valuer in accordance with the terms of the Compensation Scheme and the provisions of Part 9 of the Financial Services and Markets Act 2000 and the Financial Services and Markets Tribunal Rules 2001 (both as modified by the Compensation Scheme). You will be expected to act impartially independently and fairly in the discharge of your functions as independent valuer at all times.

An interesting condition of the valuation process is the one that provides for determination of value on the basis that Northern Rock will not receive future official assistance apart from the Bank of England's ordinary market assistance subject to its usual terms. That was the nature of the assistance that Northern Rock received initially and it is doubtful if it has ever been satisfactorily explained how that was transmuted into "tax-payer loans", necessitating the introduction of the Compensation Order. In August Northern Rock noted in its third quarter 2008 report that the B of E loans had been "novated" to the Treasury during August.

Applications were to have been made by 4th July 2008.

Although applications related to the appointment of a "valuer", it was apparent that he would require considerable backup in the execution of his duties. That seemed to point towards the appointment of a professional firm. It will be interesting to see how a professional firm reconciles its professional ethical standards and the requirement that it must be independent and have no conflicts of interest, either in relation to Northern Rock or any persons with an interest in it, or association with it, professionally or otherwise, or with HM Treasury and one would assume any other department of the government. That was a very demanding brief.

As noted above, the answer to some of those questions was provided on the 8th September 2008 when Andrew Caldwell of BDO Stoy Hayward was appointed by HM Treasury.

Throughout the next few weeks a steady flow of articles was published without adding new dimensions to the compensation topic other than that many of the articles adopted an anti-shareholder stance. Repeatedly one could have read that shareholders were just gamblers who deserved nothing from the "public purse". Alternatively they were "savvy" people who knew that when they invested they could make big profits, but equally that they could lose all. So why should an investment in Northern Rock be treated any differently?

There were releases of information intended to break that pattern, but they were selectively reported. On 8th May, SRM Global issued information on the basis of the applications for a judicial review that UKSA, SRM and RAB had each submitted. The essential points included:

- The High Court to investigate the conduct of the Government, the Bank of England, HM Treasury and the Financial Services Authority in the provision of lender of last resort support to Northern Rock as well as in the process which led to the decision to nationalize and then to impose the compensation scheme.

- that it is unprecedented for a solvent bank to be nationalized after receiving lender of last resort support.

- that the constraints imposed by the Government's compensation scheme will lead to a valuation which is far removed from Northern Rock's true value.

- Prior to the hearing, the shareholders will be asking the court to release vital documents which will shed some light on the Government's reasoning for pursuing nationalization and also publicly expose why it was imposed without fair compensation.

- Northern Rock's nationalization is *"temporary"* with the aim of making a profit for the Government.

- A contention that the Tripartite Authorities (HM Treasury, The Bank of England and the FSA) failed in their duties to protect the property of shareholders.

- The Government failed to arrest a run of depositors' funds following the leak to the media and refused to investigate the source of the leak.

- The Government introduced the concept of "value for money for the taxpayer" as the overriding principle that would justify nationalization of a solvent and profitable bank.

- It is not the role of a central bank providing LOLR facilities to make a profit for the taxpayer; this has turned the Government into financial speculators

- The Government established a compensation scheme which will not compensate shareholders for the expropriation of an asset with a book value in excess of £1.75 billion

- The Government exploited the position of the Bank of England as Lender of Last Resort for its own commercial advantage

- The Government exploited the position of the Bank of England, as Lender of Last Resort, to assume for itself the entirety of the collateral provided for the facilities.

- HM Treasury has not sought to explain why a legitimate requirement for the protection of taxpayers' interests developed into requiring sufficient value for money for the taxpayer.

- Contrary to its position last year and its public statements last month the Bank of England made available sufficient liquidity to UK financial institutions.

The foregoing is not the entire case submitted to the High Court but is illustrative of the range of factors that the shareholders' legal advisers were taking into account. There were two lengthy submissions on behalf of the shareholders that provided extensive coverage of the factors involved in the case. One by Professor Congdon and another by Philip Price, Chief Operating Officer of SRM Global Advisers. They deal with different aspects of the shareholders' case in detail and present a very credible case when taken together with all the other evidence presented.

There was an interesting government action that may well have been taken with the purpose of weakening the shareholders' case. In August 2008 HM Treasury announced that it was committed to reinforcing the bank's capital base through conversion into Ordinary shares of its holding of £400 million of Preference Shares and swapping up to £3 billion of the outstanding debt (to the Treasury) into equity. State Aid approvals were obtained from the EC.

Was the real purpose behind this move actually to make a change in the government's position *vis-à-vis* Northern Rock from lender to shareholder, thus strengthening the legal basis for its objective which was to "obtain sufficient value for the taxpayer"?

At the beginning of June 2008 there were reports that the Government had increased its team of legal advisers to Lord Grabiner QC, Philip Sales QC, a regular legal adviser to the Treasury and Clive Lewis QC a public law expert. They would be supported by a team of junior barristers and Slaughter & May. The team had been increased as the Treasury wished to achieve an early hearing of the shareholders' case. There were also reviews of the enhanced legal teams engaged by the various shareholder groups. It was anticipated that a hearing would be held in December 2008. In fact it took place from 13th to 16th January 2009.

Also reported on the 7th June was the fact that the shareholders legal team had used the Freedom of Information Act to serve demands on Northern Rock and the Government to disclose evidence relating to the decision to nationalize Northern Rock. However no evidence had been produced to them although the Treasury's solicitors had agreed to respond by the end of July to other requests for evidence made under the normal court pre-action disclosure rules.

On 19th June a website, "thelawyer.com" posted a lengthy and informative review of the appointment of legal counsel by the various parties in connection with the application for a judicial review together with comment on the grounds for the review. The review included coverage of the responses of the Treasury's legal advisers, principally to the effect that Northern Rock was effectively insolvent when it was nationalized. Insolvency describes a situation where liabilities exceed assets. That was not the case in relation to Northern Rock. In law, the state of a company is that it is either solvent or insolvent. "Effectively" insolvent is not a valid description.

If that was a valid claim, then by November 2008 there were many insolvent banks in the

UK and the rest of the world but no such claim has been made concerning them – except for Lehman Brothers.

The enormous legal expenses that will be incurred by all parties, the Government's expenses being charged to Northern Rock whether it wins or loses, are being brought about by the polarized position which HM Treasury and the Government has adopted that has forced shareholder groups to adopt an equally polarized but opposite stance. The outcome will only be resolved through one set of highly paid lawyers putting up a better argument than another set of highly paid lawyers, which is not necessarily the same thing as achieving a result based on the principles of equity, justice or human rights.

Whatever the outcome, we can be certain that the legal profession will be the real winners.

Why has this happened? There can only be one reason. The Bank of England and the Treasury (not to mention, by self-confession, the FSA) made serious mistakes in the handling of Northern Rock in September 2007 if not before but refuse to acknowledge them because it is politically inexpedient for them to do so. They must save face.

Had those entities admitted to mistakes, which were later identified by the House of Commons Select Committee, and proceeded towards a less controversial solution, the resulting problems might have been avoided. What got in the way was the introduction of the ubiquitous "taxpayer", initially by the Press but quickly taken up by the Treasury as a justification for its actions. Protecting his interests and later getting "value for money" for him and later still "getting the best possible return" for him, became a justification for everything else.

Although Northern Rock's initial difficulty was founded on a lack of liquidity, in common with many other banks as we discovered in 2008, it appears to have been transformed into one of insolvency. It has been established that the liquidity shortfall was brought about by an inability to re-finance loans in the inter-bank wholesale markets. If it had been unable to repay those loans and had no <u>lawful right of access</u> to Bank of England funding, the bank would have had to be put into administration.

But was that the whole extent of its situation? Perhaps it was not.

Administration would only have become inevitable in the event that when their loans fell due and were not repaid, the banks lending to Northern Rock sought to recover the amounts of their loans. That would have meant adopting a legal process to place the bank under administration. But how would they have adopted such a course of action? More than one bank was involved in the lending and not all the loans fell due at the same time, therefore it would have been difficult for them to adopt a common course of action at one particular time.

What alternative action could they have pursued? The loans could have been extended or restructured on different terms (including possibly at higher cost). Banks are frequently called upon to "restructure" loans, particularly corporate loans and those in the international markets. As pointed out earlier, they had been making loans to Northern Rock for a number of years, apparently perfectly satisfied with whatever collateral they required. So what caused them all to decline to renew loans to Northern Rock, all within a short period of a few months? Was it because of their own pending difficulties? Were they too afraid to renew the loans or does it take us back to the conspiracy theory?

In order to avoid a showdown of that nature with its bank lenders, Northern Rock sought and received emergency assistance from the Bank of England. It is difficult to understand the difference between what was described as "emergency assistance" and the granting of "lender of last resort" assistance, which was what the Banking Acts decreed that Northern Rock should have been able to access in the circumstances.

It follows that the proceeds of the Bank of England loans, drawn down as one after another of the inter-bank loans became repayable, did nothing more than make good the lending banks. The Bank of England knew this at the time (although the initial B of E loan was used towards repayment of some retail depositors, the balance was applied as just described).

The Bank of England's principle concern was not to save Northern Rock, the Governor made that clear at the time, but to avoid a domino effect spreading through other parts of the banking system, which might have happened if the inter-bank lenders had been faced with runs on deposits and had not received repayment from Northern Rock of what amounted by the end of 2007 to £15.238 billion, with another £11.472 billion still on the books and due for repayment within months. In all, at the end of 2007 the Bank of England had lent £26.9 billion to Northern Rock.

Also on the 19th June, "Times online" posted an article relating how Ron Sandler the recently appointed executive chairman of Northern Rock,

> *Is examining the conduct of the troubled bank's former board to see if they could be sued for compensation.*

The article noted that lawyers were of the opinion that,

> *Executives who were sued for negligence could fight back in court by trying to call members of the Tri-partite regulators as witnesses.*

Claire Canning, litigation partner with Mayer Brown International, who at her previous firm defended Ernst and Young, auditors, against Equitable Life, said that,

> *Mr. Sandler would struggle to prove his case.* She pointed out that, *The legal issues are that even if you can establish negligence, can you establish a causative link to any loss?*

The article continued,

> *A spokesman for Northern Rock said yesterday that the review was considering the bank's previous controls and processes, not the actions of individual directors.*

Lastly the article noted,

> *Shareholders said that Mr. Sandler should pursue the FSA and PriceWaterhouseCoopers, the bank's auditors, alongside the directors.*

One shareholder was quoted as having said,

> *This is a clumsy attempt by the government to divert attention from the failings of the Tripartite authorities. Mr. Sandler's role is not to indulge in speculative litigation bankrolled by the taxpayer*

That chap was back in the picture once again. Considering that "he" got his shares in Northern Rock for nothing, he could afford the legal fees but the reality was any legal costs would be paid out of Northern Rock's earnings which were still very positive.

Apart from some of the articles mentioned above, the end of November was reached with very little positive news other than the third quarter report from Northern Rock. The problems that emerged later in the year concerning other banks in the UK and globally and the solutions to them produced by governments added a new dimension to the Northern Rock shareholders' case that no doubt was studied closely by their lawyers.

The case was started on 13th January 2009 and judgement was issued on 13th February. The two judges rejected the case and declared that there was no infringement of shareholders' rights under Human Rights legislation and that the provisions made for the compensation of shareholders were not unfair. Leave to appeal was granted by the court. It was expected that an appeal would be lodged.

This ruling was despite the fact that documents obtained under the disclosure rules (and which could not be made public) showed that Northern Rock was secretly accorded a substantial valuation and demonstrated that the government knew that it was obtaining a valuable asset when it nationalised the bank. The figures also showed how much profit the government expected to make on a subsequent sale of the bank when economic conditions improved.

Watch this space, but perhaps do not hold your breath if you are a shareholder.

Other Northern Rock developments in February 2009 included an HM Treasury announcement that the bank would no longer pursue an active policy of repaying government brrowings (to date, £18 billion repaid) but would re-enter the mortgage market on normal commercial terms with a view to lending up to £14 billion over 2009-10. If necessary the Treasury would make funds available to it for this purpose.

At the same time the bank announced that it had a £1.4 billion loss in 2008 comprised of £900 million on defaulting borrowers and a further £300 million on investments. It issued figures that showed that defaulting borrowers three months in arrears had risen from 1.87% in September 2008 to 2.92% in December. Still not a bad figure when compared to Bradford and Bingley and other lenders in the US prime market.

The bank also announced that it would pay bonuses in loan notes deferred until 2010 to 100 key personnel with provisions for clawback should individual performances warrant.

The final outcome for Northern Rock is possibly still a long way off. We shall have to wait for it.

13 The Regulators and The Tripartite Standing Commitee

The run on Northern Rock deposits, which started on the morning of the 14th September 2007 was a wake-up call for the UK financial regulatory authorities and for the UK Government. It would be unfair, however, to suggest that the authorities responsible for financial stability in the United Kingdom were caught unawares, although they may not have been in effective control of the financial situation that was evolving in the UK, and appeared to have been insufficiently alerted to the global financial crisis that had been looming on the horizon for many months.

If, on the other hand, one assumes that they were aware of the global crisis heading for UK shores, they could have been much more pro-active and should have developed plans to cope with it. This is no doubt a harsh judgment, but one that was widely shared and undoubtedly had a foundation in fact. How otherwise could the financial system of the country have fallen deeper and deeper into trouble as each month passed during 2007.

The financial regulatory system and the Treasury Department of the UK Government do not deserve all the blame for the way in which the financial system became subject to severe stress, the banks and mortgage lenders brought it on themselves but as far as can be judged, whilst they were still in compliance with regulatory requirements. However, both official institutions proved inadequate in their responses to what rapidly became a major crisis after the 13th September 2007. As far as failures of the regulatory processes were concerned, an important point was that the use of derivatives that were at the root of the problems was not subject to effective regulation.

In order to understand where the regulatory system was deficient, we have to examine the purposes of the financial regulatory process and the manner in which its functions are carried out.

One point needs to be clarified first of all. The UK financial regulators are independent bodies but are answerable to the Government, and work in close co-operation with HM

Treasury. Each is responsible for carrying out its own brief. When we speak of "the UK financial regulators" we are referring to the members of the "Tripartite Standing Committee" comprised of the FSA, the Bank of England and HM Treasury.

Perhaps the simplest way of describing the link between the other regulators and HM Treasury is to quote from the Treasury website, as follows,

> *Promoting financial stability is a key objective for HM Treasury. A stable and efficient financial sector is important in its own right. But financial stability is also a crucial factor for macroeconomic stability, and is vital to the efficient conduct of monetary policy. HM Treasury, the Bank of England and the Financial Services Authority work together towards the common objective of financial stability.*

> *The Treasury's financial services objective is to secure an innovative, fair dealing, competitive and efficient market in financial services, while striking the right balance with regulation in the public interest.*

The Treasury Department has many other roles to perform, all broadly allied to financial and economic objectives but for the present we are only concerned with the regulatory role described above.

Prior to the Labour Party coming into power in 1997, supervision of the banking system was the province of the Bank of England, the UK Central Bank. That had been one of its more important roles for many years, which it had carried out very satisfactorily with only occasional glitches.

In earlier years banks, or after The Banking Act 1979, "recognized banks" and "Licensed deposit taking institutions", were the principal components of UK financial and investment services that were subject to regulation.

A later Banking Act in 1987 abolished a distinction between recognized banks and licensed deposit takers and created a single category of "authorized deposit takers". At the same time, the Act provided for the creation of a formal Board of Banking Supervision within the Bank of England. The Board was independent of the Bank of England and was comprised of six independent persons appointed by the Governor of the Bank of England who also served on the Board together with his Deputy and Senior Banking Supervision Executive.

The Board was charged with advising the Governor on all aspects of banking supervision, but the Governor was not obliged to accept its advice. However, if he did not do so, he had to explain the reason to the Chancellor of the Exchequer.

Banking and banks were only one part of the financial and investment services industries. During part of this period, a series of "self-regulatory bodies" were created to supervise the regulation of certain other financial, insurance and investment services. In addition the Securities and Investment Board Ltd (SIB) was incorporated on 7 June 1985. The Chancellor delegated certain statutory regulatory powers to it under the then Financial Services Act 1986.

After a series of scandals in the 1990s culminating in the collapse of Barings bank, there was a desire to bring the self-regulation of the financial services industry to an end and to bring regulatory responsibilities, which had been split amongst multiple regulators, under a single authority.

Consequently, SIB changed its name to the FSA on 28 October 1997 and now exercises statutory powers given to it by the Financial Services and Markets Act 2000, which replaced earlier legislation and came into force on 1 December 2001.

According to its website,

> *The Financial Services Authority (FSA) is an independent non-governmental body, given statutory powers by the Financial Services and Markets Act 2000. It is a company limited by guarantee. The Treasury appoints the FSA Board, which currently consists of a Chairman, a Chief Executive Officer, three Managing Directors, and 9 non-executive directors (including a lead non-executive member, the Deputy Chairman). This Board sets our overall policy, but day-to-day decisions and management of the staff are the responsibility of the Executive.*

> *The FSA is accountable to Treasury Ministers, and through them to Parliament. It is operationally independent of Government and is funded entirely by the firms it regulates. The FSA is an open and transparent organisation and provides full information for firms, consumers and others about its objectives, plans, policies and rules, including through its website.*

The Financial Services Authority is charged with responsibility for the regulation and supervision of a range of financial, insurance and investment services including the regulation and supervision of banks and financial markets. The breadth and range of its responsibilities should not be underestimated. It is a mammoth task, and when we come to criticize its failings that should be borne in mind.

However, The Bank of England retained, in relation to banks and banking, what it identifies as two "core purposes".

Monetary stability

Monetary stability means stable prices and confidence in the currency. Stable prices are defined by the Government's inflation target, which the Bank seeks to meet through the decisions on interest rates taken by the Monetary Policy Committee, explaining those decisions transparently and implementing them effectively in the money markets.

Financial Stability

Financial stability entails detecting and reducing threats to the financial system as a whole. Such threats are detected through the Bank's surveillance and market intelligence functions. Threats are reduced by strengthening infrastructure, and by financial and other operations, at home and abroad, including in exceptional circumstances, by acting as the lender of last resort.

The next stage in the evolution of the regulation of banking and financial services was the granting of independence to the Bank of England in 1997. The Bank of England took over responsibility for setting interest rates from HM Treasury. The second development in 1997 was the creation of a tripartite structure to act as a liason beween the three parties involved in financial regulation and the oversight of the UK financial system, with distinct roles for each of the Treasury, the Bank of England and the FSA.

The structure was called the Tripartite Standing Committee and its main purposes were set out by HM Treasury as follows,

> *"1. The Treasury, the Bank of England and the Financial Services Authority (FSA) constitute the UK's Tripartite Standing Committee that considers matters of financial stability. A published Memorandum of Understanding (MoU) sets out arrangements for co-operation between Standing Committee members in this field. The guiding principles of the MoU are that there should be clear accountability, transparency, no duplication of efforts and regular information exchange between the three parties. Standing Committee provides the regular high-level forum for such information exchange. It generally meets monthly at deputies' level with the possibility that any member authority may call a meeting at short notice if necessary. A sub-group of Standing Committee also meets monthly to consider work on contingency planning for an operational disruption and financial sector resilience.*
>
> *2. Work on financial stability conducted by the Standing Committee generally remains confidential because:-*

of constraints under EC and UK law on the disclosure of regulatory information;

publication could discourage private sector practitioners and foreign financial authorities from supplying information to HM Treasury, the Bank and the FSA on an informal basis; and

the disclosure of a Standing Committee interest in a particular issue could, in some circumstances, exacerbate problems which the Committee is seeking to avoid.

3. For these reasons, the Standing Committee's meeting agendas, papers and minutes are not normally published. However, the authorities are committed to putting considerations of financial stability matters into the public domain. For instance, the Bank of England publishes its Financial Stability Review twice a year whilst the FSA publishes its Financial Risk Outlook annually. Both the Bank and the FSA also describe their financial stability work in their annual reports.

4. As indicated by the contents of the Financial Stability Review and Financial Risk Outlook, types of issues which the Standing Committee has considered in its work include:

risks specific to a particular key financial institution, or group of similar institutions at home or abroad;

risks emerging from structural features of the financial system;

sectoral or geographical risks. For example concerning the national financial system of another country that could have implications for the UK;

risks arising from operational conditions

operational risks, such as those associated with the possibility of disruption caused by terrorist actions or other man-made or natural disasters. In some of these cases, disclosure about such risks may be less sensitive. For example, a Standing Committee website and an annual report describe aspects of its work on issues raised by potential operational disruption.

The following extracts from the Memorandum of Understanding (as updated in March 2006) which is available on HM Treasury and FSA websites, describe how it was envisaged that each of the three constituent bodies of the Tripartite Standing Committee would have its own responsibilities and how they would be carried out.

The memorandum of understanding establishes a framework for co-operation in the field of financial stability. The division of responsibilities is based on four guiding principles:

clear **accountability**. Each authority must be accountable for its actions, so each must have unambiguous and well-defined responsibilities;

transparency. Parliament, the markets and the public must know who is responsible for what;

avoidance of duplication. Each authority must have a clearly defined role, to avoid second-guessing, inefficiency and the unnecessary duplication of effort. This will help ensure proper accountability;

regular **information exchange**. This helps each authority to discharge its responsibilities as efficiently and effectively as possible.

The Bank's responsibilities

The Bank contributes to the maintenance of the stability of the financial system as a whole – one of its two core purposes. This involves :-

ensuring the stability of the monetary system as part of its monetary policy functions. It acts in the markets to deal with fluctuations in liquidity;

overseeing financial system infrastructure systemically significant to the UK.

through its involvement in markets and payments systems it may be the first to spot potential problems.

the Bank assesses the impact on monetary conditions of events in the financial sector;

undertaking, in exceptional circumstances, official financial operations in order to limit the risk of problems in or affecting particular institutions spreading to other parts of the financial system.

the bankers' bank, the Bank stands at the heart of the payments system.

It falls to the Bank to advise the Chancellor, and answer for its advice, on any major problem arising in these systems.

the Bank is also closely involved in developing and improving the infrastructure and strengthening the system to help reduce systemic risk;

The Treasury's responsibilities

4. The Treasury is responsible for:

the overall institutional structure of financial regulation and the legislation which governs it, including the negotiation of EC directives;

informing, and accounting to Parliament for the management of serious problems in the financial system and any measures used to resolve them, including any Treasury decision concerning exceptional official operations

accounting for financial sector resilience to operational disruption within government.

The Treasury has no operational responsibility for the activities of the FSA and the Bank and shall not be involved in them.

There are a variety of circumstances where the FSA and the Bank will need to alert the Treasury about possible problems.

where a serious problem arises, which could cause wider financial or economic disruption; where there is, or could be, a need for a support operation

where a problem might suggest the need for a change in the law

where a case is likely to lead to questions to Ministers in Parliament.

The following description of the resources allocated by the Treasury was given in the Select Committee report.

The Treasury normally deploys approximately 65 staff to work on financial services, as well as allocating 50% of the department's legal resource to that team. Sixteen of those 65 staff would normally work in the Financial Stability and Risk team. By October 2007, 15 additional staff had been temporarily allocated to work on these issues. We have already recommended that the Head of Financial Stability be the principal adviser to the Chancellor of the Exchequer on Financial Stability issues. The proposals in this chapter should help to ensure that, in future crises, a Chancellor of the Exchequer receives clear, consistent and authoritative advice. We believe that the reforms outlined in this chapter will reduce the reliance on the Treasury's own resources in future crises. Nevertheless, it is the responsibility of all Chancellors of the Exchequer to satisfy themselves that they and their ministerial team are fully prepared for the roles they could be called upon to play in a future period of financial instability.

During the 2007 crisis the Treasury also engaged outside professional advisers, the principal one being Goldman Sachs.

Information gathering
Through the exercise of its statutory responsibilities, the FSA gathers a wide range of information and data on the firms that it authorizes and supervises.

The Bank similarly collects information and data that it needs to discharge its responsibilities.

The FSA and the Bank work together to avoid separate collection of the same data, to minimise the burden on firms.

Where both need access to the same information, they reach agreement as to who should collect it, and how it should be transmitted to the other.

Information exchange
Free exchange of information is essential if each authority is to meet its responsibilities satisfactorily.

Information exchange is to take place on several levels. The Bank's Deputy Governor (financial stability) is a member of the FSA Board, and the FSA Chairman sits on the Court of the Bank.

At all levels, there should be close and regular contact between the FSA and the Bank, who maintain a programme of secondments between the two institutions, to strengthen the links and foster a culture of co-operation.

The FSA and the Bank maintain information-sharing arrangements, to ensure that all information which is or may be relevant to the discharge of their respective responsibilities will be shared fully and freely.

Each seeks to provide the other with relevant information as requested.

The authority receiving this information ensures that it is used only for discharging its responsibilities, and that it is not transmitted to third parties except where permitted by law.

Standing Committee

The Standing Committee on Financial Stability is chaired by the Treasury and comprises representatives of the Treasury, the Bank and the FSA.

It is the principal forum for agreeing policy and, where appropriate, coordinating or agreeing action between the three authorities.

It is also an important channel for exchanging information on threats to UK financial stability.

Standing Committee meets on a monthly basis at deputies (official) level to discuss individual cases of significance and other developments relevant to financial stability.

Meetings can be called at other times by any of the participating authorities if it considers there to be an issue which needs to be addressed urgently.

Each authority is to have nominated representatives who can be contacted, and meet, at short notice.

A sub-group of Standing Committee co-ordinates the authorities' joint work on financial sector resilience to operational disruption and maintains and tests tripartite arrangements for effective crisis management in an operational disruption.

In exceptional circumstances, for instance where a support operation is being considered, the Standing Committee meets at principals level, comprising the Chancellor of the Exchequer, the Governor of the Bank and the Chairman of the FSA (or senior alternates).

The Bank and the FSA are each to assess, from the perspective of their distinct responsibilities and expertise, the seriousness of the crisis and its potential implications for the stability of the financial system as a whole.

They will each provide their separate assessments to the Treasury, together with their views on the options available to the Chancellor.

Standing Committee may then discuss the appropriate use of measures
and ensure effective co-ordination of the response, while respecting the
formal responsibilities of the three authorities

Financial Crisis Management

In exceptional circumstances, there may be a need for an operation which
goes beyond the Bank's published framework for operations in the money
market.

such a support operation is expected to happen very rarely and would
normally only be undertaken in the case of a genuine threat to the
stability of the financial system to avoid a serious disturbance in the UK
economy.

If the Bank or the FSA identified a situation where such a support operation
might become necessary, they would immediately inform the other
authorities and invoke the co-ordination framework

ultimate responsibility for authorisation of support operations in exceptional
circumstances rests with the Chancellor.

Thereafter they would keep the Treasury informed about the developing
situation, as far as circumstances allowed.

In any such exceptional circumstances, the authorities' main aim would be
to reduce the risk of a serious problem causing wider financial or economic
disruption.

in acting to do this, they would seek to minimise both moral hazard in the
private sector and financial risk to the taxpayer arising from any support
operation.

The authorities maintain a framework for co-ordination in the management
of a financial crisis.

this includes arrangements that determine which authority would take the
lead on particular problems arising and for ensuring orderly communication
with market participants and overseas authorities.

Each authority would:

assess the situation and co-ordinate their response within the framework
agreed with the other authorities.

the form of the response would depend on the nature of the event and would be determined at the time

where possible and desirable to facilitate a solution to a problem, and hence reduce risks to wider financial stability, encourage negotiations between third parties whose agreement might be beneficial for the reduction or resolution of the issue, in its area of responsibility

Operational Crisis Management
The authorities also maintain a framework for co-ordination in the management of an operational crisis.

In a major operational disruption, the respective roles of the authorities' are as follows:-

The Treasury is to ensure that ministers are kept up-to-date on developments so as to be able to take key decisions without delay to ensure coherence between measures taken in the financial sector and the operation of public sector continuity arrangements.

The Bank is to seek to ensure the orderly functioning of the UK's financial markets, including the maintenance of adequate liquidity. - - - - this may include the provision of liquidity assistance or other support operations agreed within the tripartite framework.

The FSA is to monitor the health of institutions that fall within its regulatory remit.

- - - - It would have specific responsibility for monitoring authorized firms within the framework of the FSA's four statutory objectives.

Records
The FSA is responsible for the custody of all supervisory records. It ensures that, within the framework of the relevant legislation, the Bank has free and open access to these records.

Those are extracts from the Memorandum and they have been selected as having a relevance to the 2007 credit crisis. The Memorandum is comprehensive in its coverage of what should have been a well-designed operating structure. Unfortunately the implementation of it left much to be desired when its operational effectiveness was put to the test.

Yet another example of "I say, therefore it must be so".

That completes an outline of the evolution of financial regulation in the UK, mostly taken from official websites. It is important that we understand the evolution of the current regulatory system and how it is expected to operate before we examine how the various elements of the 2007/8 financial crisis were tackled by the regulators.

There is one more aspect which may not always be properly understood by the layman. It is the difference between regulation and supervision. Both are responsibilities of a regulatory body.

In order to regulate an activity, such as finance services, it is necessary to formulate legislation that will provide the groundwork for the desired level of control of activities within the industry. The legislation will in turn enable regulations or rules of conduct (or both) to be formulated and published. That is the basis of regulation.

Supervision consists of routines devised by the regulatory body to monitor those institutions and individuals which are subject to regulation. At its simplest, supervision means that the regulator has systems in place to monitor the activities of the regulated entity or person. Those will include meetings, often at a place of business of the regulated entity. The regulator will also call for the submission of reports and periodic returns of pertinent information sought by it or which may be required by statute law.

The UK regulatory system is broadly based on what has been called a light-touch, flexible, principles-based approach rather than a heavy-handed rules based model, as practised in the USA. In mid-2007 the UK's FSA was stated, (by Mervyn Davies, Chairman of Standard Chartered Bank and Chairman of the International Centre for Financial Regulation), "to be internationally recognised for the highest standards and integrity". This was in an article for "The Banker" magazine. He continued,

> Its distinctive strength is its application of principles-based regulation, minimising the burden of complying with detailed rules while demanding rigorous adherence to the principles of regulation. This outcome-orientated approach differs greatly from the US's desire to create rules for all eventualities.

This was written in June 2007. Whilst in principle what Mr. Davies wrote reflected the "on paper" status of UK financial regulation, the practice very soon turned out to be not up to the mark.

After some detailed discussion of the advantages and proposals relating to a new International Centre for Financial Regulation which was being set up by the UK government with the intention that it should be operational by end 2008, and form a focal point for discussion and improvement of regulatory techniques based on the *"principles based"* approach to regulation, he concluded,

> *Just as the City has attracted the world's top financial institutions, the ICFR creates the opportunity for London to become a global centre for excellence in regulation and to reinforce its position as the world's international financial centre.*

So, let us look at how the Tripartite Authorities coped with events later in 2007. As in other Chapters, we shall follow events as they were reported. Although there may be gaps between the dates selected, that does not mean that there was no media reporting or comment in between, merely that some of it was repetitive and not relative to this particular topic, regulation.

Monday 17th September 2007
The "Daily Mail" noted that the FSA had launched an investigation to discover which other banks could be toppled and accordingly mortgage lenders had been ordered by it to prove that they were solvent amid fears of a Northern Rock domino effect. The article continued,

> *One insider said the banks have been told to open their books. They need to prove they have stress-tested their finances to ensure they are prepared for the risks inherent in these market conditions.*

The paper named Bradford and Bingley, Alliance and Leicester and Paragon as three banks which had high loans-to-savings ratios, i.e., they lend out far more than they take in deposits and therefore, like Northern Rock relied on inter-bank market loans. The article recorded that the Government, Bank of England and FSA insisted that Northern Rock remained solvent, although this failed to stop the panic amongst its customers. This was a lengthy article which recorded the views of major politicians and others on the situation.

Thursday 20th September
The *"Independent"* newspaper ran an article entitled **"Tripartite regulatory system simply hadn't worked"**.

This was by Sean Farrell and recorded the views of a number of people, although only one was named. It started,

> *The Northern Rock crisis has exposed confusion at the heart of banking regulation caused by the three-way split for financial stability between the Bank of England, the FSA and the Treasury.*

A senior banker was quoted as saying,

> It was a complete and utter disaster. No one wants to take responsibility.

The paper then noted,

> The transfer in 1998 of the Bank's powers of supervision to the FSA was meant to ensure accountability, avoid duplication and avoid perceived conflicts of interest.

(this was the language used in the official explanation of the formation of the Tripartite Standing Committee). It continued,

> Critics point to lack of action by the different authorities as the credit crisis took hold. - - - - They say the crisis has been one of confidence and that restoring confidence has to be the role of one regulator.

Following other comment, the piece ended with a quote from Professor Buiter (a former member of the Monetary Policy Committee of the Bank of England, and severe critic of the tripartite arrangements) "They will have to go back to the drawing board to find a different way of sharing responsibilities"

There was much criticism from politicians, bankers and the Press of the "Tripartite" regulatory set up. Undoubtedly it did not perform well when the need arose but that was not the fault of the arrangements themselves. It was undoubtedly due to lax and ineffective implementation by officers and staffs of the Tripartite parties.

It was suggested that the same problems would not have arisen had the Bank of England been left with the responsibility for supervising banks. But would that have been so? It certainly was not the case when Bank of Credit and Commerce International collapsed in 1991, the Bank of England Banking Supervisory Division proved woefully inadequate, both in the years before the BCCI collapse and immediately following it. There were particular aspects in that case. BCCI was a Luxembourg bank and Bank of England was therefore not the main regulator. But that was not a reason for the regulatory failures that ensued, it was an excuse.

What critics fail to acknowledge is the fact that all institutions are comprised of a number of more or less self-contained divisions or departments, each charged with a particular responsibility. That was the case at the Bank of England. Those parts of the Bank that dealt with monetary and financial stability, note issue and acting as a "Banker's bank" may have performed satisfactorily but in practice they each functioned separately from the Bank Supervisory Division. They were all part of the same organisation reporting to the Governor and for that reason all the elements connected with the management and regulation of the banking system and its component banks were under one roof.

In otherwords it really made no difference whether there was a number of separate divisions concentrated in the Bank of England, or whether there was a Tripartite arrangement with a clearly identified leader. Either system would be satisfactory if those running each of the various elements carried out their functions effectively and if a person in ultimate charge ensured that they did so.

Friday 21st September

The "Financial Times" published an article by Chris Giles and Thai Larsen (who contributed a number of articles during the ensuing weeks) which related how Mervyn King believed that the first real crisis of his Bank of England leadership had been sorted out. By Tuesday morning Mr King's actions appeared to have been vindicated. The queues at Northern Rock's branches had dwindled. The share prices of banks most affected by the previous day's panic had recovered.

At a meeting the FSA and the Treasury insisted more needed to be done. Both Mr Darling and the FSA executives wanted to see the liquidity crisis in the banking system eased. The Treasury and the FSA attempted to persuade Mr King to exrtend the range of collateral acceptable to the Bank in return for its cash, but he was not convinced of the need.

This was a lengthy article which gave very good coverage of the various aspects of the involvement of the authorities up to that time and in the light of what was then known.

Aspects covered included:

a meeting at FSA with "angry and embarrassed" senior bankers wanting the Bank of England to broaden the range of collateral it was willing to accept against lending to the banks.

Hector Sants, CEO of the FSA urged the banks to "carry on providing liquidity in the inter-bank market." (Something which even a year later, the banks had still not achieved.)

A meeting of senior bankers at the Bank of England where they urged Mr King to follow other regulators and take action in the money markets. Mr King's response appears to have been a lecture on the importance of avoiding moral hazard, but that he might be willing to alter the Bank's stance.

However, the next day it was announced that the Bank would conduct a series of weekly auctions to inject liquidity into the three month money markets by lending against a wider range of collateral, including mortgages, the first being of £10 billion.

The report continued,

> *The news was greeted with disbelief at Northern Rock. Executives erupted*
> *with fury as they realised that the Bank had agreed to a move that, if it had*
> *only come a few weeks earlier, would probably have saved Northern Rock*
> *- - - - from the crisis it had just suffered.*

The article continued with some speculation about what had caused the Bank's *volte face*, one suggestion being that deep funding weaknesses still existed in other UK banks and no one wanted to risk another banking run. This, at the time, was probably the most likely reason, leaving aside possible political and banking industry pressures on Mr King.

The article then turned to the FSA., recording that the FSA stood accused of allowing Northern Rock to expand aggressively without adequate supervision and being far to close to the organisations it was supposed to regulate. We shall return to these two accusations in Chapter 14 on "Blame".

The rest of the article reviewed some political angles, much of it third hand.

Monday 24th September
The latest quarterly Bulletin from the Bank of England noted that,

> *In a review of market conditions leading up to Northern Rock's recourse to*
> *central bank emergency funding, the Bank noticed the reluctance of*
> *financial institutions to lend to each other which created the prospect of a*
> *gathering snowball of funding having to be rolled over every day in the*
> *over-night or short term money markets.*

The Bank estimated that banks could be exposed to £225 billion of loans arising from leveraged buy-out deals in Europe and the US.

Wednesday 26th September
Notwithstanding the money markets' desperate need to reinstate normal activity, it was reported that banks and building societies had shown no interest in borrowing up to £10 billion of B of E funds. There were no bidders for the money in the Bank's auction, which was held to ease strains in the money markets. It was the first such auction in the Bank's history and was designed to ensure lenders did not face the kind of funding crisis that hit Northern Rock.

Part of the answer for the lack of interest possibly lay in the interest rate on the money, 6.75%. Analysts also speculated that banks might have thought that a stigma attached to drawing on the funding at what was a punitive rate.

The bank confirmed that three more auctions would proceed, on 3, 10, and 17th October.

Tuesday 9th October

HM Treasury offered to guarantee new retail deposits at Northern Rock together with an extension of funding arrangements in order to assist a recovery. Previously the Treasury had only guaranteed retail deposits which were in the bank as at 19th September.

It should be noted that this guarantee was not offered free of charge. Northern Rock paid an unspecified fee for the facility, intended to maintain the competitiveness of other deposit takers.

This at the same time as the FSA suggested that Northern Rock may not have needed to draw on emergency funds from the B of E at all if its rescue had not been conducted in the full glare of publicity. However, the FSA also recognised that a covert operation was impossible under existing regulations. This was also the previously expressed view of Mr. King, Governor of the Bank of England although it was subsequently shown to be incorrect.

"Covert assistance" was used from time to time in earlier, and let us face it, much simpler times. On this occasion developments in European Community law which applied to the UK, and Britain's own legislation and regulations, plus the huge amount (at that time) of £30 billion estimated to be required, and the ease and rapidity with which news circulates in the City, meant that it could have been difficult to have mounted a covert aid operation.

Also, one has to keep in mind the frequent incidence of "leaked" information to news media much of which appeared to have had "sources" when it needed them.

Also on the same day, the FSA defended itself against the severe and growing criticisms of its role in the Northern Rock fiasco. Its chairman, Callum McCarthy before a House of Commons Select Committee investigation, said,

> I do not think we have failed in our supervisory duty. I think we have discharged our duties.

That was in the nature of the customary automatic defensive reaction to which chief executives and company spokespersons resort. Some weeks later he admitted that supervision had not been up to the required standard.

He also advised the Committee that the FSA, Bank of England and the Treasury were looking into reforms in areas which included deposit guarantees, and insolvency laws.

Hector Sants, CEO of the FSA, also at the Committee hearing, said,

> *The intensity of that dialogue (with Northern Rock) at the time of a February 2006 visit and subsequently, should have been more forceful. Those points were being identified by July (2007), when we were engaging in discussions on their stress-tests, but obviously at that point in time events overtook the firm. Let us remind ourselves that it is the board's responsibility (i.e. the board of Northern Rock) to run the company prudently. But - - - - we should have been in more intensive discussions with the company earlier.*

Thursday 25th October

Media reports at this time, and there were a great many, drew attention to the apparent deficiencies in the regulatory processes and discussed the level of disagreement between the FSA and Bank of England as to what should have, or could have been done and when it should have happened. There was also criticism of the Tripartite regulatory structure.

There was comment on Mr. Darling's refusal to make public letters which had passed between himself, Mr. King and Mr. McCarthy as not being in the public interest. It appears to have been his view that if such correspondence was made public it would lead in future to a reticence on the part of the various parties, who might then be disinclined to provide proper advice to each other, knowing that whatever they said may be published. This was a very reasonable and proper decision.

Later, we shall examine more closely the nature and extent of the involvement of the regulators and their perceived deficiencies.

Notwithstanding the foregoing, the Chancellor did tell the Select Committee that the regulatory set up should stay as it was, although a review of the regulatory processes in several areas needed to be undertaken.

Tuesday 6th November

A topic which had surfaced at an earlier date bcame a "hot potato" on this date when Mr King, Governor of the Bank of England gave an interview on the BBC. The subject was a proposed take-over of Northern Rock by Lloyds TSB bank which appeared to have been under final consideration during the weekend of 8/9th September 2007.

The substance of Mr King's revelations was that the Government had been approached for finance to assist with a takeover, but he had warned against the consequences of such a move. The failure of the takeover talks had resulted in the need for Northern Rock to request emergency funding from the B of E. A leak of the news of this request for "emergency funding", as we have noted in an earlier Chapter, sparked off the run on Northern Rock deposits.

Mr King disclosed that Lloyds TSB had sought a guarantee of up to £30 billion from the Bank of England to enable it to undertake the takeover. Mr King said to the Chancellor that it was not the central bank's job to fund takeovers, especially when such a large sum was involved. His view was that if the Treasury made such a facility available to one bank, it would have to be made available to any other potential bank bidder, and therefore would become public knowledge.

Such an action would have set a dangerous precedent, particularly as at the time, there were very real fears that Northern Rock might not have been the only bank in difficulties. At the very least, as noted earlier, there was unease over the situations of some of the smaller mortgage banks.

In that connection, Mr King warned that the UK financial system was likely to remain at risk from the US sub-prime mortgage crisis for several months.

It should be remembered also that at the time, the principal reason for the freezing of the inter-bank market was the uncertainty as to the extent of the exposure within UK banks to the apparently (virtually) worthless sub-prime related bonds which it was known that many of them held.

Monday 19th November
"The BBC" reported on proceedings in the House of Commons.

This chapter is concerned with regulatory matters, but in addition to HM Treasury's role as part of the regulatory system through involvement in the Tripartite Standing Committee, it represented Government and political interests.

The Treasury objective in relation to Northern Rock was to take whatever steps seemed appropriate at the time to contain the Northern Rock problems and to prevent them spreading systemically throughout the finance industry, in particular, to other banks, and then to the wider economic scene.

Its actions were not concerned with saving Northern Rock *per se*.

Very soon practically all media reporting dwelt on the "cost to the taxpayer", or the potential cost to the taxpayer Of course, this was grist to the opposition political parties' mills and they made the most of it. The Chancellor was subject to almost daily criticisms, both inside and outside parliament. Mr. Darling was frequently obliged to defend his position vigorously.

On one occasion, in the House of Commons, Mr. Darling said,

> The Government has a clear duty to protect the public interest and we will
> do that.

The response of the shadow chancellor, George Osborne, was that the "fallout from the crisis got worse each week", but Mr. Darling insisted that the government-backed loans given to Northern Rock, at that date amounting to about £24 billion, must be repaid. He said that the lending was all guaranteed against "quality assets" including mortgages.

With regard to a potential sale of Northern Rock he said that the Government would only support a proposal that protected the interests of depositors and tax-payers.

Whether or not a bidder for the company would have access to the emergency government loans after February 2008 was a point at issue, which Mr Darling clarified to some extent by saying that HM Treasury was "willing to discuss" any proposals that envisaged a continuing role for the Bank of England, the Treasury and the FSA.

As recorded earlier, there were several serious proposals under consideration by Northern Rock and its advisers with the government's knowledge. A problem which had been referred to on other occasions was that support, as provided to Northern Rock could represent state aid under EU rules and therefore could be illegal if continued indefinitely.

As everyone will have recognised by now, the political implications of the crisis had considerable significance for the Labour party, and opposition parties made the most of it. The Liberal Democrats and their caretaker leader at the time, Vince Cable, called time after time for the bank to be nationalised, stabilised and then sold off.

Wednesday 2nd January
"The Banker" magazine published an article by Howard Davies. He was the first Chairman of the FSA.

Mr Davies' theme was that,

> Regulators and governments must not make the mistake of responding in
> haste to the recent crises" (he was considering Germany and Britain in this
> context). The German government has led the way with attacks on
> "snooty" bankers (mebe it sounds more serious in German) and demands
> for new constraints on securitisation, on ratings agencies, private equity
> firms and sovereign wealth funds and, of course, demands for a cull of the
> locusts in wicked hedge funds.

Perhaps some of this rhetoric should be treated simply as political "throat-clearing.

- - - - one lesson we ought to have learnt by now is that regulations conceived in haste are often repented at leisure - - - -.

He went on to discuss the then current suggestions that the Tripartite arrangements be scrapped and to return banking supervision to the Bank of England.

As there seems to be no proof that the problem was one of co-ordination between the B of E and FSA, while there is ample evidence that understanding of Northern Rock's problems required an understanding of what was happening in securities markets; to de-link banking and securities regulation would be a curious response.

As one who has set up and managed a Financial Services Commission, albeit in a much simpler and smaller jurisdiction, Gibraltar, I agree that, properly organised and controlled, one body (in our consideration, the FSA), directly responsible for the supervision and regulation of all forms of regulated financial activities is the preferred option. The reason for this is that nowadays banks are involved in many areas of finance, insurance, securities and investment, including the "off balance-sheet" activities considered elsewhere. For the businesses of banks to be supervised by several different regulators would be totally impracticable. That was part of the problem that gave rise to ineffective regulation in the USA.

Which is not to say that the regulator cannot have three arms, properly co-ordinated, and with clearly defined responsibilities, with <u>one of them being the recognised appointed leader with ultimate control and responsibility</u>. This last requirement appears to be the one which was not adequately addressed in the Tripartite Memorandum of Understanding.

Mr. Davies discussed at length other factors leading to the crises which were not questioned by regulators anywhere and reminded us that transparency in the securities markets was very necessary.

Uncertainty about where the losses lay was a powerful factor behind the midsummer liquidity crisis.

He also covered the ratings agencies. He pointed out that regulators need to oversee their activities more closely, and finally came to liquidity. He asked if,

regulators paid too much attention to bank solvency and too little to liquidity and the risks posed to particular business models if liquidity dries up.

He suggested that in the 1970's banks typically held about 30% of their assets in highly liquid form. The current figure, he said, is nearer to 2%. (later on in 2008 this ratio was increased at FSA insistence to more than 8%. The ratio for Northern Rock in mid-2007 was 7%.

He ended by writing that,

> We should not require it (increased liquidity) without careful thought and strong justification.

He forecast that this may turn out to be the next great debate between regulators and the regulated.

Liquidity, lack of which was at the root of Northern Rock's problems can be achieved in different ways. One could assume that having sufficient liquidity actually means having cash reserves but that is not the normal method used by banks today. Adequate liquidity can be achieved by a combination of cash, reserves at the Bank of England and what are known as "open market operations" between banks and the Bank of England whereunder banks acquire short dated government stocks from the Bank of England that can be quickly sold back to the Bank of England for cash when needed. In this manner banks can maintain sufficient liquidity whilst still earning interest on their assets. If they held cash only, that cash would be "dead" money, earning no interest. That is a very much simplified description of the processes banks use to maintain liquidity.

Friday 4th January
As evidence that much work was going on behind the scenes, the Chancellor provided an update in a "Financial Times" interview. He said that the FSA would be given new powers to enable it to sieze and protect depositor's cash at a struggling bank to prevent the risk of a run and to safeguard public confidence. The Governor of the Bank of England was said to support this move. Later in the year this was more or less what it did with Bradford and Bingley depositors.

It was proposed to unveil the proposals in May 2008 and the idea was to enable the FSA to step in quickly if any bank applied to the Bank of England for an emergency loan, allowing the deposits to be secured, repaid quickly or parcelled off to another bank or the original bank if it is satisfactorily restructured. In other words, a special insolvency regime would be created for banks. Other powers would be included in the proposals.

In a separate article, the newspaper pointed out that although the proposals were needed in some form, there were flaws in them that would have to be addressed. That was more or less what Mr Davies said in his "The Banker" magazine article.

Saturday 5th January

The weekend papers were much more critical. It was suggested that Mr Darling's ideas for regulation were as much about being seen to do something as providing a serious answer to the Northern Rock disaster. The Chancellor needed something to say before he was due to appear before MPs on the Treasury Select Committee.

It was considered that vesting new powers to the FSA did not inspire great confidence. The FSA already had ample powers. What it lacked in the past was the will and foresight to use them. It was thought that nothing in Mr Darling's proposals would prevent another Northern Rock getting into trouble. That required the FSA and indeed other bank regulators to push liquidity back near the top of the supervisory agenda and to force banks to stress-test their business models with much more rigour than in the past. This was something they had started to do. In addition, the FSA, B of E and the Treasury had issued a consultation paper, the conclusions of which would be made public when they became available. In fact it was published later that month.

When forms of increased regulation are being considered it is very easy to overlook the fact that it is not necessarily the regulatory system that is at fault. Very often the deficiencies are in the <u>execution</u> of the regulatory policies. The admissions of default made by the FSA and the results of its internal review which called for at least seven significant improvements to operating procedures confirms that a hard look at staffing and management quality and performance could do much to remedy the deficiences.

By way of example, an internal FSA memorandum found on its website, from the Prudential Standards department to the Securitisation Standing Group on 4th May 2007 described a "Thematic Review of Asset backed Commercial Paper Programs" which took the whole of 2006 to carry out and which took another five months (at least) for a paper to be produced. The paper was no more than six pages long of which one page noted "Identified strengths" and another dealt with more comprehensive, "Areas for further thought". The latter, "Areas for further thought" included the following conclusions;

It was not always clear that firms had clear reporting lines to senior management in a loss situation (shades of Nick Leeson and Barings bank years before).

Some conduits may be exposed to event risks. - - - - It was not clear that the structural protection mechanisms built into transactions would always work if such an event occurred. (This no doubt referred to "credit enhancement" techniques.)

There has been a tendency for esoteric assets to be brought into conduits. - - - - Some of these assets may be more volatile in some circumstances which may mean that the firms' risk profile is greater than expected.

It became clear that conduits place emphasis on third parties (originators, auditors etc.), to manage some of the operational risks involved. We wish to understand the benefits and drawbacks of such an approach in more detail.

The three "identified strengths" were self evident matters that one would expect to find as a matter of course. It therefore took eighteen months to produce a superficial examination of securitization processes used by banks that produced no conclusion other than it identified "areas that we would like to discuss further with the industry", which would probably take at least another eighteen months.

The most appropriate comment on this review might be "Too elementary, my Dear Watson"!

Later in this chapter we shall return to the subject of reviews of the regulatory structure.

Thursday 10th January
As just noted, the FSA and the Tripartite Standing Committee (or Authority) came in for a great deal of (justified) criticism.

The turmoil in capitals markets and near collapse of Northern Rock raised far-reaching questions about FSA's ability to supervise the banking system and it was suggested that public confidence in the pragmatic, principles-based approach and the tripartite structure had been shaken.

Failure by FSA to spot Northern Rock's "shortcomings"

There was also discussion of internal changes being carried out by the FSA with particular reference to a number of senior personnel changes.

Sunday 20th January
Another topic which occupied the media was that of the vaunted "light touch" approach to financial regulation, much favoured officially up to the Northern Rock "run" in September 2007, and of course much preferred by the financial community. Although if the truth were faced, the industry would have preferred a return to the "good old" Bank of England regulatory days when a broad measure of "self-regulation" was considered to be the order of the day.

Questions were now arising as to whether the earlier campaign to encourage the EU (and others) to adopt the UK's "light touch" was still viable in view of the obvious shortcomings surrounding the supervision of Northern Rock. It is necessary to appreciate that the two expressions, "inept and inadequate" and "light touch" supervision are not synonymous. Nor is "light touch" incompatible with "active and effective supervision".

In fact "light touch" is little more than an industry euphemism that would be better forgotten.

Saturday 26th January

The House of Commons Treasury Select Committee published its report **"The run on the Rock".**

This was undoubtedly the most comprehensive, well documented and hard-hitting report produced by anyone on the Northern Rock crisis. The members of the Treasury committee were, of course, M.P's drawn from all parties, but that did not prevent them from producing a well-considered report that included positive recommendations relating to each point addressed by them, although it may have had a bias that favoured political points of view in some areas.

By way of clarification, the Treasury Select Committee is not an arm of HM Treasury, rather it is the parliamentary watchdog which monitors areas of financial activity in which the Treasury has an involvement.

Although its report dealt with the problems which overtook Northern Rock, it was also concerned with the broader repercussions affecting the whole British financial system and with the reputation of London which up to that time, had been universally regarded as one of the best run financial centres in the world.

Although, for the purposes of this book, the concentration has been on various aspects of banks and banking, the internatiomal financial activities in London go far beyond, covering insurance (including pensions), commodity futures and investment markets, including hedge funds and private equity investors. They all felt the fallout from Northern Rock, and the freezing of the inter-bank markets following the collapse of the securitisation markets.

The report ran to 163 pages and should be mandatory reading for anyone wishing to really analyze the 2007 financial crisis. However, because of its length and its comprehensiveness, it is not practical to review it here. Nevertheless, its conclusions on a number of matters are worth recording as part of our review of the regulatory system.

The picture that emerged from the report in relation to the regulatory bodies and HM Treasury was one where there was no clear leadership, and a culture which led the participants to be comfortable with policies and practices which in practice relegated too much to "the back burner", such as the review mentioned above. Too often there appears to have been something of a "laisser faire" attitude, and there can be little doubt that the sharing of information and advice, both within each of the Tripartite institutions and amongst each of them left much to be desired.

A regulatory system that does not perform its duties in a timely and comprehensive manner, irrespective of the reasons for its failure, is both useless, and equally importantly, a complete waste of money.

Monday 28th January
The Commons Treasury Select Committee report gave the media plenty on which to write and speak, generally along the following lines. The Commons Treasury Committee had issued a damning report into the Northern Rock crisis claiming that the FSA was guilty of,

> a systemic failure of duty and that the Northern Rock directors pursued a "reckless" business strategy which was excessively reliant on wholesale funding.

An FSA statement by way of a response read,

> As we have already acknowledged publicly, there were clearly supervisory failings in relation to Northern Rock and we are already addressing these (but after the horse had bolted). We will also examine carefully any further lessons that emerge form our internal review of the supervision of Northern Rock.

Another article took a different line on the same day concerning the Chancellor's proposals to strengthen the regulatory powers of the FSA by giving it tools to examine the records and liquidity of banks and to step in when institutions got into trouble. The powers held by the Treasury and the B of E would remain little changed.

Trevor Williams, Chief Economist at Lloyds TSB Group said,

> It's crucial they get this right, someone needs to take prime responsibility.

This "taking prime responsibility", as mentioned earlier, was a key factor contributing to the inadequate level of supervision.

A further quote from Michael Fallon, a member of the Treasury Select Committee,

> The FSA let us down. The FSA has a conflict of interest to carry out a rescue when it also has supervisory powers. They are the wrong people to have more power.

It should also be remembered that the FSA is funded by means of levies on those institutions that it regulates.

Other aspects of the failure of Northern Rock and the regulators were reviewed before attention turned to Sir John Gieve, Deputy Governor of the B of E, who when interviewed by the Treasury Committee was accused of not doing his job and of seeming "pretty laid back".

He defended himself, " I do not think I was asleep at the wheel." That was not a very inspiring response. Gieve's term at the B of E was due to run until 2011, so whether or not he "sleeps at the wheel" was a significant problem.

The question was resolved rather belatedly when it was announced on the 19th June 2008 that Gieve would be "stepping down" (but not until the end of the year, one cannot rush such moves). This was part of a Treasury review of regulatory responsibilities that will be examined in due course.

Mr Fallon of the Select Committee commented,

> The Deputy Governor should be someone with senior banking experience, you cannot have someone like Gieve, a civil servant without any banking experience.

This was particularly so when we are aware, with due respect to him, that Mervyn King, the Governor, is an academic economist rather than a career banker as a number of his predecessors have been.

It should be noted that Sir John Gieve was also a member of the Board of the FSA, and therefore could be said, at the very least, to have had a *de facto* co-ordinating role.

Wednesday 30th January

Turning away from the Treasury Select Committee report, "Reuters" and "Thomson Financial" both published factual explanatory articles that covered new government proposals for changes in the powers of regulators and associated topics intended to improve the protection of depositors and to prevent recurrences of the Northern Rock crash. The Government announcement was of a twelve-week consultation period on ways to improve the framework in order to preserve financial stability and to protect depositors should a bank fail.

A Treasury spokesperson was quoted as saying that the Treasury's proposals were in line with the thrust of the Treasury Select Committee's report, even if not the letter of it. Already we see the beginnings of a "watering down" of the Treasury Select Committee's recommendations.

The preliminary proposals for the better protection of depositors were naturally not welcomed by the banking community as it would have to fund it. A compensation scheme able to pay out depositors promptly in the event of a bank collapse has to be pre-funded to an extent that would enable it to meet an average size bank failure. Currently, the Depositor Compensation scheme raises money from deposit taking institutions only as and when required. Nowadays when banks in Britain count their deposits in billions of pounds, the reserve sum required would be quite substantial.

The proposals also covered ways of allowing the B of E to provide "covert " assistance to banks in trouble, as it used to be able to do, but this idea did not appeal to the Treasury Select Committee although later in the year the Bank of England with Treasury agreement carried out "covert" assistance for the banks.

Another article recorded that John Gieve, B of E Deputy Governor in charge of financial stability, got an indirect vote of confidence from the Treasury which chose not to adopt in full the proposals put forward by the Treasury Select Committee.

This same article continued with a discussion of the role of Mervyn King, Governor of the B of E, who had come in for fairly severe criticism of his performance, and noted that his term of office had been renewed by the Treasury for another five years. Another vote of confidence, this time probably more deserved.

The Government's principle concern seemed to be with the maintenance of continuity of leadership at the B of E in such troubled times. Mr. King was the most experienced member of the Monetary Policy Committee (of the B of E) having served on all 129 monthly meetings, 55 as Governor, and had been at the Bank since 1991.

Monday 4th February
"FT.com" published a letter from a Mr. Simon Hallett in Surrey that expressed an interesting viewpoint on regulation, in particular relating to the requirements formulated by the Basel 2 regime. His letter was in response to one from a Mr. Damon de Laszlo on 1st February to the paper. Mr. de Laszlo blamed part of the banking crisis on the Basel 2 regime because,

> it is rule driven, backward looking and statistical, and academic, also ascribing to it the letter-rating of risk. He then suggests that better risk management requires forward looking anticipation of trends by people who understand markets, not by box-ticking bureaucrats.

Mr. Hallett's response read,

> Just where are these far-sighted market gurus who would have kept us all

out of danger had it not been for the pettifogging bureaucrats? Well, clearly not in the offices of UBS, Morgan Stanley, Merrill Lynch and the rest.

Mr. Hallett could have justifiably added – with the possible exception of Goldman Sachs, which saw what was coming, but rather than warn the rest of us, chose to make a pile of money by betting on the falls in the sub-prime securitised markets.

A better criticism of Basel 2 might be quite the reverse: that it allowed leeway for banks to use their own models (surely not backward looking and statistical?) to assess risk.

Mr.Hallett ended by writing,

Banking has been rule-driven since the dawn of the modern economy. It has to be, given the leverage and incentives involved. I would suggest that had we all been more diligent in asking boring, box-ticking questions such as "How much equity capital do you have?" - - - - "How many loans have you made"? and " to Whom?" and "What do you know about the borrowers?" a good deal of embarrassment and money would have been saved.

Monday10th March

Returning to the FSA, we had reports of the resignations of FSA officials. It was noted that out of seven FSA supervisors who worked on Northern Rock, five had left the FSA, apparently voluntarily. However it was believed that some of them had left the FSA before the catastrophe. The high turnover of FSA staff may have been one of the reasons for the failings. Northern Rock had not been the subject of a full supervisory health check for eighteen months when it ran into difficulties.

Wednesday 19th March

The FSA issued a note to staff, made public on its website, detailing management changes within its organization. The note read,

It is with regret I announce Clive Briault is leaving the FSA by mutual agreement (which means?) *at the end of April. Clive has been an outstanding colleague who has contributed much to the organization in his time at the FSA and earlier with the Bank of England. - - - -.*

David Kenmir will take on the role as managing Director of the Retail Business Unit, in an acting capacity. The role will also be immediately advertised externally and internally (why internally, if Kenmir can only be appointed on an acting basis?). *Kathleen Reeves, Human Resources*

Director, will take on David Kenmir's current role as Chief Operating Officer, also in an acting capacity. These changes will be effective immediately.

This last appointment reminded me of a meeting I had at the Department of Trade and Industry (DTI) when I was Financial Services Commissioner in Gibraltar. One of my responsibilities was the supervision of insurance companies in Gibraltar. I visited the DTI to discuss aspects of insurance company supervision only to find that the person responsible for insurance company supervision had been, until three weeks previously, the Human Resources manager who knew less about insurance than I did.

To return to the FSA notice:

Furthermore, in order to strengthen our capacity in the key areas of large retail group supervision and financial stability, I have decided to allocate them dedicated directors. David Strachan will concentrate solely on his role as Financial Stability Sector Leader. He will join the Chief Executive's Office alongside Thomas Huertas. Clive Adamson will then take on the role of Director of Major Retail Groups, again in an acting capacity. These will be effective from 7th April. This role will also be advertised externally and internally.

It is worth drawing attention to this notice since it illustrates the extent of the weaknesses within the FSA. Three major roles could only be filled on a temporary basis by existing officers appointed in an acting capacity, which can only point to the fact that there were no appointees within the FSA's ranks that were possessed of appropriate training, ability and experience or who actually wanted those promotions.

The high level of staff turnover has been mentioned several times in the period since the spotlight shone on the activities of the FSA in September 2007. One commentator pointed out a difference between employment with the US financial and investment regulators and employment by a UK regulator.

In the USA, the perception was that employment in a (senior) regulatory capacity was a pre-cursor to a top job in one or other branches of the US finance industry. In the UK, however, the perception was that only those who could not make the top echelons of a UK financial institution would consider employment by a regulatory body. It has to be said however that the events of late 2007 may have sparked off a change in that situation, if one judges senior appointments that were announced in May / June 2008.

A problem with employment by a body such as the FSA is that with exceptions, it is difficult to motivate the incumbents. One sarcastic comment about FSA staff was that the most important consideration in the average day was to catch the 5.10 pm train home.

The same day another topic came to the fore. What was behind the topic was far from new, but came to light for a re-airing in the context of the somewhat chaotic behaviour in stock markets.

The FSA issued a warning on "market abuse" which manifested itself in the form of

> *a series of completely unfounded rumours about UK financial institutions in the London market over the last few days, sometimes accompanied by short selling. We will not tolerate market participants taking advantage of the current market conditions to commit abuse by spreading false rumours and dealing on the back of them.*

This topic was taken up by the media which identified HBOS (Halifax Bank of Scotland PLC) as bearing the brunt of the rumours, which caused its shares to fall by 17% to a record low of 398 pence at one point.

The FSA confirmed that it would probe the latest share sell-off.

The speculation was dismissed by HBOS which said that it had an "exceptionally strong balance sheet" and was continuing to access wholesale funding. The dismissal was reported at length in "The Scotsman" and other newspapers on the 20th March 2008.

The Bank of England joined in to quash the rumours by saying,

> *No meetings have taken place or been scheduled to discuss problems with any institution in the UK.*

Shortly afterwards, as we shall see in Chapter 16 the bank launched a £4 billion rights issue – to raise additional capital, despite which, six months later the bank had to be rescued by a £11.5 billion HM Treasury bailout and a takeover proposal by Lloyds TSB, which was also to receive £5.5 billion. Both sums were dependent on completion of the takeover.

There were further reports that the Authorities were concerned that speculators benefited from wild gyrations in share price and spread false information. Investors could profit by selling shares "short" before buying them back later. Shares in other banks, including Alliance and Leicester and Bradford and Bingley were also hit by the rumours. Lloyds TSB was cited as facing problems.

An example of what can generate this type of rumour was then described. The Bank

Deputy Governor John Gieve, whose remit was financial stability, had been replaced at a speech on Thursday so he could stay in London to monitor market developments. A spokesman said rumours that senior bank executives had cancelled a trip to the far east due to a possible problem were "complete fantasy".

The reporting of such rumours is capable of creating as many concerns as the rumours themselves. Until picked up by the media the rumours only circulate amongst City players, the ripples from them do not normally reach the general public. The reporting of the rumours in the media is what forms the opinions of the man in the street, the ordinary depositor or investor, and which may lead him to take precipitate action. This was a major concern of both the banks and the authorities after the run on Northern Rock.

Rumours of this type are rife in the "City" and in normal circumstances only give occasional cause for concern. In the dramatic few months at the end of 2007 and into 2008, it became difficult to distinguish between rumour and fact and as many of the City players were speculating heavily on a range of bank and other shares, not least on Northern Rock shares as we have seen, the rumour mill had more serious implications. So much so that apart from investigations by the regulators, who had difficulty on past occasions proving illegal market intervention and therefore were unlikely to be successful on this occasion, the Chancellor entered the arena.

Friday 28th March

The Chancellor had announced that he would propose legislation which would give the FSA plea-bargaining powers to be known as "specified prosecutor status" similar to those exercised by the Serious Fraud Office, and widely used in the USA.

The FSA had sought such powers for some years but discussion with the Government never produced a law. However, the Chancellor was now of the opinion that,

> I cannot allow us to get into a situation where people quite deliberately manipulate markets for personal gain with the potential to destabilize the financial system.

We have to remember that all this was happening at a time when professional market players were very "jittery" and the least thing was liable to start a panic.

To continue this Chapter on regulation and the regulators, it is appropriate to return to Wednesday 26th March 2008. The FSA published a summary of its internal review of its performance leading up to the crisis period and during it. The review identified a number of areas for improvement in the execution of supervision, which were to be advanced urgently by the FSA's management via a dedicated supervisory enhancement programme. The programme also included a number of improvements already in train.

In addition to the summary, the FSA published the recommendations made by its Internal Audit (which produced the survey), and the responses of the executive of the FSA. A full version of the report was promised for late in April 2008.

As our concern has been with the effectiveness of FSA supervision in relation to Northern Rock, and the widely expressed criticisms of it, it is worth reading the explanation of the key failings and the main features of the proposed Supervisory Enhancement Programme. These were:

Key failings
A lack of sufficient supervisory engagement with the firm (Northern Rock), in particular the failure of the supervisory team to follow up rigorously with the management of the firm on the business model vulnerability arising from changing market conditions.

A lack of adequate oversight and review by FSA line management of the quality, intensity and rigour of the firm's supervision

Inadequate specific resource directly supervising the firm.

A lack of intensity by the FSA in ensuring that all available risk information was properly utilized to inform its supervisory actions.

Supervisory enhancement programme
A new group of supervisory specialists will regularly review the supervision of all high-impact firms to ensure procedures are being rigorously adhered to.

The numbers of supervisory staff engaged with high impact firms will be increased, with a mandated minimum level of staffing for each firm.

The existing specialist prudential risk department of the FSA will be expanded following its upgrading to divisional status, as will the resource of the relevant sector teams.

The current supervisory training and competency framework for FSA staff will be upgraded.

The degree of FSA senior management involvement in direct supervision and contact with high-impact firms will be increased.

There will be more focus on liquidity, particularly in the supervision of high-impact retail firms.

There will be raised emphasis on assessing the competence of firm's
senior management.

The Board of the FSA and its Chief Executive, Hector Sants, added comments on the foregoing. Firstly, the Board noted that,

Even if supervision had been carried out at a level acceptable to the FSA,
it was by no means the case that that would have changed the outcome.

That may have been a reasonable statement if it related only to the few months prior to the run on Northern Rock, but the Northern Rock situation developed over the ten years it existed as a public company. During the whole of that period it was under supervision. It grew exponentially each year during at least half of that period. It grew at an annual rate (20%) way beyond that which its peers had managed to achieve. Its business plan had existed more or less unchanged - and unchallenged - for much of that period. Its business plan, when compared with some peer institutions, was identifiably out of line. (As we discovered later in 2008, perhaps it was not as much out of line as we were led to believe). Its assured liquidity position was tenuous, even without the intervention of extreme conditions.

The FSA review refers to "high impact retail firms" by which it meant those retail firms most at risk. Northern Rock was recognized for some years as one of those firms. Why then was so little attention given to it?

There can be little doubt that effective and conscientious regulatory supervision should have been able to identify and act on these indicators of a potential for the development of serious difficulties. Bear in mind that this was not a typical clearing bank undertaking a diversified range of business. It was essentially a mortgage lending company that happened to be categorized under the UK licensing system as a "bank" but more than 80% of its lending was long term. Many mortgage loans may in practice turn out to have an average lifespan of no more than a few years but 99% are scheduled to be amortized over twenty-five years. Unless the lending bank forecloses on the mortgagee, or mortgagees re-finance elsewhere, it will only at best see a return of a very small proportion each year of the sum lent.

A lender, relying on the inter-bank short-term wholesale market for 25% of its total funding requirements and on the securitisation markets, which had been under a spotlight in the USA for many months prior to September 2007 for a further 45% or so, in such circumstances was imprudent and should have been questioned both by the bank's own board Audit and Risk Committees (as required by their terms of reference, set by the Board) and by FSA examiners.

The bank suffered a liquidity crisis. The external factors that led to that crisis began to be apparent to those operating in the international markets, as Northern Rock was doing, from mid-2006. There is enough (although not good enough) co-operation amongst national regulators from all major countries to ensure that an effective FSA could not have been unaware of the brewing troubles. Throughout that period there were many references to the problems by US regulatory and Statutory bodies and by members of Congress and the House of Representatives. In addition, legislative proposals for greater controls to be imposed were in train in the USA.

It is not being suggested that everyone, or for that matter anyone, could have foreseen the complete seizing up of the securitisation and UK inter-bank markets at one and the same time. Nevertheless, in the light of the deteriorating situation that was very apparent in the USA, Northern Rock's extreme business model should have made it a prominent target for an assiduous regulator.

Mr Sants agreed,

> It is clear from the thorough review carried out by the Internal Audit team that our supervision of Northern Rock in the period leading up to the market instability of late last summer was not carried out to a standard that is acceptable - - - -.

He also said,

> Demonstrating our willingness to examine ourselves critically and learn lessons is central to giving the financial services industry and consumers confidence in the FSA, although, like any organization, we cannot and do not claim infallibility, and we cannot and should not, attempt to remove all risk from the system.

This last statement can be justified to a point, but we are specifically considering high-impact firms, ie, high-at-risk firms. Infallibility if related to low-impact firms which unexpectedly turn sour is one thing and acceptable, but that is not the case in respect of high-impact firms, of which Northern Rock had been recognized within the FSA as a prime example.

The systemic risks that the FSA as regulator was expected to remove from the system, or at least minimize, were quite different from those acceptable and normal business risks undertaken by most firms in any line of business.

At best this last statement from Mr Sants smacks of a reluctance to fully acknowledge the FSA's shortcomings, despite his expressions to the contrary. Before we accept that the implementation of the report will put the FSA on the right track and that future problems will therefore be unlikely, it is worth looking at other reports and reviews of its performance in earlier years.

If we go right back to the beginning when the FSA was set up in 1998, Howard Davies, its first CEO, shortly afterwards addressed a conference of the British Bankers Association (BBA) to brief them on what the changes in the regulatory structure were about.

The speech was a lengthy one and is available from the FSA archives on its web-site, but the following are points that he addressed which have a relevance to our present consideration of the FSA and its problems.

> *The overall intention is clear, to create a one stop shop arrangement for regulation and to provide better flexibility and accountability. This latter point has already attracted some attention. Is the new FSA sufficiently accountable to its paymasters, or indeed to consumers, or to Parliament?*

> *Why regulate at all?*

> *First, there is the problem of systemic risk. Left to themselves, financial systems are prone to bouts of instability and contagion. There is therefore a public policy case for the prudential supervision of institutions, especially banks with their important maturity transformation role, to ensure that they are soundly capitalized and correspondingly less vulnerable to "runs" and other market shocks.*

> *The first objective, maintaining confidence in the UK financial system, is one which can be delivered effectively only in close collaboration with the Bank (of England). The framework for that collaboration has already been set out in a Memorandum of Understanding between the Treasury, the Bank and the FSA, which established a Standing Committee to ensure that the three organisations work together effectively. That Standing Committee has now been in operation for some months and has already proved itself to be an effective forum in which emerging problems can be addressed, whether they arise in domestic or overseas markets, if they could threaten the stability of the UK financial system. I have to say that there has, in recent months, been no shortage of topics to discuss.*

> *I know that I can speak for the Governor also when I say that this aspect of the new system, which caused some concern at the outset, has so far run very smoothly indeed.*

> *We shall be carrying forward the RATE and SCALE approach to banking*

supervision which was introduced as a result of the Arthur Andersen review of supervision which I led when Deputy Governor at the Bank. We believe that that approach is already paying dividends. We have carried out a full RATE analysis for quite a large number of banks, now, and what we call desktop RATE analysis for all the institutions in our care.

In the short-term, it ought to leave us with a much clearer understanding of the shape of the institution and the risks it runs. It ought also to leave you with a much clearer understanding of our comprehension of the riskiness of your business and the aspects of it which we wish to pay attention to in our supervisory programme. In the long run, it should allow us to target our resources more effectively, paying relatively little attention to those areas of the business which we believe are low-risk, and focussing our efforts more effectively on high-risk areas.

Lastly, I do not propose to change the character of open relationships which has existed between the Bank of England supervisors and banks in the past. In my view effective supervision is built on good relationships, except where the relationships of trust break down. One of the FSA principles which we have published for consultation is that institutions must be open with their regulators. Where they are open with us we will be open with them. But of course that does not mean that we cannot and should not take effective enforcement action where principles or rules have been clearly breached, and particularly where institutions have sought to conceal things from their regulators.

With that caveat, I want to see an open and responsive relationship between you and us. That is not just because it is nice to be liked and loved, but because I am persuaded that effective supervision proceeds on the basis of a good understanding by supervisors of what banks are trying themselves to achieve. That is at the heart of the RATE process, which begins with strategy. You cannot operate that kind of regulatory system from your desk, or in a confrontational relationship between institutions. So it follows that we shall want to keep in close contact with you.

Mr. Davies talked of it being "nice to be liked and loved", but what is much more important for a regulator (and for that matter any management) is to be respected. Whether one is "liked or loved" is of little consequence. Which is not to say that the relationship should be a confrontational one, but part of the FSA's later problems was that it did not have the respect of those it regulated. Some regarded it as an (un)necessary evil to be ignored or circumvented as necessary.

> *Lastly, one plea. The FSA is a creature of the markets it regulates. We are paid by financial institutions or, perhaps, by their consumers. We will only build a better regulatory mousetrap if we do so collaboratively. I recognise that there are many more interesting things to think about than changing the regulatory framework. But we really do depend on the contribution of financial institutions and their trade associations to the work, if we are to produce a durable and market sensitive regulatory system. So it is encouraging to see so many people here today, and I hope that you will not be backward in coming forward with your constructive comments, criticisms and questions.*

The tone of this speech, to a gathering of senior bankers, could be described as "chummy", "we are all in this together" was the watchword. To some extent that is understandable. It was the first real exposure of the banking community to the new FSA. The audience would be both curious and skeptical, and not without a sizeable sprinkling of those who totally disliked the idea of the new regulatory system.

There was another element that had not been directly apparent when the B of E was responsible for the supervision of banking activities. The banks, and other regulated organizations, were going to pay for it by means of levies made by the FSA, their size calculated according to a formula. This was a burden which the regulated institutions found irksome, but one which also unwittingly placed constraints on the workings of the FSA, despite the fact it now has 2600 staff and a £323 million annual budget allocation.

One important point made by Mr. Davies was that regulation was a collaborative undertaking with the regulated. He also drew attention to the regulator's role in protecting depositors, investors and other customers of financial institutions.

As mentioned earlier in this chapter, effective regulation is a tri-partite arrangement involving the regulator, the regulated and those using the services of the regulated. If the latter do not become involved through the reasonable exercise of "caveat emptor" by making their own assessment of what they are seeking from financial institutions, the regulatory body is unlikely to achieve its objectives.

Not everyone is capable of examining what is on offer, therefore more attention needs to be paid to educating them so that they will be able to do so.

There was another review of the regulatory regime carried out by a Task Force in 2003.

The Task Force was established in February 2003 following responses to the HM Treasury Green Paper on **"The Financial System and Major Operation Disruption"**.

The Task Force examined the need for a legislative response to deal with the threat of <u>major operational disruption</u> in the UK financial system.

On 3 December 2003 the Task Force published its final report.

The Task Force found that existing contractual mechanisms and legal provisions available to market participants and infrastructures were generally sufficient to allow the financial sector to manage risks appropriately. It concluded that such mechanisms, together with co-ordinated contingency planning across the public and private sectors were best suited to the particularly international and interconnected nature of the UK's financial markets. However, the Task Force also put forward eight recommendations to further improve the UK's preparedness for dealing with major operational disruption in the financial system.

> *The conclusion that no statutory powers are needed is based not only on the work that has already been undertaken to address business continuity issues but also on the need for further improvements. In particular, the Task Force has put forward eight recommendations to help further improve the resilience of UK financial markets:*
>
> ***Recommendation 1:*** *Market participants and the financial authorities should continue to <u>place a high priority on business continuity planning.</u>*
>
> ***Recommendation 2:*** *Market participants and their trade associations should work to ensure <u>that private contracts are reviewed to take account of major operational disruption</u>. A useful starting point for such reviews is the "contracts checklist" put forward in the FMLC's report on emergency powers.*
>
> ***Recommendation 3:*** *Market infrastructures should ensure that they have specific rather than general powers to deal with major operational disruption. They should also ensure that the mechanism for invoking these powers is flexible enough to be operated successfully in a crisis.*
>
> ***Recommendation 4:*** *The UK financial authorities should continue to contribute to international efforts to develop recognised good business continuity practice for systemically important market infrastructures. Their application in the UK should recognise <u>that the prime responsibility for business continuity planning rests with the senior management of firms and market infrastructures.</u>*
>
> ***Recommendation 5:*** *Participants in significant markets should consider*

whether there would be benefits from further defining the principles on which to base claims arising from the delayed performance of contracts following major operational disruption.

Recommendation 6: *The financial authorities should aim to clarify further, and publicise, their respective roles in the event of major operational disruption.*

Recommendation 7: *The financial authorities should consider with market participants the need for a high-level committee to help ensure co-ordination across financial markets in the event of major operational disruption.*

Recommendation 8: *The UK financial authorities should continue to promote international co-operation and co-ordination in developing responses to major operational disruption.*

For each recommendation, the Task Force has suggested how it could be implemented. It has also proposed that the Tripartite Standing Committee on Financial Stability comprised of the three financial authorities — HM Treasury, FSA and Bank of England — should monitor progress in meeting the recommendations, and publish a progress report in October 2004 and annually thereafter.

Finally, it should be stated clearly that nothing in this report is intended to conflict with the wider overhaul of emergency powers being considered in connection with the Civil Contingencies Bill. Some events which could give rise to major operational disruption in the financial services sector could also give rise to urgent human and social requirements which would have to be addressed by the authorities using emergency powers.

We can see from both these reviews that "systemic risks" and "major market disruptions" were by no means an unanticipated concept before September 2007. At the same time the review was carried out following the 9/11 Twin Towers disaster in New York and it was a terrorist inspired type of disaster that the Task Force had in mind.

However, if the recommendations of the 2003 Task Force had been acted upon by the implementation of a clearly spelled out strategy, subject to direction by an appointed supremo, the authorities could have dealt with the Northern Rock crisis in a much more timely and effective manner. The underlining in the "Recommendations" highlights those aspects which, had they been effectively implemented, would have at the very least alleviated some of the September 2007 problems. It was quite clear that although an understanding of the need for a strategy existed, implementation of it was far from perfect.

Of course there is a measure of hindsight in that assessment, but time after time the Tripartite authorities discussed the need for contingency planning for a seismic event but there is very little evidence that they acted to prepare such a plan, or if they did, no evidence that their organizations were capable of implementing it.

The Northern Rock saga pin-pointed deficiencies in the UK regulatory system which could be discussed *ad infinitum* but what is more important now is to assess the future value of the improvements which are being proposed.

The first indications of the direction in which improvements would be made came In December 2007. Government plans to improve the authority of the Bank of England's financial stability section were mooted and although following a Treasury issued Consultative paper there would have been much activity behind the scenes, it was June 2008 before results started to appear in the public domain.

The first indications were of tension between the views of HM Treasury and the Bank over who should head up the Section with responsibility for monetary policy at the Bank, and to act as a Deputy Governor. Mr. King apparently wanted an economist and proposed Charles Bean, the Bank's Chief Economist. The Treasury was said to wish to see a "city heavyweight" in the post to balance Mr. King's academic economist's background. According to a public statement made by Mr. King, his opinion was that,

> This is the Deputy Governor for Monetary Policy and it is essential that it should be filled by someone with a professional background in monetary policy, particularly as the economy enters the most difficult period since 1997.

The Treasury views were expressed by Alistair Darling, the Chancellor. In a statement to Parliament he said he would,

> Learn from the example that we had with the monetary policy committee and bring in outside expertise to advise the governor and of course the appropriate deputy governor on financial stability.

The basis of the new proposals included a "beefed up" depositor protection scheme; there would be a new insolvency regime just for banks; a new body would be created to oversee the "special resolution regime" for banks in trouble, with powers to declare them insolvent and to take them over for the protection of depositors' funds.

There was much speculation in early June 2008 as to how these proposals would be "tweaked" and then implemented and who should have ultimate responsibility for their operation and results. The media had a great time guessing at what the outcome would be and in their cult of personality bashing, building up conflicts and potential conflicts between the parties.

On 10th June the Bank published a list of its "Strategic priorities for 2007/08", all very laudable, but perhaps too much in the "we have heard it all before" category.

On 11th June a bit more came into the public domain when Mr. King addressed a British Banker's Association (BBA) conference and shone light on some of the new proposals that were under consideration. In the course of his speech he introduced a possible new consumer compensation scheme that would require "some pre-funding", a very unpopular idea with the banks that were already collectively liable for up to £4 billion a year for the existing scheme.

Another point was a proposal for the creation of a new permanent funding scheme to replace the £50 billion facility put in place earlier in the year to ease the credit crunch and to which the banks had not resorted, fearful of a stigma being attached to utilization of it.

There were contributions from the audience on these and other matters of concern.

On 18th June Sir John Gieve, a deputy Governor of the Bank with responsibility for the stability of the financial system, who was heavily criticized by the Select Committee as recorded elsewhere, and who still had 2 ½ years of his term of office to run, announced that he would "step down" at the end of 2008.

On 20th June hard information began to emerge on the changes to be made in the powers of the B of E, including changes in its leadership (apart from Mr. King). A new chief economist and a new Deputy Governor, both appointees favoured by Mr. King were announced.

The proposed committee to oversee financial stability would be set up, reporting to Mr. King. This was thought to give the bank a much improved "early warning" system accompanied by specific legal powers to take action. The new committee was expected to come into being in the first half of 2009.

Some clues as to the way in which the brief for the proposed new committee might be developed came in April from Mr. King's replies to a questionnaire given to him by the Treasury Committee. His replies to Question 9 read:,

First, a lesson from Northern Rock is that the Bank needs to be directly

involved with a bank for which a support operation may be necessary prior to giving that support.

That points to adopting a model of graduated Bank involvement. In periods of calm, when financial stability risks are low, the FSA would be responsible for discussions with banks. In periods of heightened stress the Bank would join the FSA in engaging with vulnerable banks. Finally in periods of severe stress, in which support had been, or was about to be, provided, the Bank of England would take the lead with the bank(s) in question.

Second, we need to strengthen the connection between system-wide risk analysis and the outlook for individual banks and we need to communicate our analysis of the risks more sharply. It is no good identifying the right risks if no one responds to that analysis.

Third, the Bank will need to adapt its crisis management planning to take account of the new resolution regime. This will be necessary regardless of which body is given responsibility for implementing the regime.

Fourth, I intend the Bank to contribute to the design of regulatory and incentive structures for the financial system, to try to curb the excessive build-up of risk taking and credit creation which was seen ahead of the recent crisis.

There can be little doubt from the foregoing that Mr. King had correctly and fully identified the principal weaknesses in the existing Tripartite structure.

It lacked a clear leader who could act as such without regard to the internecine rivalries, jealousies or just plain apathy that appeared to plague the existing arrangements. Alternatively the situation must have been that everybody believed that someone else had ultimate responsibility. In other words everybody was passing the buck but there was nowhere for it to stop.

Provided the re-structured organizations are adequately staffed with more competent and committed people than the existing set-up and are effectively trained and managed by "hands-on" middle and senior management it should be capable of effecting substantial improvements in the supervisory role carried out by the regulatory set-up in the UK.

Mr. King's responses to the whole of this questionnaire were direct, thoughtful and purposeful. There was no sense that he was just contributing to the "I say, therefore it shall be so" executive school. His responses addressed the various topics put to him in a much more straight-forward manner than those from the FSA's senior executives when they were questioned by the Select Committee earlier. A major problem in all large institutions is that although their executive managements start out with laudable objectives, size, internal politics and eventually disillusionment amongst employees and management set in so that original intentions and enthusiasm can degenerate into mediocrity.

Regulation in the United States

So far this Chapter has concentrated on the UK regulatory system. The regulatory system in the USA was subject to a range of deficiencies, some of which had been acknowledged for many years, others were belatedly brought to light when the crises erupted in 2007/8.

The US financial regulatory system is quite different from that in the UK. It is based on prescribed "rules" rather than a "principles" based system. In addition it is much more fragmented, being a composite of State and Federally controlled regulatory bodies that are responsible for the regulation of banking, insurance, futures and investment activities. Both State and particularly Federal regulators were subject to the effects of intensive lobbying of politicians by professionals acting on behalf of regulated bodies and opposition politicians. The result was that although a number of moves were made over the years to improve the powers of regulators, they were often thwarted by political lobbying at all levels. As noted in Chapter 4, Freddie and Fannie alone spent $170 million in six years on lobbyists, thereby managing to suppress the imposition of some, if not most of the stricter regulation directed at controlling aspects of their business and that of other players in the same fields.

Another factor, particularly in relation to the subprime crisis, the associated securitisation of its mortgages and the derivatives markets generally, was that these activities were not subject to regulation. The reasons for this will be discussed in chapter 14. In addition, the mortgage companies, credit rating agencies and other institutions involved in the gathering together of the mortgages, and the packaging and selling processes were not subject to regulation.

Why was this so?

For many years the US political emphasis has been on a "laisez faire" policy in all avenues of business, freedom from government intervention had been the watchword. A leading proponent of this philosophy was Alan Greenspan during his nearly twenty years as Federal Reserve Chairman. The extent of his influence (and power) must not be underestimated. In political circles he was acknowledged as an expert in all things financial.

It is true of all democratic states that the peoples' representatives in government are, for the most part, ordinary people. If they remain in politics long enough, some will become expert in particular fields, including finance and banking but most will acknowledge that they are not experts in any particular field. They therefore look to authoritative professionals to guide them. In matters of the economy and finance, they turned to Mr.Greenspan and seemed to hang on his every word.

Mr.Greenspan was a widely recognized authority on the management of the financial and economic status of the country and adhered to long held personal views on the best way to cope with his responsibilities. For many years he believed in the wealth-creating powers of the market place and frequently defended financial institutions by saying that risks could be handled by the markets themselves without using the introduction of regulatory intervention by government in every form of activity.

His basic belief for many years was that if one encouraged a financial market system to operate on trust, the players in it would understand that the reputation of their institutions had a significant economic value and would have to be guarded with care. There was a time, both in the UK and the USA, when that was the way financial institutions operated. For many years it seemed to work but then economies grew rapidly and other factors began to have an influence.

In the USA, as discussed earlier, Presidents and political parties promoted the idea of home-ownership for all Americans. From the 1990's a burgeoning economy accompanied by very low (official) interest rates and political backing encouraged the rapid growth of building and property finance in the private sector. The need to serve its funding requirements gave rise to the development of methods of raising finance, principally through the relatively new derivative markets. As early as 1994 Mr Greenspan was quoted as saying,

> *Risks in financial markets, including derivatives markets, are being regulated by private parties. There is nothing involved in federal regulation per se which makes it superior to market regulation.*

At the same time he acknowledged that derivatives could amplify crises because they tied together the fortunes of many apparently independent institutions (counter-parties). He said,

> *The very efficiency that is involved here means that if a crisis were to occur, that crisis is transmitted at a far faster pace and with some greater virulence.*

However, he qualified that observation by adding, 'that possibility was extremely remote and risk is a part of life."

Although many observers have placed a fair measure of blame for the 2007/8 crises on Mr. Greenspan's shoulders he was carrying out the wishes of his political "masters". Nevertheless, he was very much his "own man" and whilst he made or contributed to mistakes, he appears to have acted with integrity believing, possibly erroneously, that his policies were appropriate to the circumstances.

Nevertheless had the derivative and mortgage markets been subject to regulation, even if it had not been entirely effective, at least some the major problems that arose in 2007/8 might have been foreseen or avoided. But it was not Mr. Greenspan's policies that were at the root of the problems. Many other persons and factors were involved.

The concept of allowing "*the markets*" and the players in them to self-regulate is outdated and belongs to an era when businesses could be relied upon, on the whole, to act ethically and not to be driven solely by an ever-growing need to generate profits at all costs. There is also too much of a tendency towards "short-termism" in today's business strategies that does not take into account the longer term implications. In addition, undoubtedly the culture of awarding (often to oneself) substantial monetary executive rewards (considered by many now, in early 2009, to be of an obscene size) affected behaviour in financial institutions.

The subject of financial regulation in the USA has many facets and is worthy of a much more in-depth review than the space here allows.

14 The Blame Game

Although this Chapter has been headed "The Blame Game", its objective is not to name and shame but rather to identify where blame lies with a view to learning lessons for the future.

Although it is a tempting proposition, there is no point placing blame on individuals. The reasons for the development of the sub-prime crisis, the wider freezing of bank lending and more specifically the downfall of Northern Rock, lie in the financial system as a whole and the ethos which drives it.

The activities of banks have become very diverse, particularly over the last twenty years or more. The household name banks in the UK may still have a base of "high street" branch business, to which can be added credit card lending and mortgage lending, but they have also become prominent players in many other financially orientated businesses, particularly in what used to be called merchant banking in the UK or investment banking in the USA. By way of example, these wider activities include capital markets, investment and currency dealing and holding, mergers and acquisitions, fund management, bond issues, derivatives and the securitisation processes that have featured so prominently in the 2007 credit crisis, and all kinds of insurance. Some, such as the Royal Bank of Scotland, also invested in non-financial commercial activities.

Of course the regulators charged with the responsibility of guiding the financial community along a prudent path in most of those areas have also to be brought into the equation. They must accept, and in some cases have accepted, a measure of blame.

In nearly every case there is an interaction between the different activities undertaken by banks. It follows therefore that an essential feature of financial regulation is that if banks are to be regulated, regulation and supervision must cover all of their activities. It makes no sense to concentrate on one or two activities and gloss over the rest.

One approach in seeking to ascribe blame is to identify amongst all the parties involved the degree of blame that attaches to each. We can also look out for two types of blameworthy behaviour.

The first may be described as "avoidable blame", that is to say arising from actions, or a lack of action, when it should have been evident at an earlier time that particular actions or planning of actions were necessary or appropriate. In this category can be counted non-observance of guidelines imposed by law or custom.

The second category could be dubbed "un-avoidable blame", in other words arising from events that cannot be foreseen, or at least that are not readily apparent and are not within the control of any one person, company or business sector.

With these thoughts in mind, we can examine the culpability of each of the responsible parties in turn. As the root cause of the 2007 financial problems was the sub-prime mortgage market in the USA we shall deal with it first. Although some references have been made to it in earlier chapters, the crisis that erupted in the latter half of 2008 had wider causes that will be examined in later chapters.

The Sub-prime crisis

Sub-prime mortgage lending has been around for many years but a Federal Trade Commisssion testifying on "Home Equity Lending Abuses in the Sub-prime Mortgage Industry" in March 1998 stated that 90% of sub-prime lending took place after 1996. The Commission detailed a number of abusive practices used indiscriminately by lenders against the interests of borrowers. The Commission claimed to be using its enforcement authority to "protect consumers from these abuses". Abuses that ten years later appeared to be even more rife.

Much the same story emerged in 2000 and in 2003. Even Freddie Mac commented on the same abuses. Stories about the widespread use of abusive practices by lenders surfaced frequently from then onwards. At the end of 2006 "The New York Times" ran an article forecasting that 20% of subprime loans made in the previous two years were likely to go into foreclosure. In January 2007 the F.B.I reported that fraud cases in the subprime market were rising rapidly.

By June 2007 observers were noting that although there had been a "melt down" in the subprime market it had probably been contained. The Federal Reserve Bank held a hearing in June 2007 on "what regulators could do to address aggressive abusive lending practice", the same topic as was pin-pointed by that other Commission ten years before. The Bank set new rules for subprime lending shortly afterwards.

In July 2007 the FSA also commented on its findings of "poor sales practices within the subprime market in the UK."

From the foregoing rather sketchy picture one can see a pattern that was endemic in the subprime lending market. Lenders maximizing their gains at the expense of borrowers, some of whom may have been at fault for taking up loans they knew that they could ill-afford but most of whom were honest borrowers duped by the lenders. They were offered 30-year loans at a relatively attractive interest rate for the first two years, a rate that increased substantially at the end of that period whether or not the reference rate had increased. (The reference rate was the rate obtained on certain US Treasury Bills) There were also substantial penalties if the borrower wished to transfer the loan elsewhere. Most loans were also "balloon type", i.e. there was no monthly amortization.

The circumstances just described highlight two areas of potential blame. The first lies with the lenders because of the widespread abusive practices in which they indulged. This was not a question of anecdotal stories, the practices were identified and complained about by many individuals and organizations in many parts of the USA. They were also noted and discussed by legislators and regulators, as demonstrated above, year after year with very little being done to limit the abuse. Why? The lenders' political lobbying was far too strong and the Wall Street banks were interested only in keeping the flow of mortgages coming because they were making record profits out of the associated derivatives business.

This became a predatory industry unworthy of any democratic country. Of course there was a place for it when offered by reputable lenders who cared for their clients, but those appear to have been few and far between. Not even Freddie and Fannie were immune.

The second area of blame lay with the legislators and regulators, and there were many because in the USA both Federal and State authorities had jurisdiction. Those measures that were proposed or taken were largely cosmetic. They made little difference to the underlying problems. As recently as December 2007 President Bush signed **"The Mortgage Forgiveness Debt Relief Act"**.

What did this Act do?

It reduced income taxes at the time of a foreclosure. For example, if a person bought a home for $100,000 and at the time of foreclosure it was worth $110,000, until the Act came along, that person was liable to tax on the $10,000. After the Act was passed, the foreclosure wiped out the entire debt.

What a relief for the borrower! If ever there was a case of "a double whammy" that was it!

Also in December 2007 the Federal Reserve, State and other agencies added a number of other reliefs and imposed limitations on lenders, but "The Boston Globe" summed up the new situation by writing,

> *The Fed's action was applauded by lenders for its moderation, and criticized by consumer advocates for the same reason.*

After ten years of tinkering or deliberately doing nothing, the authorities hardly covered themselves in glory.

The Securitisation process

One has to go back to the early 1990's for clues as to why the securitisation processes got out of hand. As noted in Chapter 3 there were considerable objections by both the Federal Reserve Chairman, Alan Greenspan, the Senate and the House of Representatives, not to mention more than one President, to the regulation of derivatives.

In 1997 the Commodity Futures Trading Commission, the Federal agency that regulated options and futures trading began to explore the regulation of derivatives. Its concern was that unregulated, opaque trading practices could, "threaten our regulated markets or, indeed the economy without any Federal agency knowing about it." The Commission called for greater disclosure of trades and the setting aside of reserves to cushion against losses. The Treasury Secretary was of the opinion that merely discussing new regulation threatened the derivatives market. Mr.Greenspan joined in by warning that too many rules would damage Wall Street and would prompt traders to take this business overseas. (A substantial part of the structures used were already offshore.)

The Treasury Secretary, Robert E Rubin, ex-Goldman Sachs (and who later managed Citigroup) subsequently said that he favoured the regulation of derivatives and increases in potential loss reserves when he was at the Treasury, but saw no way of achieving this at the time.

There was a widely expressed view that as this branch of investment and finance was managed by major investment banks with at that time a reputation for expertise, the industry was capable in a democratic environment of controlling itself. In 2003 Mr. Greenspan's objections were voiced as,

> *What we have found over the years in the marketplace is that derivatives have been an extraordinarily useful vehicle to transfer risk from those who shouldn't be taking it to those who are willing to and are capable of doing so. We think it would be a mistake to more deeply regulate the contracts.*

Also in 2003 Warren Buffett in an annual letter to shareholders of his investment company wrote,

> *Large amounts of risk, particularly of credit risk, have become concentrated in the hands of relatively few derivatives dealers. The troubles of one could quickly infect the others.*

By 2004/5 Mr. Greenspan's opinion was not shared by a number of prominent and successful financiers. Warren Buffett entered the fray once again. He considered that,

> *derivatives were financial weapons of mass destruction carrying dangers that, whilst now were latent, were potentially lethal.*

George Soros said he avoided using derivatives "because we do not really understand how they work". That statement gives some insight into one of the reasons for his success as an investor.

In 2008 Mr.Greenspan still held on to his views. In a speech at Georgetown University he said,

> *The problem is not that the contracts failed, rather people using them got greedy. A lack of integrity spawned the crisis.*

Whilst that was no doubt true, a lack of effective regulation enabled them to do so.

An oft-repeated complaint about the derivative markets is that they lack transparency. From the outset there have been no rules obliging institutions to disclose the size of the derivative positions that they hold nor to allocate reserves against losses that could arise, nor indeed to impose limits on the volume of this business undertaken in relation to the size of their other activities. Yet as far back as 2002 the General Accounting Office was asked by the chairman of the House sub-committee that dealt with financial matters to study the risks associated with derivatives. When that office released its report in 2004 it identified significant gaps and weaknesses in the oversight of derivatives.

It expressed the opinion that,

> *The sudden failure or abrupt withdrawal from trading of any of these large US dealers could cause liquidity problems in the markets and could pose risks to others, including federally insured banks and the financial system as a whole. In some cases intervention has and could result in a financial bailout paid for or guaranteed by taxpayers.*

With the benefit of hindsight we can see that the office foretold what could happen and what did happen in 2007 and 2008.

Securitisation in the derivatives markets is an essential service in modern economies. Markets today are global in extent. The derivatives markets enabled borrowers in one part of the world to be put in touch with lenders (i.e.investors) in another part and did much to enable strong economic growth, world wide, up to 2007. But the events of 2007, and more so of 2008 demonstrate that such a large and important market, when principally conducted by a very few major investment banks cannot be allowed to operate behind closed doors, where not even the participants know how deeply involved they have become and the extent of the risks that they have incurred. Furthermore, although intended to supply the needs of international investors, far too much of the derivatives ended up on US, UK and European bank balance sheets as assets. That has been a major reason for the financial crises suffered by individual banks.

The Wall Street investment banks

The multi-national Wall Street investment banks played a central role in the development of the credit crisis. They did so as creators, sellers and intermediaries in the securitization of assets into investment bonds. Without their involvement that business would never have got off the ground. It needed their reputation, marketing skills, contacts and global financial clout.

There was nothing wrong with it as an innovative concept that did much to accelerate economic growth globally. It also made substantial profits for the investment banks. It was hailed as the new way forward, lauded in many professional quarters, the subject of awards for excellence. It represented the new, modern, sophisticated investment and funding medium.

We are only concerned with the RMBS aspects but it had many other branches and played a part in the funding of most types of credit provision. From an international professional investors' point of view it provided better returns and greater security, at least that was how it was perceived both by its purveyors and by its investors. It was a form of alchemy devised by what were reckoned to be super-clever bankers and lawyers.

It had one very important new feature. It removed all liability for loss from the provider of the underlying security, (the "originator" in technical parlance) yet provided what was considered a cast iron guarantee for the acquirer of the bonds that were generated. It was the answer to everyone's prayers – for a few years.

So, what went wrong? Quite simply in order to increase the supply of investment bonds for an expanding and hungry market, those same Wall Street banks (and others around the world who also generated this type of derivative) paid more attention to the success of their efforts than to the source and quality of the assets that they were packaging to provide the underlying security. It did not seem to matter. Being in the USA and sourcing much of the underlying assets in the USA which had a dynamically expanding, low interest rate economy from which came the main source of the banks' raw materials, namely mortgages on new build property, the pyramid that they were creating just could not collapse. That was the perceived wisdom in all but a few minds, including in those of financial regulators and the Federal government.

That was the scene until it all began to unravel from early 2007.

Why?

Because the benign conditions in which it had flourished started to disappear one by one, blown away by one thing, substantially higher Federally imposed US interest rates. This put pressure on mortgage borrowers, at first those in the lowest income brackets, but the effect gradually spread further up the chain. Defaults by borrowers became the order of the day, reflected in the demise of some of the lenders, including some large ones. This meant that the AAA ratings which provided security for the investor's bonds in many cases became worthless. The problems grew when investors began to realize that nobody (including the banks) seemed to know where the poor quality mortgage loans had been placed. What we have to remember is that there were well in excess of 150,000 different issues of derivatives (of course only a proportion of them were RMBS backed).

What followed was a collapse in the base mortgage markets where by 2008 the default rate was actually no more than 20-25% in the sub-prime market, and much lower at about 9%, although higher than normal in the prime market, translated into 80 – 100% falls in the perceived value of the bonds purchased by investors (or held by investing banks as treasury reserves, sometimes referred to as "assets available for sale").

The reason for this catastrophic fall in value was that investors had lost all interest in acquiring securitised bonds and those that held them could not unload them because the secondary market in them ceased to function. The result was that the market "froze solid". This type of business at least for the foreseeable future was finished.

The base cause has been noted earlier as the increase in interest rates, but alongside that has to be put the greed of the bankers, those who earned fat multi-million dollar bonuses on the basis of the profits that were generated. It has been said authoritatively, although admissions of guilt are unlikely to appear, that those same bankers knew that much of what they were packaging into ever more esoteric products was "sub-prime", in other words "not of merchantable quality".

They have a lot to answer for but merely losing their jobs, as many have done, is insufficient retribution.

The monoline insurers and Credit rating agencies

The story of the monoline insurers and credit rating agencies is related in Chapter 6. Together their involvement was the key to the successful marketing of the RMBS bonds. Jointly, they created a mirage of quality around the bonds. Without their participation in the process, investors would have been obliged, if they were prudent, to look much more closely at what they were buying and the strength of its underlying mortgage securities. The Wall Street banks would have had to be much more forthcoming in their descriptions of the securities and undoubtedly would have found them much more difficult to sell.

Although those two types of institution were both closely involved in the securitization system they were not instrumental in its collapse. The credit rating agencies however quite patently did not carry out due diligence nearly as thoroughly as they should have done on the bonds that they were rating. To that extent they have to accept responsibility, not for the collapse but for ensuring the (temporary) unwarranted success of the RMBS market. They should also share the blame for its demise.

As part of a critical review by the EU's Commissioner for Internal Markets, Charlie McCreevy, he received the report of an enquiry into the activities of the Credit Rating Agencies that he had commissioned from the EU Committee of Securities Regulators. The Chairman of this committee had already voiced the opinion that the rating agencies were less culpable for the sub-prime crisis than Wall Street investment banks and investors.

Notwithstanding, Mr.McCreevy was quoted as saying that the status quo was unacceptable and that he would over-rule the findings of the Committee if he thought necessary. He also criticized the fact that the agencies are paid by those whose products they are rating, namely, the Wall Street investment banks.

Unfortunately, unless the credit rating agencies can be successfully sued by someone, they will suffer little or no loss as a result of their involvement, yet over the years they earned substantial fees for services that were since proved to have been a waste of money.

The monoline insurers possibly relied on everyone else to carry out due diligence (including the credit rating agencies). However as they contracted to pick up the pieces when it all went wrong, they will suffer, and have suffered substantial losses as a result of their involvement. It follows that they will shoulder part of the blame, whether they agree or not. Despite that, the plans of governments to buy the so-called "toxic assets" (ie. derivatives) from banks and hold them until the market recovers, or to maturity, may mean that the monoliners are rescued from the threat of major wholesale defaults.

The Media

In both the UK and the USA we are proud of our free press. It is an essential element in any democracy but there are times, and the reporting of the credit crisis and, in the UK the 2007/08 Northern Rock story was one of them, when the press does not always act responsibly. No one objects to its passion for reporting events "warts and all", but when its reporting amounts to nothing more than the creation of a "good story" or a "scoop" the media does the general public a disservice.

As far as the liquidity problems of Northern Rock were concerned, the media played no part in their creation. However after the "rescue" process began to be reported there were many inaccurate, speculative articles and sensationalist reporting that must have influenced the public perception of what was taking place because the media was the only source of information available to the man in the street. But, at the end of the day, none of it significantly affected the outcome, except perhaps the constant references to " protecting the interests of the taxpayer"

With regard to the run on Northern Rock by depositors the story is quite different. What may be referred to as the "Robert Peston story" has been related in Chapter 7. The background to it, as presented in the Report of the Select Committee included the following:

> On the afternoon of Thursday 13 September, according to the Governor of the Bank of England "rumours in the market started" in relation to the proposed operation. At 4.00 pm on that day, the Tripartite standing committee met at deputies level and <u>decided to bring forward the announcement of the operation to 7.00 am on Friday 14 September</u>. The Court of the Bank of England met on the evening of Thursday 13 September. The terms of the emergency liquidity assistance were finalised in the early hours of Friday 14 September. The announcement was made at 7.00 am that morning in the following terms,

> The Chancellor of the Exchequer has today authorized the Bank of England to provide a liquidity support facility to Northern Rock against appropriate collateral and at an interest rate premium. This liquidity facility will be available to help Northern Rock to fund its operations during the current period of turbulence in financial markets while Northern Rock

> *works to secure an orderly resolution to its current liquidity problems. The*
> *FSA judges that Northern Rock is solvent, exceeds its regulatory capital*
> *requirement and has a good quality loan book.*

Note that at this stage, this was no more than a Bank of England "liquidity support facility", it was not until later that the media brought in "the taxpayer at risk" concept which influenced all the subsequent actions and the eventual outcome in the shape of nationalization.

This was followed in a later section of the report by:

> *Before the provision of emergency liquidity assistance by the Bank of*
> *England to Northern Rock could be announced formally, the outlines of the*
> *operation were reported by the BBC—at 8.30 pm on BBC News 24 and*
> *then on other BBC media outlets. Several witnesses argued that the*
> *premature disclosure of the support operation in this way was instrumental*
> *in the run that followed. Mr Applegarth said that the leak "caused immense*
> *difficulties". He thought that, "it was the announcement of the facility being*
> *leaked that actually was the start of the run". The Chancellor of the*
> *Exchequer characterized the leak as "clearly very unhelpful". Sir Callum*
> *McCarthy told us: It was extremely unfortunate that the information leaked*
> *because it meant that instead of this being put in place as, "This is a*
> *solvent institution which has a cash flow problem and the Government is*
> *stepping in to make sure that it is saved', it became a panic measure or a*
> *response to something that was already in the making. Panic was how it*
> *was seen.*

As related earlier, Mr. Peston was adamant that his leaked "scoop" was not responsible for Northern Rock's problems. Of course not, but it certainly introduced a new dimension to them. It exacerbated them in a manner that might not have happened if the first public notification had been the official one, which as the Select Committee recorded had been scheduled for 7.00am on Friday 14th September. The decision to bring it forward from Monday 17th was made prior to the "leak" being broadcast. That is an important point since Mr.Peston, defended release of his "scoop" by saying that it would have been ingenuous to believe that the news could have been kept under covers until Monday 17th.

There is another aspect to this matter. Official announcements, and in this case including those by Northern Rock, can only be made to the media or through an internet web-site. There is no other mechanism for rapidly transmitting information directly to the public at large, and in this case, the Northern Rock depositors. The authorities are therefore in the hands of the media and have to rely on it to act responsibly.

Release of his "leaked scoop" in such a widespread manner prior to an official announcement can be viewed as a significant error of judgment, both by Mr. Peston and the BBC which after all is a public service broadcaster that is substantially funded by the public. It was quite apparent from the subsequent behaviour of both Mr. Peston and his employer that they held a different opinion. The BBC has to maintain a competitive position but should also pay attention to its responsibilities and privileged position. One could draw comparisons between this occasion and the Dr. Kelly / "Iraq weapons of mass destruction" case, although of course that episode had much more tragic consequences.

Northern Rock's management and Board

It was a commonly held opinion that primary responsibility for what happened to Northern Rock lay with its Board of Directors and its Chief Executive. However if we try to relate their responsibilities to the degree of blame for failing to carry out their responsibilities the picture becomes quite complicated. We have to examine two aspects.

Firstly, what were their statutory responsibilities and did they carry out them out professionally and effectively?

Secondly, to what extent should they have been expected to identify potential problems?

Company law dictates the overall nature of their responsibilities as company directors. They are also governed by the Combined Code for Corporate Governance 2003 and later revisions. Add to those the Listing Rules of the UK (stock exchange) Listing Authority. A company's board is required to state how it implements the various requirements and one of the ways it does so is by publishing in its Annual Report and Accounts how it conducts Corporate Governance. Northern Rock described how it did so in 5 pages of the 2006 Accounts entitled "**Corporate Governance**". They describe how the board operated, how it set up Committees of directors, including Committees responsible for overseeing Audit, Remuneration (of the directors), Risk and Internal Control. There were also an Asset and Liability Committee, a Chairman's Committee and an Executive Committee.

The responsibilities of each committee were clearly set out and were described in the Annual Report. The Board was comprised of Executive and non-executive directors, the latter forming the majority. The non-executive directors were considered (in the Report) to be independent and experienced in "a wide range of commercial or banking activities".

> *The board meets regularly throughout the year and_retains full and effective control_ over the company and its subsidiaries (the Group). It is*

collectively responsible for the success of the Group and _determines its strategy and policies_ whilst monitoring performance.

The Company had an induction and training policy for its directors,

every director should receive appropriate training when he or she is appointed to the board and subsequently as necessary. The Company's _induction process is designed to ensure that every new director understands his or her responsibilities_ as a director of the Company. Where appropriate_, the process also enables directors to build up an understanding of the Company, its business and the market in which it operates._

The initial induction programme is supported by an ongoing training programme for all directors to ensure _that they remain fully up to date with legal, regulatory and financial developments._ In addition to this programme, at Board meetings during 2006, a number of the Company's senior executives provided presentations concerning their areas of responsibility. This _ensures that the Board remains fully up to date on the Group's business._ All directors are also offered individual training on the application of the revised International accounting standards to the Company's business. The ongoing training process is enhanced by the annual appraisal process, where directors are _asked to identify areas where additional training is required._

The Chairman ensures that all directors are properly briefed on issues to be discussed at board meetings. All directors are able to obtain further advice or seek clarity on issues raised at board meetings from within the Company or from external professional sources.

In addition to this description of the implementation of Corporate Governance, the following extracts appear later in the Operating and Business Review,

The Board establishes the parameters for risk appetite for the Group through:

Setting strategic direction

Contributing to, and ultimately approving the annual operational plan

Regularly reviewing and monitoring the Group's performance in relation to risk through monthly Board reports.

> The Board delegates the articulation of risk appetite to the Management
> Board Asset and Liability Committee and ensures that this is in line with the
> strategy and the desired risk reward trade off for the Group. _Risk appetite_
> _is assessed against regular (often daily) controls and stress testing to_
> _ensure the limits are not compromised in abnormal circumstances._

Almost by definition "abnormal circumstances" are those that are least expected, such
as the closing down of the wholesale markets.

Northern Rock's analysis of the methods used for risk management is comprehensive
and covers another five pages.

When it reaches _"Liquidity Management"_ it continues,

> Liquidity risk arises from the mismatch in the cash-flows generated from
> current and expected assets, liabilities and derivatives. _The Group's_
> _liquidity policy is to ensure_ that it is able to meet retail withdrawals, _repay_
> _wholesale funds as they fall due_ **and meet current lending**
> **requirements**. _It also ensures that it meets FSA liquidity rules, which_
> _require the Group to be able to meet its Sterling obligations without_
> _recourse to the wholesale money markets for a period of at least five_
> _business days._

There were a further two paragraphs describing how Liquidity Risk was monitored and
managed.

The paragraphs dealing with liquidity management afford one clue as to where the
management's priorities may have lain in relation to liquidity, "The Group's liquidity policy
is (inter alia) to ensure - - - - (we) **meet current lending requirements**". Link that
objective to the declared policy of growing assets by +/- 20% per annum and perhaps it
became a first priority objective ahead of the maintenance of liquidity to meet the
repayment of wholesale and retail funds.

The Internal Control Committee monitors the systems of internal control.

> The system of internal control is designed to manage risk rather than
> eliminate it and in this regard _the Board considers that Northern Rock is a_
> _well-controlled risk averse business_ that _continues to adopt a prudent_
> _stance in the management of risk_. _The Board_ has reviewed the
> effectiveness of the system of internal control and _is satisfied that there_
> _is a sound system of internal control that safeguards shareholders'_
> _investments and the Company's assets._

It all sounds like a perfect set up, so why did the company hit the buffers?

Was it just another example of "I say, therefore it must be so"?

How does the Board's statement of its conduct of Corporate Governance / Risk Management square with the disaster that struck the company?

It is well established that a successful business of any kind cannot be conducted without exposure to risk and innovation. No one in business, government or regulatory circles in the case of financial businesses, disputes that fact. Difficulties arise, however when we try to analyze the nature and extent of risk that may be regarded as normal, acceptable, commercial risk-taking. Northern Rock's board was accused of pursuing an extreme business model. Yet the model it had adopted proved extremely successful and problem free for a number of years. Did it therefore qualify as acceptable risk-taking, or was it actually wilful recklessness?

After problems arose, most of the media comment and indeed the official view was that it amounted to wilful recklessness. Before real problems struck, the regulators were fully aware of the "extreme" policy and appeared to have had no problem with it. The rest of the banking and investment fraternity was perfectly comfortable with it, in fact for a number of years there were institutions, and they were major ones, which were falling over themselves to lend collectively up to £25 billion at a time to Northern Rock.

As we found out later in 2008 many household name banks, in the UK and the USA pursued "reckless" and even more extreme policies, yet were not subject by the media to the same level of criticism for doing so. Perhaps by 2008 it had come to be seen as the "norm".

Bearing in mind that Annual Reports and Accounts are published solely for the benefit of shareholders in the Company and for potential investors in it, those to whom they are addressed are entitled to expect them to express a factual situation in regard to the management of the Company. Any (ordinary) investor reading the 2006 Annual Report and Accounts could not do other than believe that all was well and that the management of the Company was in good hands. In addition, as late as August 2007, professional analysts and the investment press shared and expressed that belief.

The picture on Corporate Governance and Risk Management presented to us as just described in fact emulates the statements that appear in every set of publicly quoted company Annual accounts. They are produced by rote and sadly in most cases cannot be taken at face value. Apart from that fact the Annual Reports and Accounts of any large or even medium sized company nowadays have such a detailed and complex structure as to make it extremely difficult for even a professional to interpret the information contained in them and to really understand the true situation within the company's business.

The following extracts, admittedly referring to US companies, are from a book written in 1984, which illustrates that perhaps nothing much has changed and very few lessons have been learned.

The board of directors of any company is supposed to represent the interests of the owners – the shareholders. In doing this, the board's primary function is to oversee and evaluate the performance of the management in running the company, and if that performance is not satisfactory, to do something about it. The board's responsibility is to sit in judgment on the management, especially on the performance of the chief executive, and to reward, punish or replace the management as the board sees fit. That is what is supposed to happen. But it doesn't.

The chief executive presents an overall view of the company's activities and results. If he is so inclined he may go into details. Whatever the results, management always reports in effect how good they have been and are and will be, <u>despite whatever intolerable conditions hover over the horizon.</u>

What can an outside (non-executive) director do? He can ask a question that troubles him. It will be answered logically, if not in great detail. If he questions the answer he will be given more detail.

If he persists, he is casting himself in the role of a troublemaker, and no one likes a troublemaker. So, what does the director do, except to sit back in his chair, taste his cold coffee and desist.

Nominally, non-execs are elected by the shareholders, actually in most instances they serve at the pleasure of the chief executive.

If ever there is a conflict between board member and the chief executive, who stays and who goes?

If the Board is really there to represent the interests of shareholders, what is the chief executive doing on the board? He is the professional manager. He cannot represent the shareholders and impartially sit in judgment on himself.

In more than three-quarters of the Fortune 500 corporations (in 1984) the chief executive sits as chairman of the board.

These are extracts from a book "Managing" written in 1984 by Harold Geneen, for 17 years chief executive of ITT.

The underlining in both extracts has been added to emphasis those aspects which have a bearing on the determination of the competence of the directors in relation to the specific business strategies adopted by Northern Rock, ostensibly with their approval.

It may all sound very familiar, even today, to those who have sat in a boardroom. Not only that but in the first six months of 2008 there were many examples of CEO's and chairmen "keeping their pecker up" with glowing accounts of what they had achieved, only for us to learn sometimes only weeks later that the true facts were very different.

As noted elsewhere, the new Northern Rock Chairman, Mr Sandler examined the grounds on which one or more of the directors could be made liable for the company's present situation or for contributing to it, but later announced that there were no grounds on which an action was likely to succeed. We have also noted that others have considered the feasibility of taking legal action against the directors but this is a difficult course to pursue.

It is ironic that although Company law and other rules impacting directors' duties are all designed to afford reassurance for shareholders and others dealing with the company but at the same time when something for which the directors have clear responsibility goes wrong, it is very difficult to pin blame and to prove legal liability for damages on their part collectively as a Board or on the part of one or more of them.

The standard that generally has to be proved is that the board or a director was knowingly and wilfully negligent. Another version of that scenario is where it can be shown that a director wilfully "turned a blind eye". In this latter case of "turning a blind eye", the circumstances will be such that it can usually be assumed to have been done wilfully or deliberately.

In the case of the Northern Rock directors, the Chairman and Chief Executive have both on occasions claimed that the complete shut down of the markets was unforeseeable. But at what point in time could that be regarded as a justifiable conclusion? Was it months or days before the run on the 14th September 2007?

Neither the Bank of England nor the FSA claimed to have foreseen the looming problems much earlier, so why should the Northern Rock directors who had much less of an oversight of the markets have been expected to have "second sight"? Of course, it does not matter whether the closing down of the markets was foreseeable or not, the board claimed in its Annual Reports that "stress testing to ensure the limits are not compromised **in abnormal circumstances**" was carried out at its behest.

When interviewed by the Parliamentary Select Committee, both the Chairman, Dr Ridley and the CEO, Adam Applegarth said that in mid-September they had "two to three months funding available". Dr Ridley made the point that as at 13th September, it was the premature disclosure of the bank's approach to the Bank of England for a "back-up facility" which brought about pressure on the bank and the run on deposits, which built up to around £8 to 10 billion, and was what initially forced Northern Rock to activate the Bank of England facility.

They confirmed that they were conscious of the possibility of the wholesale markets becoming tighter, but the board was of the opinion that as they had always insisted on the maintenance of a quality mortgage book, any difficulties elsewhere would operate in their favour. They called it a "flight to quality". In most circumstances they should have been proved right but this time the markets became so jittery that no differentiation was made between the good and the bad.

Northern Rock's problems were compounded by the fact that although it is now accepted that there was a common cause, two completely different wholesale banking markets collapsed at virtually the same time, the bond securitization market and the inter-bank lending market. Northern Rock relied heavily on both for its funding needs. We shall deal with the derivatives market first.

Applegarth was said to have visited the USA six times a year. Northern Rock's own involvement in the issue of securitised bonds had been considerable (£42.6 billion by mid-2007). It had a direct and continuous involvement with seven of the major Wall Street investment banks participating in the issue of its RMBS bonds. In all probability, at various levels in Northern Rock there was daily contact.

Bear in mind also that asset backed commercial paper securitization, of which RMBS was a significant component, had for the previous three or four years been generally recognized in banking and investment circles as one of the most important and reliable funding source developments in many years. It was widely used and was said to be one of the main enabling forces behind global economic growth. Much was written in financial journals extolling its virtues. Award ceremonies celebrated the achievements of the principle players. By the end of 2005, 836 banks globally reported that they used it. The market was enormous as we have noted earlier. The major Wall Street investment banks were heavily involved and generated huge new profit flows from it. The prestigious position that those major banks enjoyed globally in financial circles, together with the approbation of the Credit Rating Agencies and Monoline insurers ensured that until some time in 2007 the whole securitisation process was accorded an aura of respectability and infallibility. It was seen as a "win – win" situation for everybody involved.

The securitization process could not have been achieved without the involvement of law firms to create the appropriate structures and to draft the documentation. Who was at the forefront of this, at least in the UK?

A long established and highly regarded firm, Allen & Overy that has always been regarded as one of the top firms for finance work, led the way throughout Europe and had a substantial presence in New York. It now has around 2600 attorneys and 28 worldwide offices. Over the years the Allen and Overy practice developed a particular position as an adviser on banking, but it is also at the forefront of other innovative legal developments.

Which firm created Northern Rock's securitization process and the Granite Master Issuer structure? Of course it was Allen and Overy. Northern Rock's board wanted nothing but the best.

Included in a list of Allen and Overy achievements was: advising Barclays Capital, Citigroup and Merrill Lynch on the establishment of Northern Rock's £20 billion Mortgage Backed Note programme. The Granite Master Issuer PLC deal, registered with the SEC (Securities and Exchange Commission, USA) was the first UK securitisation deal to obtain a shelf registration in the USA.

Another achievement attributed to Allen & Overy was to advise Barclays Bank PLC and Lehman Brothers International (Europe) as lead managers on the £423 million securitisation of the first loss piece on Northern Rock's Granite master trust transactions and stand alone deals. This was the first time an originator (Northern Rock) used the synthetic securitisation of the first loss piece on its master trust and standalone transactions as a means of transferring the risk in these deals to third party investors. It was named "MBS Deal of the Year" at the ISR Awards in 2005. The International Securitization Review (ISR) is a specialist periodical for the securitization industry.

An appropriate question that should be addressed is the extent to which Northern Rock's "expert" investment banker and legal adviser associations influenced the degree of dependency that the Board placed on wholesale funding and also influenced the degree of faith they had in its suitability.

Since 14th September 2007 Northern Rock has been accused by many not the least by Professor Willem Buiter, a founding member of the Bank of England's Monetary Policy Committee of, in his words, "an extremely aggressive and high risk strategy". Others called it "reckless". As events turned out, it may be regarded as an imprudent but not necessarily reckless policy, driven by a vision of ever increasing profits (and executive bonuses).

Applegarth has been described as the "architect" of Northern Rock's funding strategies.

But was he really the driving force behind them? When the securitization programme was commenced he was nothing more than the CEO of a modest sized, North of England ex-building society mortgage lender. He was said to be ambitious. Was he seduced by the blandishments of the aforementioned global investment banks and lawyers, in the expectation of joining them as one of the "big boys"? The investment banks were well known for their aggressive marketing tactics and they may have shown him how his ambitions could become a reality.

The gathering storms in the sub-prime market and in the securitization markets were recognized in the US many months before June 2007 and yet Applegarth's presentation of the interim accounts in July was still entirely positive and apart from reservations about the effects of increases in UK interest rates on short-term profits, made no mention of impending funding difficulties although he later claimed before the Select Committee that "they were conscious of the possibility of the wholesale markets becoming tighter". For that to have been the case, he must have had such an "awareness" at the time the 2007 Interim Accounts were issued in July 2007 and at the time he subsequently issued press releases up to September of that year. The question then arises, why did he make no mention of it?

He may genuinely not have recognized the potential seriousness of the "tightening" of the markets. He was certainly not alone in that. In its review of the FSA's supervision of Northern Rock, the FSA Internal Audit team said,

> *The extent of the market disruption that occurred in the crisis period – to wholesale funding markets, including securitization markets – was generally not foreseen by commentators. It was the crystalisation <u>of a low probability, high impact risk.</u>*

It is not clear whether the "commentators" referred to were FSA officers or media commentators (or both).

Northern Rock was so heavily committed to the securitization markets that they and their changing status must have preoccupied Applegarth for much of the time. If they did not, then was he turning a blind eye? Did he not wish to face up to the prospect that serious problems could be in prospect, or perhaps because he knew that Northern Rock / Granite issued bonds were all of good quality he hoped or believed that the majority of other bank's issues were the same? Had that actually been the case one could appreciate that he may not have had cause for real concern.

Why, apparently, were no searching questions posed to him in the boardroom on this topic? If the directors were as clued-in as the Corporate Governance pronouncements claimed, they must have been uneasy about the markets, at the very least seeking reassurances. Dr Ridley did confirm to the Treasury Select Committee that these matters "were discussed in the boardroom" but with what intensity and with what resulting action, if any, we do not know.

A key question is whether the directors took unnecessary risks by adopting a certain business strategy, and did they consciously recognize that risk? It could reasonably be maintained that they were not aware of the risk that they were taking because their perception of the risks was based on the top-level professional advice they received and it indicated that there was no significant risk.

Had events unfolded just a little more favourably, the bank would have got through the difficulties of August / September 2007 without major problems.

Those questions about the extent of potential risk involved are now being posed with hindsight. If we change tack and look at the situation differently, why should the directors have been uneasy? The board was being advised and encouraged by world leaders in the securitization based funding strategy. It was paying them handsomely for their services.   There had never been any problem funding in the inter-bank market, notwithstanding the year-by-year growth in funding requirements.   They knew that the quality of the security underpinning Northern Rock's securitized bonds was as good as it gets. The Granite programme was substantially over-collateralized by the pool of mortgages held in trust for it.   What more could be expected of the board?

The company had made exceptionally good progress for a number of years. Business and profits had been growing at about 20% per year (Applegarth claimed that a constant rate of growth had been maintained for seventeen years).   The Company had achieved a status as fifth largest mortgage lender in the UK.

One of the criticisms leveled at the FSA was that it should have questioned this rate of growth. It was claimed that it was far above the industry norm, even during a period when most of the market players were producing impressive results. The stock and housing markets had been rising for several years. Until the second half of 2007 nobody seems to have given a thought to the possibility that a crunch-time was imminent, notwithstanding that all professionals in financial markets know that markets rise and fall in a cyclical pattern.

At the end of 2006 Northern Rock was one of the darlings of the UK stock market, it was also one of the prime-rated FTSE 100 companies. Management had recommended a 33% increase in the 2007 interim dividend payable and planned a £200 million reduction in excess capital through a share buy-back. The company appeared to have a wide spread of funding sources, retail deposits from four countries (plus internet customers), wholesale deposits (of which 50% was for longer than a one year term), covered bonds, securitized bonds and capital (in different classes of stock). There can be little doubt, based on the statements made in more than one set of Annual Accounts that the Board and the CEO believed that they had achieved a good spread of funding sources as a protection against one of them proving unreliable. They had very consciously taken steps to achieve that objective. What they did not stress test for was the possibility of <u>two</u> or more principal sources of funding drying up at the same time. Something that it has to be admitted was a "low probability", as noted elsewhere.

One of the most oft-repeated criticisms of the board, and particularly of the CEO was that they had adopted a seriously flawed funding strategy, relying too much on wholesale sources. About 75% of the company's funding came from the wholesale markets, compared to less than 50% for its peers. But of that 75%, about 50% was off-balance sheet raised from securitized bonds. It should not have given rise to direct problems (and did not do so). The liability for credit risk had been shifted to the bond investors. That was the manner in which the securitization process was universally structured in the financial markets. That was also the view of the FSA and the Bank of England appeared to concur with that view. Prior to August 2007 they seemed to be unconcerned.

At all times the bank claimed to be within the regulatory liquidity and solvency requirements although a later investigation in 2008 by the FSA Internal Audit team discovered that the capital ratio requirements had been breached in April 2007 but corrected by June. Yet the FSA expressed no misgivings with the bank's strategies, and as we have noted elsewhere, had paid very little attention to Northern Rock in the previous two years. What more could the board, without the benefit of hindsight have done?

The worst that was likely to happen from the reliance on securitization was that the bank would have been unable to fund future mortgage lending in that manner if the market shut down. But why should it do so? It was a $15 trillion market, one of the largest and most widely used in the world.

In relation to the other arms of funding, Northern Rock had been steadily increasing its retail deposit base year by year and had taken what steps were available to it to maximize exposure to the retail deposit market. At £20.1 billion (end 2006) its retail deposits were in a healthy state. A sizeable part of those retail deposits were on fixed maturities of six months or more, they could not have been withdrawn without depositors suffering a penalty. That was all part of Northern Rock's strategy to reduce risk.

Its wholesale funding in the inter-bank markets amounted to £22.25 billion (end 2006) and consisted of a mix of short and medium term maturities. Up to September 2007 (or possibly a little earlier) they had been renewed as they fell due without any difficulty. Only the Northern Rock management (and possibly the Bank of England) know the identity and numbers of institutions involved but it is apparent that over a number of years they were all quite prepared to provide relatively short term funds to Northern Rock and roll them over, until the credit crunch came along bringing with it all the uncertainties surrounding the many UK banks involved in the issue and holding of securitised bonds which by then, in the general panic that developed, were all considered to be of doubtful value.

Had the uncertainties concerning the holding of securitized bonds by banks not surfaced, there was no reason why Northern Rock should not have continued to source funds in the inter-bank markets on the strength of its past performance and the perceived quality of its loan book, and of course its high credit rating.

There is one aspect that has not been mentioned so far, although the Parliamentary Select Committee made reference to it. It is regarded as good practice for banks to set up lines of credit with other banks by paying an "insurance premium" to them. That is to say, for an up-front payment a bank can ensure that for a specified period of time another bank will be committed to lending it up to a specified amount for a pre-determined period. Northern Rock said it had some "insurance" of this type, but it was an inadequate amount. The Board had to look at it on a "cost / benefit" basis as it would not have been cheap to cover £25 billion or so. They may also have been influenced by the fact that they were more or less committed to increasing profits annually at a significant rate and what could possibly be viewed as being an unnecessary expense would have detracted from that objective.

It may have made good newspaper stories to pillory the Board members and management officers of Northern Rock and their business strategies but much of it was unjustified and there were others elsewhere much more deserving of criticism.

The most comprehensive report on Northern Rock's downfall, although possibly not wholly un-biased, was posted by the Parliamentary Select Committee after it held numerous hearings and invited contributions from a variety of sources over a period of many weeks. In relation to the responsibilities of the board of Northern Rock this was its conclusion,

> *The directors of Northern Rock were the principal authors of the difficulties that the company has faced since August 2007. It is right that members of the Board of Northern Rock have been replaced, though haphazardly, since the company became dependent on liquidity support from the Bank of England. The high-risk, reckless business strategy of Northern Rock, with its reliance on short- and medium-term wholesale funding and an absence of sufficient insurance and a failure to arrange standby facility or cover that risk, meant that it was unable to cope with the liquidity pressures*

placed upon it by the freezing of international capital markets in August 2007. Given that the formulation of that strategy was a fundamental role of the Board of Northern Rock, overseen by some directors who had been there since its demutualisation, the failure of that strategy must also be attributed to the Board. The non-executive members of the Board, and in particular the Chairman of the Board, the Chairman of the Risk Committee and the senior non-executive director, failed in the case of Northern Rock to ensure that it remained liquid as well as solvent, to provide against the risks that it was taking and to act as an effective restraining force on the strategy of the executive members.

The Select Committee's verdict was positive in its identification of the areas in which Northern Rock's board should have accepted responsibility but their blameworthiness may not necessarily be as comprehensive as the media, the Committee, and even the Government would have us believe. After all, their criticisms were made with the benefit of hindsight. Many other banks played much the same game. The Select Committee may also have wished to be critical of, but not too hard on HM Treasury.

The role of the directors in this saga may have been over-emphasized in the media and by the Treasury Select Committee and perhaps they have been made a scapegoat because of the need to divert attention from the deficiencies of the government and the regulators, including the Bank of England. Furthermore the critical comments directed at the Northern Rock executive by the Treasury Select Committee should to be read bearing in mind that the members of that Committee typically have no experience of being directors of a public company of the size and complexity of Northern Rock. Whilst the report of the Committee and later public contributions by its chairman, John McFall MP were very commendable, the interview contributions by some Committee members, McCarthy style, at hearings by the Committee were less than impressive.

The Northern Rock board had duties that were clearly identified in the Report and Accounts that were issued annually with its unqualified approval. As the Select Committee identified, the board members may not have carried out their respective responsibilities in an adequate manner, despite their protestations to the contrary. However, as the book published in 1984, from which extracts are quoted above demonstrates, the Northern Rock board were by no means unique in any failure to carry out their duties adequately as we also learned later in 2008, particularly in relation to the banks that feature in Chapters 15 and16.

Until there are changes in Company Law (which, in this context, are not envisaged) and the regulators produce and police more effective rules on the subject of liquidity and risk management the situation in relation to corporate governance will remain unchanged in banks.

One external independent body, The Institute of International Finance was working (in May 2008) on a report that will recommend that the finance industry increases transparency and improves risk and liquidity management. As the Institute has 375 financial services firms as members it is well placed to produce an authoritative and widely based report provided one keeps an eye open for bias. One of the points that it regards as a key consideration is risk management, which it regards as much more than just a monitoring function. It considers that it is a core responsibility of the CEO and the entire executive management team.

It is only one of the institutions, including the Bank of England, the Treasury and the FSA, that will propose new guidelines on risk and liquidity management in 2008/9 in an effort to limit the possibility of a recurrence of the 2007/8 financial crises. It is to be hoped (although without much conviction) that they will also bring about changes that will enable errant directors and company executives of banks to be brought to account in appropriate circumstances.

The downturn in the housing market, particularly during the first half of 2008, and the tightening of the availability of mortgages brought about by the application of much higher underwriting standards by all lenders, have not been mentioned in the above review. This downturn and the consequent talk of impending recession in world economies, including the UK, was not nearly so apparent prior to September 2008, therefore although it may affect Northern Rock's recovery under nationalization, it did not play a part in its downfall.

The Northern Rock saga has been reviewed as it developed based on contemporary accounts. One has to compare what can now be considered to be the "modest" sums involved in its "bail-out", the risks to the "taxpayer" that were perceived, its nationalization, the media reporting, etc with what later came to light over a period of no more than a few weeks in September / October 2008. In the UK alone about one-third of the retail banking system would have been wiped out but for government intervention to the tune of (before and after those few weeks) £600 billion or more in the UK alone, later increased in January 2009 by $200 billion. One can see that Northern Rock and its board were unjustifiably pilloried and its shareholders shamefully treated. They were the first casualties and they became scapegoats for an ill-prepared, inexperienced and possibly incompetent officialdom.

The Regulators – an Overview

There were many differing reports about the role played by the regulators in the Northern Rock troubles but there was a general consensus that they did not acquit themselves with glory. One commentator wrote,

> *The suggestion that any public body "took control" was a sad joke. The Bank of England lectured on moral hazard, the FSA claimed to be powerless, and the Treasury dithered.*

That is hardly an encouraging starting point for an examination of their roles.

Turning to a more official viewpoint, "The Times" reported from a conference in Davos, Switzerland, that the EU's Commissioner for Internal Markets, Charlie McCreevy in a speech criticized regulators but his final comments were,

> *Managements themselves (of banks and rating agencies?) do not seem to be aware of the problems in their own organization, so it is hard to see how regulators could then be (aware). Finally, You must remember—-if you have too much regulation, you will have no innovation at all and that will kill the system.*

Killing the system through a lack of ability to innovate is an oft-repeated reason or excuse for having less regulation. Whilst it may be true that we can have too much regulation, that statement does not address the manner in which regulation should be applied. We live in a prescribed world of rules and regulations, all intended to ensure that nothing can go wrong with this or that. But despite all the rules and regulations, it does go wrong.

Why?

Firstly because all too often, for one reason or another, the rules and regulations are poorly administered by those charged with the responsibility of implementing them. Secondly, because too many of those for whom the rules and regulations were devised see them, not as "best practice" guidance, but rather as obstacles to be overcome. Financial regulation should be a tri-partite arrangement - not in the sense of the UK Tri-partite Standing Committee, but rather a compact between the regulator, the regulated financial entity and the user of the regulated financial service. Each must play an equal part, but if the regulated institutions act in a reasonable manner, based on equitable principles and justifiable trust, then the need for the consumer to be protected by masses of rules and regulations is much reduced.

Fifty years ago many of the players in the City of London financial world never considered that there was any way of providing service other than on those principles. Banks in the UK now have a published Code of Practice, approved by the FSA. Many other financial and investment firms claim to act in accordance with "best practice".

But do they actually follow the spirit of their codes of practice?

"Best practice" is a matter of adhering to established ethical and sensible business principles and giving equal weight to the interests of the customer and those of the firm. Of course we know from our first-hand experiences that all financial institutions and investment firms protest that they only operate in accordance with "best practice" and that the interests of the customer are paramount. The reality is that their motivation to increase profitability and market share usually takes precedence, driven in part by the "bonus" remuneration system that most institutions have implemented for the benefit of selected officials.

But few actually adhere to their "Codes of Practice" and "mission statements".

If it was otherwise we would not have seen in the UK a constant stream of mis-selling scandals involving split-capital trusts, annuities, endowments and unit linked endowments (both connected to the sale of mortgage loans), personal pensions, equity release schemes, product guarantee insurance and credit protection insurance, *ad nauseum*, each scandal perpetrated on a major nationwide scale.

If every firm actually observed the simple requirements stated above, which means effectively accepting and implementing "self-regulation", those scandals would be a lot less likely to occur and there would be very little need for comprehensive regulation.

The main problems facing financial regulators are the constantly changing range of business they are called upon to regulate, and the ever-increasing complexity of it. The regulatory regimes in most countries were set up in a much simpler age and although they have tried to keep abreast of developments, the fact is that the financial and investment industries, together with their high-powered legal advisers are always at least one step ahead. In many cases a conscious policy of keeping one step ahead is pursued.

It is the nature of the beast.

Until one can examine new developments, one cannot devise methods of regulating them and because the new products are increasingly complex and varied in detail, it is difficult to analyze them in sufficient depth to be certain that new regulations are necessary or that they will be effective. For that matter, does the regulator have personnel with the requisite capabilities to devise suitable regulations and supervise their observance? Not always, indeed those immediately responsible for overseeing the supervision of Northern Rock at the FSA were insurance business supervisors.

As Howard Davis pointed out when the FSA was set up, the regulator wishes to use a "light touch" but it can only do so when it is able to trust the regulated entities. There has been a substantial body of evidence produced in recent years that the primary consideration of most operators in the finance industry is not the provision of an exemplary service, but the maximization of profits and market share by any means. That militates against expectations that these financial operators are to be trusted to act prudently and within self-imposed guidelines.

A regulator must be able to apply punitive sanctions, that is to say, it must be able to penalize transgressing regulated providers of financial and investment services and ultimately it must have the power to prevent them from continuing to undertake specific activities or to insist on a change of management structure or policies in certain circumstances. If those powers, assuming they had been available and had been used appropriately at every level in the affected countries, we would not have had so many of the critical problems that faced financial markets in 2007-08. Of course, in addition we may not have enjoyed (temporarily) rapidly growing economic prosperity and higher living standards.

Unfortunately the charters under which most financial regulators have to operate leave them relatively toothless, even assuming that they are sufficiently competent to exercise effective powers in the first place. There has been ample evidence, on both sides of the Atlantic in recent times that regulators lack a mixture of competence, experience and possibly the will to act. They may also be too close to those they are responsible for regulating and they may be too inhibited by political interference. Whilst it is wholly appropriate that regulatory bodies be created and empowered by governments, they must be able to execute their daily duties without interference from political sources. At the same time, they must be answerable to government for the proper execution of their responsibilities.

In an earlier chapter the difference between "regulation" and "supervision" was discussed. It is not the quantity of regulations that matters, it is the effectiveness of the supervision of key regulations that is more important.

That is a short review of the generalities of regulation and supervision. Let us now look at the manner in which each of the Tripartite authorities dealt with the Northern Rock problem and the wider financial markets situation in 2007.

The Financial Services Authority

Northern Rock was one of more than one hundred firms that the FSA had identified as "high impact", that is to say firms that had the potential to become vulnerable to market changes and as a consequence required careful and continuous monitoring. When questioned by the Parliamentary Select Committee on the subject, Mr. Sants, the FSA's CEO confirmed that,

> *This [close and continuous supervision] is characterised by very regular dialogue with the firm on the full range of supervisory issues, through ad hoc meetings and regular telephone conversations and email traffic. Our work-streams in supervising Northern Rock over the last two years have included: reviewing strategic and business developments through discussions with the firm; attendance at result presentations; monitoring the market; assessing the ongoing validity of our risk assessment; monitoring financial data, supervisory returns and management information; reacting to specific requests from the firm—such as the Capital Requirements Directive (CRD) waiver request which was a major work-stream during this period; and undertaking the formal review process which sets the capital requirements of the firm on the basis of the risks identified by the firm and the FSA. We also carry out thematic reviews – projects to review practices in a range of firms in a specific area of their business. Northern Rock was subject to thematic reviews in the same way as other similar firms.*

The Select Committee verdict on the FSA supervision was,

> *Insofar as the FSA undertook greater "regulatory engagement" with Northern Rock, this failed to tackle the fundamental weakness in its funding model and did nothing to prevent the problems that came to the fore from August 2007 onwards. We regard this as a substantial failure of regulation.*

It transpired (some months later) that the "close and continuous" supervision actually amount to a three year cycle of visits with the last full risk assessment of Northern Rock carried out between December 2005 and February 2006. During 2005 there were no recorded visits by FSA personnel to Northern Rock. According to the FSA's own Internal Audit Enquiry into the supervision of Northern Rock the following are some of the facts that emerged:

24 firms, i.e. 63% of high-impact firms supervised had a supervisory cycle period of 18-20 months.

Northern Rock was one of four "high impact" category firms (11% of the total) that had a cycle of 36 months.

Staff turnover in the FSA was high. Between January 2005 and August 2007 two high impact firms, one of which was Northern Rock, were successively supervised by three Heads of Department, two of whom had primary responsibility for insurance firms.

Some aspects of supervision were normally carried out by means of C & C (Close and

Continuous) meetings. During the period January 2005 to August 2007 the average number of visits to Major Retail Groups (of which Northern Rock was one) was 58, and for the five largest retail banks, 143. During the same period Northern Rock had eight "visits", of which 7 were in 2007 prior to August. Two were said to be on the telephone and five were on the same day, 27th April 2007. Of those five meetings, Agendas were found for all of them, but there was only a typed record for part of one of them.

Retail Banks were also included in Risk Mitigation Programmes (RMP's). There were 37 firms classified as High Impact that were involved in RMP's. Northern Rock was the only firm not so involved.

Examinations of the supervisory meetings,

> Indicate that the supervisory team did not adequately identify and pursue risks arising in the firm as a whole and in relation to its business model and control framework. Our findings also show a level of engagement and oversight by supervisory line management below the standard we would expect for a high impact firm. This placed undue reliance on the associates.

For "associates" read "junior staff".

There was also insufficient engagement by the H o D's (Head of Department) responsible for Northern Rock. This was due, in part, to a lack of continuity (as noted, there were three HoD's in the review period, albeit one was only responsible for three months). They also had other significant demands on their time during the period, including covering gaps arising due to manager turnover. On average, they met one of their firms every week, although none met Northern Rock in the period reviewed (2005-2007). They were not pro-active in ensuring there was a robust process that meant they built up a complete picture of the issues, or (in the absence of a requirement) in holding a periodic comprehensive stock-take of each firm in their portfolios.

The B of E alerted the FSA in October 2006 to the risks inherent in Northern Rock's wholesale funding model. A senior FSA official, a Head of Department in the Major Retail Group's Division commented in an E-mail (to whom?) that, "Northern Rock's business model means it should certainly receive additional scrutiny". The Audit Team Review commented that nothing was done. The Team also recorded that officials were defensive and territorial in the face of problems. Supervisors dismissed warning signs in February and March 2007 as nothing more than blips, reassured by a Merrill Lynch broker's report in April 2007 that described Northern Rock as being "still a fantastic long term story"

It was also suggested in the Review that FSA officers were cowed by the strong and aggressive characters within Northern Rock's management team.

Turning to questions on liquidity assessment, the Review states,

> *Our understanding is that, during the review period, the FSA's approach to*
> *liquidity reflected a presumption that in the event of a crisis like that*
> *experienced in August 2007, general market liquidity provided by the Bank*
> *of England would be increased and, in extremis, liquidity would be provided*
> *for systemically important institutions.*

That was what the European Central bank and the Federal Reserve Bank in the USA did early in the second half of 2007. The Bank of England refrained from action until it was too late. However, the FSA Internal Audit statement brings out significant points in relation to liquidity. The FSA's understanding (from whom?) was that,

> *In the event of a crisis such as that experienced in August 2007 - - - - in*
> *extremis, liquidity would be provided by the Bank of England for*
> *systemically important institutions.*

There are two points here.

The first is that the crisis was recognized as having started in August 2007. The second is that the Bank of England could be expected to provide liquidity to "systemically important institutions". The reason given by the Bank of England in September 2007 when it eventually extended liquidity assistance to Northern Rock was to avoid a systemic spread of Northern Rock's problems, which means that in the scheme of things, Northern Rock was regarded as being "systemically important."

Whilst it is not considered good practice for a firm, in this case the FSA, to undertake navel-gazing by conducting its own review of its performance and effectiveness, the Internal Audit team of the FSA did a thorough job, reported in a 136 page review, part of which was of technical interest only to the FSA. The team identified 39 lessons to be learned and whilst it is too much to expect that they will all be adequately implemented to produce a perfect FSA, it is to be hoped that they will effect some very much needed major improvements. The fact that the team identified 39 deficiencies in the supervisory roles of the FSA points up a dearth of effectiveness in that body.

There was very obviously a lack of tight management oversight of operations if the country's top regulator admitted to being,

> *cowed by strong and aggressive characters within Northern Rock's*
> *management.*

That is totally unacceptable.

The FSA was or should have been firmly in the driving seat. A regulator that is not clearly seen to be in that position will achieve very little. Which is not to say that it has to respond in an aggressive or adversarial manner, but it must be firm and fair in its dealings with those that it regulates. They have to understand who has the final say.

I recall a meeting I sought with the leader of the Gibraltar Bar Association (who also held and had held many senior positions in Gibraltar), shortly after I arrived in Gibraltar as Financial Services Commissioner in 1991. The purpose of the meeting was to introduce myself and discuss prospective regulatory requirements that would affect those members of the Bar Association that undertook various regulated activities in addition to their legal practices. Some of his opening words to me were, "We are not accustomed to being regulated in Gibraltar." He and his colleagues soon found out that the situation changed with my arrival.

An examination of the information coming out of the FSA, and from other sources creates a picture of an organization with a number of major problems resulting in a unit which in the words of the Parliamentary Select Committee was "unfit for purpose".

So what were those problems?

It is tempting to start at the top, but the Chief Executive officer had to work with what he had during the latter part of the Northern Rock saga. We have to accept also that he was only appointed in July 2007, therefore the systemic problems endemic in the FSA were either accepted or created by his predecessors, and of course its Chairman. It is important to recognize that fact, particularly if one keeps in mind that the CEO, in addition to a substantial salary, (although one which was lower than the average in the commercial finance industry), had qualified for a sizeable annual bonus although only two-thirds of targets were met, as related earlier.

Staffing problems. There appears to have been a high turnover of staff at all levels. A high level of staff turnover is normally not indicative of a work overload, but of dissatisfaction with the workplace, usually brought about by a combination of poor training and bad management. Employees that are poorly trained cannot be expected to enjoy their work or to carry it out to a satisfactory standard.

Poor management means that staff are neither motivated nor adequately trained and supervised. Ample evidence has been produced to demonstrate that the FSA suffered from all of those problems. On too many occasions it sought to hide behind excuses for its shortcomings. While there can be no doubt its internal problems were real, the chief executive is paid to deal with them and the Chairman is paid to ensure that the chief executive does so. Those are their principal *raison's d'etre*.

It is not a valid excuse that too much is expected of them or that they have to work with an under-resourced organization. It is their responsibility to ensure that the organization is "fit for purpose". If it cannot be made fit for purpose within the existing framework it is the Chairman's duty to ensure that the Government creates the conditions for an appropriate framework, or resign.

The FSA Internal Audit review is worth reading for anyone with a keen interest in regulatory matters and for those involved in the banking markets that the review addressed. However there is too much material to be covered in a book of this nature. Excerpts from the review have been reproduced above and in Chapter 13.

What the review identified, however, was that despite everyone believing that it had been overseen by a comprehensive and expensive regulatory set up, Northern Rock found itself in a position where it could no longer carry on its business without assistance from the Central Bank. What purpose did the regulatory regime serve in this case?

It was yet another example following on " I say, therefore it must be so".

The Bank of England

The Bank of England fulfills a number of roles but in respect of regulation its concern is with the maintenance of financial and economic stability. As the bankers' bank and banker to the Government, the Bank stands at the heart of the payments system and controls the issue of currency. Because of those involvements in the UK financial scene and the fact that it is the UK's Central Bank, it should be well placed to monitor events taking place at both a national and international level.

It falls to the Bank to advise the Chancellor, and answer for its advice, on any major problem that may arise. It follows that when the financial system encounters problems, the principal concern of the Governor of the Bank of England is not with the immediate problems of individual firms, that is the responsibility of the FSA, but with the possibility of systemic risks spreading through the rest of the financial system.

Northern Rock was a substantial firm but when looked at in isolation it was not one that in itself would necessarily be regarded as important to the stability of the financial system as, for example, became the case when one of the five major Clearing Banks became involved. That would have been the situation in normal times.

Accordingly, the initial reaction of Mervyn King, Governor of the Bank of England when he learned on 14th August 2007 of the liquidity difficulties affecting Northern Rock was that they were caused as a result of the business strategies adopted by the bank, in other words, self-inflicted. In his opinion, shared by other observers, it was not appropriate for the Bank of England to "bail out" a firm in such circumstances. Mr.King's opinion at the time, and it was also his brief, was that central banks should only act when there were economic costs on a scale sufficient to ignore the moral hazard of the future. Avoiding "moral hazard" was a key objective. At that time he apparently did not believe that Northern Rock's problems would give rise to a systemic risk.

That was before the run on its deposits.

In order to resolve its problems Northern Rock made attempts to sell sufficient assets, but could not find buyers. The next move was that discussions were held between Northern Rock and Lloyds TSB bank with a view to a takeover of Northern Rock. Such a takeover could only be consummated if there was an injection of funds. Up to £30 billion was thought to be necessary. An approach was made to the Bank of England to provide a guarantee for this amount if required, but again Mr. King said that it was not the Bank's business to fund takeovers. However he was, apparently, prepared to make "lender of last resort " loans available at a penal interest rate. Such loans could also be made available to other bidders, if any showed an interest. The offer did not appeal to Lloyds TSB which apparently withdrew from the proposed arrangements.

Northern Rock then came to the conclusion that its only salvation was to seek "lender of last resort" assistance from the Bank. Such assistance is always available from a central bank to solvent but temporarily troubled banks.

Traditionally "lender of last resort" assistance has been carried out covertly in order to avoid exacerbating an ailing bank's problems but Mr. King later pointed out that, although that would be his preferred action, practical considerations in an electronic age dominated by "breaking news", "leaks" and laws derived from EC directives prevented covert operations from taking place.

A point that should be mentioned here is that, as noted elsewhere, on 9th August 2007 the US and EC Central Banks made substantial funds generally available and some UK banks took advantage of those facilities, but the UK authorities were said to have prohibited Northern Rock from doing so. The detail of this is unclear, but that is what was claimed in the Press.

The general perception of "lender of last resort" assistance is as a definite last resort since it is considered that a stigma attaches to it and such loans are normally at a penal rate. Nevertheless, Northern Rock had no choices left to it and by Thursday 13th September had negotiated a deal with the Bank of England, approved by the Chancellor of the Exchequer as was required due to the large amount potentially required.

All of this was accomplished in secrecy behind closed doors. It was not in the public domain. Information released some weeks later included the fact that Northern Rock claimed to have had at this time two to three months credit available to it. Its draw-down of the "lender of last resort" loans actually took place in stages over the following three months. In fact the initial draw-down in the first few days was said to be no more than £3 billion. There was no £30 billion overnight crash.

If knowledge of the Bank of England assistance had been restricted to a few in the City until the authorities made an official announcement in measured terms, there would probably have been no run on Northern Rock's deposits but the confidentiality of the arrangements was leaked prior to their finalisation.

Robert Peston of the BBC, as noted in an earlier chapter spent the entire evening of the 13th September on the BBC, broadcasting his leaked "scoop" in advance of any official announcement. The result was queues outside Northern Rock offices first thing on Friday 14th September and sufficient traffic on its internet site the previous evening / night to cause it to crash, as panicked depositors withdrew their money, possibly as much as £2 billion in the first day or two.

An official announcement of the provision of support was made at 7.00am on the 14th September, (to institutional investors and the London Stock Exchange) but in the light of what happened that day, it was inadequate and ineffective. It would also not have been generally known to the public at large but for later media reports.

Although the FSA had assured the public that Northern Rock was solvent and that if depositors wanted to get their money out they could do so, they continued to do just that. The long queues and withdrawals in volume continued until at least Tuesday of the following week despite the Chancellor's announcement that all retail deposits in Northern Rock had been accorded a 100% government guarantee.

Northern Rock, we subsequently learned, lost around £12 billion of deposits in two weeks or so and in the following weeks borrowed around £26 billion from the Bank of England to replace maturing inter-bank loans.

So where did the Bank of England go wrong?

Before seeking answers to that question, we should remind ourselves that what happened (the general freezing of credit markets) was, hopefully, a once in a lifetime event. There had been no comparable financial crises in the previous forty years or more. Other financial crises during that time were of much lesser magnitude. They also took place before the era of computerisation, satellite communication and mobile phones played a part in global financial activities.

The 2007 crisis could not escape the full glare of a news-hungry media and the rumour mill of the now many times larger financial communities in the City and other parts of the world, not to mention the enormous trading rooms operated by every major financial institution that, *inter alia*, speculated on share price and currency movements in a manner that did nothing to engender faith in the stability of the financial or stock markets. The scale of what happened globally seemed beyond comprehension. Nearly every event that one examined was counted not in millions but in billions and tens of billions, whether of Dollars, Euros or Sterling hardly matters. However, as stated earlier, the crisis that arose in 2007 was dwarfed by the one that erupted a year later, as we shall see.

The Bank of England's principle regulatory responsibility is to maintain the stability of the UK financial system, but London is a premier international financial center. It follows that the Bank of England must therefore have regard to what happens elsewhere and its possible impact on the domestic financial markets.

It was apparent in the USA and Europe (including the UK) from at least mid-2007 that transactions between banks were becoming subject to more stringent requirements and more difficult to achieve. The reason for this was increasing unease about the quality of securitised bond issues associated with the sub-prime mortgage market in the USA. Eventually, in August-September 2007, the securitisation markets rapidly ground to a halt.

What were the central banks doing during this period?

On 9th August 2007 the European Central Bank injected 94.8 billion Euros into its markets in an effort to ease the credit squeeze. The Federal Reserve in the USA followed suit with a $ 24 billion injection into the US markets. Globally, over a few days Central Banks injected the equivalent of $290 billion into markets. The Bank of England appeared to take the view that the problems were created by the banks and they should be left to find a way to solve them even if as a result it cost them dearly. The Bank of England only supplied £4 billion or so in August and did not assist the banks by injecting new funds into the UK market until 19th September 2007 when it offered £10 billion of three-month funds. Unexpectedly, when the £10 billion was made available at auction, there were no takers, partly because the interest rate had been fixed at 6.75% and the three month commercial rates had fallen substantially from their previous week peak and partly because banks did not wish to be seen in the financial climate at that time to apparently require emergency assistance.

Notwithstanding, the Bank of England simultaneously announced that it would hold similar weekly auctions for three weeks beginning 3rd October 2007.

There are points that need to be understood about Central Bank injections of new funds into financial markets. Firstly, a Central Bank does not lay the money on the counter to be picked up by any bank that wishes to take it. The money is only made available against security satisfactory to the central Bank. Until the 2007 crisis brought about a need to relax the security requirements, mortgage loans (and many other assets) were not regarded by the B of E as suitable security. The range of assets acceptable as security was quite narrow. However in the light of the severity of the financial crisis, the three Central Banks that were most closely involved relaxed the rules and accepted packages of mortgage loans and other assets as security. This was an important concession, bearing in mind that one of the reasons banks needed funds from the central bank was because commercial banks did not recognize such assets as being acceptable security for inter-bank borrowings.

The second factor was that Central bank aid comes at a price, which made it unattractive, particularly if large amounts were involved.

Such injections of funds were not intended by the Bank of England to enable banks to expand business or even to maintain a current level of business, but rather they were intended to help correct capital shortfalls in some banks and to "oil the wheels" of the financial markets and restore confidence in them. In this case it has to be acknowledged that they did not achieve either objective, the problems were too deep.

Over the ensuing six months or more, further injections of funds were made by the Central banks, this time including the Bank of England. The list may not be complete, but it illustrates the extent of the funds involved.

In December 2007 five Central Banks produced up to $110 billion.

In February 2008 the US Federal Reserve Bank made $168 billion available and in March 2008, it produced a further $200 billion.

On 2nd May 2008 the Federal Reserve, the ECB and the Swiss National Bank joined forces to put up another $76 billion. The availability of these sums was in addition to bi-weekly funding auctions in the USA of $50 billion, raised to $75 billion in May 2008

The Bank of England announced a "Special Liquidity Scheme" on21st April 2008 that was intended to relieve the "log jam" that still existed in UK inter-bank transactions. The Bank said that up to £200 billion could be made available.

The basis of the scheme was to allow banks to temporarily swap illiquid assets of sufficiently high quality for Treasury stocks. Responsibility for losses on their loans stayed with the banks. The scheme had a number of key features:

•   The asset swaps would be for long terms. Each swap would be for a period of one year and could be renewed for up to three years.

- The risk of losses on their loans remained with the banks

- The swaps were available only for assets existing at the end of 2007 and could not be used to finance new lending.

- Banks would need at all times to provide the Bank of England with assets of significantly greater value than the Treasury Bills they received. If the value of the assets falls, the banks would have to "top up"

There were other conditions attaching to the scheme and it is quite obvious that it was not intended as a "free lunch". Mr. King, the Bank's Governor was quoted as saying,

> This is not a bail out for banks. The objective is not to protect the banks. It is to protect the public from the banks.

It is worth noting *en passant* that this scheme is virtually the same as one proposed by the advisers to HM Treasury as a solution to Northern Rock's problems in December 2007 but which was not implemented.

For several months after September 14th the Bank of England, its Governor and Deputy Governor (who was directly responsible for overseeing financial stability of the UK banking system) were subject to much criticism in common with the FSA and the Tripartite Standing Committee.

One of the criticisms leveled at Mervyn King, the Governor, was that he was not a banker, he was an economist, whereas his predecessors were usually career bankers who had held top spots in their banks. But this criticism does not take account of the changes that have taken place in the role of the Bank of England. The key responsibilities of the Bank of England are now the maintenance of monetary and of economic stability in the UK. In the performance of those roles the Bank participates as one of the Tripartite Regulatory Authorities. Its former responsibility to monitor individual banks in the banking system was taken over by the FSA.

Arguments have raged as to whether this was an appropriate change to make, since the parties to the Tripartite arrangements did not acquit themselves with glory when the crunch-time occurred in 2007. However that was not necessarily the fault of the Tripartite structure *per se,* the fault lay in the poor quality of execution of responsibilities by each part of it, a fault which lies at the door of its managements.

It has also been pointed out that in 2007 some other central banks pumped substantial sums of money into their banking systems to avert possible systemic failures. Mr. King, and the responsibility for doing so was his, did not. Why not? Possibly because in the period June to September when that was happening, the financial problems directly affecting the UK market place were neither so obvious nor as large as, for example, in the USA. Perhaps another reason was that the FSA was not sufficiently alert to identify them.

Northern Rock was looked upon as being at the center of the problems and it had been recognized for several months that it had a potential to run into difficulties in consequence of the adverse conditions that were becoming more and more apparent in the financial markets. But Northern Rock was not initially seen as a major financial institution likely, on its own, to cause immediate systemic risk in the rest of the banking system.

His decision, until events brought about by the panic run on Northern Rock by its depositors overtook him, was not to intervene. Why not? He considered that the Bank should only intervene when there were economic costs on a scale sufficient to ignore the moral hazard of saving an individual bank from the result of its folly.

That must have been a difficult decision for him, but was one which he made after due consideration and in good faith based on the facts as he and his team interpreted them at the time.

In a later BBC interview in November 2007, Mr. King said,

> The role of the Bank of England is not to do what banks ask us to do, it is to do what's in the interests of the country as a whole.

Later in 2008/9 this distinction appeared to have become blurred.

The run on Northern Rock, and more particularly the lurid reporting of it, completely changed the circumstances when allied to the fact that after the run rumours were rife, and being sensationalized by the media, that other banks were also about to run into trouble. At that point Mr. King declared that the Bank would make funds available to improve market liquidity. The media (and politicians) were then able to claim that Mr. King had made a "humiliating U-turn" and that his credibility had been completely destroyed. There were calls for his resignation. Such is today's world in which those with heavy responsibilities have to carry them out.

Critics are ten a penny, and that is about their worth at times.

One commentator viewed the situation as,

> It would seem that the Bank of England is independent of the UK

government when it is pursuing government policy. However, if it pursues policies which it deems in the interests of the UK economy, yet are contrary to short term political expediency, then this independence is an illusion.

Possibly a reference to the need to refer to the Chancellor before significant actions could be taken

A key factor in the events of mid-September 2007 was the speed at which they happened. The B of E became directly aware of definite problems at Northern Rock on 14th August. A watching brief was kept on the bank by the FSA during the following period, but there was no intervention other than (it is believed) to encourage it to seek a solution through a takeover by another bank. The bank did so and negotiations took place between it and Lloyds TSB with the assistance of the FSA. About 8–9th September the negotiations culminated in a request to the B of E to make available a guarantee of up to £30 billion, if required, to assist with the purchase by Lloyds TSB. Mr. King took the view that it was not part of the business of the B of E to finance private takeovers, at the same time assuming risk. Another consideration was that such assistance would have been interpreted by the EC as constituting unacceptable State Aid. Without such assistance, Lloyds TSB appeared unable to put together a deal that would have made sense to it.

Under the leadership of its Chief Executive Eric Daniels, Lloyds TSB was one of the few British banks that avoided the blandishments of the securitization and other esoteric markets. He was quoted as saying,

> *I had a strong conviction - and colleagues shared it - that we were doing the right thing, not pushing the risk envelope, not stretching our capital too far. Economies and markets are by nature cyclical, and if you set a prudent policy it gives you much better consistency and much less volatility. At some point I think there will be recognition that those kind of values are worth something.*

How right he was. In fact, as quoted in chapter 16, George Rae in "The Country Banker" said much the same thing in 1885!

Lloyds TSB tended to be seen in stock markets as the lack-lustre institution amongst the British high-street banks. Perhaps its critics should have paid more attention to the parable of the tortoise and the hare. Unfortunately it was a pity he did not stick to his philosophy instead of bidding for the sinking HBOS later in the year.

Why did the B of E not take more direct action? Mr. King was quoted as saying, firstly, that earlier intervention would have been very damaging to Northern Rock, bearing in mind that it was only beginning to experience difficulty renewing or replacing some of its inter-bank wholesale loans. The full extent of the problems had yet to become apparent. The markets had slowed down but they had not frozen solid. Had he been able to do so covertly, he would have extended "lender of last resort" facilities to Northern Rock at that time. But he felt unable to do so because of the Market Abuse Directive and inter-action with other legislation.

Additionally it was considered that it would have been impossible in the circumstances that arose for him to have acted covertly – some in the City (including those shorting Northern Rock shares) were keeping too close an eye on Northern Rock's fortunes. We shall return to this topic of "covert assistance" later when we review the proposals that were announced in August 2008 for assistance to banks.

It is quite probable that if Mr. King had been able to act with the benefit of the experience and hindsight he had acquired by mid-2008, he might have adopted a different course of action.

H M Treasury and The Chancellor of the Exchequer

Where does H M Treasury fit into the Tripartite financial regulatory structure?

It has responsibility for the institutional structure of the financial regulatory system, and the legislation behind it. It forms the liaison point between the other two parties and the Government. Its principal concerns are to ensure the wider financial stability of the financial system, the protection of both bank depositors and the interests of taxpayers in any decisions it is called upon to make as one of the Tripartite regulators.

In terms of everyday involvement the Treasury played a passive role in the application of the regulatory framework once its role in its creation had been accomplished. It does, however, come back into play when a serious crisis in the economy or the financial system occurs. As an agency of Government it will also formulate, and once approved implement the government's policies on the maintenance of financial stability through the regulatory system.

In relation to the Northern Rock collapse the Treasury was responsible for the offers to guarantee deposits in Northern Rock and it also approved the funding arrangements provided by the Bank of England, including the types of collateral that would be accepted as security.

Although the FSA and B of E have their own specific responsibilities, the Tripartite Standing Committee provides a conduit through which they can keep the Treasury "in the loop". In this way Mr. King on several occasions discussed with the Chancellor, as head of the Treasury, his decision not to assist Lloyds TSB with guarantees for the takeover of Northern Rock. The Chancellor later confirmed that he had agreed with Mr. King's decision.

As the Northern Rock post-September 14th story unfolded, most of what emerged from the Treasury through the Chancellor, Alistair Darling, amounted to reassurances to Parliament and the public that the Treasury's principal concern was to ensure an outcome that solved Northern Rock's liquidity problems, one way or another and which ensured full repayment of the B of E loans at the earliest possible time, together with an appropriate amount of interest so that the "interests of the taxpayer were fully protected."

Time after time the Chancellor's statements stressed the need to look after taxpayer interests in a manner that would ensure that benefits resulting from the fact that the government / Bank of England loans had saved northern Rock would accrue to "the taxpayer" and not to private sector interests.

Whilst no one can quarrel with Mr Darling's determination to look after "the taxpayer", questions were raised after he had arranged for the nationalization of Northern Rock as to the legality of "the taxpayer" acquiring equity rights in Northern Rock equal to total ownership and intended to be at no cost, in addition to a penal rate of interest on the government's loans and fees for the provision of depositor and other guarantees. Bear in mind also that the B of E loans were fully secured by Northern Rock assets acceptable to the Bank that were of a higher book value than the loans, thus making "risk to the taxpayer" highly unlikely.

Those topics have been covered elsewhere in earlier chapters and do not have a direct relevance in a consideration of the extent, if any, to which blame for the inadequate handling of Northern Rock's situation should be apportioned to the Treasury and the Chancellor.

What the Chancellor readily recognized, however, was that there were unsatisfactory elements in the regulatory supervision of Northern Rock that had to be tackled. His proposals for improvements to the organization of the regulatory structure have been discussed earlier.

Any consideration of the fall of Northern Rock must separate two elements – the fundamental problems relating to liquidity and those relating to the run on deposits. Initially the Treasury was only incidentally involved in the first. However it was directly involved in dealing with the second, the run on deposits.

There was criticism from all quarters of the delays that took place before the Chancellor announced that the Treasury would guarantee all deposits in Northern Rock after the run commenced. The run started sometime on the evening of Thursday 13th September (internet deposits). This would not have been common knowledge until the following morning, Friday. The bank opened to find queues of depositors formed outside branches, followed very soon afterwards by media cameras.

The Select Committee commented on the delay as follows:

> *A swift announcement would have been assisted by early preparation of such an announcement. In that context, we find it surprising that high level discussions between the Bank of England and Northern Rock about the support facility did not take place prior to 10 September.*

There were queues outside branches of Northern Rock for the rest of that first day despite reassurances coming from a variety of sources, FSA, Chancellor, British Bankers Association (BBA), Northern Rock, etc, that there was no cause for alarm. The BBA said,

> *Everyone should calm down and refrain from making simplistic comments on a very complex area which just causes unnecessary worry and concern. Northern Rock is a sound and safe bank and there is absolutely no reason for either mortgage customers or savers to worry.*

But none of it stopped the panic.

Why not? Partly because we have reached a time when with considerable justification the pronouncements from corporations of any kind, or trade associations, or official bodies are no longer accepted by the public at face value. The only reassurance that depositors were likely to accept was an unequivocable 100% guarantee from the Government.

Northern Rock opened for business on Saturday morning, 15th September and appeared to have been more or less capable of dealing with all withdrawals made. It also made arrangements to extend its opening hours. The run continued and resumed on Monday morning, 17th September, notwithstanding that many depositors suffered a contractual penalty for withdrawing their money. News media on Saturday 15th had a field day, speculating on the problems and future of Northern Rock on page after page. TV and radio news bulletins joined in.

The Parliamentary Select Committee in its report covered the provision of a deposit guarantee in depth, possibly the only source of comprehensive coverage of the circumstances surrounding the announcement of a government guarantee. The following are extracts from the report :

The Governor of the Bank of England stated (to the Chancellor) that the only way to halt the run was to provide a Government guarantee of deposits in Northern Rock. The Chancellor of the Exchequer "became convinced" on Sunday 16 September that action along these lines was necessary.

The announcement of the guarantee took place during a press conference that the Chancellor of the Exchequer held <u>after 5.00 pm on Monday 17 September</u>.

The announcement was that,

Following discussions with the Governor and the Chairman of the FSA, <u>should it be necessary</u>, we, with the Bank of England, would put in place arrangements that would guarantee all the existing deposits in Northern Rock during the current instability in the financial markets. This means that people can continue to take their money out of Northern Rock. But if they choose to leave their money in Northern Rock, it will be guaranteed safe and secure.

The announcement late on Monday 17 September had a partial effect. The momentum of the run was slowed down but not stopped.

The report then considered the timing of the announcement, now summarized as :

During our inquiry, we examined in detail the questions of when the Government guarantee of Northern Rock deposits was first considered, whether it should have been announced earlier and whether preparations of such an announcement could have been put in hand at an earlier stage.

The participants in the discussions that considered the liquidity facility to Northern Rock emphasized the difficulty that they faced in predicting the effect of its announcement.

Sir John Gieve told us:

We knew when we did that that the announcement of that would have two effects: a good effect because it would show they had a new source of finance but a bad effect because it would send the market a signal that they really needed a new source of finance. In the event we knew that there was a risk that that balance would go the wrong way and it did.

The Governor of the Bank of England told us that he did not view a bank run as "inevitable" on Thursday 13 September, when the date of the announcement of the support operation was brought forward because of market rumours.

The nature of a bank run is that it is a knife edge: it might happen, it might not. That is exactly why a bank run is so difficult to handle.

He emphasized that the provision of the support facility might have had a reassuring effect on depositors, and went on to say: I do not think anyone could have known with any certainty at all what would have been the consequences on retail depositors of the announcement.

Sir Callum McCarthy (Chairman, FSA) supported the view of the Governor of the Bank of England that the likely effect of the announcement of liquidity support was not "obvious".

The then Chairman of Northern Rock also emphasized the unexpectedness of the run,

I think it is worth reflecting that all of us, both here and in the authorities, were surprised by the degree to which the announcement of a facility from the Bank of England—not the use of it but the existence of a facility—and the reassurances that went with it about us being a solvent and profitable business did not have a sufficiently reassuring effect on customers.

In view of the awareness apparent within the Tripartite authorities and within Northern Rock's Board that a retail run was one possible consequence of the announcement of the Bank of England's liquidity support, we asked witnesses from the Tripartite authorities about the extent to which a Government guarantee—the device that was used on Monday 17 September to halt the run—had been the subject of prior consideration.

Sir John Gieve implied in his evidence in September that the possibility of announcing a Government guarantee alongside announcement of the support facility was at least considered, and was consciously rejected.

In terms of the crisis, the key question that underlies your questions is was it worth on Friday announcing that the Bank was making a facility available or should we have said at the same time that the Government guaranteed all the deposits? We did realise there was a risk that, if you like, the shock effect of an announcement would overwhelm the positive effect of saying the Bank was standing by with some money. We knew that was a risk but we thought that it was not an overwhelming risk and it was worth taking that step.

He reinforced the impression of prior consideration of the Government guarantee when he next gave evidence:

The initial Government guarantee on Northern Rock deposits was announced on Monday 17 September in circumstances we considered earlier. The announcement did not take place until late that day even though the decision in principle to provide it had been reached the previous day because, in the Chancellor of the Exchequer's words,

> When I announced the guarantee, I wanted to be pretty clear what exactly I was announcing because people would want to know beyond doubt what the position was.

The objective of the Select Committee investigation was to create a picture of all the circumstances that was as near to the truth as could be achieved. For that reason their consideration of the circumstances surrounding the issue of the deposit guarantee have been set out at length above. From the Committee's investigation, it can be seen that although it may have seemed to the casual observer (and there were many with opinions) that the Treasury should have jumped in immediately on the morning of Friday 14th to squash the run, those closest to the need to take action may not have made the most appropriate decision but they acted in good faith and after due consideration. That interpretation can be, and has been challenged in the Press, but only with the benefit of that great solver of problems, hindsight.

The other aspect of H M Treasury's involvement was the long running saga of what to do about recovering the Bank of England loans expeditiously and completely. The Chancellor was seeking a private sector solution, of which several were presented to the Treasury, the one most favoured by the Treasury (and presumably supported by the Treasury's adviser) was that from Branson and his Virgin consortium.

All suffered from the same problem, where to find the £26 billion or so required to repay the B of E loans. Branson from an early stage appeared to be the most favoured, except by Northern Rock shareholders. The reason why it was the favourite was subject to speculation, crony-ism with the Prime Minister being one suggestion.

To help solve the central problem the Chancellor indicated that a successful bidder that managed to meet the Treasury requirements (probably devised by Goldman Sachs) could have access to a continuation of the Bank of England loans for up to three years.

At a late stage, towards the end of December 2007, an in-house Northern Rock plan was presented which appeared to have in it the elements that the Treasury had stipulated but was thought by the Treasury's advisers to be inadequately devised, notwithstanding that it proposed an almost identical strategy to that implemented by the Treasury after nationalization.

So why was it rejected as inadequate?

Initially the government claimed that it was because it did not offer the *"best value"* – to the taxpayer. Subsequently it added that nationalization would result in the "least subsidy" in comparison with the private sector solutions. Critics (amongst the shareholders) believed it was chosen because by wiping out the shareholders and by paying them nothing, a profit for the government (and of course "the taxpayer") would be maximized.

Other reasons have been suggested such as:-

Firstly,a determination to ensure that RAB and SRM did not profit from their investment.

Secondly, because it had become obvious that shareholders would never vote for and therefore would thwart the Branson bid. (There were suggestions that this reason may have emanated from No 10 Downing Street).

The Treasury appeared determined that the government's views would prevail and that a Treasury decision would decide the fate of Northern Rock. It consistently ignored the shareholders (as noted earlier) and indeed the directors of the company (except perhaps for its own implanted chairman) and although shareholders and their representatives sought meetings, the Treasury had no meetings with them although it met on a number of occasions with Virgin and the other bidders. It appears to have been a conscious Treasury strategy to act unilaterally as we shall see when we consider its actions later in 2008 in respect of other banks.

The UK Shareholders Association sent a letter to the Chancellor on 10th February 2008, in other words, not long before the final decision was taken to nationalize, it read,

> *I have enclosed a copy of a note we have just issued to shareholders in the company that explains what we feel about the current position. I would urge you to take a more reasonable attitude to the issue of how to enable the company to recover – for example by ensuring that it is reasonably able to compete in its chosen market. This will best preserve the jobs of employees, and will of course also ensure some certainty that the company can repay the debts that it owes.*

> *I would also reiterate the views expressed to me by many shareholders- namely that they oppose the proposal from Mr. Branson and Virgin Group on a large number of grounds. Indeed the only negative feedback I have received to the note enclosed from the several thousands of people to whom it was sent was the comment by one person who felt that*

southerners were being disparaged if I assumed they would support the Virgin offer!

So I must point out that if the Government tries to force the Virgin proposal onto shareholders, you may well find that we reject it anyway. There is sufficient strength of feeling against Mr. Branson and Virgin that people might choose to do that despite the threat of nationalization.

The letter was signed by Roger Lawson, Communications Director, UKSA.

Conclusions

If we are to sum up the extent of blame that could be apportioned to the regulatory bodies, it would be as follows:

The FSA proved ineffective as a regulator of banks.

It was remiss in its supervision of Northern Rock (and of other banks in view of the number of them that have since fallen on their swords). The culprit was a lax senior management that failed to ensure that it managed an organization "fit for purpose" and which had no prepared plan to deal with a credit crisis of major proportions.

It suffered from inadequate and poorly managed internal structures and a lack of adequate staff training, possible exacerbated by high staff turnover; a poor implementation of policies relative to the supervision of "high impact" firms and a poor standard of liaison with its fellows in the Tripartite Committee. There were many who blamed the Tripartite arrangement for the shortcomings of FSA supervision. However, it was not the Tripartite structure that was to blame, it was the administration of it.

The FSA required a top to bottom review of its effectiveness. At the same time it should not be forgotten that it is a big institution with responsibility for the regulation of a wide range of financial activities. The FSA did not ensure that it knew and understood the implications of what was going on inside all the banks for which it had regulatory responsibility.

The FSA is now so big and so diverse in its responsibilities that it is understandably difficult to implement and ensure consistent, effective management and performance.

Are the deficiencies the fault of government?

No. They are the responsibility of FSA's management, at all levels. However it is now government's job to ensure that more effective regulation, and more importantly effective supervision by the regulators of those bodies for which they have regulatory responsibility, is implemented and maintained.

The Bank of England had primary responsibility for the prevention of systemic spread of risk in a financial crisis. It was operating at what proved to be the end of a long period when everyone - players, regulators and the public - thought that the only path for the City and financial institutions was onwards and upwards. Northern Rock could be regarded as a largely unanticipated shock.

The Bank of England, although not responsible for the day-to-day supervision of individual financial institutions, has to become more involved at that level in times when extreme stress in the financial system appears imminent. That has been proposed as part of an overhaul of its duties and the execution of them.

Although Mr. King's responses to the Northern rock liquidity problems were subsequently proved to be inadequate and a mistake, he was faced with a dilemma on which, after due consideration and in good faith he unfortunately made the wrong decision.

However, he does need to ensure that the Bank has adequate contingency plans in place and that there are more effective communication channels between the B of E, the FSA and HM Treasury. By October 2008 he had initiated a review of those and other administrative matters.

His responses to the 2008 problems could be viewed as having excused him for making that first mistake.

The Treasury and the Chancellor had to become involved as the Treasury was one of the Tripartite regulators. Presumably at the instance of the Chancellor, Goldman Sachs advised the Treasury on its approach to a Northern Rock solution. One can assume therefore that the ideas and decisions that emanated from the Treasury were recommended by Goldman Sachs although they were presented by the Chancellor.

Although Northern Rock was nationalized at the end of the process, that may not have been the Chancellor's preferred option. Perhaps he was influenced too much by political imperatives.

The Treasury was initially involved only on the side-lines. However it quickly became the central player in the Triumvirate but was faced with a situation for which no plan of action had been drawn up in advance.

The Treasury allowed attempts to find a wholly private sector solution to drag on for far too long in circumstances where it could be readily seen that until the inter-bank market was "unfrozen" - which it and the B of E tried ineffectually to achieve – a private sector solution without the continuance of substantial Treasury / Bank of England financial assistance would not be achieved.

There was an obsession with one facet of the search for a solution – to obtain maximum value for "the tax-payer". That objective appeared to over-ride all other considerations and may have emanated from Goldman Sachs. We shall never know because the Chancellor refused to reveal details of the basis on which the Treasury's nationalization decision was reached.

Greater emphasis may have been placed on nationalization because it was a way to prevent the two hedge fund investors from benefiting from their investment in Northern Rock. What appeared to have been given no consideration was the fact that all the other shareholders owning around 70% of the company, including pension funds and insurance companies would be wiped out at the same time.

The adoption of nationalization as a solution was one thing, however the government's insistence that the company had to be valued on the basis that it was insolvent, when it was clearly operating as a "going concern" was a serious error of judgment and grossly unfair to the shareholders.

Subsequently, during 2008, the government was prepared to provide the banking system with a £600 billion bail out - or more if necessary – in order to prevent the collapse of other banks much less deserving of assistance than Northern Rock. The banks receiving the assistance unthinkingly acquired hundreds of billions of pounds worth of sub-prime assets that currently have been reduced to a nominal value. As a result, and because of injudicious lending policies they also wrote off sixty or more billion pounds of their shareholders' funds and depleted their capital funds below an acceptable level by pursuing those ill-conceived policies.

The provisions made in Northern Rock's 2007 Accounts for losses, most of which had still to materialize, were minimal by comparison.

What was the justification for the government's actions later in 2008? It acted to avoid a complete collapse of much of the UK banking system. Undoubtedly this was a very valid reason but it was one that demonstrated the inequity of the treatment meted out to Northern Rock's shareholders.

The shareholders in Northern Rock played no part in its downfall, either before or after 14th September 2007. The government's proposed treatment of them can only be described as shameful. In the light of all that has happened since in the financial sector, the cost of compensating shareholders in a reasonable and professionally assessed manner would be a small price for it to be seen to have acted honourably and fairly, a frequently declared objective of the Labour Government. Such a course of action would not be difficult to justify since the relatively modest cost would be recovered when the nationalized business is sold on, something that is likely to be achieved at a favourable valuation much sooner than was anticipated due to the fact that it has been proved that Northern Rock is not the basket-case it was made out to be.

Eighteen months on from September 2007 "the taxpayer" had not lost a penny on his involvement with Northern Rock and under Treasury plans his government will not only be properly paid for all the assistance given, it hopes to make a substantial profit in addition, only for his benefit, of course.

The case for a judicial review as submitted by the UK Shareholders Association, RAB Capital and SRM is a strong one as can be seen from an examination of the papers submitted to support it. The outcome of the appeal will be interesting.

Will the "son of the manse" make a U-turn? Or is it more important to save face?

Time will tell.

The subprime debacle in the USA was an undoubted catalyst in the crisis because those supplying the mortgages were more interested in the amount of profit that could be made from them than ensuring a proper quality standard. They were encouraged to keep at it by the politicians and even a succession of Presidents all of whom were anxious to propagate the American dream of being a property owner. Many mortgage brokers and mortgage-lending firms must share the blame for the creation of the financial crisis.

This is a necessary sector of the mortgage market but it requires implementation of a much-enhanced regulatory regime to ensure that its excesses are not repeated.

Derivatives and the securitization process played a major part in the development of the global crisis but principally because of the actions of the Wall Street banks. The process itself was not necessarily at fault. Northern Rock demonstrated that. The quality of the loans that it securitized required no artificial enhancement (although they received it because investors thought that it was a good thing for them). Although we have concentrated on the RMBS based derivatives, they were only part of the problem. Derivatives based on other assets also turned sour. It was estimated in early 2009 that up to $757 billion of outstanding synthetic Collateralised Debt Obligations based on corporate debt and issued in 2006/7 were being downgraded and could add to the general problems.

The securitization process, at least for the time being and in its current form, is no more.

The Wall Street investment banks that devised the process were undoubtedly instrumental in fomenting the two crises in 2007/8. Their principal faults were the reckless, possibly criminal lack of attention to the quality of loans that were parceled into what were then described as AAA rated securities and their obsession with ever greater profit margins and the resulting executive bonuses.

They have all paid a price, particularly those most involved. Unfortunately at the end of the day, it was their shareholders who bore most of the pain. The executive management of those institutions walked away.

The monoline insurers and the credit rating agencies were spurred on by the investment banks and motivated by the apparently easy profits to be made. They were reckless in the nature and extent of their involvement.

The monoliners have done, and will suffer more losses. They have had their fingers burnt, some much more badly than others. At the same time, the government rescue packages that are being offered in a number of countries will moderate the extent of their liabilities.

The credit rating agencies that play an important role in investment markets were very remiss because they did not ensure that they had sufficient information on which to accurately base their assessments. As a result they misled investors.

Effective regulation of credit rating agencies and the monoliners should become a priority.

The media played no part in the origination of the crisis other than that Robert Peston's BBC broadcasts on the 13th September 2007 started a panic by depositors that exacerbated Northern Rock's problems and played a major role in the creation of the losses suffered by Northern Rock investors. The frequent sensationalism and inaccuracy of media reporting was less than helpful as the crisis developed.

The Chancellor refused to investigate the source of the leaked information Peston used and as the Press is a law unto itself in a democracy, it will be free to repeat its performance when the next crisis arises. Nevertheless we have to be very grateful that we enjoy a free press otherwise we would learn even less about the troubles brewing around us.

The Northern Rock board pursued a policy that nearly every commentator regarded as "reckless". But that assessment was only made after the event. Prior to the run on the bank, there was no criticism of its policies, in fact Northern Rock was declared to be progressive, well-run and an excellent long term investment.

Perhaps the most appropriate comment is that in relation to risk, it pursued a "low probability, high impact" strategy but one that was disastrous for its shareholders, and will be even more so unless the government has a change of heart.

Those then were the parties at whose door blame lay. But were the people and organizations involved deserving of blame? With hindsight we can say of course they were. Apportioning the extent of blame applicable to each is a much more difficult determination on which there will be many differing opinions.

Perhaps after reading the history of the financial crisis that has been set out so far and in ensuing chapters, the reader – using the benefit of the hindsight that the story provides – will be able to make his own judgment as to how blame should be apportioned.

15 The Wider Picture in the USA

The centre piece of our study has been the effect of the financial crisis on Northern Rock, but the problems rippled out much further to seriously affect many other banks and financial institutions in the UK, USA and elsewhere.

The losses suffered in the banking industry were substantial and stemmed from a combination of the sub-prime mortgage crisis in the USA, the securitization processes carried out principally through five big Wall Street banks and over-trading by those banks. Although in many cases the losses were so substantial that a few sizeable banks collapsed, up to September 2008 the losses were not sufficiently large to bring about a collapse of the global banking system, although it could be said to have had its fingers severely burned.

As far as the UK was concerned, the crisis surfaced in August 2007, with occasional lulls thereafter. However in September 2008 it flared up again in a big way, as we shall see. The effects of the 2008 crisis extended beyond the banks and into the economies and stock markets of a number of countries so that there was constant talk of economic recession and hard times ahead.

The concern of central Banks in the USA, UK, Europe and elsewhere was to contain the crises as far as possible and to mitigate any fall-out. At the time of writing in November 2008 it remains to be seen how far they will be able to achieve that objective as yet another aspect of the crisis manifests itself.

Perhaps the most notable impact was on the banks themselves. A major contribution to the 2007crisis as it related to the UK was the uncertainty as to what was really going on within individual banks. It was known in the City that many banks had been affected by the collapse of the sub-prime and securitization markets. What was not known was the extent to which individual banks were exposed. Part of the reason for this, as recorded elsewhere, was that the valuation system applied to such assets allowed each bank to determine the extent of the "impairment of its assets" it considered appropriate to write down. In other words, they were allowed to individually determine the extent of their losses at different times of their choosing and the results were not always made public until much later.

A significant problem facing bank managements relates to when and to what extent they should make full disclosures. They are supposed to do so if they identify a situation at any time that gives rise to stock market sensitive information. It could be said that they are obliged to do so when their half-yearly and annual accounts are published but they do not necessarily tell the whole story, or if they do, it is too complicated a story for most people to try to unravel. CEO's are therefore put in a quandary. If they are not upbeat about the status of current and projected activities, they risk a poor press and a concomitant decline in share price. If they do not disclose until the balloon is about to go up, at worst they are being dishonest. History (not just recent events) tells us that they invariably keep to the "up-beat" scenario, waiting until the crash speaks for itself.

Uncertainty, and the actual impairment and write off charges when published had a disastrous affect on the share prices of many British banks. Table 18 details a number of examples.

Share prices over the year were very volatile. The figures quoted record a price at the beginning and end of a twelve-month period plus the prices on 18th September 2008 after turbulent days. As can be seen the banks suffered disastrous reductions in quoted share prices. The US banks and Fannie and Freddie fared no better. It should be noted that most banks suffered further falls as the threat of recession and further losses grew. By 18th January 2009 Royal Bank of Scotland dropped as low as 10.30 pence. LLoyds Bank after its takeover of HBOS dropped to 45 pence. Barclays fell to 47.30 pence but recovered to 66.10 pence. HSBC also dropped to 513.75 pence but was the only British bank to retain much of its former value.

Table 18

	% fall (June 2007 – Sept 2008)	**Share Prices** (pence)		
		June 2007	June 2008	18 Sept 2008
Barclays Bank	56.55%	672	285	292
HBOS	79%	875	249	185.3
HSBC	12%	972	676	854.5
Royal Bank of Scotland	72.7%	602	204	164.3
LloydsTSB	58%	585	326	247
Alliance and Leicester	75.25%	1083	302	267.75
Bradford and Bingley	91.2%	323	60	28.5

A second measure of the effect of the credit crisis on banks was the extent of the write-downs that they eventually published, although in some cases they were released piecemeal. As a result this table is not warranted to be wholly accurate.

The following list in Table 19 records the losses suffered up to September 2008. It does not present a complete picture as it relates principally to the larger US and UK banks but it does illustrate that the losses were substantial and wide spread.

Table 19 provides an indication of the extent of the losses by major banks up to mid-2008. It does not include the losses suffered by lesser banks, particularly in the USA. Further losses were published later in 2008 and early 2009. From the US Treasury Department "bail-out" of $700 billion in late 2008, £350 billion was distributed amongst a total of 279 banks and financial institutions in the USA. The remainder had still to be dealt with early in 2009.

In addition, by October 2008, a total of 16 banks had failed in the USA, not counting numerous unregulated mortgage-lending companies, some of significant size.

Table 19

US Banks (and others)		UK Banks	
	(billion dollars)		(billion pounds Stg)
Merrill Lynch	52.2	Roy B of Scotland	4.3
UBS (Swiss)	44.2		(+32 bn in early 2009)
Citigroup	55.1	HSBC	5.9
SocGen(France)	9.6	Barclays	3.65
Morgan Stanley	12.6	HBOS	3.0
Bank of China	9		
West LB (Germany)	7.2		
J P Morgan	5.1		
Wachovia	4.4		
Deutsche bank	3.2		
Bank of America	3		
Goldman Sachs	3		
Lehman Bros	2.8		
Wells Fargo	2		
CIBC (Canada)	2		
Credit Suisse (Swiss)	1.9		
Bear Stearns	1.9		
Nomura (Japan)	1.4		

The estimated global total for bank losses or write-downs as at August 2008 was estimated at $300 billion but that soon proved to be an optimistic figure. The International Monetary Fund estimated that total losses could amount, in time, to one Trillion dollars. That was thought to be a"worst-case" scenario but as each week passed in the fourth quarter of 2008 reported losses were heading beyond that figure. When making an assessment of the potential total losses that may be incurred there are conflicting methods of arriving at an answer.

Accounting rules require "impairment charges" to be sufficient to write down the value of an asset to "fair value" or "market value". In normal times the market value method is probably the one that gives the most realistic picture but when no market exists for a particular category of asset, in this case RMBS and other similar bonds, the value of the asset becomes zero, or some figure close to it, but that takes no account of an eventual re-opening of the market. The alternative is to mark to "fair value". Under that method a company's board has to determine what, in all the circumstances represents fair value. A problem with such an evaluation is that the results will not necessarily be consistent for similar assets held by a variety of companies. By way of example, in September 2008, Lehman Brothers placed a fair value of 39 cents per dollar on its RMBS portfolio, whereas at much the same time, AIG, the world's largest insurance company (until its collapse a few days later) valued its RMBS holdings at 69 cents in the dollar.

Points that seem to have been discounted when placing a "fair value" on impaired RMBS assets are that the issues were all (or mostly) guaranteed by insurers through Credit Default Swap contracts, although the wholesale losses that the insurers could incur might be beyond their capacity to meet. The second point was that the default rate in the subprime market was only around 20% on average, therefore one would expect the possible losses to have been limited to around 20% of the loans outstanding but the factor that seemed to have most influence on the "fair value" calculations was fear of a worst possible scenario.

In the prime markets, if we look at Freddie and Fannie's figures we find that Freddie's overall delinquency rate (i.e. over three months in arrears) rose from 0.5% in June 2007 to 1.22%, and 28,000 repossessions in September 2008. Fannie's rates went from 0.78% in September 2007 to 1.72% a year later.

It is important to realise the size of the US housing market if the extent of the problems is to be understood. There were said to have been 2.2 million foreclosures in 2008 and it was estimated that this figure could rise to 4 million in 2009, which is why the new Obama administration diverted some of its bank bail-out efforts to assisting home owners to avoid foreclosure proceedings. It has been reported that there has been a 25% fall in US house prices since 2006 and that has resulted in a loss of wealth for homeowners of $6 Trillion which partly demonstrates why defaults on mortgages have become a major problem.

As recorded earlier, the subprime market was about $1300 billion and the prime market processed by Freddie and Fannie $5.7 trillion or $5,700 billion out of a total prime market of $11.5 trillion. If we apply the delinquency rates quoted above and assume that there will be no recoveries from repossessed properties we can obtain an approximation of the write-offs that Fannie and Freddie should have to suffer, namely $83 billion. However it is difficult to reconcile that estimate with the write-off figures being applied by those two companies or with the sums that they are obtaining in government aid.

It would appear that Freddie and Fannie and other major banks are writing down or disposing of their so-called "toxic assets" at values that are much lower than their eventual worth may prove to be. This would seem to indicate that some people, somewhere, are going to make a lot of money out of purchases made at distressed sale prices (and that includes governments).

At the same time it has to be remembered that the bail-outs being offered by governments around the world are not hand-outs. The cash is in exchange for bundles of those "toxic assets". The important point is, at what price are these assets being exchanged for cash? This is not a topic that has received publicity. If the value placed on the assets is too high, governments (and of course taxpayers) will suffer losses eventually. If the price is too low, there is little incentive for financial institutions to take up the government money.

Another aspect of the credit crunch was the impact on employment levels. There have been substantial cuts in staffing by banks globally and after the turmoil during the weekend of 14th September 2008, the figures quoted in Table 20, which set out the situation in mid-2008, are likely to pale into insignificance when the final figure is known, for example as a result of the takeovers that took place in the UK, Europe and the USA in the fourth quarter of 2008 and a later announcement by Citigroup in November 2008 that it planned another 53,000 redundancies globally. The collapse of Lehman Bros left 25000 employees out of work although Barclays Bank acquired part of the business and about 10000 of the employees. Table 20 gives some idea of the extent of job losses up to October 2008 although they are only representative of major institutions.

Hedge Funds

In addition to bank losses, hedge funds (and therefore their investors) also lost billions of dollars. Since the beginning of 2008 the industry suffered several high-profile failures, including Peloton, the $2 billion bond fund set up by former Goldman Sachs bankers that collapsed with heavy losses in January 2008. In the first quarter of 2008, 170 hedge funds collapsed. At the same time 247 new funds were set up although they only pulled

Table 20

Bank of America	3000
Citigroup	30000
Royal Bank of Scotland	7000
	(partly resulting from the ABN Amro acquisition
	plus 2000 in early 2009)
Merrill Lynch	4000
Morgan Stanley	2900
UBS	2200
Northern Rock	2000
Bear Stearns	1500
	(before take-over by JP Morgan Stanley)
Goldman Sachs	1500
HSBC	750
Credit Suise	320
Deutsche bank	300

in a net $2.6 billion of new capital. It may seem a large amount but it was down 81% from the previous quarter total of $13.7 billion.

A complicating factor with hedge funds is the manner in which they are structured. The managers are often in one country, the assets in another, and where investments related to subprime mortgages are concerned, that means the USA. The funds themselves are frequently set up in an offshore jurisdiction, Grand Cayman being a frequent choice. What this means is that when the funds run into serious financial decline, the question of the legal jurisdiction in which creditors or the managers should take steps to recover or protect assets becomes complicated.

By way of an example, in August 2007, Basis Capital Management, an Australian based firm that ran Basis Yield Alpha hedge fund suffered an 80% loss in asset value of the fund. It sought approval from the Cayman Island Court to liquidate its assets, but as the principal creditors were in the USA, it filed an application with a Federal bankruptcy judge for bankruptcy protection against US creditors. A Federal judge had earlier in the month refused to grant protection to two Bear Stearns funds based in Grand Cayman Island as he was not satisfied that the Cayman island was the proper jurisdiction to control a liquidation of assets that were mostly domiciled in the USA.

There are many hedge fund stories that could be related but as we shall be examining the fall of Bear Stearns, the fifth largest investment bank on Wall Street, it is appropriate to look at the fate of two of the hedge funds managed by Bear Stearns. They were known as the High-Grade Structured Credit Strategies Enhanced Leverage Fund (the "Enhanced Fund") and the High-Grade Structured Credit Fund (the "High-Grade Fund"). Those names were somewhat ironic in view of what happened to both funds.

In May 2007, when investors tried to get out of the funds after learning that losses far exceeded the amounts that had been reported earlier, Bear Stearns halted redemptions. In June, it told clients that the High-Grade fund was down 91% and the Enhanced Fund also had suffered a sharp decline. Two months later, in a July letter to investors, Bear Stearns acknowledged that "there is effectively no value left" in the Enhanced Fund and "very little value left" in the High-Grade Fund. The two funds, which had an estimated aggregate value of $1.5 billion at the end of 2006 were now essentially worthless. A letter to investors stated that,

> unprecedented declines in the valuations of a number of highly rated (AA and AAA) securities, contributed to the funds' devastating losses.

In view of the relatively short life of both funds, one has to question how the particular investments in those funds could ever have deserved to be rated AA or AAA.

In addition to all that, Massachusetts securities regulators were examining whether Bear Stearns traded mortgage-backed securities for its own account with the two hedge funds without first notifying the funds' independent directors. Federal securities law requires that any investment adviser whose affiliates engage in principal trading with clients must obtain their written consent in advance. If the investigation reveals that Bear Stearns failed to give this proper disclosure and engaged in conflicted trading, the fund managers could be accused of breaching their fiduciary duty to investors.

At the same time Federal prosecutors and the Securities and Exchange Commission were conducting their own investigations of the Enhanced Fund and High-Grade Fund, focusing on the circumstances that led to their implosion. Although it is right that such matters be subjected to scrutiny by the regulators such cases are notoriously difficult to bring to a satisfactory conclusion.

The funds not only used enormous amounts of leverage, or borrowed money, they also relied on accounting practices that allowed them to base the value of securities in their portfolios on "fair value," or estimated value, rather than the true market price. Although only 25% of the High-Grade Fund's assets were based on fair value in 2004, two years later over 70% of its assets — $616 million — were calculated on this basis. For the Enhanced Fund, 63% of its assets in 2006 — $589 million — were assessed at fair value. Prior to their July 2007 bankruptcies, more than 60% percent of the two funds' net worth consisted of complex exotic securities with a worth calculated on a fair value basis. In a note to the Enhanced Fund's 2006 financial statements, Deloitte & Touche, the funds' auditor, warned investors that the value of the majority of the fund's net assets had been estimated by its own managers. Add to that the facts that Bear Stearns did not release the 2006 audited financials until mid-May 2007, only two weeks before the firm suspended redemptions in the Enhanced Fund, and also that many investors claim that they never received a copy of the Deloitte report.

All of that was possibly not untypical of many other hedge fund stories but the Bear Stearns funds had an extra twist. The Enhanced Fund had an unusual arrangement with Barclays Bank, an arrangement that gave the bank advantages over the interests of other investors. In exchange for Barclays providing approximately $275 million in capital to help launch the Enhanced Fund in <u>August 2006</u>, Bear Stearns designated Barclays as the fund's sole equity investor. Other investors in the fund merely held a stake in a complicated derivative contract that mimicked the fund's gains or losses, but conferred no actual ownership rights.

It is understood that the Enhanced Fund's offering memorandum included an oblique mention of the fact that Barclays' interests "might conflict" with those of other shareholders, but it was thought doubtful that other investors would have picked up on the significance of it, equally it could be said that Bear Stearns had little incentive to provide a clear explanation of the arrangement.

In late December 2007 Barclays bank lodged a lawsuit against Bear Stearns seeking compensation of $300 million or more, alleging that two senior officers responsible for the fund's investment policies had known for some time that the underlying assets had a much lower value that that stated earlier in 2007.

Following the collapse of the two funds in detail would be a story in itself but a year after the collapse, in June 2008, the two fund officers were arrested and charged with securities fraud by Federal authorities. It may be some time before we learn if the charges will result in convictions. As so often is the fact in such cases involving financial markets there are others in Bear Stearns who are just as culpable as the two managers. That was the case, for example in the downfall of Baring Brothers in London in the 1990's. The only person convicted was the Singapore trader, Nick Leeson, but those who enabled and authorized him to play the markets by providing him with the equivalent of the entire capital of that bank were never brought to account.

Although those figures paint a bleak picture they have to be viewed in the context of the hedge fund industry total funds, estimated at around $2000 billion ($2 Trillion). About one-half of this sum is held in the top 350 funds, each of which had taken in more than $1billion. Collectively they accounted for $950 billion of the total. Petrac Financial produced those figures in a survey. The company also put the total number of funds at end 2007 at 15,250. The industry has only posted one loss-making year, in 2002, but figures so far this year (to July 2008) suggest 2008 may end that six-year winning record and its accompanying multi-million dollar bonuses for the managers. As noted elsewhere, a large part of the strategy of hedge funds is to "short" shares.

Short Selling

In the USA during September 2008 shares in the last two of the big Wall Street Investment banks, Morgan Stanley and Goldman Sachs, were aggressively attacked by short sellers driving down their prices amid rumours that they would be unable to survive on their own. To counter those short-selling activities, on 17th September the US Securities and Exchange Commission introduced rules requiring short sellers and their broker/dealers to deliver securities by the close of business on the settlement date, normally three days after the sale. The following day the FSA announced a temporary ban on short selling financial stocks with immediate effect.

The New York attorney general also launched a criminal investigation into traders who made millions, after his office received a significant number of complaints that traders used illegal practices to drive down prices.

What has to be remembered is that the restrictions on shorting imposed in the UK, USA and many other countries at the same time were only imposed on trading in the shares of certain financial institutions, there was no imposition of blanket prohibitions. In all countries with sizeable banking industries it was recognised that there was a need to protect the stability of the financial system that over-rode other considerations.

Those actions appeared to have the desired effect. The two investment banks' shares in the US recovered initially by 10% and in the UK all the banks showed substantial gains when trading opened the following morning.

If we return to earlier in the year, in addition to direct losses and write-downs brought about by their involvement as investors in, and purveyors of securitised bonds there were other institutions that suffered from the "knock-on" effects. Northern Rock was the UK's high profile casualty. In the USA, Bear Stearns was its opposite number. Its story surfaced in late December 2007 but it ended very differently.

Bear Stearns

The first announcement was of a loss of $854 million in the fourth quarter of 2007 following a write-down of $1.9 billion related to its holdings of mortgage backed securities. Bear Stearns was known as one of the biggest players in the packaging of mortgages into mortgage backed securities. Other aspects of its business also saw a decline and contributed to the overall loss.

It seemed to be "business as usual" until early march 2008 when the deterioration in the markets resulted in difficulties for Bear Stearns as it had been a major lender to hedge funds that themselves were facing increasing difficulties. All this sparked off market-place rumours as to the solvency of Bear Stearns particularly after a hedge fund Carlyle Capital Corporation to which Bear Stearns had lent $1.6 billion, collapsed. It appears that in addition to those woes, lenders to Bear Stearns were seeking repayment of their loans. Effectively, although it may not have been apparent in the public arena, there was a run on Bear Stearns. It later transpired that the bank had lost $10 billion of its available liquid funds in one day. The bank then sought emergency short term funding from J P Morgan Chase bank and the New York Federal Reserve Bank.

Bear Stearns was recognised as one of the largest global custodian banks and this fact influenced the Federal authorities in their response to the bank's problems. The collapse of a substantial bank, so heavily involved as a custodian with many counter-parties would have severe repercussions in the financial world. The bank had also been very active in the prime brokerage area, through the provision of trading, lending and administrative services to hedge funds and other investors.

There was much speculation over the future of Bear Stearns for several days in March 2008 until, somewhat reluctantly, J P Morgan Chase changed from offers of temporary financial assistance to a buy out bid at $2 per share, considered to be much less than the book value of the bank. The Morgan Chase bid was backed by the Federal Reserve which guaranteed $29 billion of Bear Stearns illiquid assets. This gave rise to a Senate Banking Committee enquiry and raised questions in the Senate where members queried why it was that the US Treasury was prepared to rescue a failing bank but did nothing to help the multitude of home-owners facing foreclosure.

Perhaps part of the answer may be found in the close relationships that exist between government and the finance industry. By way of example here are some career paths that over a period stemmed from Goldman Sachs ranks:

Henry M Paulson Jr	Treasury Secretary
Robert E Rubin	Treasury Secretary under President Clinton, now Citigroup Chairman
Joshua B Bolton	White House Chief of Staff
John Thain	President and Chief Operating Officer, Goldman Sachs, then head of New York Stock Exchange, then CEO Merrill Lynch until his departure in 2008

There are other senior appointments filled by Goldman Sachs former executives that could be identified. It is not suggested here that any of these gentlemen were guilty of any impropriety, the list only illustrates that at the top of government and the US financial scene there is a fairly close-knit community. It must also be recognised that as far as the examples mentioned are concerned, they all probably achieved their respective posts because Goldman Sachs had a reputation as an excellent training ground for some of the brightest people in finance.

A twist to the Goldman Sachs executives' story came in November 2008 when a US Senator, Chuck Grassley, the most senior Republican on the Senate finance committee, requested the Inspector General of the US Treasury to investigate potential conflicts of interest among former Goldman Sachs executives serving at the Treasury. His concerns arose following the acquisition of Wachovia Bank (see later in this chapter) by Wells Fargo Bank. Mr. Grassley was concerned that relationships between Treasury officials and board members at both Wachovia and Wells Fargo gave an appearance of preferential treatment of the takeover. He particularly had in mind that the CEO of Wachovia had worked for Mr. Paulson at Goldman.

Perhaps all was not as it should have been.

Criticism of banking regulators was also expressed in the Senate and suggestions made that regulators needed to look at their performance and come up with a much improved standard of regulation. As we have seen in Chapter 13 this was a recurring criticism.

Shareholders protested strongly about the $2 bid and within a few days Morgan Chase was obliged to raise its offer to $10 per share. It is illustrative of the depths to which Bear Stearns had plunged that only a year before its shares had traded at $171.

The Senate Banking Committee acted swiftly to hold a hearing on 3rd April 2008 investigating the bank's collapse. The Federal Reserve Boards, Treasury Department and SEC were called upon to defend their part in the affair. They were all of the opinion that there were no choices available to them. They had to act for the broader good of the markets and the economy. The opinion of the president of the Federal Reserve Bank of New York was that a failure of Bear Stearns would have resulted in a greater probability of widespread insolvencies, severe and protracted damage to the financial system and the economy as a whole.

The hearing also produced the fact that regulators were unaware of Bear Stearns precarious situation and did not know until the afternoon of 13th March 2008 that the bank was planning to file for bankruptcy protection the following morning. Another interesting fact that emerged was that Henry M Paulson, Jr. Treasury Secretary, appears to have suggested during the negotiations between Bear Stearns and Morgan Chase that the share offer price should be low because the deal was being supported by a $30 billion "tax-payer" loan. He said further that a lower price was desirable to make the broader point to the markets that by rescuing the bank the government did not want to encourage risky behaviour by other large institutions, a concept known as "moral hazard", as we saw in relation to Northern Rock and the Bank of England.

It was anticipated that there would be other official enquiries, The SEC started one but did not complete it and turned aside Congressional requests for a reason to be given as to why it did not do so.

It is worth spending some time on the Bear Stearns saga since there were many echoes of the reasoning behind the actions taken in respect of Northern Rock, except that the US government actions were on a much more accelerated basis. Other points of interest included:

J P Morgan Chase would absorb the first $1 billion of any losses on the security behind the Federal reserve loans.

The loans were secured by investment grade securities and collateralised mortgage obligations, the majority of which were from institutions like Freddie Mac.

The Fed would have 10 years to dispose of the assets, thus avoiding any "fire-sale" problems.

Bear Stearns was given only four days to accept the Morgan Chase offer. The only alternative facing it would have been to file for bankruptcy which would have wiped out shareholders, some of its creditors and its employees.

How did other banks fare in the credit crisis?

Goldman Sachs

The investment bank that fared best was undoubtedly Goldman Sachs. Late in 2006 at a time when most of Goldman Sachs' competitors were becoming more and more involved in the mortgage markets, packaging and trading securitised bonds and other complex related products, Goldman began to reduce its involvement and, at a cost, purchased insurance against losses in the mortgage-related securities it continued to hold. As a result when those markets froze in the second half of 2007, Goldman Sachs was far better placed than its competitors to not only survive the storm, but to maintain profitability. This is borne out by Goldman Sachs' performance throughout the credit crisis. Goldman was acknowledged to be one of the most profitable financial firms in the world.

How did it achieve this?

Its President said that it concentrated on making fewer mistakes. That it made fewer mistakes than its competitors was borne out in mid-2008 when, although it had suffered modest losses of $3 billion, it was still showing satisfactory earnings results when others were posting multi-billion dollar losses. Nevertheless as the year progressed Goldman's position began to look shaky. It and Morgan Stanley managed to retain their independence by applying in September 2008 to convert themselves into regulated bank holding companies. This transformation meant that they would be unable to conduct some of their activities and others would be subject to restriction under the tougher regulatory regime to which they will be subjected. At the same time that regulatory regime did not prevent all the other bank collapses related in this Chapter. On the other hand the banks gained in other ways from the change in status.

In September Warren Buffett acknowledged Goldman's improved situation by investing $5 billion. In November 2008 the US Treasury bail-out plan allocated $125 billion to nine major banks, including Goldman which received $10 billion just as analysts had calculated that the bank was about to declare its first ever quarterly loss.

The terms of the government aid to those banks was that the banks would issue Preferred Stock to the Treasury that will pay special dividends at 5% for the first five years and 9% thereafter. In addition the Treasury would receive convertible warrants for shares in each bank. Should share prices improve, the government / taxpayer would benefit, if not, the warrants would have no value.

In consequence of these events seven senior Goldman executives agreed that no bonuses would be received by them for 2008. Compare that with $68.5 million to the CEO and two co-presidents who each had around $67.5 million for 2007. As they will still have substantial salaries, foregoing bonuses will not put them in the poorhouse as is likely to happen to many other bank employees in 2008.

Lehman Brothers

Another New York bank that was listed as fourth largest in the US, Lehman Brothers, dating back to 1850 (with 25,000 employees) had been trying unsuccessfully for some months to resolve its problems but by September 2008 the bank's options were narrowing. It had been trying to negotiate a substantial capital investment from Korea Investment Bank (KDP) but by early September it appeared that a participation by KDP was unlikely. Other avenues pursued by the bank included trying to sell off its investment division for around $6 billion, a price that was not acceptable to prospective bidders. Other parts of the bank included $30 billion of commercial real estate assets of debatable value. The bank had been working on another plan to transfer those assets to a separate company, owned by Lehman shareholders and financed by debt and equity from the bank. This plan was not concluded.

Part of the problem appears to have been that the bank's CEO did not believe that its problems were serious enough to require it to conduct a fire sale of its various parts, particularly as it had access to an emergency lending facility from the Federal Reserve. Its CEO, Dick Fuld was in denial. Mr Fuld had spent 30 years at the bank. It was suggested that he had the typical hubris that affected long term CEO's,

I built this thing and it has more value than the market place understands.

During June 2008 Lehman's shares were subject to heavy short-selling on the back of widespread rumours that Barclays Bank was about to acquire Lehman Brothers at a steep discount, rumoured to be up to $15 per share. The rumour was so widespread that it drove Lehman's share price down to $19.80, its lowest in ten years. Neither bank would comment on the rumours on the basis that even to comment would give credence to a "no smoke without fire" scenario. Some Press reporting made the point that there would be no sense in such a merger for Barclays as there would be a substantial overlap in their fixed-income departments and other areas. The prominence and implausibility of the rumour convinced Lehman's CEO, Dick Fuld that the bank was the object of a short-selling conspiracy

Within a month or so at the instance of Federal officials, the bank put itself up for sale. Bank of America and Barclays were named as interested bidders, but it appeared that any acquisition would require Federal Reserve support, as had been given to Bear Stearns.

Lehman's problems increased week by week as the credit crisis continued. Its credit ratings were threatened, other banks became reluctant to lend to it, its shareholders did not trust management, all of which resulted in a sliding share price that dropped 93% in a year to a low of under $4. Despite all this, Mr.Fuld was awarded and retained a $22 million bonus for 2007, admittedly a year when the bank produced a record profit.

In view of the downfall recorded in the next paragraph, it is worth noting the opinions of a Standard and Poors analyst, Scott Sprinzen, on Friday 12th September,

We don't expect Lehman to fail. Lehman was pretty conservatively positioned all along. It can survive given the strength of its near-term liquidity, including its access to existing Fed facilities.

Another S&P statement the same day said that,

It was evaluating its rating on Lehman following reports that the bank is in discussions to be potentially acquired.

No wonder the credit rating agencies were so far adrift in their rating of RMBS bonds.

It was reported that on 12th September J P Morgan Chase Bank had blocked $17 billion of cash and securities that it held belonging to Lehman Brothers.

That was the straw that broke the camel's back.

On the weekend of 13-14th September 2008, a year to the day after the collapse of Northern Rock, Mr.Paulson, the US Treasury Secretary made it clear that government assistance would not be extended to a successful bidder for Lehman Brothers as had been done for Bear Stearns. In the UK it was suggested that Barclays did not have sufficient strength to indulge in a takeover of what was seen to be a basket case bank. On the 15th September Barclays' version of the story was that,

It was unable to secure an agreement that was in the best interests of its shareholders.

On Sunday both Bank of America and Barclays Bank withdrew their interest and Lehman Brothers found that it had no other option but to file for bankruptcy protection in the US and place its UK operations in administration. The bank closed for business.

Its stock price sank to 29 cents. Lehman did not have a retail business in the same way as many other banks. Being primarily an investment bank it relied on a line of $188 billion in the wholesale money markets for funding and it conducted a wide range of activities with other banks that would be counter-parties in deals. It was considered that on a global basis nearly every major bank and insurance company would be a creditor of Lehman Brothers.

Concern about the adverse effects that such deals could have on other banks caused a considerable disturbance on stock markets and in particular affected the share prices of banks. Citigroup immediately issued a press release to the effect that Lehman's demise would not cause it concern. Despite its own troubles it had increased its capital funds by US$50 billion and announced that it had over $800 billion in deposits worldwide. In the UK on Monday 15th September the banks that were believed might be most at risk were immediately marked down at the opening of trading. After some fluctuations, by 2.30pm RBS had fallen by 13.5%; HBOS, 21.5%; Barclays 12.7%; and Lloyds TSB, 8%. Trading volumes were much higher than normal.

On 16th September it was reported that Barclays had agreed to buy the broker/dealer and merger and debt advisory businesses of Lehman Brothers in New York. Those areas of the bank employed 10,000 people. Barclays acted swiftly in order to retain the best employees that were essential to the worth of Lehman's operations to it and who otherwise could have been poached by other institutions.

On 17th September Press reports related how Lehman in New York had moved $8.2 billion from its London operation on Friday 12th September before it filed for bankruptcy. It appeared at first that this was a normal weekly transfer to fund US assets over the weekend and the transfer was customarily reversed on the following Monday. On this occasion the funds were not returned and the London office was left with no cash on which to continue to operate, or for that matter, pay the month's salaries of the 5,200 London employees that were due for payment. The London staff was not included in the Barclays' deal. However, 1100 were retained to assist Price Waterhouse Coopers with its audit, 2500 were taken on by Nomura Securities London, a major brokerage firm with business similar to that of Lehman's London office, 1000 more were laid off and 500 resigned.

On 20th September it was reported that the Prime Minister was working with the US authorities to obtain the return of the money, the point being that the Chapter 11 bankruptcy proceedings in the US were separate from the administration being carried out in London by Price Waterhouse Coopers which had filed an 83 page document also calling for the repatriation of the London funds.

The US Treasury decision not to provide support for Lehman was very controversial and was still being debated in official circles months later. It was supposed to reinforce the point that the government would not automatically bail-out every bank that got itself into trouble. However the decision not to assist had wide-ranging consequences. In mid-November 2008 about 1000 corporate creditors attended a meeting in London at what used to be known as "The Dome" so that the administrators could review the progress they were making and also explain that it would take many years to sort out a distribution of assets. They said that after nine weeks work they had been unable to fully identify the extent of the bank's assets and liabilities. They also announced that it was likely that creditors would lose money. The key lay in the size of the problems they had to resolve, having identified 11,500 creditors and counter-parties in Lehman's European business, which was all that Price Waterhouse Coopers controlled. The meeting was told that the administrator's fees and costs were amounting to £4 million per week. If the administration lasts for several years as projected, there could be little left to distribute at the end of it all.

Lehman Brothers was not the only major shock in the financial world that weekend.

Merrill Lynch

Merrill Lynch, the major Wall Street investment bank and stock broker was not immune to credit crisis woes, in fact it suffered very badly as can be seen from Table 19. The bank's wealth management unit remained profitable with earnings of $720 million in the first quarter of 2008, but its global markets and investment banking units recorded a pre-tax loss of $4 billion and "negative revenue" of $690 million in the same period. Although the wealth management unit remained profitable, one wonders if its clients were as fortunate. The "Chinese Wall" that should have existed between its investment banking unit and its wealth management unit does not seem to have been as effective as its counter-part, the Great Wall of China.

Merrill followed other banks during the first half of 2008 and raised $7 billion from bond sales but at a cost, 3.20 –3.25 percentage points over US Treasury rates, to assist its ailing capital position, further improved by sales of assets other than its distressed mortgage backed securities. However in August a deal was struck to sell $30 billion of those to a private equity firm at a discount, it is believed, of $5 billion.

Merrill Lynch's stock price declined steadily, partly because the market perception was that after Bear Stearns and Lehman Brothers, it could be number three. This was symptomatic of what was driving markets in bank shares. Earlier, on 8th march 2008 Patrick Hosking of the UK "The Times" newspaper, as a commentary on a report of the US Federal Reserve making available a further $200 billion into the markets, wrote,

> *(it) will provide extra lubricant to a banking system paralysed in places. However, it will not alter sentiment. Bankers are in a funk. The sensible thing might be to act co-operatively, to give over-borrowed clients breathing space, to agree standstill arrangements, to offer a bit of slack to prevent fire sales. But competition does not work like that and the sheer number of creditors often makes such deals impractical. Once one bank pulls the plug, or just looks like it might, others have little choice but to follow, or preferably to anticipate the capitulation and get out first.*

This piece was a good assessment of what central banks are up against in trying to assist with solutions, and confirms that what really matters is not the true situation, but the market perception of it. The Fed kept trying and released a further $76 billion into the system at the beginning of May 2008.

Merrill Lynch ended its career on Sunday 14th September 2008 as an independent and well regarded brokerage firm when it announced that it had agreed to sell itself to Bank of America for $50.3 billion in stock, valuing its shares at $29. It appeared that the firm would not die completely as it would have a reincarnation as Merrill Lynch Wealth management within Bank of America, managed by some of its former wealth management executives who were not involved in the mortgage-related assets melt down. Later it was announced that they would qualify for bonuses to encourage them to stay in their new environment.

With banks crashing all round them nobody seems to have considered that they probably would have nowhere else to go.

As far as the Merrill Lynch CEO, John Thain and the Head of trading, Thomas Montag were concerned, they had adequate protection if they either left the bank on the takeover or accepted lesser jobs from B of A. Thain, who had only been CEO since December 2007, when he received his "golden hello" of $15 million, would be entitled (at the takeover price) to $11 million of free shares. Montag (he and Thain were formerly colleagues at Goldman Sachs) would be eligible for $30million in stock awards and $6.4 million in options.

The acquisition of Merrill Lynch may well prove to be a headache for Bank of America. Early in 2009 the extent of the losses buried in Merrill Lynch began to emerge. 4th Quarter 2008 losses were declared at $15.3 billion, resulting in the departure of its former chief, John A Thain who was said to have sought a $30 million bonus although in the end he did not receive one. At the same time, earlier in the year he controversially refurbished his personal New York offices for $1.2 million and at a time in December 2008 (notwithstanding the $15.3 billion of losses), paid out substantial bonuses amounting to $3.6 billion to executive officers and a total of 39,000 employees, payments that in February 2009 were being investigated by the New York Attorney General's office.

Nevertheless Thain's personal rewards for running a company for only nine months before it had to be rescued from his management efforts were considerable.

Notwithstanding all that, by February 2009 the US government had injected $45 billion in cash into B of A and agreed to provide a backstop for up to $120 billion of more dicey Merrill assets, plus help to cover another $30 billion of potential losses on B of A assets. As part of the deal, B of A agreed to give the government an additional $4 billion in preferred stock, cut its quarterly dividend to one cent (from 32 cents), accept a loan modification programme and place restrictions on executive pay.

Despite all this, analysts were of the opinion that B of A's troubles were not over.

Washington Mutual Savings & Loan

Washington Mutual (WaMu) started life in Washington, Oregon in 1885 and grew to be the largest mortgage lender in the USA with assets of $307 billion and deposits amounting to $188 billion. During 2007 it was seriously affected by the fallout from the subprime crisis and in the fourth quarter posted a loss of $1.87 billion, followed by further losses culminating in a second quarter 2008 loss which was its biggest ever and which drove its share price down to $3. For a number of years WaMu had concentrated its operations on lower-income urban borrowers, in other words, sub-prime. This category of lending encompassed both its mortgage and credit card business.

In June 2008 changes were made to the bank's board and the roles of Chairman and CEO, both of which had been held by Kerry K Killinger for eighteen years, were split and a new chairman, Stephen E Frank appointed. On 8th September 2008 Killinger was apparently told that the board had decided he must retire. This decision may have been connected to a memorandum of understanding that the bank signed with the Office of Thrift Supervision (OTS), its principal regulator. The OTS required the bank to improve its risk management and compliance procedures. A new CEO, Alan H Fishman was appointed. His terms of engagement were extremely generous for a bank that might have been too far-gone for him to effect a turn-round. He had a "hello" cash bonus of $7.45 million, plus 612,000 of restricted stock shares, 5 million stock options (for which he would have to work pretty hard), a $1 million salary supplemented by annual bonuses aimed at reaching $3.65 million and annual stock-grants (not options) of at least $8 million.

Despite the fact that WaMu was heading for the rocks after Mr. Killinger's eighteen years at the helm, it was said that his "exit package" could amount to $23.5 million, a fact which if true contrasted with the fate of the 4200 employees that had been terminated since the beginning of 2008.

A few days later, 11th September 2008, the share price fell to $2 as investors became concerned at the bank's situation and that it would be unable to raise new capital or find a white knight to rescue it.

Earlier in the year, in January, there had been talk of a deal with J P Morgan Chase bank (JPM) and some accounts reported that JPM had made an offer that was considered inadequate. Reports also circulated that whilst JPM was interested in an expansion of its mortgage activities to the West Coast, the bank was not about to pay a premium to acquire WaMu, notwithstanding that its then market value of $13 billion was less than a third of what it had been six months earlier.

It has been said that in March 2008, JPM returned with an offer, but the WaMu board rejected it. Shortly afterwards, in April, a deal was struck with a private equity fund, TPG, to make a purchase of $7.2 billion of new WaMu shares. TPG had previous dealings with WaMu and took advantage of the distressed market price to pick up what it regarded as a bargain in a bank that, whilst it had a measure of capital inadequacy, was perceived to have no solvency issues. It acquired 822 million shares thereby diluting existing shareholders' rights by about 50%. It paid $8.75 per share and included in the deal a right to revise it if there was dilution of its interests following any other issue of shares. A seat on the board for Mr. Bonderman, a co-founder of TPG was also obtained. This appears to have been TPG's normal ploy as it did the same later in 2008 when it proposed a share acquisition in Bradford and Bingley (a story related in Chapter 16).

Events were beginning to accelerate at WaMu in September. Moodies and Standard and Poors cut its credit rating, in consequence the rates for insuring its debt hit a record high and it had $44 billion of debt due for repayment by end 2008. Between 15th and 24th September it suffered a loss of deposits amounting to $16.7 billion, a sure sign of a lack of confidence in the bank, the outflow increased after the collapse of Lehman Brothers just days earlier.

During this same period WaMu engaged Goldman Sachs to advise it and find a buyer. It was reported that Goldman had approached Wells Fargo, J P Morgan Chase and HSBC. It was also suggested that if a buyer could not be found, the government would be obliged to put WaMu into "conservatorship", as it had done earlier in the year with IndyMac bank.

By 25th September Federal regulators were working to broker a deal to save WaMu in the light of speculation that the bank could have racked up losses amounting to $30 billion or more. Later that day the bank was taken over by its Federal regulators giving rise to what was the biggest bank failure in US history. The regulators had also arranged a deal under which J P Morgan Chase could acquire the bank for $1.9 billion. This deal avoided the need to take the bank into public ownership, an undesirable outcome as the $700 billion bail-out package being put together by Mr. Paulson, Secretary to the Treasury, had failed to gain the approval of Federal legislators.

This deal also removed a potential $31 billion of losses that may otherwise have fallen on the Federal Deposit Insurance Corporation (FDIC) and would now be borne by J P Morgan Chase. The latter bank had thus acquired an enormous expansion of its business potential. Taking over WaMu gave JPM around 5400 branches spread across the country. It was thought that the resultant duplication of branches would result in about 10% of them being shut down.

The deal removed a serious threat to the FDIC which had become alarmed at the extent of WaMu's problems. An unusual feature of this whole process was that it was carried out in secret without the knowledge of the WaMu board, possibly because of its continued insistence that WaMu was well capitalised and could weather the storm.

Although the deal solved problems for the government, it did nothing for WaMu's ordinary and preference shareholders. They were wiped out.

That included TPG. It was a poor outcome for a $7.2 billion investment that lasted only five months. Mr. Bonderman wrote in a newsletter to his investors,

> *We have never run across a situation where the combination of regulatory uncertainty and market disruption have combined to swiftly and decisively overtake the fundamental aspects of an investment. We are clearly perplexed by this turn of events.*

In all the circumstances at the time, with major banks going down like nine-pins in the USA, Europe and Britain during September after months of uncertainty, that sounds like a very roundabout way of saying, "I got it wrong".

Apparently the WaMu story will not end there. A joint investigation by FBI, FDIC, SEC and IRS (Revenue Service) was commenced to determine if there was any wrong-doing at WaMu prior to it being taken over by J P Morgan Chase, in particular, they wished to ascertain what had caused regulators to act so quickly to close down the bank.

Other stories that emerged about WaMu in early November 2008 came from employees and customers. A senior mortgage underwriter who had been employed by WaMu stated,

> *At WaMu it was not about the quality of loans, it was about numbers. They did not care if we were giving loans to people that did not qualify. Instead it was about how many loans did you guys close and fund?*

Apparently this employee was one of 89 whose stories were used in a complaint filed against officers of the company by the Ontario Teachers Pension Plan Board, a big shareholder. The shareholder complaint depicts WaMu's mortgage lending operation as a "boiler room" where volume was paramount and questionable loans were pushed through because they were considered to be more profitable to the company.

Staff mortgage sellers were rewarded when they achieved high loan volumes. One was awarded a holiday in Jamaica for a month because he closed $3.5 million in loans in a month. The WaMu employee who related her story gave many examples of the culture that had been forced upon her despite frequent protestations on her part, until eventually she was made redundant.

The lawyers acting for their Ontario and other clients were reported as saying,

> *Killinger pocketed millions of dollars from WaMu, while investors were left with worthless stock. With WaMu gone it is all the more important that Killinger and his co-defendants are held accountable.*

The WaMu officer's story was not untypical of experience in many other financial institutions. Here is another illustration that the imperative of meeting monthly sales targets that was imposed on staff was not a recent phenomenon. This example was recorded in a newspaper report in September 2005. It concerned a Royal Bank of Scotland branch,

> *The trade union Amicus demanded immediate action after a Branch manager in Glasgow publicly humiliated a junior member of staff for an apparent failure to sell enough mortgage products. The employee had a cabbage, complete with a drawing of his face, placed on his desk in full view of the branches' customers apparently as a motivational strategy. It would have remained there until it could be moved to another employee with a poorer performance. - - - - The union called for a company–wide investigation into claims that bullying and intimidation is rife in an attempt to force staff to meet monthly sales targets. Amicus claimed that a branch manager refused to remove the vegetable from his desk and even fished it out of a waste-paper basket when the employee thought that that he had made enough mortgage leads. The bank worked a complicated points system which meant that staff earned points for establishing possible mortgage leads and other staff earned points for selling the lead. - - - -*

Amicus added,

> *We have had all sorts of complaints from members over the years including schemes involving donkey ears.*

There is nothing wrong with reasonable incentives to improve employee performance. However, the experience of many front-line employees at lower levels was that they were pressed unreasonably to produce profits for their institutions, profits from which they received very little reward in contrast to executive officers of those institutions who pocketed millions in recognition of their (temporary) success on the backs of their employees.

Wachovia Corporation

In April 2008 Wachovia shook the analysts on Wall Street when it announced a first quarter loss of $350 million. Its level of capital funds had also fallen, partly as a result of an ill-timed acquisition of Golden West Financial (a large California lender) at the peak of the housing boom. Golden West had about $120 billion of "option rate-adjustable" mortgages on its books. These were considered to be riskier than average as borrowers could exercise an option from time to time not to make monthly interest payments and to have the missed payments added to the sum borrowed, a procedure that would adversely affect the loan-to-value ratio.

In order to strengthen its capital position after the take-over, Wachovia announced plans to raise $7 billion through the issue of preferred stock together with common stock at $24 per share, a discount of 14% to its quoted share price.

There was very little other media coverage of Wachovia until 18th September 2008 when there was a report that Wachovia had made an approach to Morgan Stanley regarding a possible merger and that the Wall Street investment bank, was considering it.

Why was Morgan Stanley interested in a merger with another bank? Because it was one of the only two Wall Street investment banks left as independents. Although Morgan Stanley did not admit to any problems, analysts were expressing doubts about it.

Within days, however, Wachovia was the centre of attention, not Morgan Stanley. Within just over a week, on 26th September Wachovia appeared to have dropped its talks with Morgan Stanley and commenced negotiations with Citigroup. At the same time it seems to have made approaches to Wells Fargo and Bank Santander of Spain. Santander appeared to be disinterested and Wells Fargo withdrew initial interest fairly quickly.

This flurry of activity on the part of Wachovia has to be seen against the backdrop of what was happening elsewhere at that time. The Treasury proposed $700 billion relief package that would have resolved its problems, at least in the short term, had stalled, other major banks were merging or collapsing. Wachovia's stock price had fallen 78% in the previous twelve months and on the 26th September suffered a 38% drop within days. The bank was under severe market pressures and had to act quickly.

Federal regulators became involved and worked night and day through the weekend with Citigroup and Wachovia. By the 30th September an "agreement in principle" had been hammered out. Citigroup would pay $2.2 billion, equivalent to $1 per share to acquire the banking operations of Wachovia. Citi would assume the first $42billion of any losses arising on Wachovia's riskiest mortgages (inherited from Golden West). It would also issue $12 billion in preferred stock and warrants to Federal Deposit Insurance Corporation, in exchange for which FDIC would assume all losses above $42 billion.

This was a good deal for Citi. It greatly extended its retail banking operations in the USA at a bargain price, the FDIC carrying the unknown risks. Everyone, including the regulators, was so anxious to complete a deal that the terms were not questioned. It was considered, by Citi, the regulators and FDIC to be a "done deal" on Tuesday 30th September.

But it wasn't.

Wells Fargo came back into the picture and on Friday, 3rd October announced that it would merge with Wachovia in a $15.1 billion all-stock deal with no FDIC or government assistance. Wells Fargo would raise $20 billion in an issue of new shares. Wachovia shares had dropped to $2 before the Citi deal was announced. The Wells Fargo deal was worth about $7 per share.

As one would expect, this sudden change of direction by Wachovia put the cat amongst the pigeons! By all accounts Citi's executives were furious.

Citi immediately applied to a New York judge for an order to put a temporary block on the Wells Fargo deal. It also proposed to seek $60 billion in damages from Wells Fargo. The judge issued the order over the weekend, but legal action could not be pursued until the Courts opened on Monday. The stage was set for a battle royal between the two banks. Wachovia defended its decision on the grounds that its board had a fiduciary duty to ensure the best deal for its shareholders.

The Federal Reserve chairman personally intervened to encourage the two banks to try for a compromise. By the 9th October there was talk of a compromise being reached but on the 10th October Federal anti-trust regulators approved the acquisition of Wachovia by Wells Fargo and Citigroup withdrew from the battle. Perhaps Citi was having second thoughts about the potential losses that could be dormant in Wachovia. Nevertheless its CEO, Vikram S. Pandit said,

> *Our shareholders have been unjustly and illegally deprived of the opportunity the transaction created.*

It would also have had a noticeable effect on his bonus entitlements.

On 23rd October Wachovia announced a $23.9 billion loss for third quarter 2008 and projected $26.1 billion in mortgage related losses in 2009, so perhaps Mr. Vikram knew more than he was saying.

When one reads of all this involving the futures of three of the largest banks in the USA that were settled within a matter of a few days, one has to wonder as to the extent to which it was possible to carry out effective due diligence and make a proper assessment of the benefits to each party. It smacks more of an opportunistic raid in troubled times.

Another major catastrophe needs to be recorded although this time it was an insurance company rather than a bank.

American International Group

Although earlier in the year the insurer, American International Group (AIG) had raised $20billion in new capital funds and it had subsequently been in talks with several private equity firms regarding injections of capital, they all withdrew due to anxiety about the state of AIG's finances. Its troubles took another turn in September 2008 when its credit rating was threatened with downgrading by the rating agencies on 15th September. This threat caused it to seek, unsuccessfully, an immediate injection of funds by way of a bridging loan of $40 billion from the Federal Reserve.

This was on the weekend when Lehman Brothers filed for bankruptcy and Merrill Lynch was bought by Bank of America and it looked as if AIG was in an even more serious situation since its share price had fallen 46% in the previous week. Its problems had increased due to a need to mark-down the values of its large holdings of mortgage related bonds and other similar assets. It also had substantial potential commitments on credit default swaps that had to be covered.

By the 16th September AIG was working with Federal Reserve officials, Goldman Sachs and J P Morgan Chase to put together an increased $75 billion line of credit. The background to AIG's problems was complicated as was the interplay between its various units, operating as they did in a variety of insurance markets all subject to different regulatory rules. A major problem had been that the credit rating downgrades had triggered contractual obligations to place billions of dollars with various counter-party trading partners. The Fed loan was required immediately to meet those obligations.

By 4th October, an $85 billion emergency loan, to be repaid within two years, had been negotiated and $61 billion had been drawn down. Repayment was expected to come over time from the sale of large parts of AIG's business but the deal also gave the government warrants convertible into ordinary stock that would give the government an 80% controlling interest in AIG. This did not wipe out the shareholders, but left them with very little.

On 9th October the Fed agreed to provide up to another $37.8 billion of cash in exchange for a similar amount of fixed income securities held by AIG's regulated life assurance subsidiaries. The money was to be used, not to improve AIG's capital and reserves position, but to improve liquidity in its securities lending business. (Securities lending was explained in the section on "shorting of shares").

So what was the problem that had to be resolved?

AIG's subsidiaries lent securities to investors, such as hedge funds, and received both the value of the securities and a fee in return. The insurers then invested those funds in other instruments, such as mortgage-backed securities. Because the value of mortgage-backed securities had plummeted, AIG's insurance subsidiaries did not have the money to repay their securities-lending partners when they brought back the securities they had borrowed and wanted their money back.

That was only one facet of AIG's problems.

By the nature of their business insurance companies can incur huge potential liabilities relative to the size of the insurance premiums they receive. In the normal course of events only a percentage of those potential liabilities actually materialise. However a part of AIG's business, and it was a substantial proportion of the total, related to its credit default swap (CDS) business under which it insured banks against losses arising from their corporate and mortgage loans. That business was now in trouble. When financial markets and property prices were rising, as they had been doing for some years, the insurance risks were deemed to be slight. However when one aspect after another of global financial activities turned sour, the risks underwritten by the insurers became very real. AIG was one of the biggest of those insurers, therefore it was one with a substantial exposure. The fears that permeated financial markets at that time caused the pressures on AIG to build up very rapidly.

The systemic risks were so great that AIG could not be allowed to fail, hence the government intervention for such an enormous amount. Very shortly afterwards, the Treasury Secretary, Mr.Paulson obtained the go-ahead on his $700 billion bail-out fund for ailing banks that dwarfed the AIG government package.

It will be examined later, as its objectives were changed very soon after being approved.

Citigroup

Another US bank that suffered in the credit crisis was Citigroup.

It was the biggest and possibly the one least likely to collapse. At the same time, it was not altogether surprising as Citi had for many years been recognised in banking circles as the most aggressive of all the majors, constantly pushing the boundaries. The fact that it suffered so much from the subprime crisis has to be weighed against the fact that it was also the biggest international bank in the world, considerably larger than most of its global competitors. It employed 374,000 staff members that were spread around the globe and it was represented in over 100 countries. This wide spread of interests meant that it had more difficulty containing its expense / earnings ratios than did its competitors. In order to improve this situation, the bank planned in March 2007 to cut 10,000 jobs worldwide.

Towards the end of 2007, staffing concerns and expense ratios were not Citigroup's only problems. The bank held $43 billion of mortgage-backed securities of questionable value. By March 2008, write downs amounted to $22 billion as noted in Table 22. The result was a first quarter 2008 net loss of $5.1 billion. These losses forced the resignation of Charles O. Prince, the bank's CEO and Chairman. Unbelievably, he left with a $40 million payout that included a $10 million bonus! All despite the fact that in the previous nine months Citi's share price more than halved in value.

Vikram S.Pandit, his successor as CEO was awarded $102 million in January 2008 before he had proved anything. That included a $2.5 million retention equity award, $27 million of stock and 3 million stock options worth at the time $73 million. A very nice "golden hello" that does not appear to have been earned when one examines the 2008 performance of the bank and its shares.

The third quarter results published by Citi in October 2008 recorded another $13 billion write off. It also transpired that the US government would take a $25 billion equity stake in Citigroup.

During 2008 Citi added another 23,000 job losses before it announced in November 2008 plans to reduce staffing by a further 52,000 worldwide. It planned to achieve this last reduction principally through a sale of units and by natural attrition.

By mid-November, its share price had sunk by 70% to $9.08 after reporting four consecutive quarter losses culminating in a third quarter 2008 loss of $2.8 billion. There was speculation about the effectiveness of the Chairman, Sir Win Bischoff largely because it was considered that he had no first-hand capital markets trading experience and had not exercised enough oversight of the bank's business as it tried to weather the financial storms. Later in the month it was announced that Citi would start to exit some of its riskier businesses.

From mid-October, when its shares stood at around $22, Citi's shares dropped further to $3.87 by 21st November and a board meeting was held to consider what options were available to the bank. It was believed that disposals of all or parts of the bank were under consideration. Once again rumour had it that J P Morgan Chase could merge with Citi. Other possibilities included Morgan Stanley and Goldman Sachs but none of them stepped forward.

At the same time the official line from the bank was that it had,

> A very strong capital and liquidity position and a unique global franchise.

A Saudi investor, Prince Alwaleed bin Talal said the shares were undervalued and announced an increase in his investment to 5% of the bank's equity but this was not sufficient to quell the market rumours about the bank's situation. Those rumours were to the effect that Citigroup would need up to a further $100 billion of government aid over the ensuing eighteen months as its losses mounted. There were many other speculative comments about the extent of the bank's woes. This was all reflected in the fact that the bank's market equity capitalization had fallen from a figure of about $300 billion in 2006 to $26 billion, in other words little more than the $25 billion aid package it had received from the government in October.

Citi was also concerned at the effect of "shorting" on its share price and lobbied the SEC to reinstate the ban that had been temporarily imposed earlier in the year.

Citi had raised $50 billion from sovereign wealth funds during the year, and $25billion from the government bail-out programme but it also suffered write-downs and took the remaining $17.4 billion of assets held in its derivative structured vehicles back on to its balance sheet, partially offsetting the benefit of the increased capital funds.

On Friday 21st November 2008 the Chairman and CEO had discussions with the authorities and decided to take extensive advertising over the weekend on the lines of,

> *The bank has a broad range of businesses and enough management expertise to pull through. That is why now, more than ever, you can feel confident that Citi never sleeps.*

That weekend there was a great deal of other Press speculation about what could or should be done to solve Citi's problems

On Monday 24th November the government stepped in. Its plan was for Citigroup to issue $27 billion in preferred shares to the US Treasury and the Federal Deposit Insurance Corporation (FDIC). In return the Federal Reserve, Treasury and FDIC would absorb most of the potential losses on Citi's $306 billion portfolio of debt assets after Citi assumed responsibility for the first $29 billion of losses.

Considering how much of its debt assets had already been written off, it was perhaps surprising that Citi still had $306 billion on its books. The fact was that the earlier write offs related to its mortgage-backed securities holdings whereas now credit card, real estate and other securitised debt had also (and perhaps, at last) been taken into account.

By February 2009 the government had put a total of $45 billion into Citi in the form of Preference capital alongside similar preference share investments by sovereign wealth funds. Also in February Citi announced that its 2008 losses amounted to $27.7 billion and that it still had $306 billion of troubled assets on its books. Overall the bank needed more financial aid. This was achieved by reaching an agreement with the government and the foreign wealth funds that they would convert part of the preference share holdings into common shares. In this way the bank could increase its cash position by eliminating the need to pay the 9% dividend on the preference shares. It currently does not pay a dividend on its common stock, and is unlikely to do so for some years. The government agreed to convert up to $25 billion in this way and the bank offered its foreign wealth fund holders the same facility on up to £27.5 billion at a premium price of $3.25 per share. That compared with a market price of $1.80 per share.

Those moves would increase the government's stake to 36% of the bank and would dilute existing shareholders stake to 26%, the balance being attributed to the foreign wealth funds. At the same time they did not remove the toxic assets from Citi's books. The bank's underlying problem was that it may not have the earning power to meet the increase in consumer loan losses expected over the next year or two. The continued existence of the toxic assets will inhibit the bank's ability to raise new capital from investors.

As at the end of February 2009 Citigroup had been saved from slaughter but it is illustrative of the folly and recklessness of bank managements that the world's largest and most progressive bank could have been placed in a position of near total collapse.

16 The Wider Picture Europe and the UK

The credit crisis may have had its origins in the USA but it soon spread to the rest of the world, the UK and Europe being the worst affected financial markets. The full extent of the severity of the crisis took some months to emerge after the initial problems experienced by Northern Rock. But that was a delusion. The problems were undisclosed but they were there all the time.

Whereas, in general, the approach of banks' executives (and those of Freddie and Fannie) was at first to deny that any real problem existed; then after a time admit that their bank may be experiencing problems (but not of their making); the next step was to include in a report for analysts or quarterly reports an indication of the extent of its problems, generally weeks or months after losses were first recognized, and even then they possibly did not acknowledge the full potential extent of losses or write-downs. Of course, rapidly changing events played a part in that scenario.

In all but a few cases the CEO's, directors and other senior officers all survived (at the very least, for too long) and continued to receive their remuneration, including bonus payments. Many of those CEO's who lost their jobs managed to hang on to all of their usually generous contractual "golden parachute" packages. The most that was published by them were lame excuses or indirect references to the problems. Hardly any of them ever used the expression "losses" or "substantial losses", preferring such expressions as "negative income", "value dilutive", "difficult market conditions", "global downturn", etc.

We commence our review of European banks in Switzerland.

Union Bank of Switzerland

The Union Bank of Swizerland was possibly the first global bank to admit that all was not well. At first, UBS followed the general behaviour of bank managements. In October 2007 it wrote off $4.4 billion. In December 2007 it acknowledged another $10 billion loss and wrote it off. At the same time it made moves to raise new capital and issued a profits warning that it was possible that it would show a loss for the full year (2007), the first in its history. It was due to publish its annual accounts on 14th February 2008, ahead of an Extraordinary General Meeting of shareholders on 27th February. In a Press interview in early January 2008, the CEO, Marcel Rohner, suggested (rather optimistically) that the problems in the subprime markets had stabilised.

At no time did the bank or the Swiss regulatory authorities suggest that the bank was other than basically sound and in no danger. Nevertheless, the EGM in February was a very stormy meeting at which, *inter alia*, the Chairman, Marcel Ospel, had his proposed term of office cut from three years to one year but there were also calls for his immediate resignation. In fact he stepped down at the AGM held on 23rd April. The Annual Report disclosed that his remuneration was cut by 90% for 2007 and he confirmed that he would not receive a bonus for the year. The cut was from SwF 26.6 million in 2006 to SwF 2.5 million in 2007, so he was not exactly left destitute.

He was to be succeeded by Peter Kurer, the bank's in-house legal counsel. A strong objection was raised by Luqman Arnold, a previous Chairman of UBS and substantial shareholder in the bank, who now ran his own investment company, Olivant, (and was one of the bidders for Northern Rock). His grounds were that Mr Kurer did not have the requisite experience of investment banking and markets that was essential for a holder of the chairmanship.

Although UBS did not recognise or acknowledge in the early stages the full extent of its problems, it did so under pressure before the AGM was due and issued a 70 page report describing its situation, the losses incurred and also the deficiencies in its organisation and operating methods that had resulted in management being unaware that in total UBS had acquired more than $70 billion of exposure in the RMBS and CDO markets. The report only covered the situation up to the end of 2007. Further write-downs in the first quarter of 2008 took the total for the whole period to $37.4 billion. It was calculated at that time that UBS had wiped out the equivalent of all the profits it had made since 2004.

The published report was no more than a summary of the much more comprehensive report that the bank had been required to submit to the Swiss Federal Banking Commission (EBK). The admissions included the following:-

•   A blind drive for revenue led it to take more risks than it should have.

•   It admitted to poor risk control and an overly fast build-up of its investment banking
        activities and a lack of clear management structures.

•   The oversight of investment banking " lacked effectiveness" and "focussed too much on the maximisation of revenue growth".

- Senior management did not sufficiently challenge each other.

- There was a lack of reaction to changing markets. (In other words they should have seen what was coming. The signs were there from 2006 in the USA).

This report was quite unique in that it was the only public admission of management shortcomings made by the managements of any of the many troubled banks whose stories have been noted in this and other chapters. No other management unilaterally admitted to mistakes or deficiencies.

By end May 2008 the bank warned of further losses to come from its holdings of $45 billion US mortgage-backed securities, $8.6 billion in leveraged finance commitments and $10.4 billion in US student loans. (The student loans arose from a securitisation process similar to that of the RMBS loans, but formed a separate market.)

UBS was still able to access additional funding from a variety of investor sources, including sovereign wealth funds, and by those means was able to partially replenish its depleted capital. It needed to do so as the final total of its losses (as at early September 2008) amounted to $43 billion).

One of the reasons why UBS ran up such large positions in securitised loans was that it operated through three divisions, private client banking, asset management and investment banking, but the management of each division did not have autonomy or more importantly ultimate responsibility for its performance. As a result of the ineffective management controls noted above, it transpired that each division had individually acquired substantial amounts of the US securitised loans, a fact that escaped the notice of senior central management. As part of its recovery plan the bank announced that it would create separate units for each activity, under autonomous and accountable management but reporting through improved communication channels to the central management and board of the bank. The Chairman acknowledged that these proposals were no more than a start to putting the bank back on track and rebuilding its earlier reputation as one of the world's top banks.

As the global financial and economic situation deteriorated during October 2008, UBS accepted a Swiss National Bank (SNB) bail-out. Part of the arrangement was that UBS would transfer $60 billion of debt linked to subprime and Alt-A mortgages, commercial real estate and US student loans. The transfer was to a fund owned by SNB that would provide funding of $54 billion whilst UBS contributed $6 billion. The plan was that as and when the securitisation markets recover SNB would sell off the bonds and any profit would be shared with UBS, presumably on a *pro rata* basis. SNB would also provide

UBS with 6 billion of new capital in Swiss francs. SNB would receive Convertible preference shares in UBS that could be converted into ordinary non-voting shares and would then represent 9% of UBS ordinary share capital.

Also in October 2008, UBS planned another 2000 job cuts, making a total of 6000 since 2007.

The UK scene

Northern Rock was not the only British bank that experienced problems arising from the US subprime crisis that gave rise to the "freezing" of the inter-bank markets but it had the distinction of being the first to have its weaknesses publicly disclosed. Northern Rock had been vulnerable because it had depended too much on the renewal of its inter-bank loans as they matured. However, it was known that other banks also had a dependence on these markets. Add the fact that shortly afterwards it became apparent that most British banks were heavily involved in the US RMBS markets and held substantial amounts of those bonds as assets. Those two concerns were sufficient to cause the authorities to fear a systemic knock-on effect if Northern Rock was not rescued.

At that time, apart from Bradford & Bingley and Alliance and Leicester, both of which were mortgage banks and former Building Societies, there were no immediate publicly reported signs of serious troubles within the banking system. Those did not start to emerge until late in 2007.

Royal Bank of Scotland

Media reports in early December 2007 focused on Royal Bank of Scotland (RBS) and its CEO, Sir Fred Goodwin. RBS had not long before entered into the final stages of an acquisition of ABN Amro Bank (ABN, a Dutch bank) in conjunction with other bank members of a consortium (Fortis bank of Belgium and Santander of Spain) at a total cost of 72 billion Euros, of which 93% or 66 billion Euros was cash.

RBS was to take over the global wholesale and International retail businesses of ABN for 27.2 billion Euros as its 38.3% share. RBS said that this would create a strengthened platform for growth outside the UK, a leading corporate and institutional bank globally, a leading retail and commercial bank in the US and accelerated opportunities in Asia.

RBS expected to generate substantial transaction benefits:

•   Aggregate estimated cost savings of €4.23 billion by the end of 2010

- Aggregate estimated profit enhancements from revenue benefits of €1.22 billion by the end of 2010

- Benefits well balanced across activities and geographic regions.

RBS also claimed that the Banks' extensive experience and proven track records would reduce integration risk through:

- its extensive knowledge of markets in which ABN AMRO had major businesses

- its strong track records in large scale integration (Nat West?)

- Projected synergies based on achievable objectives.

In addition it expected to enhance adjusted Earnings Per Share by 7.3% by the end of 2010 and expected a return on investment of 13.2% in 2010.

Pending the break-up of ABN AMRO and because RBS was the lead bank in the takeover, regulators required RBS to take full responsibility for the whole of ABN Amro until the completion of the break-up.

This had been a long running takeover battle against Barclays bank. The RBS consortium bid 13.7% more than Barclays and, although it may not have been evident at the outset, it was an expensive battle completed at the top of the market just prior to substantial falls in stock markets, particularly of bank shares, as a result of the growing credit crisis.

Sir Fred said in July 2007,

> *The acquisition of the ABN AMRO businesses remains compelling from a financial point of view, ———- the businesses we are acquiring open up many new markets and growth opportunities, enabling us to significantly accelerate our strategic development".*

At the same time his statement, and others in the Press release, were hedged by extensive " Forward-looking Statement " caveats.

The takeover had been the subject of media comment for many months during 2007. On its finalisation early in October 2007 Sir Fred Goodwin was feted for having achieved what many had regarded as the impossible. In the light of the problems then besetting the financial world it may have been more appropriate to have viewed it as an ego trip rather than as a masterpiece of financial engineering, one which as we shall see, cost

RBS (and Sir Fred) dearly. It was said afterwards that there were plenty of reports coming from other RBS executives to Sir Fred that pointed to the ABN Amro takeover as being a bad deal. After the run on Northern Rock, commentators were also concerned about the exposure of RBS to US subprime mortgage and other leveraged finance assets. Analysts recognised that RBS would have to take write-downs of those assets, and estimated that provisions would amount to around £1.5 billion.

Such a write-down, coupled with the ABN acquisition seriously weakened the Tier One capital position of RBS below 4.25%, close to the recognised minimum level. A norm was expected to be above 6%. This meant that RBS would have to raise additional capital. Nevertheless, in January 2008 Sir Fred Goodwin dismissed accusations that the bank was short of capital and would have to write down more of its holdings of subprime related assets, insisting that the bank was "comfortably meeting its capital targets".

This was despite the subprime problems that emerged from ABN Amro and landed in his lap.

Rumours and counter rumours persisted until 18th April when the bank confirmed that it was preparing to raise new capital through a rights issue. Analysts speculated that about £9 billion would be required and other rumours suggested £12 billion, which proved to be accurate. At the same time institutional shareholders of the bank were pressing for asset sales as a preferred alternative source of funds. The bank had a number of valuable subsidiary businesses that were not part of its core banking activities and consideration was being given to disposals – at the right price.

Calls for Sir Fred's resignation were related frequently and in full in the media, some calling for immediate action, others for delayed action to give him time to integrate ABN. In answer to the calls the Chairman, Sir Tom McKillop, said,

> The board unanimously believe that our executive team has all the ability to steer the bank successfully through this tricky period in financial markets.

He would say that wouldn't he?

The £12 billion fully underwritten rights issue went ahead at 200 pence per share, a record amount in Britain for such an issue. (At a cost of £210 million in fees to Merrill Lynch, Goldman Sachs and UBS) It was successful, 85% of the new shares were taken up (5,823,635,440 shares) and the underwriters were left with no more than £1.7 billion to dispose of afterwards. At the Annual General meeting at which the details were put to shareholders, at least one major institutional investor expressed fury that shareholders were being expected to approve payment of a £2.86 million bonus for Sir Fred. Another said,

> Of course he should go. He is a megalomaniac. He got one thing right,

> *National Westminster bank* (acquisition). *Everything else he has done has been catastrophic.*

To put this last accusation in context, RBS completed 23 acquisitions during Sir Fred's tenure of office notwithstanding that on several occasions he stated that "organic growth" rather than acquisitions was RBS's strength.

The bank issued a statement that the Chairman, Sir Tom McKillop proposed to present at the AGM of the bank concerning principally the need for the Rights Issue of £12 billion. The following are the more significant extracts.

> *I would like to take you through the thinking behind this fundamental shift in RBS's financial strategy.*
>
> *In summary, our view is that the world has changed. The further deterioration we have seen in credit markets this year; the examples of quite extreme stress we have seen in some of our financial counterparties; the worsening of the economic outlook - all these factors have brought us to the conclusion that we needed to carry more capital in our business than we have chosen to do in recent years, when the economic environment was more stable.*
>
> *We have therefore raised our target range for Tier 1 capital to between 7.5% and 8.5%. We also believe that in this less certain business climate it is appropriate to attach greater weight to the narrower measure of Core Tier 1 capital, and have therefore set a new target for this ratio to exceed 6%.*
>
> *The Board believed that it was important to take a prudent view of the potential for further write-downs on our credit market exposures, so we have carried out a thorough assessment of these, and have currently estimated for our capital planning purposes that the effect on our capital of write-downs could be £4.3 billion net of tax, or £5.9 billion before tax.*
>
> *Many financial institutions have been affected by such write-downs on structured credit assets. Nevertheless, we take the lessons that we have learnt from this experience very seriously and have discontinued some of these activities. We have also taken steps to strengthen the control environment in our Global Banking & Markets division.*

He went on to describe the possibilities of selling off assets such as the bank's two insurance companies. He then discussed dividend policies.

For the future, the Board believes that the Group's strength and diversity mean that the 2007 dividend payout ratio of around 45% of earnings remains sustainable in the medium term. Whilst the Board must take each dividend decision in the light of the circumstances prevailing at the time, we would expect in future years to continue to pay approximately that proportion of the Group's earnings as dividends.

Looking ahead, RBS is now well-placed to generate growth from its businesses, and our ability to deliver on this potential will be the crucial test of our organisation. RBS has always prided itself on delivery - we have successfully achieved this in the past, and I and the leadership team are determined that we will not fall short this time.

With a stronger capital base we will be better protected against an economic environment that remains uncertain, and will be better positioned to maintain the momentum in our core businesses. And I am confident that we will be able to maintain this momentum; although this environment is not without risk, those risks are now being rewarded with a greater premium than we have seen for some time, and we have been able to begin to rebuild margins in a number of businesses.

And of course, we must deliver the benefits from the ABN AMRO integration - benefits that we now expect to total almost €2.3 billion a year, a third greater than our original expectation. Our management remains firmly focused on this task.

We are also extending our successful Manufacturing model globally, and as we roll this out across the Group we are confident we can take advantage of our greater scale and achieve significant improvements in efficiency throughout RBS.

But more than this, we have taken a huge step in the development of the RBS Group, building a global banking platform with all the attributes necessary to achieve good, sustainable growth.

But we have also greatly enhanced our position in these key respects:

- *We have enhanced our diversification, both by product and by geography through the ABN acquisition - and we are grateful for your support for this last year.*

- *We have enhanced our customer franchises around the world,*

*with outstanding retail customer bases in the UK and
the US and leading corporate customer franchises in all of the
major regions.*

- *We have enhanced our product set, with competitive and
attractive products that our customers want to buy.*

- *We have a full range of distribution channels through which to
sell these products, and this range has been enhanced in
particular by ABN AMRO's world class payments and cash
management platform.*

*And finally, we have outstanding people working for the Group, here and
around the world, and it is a great delight as Chairman to go around the
Group and see the passion of our employees. As I travel to some of our
newer businesses in Asia and the Middle East I have found exactly the
same commitment from our people as I see here in the UK, and I have
every confidence in their ability to deliver on the opportunities before us.*

*So we have built the platform we need, and with our new financial strategy
embedded we will be better placed than ever to capitalise on that platform.
I am conscious that in raising our capital targets we are asking our
shareholders to make a very significant commitment in support of that
strategy, and we are grateful for your support. It is incumbent upon me and
upon the executive team to deliver, and that is what we intend to do. I
believe we have the franchises, the products and the people to Make it
happen.*

Wouldn't anyone feel proud and lucky to be a shareholder in such an organisation with
such a management?

This was a lengthy speech by the Chairman and one can only view it as being intended
to be very reassuring for shareholders and the stock markets, for that reason most of it
has been repeated here since it gave no indication of the problems to come, particularly
in relation to the ABN acquisition and the £325 billion holdings of shaky derivatives, as
we shall discover shortly.

Nevertheless, throughout the summer of 2008 there were many criticisms of Sir Fred's
tenure as CEO. The press sometimes referred to him as "Fred the shred", in view of his
cost-cutting propensities, originally practised when he was CEO of the Clydesdale Bank
in Scotland. Nevertheless, he and the Chairman survived, although changes were made
to the non-executive directors in a move to strengthen their ranks with more senior,

experienced persons, who might be expected to question the Chairman and CEO's seemingly unfettered actions. Their ability to do so would only come about if they showed a willingness to act when necessary, using their ratio of 12 non-executives to 5 executive directors on the board.

Also in May 2008 it was reported that the US Securities and Exchange Commission (SEC) was investigating RBS concerning its exposure to subprime mortgages and residential mortgages provided by its US subsidiaries. This was only one of about forty investigations on which the SEC embarked from late 2007 into 2008. It was a pity that the SEC and other regulatory bodies had not taken a much greater interest in such matters a year or two earlier, instead of ignoring all the warning signals of the impending crisis.

RBS continued unsuccessfully throughout the summer in its efforts to sell various subsidiary companies, the principal ones being Direct Line and Churchill, two insurance companies from which it hoped to raise about £7 billion.

At the beginning of August 2008, analysts were predicting a pre-tax loss for the first-half year of £1.7 billion as a result of write-downs, principally of mortgage-backed assets. At the same time they projected underlying profits of £6.3 billion, an indication that earnings were still strong if only the write-downs had not been necessary. At the same time, it was being suggested that those write-downs may not all turn out to be "real" losses if the underlying securities recover in value and the market for them re-opens.

All of this was against a background where RBS had been crowned "Securitization Bank of the Year 2006".

The criticisms of the leadership of RBS, and Sir Fred in particular are justifiable, particularly when one considers that the ordinary share price fell from 602 pence to 194 pence in twelve months; by November 2008 it had dropped as low as 47 pence and by 18th January 2009 it reached an all time low of 10.3 pence coupled with speculation that the government would complete the nationalisation of the bank. In February 2009 the share price fluctuated around 20 - 26 pence. However, one has also to take into account that, mostly during his tenure, RBS grew from a predominantly Scottish regional bank into the number two bank (by size) in Europe and number five in the world. Goodwin concentrated on investment banking activities and global expansion, particularly in the USA. RBS was one of the largest employers in Scotland and its name appeared everywhere. It became an international bank on the back of leveraged deals in its investment and capital markets activities, although in doing so it became much too over-extended in relation to its capital funds and those very activities were to become the principal cause of its downfall.

In its Financial Stability Report on 28th October 2008 the Bank of England noted that in

2001 customer lending by banks in Britain was roughly equal to the amount of customer deposits. By 2008 banks were lending £700 billion more than the deposits that they were taking in. It also noted that whereas up to 2002 the leveraging ratio (total assets divided by total equity capital) was around 30%. By 2008 this had doubled to 60%.

Price gyrations in RBS shares may not have suited the shareholders, but others appeared to revel in them. By way of example, on 16th July 2008, 166,530,545 shares were purchased and 191,244,448 sold, a total of 357,774,993 shares dealt in 28,874 trades, in which, for example, there were 49 sales of 10,000 shares within a 10 second period. Few of those trades can have been related to true long-term investment decisions in the volatile and depressed bank shares' market.

If we look back beyond 2007, the headlines were quite different. "The Times" newspaper on 4th August 2006 read, "Profits boom at Royal Bank of Scotland". It related that first-half profits had jumped 23 % to more than £4.5 billion. Sir Fred was quoted as saying,

> RBS has maintained its growth momentum for five solid years and growth in the last has been entirely organic. (compared with growth from acquisitions in earlier years). We have always placed great emphasis on organic income growth, operating efficiency and risk management and these are again visible hallmarks of the Group's results.

Six months later, with Fortis Bank and Banco Santander he led the consortium acquisition of ABN Amro for 72 billion Euros, only part of which had to be met by RBS for its share of ABN as noted above.

Sir Fred has been criticised for being autocratic but perhaps the CEO's of companies that appear to achieve most do so for that reason. He ruled RBS for nine years and indeed in 2008 was said to be the longest serving bank CEO in the UK. His achievements, seriously flawed as they subsequently proved to be, were acknowledged. In December 2002 Forbes Magazine named him "Businessman of the Year", describing him as,

> an original thinker with a fast-forward frame of mind who had transformed RBS from a nonentity into a global name.

In 2003 he was named "No1 in Scotland" by a Scottish newspaper. At the end of 2003 he was declared "European Banker of the Year." In 2004 he was knighted for "his services to banking". In recognition of all that, from 2004 to 2007 Sir Fred was paid, in salary and bonuses, the equivalent of £15.5 million.

Fred Goodwin undoubtedly had a talent as a "shaker and mover" but his Achilles heel may have been ambition and a belief in his own infallibility. So, when things go wrong the autocrat should bear the blame as the decision making input from most other management officers is likely to have been minimal or ignored.

In July 2008 there were reports that Stephen Hester, CEO of British Land had joined the bank as a non-executive director, at the same time he was being tipped as Sir Fred's successor.

On 5th August 2008 "The Times" published an article by Magnus Linklater that demonstrated how without the benefit of hindsight it is difficult to reach an accurate assessment of a company's true situation. In this article he wrote,

> *Figures that look stark in a headline, however, are not necessarily the best indicators of a bank's underlying position. - - - - Most analysts make the point that the bank is still profitable, that the £1 billion plus (loss) figure analysts predict does not represent an actual loss, more a potential one, and that, against the background of the global credit crunch, it might in fact turn out to be a pretty good result. What have changed since the last downturn are the bank and the state of the economy. RBS is now a far more widely diversified business than it ever was, with its activities spread across America, Europe and the Far East. Its managers believe that the bank is well set up to withstand a tough year ahead, and that it (or was it Fred?) has the confidence in its own ability to steer a course through the storm to influence financial opinion within Scotland and the rest of the UK. It has not yet had to stop lending money, and it continues to deal in mortgages and to support businesses. With £12 billion in the bank, it can afford to.*

The same day another commentator, Owen Kelly, CEO of Scottish Financial Enterprise added,

> *You really have to look at the underlying strength of the company, rather than figures based on accounting requirements.*

It is difficult to reconcile this statement with company external auditors' declarations that the published accounts presented "a true and fair " view. Those two comments proved within weeks to be way off the mark when the true picture emerged.

Although there were other media comments on RBS and its directors, we have to reach 7th October 2008 before more really bad news emerged. RBS shares took another severe tumble, falling up to 40% at one point amidst general turmoil in stock markets, not only in Britain, but worldwide. There was also a report on a meeting held between the CEO's of a number of banks, including RBS, Barclays, Lloyds TSB and the

Chancellor at which they were said to be seeking Treasury support for the financial markets – or for themselves? This latter suggestion was denied.

The 8th October brought announcements of projected increases in the amount that would be guaranteed on deposits in the UK and a number of other European countries. In the UK the protection was extended to £50,000 from £34,000. Nevertheless depositors had to bear in mind that the limit on protection applied to all deposits held with a licence holder. The point here being that some banks operated through several apparently separate companies that were all covered by the same licence. For example we have Halifax Bank, Bank of Scotland and Birmingham Midshires but all three operate under a single HBOS licence.

Another speculation on 8th October was that the UK government would shortly announce a plan to provide up to £50 billion in capital injections to a number of banks, one of them being RBS, and would also make available to the financial markets up to £200 billion of new funds.

Move on to 13th October 2008 when RBS announced a profit warning and gave details of a proposed £20 billion capital increase. This was comprised of £5 billion of 12% Preference shares taken up by the UK government, accompanied by an agreement from the bank not to pay a dividend until the Preference shares had been repaid, which it hoped to achieve by 2010 as was later disclosed. RBS planned to issue another £15 billion worth of new ordinary shares, underwritten by HM Treasury at 65½ pence. If the government became obliged to take up the whole issue, in the absence of other investors, it would end up with a 57% equity holding in the bank. The issue of new shares was not approved until a meeting of shareholders on 20th November 2008 by which time the share price had dipped to 47 pence. By 28th November existing shareholders failed to subscribe for more than 55,977,458 shares and the government completed its commitment, acquiring 22,853,798,818 new shares. Adding in the preference shares resulted in the government (or the taxpayer?) owning 70% of RBS. This meant that RBS had been as good as "nationalised", although the government was at pains to say that it wished RBS to stay in the private sector.

About the only shareholder who took up his allotment was Sir Fred. He subscribed for his entitlement of 1.59 million shares. Was that a way of saying sorry, was it an act of faith, or was it just an astute longer term investment?

What does not always emerge in considerations of the bank's problems is its sheer size. RBS had £2 trillion of assets in its Group accounts. Its issued ordinary share capital in 2007 amounted to 10,006,215,000 shares of 25 pence each, add to this the rights issue in June 2008 of 6,123,010,462 shares and in November a further 22,909,776,276 shares, making a grand total of 39,039,001,738 shares.

In June 2007 a representative market value of RBS ordinary shares was £60.372 billion. By end February 2009 that figure had become £7.886 billion, of which the government owned shares were worth about £2.596 billion for which the taxpayer (!) had paid £14.969 billion barely three months earlier.

Those figures give some indication of the size of the problems faced in banks, and by governments, bearing in mind that there are many other banks in similar circumstances in the UK, USA and Europe, not to mention the Far East and South America.

Relate those figures to the experience of a "small shareholder" in the bank with, say, 1000 shares. In June 2007 they were worth £6000. By February 2009 they were only worth around £200. Such was the damage that the board inflicted on the shareholders whose interests it was supposed to protect.

The *quid pro quo* for government aid in October 2008 was a commitment to continue to lend on mortgages and to small businesses at least at the same rate as it did in 2007. Within days various interpretations of what that really meant were being bandied about. Whether the bank was trying to "wriggle out" of a firm commitment or not, was not established. It was also a requirement that the bank would cut back on its more risky activities in its global market activities and significantly downsize its capital-intensive businesses. There would also be government representation on the board. Later in November 2008 the bank announced a cut-back in staff of about 3000, most of which would result from a cull in the investment banking activities of the bank.

The resignations of the Chairman, Sir Fred and the head of global markets were announced in October and confirmed at the November shareholder meeting. Unlike many of his contemporaries in the same position, Sir Fred waived his entitlement to compensation, including his profit sharing package. Nevertheless he was asked to stay on into January *"to help with an orderly transition"* for which he would be paid £300,000! At the meeting a shareholder managed to obtain a reluctant apology from him for the state to which he had reduced the bank. His apology was not volunteered. Later, in January 2009 he was said to be the worst banker in the world and there were calls for him to be banned from company directorship and the finance industry, and for him to be stripped of his title.

Towards the end of February 2009 it emerged that the Board of RBS had agreed to double Sir Fred's pension pot to £16 million so that his full pension of £693,000 could start to be paid immediately rather than have him wait another ten years until his 60th birthday, as anyone else would have to do. This became the central topic for newspaper front pages and every newscast. Sir Fred became the most vilified banker in Britain, if not the world.

Justified?

Perhaps, but there was no mention whatever of Sir Tom McKillop who, as Chairman of the bank since September 2005 had been the person responsible for monitoring and approving the actions of the executive management of the bank. Nor was there any mention of the extent of his pension or other financial recompense.

The news media concentrated on another aspect of the pension row, Sir Fred and RBS maintained that it had been approved by the government minister responsible, Lord Myners, in October 2008 and Sir Fred made it clear that he had no intention of surrendering it or volunteering a material reduction in it, particularly as he had made agreed "gestures" by waiving his entitlement to one year's salary, share related rewards and at the same time he subscribed for his full allocation of shares in the November 2008 rights issue.

So what was at the heart of this matter?

The government had been adamant in relation to remuneration and bonus payments generally that there should be "no reward for failure" but accepted that contractual obligations would have to be honoured. So, what was the situation in Sir Fred's case?

The government's argument was that ministers had not appreciated that there was a discretionary element in the total amount of Sir Fred's pension. It emerged that the pension pot for Sir Fred had been £8 million, the amount required to provide his "final salary" pension from age 60. However, as he was taking voluntary retirement at age 50, the pot had to be doubled to finance his pension from the earlier age and the board decided to do so. It must therefore have exercised its discretion when it brought forward his effective retirement date. Why were the government ministers involved not aware of those facts in October 2008? They obviously did not take the trouble to examine the proposals properly. In other words, they were incompetent.

What excuse was given? They had more important problems on their collective minds.

By the time readers can reach this point in the book, they will probably be aware of the final outcome. It was a considerable embarassment to the government and the Prime Minister but it highlights yet again what is wrong with company governance. Executives are given unbreakable one-sided contracts of a kind that no other employees enjoy. They are virtually unsackable unless they commit a criminal offence against the company. Sir Fred may not have committed a criminal offence but for very much less than what he, not necessarily alone, did to the bank, any other normal employee would have been summarily dismissed.

In every case of a recent bank collapse, here and in the USA, senior executives have enjoyed the protection of one-sided, unchallengable contracts.

In November 2008 Steven Hestor, the new CEO of the bank had announced that a loss was anticipated for the whole of 2008. In February 2009 it was confirmed as being £24.1 billion, pre-tax, the biggest single loss ever suffered by a UK company. Components of the loss included £7 billion in bad debt charges and £16.2 billion written off the ABN AMRO acquisition and the operations of the bank in the USA. The share price sank to 10.3 pence but recovered to around 20 pence.

Readers should compare these results with the up-beat statement the Chairman made only four months before as related earlier in this chapter.

Once again we have an example of the "I say, therefore it must be so" syndrome.

This disclosure meant that further government aid was required and a third capital injection amounting to £25 billion was agreed together with £325 billion of "toxic assets" that would be brought into the government's latest insurance programme, its Asset Protection Scheme (APS).

Under this programme, banks in need of assistance could enjoy a government guarantee of their dicey assets for a fee and provided they met other conditions that would be tailored to suit the circumstances of each indivdual bank. It was stressed that there was no automatic right of entry to the scheme. In the case of RBS, the terms were that the bank would absorb the first £19.5 billion of losses incurred, plus 10% of any losses over that amount. The bank would also lend £25 billion to customers over the following twelve months and a similar amount in 2010.

Meanwhile, RBS again fell 20 per cent to 20.2p as traders belatedly picked up on news that its use of the APS required the cancellation of deferred tax assets, which effectively doubled the participation fee to 4 per cent, equal to £130 million, although this was not an all cash deal since RBS used "B" shares carrying preferential dividend rights to help defray the costs of the fee.

It will be worth remembering those figures when we know the end result in a few years time.

Press comment indicated that the solution described above did not involve as much aid as RBS would have liked. Part of the problem of increasing the injection of funds into the bank was that under this plan, the government's effective stake in the bank would become about 95%, therefore any additional injection of funds could have required full nationalisation, something that the government wished to avoid.

Derek Simpson, joint leader of the Unite union commented on the situation,

These historic and humiliating losses bring into sharp focus just how

reckless RBS's former management team behaved. The whole country is paying the price through job cuts and repossessions on a massive scale. It is time to take control and fully nationalise this bank.

Stephen Hestor, the bank's new CEO said that the key elements for the bank were recapitalisation, management changes, identification of problem areas and formation of a new strategy, including taking part in the APS programme to provide a measure of stability. It was also essential to have an improving economic climate.

In "The Country Banker" George Rae wrote the following in 1885 about the need for banks to maintain adequate capital reserves.

*My counsel to you, therefore, for what it may be worth, would be to maintain your finances at all times and under all circumstances, in a position of impregnable strength; because panic, when it comes, will travel like other things nowadays on electric wings. (*a reference to the recently invented telegraph)*. Be less anxious for your dividend than solicitous about your financial safety. Let that be assured, whatever the immediate effects on your profits may be. A dividend based on financial strength, may suffer occasional abatement; but one earned by a more adventurous policy, at the cost of financial weakness, is a precarious one at best; at worst, it may fail you altogether some day, and dividend, bank, and Manager simultaneously disappear.*

So what is new? How right he was. Sir Fred, Sir Tom McKillop and RBS certainly lived up to the bank's advertising slogan "**Make it happen**".

The 2007-09 story of RBS has been selected as one example of what was happening to British banks, and because it was believed to have been more deeply involved in subprime and similar securities than the others. But it certainly did not have a monopoly of the problems. If we think back to Northern Rock and the B of E bail-out, it was stated then that the principal reason for extending government aid was not to save it, but to prevent contagion spreading throughout the British banking system. Because of the lack of transparency relating to holdings of subprime related assets by our banks, there was a real concern that there could be a systemic collapse.

Several other well-known British banks were subject to rumours regarding illiquidity and even their solvency. Several eventually disclosed losses and write-downs on their assets, and also raised new capital through rights issues. At the same time their share prices suffered catastrophic declines.

HBOS, LLoyds TSB, Barclays, Alliance and Leicester and Bradford & Bingley kept the headline writers busy for several months. With the exception of A&L they all had to make rights issues to cover losses and boost capital. A&L avoided doing so by arranging a £4 billion two-year facility from Credit Suisse and was eventually taken over later in 2008 by Banco Santander, this meant that Santander owned A & L as well as Abbey, thus securing a large share of the UK mortgage market. Bradford and Bingley's woes were perhaps worse than those of the other banks, even although they were smaller in size.

Bradford and Bingley

The background to B&B's woes lay in its business model. Northern Rock had suffered from a liquidity crisis but, according to everyone involved with it including the B of E and FSA, it had a good quality loan book. The problems at B&B on the other hand stemmed firstly from a lack of senior management control over what were effectively vulnerable assets, subject to higher than average default ratios. The bank had made itself into a specialist "*buy to let*" lender where borrowers tended to look for 100% mortgages and to leverage their investment portfolios by using appreciation on one property to support borrowing on the next. The buy to let market is also very vulnerable to changes to the economic situation in the country.

Some institutional shareholders and City commentators referred to the management of B&B as a shambles. In its half-yearly report for 2008 B&B reported three-month arrears on two classes of loans. The first were "organic" loans, in other words, loans it generated itself. The default rate was 1.78%. The second category was "acquired loans", those purchased from "packagers", such as other lending companies and brokers, most significantly from GMAC (a UK company affiliated with General Motors, a US company) with which it had contracted to take over £350 million of mortgages every quarter until the end of 2009. The default rate here was higher at 5.11%. This deal, which proved to be a bad one, was struck by B&B as part of its efforts to increase its business volume. Later, after nationalisation, it appeared that the deal would continue and that by April 2009 the government owners of B&B could be holding up to £7 billion of inferior quality mortgages from this source.

The default rate on its loan book as a whole was 2.29% well above the average of 1.3% for the industry. A second source of problems lay in its practice of accepting "self certification loans", previously taken on at up to 90% loan to value ratio, but reduced in 2008 to 75%. Loans processed on this basis afforded borrowers an ability to "massage" their income figures, assuming that they were asked for them in the first place.

The collapse of Bradford and Bingley has to be studied in detail if one is to fully comprehend the reasons why it was such a disastrous story. It is a story that demonstrates very clearly why it is difficult to take company executives, their pronouncements and published accounts at face value. In B&B's case, the timetable of events was particularly significant.

13th April 2008
The CEO denied rumours of a need for a rights issue.

14th May 2008
A rights issue of ordinary shares at 82 pence per share, underwritten by Citigroup and UBS was announced subject to approval at a shareholders' meeting.

2nd June 2008
By this time the quoted share price of B & B shares had fallen to 67.25pence following a profit warning from its CEO. It was then variously reported that :-

the underwriters were withdrawing from their commitment on the basis that they, "believed that material information on the group had been omitted when they signed the underwriting agreement two weeks ago."

B & B announced that it was scrapping that rights issue.

In addition it was announced that Steven Crawshaw, its CEO was "standing down" due to a serious cardiovascular problem. That took him away from the bank's problems. The chairman, Rod Kent, was appointed temporary CEO.

It was also announced that a US investment group, Texas Pacific Group (TPG) was taking a 23% stake in the capital of the bank for £179 million at a price of 55 pence per share. In addition it would obtain the right to appoint two directors and had a "non-dilutive" clause in its agreement, protecting its 23% stake.

Problem. This injection of capital was dependent upon another rights issue but according to normal City practice, shareholders had a prior right to take up a rights issue before outside parties became involved. The bank therefore had to price a second rights issue at 55 pence, to raise another £258 million, making £400 million in total after expenses. Shareholders were less than pleased, not least because of the new terms of the issue.

16th June 2008
The UK Shareholders Association, (UKSA) on behalf of shareholders in the bank indicated that the deal was a good one for TPG but less good for the shareholders. It also questioned the withdrawal of the underwriters from the first deal. The underwriters came back for this second rights issue and were paid a £3 million commitment fee.

The Association of British Insurers (ABI) was highly critical of the TPG deal. Several of its insurance company members were substantial shareholders in B & B. and they were less than pleased by the turn of events. They considered calling for the resignations of the chairman and finance director who had worked on the deal.

20-26th June 2008
In the midst of all this, institutional shareholders in the bank joined with an acquisition vehicle, Resolution, in an alternative proposal for them to back Resolution and inject £400 million for a placement of new shares at 72 pence and for Resolution to take control of the bank on the back of what would have been a 55% interest in the capital of the bank. The proposal included an undertaking from Resolution that although it would have a 55% stake in the bank, it would limit its voting rights to 29.9%. After representations from UKSA, Resolution improved the terms of its offer which was subject to obtaining "due diligence" on B&B. On 25th June the B&B board rejected the Resolution offer on the basis that Resolution could not give a firm commitment until early in July and that it ceded too much control to Resolution. Mr Kent apparently also refused to allow access to B&B's books to enable the due diligence to take place.

27th June 2008
Resolution withdrew its offer. B&B issued comments on the Resolution proposals that included,

> *The indicative proposal did not meet requirements concerning certainty, clarity, change of control* (this might have been the real sticking point) *and price.*

8th July 2008
It was reported that, no doubt for reasons of its own (apart from the delay), TPG had withdrawn its offer, possibly also because Moodies had just downgraded B&B. Moodies also gave the bank 30 days to prevent a further downgrading by injecting unspecified tens of millions of pounds into its securitization conduit, Aire Valley, which had £8 billion of notes in issue.

All this meant that the rights issue had to be re-structured for the third time in order to raise the full £400 million now required. The underwriters stepped up again, this time at an increased cost because of all the uncertainties surrounding B&B and its true value. The increased cost of the issue rose to £55 million or 13.75% of the £400 million to be raised. The increased cost included the underwriting fees, enhanced legal costs and other expenses but most of it went to the underwriters.

However, that was not the whole story.

Earlier, four institutional shareholders in B&B namely Insight, Legal and General, M & G and Standard Life had agreed to take up their share of the rights issue. In addition, the FSA had cajoled six high street banks to act as sub-underwriters to the proposed extent of £20 million each. (Bear in mind that at this time some of those banks had their own serious capital inadequacy problems). It appears that Santander also signed up for £20 million.

On the 7th July, B&B's stock price fell to 42 pence, 13 pence below the rights issue price.

23rd August 2008
The rights issue went ahead. Shareholders (principally the four institutions mentioned above who subscribed £93.5 million, although this figure may be understated – there were a number of conflicting reports) took up 28% of the issue, leaving the underwriters and the six banks with £195 million. Of that, the banks contributed £120 million, leaving the two lead underwriters with £75 million. As sub-underwriters the banks shared the underwriting fees, therefore their net costs were less than £120 million.

Towards the end of August, at a presentation for analysts, a B&B spokesman declared losses for the previous six months of £26.7 million but at the same time told them that B&B was the best capitalised bank in the UK.

So B&B's troubles were over? Well no, they weren't, not quite.

20th September 2008
it was reported that the FSA was involved in secret takeover talks with three banks, Santander, ING Bank and National Australia Bank (the latter owned Clydesdale Bank in Scotland and Yorkshire Bank in England). They must have been secret because in the same report "sources" at B&B were quoted as saying that it was not currently in takeover talks, there was no deal imminent, the bank was adequately capitalised and depositors were safe.

22nd September 2008
There were reports that the FSA talks were "floundering" and that the share price was down to 27 pence.

28th September 2008
UKSA issued a Press release in which it declared its opposition (on behalf of shareholder members) to the nationalisation of B&B on the grounds that there may have been better alternatives to protect the interests of all stakeholders (including the shareholders). The release comprehensively listed UKSA's reasons.

"The Times" suggested that the fate of B&B would be decided that day. It reported that Santander was in negotiations to buy the bank but that it was setting stringent conditions.

It also related that the FSA was considering a carve-up by selling the £20 billion of retail deposits and the 197 branches.

Withdrawals of deposits and queues at branches were noted.

Monday, 29th September 2008
The FSA announced that it had determined on Saturday morning that,

> the firm no longer met its threshold conditions for operating as a deposit taker - - - - under the rules.

No detailed reasons for this determination were given. B&B shares were suspended on the London Stock Exchange at 20 pence and the deposits and branches sold to Abbey, a subsidiary of Santander.

How was this achieved?

On the same day, HM Treasury issued two newsroom releases from which the following are extracts. Under the Banking (Special Provisions) Act 2008 the Chancellor announced a Transfer Order that transferred B&B's UK retail deposit business together with that in the Isle of Man and the branch network to Abbey National. The transfer followed a competitive sale process for this part of the business, conducted by Morgan Stanley on behalf of HM Treasury. (The names of any other parties involved in the competitive sale process were not disclosed) The remainder of the business (i.e. its headquarters and staff, treasury assets, wholesale liabilities, mortgage book and personal loan book) were all taken into public ownership, i.e. nationalised.

The notice stressed that as far as customers were concerned, it was business as usual, except that they would be customers of Abbey but at the same B&B branch as before.

It also explained the key point behind this rather complex solution. The transfer of the retail deposit business was backed (i.e. funded) by cash from HM Treasury and the Financial Services Compensation Scheme (FSCS) which would (eventually) recover their outlay by having priority "in the wind-down of B&B".

Here comes the best bit!

The release described how the FSCS involvement was triggered (into liability for the first £50,000 of each deposit) because the FSA determined that B&B was unable or likely to be unable to satisfy claims against it, prior to the making the Transfer Order. Which, if either, was the true situation?

How did this work?

Under the Order the FSCS paid out approximately £14 billion pounds to facilitate the transfer to Abbey, and HM Treasury paid out approximately £4 billion in respect of the deposits not covered by the FSCS. In exchange, the FSCS and Treasury acquired rights in the proceeds of the "wind-down" and in the realisation of the assets of the remaining business of B&B in public ownership. As £20 billion of deposits were transferred it can be presumed that £2 billion was the cost of the branch network and whatever else Abbey acquired.

But that was not all, oh no!

The FSCS financed its share through a "short term loan" from the Bank of England that would be replaced with a loan from the Government after a short period of time (it turned out to be no more than three months). The repayment terms of the loan provided for the payment of interest at a rate of one-year LIBOR plus 0.32 % for the first three years and LIBOR plus 1.0% for "the following years" (that could be 20 or more!). In addition to those interest payments the Government will be repaid from any recoverables accruing to the FSCS from the wind-down, etc. The first year's interest had been calculated at £450 million.

Because this was a somewhat onerous burden for the FSCS to bear, the government said that,

> it stands behind the FSCS so it can be relied upon to be able to play its role in meeting future claims that arise.

Eureka!

HM Treasury had engineered the nationalisation of B & B at very little cost to the "taxpayer" but of course, it was only a potential cost anyway. The cost to the FSCS was, however, very real.

The press release from HM Treasury continued with other administrative details, of much the same character as when Northern Rock was nationalised, including a statement that a valuer would be appointed (under the same rules and instructions) to place a valuation on the shares immediately prior to "nationalisation".

The second news release from the Treasury dealt with various Guarantee arrangements that the Treasury was making for other aspects of B & B's business.

So that was the story? Actually no, it was not the whole story. The rest of it relates to the affect on other parties.

UKSA, the big institutional shareholders and others all deplored the government's seemingly inexplicable actions when the bank appeared to be well capitalised and probable capable of trading its way through its difficulties, possibly with the help of a new management team. They were also of the opinion that with all the money (£200 billion) that the Treasury was making available to banks in exchange for so-called "toxic" assets, that mechanism could have been extended to B & B.

The big institutional investors had stood behind the rights issue, and stated in advance that they would do so. They now had their entire shareholdings, including the £93 million subscribed a few weeks previously, wiped out if the post-nationalisation valuer followed the rules set by the Treasury.

The six banks that had taken up their allotment costing £120 million as sub-underwriters (at the FSA's behest) also stood to lose the lot. This was hardly an appropriate reward for trying to help the Treasury solve one of its problems. But that was not the only pain these banks were to suffer.

The FSCS is funded, not by government (or the taxpayer) but by levies on all licenced deposit takers. The size of the levies paid by institutions is related to the size of its deposit base. As the six banks involved in the sub-underwriting are six of the biggest, it follows that they will be called upon to contribute the largest amounts. In the (unlikely) event that the Treasury does not recover from B & B all of the £14 billion owed to the Treasury by the FSCS, the banks will no doubt be called upon to make good the deficiency. That may be theoretical at present, but paying the annual interest is not and could amount to tens of millions each year for each bank.

B & B executives failed to acknowledge the seriousness of their bank's situation and in view of the very short time-span involved, three months or so from first proclaiming that the bank had no real problems to its demise, one has to question the competence and veracity of its senior management. Three consecutive CEO's all gave much the same assurances during that period. The last was Richard Pym, formerly the CEO of Alliance & Leicester who "stepped down" a few weeks before it had to accept a takeover by Banco Santander. He was appointed to B&B on 18th August 2008 at a base salary of £750,000 for at least two years, plus a bonus for the second half of 2008 (in fact the actual period was four months and fifteen days) variously reported as £375,000 and £139,000. He was then guaranteed another cash bonus of £375,000 or possibly £187,000 for the first half of 2009 plus share options that would have had a worth of £1.5 million but for the fact that the government as good as declared shares in the company to be valueless.

"The Times" newspaper published an article by Peter Hosking on 19th November 2008 that covered a Treasury Select Committee examination of the Bradford and Bingley collapse. Mr Pym's responses were not calculated to inspire confidence in his performance at B&B.

The article recorded,

> Forty-eight hours after saying that B&B was strong and fit for purpose on 25th September, Mr Pym agreed with the FSA that the bank was so weak that it had to be nationalised, devastating shareholders.

It then quoted Mr Pym as saying,

> That's dramatic, I can sympathise with people who say I may have been misleading. Later, Poor little B&B was the last mortgage bank standing and was always going to be the centre of media attention, and there was a loss of (depositor) confidence. He was then quoted, We saw Robert Peston's blog at 4.50 pm (on 26th September) and I think we realised things weren't looking that good.

So, a man paid up to £1.5 million a year to sort out B&B's problems as good as admitted that he did not realise how bad the situation was until he read a journalist's blog on the company's prospects.

Also at this hearing Mr Kent was quoted as defending 2007 payments of £3.77 million to directors,

> At the time we were trading quite well

Even if it was, and we can see now that it must have been an illusion, how could "poor little B&B" afford or justify such payments to executives in any circumstances? On 14th November, Mr Kent and three other non-executive directors resigned, (without "pay offs") leaving Pym as executive chairman with a "skeleton" board.

The answer to the pay question is quite simple, the executives decide what they will pay themselves. Forget about "remuneration committees " etc, they are a sham in most cases.

Although the company in its normal form ceased to exist on 18th August, Mr Pym will be able to enjoy his cash salary and bonuses as he has been retained to assist the government to wind down the assets in the company. He will have no liabilities to manage as they have been sold to Santander as noted above.

Note also that once again HM Treasury appears to have relied totally on the advice of two of the Wall Street investment banks that played significant roles in the creation of the global crisis in the first place, and barely survived it themselves. Why was it not considered more appropriate for HM Treasury to be advised by a major British firm of Chartered Accountants that audits banks and therefore is familiar with the UK financial scene and possibly more qualified to give sound, impartial advice?

Perhaps it was because our bank external auditors have not covered themselves in glory either.

Of all the tales of woe that have emerged in the course of the period after September 2007, this must be the sorriest and most anger inducing. The directors were incompetent and the government appeared to have behaved in a cavalier manner with a total disregard for some of the results of its actions.

HBOS

Of all the bank problems that finally emerged in September 2008, HBOS was the most serious. Halifax and Bank of Scotland merged in 2001 under a holding company that was named HBOS. The merger created the fifth largest bank in the UK measured by capitalisation, now commonly referred to as "HBOS". Both entities continued to trade under their separate names, Bank of Scotland principally in corporate banking and wealth management and Halifax as a retail deposit taker and retail loans and mortgage lender. For many years each had been a household name throughout the UK, indeed Bank of Scotland was the oldest bank in Britain. To the public and to its retail customers it was unthinkable that the HBOS duo, together with its big name insurance subsidiary Clerical & Medical and its mortgage lending subsidiary, Birmingham Midshires, were other than totally dependable, providing as high a level of security to its retail customers as one could wish for. Later it transpired that Birmingham Midshires and its affiliated BM Solutions actively promoted loans of up to 125% of property values.

In the early part of 2008 HBOS and most other banks in the UK suffered from the growing credit crisis and turbulent stock markets. Ever since the liquidity problems of Northern Rock emerged in September 2007, financial markets were subject to a succession of rumours. In March 2008 short-selling caused HBOS shares to fall 17% on false rumours that it had sought emergency funding from the Bank of England. The FSA conducted an investigation to establish if there were links between the short-selling and the rumours but it produced no firm conclusions, which was par for the course.

Shortly afterwards Royal Bank of Scotland announced that it would raise £12 billion through a rights issue of ordinary shares. On 19th March 2008 there was newspaper speculation that Barclays Bank and HBOS would soon also seek to raise new capital.

Speculation was that HBOS' high exposure to the effect of declines in both the housing and commercial property markets meant that its capital ratios would be adversely affected and this would create a need to raise new capital. Despite the fact that statements from the bank up till then were to the effect that the bank had no serious problems that could not be resolved with the passage of time the rumours continued until the end of the month when they changed into an announcement that the bank would seek to raise £4 billion by means of a rights issue of two shares for every five held.

It is worth looking at the share price history. In February 2007 the shares reached £11.67 pence and by summer 2007 HBOS shares traded steadily at between 800 and 900 pence. By the beginning of May 2008 when the rights issue was announced, the price had dropped to 485 pence in common with the falls in most other bank shares. The rights issue was priced at 275 pence thus providing a substantial discount. By 10th June the share price had dropped to 258 pence, that is by 48% since the rights issue was announced. However, the issue was fully underwritten and went ahead although investors only took up 8.3% of the issue leaving the underwriters with the balance.

Towards the end of July 2008 more rumours emerged of possible takeovers of HBOS. One was said to involve J P Morgan Chase which was forming a consortium to "break-up" HBOS (according to the UK and US Press, JPM seemed to be involved in offering for everything that needed an offer), National Australia Bank (the owner of Clydesdale / Yorkshire Banks), and of course, Santander Bank. None of these rumours came to fruition, although they kept the share price of HBOS on the move.

As the housing markets slowed down HBOS was forced in late August to announce the proposed closure of 53 of its estate agent branches by the end of the year as part of an effort to reduce costs.

The crisis for HBOS started in earnest on 17th September 2008 shortly after Lehman Brothers was allowed to collapse in New York. Despite FSA assurances as to its liquidity adequacy and the extent of its exposure to the credit crunch, HBOS share price fluctuated wildly between 220 pence and 88 pence. Later in the day the ubiquitous Mr Peston of the BBC "revealed" (his word) that HBOS was in advanced talks with Lloyds TSB to create a "super-bank" (again his words) with 38 million customers. It was suggested that HBOS shareholders would be offered around £3 per share, causing the share price to rise, but this statement was later withdrawn and later in the day an official announcement was made by Lloyds TSB that the price had been set at 0.83 Lloyds shares for each HBOS share, placing a value of 232 pence on them. This was an all-share offer.

Full confirmation that HBOS and Lloyds TSB had reached an agreement to enable Lloyds TSB to takeover HBOS was not announced until 18th September 2008 when it was confirmed that Lloyds TSB had approached HBOS six weeks earlier. The price agreed was £12.2 billion. The new bank would be the biggest in the UK.

As the government was anxious to avoid a repetition of the Northern Rock saga, it confirmed that should the takeover go ahead, it would overrule competition law requirements that restricted the market share of any one company to 25%, which it was known that the merged companies would exceed.

As has been recorded elsewhere this was a week in which financial markets were in their greatest turmoil, rife with global failures and takeovers of banks. The collapse of Lehman Brothers caused particular concern as it was heavily involved in the subprime and other securitization markets. If there was a forced sale of those distressed assets at "fire-sale" prices, there could be a knock-on effect on other banks, such as HBOS, which would have to mark-down the values of their treasury holdings of such assets and in so doing, reduce capital funds. This affected their share prices adversely.

Although there had been little or no mention of it until this point, HBOS had a funding strategy similar to the one that brought down Northern Rock. Although it had a good retail deposit base of £250 billion, it also relied heavily on the inter-bank markets and had wholesale funding commitments of £278 billion. Of that sum, £164.1 billion had short-term maturities of less than one year. This type of funding was used to bolster the build up of a £236.5 billion mortgage book and £120 billion of corporate loans of which 40% was in commercial property.

The FSA declared that HBOS was "funding itself satisfactorily" and the bank confirmed this in its own statement. Yet the financial and stock markets did not reflect that opinion. Concerns were felt about the bank's exposure to structured credit assets, higher funding costs and a heavy exposure to the deteriorating UK housing and commercial property markets. Commentators' estimates projected total losses of about £4 billion. Standard and Poors followed up by downgrading HBOS, declaring that,

> It was less well positioned to manage the deteriorating operating environment than its rivals.

The situation changed again by 12th October 2008 when it was announced that HBOS was seeking £10 billion by way of an emergency capital injection from the UK government which would receive ordinary shares in exchange. It was estimated that such a deal would give the government a 70% stake in the bank. There were also suggestions that Lloyds TSB would seek to renegotiate its takeover which was said by both parties to be "progressing and on track".

On 14th October it was reported that Lloyds TSB had cut the terms of its offer by 27% to take account of the deterioration in HBOS situation. The revised offer gave HBOS shareholders 0.605 Lloyds' shares for each HBOS share. The respective share prices that day were, HBOS 90 pence, Lloyds TSB 162 pence. At the same time the two banks jointly sought £17 billion in new funding from HM Treasury. The HBOS proposal was for £11.5 billion made up of £3 billion Preference shares paying 12% and £8.5 billion of ordinary shares issued at 113.6 pence. Lloyds TSB proposed £1 billion of Preference shares and £4.5 billion of ordinary shares at 173.3 pence each. The Ordinary shares would be issued on the basis that if institutional shareholders did not subscribe, the government would take up the shares but only on condition that the two banks merged.

It was also announced that Andy Hornby, CEO of HBOS and its chairman Lord Stevenson would depart after the merger. This was quite contrary to what had been publicised less than a month earlier when Eric Daniels, Lloyds TSB CEO was quoted as having said he was,

> *Looking forward to welcoming Andy*, who was *phenomenal and brilliant, and that they had become close colleagues.*

This was about the man who for three years presided over the completion of the wrecking of HBOS that had started in Sir James Cosby's time as CEO. Yet another example of why the public have ceased to trust the pronouncements of senior company executives.

Incidentlly in 2006 Sir James Cosby on "stepping down" early (which means?) from HBOS was already a non-executive director of the Financial Services Authority and was appointed Deputy Chairman of the FSA in 2007. He was also appointed in April 2008 by the Prime Minister to provide advice to the Government on options for improving the function of mortgage finance markets, working closely with mortgage industry experts. That was all until it came to light in February 2009 that the FSA had had concerns about HBOS's business model since 2002 and that in 2004 Sir James had sacked and gagged Paul Moore, an HBOS senior risk manager who had expressed his opinion on more than one occasion, including to the FSA, that HBOS strategies were too sales orientated at the expense of prudent risk management, a claim that seems to have been borne out when Sir James selected a sales manager in the bank to head up risk management.

None of this was in the public domain until Paul Moore decided in February 2009 to speak out and sent a lengthy memo about the concerns he had expressed in 2004 to the Treasury Select Committee which made much of it when questioning the HBOS Chairman and CEO in that month. Both gentlemen said they were satisfied that Mr Moore's complaints had been fully and "independently" examined and that they were satisfied at the time that there was no case to answer. The "independent" examiners turned out to be KPMG, the bank's auditors and advisers.

Some support for Mr Moore's contentions can be gleaned from the story of Benny Higgins, a £1 million a year retail banker hired from RBS in 2006. It appears that he may have been responsible for a slow-down in new mortgage business in the first six months of 2007 to an 8% share of the UK new loan mortgage market, due possibly to the fact that he had cut the commissions paid to mortgage brokers and financial advisers for selling HBOS products.

So much for their vaunted "independent financial adviser" status.

In August 2007 the CEO, Andy Hornby ousted him in what was described as a sudden and unexpected boardroom clearout. It appears that HBOS returned to its former aggressive selling and within six months regained a 22% share of the new mortgages market.

By the 25th October 2008 doubts were being expressed about the completion of the takeover as HBOS shares had fallen by 18% to 59.9 pence, caught up in a general slide in bank shares. Both banks denied that there was a prospect that there could be a second re-negotiation.

Towards the end of October it was announced that only two of HBOS' top executives would join Lloyds TSB senior management after the takeover. It was also reported that five HBOS executives had a contractual right to £2.7 million in compensation should they not be accommodated after the merger. The Chairman and CEO had earlier announced that they would waive their right to compensation.

There were mutterings that HBOS would secretly make pay-offs to those executives entitled. This caused Michael Fallon, a member of the Treasury Select Committee to say,

> The public have a right to know about rewards for failure. We'd expect any package to be disclosed and if they are not, we have the power to require that they are.

(Later in February 2009 LLoyds refused to confirm whether the deposed HBOS executives had received enhanced pension arrangements.)

Another new twist happened on 2nd November 2008 when it was reported that Jim Spowart who had founded HBOS' internet bank, Intelligent Finance, revealed that he was working with an un-named foreign bank with a 50/50 chance that it might introduce a counter-bid for HBOS. (Mr. Peston popped up again to "reveal" that the possible bidder was Bank of China, but he did not think that a deal would be struck.)

Mr Spowart later said that he had been approached by an investment bank as agent for the interested party but refused to confirm the name of the possible bidder. Although one should not doubt the sincerity of Mr Spowart's efforts, the whole episode may have been yet another red-herring as it is difficult to see how the necessary due diligence in a deteriorating financial environment could have been carried out before Lloyds TSB shareholders voted on its bid on 19th November 2008.

Apart from that, government support at the level proposed was contingent on the Lloyds deal going through. The Treasury had made it clear that there was no automatic right of entry to the bail-out scheme and that the terms for future bail-outs would not necessarily be as good. This statement also applied to the Lloyds TSB / HBOS merger if there was any attempt to alter the terms already agreed between the banks.

It was also unlikely that the HBOS board would have recommended a competing offer in view of the fact that they had undertaken to Lloyds TSB to pay,

> an inducement fee of 1% of the offer price if, inter alia a Competing Proposal is announced prior to the Scheme lapsing or being withdrawn, which Competing Proposal subsequently becomes or is declared wholly unconditional or is completed.

However, it was thought that the Scottish Parliament would try to influence the final outcome in order to protect Scottish interests as there were pronounced nationalistic aspects to the demise of Scotland's oldest bank.

On 3rd November Lloyds TSB officially sent its shareholders details of the proposed takeover and government funding of the new combined bank, to be known as "Lloyds Banking Group PLC". The shareholder circular included the following extracts,

> Importantly, the combination will also drive significant synergy benefits; the Lloyds TSB Board believes it will deliver total annual pre-tax cost savings greater than £1.5 billion by the end of 2011.

> When combined with the new capital being raised by HBOS, the Proposed Government Funding is designed to provide the Enlarged Group with the capital strength and the funding capabilities to meet the short-term challenges that current markets present and support the longer-term creation of shareholder value. Lloyds TSB believes that HM Treasury will, in accordance with its public statements, act as a value-oriented shareholder with regard to the strategic development of the Enlarged Group and will recognise the importance of delivering the significant cost synergies highlighted above.

> Subject to this, at the Lloyds TSB Board's request, HM Treasury has

confirmed that it currently has no intentions or strategic plans concerning the Enlarged Group or its business or employees.

The Lloyds TSB Directors believe that the combination of Lloyds TSB and HBOS, including the required capital raising by both companies, is in the best interests of the Company and Lloyds TSB Shareholders as a whole. The Lloyds TSB Board believes the turbulence in current markets has presented a unique opportunity to pursue the Acquisition, and unanimously recommends that Lloyds TSB shareholders vote in favour of the Acquisition and the Resolutions associated with the Proposed Government Funding.

The underlined phrases are worth noting. The first is that HM Treasury will act as a value orientated shareholder and secondly, it has no intentions or strategic plans concerning - - - - (HBOS) employees.

What does that really mean? One interpretation was that the government accepted that a major component in achieving them will be staff redundancies. Nowhere in the description of the manner in which the cost-savings will be achieved is staff reduction mentioned. The nearest wording was, "removing duplicated roles".   Speculative estimates by other commentators put the reduction of staff numbers at upwards of 30,000. The banks each employed about 70,000 people at the time of the takeover

Upon the assumption that the takeover would be approved by shareholders and would proceed as planned, ownership of the new bank group was calculated as follows:

Lloyds TSB shareholders:	36.5%
HBOS shareholders:	20%
HM Treasury:	43.5%

Although the impression given was that the London government accepted the need for redundancies (which could add substantially to the government's "unemployment benefit costs"), the Scottish parliament expressed deep concern at the prospect. Alex Salmond, the Scottish Nationalist First Minister (formerly a bank economist), was particularly active in the pursuit of meetings with all the parties involved, seeking assurances that as far as possible the new bank would maintain its presence in Scotland as a significant contributor to the Scottish economy. Bearing in mind that RBS was also in a shaky state there was concern that the status of Edinburgh as an important international financial center could be damaged. There was also a concern to minimize the effect of redundancies in Scotland.

Because of the merging of what was essentially a Scottish bank with an English one (although Lloyds TSB was very active as a corporate banker in Scotland and had its Registered Office in Edinburgh) the political considerations were extremely important.

In the midst of all this in early November 2008, Sir George Mathewson, former CEO and Chairman of RBS joined with Sir Peter Burt, a former Chairman of HBOS to produce a counter proposal. This one did not involve cash. All they said, very publicly was,

> *Get rid of the present Chairman and CEO who were apathetic and secretive and appoint us in their place and we will sort HBOS' problems.*

They gave no indication as to how they would achieve a turn-round of the bank, particularly when they had no access to HBOS' books and made no discernible attempt to discover the true underlying state of the bank. They apparently sent a letter to the HBOS Chairman and CEO demanding the resignations of both and their appointment as replacements. The bank's response was reported as,

> *You do not describe any specific aspect whatsoever in this plan. Nor do you set out a value proposition for shareholders, or address how your idea would provide certainty or stability for HBOS and its shareholders and customers. There is no basis for further discussion.*

The two ex-chiefs failed to convince shareholders, despite their wide connections in the financial community in London and Scotland. Their solution never was a "flyer" but it gave the media something new to pursue, which they did at every opportunity. One newspaper described it as "Highly entertaining, but doomed to fail". It was seen as much as anything to be an ego trip by two aging "Don Quixote" characters but with tartan overtones. Their contention that HBOS shareholders were getting a raw deal was no doubt correct but that was about as far as their challenge went.

Later in the month Sir Peter Burt disclosed that he had personally lost over £1 million as a result of the collapse in the HBOS share price. As his shares were probably part of his reward for setting HBOS on its path to doom bearing in mind that the main events of his Governorship were said to be the failed takeover bid for the Natwest Bank and the merger with Halifax PLC to form HBOS, this could be regarded as poetic justice.

There was another disclosure in mid-November. It was that HBOS had suffered heavy withdrawals by depositors earlier in September. The bank refused to confirm the extent of the withdrawals, which had obviously concerned government that another Northern Rock type run may have been imminent. Analysts estimated the extent of withdrawals by personal and corporate customers at 10% of deposits or £30 billion.

There was another HBOS story that was reported in the "Daily Mail" on 21st September. It concerned suspected trading in the bank's shares with insider knowledge on the morning of 17th September. The story was that Robert Peston (yet again) announced details of takeover talks between Lloyds TSB and HBOS at precisely 9.00 am on BBC news, four hours before HBOS officially confirmed the news. Between 8.00am when trading commenced and 9.00am, the HBOS share price fluctuated from 200 pence at opening down to about 88 pence. Between 8.57 and 8.58 am there were a number of massive deals involving about 160 million shares, the two largest being purchases of 10 and 12.4 million shares at 96 pence. Peston broadcast his "leaked" information at 9.00am precisely. The price started to rise rapidly immediately after Peston's broadcast of what was generally regarded as good news for the bank's prospects and by 9.45 am the shares had risen to 215 pence.

It was calculated that the buyers of those shares would have made around £190 million in less than an hour. A leak of the information shortly before 9.00am was suspected although Peston maintained that his information was tightly held. He described the frenzy of dealing as "scary." A hedge fund manager was quoted as saying,

> I am sure there are hedge funds that insider-deal but there are just as many banks whose trading desks are up to no good.

Although some commentators put it down to "coincidence" a more credible reason would have been that the person who "leaked" the news did so to others as well as to Peston.

There were no later reports of the FSA either having investigated or having identified those involved. Again, this was par for the course.

Lloyds TSB shareholders approved the merger at an EGM in Glasgow on 19th November. HBOS shareholders were recommended to approve it at a general meeting to be held on 12th December at the NEC, Birmingham, a strange place for a shareholder meeting of what was viewed as a Scottish bank. In order to ensure that its shareholders were well briefed on the proposed merger, on 14th November the bank sent them all a 349 page Explanatory Statement, almost as big as a telephone directory. It was introduced by the Chairman who wrote,

> Please read carefully the rest of my letter (12 pages) and the contents of this document.

If any shareholder managed to read it all, which is doubtful, he would probably be more confused than he was before doing so, particularly after reading the fourteen pages of Part 8, **"Lloyds TSB and enlarged group risk factors"**.

By 14th February 2009 it was announced by the new LLoyds Banking Group that its newly acquired HBOS segment had made losses of £10 billion in 2008, of which £7 billion had been in corporate lending of which £48 billion had been to property companies. There was general amazement and indignation that three days before this announcement, Eric Daniels, CEO of LLoyds banking Group made no mention of the possibility of such a loss when he was grilled before the Treasury Select Committee on finance.

The corporate lending sector had been run by Peter Cummings, the bank's highest paid executive who left in January 2009 with a £660,000 pay-off and a £6 million pension pot. There were later calls for those to be recovered. Let us not hold our breath!

As with RBS, it became clear as time passed that any picture we may have had of HBOS as a great and successful institution was way off the mark, although of course the deteriorating economic situation in the country added a new dimension.

A continuing decline in the housing market meant that more people were falling into negative equity. Taken on its own that may not be too important as long as the borrowers can maintain their monthly payments. It only becomes a problem if the property has to be sold and as we moved into 2009 the incidence of three month arrears became greater. In the case of HBOS which had written off £28 million in mortgages losses in 2007, the figure increased to £1.12 billion for 2008. For LLoyds TSB the figures were £16 million in 2007 and £167 million in 2008. What may not be clear however is just how much of the 2008 figures are impairment charges for estimates of projected losses since LLoyds claimed to have applied stricter assessment criteria than HBOS had been doing.

Nevertheless by the end of February 2009 the new LLoyds banking Group was in negotiations with the government to ring-fence £250 billion of what were HBOS' toxic assets and doubtful commercial property loans. However, in view of the perceived higher risks attaching to ex-HBOS assets, LLoyds had a problem negotiating an acceptable fee and associated terms.

Part of the problem was an admission by LLoyds that about £165billion of HBOS' £432 billion loan book was outside LLoyds' normal risk appetite parameters and of those, £80 billion were regarded as being in a "higher risk" category. To cope with them LLoyds was transferring them to a special unit where it planned to increase the staff supervising them from 240 to 720, an expensive exercise.

That was the convoluted story of HBOS'collapse as far as it was made public up to February 2009 but it probably has a long way to run yet.

Barclays Bank

Barclays was another British bank that found itself in the headlines, although not nearly to such an extent as the others covered in this Chapter. In May 2008 it announced a net £1 billion drop in profits due to the credit crunch and said that it was looking at various ways of improving its capital ratios. A rights issue was not considered imminent but it was an option.

By October 2008, when other banks, as noted above, had to turn to HM Treasury for assistance, Barclays announced that it would raise £6.6 billion new capital but that it would do so from investors without resorting to government aid. The proposals included the issuance of £3 billion of Preference shares before the end of 2008 and a further £3 billion from an issue of Ordinary shares to be completed by the end of March 2009. Other fund-raising included an immediate £600 million from new shares to pay for its acquisition of Lehman Brothers North American business; withholding a final dividend payable in April 2009 and cost-savings of £1.5 billion.

Barclays' proposals had been approved by the FSA but by 2nd November it had changed its tactics. Barclays has always been an internationally orientated bank, which was one reason for getting in first to acquire Lehman Brothers' New York office. In particular, John Varley, CEO of Barclays was interested in developing business and connections in the Arab Middle East. An introduction was made by an independent company PCP Capital Partners and in particular by one of its owners, Amanda Staveley. M/s. Staveley had spent many years developing close contacts with ruling families in the Gulf States. This enabled her to introduce them to direct investment opportunities in the UK including Barclays' need for capital investment.

Barclays welcomed the opportunity to avoid an approach to HM Treasury for funding and thereby losing at least part of its ability to choose its own policies. Of equal importance, it was enabled to build closer ties with Abu Dhabi and Qatar. However, there was a price to pay. UK Government funding could have been achieved at a 12% maximum interest cost with strings attached. The Arab States funding came through the issue of reserve capital instruments and mandatory convertible notes, convertible into equity at a 23% discount to a much depressed Barclays share price at the time of the funding.

This raising of new capital was not popular with institutional shareholders in Barclays and by mid- November 2008 the Association of British Insurers (ABI), acting on behalf of a group of investment fund managers, expressed concern at the manner in which Barclays had made available preferential investment terms to the new Middle-East investors without offering similar terms to existing investors.

Barclays tried to resolve the problem by requesting the Arab investors to give up £500 million worth of their reserve capital instruments which it then made available to existing investors on the same terms. In addition the entire board of Barclays would offer itself for re-election in April 2009 at its AGM and confirmed that there would be no executive bonuses for 2008, a noble gesture considering that for 2007, Bob Diamond, its highest paid executive received £21 million in cash and shares, his basic salary being only £250,000. That was all that was proposed for him for 2008. Notwithstanding those concessions, Barclays' share price dipped by about 9%, although this was also part of general day-to-day fluctuations affecting bank shares.

At the time of writing (November 2008) there were no published details of the reserve capital instruments but it is thought that the Arab investors would require them in preference to ordinary shares as they have a higher priority in a wind-up situation than ordinary share capital. The reserve capital instruments carry a coupon of 14% and the convertible notes, 9.75%. Arab investors were driving a hard bargain because in recent times the Wall Street banks had encouraged them to invest in products that had proved disastrous. Once bitten, twice shy.

Another bone of contention with UK institutional investors in the bank was the cost of these issues, around £300 million.

Why did the bank agree to such onerous terms? Simply because it had no other option if it was to avoid UK government funding aid. Existing UK institutional investors were previously offered £1.5 billion of notes (with an undisclosed coupon which must have been less than 14% to create such a furore as later arose) but investors only subscribed to £1.25 billion. The bank could not have raised as much as it needed from UK investors in the investment climate at the time, without providing a substantial carrot.

Those arrangements when completed will give the new Arab investors a 31% interest in the bank. At the same time, clauses in the agreement with the Arab States will make it very difficult for Barclays to receive government aid on the terms that the UK government is likely to offer. It will also create difficulties should Barclays seek to raise further capital funds in the markets.

It is unlikely that those arrangements will be sufficient to cope with its problems which by January 2009 seemed to be re-emerging. To assuage concerns, Barclays made an advance announcement at the end of January of some of its year's results which included a profit of just over £5 billion after writedowns of £8 billion.

By end-February 2009 there were also reports that Barclays had submitted three portfolios of loans to the Treasury for assessment as part of the Asset Protection Scheme. The amount involved was said to be no more than £10 billion

Icelandic Banks

Early in October 2008 Icelandic banks also featured in that the Icelandic government had been involved in the rescue of Glitnir Bank and then Landsbanki.

Iceland being if anything rather isolated, the rest of the world appeared oblivious to its economic situation. That should not necessarily have been the case. In March 2006 US institutions that had made funding available to three of the Icelandic banks decided to withdraw the facilities that were comprised of short-term extendable notes. These were notes that were renewable monthly for a period of up to five years. Kaupthing Bank had $600 million of notes withdrawn, Landesbanki, $200 million and Glitner Bank also had its facilities cancelled.

Why did the US institutions take those actions?

A Merrill Lynch analyst, Richard Thomas said,

> We are seeing the classic signs of an over-leveraged banking system and this has flashed the red alarm signal. The banks are extremely vulnerable and it is clear that the sentiment is shifting against them. Iceland's banks have grown so fast in the past three years that the loans they have made are now three times as great as their deposits. A solid European bank would typically have a loan value of between one and one-and-a-half times its deposits.

(perhaps that was the situation then but it very quickly ceased to be the case, as we now know to our cost).

A Kaupthing spokesman was quoted as saying, *The US lenders in question have limited investment criteria. I cannot see that this will have an impact on our situation in Europe.*

The US institutions may have given an impression of " limited investment criteria", but they were on the ball and in fact they were two years ahead of the game.

In October 2008 the Icelandic government was obliged to acquire a 75% stake in Glitner for $600 million to prevent it going bankrupt. In addition an investment bank, Straumur-Burdaras purchased part of Landsbanki's operations in the UK, Ireland and Europe for £300 million.

The problems of the banks could be viewed against an economic collapse in Iceland following on soaring wage and price inflation, an overheated economy and a collapsing currency. Rising interest rates (in Iceland the Central bank raised its rate to 15.5% and later to 18%) made it difficult for Icelandic banks to fund their business needs, particularly in view of the general financial crisis spreading across the world at the time.

By October 2008 the Icelandic banks had been very active in their deposit raising activities in the UK and elsewhere in Europe. Landsbanki owned Heritable Bank with a deposit raising office in England. Kaupthing advertised for internet deposits very aggressively using the Singer & Friedlander name (it had bought this British merchant bank earlier). There was also Icesave, an internet deposit taker which was not subject to UK regulation and therefore its British depositors were outside the scope of the UK depositor protection provisions. However, the UK government later declared that it would guarantee the whole deposit of any retail savers with Icesave in the event of default. UK depositors in Kaupthing bank were rescued by the Netherlands ING Bank which took over the retail depositors of Kaupthing.

"Retail" depositors have been highlighted because it soon transpired that 123 local government Councils had deposited £900 million with the Icelandic banks. The UK Government guarantee did not cover them. This caused much consternation. The rules that governed investment of Council monies in foreign banks related back to 2004 at which time they were relaxed to allow Councils to place funds with any foreign bank that was subject to UK regulation. Previously there had been a restriction that funds could not be placed for more than one year.

In the case of the Icelandic deposits, much of the Council funds had been placed for two to three years in order to earn higher rates of return. Those deposits were normally subject to interest penalties if withdrawn before maturity. The Councils protested that for them to have done otherwise would have been to the disadvantage of their taxpayers. The government's response appeared to have been that they should have examined the risk / return ratio and acted sensibly, not just with an aim to maximise returns.

One would have thought that those same councils that had been badly burned when they invested in Bank of Credit and Commerce International (BCCI) in the 1990's would have by 2008 learned a lesson and would have been more cautious.

The Icelandic episode was the object of much ill-feeling from the Icelandic government to the British government that had accused it of gross mismanagement of its economy. That was an incontrovertible fact. Loans made by the Icelandic banks were three times the sum claimed by the British government as the cost of its guarantee of 100% of the deposits of British retail depositors. It was considered that the Icelandic government was responsible, under EC Rules, for payments of up to £16,500 under its compensation scheme. The amount involved was calculated at £4.5 billion, many times the size of Iceland's compensation fund.

In order to assist the Icelandic government to stabilise its economy the International Monetary Fund provided $2 billion. The Icelandic government believed that was only one-third of what was required to restore its economy.

Later in October came threats of legal action by means of a judicial review against the British government that was accused of exceeding its powers by seizing the UK assets of the Icelandic banks - shades of Northern Rock. Later the Icelandic government stated that international banking would not become a major industry in Iceland any time soon. Yet another government had learned the lesson the hard way not to "let the good times roll".

A postscript to British depositors' love affair with Icelandic banks came in November 2008 from the Building Societies Association (BSA). Its Chairman, John Goodfellow thought that it was unfair that the building societies (as licensed deposit takers and therefore members of the Financial Services Compensation Scheme, FSCS) should be expected to contribute in a substantial manner in order for the scheme to pay out the depositors of less prudent financial institutions that included the Icelandic banks, Heritable Bank, Singer and Friedlander and Bradford and Bingley.

By way of example, the amount payable by the FSCS to 240,000 Icesave depositors was calculated at £1.4 billion, funded initially by a Bank of England loan. HM Treasury provided a further £800 million to cover deposits over £50,000. Not only would licenced deposit takers be required to repay the loans made to the FSCS, but they would have to pay interest on them to the B of E.

That still left the local Councils out in the cold.

Time now to turn to other parts of Europe.

Fortis Bank

The weekend of 27-28th September 2008 brought other unanticipated bank disasters in Europe that have to be viewed in the light of global events that weekend. The first was the Belgian Fortis Bank that had its main operations in Belgium, Netherlands and Luxembourg, a 540 billion Euro balance sheet total and 2500 branches across Europe.

Fortis had to deny speculation that it was about to collapse following five consecutive days in which its share price fell and it had announced plans to sell up to 10 billion Euros worth of assets. In the light of the announcement that Lehman Brothers had shut down in the US, Fortis interim CEO, Herman Verwilst, declared

There is not a single chance that we will face an issue in that respect.

There followed rumours that depositors were withdrawing funds but the bank said this amounted to no more than 3% of the total. The bank also declared that whilst it was seeking new funds, additional capital would not be required until well into 2009.

Also on this weekend it was reported that ING, a major Dutch bank, and BNP Paribas of France were in negotiations to acquire all or parts of Fortis' business but they would require government guarantees covering the bank's subprime and other problem assets.

Behind the concern was the fact that by the following year Fortis had to find 24 billion Euros to complete its share of the ABN Amro takeover. At the same time its own capitalisation was no more than 12.3 billion Euros, a figure that was subject to fluctuations almost daily and which had fallen by 70% in a few months. Fortis had also suffered write-downs amounting to 2.9 billion Euros arising from subprime exposure.

Working on their own plans as a back-up were the Belgian government, the Netherlands Central bank and regulators. As part of their efforts, assurances were given that no depositors in the bank would be allowed to suffer loss.

On Monday 29th September 2008 the governments of Belgium, Netherlands and Luxembourg announced an 11.2 billion Euros rescue package that would see each of these countries taking a 49% stake in the business of the bank in its own country. The Fortis chairman would resign and the bank would be required to dispose of its ABN Amro commitment. It was understood that Jean-Claude Trichet, the EU Central Bank president presided over the talks that led to this result.

On the 6th October it was announced that BNP Paribas had agreed a deal to pay 14.5 billion Euros in cash and shares for Fortis' banking businesses in Belgium and Luxembourg and its insurance business in Belgium. This deal made the Belgian government the largest shareholder in Paribas with an 11.7% stake and gave Paribas a 75% share of Fortis in the two countries. Although the two governments had reduced their financial stakes in Fortis, they retained a blocking vote in respect of the bank's activities in their respective countries.

Dexia Bank

Another bank in trouble over the weekend of 27-28th September 2008 was the Belgian Dexia Bank. This was an example of how contagious the global financial problems had become. Dexia had been subject to reports that it was seeking an increase in its capital. Its shares had dropped 24% in one day. A spokes-person for Dexia said that,

Its liquidity was very good and that the group was solid at a capital level.

To calm the situation, the Belgian government made the same depositor guarantee that it had given to Fortis depositors. The French government also became involved as Dexia operated in France and specialised in local government finance, an added incentive for the central government to become involved.

On 30th September 2008 it was announced that Belgium, France and Luxembourg proposed to provide 6.4 billion Euros to bolster up Dexia. Shares in the bank had fallen by 28% the previous day and trading was suspended. In order to support the Group's activity and to strengthen its development, the three Governments jointly undertook, until October 31, 2009, to guarantee new inter-bank and institutional deposits and financing as well as new bond issuance intended for institutional investors, with a maximum maturity of three years. The guarantee would be paid for by the bank and gave an assurance to depositors that Dexia would have sufficient liquidity to meet its obligations towards all its clients.

KBC Bank

The Belgian government announced yet another bank rescue deal on 27th October 2008 to support KBC Bank the shares in which had fallen by 74% during 2008. Although the bank did not appear to have serious immediate problems, its CEO stated that,

It is prudent to proactively strengthen our excess capital further.

Perhaps the biggest reason for doing so was that so many other banks were taking government aid to improve their capital and liquidity positions that he did not want to be seen as "odd man out".

Hypo Real Estate

This major German commercial property lender was said on 5th October 2008 to be on the brink of collapse because a consortium of banks decided not to proceed with their contribution of an 8.5 billion Euros line of credit in a 35 billion Euros bailout deal brokered by the German government. This deal fell through and on 31st October another bail-out was completed when the German Government provided 50 billion Euros and the bank received a further 15 billion Euros guarantee from Soffin, the Financial Markets Stabilization Fund, to cover short–term cash requirements.

This latest bailout came from a 500 billion Euros German government rescue plan to provide loan guarantees and capital funds to approved banks in distress. Hypo was the first institution to make use of the facilities but other German banks followed, although not to the same extent.

There were other problem banks in Europe, Russia and elsewhere but the foregoing describes those with the most severe problems.

This chapter and Chapter 15 relate the fortunes (or lack of them) of major banks in a number of countries. There are three very significant facts that link them all.

Nobody foresaw the full extent of the problems that were to beset the financial world in 2008.

The downfall of each of the banks that was principally affected was brought about for the same reasons, too great an involvement in the derivatives markets relative to their other activities and the closing-down of the interbank markets.

Their managements were all mesmerised by the profitable times they had enjoyed and none of them thought to look below the surface and make a proper assessment of the potential risks that they had occurred.

Neither did the regulators.

17 Government Intervention in Financial Markets

The first real sign of government intervention in the UK was when the Bank of England made available emergency liquidity assistance to Northern Rock in September 2007. Initially the amount involved was about £3 billion, but over several weeks it grew to £26 billion or so. At the time it was a huge shock to the banking system, the government, the opposition parties and the public generally, not to forget the shareholders in Northern Rock.

Media comment, and opposition political party members concentrated on this as putting a huge amount of "taxpayers" money at risk. It was reported as being the equivalent of £2000 owing to each taxpayer in the country and much publicity was given to it.

It may be true to say that politicians, media and public were stunned at the thought of such a large bail-out being given to any institution. "Billions" did not feature much in daily life except perhaps for a select coterie of bankers in the City. How naïve they all were when we look, only a year later at the many hundreds of billions of £, $ and Euros that the authorities have been obliged to make available to the banking world. Much of it although said to be available, has not been disbursed as at end 2008. If we allocate to the poor "taxpayer" the total government aid from the UK government to banks on the same basis as the media used for Northern Rock's aid, we would arrive at £44,000 per taxpayer, yet there was no mention of it in those terms, possibly because it would sound ridiculous.

It is difficult to trace all the funds that governments are pouring into banks and swapping for what it is to be hoped are temporarily unsaleable assets as has been done piecemeal by the USA, UK, European Union, Japan and other governments. Later, in February 2009 emphasis changed to the provision, at a price, of government guarantees rather than the absorption by governments of "toxic" assets into so-called "bad banks". This change was taking place in the UK and in the USA.

A ball-park figure of global government commitments and disbursements is probably in excess of $2000 billion which puts the Northern Rock bail-out in the peanuts category.

Government intervention has been structured in a number of different ways to meet differing circumstances at different times. It falls into several categories :-

1.   Exchange of illiquid assets for cash or government securities.

2.   Taking a participation in a distressed institution either through an issue to the government of preference shares or ordinary shares.

3.   Part or complete (temporary) nationalisation. Not always identified as such, the US uses the term *"conservatorship"* which may be more politically acceptable in its "free enterprise" economy.

4.   Assisting or exhorting private sector rescues or takeovers.

5.   Providing added protection for depositors.

6.   Providing insurance against losses on depreciated assets.

There were two principal reasons why financial institutions required state aid. The first was that in 2007 the subprime mortgage market in the US imploded which caused the securitized bond or derivative markets to close down, as described in Chapters 2, 3 and elsewhere. That gave rise to a lack of liquidity in bank assets that otherwise would have been marketable. As banks did not know exactly where these problem securities were held, and in what quantities individual banks held them, the uncertainty caused inter-bank markets in many countries to shut down. Activity in inter-bank markets was further diminished as the normal flow of funds into UK and US banks from foreign governments and investors also dried up because of fears as to the security of our banks and also concern about Sterling and dollar currency depreciation. Those events gave rise to a spiralling credit crisis as the facts came to light.

Those happenings meant that the two principal sources of liquidity ceased to exist, at least temporarily. The third source, retail deposits, was somewhat finite in nature and could not be expanded to the extent necessary to make up the shortfall brought about by the closure of the other two sources of funds. Apart from any other consideration, depositors were disinclined to trust their savings to banks after all the problems into which the banks had got themselves.

The second reason for requiring funds was that the collapse of the securitized bond markets left banks holding large amounts of assets that could not be disposed of and which therefore could not be valued at a market price until such time as a market in them could be re-established or until they reached maturity. Writing down the value of those assets and other losses arising out of the deteriorating economic and financial situation weakened the capital position of the banks. The authorities indicated but in most cases required that capital funds should be strengthened in order to enable the banks to operate safely and effectively. As there was only a very limited investor appetite for the provision of new capital funds, governments had to make them available.

Another point worth considering since it is at the heart of the crisis is the size of the problem. The breakdown in the markets for credit derivatives was largely responsible for the primary problems. Those markets were unregulated and had a total value estimated at up to $62,000 billion, that is $62 trillion. When that figure is taken into account it is not difficult to see why even a small proportion of that market in default gives rise to substantial problems. If we are to put it in some sort of context, the borrowing limit of the US Federal government is less than $11 trillion.

In earlier chapters the manner in which governments and their agencies provided assistance in specific cases has been described. In this Chapter we shall examine some of the broader policies and outcomes as they happened in the USA and in the UK.

USA

During the last part of 2007 the US authorities started to make tranches of funds available to banks in exchange for their illiquid securities. A security margin was required and this could be as high as 100%, depending on the status of the institution and the quality of the security it provided. This continued at intervals until in March 2008 the New York Federal Authority worked on the creation of new lending entities that made up the Term Securities Lending Facility, collectively enabling banks and financial firms such as brokers to access upwards of $350 billion for as long as the relative securities markets remained inoperative. Although there was an ultimate potential risk that might fall on the public purse, the borrowers using the facility remained liable for any losses incurred should the deposited security fall short when it becomes possible to realize it.

In early September 2008 the US Treasury decided that a rescue package for Freddie and Fannie was required in order to keep up the popular belief amongst investors that their bonds were as good as US Treasuries and as between them they had $5.2 trillion of debt it was an important consideration. The Treasury said that it took this step because,

> Freddie and Fannie securities are held by central banks and investors around the world. Investors have purchased those securities in part because the ambiguities in their congressional charters created a perception of government backing.

In all the government made a guarantee facility of up to $200 billion to the two entities and they became effectively nationalised, which is, of course, where they started 75 years or so ago. This was not a "handout", the Treasury immediately acquired a 79.9% stake in the two companies that would be increased if the facility was called into play. Although the shareholders were not wiped out, they were left with only a small percentage of each of the companies and shares with a minimal market value.

By 20th September 2008 the stakes had grown. Mr. Paulson, Treasury Secretary, The Federal Reserve Chairman, Ben Bernancke and George W Bush, the US President, declared that a major taxpayer financed relief programme was required to cope with the financial crisis that seemed to grow daily. The plan was to be known as the "Troubled Asset Relief Programme" (TARP). The programme was said to be not primarily for the benefit of "fat cat" Wall Street financiers, its main purpose was declared to be the protection of the retirement savings, home values and savings of "Main Street Americans". It amounted to $700 billion and it was required to be put in place immediately but subject first to the approval of Congress. That was thought to be a formality in view of its sponsorship. However Congress turned it down and it was not until two weeks later that it was approved by Congress on its second time round, with some amendments that would benefit troubled mortgage borrowers directly. As we saw in Chapter 15 all this was going on against a background of the problems in AIG, WaMu, Wachovia and elsewhere.

There was a sense of panic in the air.

The $700 billion package would be released against the usual deposit of acceptable security and margin requirements, the object being to clear the log-jam in the inter-bank market. The expectation was that the first swaps would not take place until after the Presidential election in early November 2008. Previously the US government had also been reluctant to guarantee inter-bank loans on the grounds that it would give banks a competitive advantage over other institutions.

By mid-October Mr. Paulson was revising his $700 billion package to include taking equity stakes in banks. He appeared on American television networks to defend his revamped bank rescue, admitting it was "objectionable" for the government to own stakes in private banks and that he regretted having to make the decision.

As a firm believer in free markets he said it was tough for him to make the decision to buy a piece of nine of the country's largest banks, including Goldman Sachs, the Wall Street firm he headed before joining the Bush administration.

> *It's always difficult when you come from a country like ours that's based on markets to be in a situation where intervention is necessary*, he said. *This is only about the American people, only about Main Street.*

Perhaps if the Treasury Department had paid more attention to ensuring that there had been effective regulatory intervention in earlier times there would have been less need for Mr. Paulson's intervention.

In September, President Bush was less troubled by the need to intervene,

> *Our system of free enterprise rests on the conviction that the federal government should interfere in the market place only when necessary. Given the precarious state of today's financial markets and their vital importance to the daily lives of the American people, government intervention is not only warranted, it is essential.*

There were interesting aspects to the proposed operation of the bail-out package. Because It involved such a huge sum the central control of it would be by a staff of twenty-five or so people, recruited for their skills in asset management, accounting and legal issues plus Treasury officials. Surprise, some of the new advisers were former colleagues of Mr. Paulson at Goldman Sachs, but only, one assumes, because as noted elsewhere it was seen as a breeding ground for financial experts.

The proposal was that this central cadre would out-source much of the day-to-day administration of the programme and its assets to upwards of ten asset management firms. Those firms would be paid fees for their services, determined in part through a competitive bidding process for inclusion as administrators. Asset management firms typically charge 1% of assets under management, therefore the chosen few stand to make a lot of money if that level of fee could be negotiated. There was also the question of conflicts of interest arising. This was addressed by the Treasury which planned to provide a policy manual on dealing with conflicts of interest.

By the beginning of October 2008, before the scheme had been fully launched, lobbyists for interest groups were active on behalf of their principals, possibly with scant regard for principles. They seemed to be scrambling all over Capitol Hill and the Treasury like 19th century carpet-baggers, all vying with each other and fighting for a piece of the $350 billion pie. If the whole situation was not so deadly serious involving as it did the whole future of the USA, their antics and the arguments they used in support of a myriad of different claims, would have been laughable.

This huge bail-out programme that many considered essential to a recovery of not only financial firms but the US economy as a whole, was complex and gave rise to many other issues. However, even before implementation of its provisions got under way, its structure was changed. It was planned to release aid in two tranches of $350 billion. Mr Paulson started with the first in October 2008. He used $125 billion to invest in nine major banks and another $125 billion was spread through other needy banks, (remember, the USA has several thousand individual banks spread throughout the nation). In all it was believed that about twenty-five banks benefited directly. The purpose of this strategy was to improve the capitalisation of banks and restart the inter-bank markets and general lending to customers. At first it seemed to improve matters somewhat but soon the banks raised inter-bank lending rates and consumer borrowing costs for such business as they conducted. However, the volume of business re-instituted by the banks was nowhere near as much as was required or much as the government had expected.

The UK government bail-out intervention came at a relatively high cost to the banks, 12%, together with restrictions on payment of dividends and executive pay plus government representation on the boards of banks receiving assistance and a requirement to undertake a level of lending to customers at least equal to that of 2007. Although that level of lending was a pre-condition, the banks appeared to have ignored the requirement and did little to increase lending. The rate of interest chargeable and the restrictions on dividends for five years were considered to be harsh by those speaking for shareholders. It was also suggested that such onerous terms would inhibit the ability of the banks to recover and it penalised those who depended on dividends for income. That included pension funds and life insurance companies. Whilst it is not difficult to see a need for banks to be penalised in some degree, most of the pain would be borne by innocent parties, the shareholders.

The US scheme was much more lenient. 5% interest rate, no restrictions on dividends and only mild restrictions on executive pay, until after the inauguration of the new President Obama who, in February 2009, imposed a ceiling of $500,000 on executive pay. The result appeared to have been that banks have felt free to retain the funds as treasury assets or buy other banks with it and did very little to lend more to consumers and small businesses, those most in need of a pass-through of the funds, the very purpose behind the plans.

By mid-November 2008 a general opinion was coming to the fore that Mr Paulson had no clear strategy for the rescue plans. They seemed to change weekly, if not daily. Not only did he veer from the original plan to purchase "toxic" bank assets, he added another $40 billion to the bail-out of the insurer, American International Group (AIG) that had already received $85 billion in government money. There was a comment at the time that if government officials knew where all that money was going, they weren't sharing it with the public. The inference being that it probably was not being used for the purposes for which it was given.

The following week Paulson abandoned the plan to buy bank's bad assets as it was apparent that so far it had achieved very few of its intended objectives. Instead Mr. Paulson indicated that the bailout would be expanded to include non-bank financial companies such as GMAC, which, as we learned in an earlier chapter, was the financing arm of General Motors. He also included the finance companies of other auto-lenders. The reason for this approach may have been to indirectly make funds available to the auto manufacturers since direct aid to them was considered a bad idea (back to the free enterprise economy), except that the President Elect, Mr Obama had signified that he favoured assistance for the auto-makers, (they were later given financial assistance). It was also announced that the Treasury and Federal Reserve were contemplating a plan to kick-start consumer lending through credit cards, car loans and student loans.

The one approach that Mr Paulson resolutely refused to countenance was direct help to troubled home-owners with their mortgages. His reason was expressed as a need to use the available funds to stabilize the financial system, this despite the fact that everyone saw the root of the instability in the collapse of the housing market. Once again, the new President Obama stepped in to organise meaningful help for troubled mortgage holders, albeit with strings attached and at a certain cost.

In January2009 the "New York Times" published a list of those financial institutions that had received part of the $700 bail-out package. The list covered 297 institutions that individually received amounts varying from $50 billion down to $1 million. One is left to wonder just how accurately the needs of 297 separate institutions could be assessed in such a short period of time.

The UK

Although responsible as lender of last resort for the provision of emergency funds the Bank of England, until September 2007, resisted following the European Central Bank and the Fed in the US in making funds available to ease the growing problems in their financial markets. It resisted the idea of making funds available prior to the Northern Rock crisis on the grounds that the banks' problems were self-inflicted and it was not its job to bail them out in such circumstances. Other Central Banks appear to have taken the view that unless they did so they risked creating a systemic collapse of the financial market place.

Mr King, Bank of England governor was criticised for his lack of action.

Northern Rock changed the picture and the spectre of a systemic collapse made Mr. King change his mind. However, he was only talking about £10 billion of funds each week for three weeks. In the event his offers were not taken up. At that time the CEO's of the major banks preferred not to be seen to apparently need funds. There was considered to be a stigma attached that might cause a run on deposits and / or on their share prices. Up to that time it was thought impossible to provide a bank covertly with funds. Another problem was that the B of E accepted deposit of a very narrow range of top class securities as back-up for its loans. The B of E subsequently made more funds available from time to time in larger amounts but this did nothing to ease the inter-bank markets which remained closed.

Until March / April 2008 there was no sign coming publicly from any bank that it had problems although the Northern Rock episode had shown that there could be weaknesses in the financial structure of several banks.

In April 2008, in anticipation of a need arising, probably as a result of a much enhanced monitoring programme instituted by the FSA, the Bank of England announced a new "Special Liquidity Scheme". The main terms of the scheme were as follows,

> *banks could, for a period of six months, swap sufficiently high quality illiquid assets plus a margin for Treasury Bills. The asset swaps would be for long terms. Each swap would be for a period of one year, renewable for a total of up to three years.*
>
> *The risk of losses on the loans remained with the banks.*
>
> *The swaps were available only for assets existing at the end of 2007 and could not be used to finance new lending.*
>
> *A fee was payable, based on 3-month LIBOR during the lifetime of the swap.*
>
> *The initial availablility of the scheme would be a total of $50 billion which was later increased to £100 billion and later still, to £200 billion.*

Applications would be on a strictly confidential basis. No borrower names nor any indication of the total borrowed under the scheme would be made public until after the scheme closed.

On 12th September 2008 Mr. King ruled out the possibility of an extension after the scheme ended in October 2008 and cautioned the government against putting forward a guarantee programme for home loans. That announcement was made at the same time as Mr. King introduced a new scheme intended to provide short-term support of up to three months to ease liquidity problems. It was not intended to be a source of funding for new lending. It was specifically aimed at opening up the inter-bank market but it had very little affect.

On 19th September Mr. King announced a three-month extension to the Special Liquidity Scheme, reversing his statement of a week earlier.

Turning away from liquidity problems, the FSA in October announced a comprehensive review of banks' capitalisation and new requirements for improved capital / asset ratios that were non-negotiable and would take UK bank capitalization above levels that had previously been regarded in recent years as adequate. Of course this new requirement was unwelcome as far as the banks were concerned and there were noises that it would impact on their international competitiveness.

It was not before time that the FSA started to assert itself in this manner.

The next instance of government intervention also came on 7th October when it was announced that the government was to buy stakes in Royal Bank of Scotland, Lloyds TSB and HBOS. Its involvement with these banks and Bradford & Bingley has been covered in Chapter 16.

In a Treasury Statement on 13th October it was announced that up to £25 billion would be made available to banks to assist them to meet the new capital requirements. Funds would be made available in exchange for preference shares. Apart from the first three banks mentioned above that were collectively to receive investment of £37 billion, five others were said to be interested. In addition to this facility, the Treasury proposed to make available guarantees of up to £250 billion of short-term borrowings from other financial institutions (i.e. inter-bank transactions). This was directly aimed at freeing up the inter-bank markets.

Those banks that were to be supported by the recapitalisation scheme agreed to subscribe to a range of commitments covering:

* maintain, over the next three years, the availability and active marketing of competitively-priced lending to homeowners and to small businesses at 2007 levels;

* support for schemes to help people struggling with mortgage payments to stay in their homes, and to support the expansion of financial capability initiatives;

* remuneration of senior executives - both for 2008 (when the Government expects no cash bonuses to be paid to board members) and for remuneration policy going forward (where incentive schemes will be reviewed and linked to long-term value creation, taking account of risk; and restricting the potential for "*rewards for failure*");

* the right for the Government to agree with boards the appointment of new independent non-executive directors; and dividend policy.

The government created a company, UK Financial Investments Ltd, to manage its investments in the three banks. It would be under the control of a Treasury official, John Kingman who handled the nationalisations of Northern Rock and Bradford & Bingley and also the bank bailouts.

The Prime Minister, Gordon Brown, told a Press conference in London that,

> *The action we are taking is unprecedented but essential for us and is intended to build the trust and confidence we need.*

He also said that he expected other countries to adopt much the same policies.

Whilst some banks and commentators considered that the terms the UK government had set for its bank aid were harsh, the government was undertaking risk and there was nobody else who could bail banks out of the problems they had created for themselves. Northern Rock was caught out when its wholesale funding sources shut down. Otherwise it had well managed quality control and after it was nationalised the write-downs that its new board undertook in the 2007 accounts were manageable within its resources and were more concerned with potential future losses than actual realised losses.

It did not deserve to be nationalised in light of all the other liquidity solutions that the B of E and Treasury subsequently devised and could have applied instead of nationalisation. On the other hand those banks that subsequently received a government bailout and / or guarantees had pursued injudicious policies that got them into problems that would not necessarily all have been solved when the inter-bank markets resumed operation. Nearly all of them were obliged to write off or make provision for billions of pounds of losses. They all needed substantial enhancements of their capital positions.

European Union

By September 2008 European national governments were faced with similar problems to those that had arisen in the UK. Mr. Brown attended a meeting of European Heads of State in Paris that sought to agree a uniform method of approach to easing the problems in banking. The outcome was that initially European countries followed the UK approach, although the individual terms varied and the degree of compliance diminished after a time.

They pledged that funds would be made available as necessary against acceptable security and that they would guarantee bank debt for periods up to five years. Adjustments of varying degrees were made to the depositor protection limits applied in most of the countries involved. Ireland and Greece increased their protection to 100%.

In Chapter 16 we covered most of the major interventions, but there were others, particularly in Germany and Austria. Possibly the only EC country whose banks were largely directly unaffected by the global problems was France.

18 Learning the Lessons

"I believe that banking institutions are more dangerous to our liberties than standing armies"
Thomas Jefferson (1816)

2007 started off as typical of the previous ten years or so in terms of the financial world. In the UK the only cloud on the horizon was a not very seriously treated warning that there was too much lending to consumers by way of personal and mortgage loans. Nobody appeared to realize that there was an underlying problem waiting to surface, one that would change and in fact virtually decimate much of the financial world.

There was no recognition of the danger possibly because the thought never occurred to the global banking fraternity that it could self-destruct. As we have seen it took just over twelve months for it to do so to an extent not seen since the1930's, aided by irresponsible lending by banks and borrowing by customers, a lack of adequate regulation and governments that were blinded by the apparent success of their economies. Everything was rising, living standards, (at least in all developed countries), personal wealth, stock markets, international trade, business output and personal consumption. There was only one negative factor - the high price of oil and that lasted for less than a year.

There was another factor and it was one that the authorities, at the insistence of the community at large must now tackle and ensure that, as we say about so many things that go wrong, it "must not be allowed to happen again". It was the recklessness of top bankers and financiers who seemed oblivious to a need for the management of risk and who appeared to believe that the good times could not end, including their high levels of total remuneration, in other words, "the bonus culture" backed up by one-sided cast-iron employment contracts.

We now need to recognize the mistakes that were made and devise ways of protecting ourselves from a repetition. That does not necessarily mean imposing draconian regulatory rules. Nor does it mean that we must completely stifle innovation in the financial world. However, we must pin-point the weaknesses that came to light during 2007/08 and do what we can to correct them.

One point that became very clear was that we live in an irreversibly global world. No one country can effect the necessary changes for its own benefit, however willing or able it may appear to be. We have lived through a long period where the USA has forged its own path and seemed to rule the world, at least in financial terms. It no longer does so although it is still a global powerhouse, despite all the problems it has suffered. For several centuries Great Britain also seemed to rule the world of trade and finance. It no longer does so, but still has a significant role to play in global financial affairs.

Over the last fifty years the European Economic Community has grown stronger (some may consider too strong) and the EC has emerged as a powerful third force in the financial world, chipping away at the nationalism that was a feature of its member countries. We could also mention China and India, but they are for the future more than the present.

What all this means, as Prime Minister Gordon Brown has stressed, is that in terms of trade and finance the world must act as one. There is no longer any justification or place for countries to try to act individually. We know from the past that such an approach only encourages those in business and finance to play one country's systems against another to the advantage of individual players.

Bankers have also been accused of greed but that is a generalization. Yes there were a few hundred people at or near the top of financial institutions who have been egotistical, reckless and who have shown avarice. So also have many of a generation of currency and investment traders, employees who through the introduction of computer networks have been afforded an ability to make vast amounts of money for their firms and themselves that are disproportionate to their contribution to the community at large. Although they only account for a few thousands out of the billions of workers around the world, in some countries and most noticeably in London they have been elevated to a celebrity status that has no doubt pleased their egos judging from the extravagant lifestyles they have been enabled to lead. At the end of the day, with a few exceptions, none of them are important to the rest of us in the scheme of things.

So, what are the problems that have to be tackled? Everyone will no doubt have his or her own ideas but here are some that would make a good start.

The Management of financial Institutions

There can be little doubt that a good starting place would be to examine the manner in which financial institutions are managed, and that encompasses a wider spectrum than merely banks. The management of any large company nowadays is a complex business. It takes a good staff under the direction of competent and committed middle management to generate success. It follows that it is not appropriate to attribute the success of a company to one CEO or Chairman on his own. However, a culture has developed that pre-supposes that he will be a highly paid, high profile individual who also benefits substantially from the *"bonus culture"*, all intended to lead one to the conclusion that the successful operation of a company is down to him alone. That certainly is not the case, as we learn when things go seriously wrong. It is then the custom for him to walk away, frequently with a substantial "farewell" financial package and leave others to cope with the problems. He seldom acknowledges that the failures are his fault.

The rapid growth of the global finance industry and the expansion of individual institutions within it created something that became very apparent during 2007/8 – a skills shortage that also means a lack of experience. There were too many people in positions at all management levels that had no prior experience of other than "good times". That must explain, at least in part, how they managed to create such a major series of financial disasters. Many achieved management positions because of a dearth of suitable candidates, not because they were experienced and well trained.

It is perhaps a jaundiced personal view, but one based on first-hand experience, that banks' problems grew after they started to be led by accountants and not by career bankers. Part of the blame for this lies with the bankers themselves, for far too many years the professional diplomas of the Chartered Institute of Bankers, (now the Institute of Financial Services), although of university degree standard and the equivalent of professional qualifications in other fields, have been undervalued by bank employers generally. Very little emphasis has been placed on the need to acquire qualifications. Traditionally, time and training on the job or management experience in some other enterprise were considered adequate formal qualifications.

That may have been acceptable, up to a point, in a simpler age when staff worked their way through the branch and Head Office systems, exposed to a wide variety of jobs appropriate to the extent of their experience but that has not been the case for the best part of twenty years. Staff tend to be trained in one task only, or to achieve a single technical qualification that is more often than not "sales orientated". Not only that, but banking for many employees has become nothing more than another job. It has ceased to be the life-long progressive career that it once was. That follows the pattern that has existed in the USA and Canada for many years.

Accountants tend to have an eye on one aspect of business, the "bottom line". They chase profits, "shareholder value", "efficiency" and of course bonuses, to the exclusion of caution, public service and other traditional banking values, including specific technical banking expertise. Interestingly, when the Treasury Select Committee interviewed the Chairmen and CEO's of HBOS and RBS, all four had to admit that they did not hold a professional banking qualification. Would we accept the same situation in the medical profession, or for that matter amongst partners in an accountancy firm?

A perception has arisen that it is sufficient for executive officers to understand "management", leaving technical expertise to others. Unfortunately, as suggested above, "the others" have in many cases failed to acquire an appropriate level of technical expertise. It is important to recognize that in today's banks (and until some structural reorganisation of them is carried out) many specialist technical skills are required and it is beyond the capacity of any one person to adequately acquire skills in more than one or two specialties. What that means is that CEO's must not act autocratically, they must act in conjunction with the guidance of their properly trained and experienced specialist senior colleagues.

Of course profitability is important but we have been reminded at intervals during the financial crises described in this book that banks are different from other businesses. Of course they are. They are at the centre of the social and economic well-being of a nation. No developed country can function without a trustworthy and stable banking system.

What has happened, at an accelerating pace over the last twenty-five years or so has been a transformation in the banking and wider financial systems in many countries, not to mention in the degree of internationalization of banking and finance. Much of this transformation has been essential and beneficial. However the events of 2007/8 have highlighted the downside of some of those developments.

Part of the problem has been that banks have been transformed into "one stop shops" for all manner of financial transactions. In some ways this is advantageous for the consumer of financial services but it makes it much more difficult to assess the true financial standing of a bank and to ensure that its executive officers have the requisite skills. The ability to make such a judgment of financial standing – by either the management of the bank, official regulators, governments and the public that makes up its customers and shareholders – is diminished. It is also made difficult by the high volumes of speculative foreign exchange, stock and derivative trading that many banks now undertake as a significant part of their everyday business. Banks have long ceased to be the relatively simple institutions that existed in the first half of the twentieth century and earlier and which were mindful of their public service role.

It is not suggested that we should return to that model, it would be inadequate in today's much more complex business world. However, it is appropriate that there must be a return to some of its values. Take, for example, the commonly used expression fifty-years ago in the City of London, common to all financial and investment firms in the City, "my word is my bond". Ask almost anyone today if he or she trusts his or her bank or financial services provider. The answer will almost certainly be a resounding " **NO**".

Why not? One reason can be found in the widespread exposure of consumers to the numerous mis-selling scandals mentioned elsewhere in which financial institutions have been, and still are involved.

Is it important? Of course it is.

The foundations of all banking activity are trust and confidence. When those are in doubt the whole structure of banking is liable to collapse as we have seen only too well in earlier chapters. During 2007/8 we saw that not only did their customers lose confidence in them, banks did not even trust each other. In some cases banks that had existed for one hundred and fifty years and more were brought down by the policies of their recent managements within a matter of a few months.

What brought them tumbling down? A significant factor was inadequate oversight by boards of directors.

The Board of Directors

The two principal elements in the management of corporations are the duties and responsibilities of the Chief Executive Officer, CEO, (he may have other titles that identify him as the senior operating officer) and those of the Board of Directors.

In Chapter 14 attention was paid to the respective roles of the CEO and the board of directors particularly in relation to Northern Rock. Company Laws detail the manner in which they should carry out their respective functions but the practice is usually quite different as related in that chapter. Let us start with the directors and although what we are about to discuss should apply to all company directors we shall confine our consideration to bank directors as that is where the most urgent current problems lie.

In most, if not all banks, the board of directors is comprised firstly of a chairman, a deputy chairman, either or both of whom may have been appointed from outside the bank or possibly from the executive ranks of the bank. The remainder of the board membership is comprised of a mix of executive directors and non-executive directors. The executive directors will usually be drawn from the ranks of the full-time senior operating officers of the bank, the CEO, financial chief executive, marketing chief executive, etc.

The non-executive directors will be drawn from outside the bank, preferably from those with a banking or business background but also from academic or ex-political backgrounds, or perhaps with just a "Sir" or "Lord" in their title. There may also be a non-executive director representing the staff. It is also worth keeping in mind that many non-executive directors and chairmen are on the boards of a number of companies, which leads one to question their ability to keep several balls in the air at any one time.

In law, all directors carry equal responsibility for the execution of their functions. There is no distinction drawn between executive and non-executive directors. So what are the functions of a board of directors? The board has been appointed ostensibly by the shareholders to protect their interests and assess how well the operating officers manage the affairs of the company. They are not responsible for the day to day running of the company's business. That is the responsibility of the executive officers of the company appointed by them. That being the case, it raises the question as to why executive management officers are normally included in the board of directors.

The problem here is that there are potential, and very real conflicts of interest between the responsibilities of the executive management and the role of the board. How can a board that is comprised equally or almost equally of executive management officers and non-executive directors, as may often be the case, function properly and impartially? There is frequently a perception by the non-executive directors that the executive directors are in the driving seat. They must know best, therefore it is difficult to challenge them. There can be very few companies today wherein the non-executive directors are able or willing or given the opportunity to carry out their full responsibilities as directors. In all too many cases the boardroom is treated as a forum in which the CEO's (and possibly the Chairman's) plans are slavishly endorsed.

There is an overwhelming case for keeping the executive management away from board membership. That is not to say that they are kept out of the board-room but when they are there it should be because they are summoned to report on the running of the company and the state of its business, etc. The board should then consider the reports and question management officers as they see fit. In particular consideration should be given to the exclusion of CEOs from board membership by law. At the very least the combination of the roles of CEO and Chairman should be prohibited.

Board members are the representatives of the shareholders. Executives are employees of the company.

Those are controversial matters but for far too long, in fact probably since the creation of shareholder ownership of stock market quoted companies, it can be shown that boards of directors that are subject to the will of the CEO, particularly if he is a protégé of the Chairman, are themselves ineffectual. That is a well-established fact that must be changed, by law if necessary, if we are to eliminate some of the management mistakes that gave rise to the 2007/8 financial crises. Part of the problem is that the basis of company law has changed very little since it was first introduced in the 19th Century. At that time shareholders and directors were often family members or from a localized community, in other words they were more closely involved with the company and its directors than today's institutional and personal investors.

It has been said that non-executives are paid too much for what they do and far too little for what they are supposed to do.

Although the law imposes duties on them, in practice the Courts deal very lightly with claims against directors for dereliction of duty. As most people pay a lot more attention when their pocket is affected it has been suggested that directors should be subject to fines of a restricted but meaningful nature when it can be shown that they have failed without good reason to carry out their duties. A proposal was that the fines could be related to the amount of their fees, say a maximum amount of ten times annual fees. (There would have to be a law prohibiting the company from reimbursing such fines.)

There have been reviews of directors' responsibilities from time to time but none seem to have changed the effective status quo of directors or more importantly, improved company governance. This is a serious matter. Nearly every one of the banks that ran into serious difficulties or collapsed altogether had boards of directors that could be shown to have been ineffectual. Bradford & Bingley's board supervision was described as a shambles.

It is one thing to call for increased transparency by banks and for improved risk management but how will we know that they have taken place? Perhaps there is a need for better "minute keeping" of board meetings but how does one allow access to the minutes, or an edited version of them, whilst still retaining the confidentiality of commercially sensitive information? There is no obvious solution to that problem, which leaves us with a need to ensure that when we are shareholders we must hold boards of directors fully accountable.

Difficult? Yes, but a significant factor in the development of the current financial crisis was that nobody, including regulators, governments and shareholders did so.

Until we have proper enforcement of effective changes in the practice of public company governance we shall continue to suffer unnecessarily from periodic financial disasters. More attention needs to be paid to the contributions of all staff and management as well as that of CEOs. Of course, in defence of company governance it will be maintained that systems and reviews are in place to monitor performance but the reality is that these are rarely as effective as they need to be. Throughout this book I have repeated the expression "I say, therefore it must be so" in order to highlight situations where the reality is different from the stated situation.

Executive Remuneration

It is one of the duties of a board of directors to set remuneration and remuneration policies. So how do they usually go about doing so? Let us concentrate on CEO remuneration since it has been the subject of a great deal of media and public attention.

In most cases, the board contracts out the fixing of CEO remuneration to a professional consulting firm and accepts its recommendations. How do such firms assess the appropriate level of remuneration? They generally do not look only at personal performance but rather at the size of the company, its public image and what is being paid for similar jobs elsewhere. In the case of a new recruit CEO, there will be something added to attract him to the job. In that way we have a spiral that keeps winding upwards as each new salary is set at a higher level. That this has been the case is quite evident if we compare the current level of salaries of CEOs with those of ten years ago.

For example, let us look at RBS. Dr George Mathewson, CEO in 1998 had a salary of £438,000, performance related bonuses of £260,000, profit sharing and benefits of £55,000 and pension contributions of £56,000, making total remuneration of £809,000.

Compare that with Sir Fred Goodwin's remuneration for 2007. Salary, £1,290,000, performance bonus £2,860,000, benefits of £ 40,000 (no pension allowance recorded for that year), making a total of £4,190.000.

Salary is only one element of CEO remuneration, in many cases, a relatively minor element. We have to add cash bonuses, golden hellos, golden exit parachutes, stock allocations, stock options and of course generous pension rights that bear no relationship to employee pension plans. In the annual reports of major companies, this topic can occupy many pages. It is common practice to "pick and mix" the range of executive rewards to create an almost unlimited number of combinations, so much so that it can take a considerable amount of study to determine the total effective remuneration received by many executives, and impossible to relate it to the remuneration in other companies. Additionally it seems to become more complex in each succeeding year.

How far are existing remuneration policies justified?

The argument usually put forward is that one has to remunerate adequately to "attract the right person" for the job – or to keep him in it as bidding wars for CEOs (and other senior executives) are fairly common, bearing in mind that many CEOs only spend 3-5 years in one company. It is a competitive environment and there is some justification for that approach. The problem comes when too much has been awarded up front and the CEO does not perform as expected. Generally he has also been awarded a contract of employment that makes it difficult and / or expensive to change him for someone else. So he is kept on and the board has to live with it.

Despite the obvious shortcomings of so many financial institution CEOs during the period 2007/9 there are still those who stress the need to pay well to "attract the right people", notwithstanding that it has been shown time after time that those CEOs could not have been the right people and that paying high remuneration did not necessarily achieve that objective.

Much critical publicity was given to CEO remuneration during 2007/8 as one disaster after another unfolded and the public discovered how much the responsible CEOs had been paid. Governments that extended financial aid or invested in failing banks initially made it a condition of their involvement that executive remuneration would be reviewed and kept in check and that executive "performance" bonuses would not be paid whilst the aid was in place. Unfortunately governments seem to have backed off this requirement on the grounds that in most cases the remuneration terms are contractual and cannot be set aside.

There were also public calls, related in media reports for legislation to control remuneration policies and much talk about "rewards for failure". However whilst imposing the restrictions just noted, governments considered that it was the responsibility of company boards to determine remuneration within their company and for shareholders to sack the board if they were not satisfied with their actions.

Another frequent criticism of remuneration policies, particularly of "performance bonuses" was that they reward short-term performance, usually assessed on a year-by-year basis. This means that bonuses are paid in respect of a single good year, but are not removed if the following years are poor in performance terms. New guidelines are needed to relate such bonuses to longer-term performance by delaying the vesting of a bonus for, say, three years. Stock options tend to do this automatically as the share price has to keep rising for realistically priced options to have a value at their vesting dates. There is a good case for rewarding performance only through options and eliminating cash bonuses and grants of shares altogether. In that way those in receipt of stock options have a vested interest in ensuring the continuing health of their company.

However even stock options can be altered to benefit executives. In April 2008, when it became apparent that HBOS executives were unlikely to benefit from the exercise price set on their share options, the board (comprised of seven executive officers, a chairman and seven non-executives) reset the exercise price at a lower level.

There is another aspect of the bonus remuneration system that is often overlooked. It was created partly to offset rising ancillary employment costs. Bonuses, being annual and discretionary in amount do not count for pension entitlement. They therefore enable a company to substantially increase current rewards without incurring future pension liabilities.

The need for appropriate levels of executive remuneration is not disputed but there has also to be recognition of the fact that executive officers of a company are not entrepreneurial owners of the company. They do not suffer financially when they get policies wrong. It is shareholders, stakeholders and employees of the company that suffer. Nobody can object to an entrepreneur making substantial gains when his own fortune is at stake in a company, and when he personally bears losses when he creates them by mis-managing his company or suffers them in a general business downturn.

Who should impose such changes as are considered necessary? Primary responsibility lies with the shareholders but if they are to have a meaningful input there have to be some legislative changes that improve their ability to act. In theory they can currently exercise all the authority that they need, in practice that is far from the case. In particular it makes no sense that the managements of pension funds, investment holding companies and unit trusts who collectively control majority stakes in banks and other companies should have the ability to out-vote other smaller shareholders since they can vote such shares to suit their own purposes rather than in accordance with the interests of their own underlying investors. They may also fail to vote their shares and therefore make it impossible for the votes of minority shareholders to imfluence control over the directors.

An organisation such as the UK Shareholders Association provides a useful platform for "small" shareholders to improve their situation by having a combined representation but it is a voluntary organisation with limited resources that can only achieve a more effective voice through a much increased membership. It is very much in the interests of "small" investors to have access to such a body as it is the only viable way in which they will be able to make their voices heard. It also gives them access to a level of professionalism that individually they are unlikely to possess.

Current company law on corporate governance is not "fit for purpose". Changes are required to imbue shareholders with more effective control over their companies. It should not be the responsibility of regulators to monitor bank remuneration policies or the general business strategies of companies.

External Auditors

The perception of the accuracy of company annual accounts is enhanced by the fact that they have been audited by an external professional accounting firm which, if it is satisfied with the results of its examination of the year's financial activities undertaken by its client company, endorses the accounts, inter alia, with a statement that in its opinion the accounts represent a "true and fair view". Following the succession of horror stories that emerged with the bank annual accounts in 2008/9 questions arose as to the value of the external audit certification, particularly when it has to be recognized that it is no more than a "snapshot view" of the company's affairs based on sampling.

Two concerns were aired. The first was the same as with the credit rating agencies, the client was the audited bank, whereas the audit is intended for the benefit of shareholders and other parties dealing with the bank. The second concern was that the accounting firms carrying out the audit were increasingly providing other consulting services to the audited bank. This could give rise to a conflict of interest in that the same firm that was advising the bank how to structure parts of its business was confirming that the business had been conducted satisfactorily. As the amounts involved for several of the larger British banks was running into tens of millions of pounds annually for each of the auditing and advisory services, one has to question whether that is a desirable state of affairs.

Auditors regard their work as confidential to their client, i.e the audited bank, however a case can be made for requiring external auditors to confidentially report significant concerns they may have to the bank's official regulator particularly where they identify breaches or potential breaches of regulatory requirements.

There will be differing views on that suggestion, but it is one that I imposed in Gibraltar.

The next area that deserves attention is:

Derivatives and Securitisation

Over investment in derivatives of doubtful worth and the "freezing" of markets in them have been cited as primary contributors to the credit crisis.

The creation, circulation and selling of some forms of derivative investments is a satisfactory modern method of raising funds. The flaw lies in its uninhibited use with a flagrant disregard for the true value of the underlying securities that form the backup. As explained elsewhere, deficiencies that lay in underlying value were ignored or inadequately assessed by the packagers and pasted over by "credit enhancement", a very reassuring description for an artificial creation of security, bolstered further by reliance on credit ratings applied by supposedly world class specialist agencies that were paid by the issuers of those securities and whose competence and impartiality went unquestioned for far too long.

The basic problem with the marketing of derivative bonds was that the chain by means of which they were created was so extended that the end purchaser (or anyone else for that matter) could not identify the worth of the assets that were his security. Purchasers had to rely on the probity of the sellers and what proved to be indifferent quality assessments that initially gave almost every issue a high credit rating. It should not be forgotten however that all the problems involving derivatives arose despite the fact that every detail of the hundreds of pages of documentation relating to every issue was registered with the SEC (and for UK issues, with the FSA) and ostensibly received approval.

It must also be noted that derivatives were sold on exclusively to professional and institutional investors who should have been capablr of satisfying themselves as to the inherent risks in what they were acquiring.

Securitisation, if used as a means of using assets as security to raise more capital, is a legitimate activity. What is not legitimate and what has become a driving force has been the creation of ever more complex instruments such as synthetic derivatives, deliberately constructed in opaque ways, whose principal purpose is to enable fees and commissions to be earned by intermediaries. In particular, there has to be a simplification of the new processes and a return to first principles.

Derivatives have to be seen as a secure method of raising finance. Secure both from the points of view of the investors in them and those raising the finance.

Although derivatives are regarded as a relatively recent introduction there were forerunners that sold on the basis of their simplicity and total security.

After German Land Mortgage Bank Bonds had been in existence for fifty years they began to be marketed internationally in 1925. The bonds were issued by regional mortgage banks and traded through markets in London, Amsterdam and later, New York.

They were issued in the days when we had a Gold Standard to which currencies were tied. They therefore had a fixed par value based on a given weight of gold that was recognized universally therefore currency risks were effectively negated. They were long term bonds issued for thirty years or so, but redeemable earlier at the option of the issuer. Investors obtained protection by the following means:

They were issued subject to German Mortgage Bank Law

All issuing banks were subject to State control

A Trustee appointed by the German government had to approve all issues, and held the mortgages against which the bonds were issued and secured.

The trustee was responsible to ensure that the legal cover for the bonds remained intact and that the mortgages were officially recorded.

The bonds issued by a mortgage bank were guaranteed unconditionally and irrevocably by the Associated German Mortgage Banks. In all there were eight mortgage banks.

Perhaps the last guarantee provides a clue as to how modern derivatives could be improved by requiring all the banks involved as issuers to collectively guarantee all issues. This is not such an outlandish idea, after all that is the way in which deposits in our banks are guaranteed (with limitations).

There would be several advantages:

- It would make banks more careful about ensuring adequate underlying security

- It would be more dependable than the present credit rating by agencies

- It would restrict the use of derivatives to a reasonable volume.

German laws provided further protections. Mortgage banks were not allowed to undertake any business other than:

- To grant loans secured by first mortgages

- To issue bonds secured on those mortgages

There were two other supplementary types of business allowed, but they were very restricted in scope and in areas that were considered very safe.

Of course that is a description of a fairly simplistic type of business formula but perhaps that is what is needed in the mortgage world. After all when mortgages in the UK were principally obtainable from Building Societies we never had a failure of a building society. Admittedly it would have been difficult for them to have followed their business models and still have kept up with an ever-increasing need for mortgage loans. That is not to say that it could not have been achieved by adapting the German 1925 model to building societies as a way of enabling them to raise additional funding.

A major difference between the German Mortgage Bank Bonds and present day derivatives was that the German bonds were completely transparent and safe, which today's derivatives patently are not.

The topic of derivatives including their regulation and the problems surrounding them has been dealt with fairly fully in earlier chapters. Derivatives are essentially global in their appeal. What now needs to be done is to devise better methods of structuring and controlling their issue that are applied globally. For the present the issue and secondary markets in derivatives are virtually non-existent and many of those securities have been marked down to a fraction of their issue prices. As at the beginning of 2009 there is talk of new forms of securitisation being devised to replace the discredited forms that gave rise to the credit crisis. Governments and regulators need to be proactive in monitoring those developments. It is currently necessary to decide whether or not the derivatives market is to be revived and if so on what terms and conditions. That probably means new laws applied internationally and backed up by meaningful penalties.

A significant problem with the present derivatives markets is that there has been insufficient identification of the quality of the underlying investments. Instead, reliance was placed on an artificially applied credit rating backed up by Credit Default Swap (CDS) guarantees. What we need to consider is creating a more transparent variety of products ranging from totally secure, backed by a government guarantee paid for by the issuers to less secure issues clearly identified as such in a way that investors cannot deny that they are unaware of the potential risks involved in them.

The structure of a new market in derivatives will be different if only because the principal players in it, the Wall Street investment banks have all but ceased to exist.

However, it is deceptive to belief that simplistic solutions can be proposed. Derivatives are probably one of the most complex financial instruments ever devised. As we have seen, they have been issued in amounts that were unheard of in financial markets less than twenty-years ago. If a successful and trusted market is to be resurrected it will have to be much simpler in concept, subject to effective regulation and when used for funding its size will have to be proportionate to the size of other funding methods used by financial institutions.

Another important factor must be that there is no artificial device for removing the liability on underlying assets off bank balance sheets. It makes very little sense to "insure" the risk with insurers that are no better capitalised to cope with the risk than the banks themselves. It may be possible to confer some advantages to banks by allowing a "risk weighting" on derivatives in much the same way as it is applied to other assets but one that depends on the nature and quality of the underlying assets.

Much of the problem that has given rise to the need for governments to make available enormous amounts of financial aid to banks arises from the extreme leveraging effect that derivatives enabled banks to use. The consequence has been that the liquidity ratios and capital structures of banks have been considerably weakened.

Banks are only interested in leveraging and minimizing liquidity ratios for one reason – to increase the level of profitability derived from a given amount of assets and capital. Both aspects require to be subjected to better co-ordinated control by global regulatory authorities in order to provide reassurance to investors concerning the quality of their investments in derivatives.

Stock Markets

Stock markets are the instruments through which investment activities are facilitated. For many years stock market investment in company shares has been regarded as the most effective way of protecting the value of funds in the long term. Stock markets provide opportunities for individuals and corporations, both nationally and internationally to invest funds. They are essential to the investment process. Our savings, pensions, insurance and corporate reserves are all involved.

Their importance is such that we must ensure that they operate smoothly, effectively and with an integrity that can be trusted by investors. That brings into question the validity of short selling strategies. The proponents of short selling claim that it is a strategy for protecting oneself against inefficient managements. That may be so when it is used moderately as part of an overall investment strategy in appropriate circumstances. However, short selling does not always constitute investment, it can quite simply be gambling, but with a difference. When particular shares are "shorted" in large quantities, for all practical purposes the gamble becomes a one-way bet. Furthermore short selling of shares in specific companies can very rapidly become a deliberate attack on that company's share price, driving it down.

Share lending and shorting have been dealt with in depth in earlier chapters. Our consideration here is whether or not the practice should be allowed to continue. Events in 2007/8 have demonstrated that when bank shares are subjected to such attacks in times of financial stress, short selling exacerbates a bank's other problems and can have an impact beyond the bank whose shares are being traded.

If we add to this the fact that the authorities have difficulty identifying short selling activity that appears to be associated with the spread of unfounded rumours, a case for banning or at least restricting such activities when bank shares are involved becomes very strong. That is a fact that was recognised by George Rae in his book "The Country Banker" in the 19th Century, as noted elsewhere.

In both the UK and USA, short selling of bank shares was temporarily banned during 2008. There is a very good case for either a permanent ban or the placing of limitations on the practice. An outright ban would not be difficult to police, however trying to place limitations on the shorting of shares in any one company could be very difficult to achieve.

Elsewhere in this book an indication of the involvement of hedge funds and the extent of short selling that is carried out in any one day has been described. It must be kept in mind that the volumes are often huge, producing significant side effects.

Short selling, insider trading and rumour mongering can be interconnected and are matters affecting the public interest. They are also a source of considerable profit to those indulging in them. We cannot expect those involved to voluntarily restrict their activities. It follows that those are matters that must be tackled much more effectively by government and regulatory authorities. Notwithstanding, the UK government announced in January 2009 that it would lift the restrictions on "shorting" of financial company shares but that the reporting of short-sales on all traded shares was under consideration. The very next day Barclays, Lloyds and RBS shares were shorted following bad banking sector news and lost 10%, 35% and 67% respectively.

Those are all important considerations. The average person does not appreciate the growth in the volumes of activity on stock exchanges. For example, the London Stock Exchange, which is large but by no means the most active, has seen an increase in stock market activity over the last twenty years that has resulted in the average monthly value of shares traded increasing from £27,025,000,000 in 1988 to £216,927,000,000 in 2008, in other words, an eight-fold increase.

Those volumes of activity can generate a substantial volume of fees and commissions for brokers and the stock exchanges, therefore there is no incentive for a voluntary reduction in trading volumes that a cessation of short selling would bring about.

Regulation and supervision

Regulators, particularly in the USA and UK have been subject to much criticism during 2007/8, some of it justified but part of it was down to placing blame somewhere. One of the problems faced by regulators is that they do not always have full political backing, even if the authority vested in them by government appears to be adequate.

Many financial institutions, although they will protest to the contrary, see regulation as inhibiting business growth and as a diversion of resources from their profit generating goals. There is a virtual industry devoted to finding ways of circumventing rules or utilising "loop-holes" in them. The derivatives that have been at the root of recent problems were devised for that purpose as much as for any other reason, namely to remove liabilities from bank balance sheets.

We also have two different approaches to regulation. The US approach is to devise specific rules to prescribe the conduct of as many aspects of financial activity as is considered necessary. The problem with this approach is that it always lags behind new business developments that may not be brought within the regulatory regime until something goes wrong. It is also impossible for management and employees at all levels in a financial institution (or for that matter within the regulators) to remain conversant with all the rules. By way of example one US regulatory authority was said to have a 9000-page rule-book.

In the UK, "light touch" regulation was developed. This means fewer prescriptive rules combined with enhanced general supervision that should be aimed particularly at those financial institutions that are considered to be in a higher risk category. It relies to some extent on rules that tend to be regarded as optionally applied advisory guidelines because they are inadequately policed.

It is a form of regulation that is very dependent upon co-operation by regulated financial institutions and on a willingness on their part to follow the spirit of the regulatory guidance rather than the possibly inadequate letter of the law. Where it proved unsatisfactory in the UK context was that effective supervision by experienced senior officers was not carried out adequately.

Effective regulation is closely allied to good corporate governance. The proper conduct of its business is the responsibility of a company's board of directors. The buck stops with them. Imposed regulation should be seen as assisting them to make the right decisions within the regulatory framework. It is not intended as a method of absolving them from responsibility for their actions or of making business decisions for them. Many of the rules we have are aimed at nothing more than ensuring fair and sensible behaviour.

An unwillingness to responsibly observe the spirit of regulatory requirements has been very apparent in recent years and it played a substantial role in the collapse of financial systems in 2007/8. Until such time as financial institutions are prepared to self-regulate their activities in a meaningful manner, it will be very difficult to impose effective regulation.

It is interesting to note that although there was a substantial amount of criticism of the Bank of England and the FSA when what can now be described as Northern Rock's relatively modest liquidity problems arose and were not pre-identified by the regulators, there has been practically no criticism of the regulators in relation to the much more serious total collapses of Bradford and Bingley, HBOS, RBS and the Icelandic banks operating in the UK. Those all collapsed, not because their managements failed to recognize what was described as a "low probability" event but because they pursued undeniably reckless strategies with a disregard for risk management principles that company boards claimed to espouse. The regulators either allowed them to do so or failed to spot what they were doing but in either event there has been hardly a word of public or official criticism of the regulatory failings and the regulators have not owned up to any such failings.

There has been a tendency in the UK to over-stress the value of regulation. Every piece of paper or advertisement of its services that is issued by a licensed financial firm must by law contain a statement that it is regulated by the FSA. That encourages a false sense of security in the minds of those using the financial services. They view it as a guarantee that it is safe to deal with that firm in all circumstances without further enquiry. Whilst it is important that investors and other customers should be aware that the firm is subject to regulation there needs to be some sort of accompanying warning such as we find on cigarette packets – although perhaps not quite such a doom-laden message.

In what are sometimes referred to as the "good old days" of UK banking, an eyebrow raised by the Governor of the Bank of England was considered sufficient to bring an errant bank into line. Today's globalised financial markets are too large, too competitive and too complex for that to be effective. We may need some new regulations but we also need better observation of existing rules particularly in relation to the identification and management of risk. Only a mixture of encouragement, meaningful penalties for transgression, which could include a requirement for a company to change its management, and better quality supervision will improve compliance. In an earlier chapter a distinction was drawn between "regulation" and "supervision". Whilst we need an effective armoury of regulatory rules, they are useless if their implementation is not properly supervised.

This must be done, not only on a national basis, but with a high degree of international cooperation. Stimulating effective international cooperation has been a goal of the Prime Minister, Gordon Brown in recent times. In February 2009 at the Labour Party's National Policy Forum meeting he called for more rigorous global supervision of the banking system and of hedge funds and tax havens. In particular he said that he wanted to have global supervision of what was a shadow global system. He wanted there to be no hiding place for special investment vehicles, for hedge funds or tax havens. He said also that some practices were indefensible and that they have got to be cleaned up now. It was time to set new rules for the banks of all countries.

It would be a mistake however to put all the concentration of international supervisory efforts on hedge funds and tax havens. They may have contributed to the financial turmoil but were not at the centre of it. Financial institutions service international trade and investment and to do so they have to be spread around the world. If they are to be monitored effectively it can only be through properly coordinated regulation and supervision. That does not necessarily presuppose a central global supervisory body. It is an objective that can be achieved by meaningful cooperation amongst national regulators, meeting regularly and exchanging information freely. That was what was done in the case of Bank of Commerce and Credit International in the early-1990's.

A "College of Supervisors" from those countries in which the bank had its most significant operations was formed to monitor the bank's activities and to ensure that each member of the college was kept informed of any new developments. However for many years, other than on that occasion, we have had a less than satisfactory degree of international co-operation amongst national regulatory authorities. There are a number of reasons for this but human nature is probably the most significant.

The spirit was willing, but the flesh was weak and still is so.

Governments and regulatory authorities from many countries are now said to be combining forces to examine the weaknesses in the regulation of financial activities and considering how to create a co-ordinated and appropriate structure. That will not be easy to implement unless inter-government co-operation is brought to bear. The UK authorities have already issued consultative papers and there can be little doubt that some elements of the regulatory structure will be changed, in the UK and elsewhere. They have to do so.

However it is a mistake to believe that an official regulator can adequately police the complex business models that are used by today's financial institutions. As with external auditors, regulators can only take "snapshots" of an institution' s activities. With the limited resources available to it, a regulator cannot continuously monitor every aspect of a bank's business. That is the job of the management of a bank. The best a regulator can hope to achieve is to set and monitor basic ground-rules. What it must do, however, is to make sure that as far as possible it does so in a timely, effective manner and on a globally applied basis. That was not the case prior to and during the recent financial crises.

In relation to Northern Rock it was shown that FSA senior management had little or no direct involvement in its supervision. It is most important that senior management of the regulator is directly involved in supervision, particularly when meetings are being held with the senior management of regulated institutions otherwise the regulator will be unable to command respect. If an increase in the numbers of competent, experienced senior officers is required to fulfil that requirement, then that has to be arranged. Nothing less will achieve a satisfactory supervisory regime.

There was another aspect in which the regulatory authorities, in the UK and elsewhere were deficient. They were unprepared for the recent financial crises. In truth until they happened nobody foresaw the possibility that the financial disasters could be so extensive. We are accustomed to business cycles but they have had a modest impact compared with the 2007/8 crises that developed, particularly as they developed in two separate phases, the second some time after the first and of a severity that was not foreseen.

Because the events were unanticipated and inadequate contingency plans were in place everything was tackled in a hurry. There was a lot of shooting from the hip, both in the UK and the USA and the phrase "running about like headless chickens" comes to mind. That was understandable up to a point. It also brought about a number of changes of mind within days or a week or two on very important decisions - indicative of a lack of proper analysis and planning. The October 2008 US Treasury plan involving $700 billion was a good example. Not only were the objectives of the plan changed more than once, it was very soon supplemented with a second tranche of economic aid amounting to another $800 billion.

We cannot expect to pre-plan a perfect solution for every eventuality but now that a major financial collapse has been experienced we should expect the authorities – regulators and governments—plus financial institutions themselves to prepare contingency plans to cope with any repetitions of what were the most significant factors in the recent crises. Governments and regulators have to ensure that a much more effective "early warning" system is created.

A serious contributor to the depth of the financial crises and the economic downturns stemming from them has been the reluctance of banks to reactivate the wholesale financial markets and to act as lenders to their customers. They have a duty to find ways to quickly resolve that situation and to avoid any repetition in future.

The nature of banks

What is a bank?

Unfortunately we have no comprehensive definition of what constitutes a bank, the nearest we get is that a bank is an institution carrying on the business of banking. As noted in chapter 13 the 1979 Banking Act provided that a bank could only be described as such if it was recognized by the Bank of England under the Banking Act 1979, Sec 36 as a bank. Later, in 1987 another Banking Act established that if an institution accepted deposits (from the public), then it was a bank for the purposes of regulation.

Banks therefore are a bit like caterpillars, they come in all shapes and sizes. It is dificult to describe one precisely, but we all know one when we see it.

So, if a bank accepts deposits, what does it do with them?

It uses them, one way or another, to generate an income, principally by lending. The minute it starts to use its deposits, it incurs risk and that is the key to the proper management of a bank. Bank managements must make, and be capable of making, an accurate risk assessment. This is not just an evaluation of the risk / reward ratio, it also has to take into account economic and social factors.

We saw this in the USA. The rapid growth of the mortgage market there, whilst it was enabled, as we have seen, by the development of the securitisation processes, it was driven by a political desire to spread home-ownership throughout the nation.

It is also a well-established principle in banking that "the higher the reward, the greater the risk".

Striking the right risk / reward ratio does not necessarily mean that high-risk activities have to be completely eschewed but what it does mean is that the amount of high-risk business undertaken must be restricted so that it does not create an imbalance in the acceptable overall risk / reward ratio for each individual bank. A failure to fully identify the potential risks that had been incurred and to ensure that they did not create an unacceptable risk / reward ratio was a fundamental cause of much of the recent financial crisis.

Banks, as we have noted, have developed into very complex institutions. We now have to determine the extent to which they should continue to engage in a wide range of activities and if so, how can we more effectively regulate them to avoid the excesses that created recent problems.

The Structure of banks

The structure of banks globally has changed greatly over the years, as have their objectives. Those of us who have experience of banking, either from within or without over the last fifty years are very conscious of that fact. There is no suggestion that banks were better in the past than they are today but they were more "fit for purpose". That is to say, if their purpose was to provide conventional financial services for the communities in which they operated.

What we have seen during 2007/8 is that banks appear to have two business streams.

One is the provision of "high street" banking services for customers including money transfer, savings, credit, mortgages, supplemented in some cases by the provision of unit trusts, insurance, estate agency and consultancy services.

The other is dealing in wholesale capital markets including mergers and acquisitions, creation of derivatives and speculative trading in the currency and investment markets. Those have all been regarded as legitimate activities for a bank, indeed nowhere has there been a legislative attempt to modify them. In fact, quite the opposite is the case. Regulatory control has been made more liberal.

As the recent crisis has demonstrated, the second area of business can have very adverse effects on the more traditional activities. That is brought about by an imbalance between the two types of activity and the higher element of risk attaching to the second range of activities. The questions have to be put, is it appropriate for a bank to operate in both fields, alternatively, how can it be stopped from doing so?

Serious consideration needs to be given to those matters. If we go back forty years or so they were dealt with, both in the UK and the USA by having different types of bank. In the UK we had "merchant banks", "discount houses" and "high-street" banks. In the US there were "investment banks", which undertook various combinations of capital market / investment management and wholesale banking activities. Their deposit / lending activities were more or less restricted to the corporate and high net worth ends of the market, in other words with people who could be regarded as financially literate and able to assess and assume risk. We also had what were referred to in the USA as "main-street" or retail banks. In the US the two categories were for many years separated by law. This was achieved by the Banking Act 1933, also known as the Glass-Steagal Act which was repealed in 1999 as part of liberalisation of banking and financial services.

As the UK retail banks grew in size, they spread their range of activities by absorbing stock broking firms, retail finance companies, insurance companies, merchant banks and other commercial interests. Alternatively they assumed many of the functions of such firms and rapidly expanded their activities in other directions, as noted in the previous paragraph. If there was a mistake made it was in their managements believing that they were equipped (i.e. the managements, not the banks) to conduct any type of financial activity despite in varying degrees an incomplete understanding of the level of risk involved and the complexity of the products with which they became involved.

This was vividly illustrated in the outcome of what latterly became too great an involvement with derivatives. It was somewhat ironic that banks, having created and sold their own derivatives and in so doing, removed liabilities from their balance sheets, in many cases then proceeded to acquire as assets other banks' derivatives. In so doing they brought un-assessed risks back onto their balance sheets. This has been one of the major reasons for the need for government intervention to prop up bank balance sheets.

Why did they do it? For one reason only, they were chasing a slightly better "bottom line" result.

The wide spread of retail activities conducted by today's banks has many advantages for consumers, but only if banks strike an appropriate balance between their own interest which is to operate profitably, and an obligation to deal fairly and transparently with their customers.

The big question is whether they should be permitted to engage in the second range of activities noted above or whether only in some of them. Assuming that the conclusion is that they should not do so, how does one stop them? Very few banks nowadays operate through only one company. They conduct different facets of business through subsidiaries. It may be thought possible therefore to separate the wholesale and higher risk activities from the every-day "high street" activities. It sounds simple, but some of those bank corporate structures are very complex. It is difficult to know just what is going on within them all. How does one ensure that they remain as watertight compartments within "chinese walls" with only closely prescribed inter-company dealings? When I was in Gibraltar I was faced with an application for a banking licence from a well-established overseas bank that had thirty-eight separate companies in its Group. I turned down the application because I realized that I would never be able to keep track of how all those subsidiaries were inter-acting with the proposed Gibraltar subsidiary.

The point of all this can be related to what happened to Northern Rock. It was a perfectly sound mortgage bank with one weakness in its business plan, too much reliance on wholesale markets. But when disaster struck, it was the bank's retail deposit customers and shareholders that were worst hit, although government intervention ensured that depositors did not actually lose a penny. At the same time the intervention was designed to ensure that the shareholders would lose everything.

Even if regulation manages to keep the various elements separate, what is to prevent one bank lending its depositors' funds through the inter-bank markets to other banks permitted to invest them in higher risk business?

Perhaps a partial answer is to place individual limits on the amounts of higher risk activities a bank may engage in relative to its primary retail business activity. Of course, in relation to the use of derivatives, they do not necessarily have to be classified as "high risk" assets if they are transparently and honestly structured.

There is no simple answer to those questions but one thing is certain, ways have to be devised to ensure that retail deposits in a bank are not used to fund high-risk activities with a disregard for the fundamental rules of banking. It is totally wrong that governments are left to pick up the pieces and be ultimately responsible for the protection of depositors.

There is another fact that has changed the nature of banking, particularly in the UK. Banks have become bigger and fewer in number. We have lost the diversification of risk that a larger number of smaller (but still not "small" banks) provided. This change was heralded as improving efficiency and enabling banks to cope globally with larger transactions.

We can see now where that got us!

One has to question whether the takeover of HBOS by LLoydsTSB to create the new LLoyds Banking Group, essential as it may have seemed at the time, is not yet another step in the wrong direction.

Finale

We are coming to the end of the story as it has been recorded here. However the full story has a long way to run yet and there are many other avenues that could be explored. There will be other (unforeseen) developments from time to time and the full economic consequences have yet to be experienced. Unfortunately they will have to be recorded elsewhere. Every author who writes about current events has to draw a line at some point and that point, early in 2009, has been reached in this instance.

The object of this chapter is not to provide some kind of blueprint for the future by identifying solutions. No single person can produce satisfactory solutions to shortcomings in the finance industry. Instead the intention has been to identify some of the areas where action is required. The 2008 financial collapse appeared to come out of the blue. If we are to avoid a repetition it is essential that we learn some lessons from recent experiences.

Are we likely to create a foolproof global financial world? It is highly unlikely. The best we can hope to achieve is to eliminate the principal weaknesses and excesses that gave rise to the worst events of 2007/8.

Perhaps the following assessment made in 1885 by George Rae, in his book "The Country Banker" is as appropriate as any we may guess at now! It proved to be correct in 2008, so why not yet again on some future date?

The question that we have to ask is ——Have we seen the last of over-

trading and speculation? We might as well ask have we seen the last of human nature. We have not seen the last of these things. On the contrary, when they next take place they will probably be on a larger scale than heretofore – a scale proportional to the enormous increase in our commercial and monetary transactions. It is possible indeed to imagine such a conjunction of disturbing events and adverse influences, at some critical point in the future, as may result in more intense pressure upon our monetary system than it has ever suffered in the past.

Index